American Presbyterian Review
by Henry Boynton Smith

Address:
HardPress
8345 NW 66TH ST #2561
MIAMI FL 33166-2626
USA
Email: info@hardpress.net

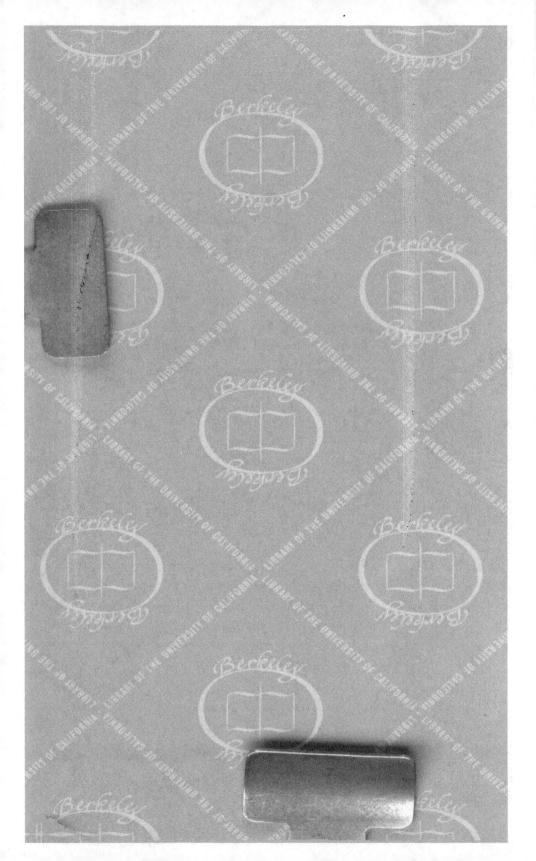

THE

AMERICAN

RESBYTERIAN AND THEOLOGICAL

REVIEW.

EDITORS:

ENRY B. SMITH AND J. M. SHERWOOD.

Associate Editors:

ALBERT BARNES,
THOMAS BRAINERD, }Philadelphia.
JOHN JENKINS,
ROSWELL D. HITCHCOCK, Union Theological Seminary, N. Y.
JONATHAN B. CONDIT, Auburn Theological Seminary, N. Y.
GEORGE E. DAY, Lane Theological Seminary, O.

NEW SERIES, VOL. I.

1863.

NEW-YORK:
J. M. SHERWOOD, No. 5 BEEKMAN STREET.
PHILADELPHIA:
PRESBYTERIAN BOOKSTORE, 1334 CHESTNUT STREET.
EDINBURGH: OGLE & MURRAY.

THE
AMERICAN PRESBYTERIAN

AND

THEOLOGICAL REVIEW.

NEW SERIES, No. I.

JANUARY, 1863.

Art. I.—HARD MATTER.

By Tayler Lewis, LL.D., of Union College, New York.

Is there an external world? Certainly, says Dr. Hickok, there is such a reality, beyond all question. Certainly, says Dr. Hall,*—an external world there is, and of hard matter too; are we not every day coming in contact with it? But how do we know it — that is, how do we know it as external? Here is another question, and on this they differ. How do we know it, says Dr. Hickok; why, we know it from our reason. It stands to reason that there is something outside of us, when there are effects produced within us of which we are conscious, but which we are sure did not come from any willing, or any internal self-originated activity of our own. The reason, as a higher comprehending, overlooking faculty, comprehends the one universal time and space which never could have been found in the chaotic sea of individual sensations,

* [See Dr.Hall's article on the Rational Psychology and its Vindications, in the AMERICAN THEOLOGICAL REVIEW, Oct. 1862.]

1

and without which such sensations could never be certainly known to have a common objective reality existing in the one space and time that belongs alike to all. It is only by reason that we can be quite sure we are not dreaming. We state his argument very partially and defectively. There is much more of it; but this is sufficient for the purposes of the present contrast. We know it, says Dr. Hickok, by our reason. Dr. Hall, too, sometimes forgets himself, and attempts to prove it in a way which shows that he has a little unconscious distrust, occasionally, of the sense; but in general he has another, and, as he thinks, far more direct way of settling the matter. How do we *positively* know that there is such a real outside world? Why, we smell it, Dr. Hall maintains; we take cognizance of it in the spiritual olfactory, and all reasoning about it is superfluous, besides being a treasonable denial of something better and more religious. Reason and reasoning will make us pantheists, but sense is orthodox; it is the only sure foundation for a right faith.

In stating Dr. Hall's position, we have chosen this sense of smell, not for the purpose of an unjust or partial caricature, but because, in this matter, any one sense is a representative of all the rest, and, therefore, the grosser presents the most direct and plainest issue. If we were confined to this sense, we could, doubtless, though with more difficulty, get from it much, if not all the knowledge we derive from the others, any or all of them. Greatly quickened, as it doubtless would be in that case, we might get, from its varying intensities, distance, direct and lateral; hence, extension, bound, figure. Modification in such intensities might correspond to hardness, softness, solidity. Other differences of odor might *represent* to us something like colors. Long use might make these seem like direct and inseparable perceptions, so that it would cease to be absurd to say, it smells hard, or long, or round, or square, or hollow, or solid, or even red, and green. We might have not only a smell of some huge, indefinite thing outside of us, but of a well furnished world of greatly varied perceptions. All this knowledge we might get, through this one avenue; or rather, to use more correct language, the mind

from its own rich stores might cloth these dull sensations, or
the infinitely varying intensities of them, with manifold ideas,
so that it might be truly said that a being endowed with reason, and a nose only, would smell out more knowledge from
the external world, than a being without reason, that is, without ideas, would get from the highest sense-organization, including, as is perfectly conceivable, many more sense avenues
than have ever been given to man. But this is a digression,
since Dr. Hall does not believe in any such mental furnishing
of ideas, and we took this sense of smell because it represents
his doctrine as precisely as any or all the rest.

In a previous article we made use of the sense of hearing
in an attempt to show that we are not directly conscious of the
external thing, but only of our own sensation. Dr. Hall is
surprised at that, for he says that "Professor Lewis argues as
though he really supposed that those of a different philosophy
maintain that we perceive the bell by hearing alone" (p. 614).
We are surprised at Dr. Hall. The argument about the hearing was meant to be applicable, and truly is applicable, to all
the senses. And so it was expressly said. The sense of hearing was taken because it was so much slower in its process
than the sight, and we could, therefore, the more easily trace
the steps. It was like taking a magnified object, or a slow
motion, when we know that the law of its continuance is the
same with that of the lightning telegraph. "No advocate of
natural realism", says Dr. Hall, "pretends that hearing *alone*
would give knowledge of a bell; the hearing is limited to the
sensation". "Nor is it every sense", he says further, "that
gives immediate intuition of an outward object". In conceding this, he concedes all. It is not a mere question of ac-
cumulative testimony. Senses themselves defective cannot
help other senses. Besides, to resort to this looks very much
like an attempt to prove it by reason; as when Dr. Hall says,
just below, "For sufficient reasons we *judge* these causes to
be qualities in the object". Here, again, is that irreligious
reason or reasoning, involving a distrust of the sense, and
opening the door to all the horrid spectres of pantheism. But
there is one sense, it seems, that is unerring. "The natural

Realist ", we are told, " holds that in touch, or rather in the muscular sense of resistance commonly included in touch, we are presented *face to face with outward objects having exten- sion and solidity* ". This is from Sir William Hamilton, and it really is very remarkable language. If Dr. Hall means by it the sense of touch as distinguished from the others, then sight goes along with smelling and hearing, as among those that " do not give immediate intuition of an outward object". But if all the senses are ultimately touch, then the distinction between primary and secondary qualities *in sensation* falls to the ground. With all respect for Sir William Hamilton, this we affirm and proceed to prove. But first a few preliminaries.

The sense of touch differs not essentially, in this respect of nearness from sight and hearing. It does not bridge the chasm between matter and spirit, any more than they do. As there is an *imago figuræ*, an *imago vocis*, so, also, is there an *imago tactus*. One is as much representative as the others. Our consciousness of repellency takes us no more *out of our- selves* than those lighter contacts of some lighter medium which we call sound and hearing, or sight and seeing. Lan- guage itself, which, when freely developed, is reason itself, and will not permit us to talk nonsense, tells us that con- sciousness can only be of that which is *within* the soul. It is self-consciousness, and can be nothing else. Take this away, and there is no difference between it and *scientia*, and no call for a different word. But how to get within the soul by touch rather than in any other way of sense — this is the difficulty. The chasm may have but the breadth of a hair- line, but it presents no easier passage than though it had the width of infinity. In truth it is infinite; and *tactus* can no more spring across, or climb over, than smelling or hearing. Sir William Hamilton's ladder of " primary and secondary qualities " can give it no aid in doing this, as we proceed to show.

We say, first, that this distinction will not do, because what are called secondary qualities are but modifications of the primary so named. As bodies cannot exist without the first, so the first cannot exist without the second, or the grounds of the second, inhering as they do in the first, and ever ready to manifest themselves whenever the sentient comes to which they are adapted. That which cannot exist without *something*, cannot exist without having (*in effectu*) all the things that have their ground inhering in that first sómething. Color, for example, has its ground in the inner organization of bodies,—in the extent, number, site, size, distance, force, ratio, of the elementary parts, be they what they may, of the body color- ed. When we see color, then, it is also a touching (we use the language of this school), an ultimate touching, by the soul, of those " primary qualities " in which its sentiency inheres. We need not stop to show that the same reasoning applies to sounds and odors, or to hearing, taste and smell. The distinction of " primary and secondary " falls away in like manner in re- spect to all of them. They all come from a certain disposi- tion of the elements and forces of the bodies that give rise to the sensation, and these run immediately down to the primary notions of force, quantity, and extent. Hence we may truly say that a body can no more exist without color, than without figure. There may not be a sentient to perceive either, but the *intensity* of the one feeling, which is the source of the color-sensation, has its ground in the causing body, as much as the *extensity* of the other, for intensity in degree is but ex- tent in another aspect and direction. In other words, it in- heres in those modifications of extent and force which will make it *appear* to an adapted sentient. Go to the bottom of matter; traverse it by the sense, the imagination, or the rea- son, and we have these elemental bones, these " primary qualities "—nothing more or less. *Qualities*, we say, by way of accommodation; but they are, all in themselves, strictly *quantities*, matters wholly of more and less. All else are affec- tions in us, however caused, or however far it be true or not that the mind creates them. We can see nothing else, think nothing else, in which one material object differs from another, until the mind comes, and, out of these varieties of resistance and differences of quantity (which it comprehends in some strange and ineffable way through some prior knowledge of its own), raises its splendid temple of qualities, all real, but real only as they are spiritual.

All quality is spiritual, and spiritually perceived. On the other hand, says Comte, who knows nothing of spirit, " *all is quantity* ". No man ever explored this material ground of sensation more acutely than this French atheist. Denying everything spiritual, whether as a blank power, or an *à priori* intelligence, holding that mind added nothing here,—denying, in fact, all soul or mind, except as thinking matter,—he carried out most rigidly and most consistently this materialising atheistic theory of contacts of which Dr. Hall is so fond. We love to read Hobbes or Comte. They are so thorough, so unshrinking, and, withal, so clear. When pressed with some of the difficulties of spiritualism, we find relief in their square, logical mason-work; for they show a man what he must come to if he departs a hair's breadth from the belief that the soul has a knowledge of its own; and as we cannot accept their darkness, though it be a darkness visible, so are we the more content with the light we have, notwithstanding its necessarily accompanying shadows. Now, Comte denies, and, on his theory of materialism, truthfully denies, that there is anything in matter, anything in the outer world, but quantity. Quality is wholly spiritual, and, therefore, to him a delusion and a nonentity. There is no ποῖον except as a cheating name for differences and diversities of πόσον. Its place must be wholly erased from the list of the categories. All qualities, so called, are but varied exhibitions or *more or less* among the primary numbers, figures, distances, forces, and intensities, that are in the ultimate constitution of matter. There are no qualities, so called, but what may be expressed arithmetically; and, therefore, they are strictly quantity, and nothing else. So holds Comte. But we do know that there *is* quality as a pure spiritual entity, and that is the way, and the only way, in which we know that Comte is false. There lie before us, for example, two musical strings. They differ in length as four fifths and five sixths. There is nothing here, as yet, but quantity; and there is just such a difference of quantity in the outward sounds and undulations they produce. There is just this difference of quantity in the sensation felt from them; just this and nothing more. But listen to them, and hear how they speak to the soul, or, rather, how the soul speaks through them, when it *qualifies* them, or puts its quality into them. One is now the sad melting minor, the other the joyful major strain. Whence comes it? There is a mighty difference of quality, we say, but this is from the spirit alone, and its eternal harmony. All the mathematics and all the dynamics of the schools could not find it in the strings, or in any motions or bare sensations from the strings. There is nothing there but number, tensions, and intensities,—nothing but bare quantities, and that is all a soul would get, or a blank spiritual power would get, which, having no ideas of its own, could only "stand face to face with outward objects", meeting them fair and square, "in touch and the sense of muscular resistance". Tact would meet tact; tension would meet tension, and the offspring would be a sensation of tact and tension, having so much quantity,—just this and nothing more.

·But how to get even this primary quality (yielding the name) with which the soul is thus said to "stand face to face" in direct and immediate consciousness. This is not so easy as the plausible plainness of the theory might lead one to suppose. I have a single sensation. Let it be the puncture of a sharp instrument in that part of the material sensorium that lies nearest to the spiritual. It is hard telling what I perceive in that, except a change in my being. There is being and not being—there is *is* and *was*. I can hardly think of anything else I could predicate of it, or any other idea in my mind which it wakes up, and which I bring as a lamp to its cogniture. Again—I have a second sensation. It is like the first. So far as sense is concerned, it can give me nothing different from the first in kind, but only in quantity. There is something, however, something different in kind, which was not in the first. Not one, or two only, but a host of ideas now start up, not one of which can be said to be in that second sensation, any more than in the first; for, as sensations, they differed not at all, or only in quantity. But here a wide spiritual space (we cannot talk here without a metaphor), is illumined by the flash within which this outside spark hath lit up in my mental consciousness. Here there is not only being and not being, but there is time, there is movement; there is unity, duality, and, from them, plurality; there is, virtually, the whole infinite world of number; there is presentness and pastness, and a glimpse of futurity; there is difference and identity; there is quality; there is quantity, moreover, not in the sensation merely, but as an idea of the mind. Should any one say that all this comes from memory and comparison, through a connecting of the former sensation with the present; true, we answer, but how does that solve the mystery of memory and judgment themselves? How is memory conceivable without the previous idea of time? how can there be comparison without number and ratio? how can there be measure or measurement without a rule? Again, the first sensation, it may be asserted, remains in the sensorium, and this, connected with the second, gives birth to the new knowledge that is not in either singly. To this we say, the first, if it remains at all, can only remain simply as it was, so *much* felt force, so much quantity; and this, added to the second, can only make so much additional quantity. It can add a *more or less* to the old sensation, or the two together may make a sum total of more or less *motion* in the material sensorium, and of more or less *feeling* in the spiritual sensorium, but whence the new knowledge?

To go back again. I feel a single puncture of sensation. There is no extension in it. A second comes, but it cannot give it. The two are put together. They are only felt as additional quantity. Unless the soul brings to it the idea of space, there cannot be distance here, any more than memory in the other case of successive sentiencies. There can be no felt distance of one from the other, unless it be in the sensorium, that is, the spiritual sensorium, and there it can only exist as a knowledge, a spiritual idea; for if we make a space distance in the soul, spiritually felt as such, we thereby give soul itself extension, and plunge immediately into a returnless sea of materialism. It can only come there as represented, and that can only be by something which can dwell on either side of the line, some quantity of force or number which can be predicated of spirit as well as of matter. It is in this way, and, as thus represented, through some unknown process, that the quantity or *intensity* in the sense (and in what avenue of sense makes no difference) is built up by us, or builds itself up, into this seminal idea of extension, and the immediately related ideas of outward space, form, or figure.

Sir William Hamilton has somewhere, if we are not mistaken, refuted Aristotle's doctrine of "occult qualities", as they were called ; that is, the supposition that there might be different *qualities* in bodies whose *quantities*, and quantitative arrangements, were precisely alike. With all his great learning, of which, as we cannot help thinking, he often makes an unnecessary show, he has fallen in his distinction of primary and secondary qualities, as applied to sensation, into precisely the same error.

This doctrine of Sir William Hamilton, as Dr. Hall cites him, of soul "*touching*" matter, or "coming face to face with outward objects having extension and solidity", becomes very easy on one theory, which, although it has a terrible mystery at the entrance, is all the plainest of sailing ever after. Matter thinking is a thing unthinkable to the true spiritualist, but only get over this, and psychology becomes the smoothest of the sciences, the most "exact of the sciences". So it was to Comte as an avowed materialist. With him matter is the only thing in the universe. Matter is not simply thought about; it thinks, and so the thinking and the thing thought about become identical. One is just as long, and as wide, and as deep as the other. This clears up, at once, a host of difficulties. The chasms are all bridged, or, rather, they are all filled up, and "touch" and "muscular sense of resistance" go right over. This language of Dr. Hall and Sir William Hamilton, this talk of soul "touching" matter, and "standing face to face" with matter, and thus taking an impression of its primary qualities of extension, etc., right from the matter itself, and being "directly conscious of things themselves", becomes as simple as geography ; psychology is as easy as the study of a town map, or the brain lots of phrenology. To get over the awful chasm from extension, and touch, and space, and motion, to that which has no place, and no touch, and no extension, and no motion, that is hard indeed; but only concede that matter thinks, and all trouble vanishes. That which thinks, and that which is thought, are one. The soul is matter, and matter thinks itself. Being extension, it thinks extension; being figure, it thinks figure; being touch, it can "stand face to face with solidity" and all outwardness. It is directly "conscious of the things themselves", for it is *the things themselves*, and, therefore, its consciousness of matter is self-consciousness. The old Democritic, Epicurean, and Lucretian dogma of "like feeling like", ὅμοιον τῷ ὁμοίῳ—carries us over at once. This explains all; but it makes the converse equally true, and therefore we say, unhesitatingly, that this Hamiltonian dogma of soul-contact, and "muscular resistance", and the soul, through it, "standing face to face with outward objects having extension and solidity",—this must be given up, or the doctrine of Comte and Hobbes must come in to make it intelligible. At all events, its advocates must be a little more modest in claiming it to be the peculiarly religious doctrine, and in branding those who hold that the soul has a knowledge of its own, and ideas of its own, as running into pantheism and impiety.

But this suspicion of materialism, or a tendency to materialism, they indignantly repel. They can talk *à priori* too, sometimes, notwithstanding the "flowing horse", and the very fresh joke of "the Hibernian, who began to build houses at the top". *A priori*, after all, is respectable, and with all their attempts to jest about it, they get an inkling, sometimes, that what is absurd to the sense, may be the highest truth in another sphere. There is a knowledge which builds from above, whether the Hibernian can comprehend it or not. "Sense can give nothing but objects of sense." This admission sounds very well indeed. But then, to make it worth anything, it should be remembered that the only pure objects of sense are intensities of sensation. All else in thought must come from another sphere; it must be "a building down". Again, hear how well men, whose vernacular is the speech of

Ashdod, can talk the Jews language: "It is reason that rises to necessary principles and truths, and that discerns in objects of sense more than sense reveals". This is an improvement. But really what is meant by these fine words? Either there is no thought in them, or they furnish an entrance large enough for the whole Rational Psychology to come in. Let us interrogate them. "Discerns in sense more than sense reveals." Where does it get this *more*? Has the soul always had it, or has there been a special revelation made to it for that purpose? They are no Sadducees; they believe in spirit; but it is a blank spirituality, rising by hardly a perceptible grade above Comte's panhylism, or pansomatism. For that which has only a *power* of thinking what matter or experience gives it, is barely distinguishable from matter thinking matter. A reason, too, they would have; but what is this but a blank reason, determined by no knowledge of its own, conditioned by no ideas? There is, indeed, some demand for these words. Naked materialism, beside having a very unorthodox look, is, at present, philosophically vulgar. Such brave men as Comte, to be sure, care nothing about its vulgarity; they have no spiritualism to take care of. But their orthodox colaborers have not nerve enough for that; they, too, would talk a little transcendentalism now and then; or to do them more justice, they have too much sincere religion, too much of the spirit of the Bible, to carry it out. They have, it is true, left the old philosophy of the Church, but its spirit and its Scriptures hold them back from the perilous places where Comte and Hobbes walk so fearlessly. Along with this there is another feeling, perhaps, which is not so spiritual. *A priori*, and reason, and Rational Psychology, are, after all, very respectable things. Ideas are bugbears, they are τερατώδεις, as Aristotle called them long ago; their old, bright Platonic stamp has been sadly marred by modern usage, yet still "*ideas*" can never be vulgar; they can never lose their look of intelligence, or cease to belong to the choice language of philosophy. The worst radicals in our land are now claiming to themselves that respectable word, conservative, and doing immense mischief under it. It is not this exactly, but something like it, which unconsciously draws men of the hard-matter school, or the believers in soul-contact and "immediate sense consciousness of things themselves", to use, now and then, a little of the *à priori* dialect.

A blank spiritual power, whether we call it a faculty or a reason,—a blank soul activity, undetermined by ideas, unconditioned by any innate knowledge, we say again, rises by a hardly perceptible grade above thinking matter. Such a soul, or spiritual entity, having nothing *à priori* to determine it to know one thing more than another, or to think one thing more than another, or to believe one thing more than another, can only be a recipient of what the world of sense and matter is pouring into it, without any power to modify or to add. It is simply δεκτικόν τι, a "capacity", a thing that holds—measuring nothing, *qualifying* nothing, but ever itself measured by the quantities of sensation it contains. Should any say that this blank power is determined by truth, as the mighty locomotive is determined by the rail, the short answer immediately rises, truth has no being separate from mind; it cannot be conceived except as thought and knowledge. It dwells in soul, even as matter dwells in space. The one is ἐν νῷ, even as the other is ἐν τόπῳ. It dwells in the eternal mind. It is absolute because the Eternal Soul is absolute. It is seen by men, however dimly, because men are made in the image of God—we may startle Dr. Hall here again, but we cannot help it—because men were made in the image of God, and through that image have a vision of the divine, the absolute, and the immortal ideas. Truth can only determine in so far as the soul carries with it a knowledge, or something else, that corresponds to the truth itself. It is the "*self-determination*" of the soul to truth. The famous phrase has far more application to that spiritual activity we call the intelligence, or the reason, than it has to the *motive* determined and motive determining will.

We have said that consciousness could only be of that which is in the soul. And most solemn is the declaration; for if it can cross this barrier, then, as we have proved before, there is no limit short of the outermost bound of nature. On this side is the material sensorium. How far it extends we cannot say. Some parts of the body have barely an organic connection of vegetable growth. In regard, however, to continuance of motion and physical effect, there is no severance of such continuance between the body and all outward nature. That motion which terminates, on the one hand, in the sensation of which I am conscious after it has passed the last matter of the material and entered the spiritual sensorium,— that same motion, on the other hand, and in the other direction, has no break until it dies away in the last matter of the material universe. Once let consciousness pass this line between the spiritual and the material, and we pass it without any calculable limit in time and space. We have pan-psychism, *all-soulism;* we are lost in a world-consciousness,—a heresy which has as bad a look, and is equally dangerous, if not rather identical with that pantheism of which Dr. Hall seems so much afraid. The holy boundary is broken, the sacred precinct is invaded, the separate human personality is gone. But we have already dwelt on this. Dr. Hall might, perhaps, call it a play upon the word consciousness. By being conscious of an external object, there is meant, he might say, the knowing an external object through consciousness, or by means of consciousness — that is, a consciousness of its representative. But that, if it means anything, means a knowing it by a *reasoning* from consciousness. This, to be sure, is a very different thing from a direct consciousness of it. But if he thinks the difference small, what is all his clamor about? What mean these persevering attempts to excite the unthinking theological odium against men as orthodox, as pious, and as humble as himself? Why this outcry of pantheism, atheism, and every other horrible ism that he maintains must come from saying that we are not conscious of external things themselves, but of the impressions or sensations that from any outward cause or object are produced in our spiritual region ?

But Dr. Hickok has tried to prove an external world. The heresy consists in the assumption that this needed proof, or was not as plain as "muscular resistance" could make it. Surely Dr. Hall's own quotation, from Edwards, ought to have shown him that there was some little difficulty here. Edwards was not a man who loved absurdity *per se*, or adopted opinions which "a moment's reflection" would show to be false. Neither was Edwards heretical, or a teacher of dangerous dogmas, because, as Dr. Hall intimates, he could not see the tendency of his own reasoning. There was as much light in old Northampton, as there is now in the chair of theology at Auburn. Neither do we think that there is anything in the latter position which enables its holder to look clear over Edwards, as from some high plain, and tell us, so confidently, how he came by his notions of "*being*" and "*becoming*", and of the comparative unreality of matter in its relation to a higher and more real world of truth and ideas, where all things *stand* and nothing *flows*. Edwards, he says, got this notion from Sir Isaac Newton, and Newton was befogged by holding this dogma which had come down to him through the Church and the Schoolmen, that in perception we are conscious only of our own sensations.

Again,—all that Newton could see in matter, or, rather, think in matter, was that " God, by his power, renders a certain portion of space impenetrable to another portion of space rendered likewise impenetrable"; a doctrine which very much resembles Dr. Hickok's space-filling force, at least so far as the pantheistic heresy is concerned. Edwards, too, although he is allowed to have a little more acuteness than Newton, and to have had a glimpse of what was coming, is at last brought to a stand in a similar wild absurdity. Finally, Dr. Hall, from his higher place, has a clairvoyant vision. He sees these benighted men struggling with their own absurdities, until at last, along with Berkeley and Kant, they are all " swept by the same resistless tide to the shores of a dreary pantheism". Appalling catastrophe! "And now Dr. Hickok", says the reviewer, "assumes the same principle". Unwarned by all this "resistless drifting", which had made such a sad wreck of Newton and Edwards, he still "holds that the phenomena of the sense are all thoroughly subjective". A man so incorrigible as this can expect no mercy, and so our clairvoyant proceeds to show "that in Dr. Hickok's hands also, this principle still yields its necessary results of pantheism". Ever more this same horrid pantheism, how it haunts the seer's terrified imagination !

But let us go back to Newton, and see what is the real absurdity and real danger of his position. As far as the pantheism is concerned, it is the same with that of Dr. Hickok. Newton had a difficulty about matter. In this respect he differs from Dr. Hall, who regards it as the simplest and plainest thing in the universe. It puzzled him, this hard thing, which is something aside from force and resistance, this dead thing, in which force and resistance inhere. Perhaps it was owing to some idiosyncratic defect in this great man's thinking ; but all that he could see in matter, and all that he could say about matter, was this, that " God, by his power, renders a certain portion of space impenetrable to another portion of space rendered likewise impenetrable ". Thus far the sentence given is a true representation of Newton's view, but Dr. Hall, as usual, must put in something of his own, and thereby make nonsense of it. He adds immediately after Newton's statement, these words :. *both spaces continuing absolutely void as before.* Here he has a *void*, and not only a void, but an " absolute void ", foisted upon Newton, a man who, of all men among the moderns, " had a horror of a vacuum ", who contended that the universe was a plenum having no void, and this simply because he could not surrender that teaching of the *à priori* reason that nothing can act but *when* it is and *where* it is. A man who goes alone by a seeming experience, and who rejects an *à priori* reason, might believe that, but Newton could not. Hence he could not conceive of gravitation except as force pervading, or a real something at every point of cosmical space. It was not a power at two distant points with nothing between them — that is, the hard-matter-man's idea — but a continuity, a continuity of force. Force was something ; force was matter ; what we call gravity was its most primary state, as far as we know, and this was everywhere. This great man, in not being able to think matter at all, except as force or space impenetrability, must have lacked a mental power which Dr. Hall claims to possess in abundance. But may not a man differ from Newton? Certainly; but then he should do so very modestly, and not talk about a " moment's reflection " being sufficient to show the false and dangerous tendency of Newton's views, or declaim so volubly about being " swept down the tide of pantheism ", as though there had really been some new light cast upon this " matter " which Newton did not possess.

In putting these words, " *both spaces continuing absolutely void as before* ", into Newton's terse definition, Dr. Hall makes him not only contradict himself, but talk inconceivable nonsense. These two mutually impenetrable " spaces remaining an absolute void as before " ! That is, the impenetrability is nothing, the resistance is nothing, the force is nothing. They are all a show, a mighty show indeed, for all the powers of the universe might be there, the sumless strength of the strong Jehovah might be there, but if this *absolute* hard matter, which is something else, be not there, then there is an *absolute* void all the time. How fond Dr. Hall is, we cannot help remarking, of this word *absolute*, as applied to matter and voidness, when he would make an unmeaning jest of its holier sense: "The Absolute ", he says (p. 634), " the transcendental name for God"!

And this he would call the religious doctrine ! Never did the poor African seem more attached to his fetish, and more determined not to let it go, than Dr. Hall clings to this hard matter. If we let it go, we are all gone, he thinks. There is nothing left but names, ideas, laws. Ask him what is more real than an idea dwelling in the mind of God; what is stronger than the power of God which makes that idea to dwell as an abiding outward law in space ? He shakes his head. There is nothing there, he still insists, unless we have that inconceivable *something else*, which is over and above the idea, the law, and the force. We know of no one, since the days of Protagoras, who seems better entitled to Plato's most descriptive epithet, ἀντίτυπος ἀνήρ, a repelling, resistant, absolute, hard-matter man. Saint Paul seems to find the ground

of all religion in "the unseen" or unseeable; our reviewer
finds the deep root of reverence in his hard matter, all irreverence, all irreligion, in the least departure from this inconceivable conception, this idealess idea.

Now, we are not so much concerned, at present, to debate
this absolute hard-matter question *per se*, as to test its religious
or irreligious aspect, especially as that has been so prominently thrust into what ought to have remained, and might otherwise have remained, a purely speculative discussion.   Let us
try it, then, on this charge of irreverence, and see on which
side the imputation most clearly lies.   Newton supposed that
God, by his power, renders a certain portion of space impenetrable to another portion of space rendered likewise impenetrable.   Any one who chooses to say that Newton talked nonsense, may do so if he has the hardihood; but to the irreligion,
the dangerous tendency.   Newton supposed so and so.   Now
certainly the thing is conceivable.   It involves no contradiction of idea.   Not only can we imagine something very much
like it, on a smaller scale, but actually, to some extent, reduce
it to practice.   Let us just imagine magnets so arranged, that
the repellent power, stronger or weaker, is brought to bear on
certain points and lines, in an ordinary vacuum, so that the
space in which the resisting influence is exerted, may be said
to have bound and figure.   It is *a certain space*, and, under
such arrangements, iron particles cannot freely enter it; they
are repelled; to them it is impenetrable.   Is there anything
there, or is it an absolute void?   Some might talk of magnetic fluids, but that is a thing of which they know nothing;
it has not yet been proved, and fluid remains but a name for
unexplained phenomena.   Besides, it would not interfere with
our question of conceivability, which is all that we are, at
present, concerned about.   Within this space there is force,
there is resistance, there may be varying diversities of force
and resistance, such as those that give rise to the secondary
qualities of Sir William Hamilton.   Let the magnetic or elec-
trical repellences be conceived as affecting the human repellences of nerve or muscle, instead of points of iron, and there
may arise in that space colors, odors, sounds.   Yet still, says

2

the hard-matter man, it is an absolute void, there is nothing
there.

Now, if the conception can be thus indulged in regard to
supposed human arrangements of human wills, certainly may
it be entertained in respect to the power and will of God.
Will Dr. Hall say that God cannot, simply by the activity of
his will, so make a certain space affected, that he, Dr. Hall,
cannot enter it without being driven back? Such a denial
would surely look like " running on the thick bosses of the
Almighty's buckler ". Or, which is the same thing, will he
say that God cannot fill such space with such resisting power,
without at the same time putting there hard or soft matter
which is not such resisting power, but a distinct substance or
entity by itself?

Now, the perfect conceivability is the possibility; and this
being admitted, which it would be blasphemy to deny, let
us reverently suppose it actually accomplished. " It is spoken
and it is done; it is commanded and it immediately stands
fast ", resisting and impenetrable. Here are spaces filled with
power, excluding other spaces in like manner filled. These
spaces are transferable, or, which is the same thing, if the
other language be objected to, these resistances are transferred
from space to space, so that the space before impenetrable,
now ceases to be so, or in the same degree of intensity, and
another becomes such. This would fully answer all the phenomena of motion, and motive force, which have always been
found, under any theory, so difficult of definition. It would
present every conceivable aspect of matter as it can be felt
by the sense, perceived by the perception, imagined by the
conceiving faculty, or thought as an idea of the reason. All
the hard-matter men on earth may be challenged to point out
a single logical differentia. Such resistances thus occupying
spaces would have bound and figure; they would have relation to each other of more or less of distance. There might
thus arise worlds, and planets, and systems, and human
bodies — spirit, of course, remaining unaffected as on any
other view of matter. Along with these resistances and varying intensities of force, there might be a world of sentient

beings receiving affections from them ; of moral beings finding in them motives and reasons of action ; of rational beings
comprehending their sequences of cause and of effect ; of religious beings adoring the Great God, who, by the creative
energies of his "Word of *power*", had so manifested himself
to them in time and space. This manifestation might remain
just so long as the immanent divine power remained through
which such phenomena came, upheld as this power upheld
them, modified as it changed, and ceasing wholly when it
should be withdrawn.

Would it be a real world? No, says Dr. Hall ; it would be
all a cheat ; there would be no hard matter in it. These spaces,
though filled with resistances and impenetrabilities, according
to Newton's conception, or space-filling forces, to use some of
Dr. Hickok's language, would, after all, be absolutely void.
How so? Why so? Because Dr. Hall cannot conceive any
such thing, cannot think any such thing. These resistances
are, to him, resistances of nothing ; it is nothing resisting
nothing. But shall his difficulty of thinking be the limit of
all other men's thinking, as it is even made the limit of God's
power? Some of the Germans are charged with blasphemy,
because they would fit up a world by their thinking. Dr.
Hickok is charged in the same way, in spite of his protesta-
tion and his proof that his " profane attempt ", so-called, is
simply a humble effort, and we believe it a very devout as
well as able effort, to trace God's necessary thinking by the
intuitive reason which he has given to us. But here we have
a denial of reality to that which has every thinkable element
of reality, merely because Dr. Hall cannot conceive how it can
be, unless over and above, and under and below, and around
and besides all this, there is a something which he calls hard
matter, but which something, by itself, he, like all other men,
is utterly unable to think or define. We candidly think that
the German irreverence is far outdone in this.

We can form a clear idea of Newton's theory. We see how
a most real and substantial world could arise out of it. But
this something, which is wholly aside from force and resistance, is as utterly inconceivable as it is unthinkable. The

sense conception is ever slipping off; the reason cannot hold it, for it presents nothing—not even an ideal nothingness —to its grasp.

Ah! but the pantheism! This force you talk of is God's force, and so there is no matter aside from God. We are not careful to answer Dr. Hall in this matter. By the help of Scripture we cut the Gordian knot, and he can do no more. The Bible says: "In God we live and *are*". Our being is *in* his being. The same Scripture saith: "He dwelleth in light unapproachable". The Bible says: "God *is* all and *in* all". The same Scripture represents him as far off. "He is holy, most holy",—*separate* as the Hebrew word literally means, by himself, without contact or mixture with other things. He is far apart. "The heavens are not pure in his sight." We most reverently and literally believe both these representations. But as against this outcry of pantheism, it is enough to show that Dr. Hall no more escapes it, logically, than others. He is too good a theist to maintain that his matter, be it ever so hard, could remain one instant without the immanent power of God, and present will of God, pervading every part and particle,—that is, being *in*, and *through*, and inseparable from, and, therefore, both spatially and dynamically identical with, the whole and every part of every part. Take away, then, this divine power from the space where, and the time when, this hard matter is, and immediately there is nothing left. It would seem, therefore, like an axiom in the mathematics, that there could have been nothing there before beside that which is taken away, and that is divine, that is God. Here, then, is the pantheism all back again, unless we adopt the inconceivable supposition, that in the very moment of withdrawing the supporting and constituting force, God annihilates the hard matter as an extra work. But then this extra work, besides its want of all reason, brings us right up to the same difficulty again ; for it seems to imply, if there was a real need of it, that there was some kind of resistance to be resisted, still remaining; or, if not, that then the hard matter, which would otherwise be left, having now no force, no resistance, no hardness of any degree, nothing by which it could be felt by any sentiency, or thought by any reason, must be a very useless thing, if thing it could be called at all,—something which would never be missed, nor make any kind of difference in the universe, whether it was or was not.

We believe in creation, pure and simple, as well as Dr. Hall. "The things that are seen are temporal"; they all had a beginning in time. By the things that are seen, we mean all things that occupy space, and that are, or may be, sensible to any possible sentiency, or sense conception, in the universe. We think this is orthodox and scriptural. It saves the great truth, although we can hardly expect that our manner of stating it will be satisfactory to those of a radically different way of thinking. But let us try. Matter and form make up the universe. Of course we use form here in the scholastic or Aristotelian sense, not as the mere outside phantom, but as the εἶδος, the idea, law, or that which makes each thing what it *is*. Matter and form; matter is the thing, and the form is the form of it. That is one way of saying it, but it involves a contradiction for the reason. It is not a *thing* until it has a form, or, in other words, it is not a thing at all until it is a *thing formed*. That which is regarded as the matter, is only a thing so far as it has form, and then we must have another matter or mass to it, of which it is the form. "The bread is the form of the dough"—we quote the familiar illustration of a curious Arabic work, called the Book of the Pure Brethren*, — "The bread is the form of the dough, and the dough is the matter to it". Or to give his language more truly, "the bread is the quality of the dough, and the dough is *mass* or quantity to it. The dough, again, is the form of the meal, and the meal is the matter or quantity to it; the meal is the form of the grain, and the grain is the mass or matter to it"; and so on. In a similar manner "the garment is the form of

---

* Ach-wan-u-safa. A translation has been made in a work entitled, *Die Natur-anschauung und Naturphilosophie der Araber im zehnten Jahrhundert*. Dr. Fr. Dieterici. Berlin. 1861. The Arabic treatise is a strange mixture of the Aristotelian and Platonic philosophies, with many thoughts and illustrations peculiarly Oriental. It is No. 1011 of the second volume of Zenker's *Bibliotheca Orientalis*. Calcutta. 1846.

the cloth, the cloth the form of the yarn, the yarn the form of
the flax ", until, as in the other example, we come to what
the writer calls the element or elements, and still " this is the
form of the hyle (or ur-grund), and the hyle is mass to it".
But " this last thing, of course, is *form-less* ", or, if not, then
we have to march on to another last thing, which shall be
matter or mass to this form, and so on *ad infinitum*. It must
be sense-less and reason-less, that is, it cannot be taken by the
sense or by the reason, for if either could take it, it would become itself quality or idea. We should have to take another
turn on Proteus, and still another, to hold him fast, and then
we could not do it. This last thing, then, is " without form
and void ". It is no thing for the sense of any sentiency ; it
is no thing for the reason. To us, therefore, it is nulla res, not
a res—it is un-real—it is nothing. This is the inevitable consequence in that direction. It can have no place in our sense-
world, or in our thought-world, unless we adopt Dr. Hickok's
idea (for this purpose substantially that of Newton), that this
last thing is force, pure and simple, in which power and idea,
substance and form, matter and thing, become one and the
same thing ; so that if such first pure force could become perceptible to the sense of any possible sentient (which is very
conceivable), then the sense would *feel* exactly what the reason *thinks*. The thought and the sense would be one ; both
mutually realizing, and both being equally real. Here we
start, and then, in all the process above this, ever after, that
which is lowest for the reason, is matter or material to the
form which lies above, until we come to the highest forms, or
most real things in the universe. But all through the forms
are the real and realizing—that is, real-making things,—more
real each than all the forms below which serve as material to
each successive stage. To silence all cavil, it need only be
said that this pure force which before was not in space, God
causes to be in space, when, and where, and so much, and so
long as it pleases him—that is, solely " according to the counsel of his will ".

But it is contended that we *must* have a first something, a
prime matter, beyond all this, even though it be sense-less and

reason-less, formless and void.   We must have it whether or
no.   We must have it as a logical conception to stand upon.
We must think of it, so and so, if we can ; but alas, we cannot think of it at all.   We can no more get a thought here
than the clown whom the Aristophanic Socrates is forcing to
think "out of himself" "the abstracting idea".   We cannot think of it but by way of something that makes it form,
demanding another mass or matter, and there we are.   Our
ur-grund is no ur-grund at all.   Proteus is back again.

Hamilton and his school deny that we can have any idea of
the Infinite and the Absolute.   Matter is the thing for us in
our human sphere.   That is something we can understand.
Hard matter is Dr. Hall's fulcrum ; it is his ποῦ στῶ whence to
begin a world making.   What can be more simple than such
a principium ?   But try and think it then, and see how we
must ever fall back upon forms and ideas, even the ideas of the
Infinite and the Absolute, for relief.   And so it is found that
the utterly unthinkable is actually at the other end of the
scale.   The infinite is doubtless very high, though we would
still maintain that the human soul has a God-given idea of it ;
but this hard matter is unthinkable, from its falling utterly
below our thought.

But, after all, what is the religious worth of this thing, be
it what it may, which is nothing for the sense and the reason ?
If it is unthinkable, why think we at all about it ?   Why
make we such ado, and call everybody pantheist or atheist,
who in the least questions its moral or intellectual value ?
Let us go to the Scripture.   As we read the Bible we find the
very reverse of this modern philosophising.   Not the first
matter, be it what it may, but the building the Heavens and
the Earth, the firmaments, the spheres, the seas, the lands, the
trees seeding seed each after its kind, the living things each
after its idea,—in other words, the giving their forms to things
as they so sublimely rise in the order of reality,—this is the
work, the great work of God the Κτιστής*, God the Architect,
the Former†, the Great Master-Builder.   That which this

---

* *Eph.* iii, 9 ; *Col.* i, 16 ; *Rev.* iv, 11—x, 16.

† The Hebrew יוֹצֵר, *The Former,* is one of the most frequent and significant of
the epithets applied to God as Creator.

modern speculation is so concerned about, the making the mass or masses out of nothing, is not mentioned at all in the sense it wants. The things that were not, of which the Prophet speaks, are the forms that were not. The new thing, בריאה, is the event or doing that had never before been manifested in time and space. The first matter, the hyle, formless, sense-less, reason-less, is not dwelt upon at all, unless it be meant by the Tohu and Bohu, which are the nearest Hebrew words to nothingness. This would be making God, Dr. Hall might say, a *mere* form-giver, a *mere* artist, but this is just what the Bible does, leaving out the diminutively qualifying adjective. Whether the old Hebrews, in reading their simple, yet majestic Scriptures, got the conception of a first matter or not, yet this is certain, that instead of being dwelt upon as though it were so religious, and such a shield against pantheism, it is thrown altogether into the background, never made prominent as Dr. Hall would have it. Be it force, then, be it hyle, be it matter, be it what it may, this first thing is the easiest for God; it is the lowest, least thought of, least mentioned thing in the Scriptural creation.

And so is it with the earliest Christian writers. They received the doctrine of a pure creation from a previous nonexistence both of mass and form. In what they say, however, of creation as a process or work, they differ strikingly from our modern schools. They dwell much more on the hypostatic Wisdom—the Word or Logos in nature. Hence their talk is more of *forms* and *ideas*, than of *causes* and *effects*. They made much of certain texts which are now hardly ever employed in such a way. The Scriptures, in a number of places, most explicitly teach that God made the worlds (τοὺς αἰῶνας) in and through the Son, the Logos; nay more, that "in Him all things consist" (συνέστηκε), stand together, have their present reality of being. (See *John* i, 3 ; *Col.* i, 15, 16, 17 ; *Heb.* i, 3—xi, 3 ; *Prov.* viii, 30*. To these remarkable passages

---

* The translation of the word אָמוֹן here, " *as one brought up with him* ", is all wrong. It means the *Architect*. So the Syriac word from the same radix. It is from the radical sense of the universal Shemitic root, אמן, which everywhere carries the sense of constructive firmness and security, as, to be secure, to make se-

we give but little meaning, because it is felt that, somehow, our philosophy is not in harmony. Hence we seldom use these texts, except in a polemical way against the Unitarians, in order to fix the rank of the Logos, not to assist our ideas of creation and the world's subsistence. We think of the Logos as an instrumental *cause*, or, at most, as a *causa efficiens*, yet still as a mere mechanical or force-working power, making things so and so. According to this earlier idea, the Logos creates all things by giving them *form*, he himself being Forma Dei, *Phil.* ii, 16, Εἰκὼν τοῦ Θεοῦ ἀοράτου, the Great " Form of the unseen God ", *Col.* i, 15.` He is " the Outshining ", the Χαρακτὴρ ὑποστάσεως, the " Express, or perfect image ", Figura substantiae ejus, *Heb.* i, 3. As being thus Μορφὴ Θεοῦ, Forma Dei, he is the great source of form, *or formal cause*, to things, which are thus made things, not through a force causality solely, but in and through the in-forming Word. This is Scripture doctrine, whether we fully comprehend it or not ; and in what perfect harmony is the Bible-teaching here ! This same Logos, *in* whom πάντα ἐκτίσθη, " all things were built or formed ", is " the light that lighteth every man " (*John* i, 9), that giveth form and idea to our souls. Thus *John* i, 9, in connection with *Col.* i, 5, and *Heb.* i, 3, is the interpretation of *Gen.* i, 27. From the Eternal Εἰκὼν Θεοῦ, the " express ", or perfect Image, comes the human image of God, imperfect, finite, faint, and far away, yet through which man sees the ideas or forms in nature, reads them (ἀναγιγνωσκει), knows them again, remembers them as the thoughts of God, given to him in this image. The Logos in nature and in man ; the early Christian theology made much of it, though held with but little science. It came from the Scriptures ; it made their philosophy, and was not made by it. It must be revived again if we would have

---

cure, to make " to stand " in distinction from the flowing, the chaotic, the void which has no form nor constitution. Hence אֱמֶן *faith*, Isaiah xxv, 1, and the common word for truth אֱמֶת *firmitas, perennitas, veritas*. It admirably corresponds to the description of the Logos, given elsewhere as the Former, he who gives form, idea, truth, that which gives a thing reality, or makes it something for the mind. The LXX render it ἁρμόζουσα—the Vulgate, *cuncta componens*, the Syriac, *me-tak-no*, the *artificer*. Compare κατηρτίσθαι, Heb. xi, 3.

science religious; it must again take its place in the Church
if we would have theology truly philosophical and scientific.

The dangerous pantheism is that which denies the divine
personality. But how is this done by the doctrine that matter is divine force made immanent in space, as Newton holds?
Have we not still a personal God with will, and wisdom, and
moral attributes? Have we not all that is necessary to religion? Have we not personal spirits, men, angels, devils?
Have we not moral government, law, justice, retribution, reward, love, holiness, prayer, providence, revelation? Have
we not a finite manifestation, and have we not reason by
which we can separate this finite manifestation from the Infinite Manifester and from the Infinite Manifested? There is
another kind of pantheism. It does not, like that charged
upon Dr. Hickok, "build down" *à priori* from the will, wisdom, and power of a personal God (making a world which is
the outworking, or manifestation in space and time of this will
and wisdom), but is a development, *à posteriori*, of feeling
and thinking matter, directly "conscious of matter", and rising up, through different stages of life, to the great development of a universal, impersonal soul of the world. This is
the really frightful pantheism; but whether the inductive or
Baconian thinking, as it is called, which derives all knowledge
from experience, be more favorable to this than the *à priori*
or rational psychology, is a question we cannot now discuss.
We would merely say that Church history, and a knowledge
of the tendencies exhibited by the most spiritual minds in the
Church, would go far to settle it. Were Augustine, Anselm,
Wickliffe, the martyr Huss, all spiritual realists, less holy,
heavenly minded, spiritually minded, than the nominalists of
the middle ages? Were Howe, and Leighton, and Edwards,
if we regard his own peculiar thinking more than that which
he derived from the schools of his day, less saintly, unearthly,
godly, than Locke, or Dugald Stewart, or even Sir William
Hamilton? We would be willing to rest the whole question
of tendency on the right answer to these inquiries.

The truth is, this whole difficulty of pantheism, transcending as it does every human effort to solve it, is, in this respect,

precisely similar to that other great analogous problem of evil. How shall we separate the power and being of God from the force and being of the world, without making the latter independent? How shall we separate the truth and goodness of God from the evil that is in the world, without making the evil absolute and eternal? We do not say that either problem can be solved; but this may be affirmed, and the history of these controversies in all ages shows it, that whoever, on either question, and on either side of it, chooses to take the safe position of assailant, can raise objections, and ask questions, which the other party will find it difficult to answer, if he can answer them at all. Let him choose his own stand-point, and he can almost always drive his antagonist to the wall. But then this antagonist, if he chooses, can turn right round, and by taking *his* stand-point, and putting *his* questions in *his* way, drive the other back to the wall again in like manner; and so on as long as they are mutually fond of such amusement. Dr. Hall believes in an ante-mundane state when God was all. Let us repeat to him the question given a little way back: Has God ceased to be all? Then the all is more than it was, or God has become less. In either case he is comparatively finite. Now, where would Dr. Hall stand in answer to such a perfectly clear mathematical statement? Why, with his back to the wall, crying, mystery, mystery, "O the depths", etc,—O vain and boasting reason, "strive for the faith once delivered to the saints", — "because lest any man spoil you through philosophy and vain deceit". If, then, the difficulty in his own view, so far as it has any consistent meaning, is just as great, to say the least, as that of the one whom he so causelessly assails, why does he get up such an uproar about pantheism, that there is hardly a paragraph in which this bugbear word does not stare you in the face, with all the changes rung upon it that the dialect of polemics could furnish? We would not wish to be uncharitable here; but if we may regard the known as the intended effect, it does look as though this frequent word had been selected, and these ringing epithets ranged around it for the purpose of exciting the unreasoning *odium theologicum* against one who, though deeply philosophical, is, perhaps, the least controversial, the least polemical, among all the thinkers and writers of our land.

We cannot follow Dr. Hall in all the places where he has been muddying the waters, but there is one question which he so utterly fails to comprehend, that we must ask the reader's indulgence when we attempt to put it in its true light.

What is reality, or if there are different degrees of it, what is the highest reality ?   We may take a production of human art, or we may take a work of nature, that is, of divine art.   In the first we have matter and idea,—that which is for the sense, and that which is for the mind or reason,— the one *felt*, the other *thought*. The matter may be changed, or changing, and yet the idea remain the same. The matter may all pass away, and other matter take its place, and yet it is the same *thing, res, reality*. Again—all the matter may remain in quantity, whilst through disorganization, the idea departs.   It is no longer the same *thing* that it was ; it ·is another thing. If all idea is gone, if there is nothing for the mind, nothing thinkable (unless we may regard mere quantity, without any thinkable quality, as the lowest form of an idea), then it is no longer a thing at all, no longer a *res* or reality. Without quality, or idea, it may be for the sense, but the mind sees in it nothing to think about, nothing by which to separate it from the general mass of the sense world, and make it a thing *by itself*.   In a work of human art, then, such as a chair, or a watch, or a structure of any kind, the idea is the reality.   It would be the *reason* of the thing subjectively, if it had a conscious soul ; it would be the reason objectively, if it had only an organic life.   Having neither of these, it is the idea of the mind that creates it, and this is its reality, that which makes it a thing, a thing for the mind.

Again — take a natural object, or work of divine art.   It differs from the other in this, that by the divine power, its idea is made an organic, reproducing, vital law, or life.   Let it be a tree.   Here, too, the matter is ever changing, more slowly, but just as truly as the water in the flowing river. The leaves and bark disappear, and are replaced at short intervals; the whole matter goes and other matter comes in at longer intervals, but it is the same tree, because it is the same life, the same idea, the same vitalized law. On the other hand, take this away, or change it, and though all the matter remain, it is no longer *the* thing. When reduced to formless quantity, without anything for the mind to think, it is no longer a thing at all. The idea and the life here are the same. It is a spiritual force working on outward material, gathering and building it up for its material manifestation.

In either case, the idea, whether as artistic, organic, or vital, is the *res* or reality, the real thing; for it is that which makes it what it *is*, — its οὐσία, essence, *is-ity*, or being, — the verb *IS*, as thus used, being something more than the bare logical copula, and having a real predicative force. It is what Aristotle* defines as the τὸ τί ἦν εἶναι, " the being what it *is* ", or the being something — that is, something for the mind, a reality — the thing itself. The true thought of reality, or what makes a thing, is so simple, that we overlook it on that very account.

With these preliminaries, we proceed to another very serious matter, though Dr. Hall treats it very lightly. He is so delighted with his " honest Hibernian ", and his " flowing horse ", and other facetiæ of a similar kind, that he does not seem to be aware how very solemn a question this is. It has been held by some great minds, and by very many devout, though unspeculating minds, that throughout the worlds of nature and matter, the thing of sense, or "that which is seen", is ever " becoming ", but never truly *is ;* whilst the " thing unseen " is *the* thing, the real thing, the reality. There has been much of speculation on this question ; there is room for argument on both sides ; but we doubt whether ever before it has seemed to any one a good subject for a jest. What is shadow, what is substance? From the days of Abraham, " who sought a city which had foundations ", it has ever been

---

* *Metaphysica* VI, 6 : Where there is discussed the question, πότερον ταὐτό ἐστιν ἢ ἕτερον τό τί ἦν εἶναι καὶ ἕκαστον, "whether this τὸ τί ἦν εἶναι, the constituting idea, and the individual mass (which it qualifies, that is, makes ποιόν τι) are the same thing. "

the inquiry, not more of serious philosophy than of true religion.   The peculiar language of the question has come down
to us from the early Greeks ; but in the East, as in the West,
by devout Buddhist, devout Mohammedan, and, most of all,
by devout Christian, has it been solemnly asked : " Do all
things *flow*, or do some things *stand* " ?   If anything can be
said to have come out of the pure common sense and common thinking of the human soul, it is this question   It arose
before schools were formed, before books were written, before
science was heard of, or philosophy had a name.   First as a
devout sentiment having great depth of thought and feeling
without precision or logical form, next as a scholastic or speculative theorem, did the human mind inquire : Is there a
fixed being in nature, aside from the ideas and laws of nature
which its flowing forces represent ?   This question affords
matter of merriment to Dr. Hall.   He cannot understand how
a sensible man can entertain it.   He has a very summary way
of dealing with all such transcendental nonsense.   To say that
" quality as educed from sensation " is the true reality by
which the " phenomenal being is particularized from all
others ", is with him too unmeaning and absurd for argument.
Such moonshine as that need only be answered by dashes, and
italicised exclamations, and imitations of slow oracular utterance — (*sic*) : " *The sensation — becomes — quality !* quality of
an outer material thing.   What mystic muttering of robed
priest ; what hocus pocus of a conjurer ever wrought a more
marvellous transformation ! "   To say, again, that material
things are " becoming ", or that " the realities are above the
world of sense for evermore ", is a mystical raving still more
unworthy of a sober man's notice.   If any reply is needed, Dr.
Hall has one that is conclusive : " Where, then, did he find
his Bible ?   If he believes it as he interprets it, then he believes there is no Bible ".   It is only a phenomenal Bible, a
book becoming.   There, answer me that.   Surely such a reply must be an extinguisher.

" Do all things *flow*, or do some things *stand* " ?   From the
way he treats this question, it would almost seem as though
the reviewer regarded its very peculiar and somewhat strange

phraseology, as coming from Dr. Hickok. He may have thought that it was one of those " affectations of style ", with which some of his critics have charged him. That word " flow " is so very comical, that, like some of the catch-words that Dickens puts into the mouth of certain of his characters, he never can cease repeating it. He will find, however, that some of the first cotemporaries of this very odd question had their jokes, too, about its quaint diction, and still more singular thought, as it appeared to their hard materialism. They were fond of telling the story of old Cratylus*, who " heraclitized " to such an extent, they said, that finally he determined to say nothing at all, but, to every question, only moved his finger. Things were changing in the very moment of utterance, and, therefore, as a man could not speak without telling a lie, or the thing that was not, he had better hold his tongue altogether. It was this same "honest Hibernian" who found fault with his master, Heraclitus, for saying that a man could not twice jump the same stream. Not even once, said he, for it is a different stream before he gets over. The case differs from that of Dr. Hall, in the fact that there was some real Attic salt in these old repartees. It should be borne in mind, too, that these men, who are thus ridiculed, were not the idealists, but the downright atheists, materialists, and nominalists of their day. The Eleatic followers of Parmenides, on the other hand, reasoned from this imperfect, *never-abiding*, being of nature, to the necessity of something immovable, only to be found in a world of *à priori* truth and eternal ideas. The disciples of Heraclitus believed in the flowing,—all thinking men did,— for though atheists they were no jesters, but earnest inquirers after truth, — deeply thoughtful as an atheist may well be,— but they could not believe in anything *à priori*, or that anything stands, and so they were very melancholy men. Their awful position made them serious. They had a solemnity, these old Ionic atheists, which would not be out of place in some of the Synods, Conventions, or General Assemblies, of

* There is a very full and interesting account of these odd matters, given by Aristotle in his *Metaphysica*, lib. iii, ch. 5.

modern polemics. Heraclitus, their master, was called the
weeping philosopher. He could never smile at his own ghast-
ly theory of a God-less, idea-less world. It may be said, too,
that though materialists, they were not *hard-matter*-men like
Dr. Hall.   Matter, with them, was *all ;* but it was in an everlasting flow ; there was nothing about it which " *stood* ", nothing that was hard, and solid, and substantial, in the sense of
immovable, nothing that was not continually changing and
" becoming ", as much so in fact, — however differing in appearance or rate of movement — as the " water spilled upon
the ground which cannot be gathered up again ", or the disappearing smoke to which the Hebrew prophet compares the
ever dissolving Earth and Heavens.   This was their view of
matter and nature, the true view, as it came out of the far-
reaching thought of the ancient mind ; the view, too, to which
modern science, by its slow yet sure induction, is steadily advancing.   Thus, thinking of matter, it may be said that so far
they were prepared to be spiritualists. They must have wished
to believe in something that did not flow, and that, therefore,
stood above this flowing world.*   But they stumbled at *ideas*,

---

* We see here the difference between the Platonic or Eleatic and the Hebrew aspect of the great thought.   With the Greek it had more of the intellectual ; with the
Jew more of the moral idealism.   " Matter *flows*, but ideas *stand* ", said the one.
" Heaven and Earth dissolve, but God's righteousness standeth fast forever ", is the
rapt language of the other.   See *Isaiah* li, 6 : " *Lift up to the Heavens your eyes,
and look upon the Earth below ; for the Heavens, like vapor, are melting away, and
the Earth is wasting like a garment, but my salvation is forever, and my righteousness faileth not* ".   Some might think such a citation of Scripture extravagant, except as made by way of figurative accommodation.   It is doubtless true that each
man's habit of thought affects very much the ideas he gets from the Bible.   But
may not this be one of the designs in the peculiar construction of this most *suggestive* book ?   The language here is certainly highly suggestive of the Eleatic
thought and diction.   When we speak of different aspects of a passage, we mean
not a double sense, or a mystical sense, or a philosophical sense, but the same essential thought expanding in different degrees for different minds, as it rises up toward that thought of the infinite Author, which is ineffable for all finite minds.   We
believe that the rudiments of this old world conception of nature's ceaseless flow
were in the Prophet's mind.   It lay not there philosophically formed.   He had it
as belonging to the common thoughtful mind of all ages.   The style of expression
is not far from that of the Greek thought, even as the Prophet himself was not far
from being the cotemporary of some who were most fond of uttering it.   There

that τέρας, τερατῶδες, or bugbear, as Aristotle calls it. They could not *see* how these could be truly *res*, realities, or "*real things*", to use our modern tautological language, and so they rejected theism. They were too consistent to believe in a lonely "god of forces", without a world of eternal *immovable* ideas, in which he dwells for evermore. They already had an eternal, physical power, and as long, therefore, as they rejected the Eleatic ideal world, they did not, as consistent men, care much whether this was called a deity or not. In the same way Aristotle, in rejecting the Platonic ideas, could only believe in an impersonal God.

This old-world thought had its birth in a time to which the historical memory runneth not. But whether born on the Ganges, or the Nile, or in the mountains of Palestine, or first brought by Noah's grandson Javan to the shores of the Ægean, it has come down to our time, and still haunts the souls of men. No jesting will ever drive out this mode of thinking, and this talk of the "being and the becoming". There are minds that can find no religion, no higher world, no immortality of the human soul, if they once let go this very

---

was, too, the same mode of thinking and speaking in the early East, as we learn, not only from the writings of their Sages, but from peculiar expressions in language that must have been of ancient formation. Thus one of the old Arabic names for the flowing world, was עָאגֵל literally "*the hastening*", the *quick-going—mundus caducus—see Koran* xvii, 19—very much the same with the Hebrew חֶלֶד *die schnell entschlüpfende* (*Gesenius*), the *gliding, slipping world. Ps.* xvii, 14—xlix, 2.

The resemblance in expression is seen especially in the verb נִמְלָחוּ, a denominative verb from the noun for salt — literally, "shall dissolve" like the flowing salt. The Prophet had never seen the vivid picture of this process under the immense magnifying power of the solar microscope, where the *melting* crystals *seem* like the flowing down of granite mountains, but he could conceive it in his mind, and there was that in all nature around which would suggest the conception. So the *Vulgate—coeli sicut fumus liquescent.*

The same conception is expressed in nearly the same language, *Ps.* cii, 27 : "*They are flowing, but thou abidest*". We must give יאבדו here this sense to make it parallel with תעמד, "but thou shalt *stand*, or standest—*tu autem permancs*, "thou abidest *through*"—that is, through all cosmical change.

In both passages the evident pictorial design of the language requires that all the Hebrew verbs should be rendered in the present tense. It is not prediction strictly, but that which is now, and constantly going on. The *flowing*, and the *abiding*, or *standing*, are coëxistent.

old distinction. They trace in the Scriptures, too, much
which, if it does not philosophically or logically prove, does
at least make them often think about it. "The fashion of the
world", το σχῆμα τοῦ κοσμου τόυτου, its *outside**, all that falls
under the knowledge of sense, παράγει, "is passing off,"—passing away,—evermore passing away. It is the same thought.
We do not say that Paul uses it philosophically, although he
must have often heard this word σχῆμα thus employed in the
wrangling schools of Tarsus, whither Greek philosophy migrated after it had left Athens and Alexandria. He must
have known how they used it for the outside of things, in
other words, the material, for it was the greatest philosopher
among the Greeks who taught that matter, in its most remote
analysis, must be all outside, having strictly nothing interior, as
it had no real solidity. But we are not required to suppose any
such technicality in the Apostle. It was that deeper musing
of the soul, unscientific and unphilosophical, but out of which
all true philosophy is born. The full round thought of the
σχῆμα here, is not any particular fashion of the world, but the
world itself†, all that is matter of sense, the "things that are
seen" and touched, they are passing off, evermore passing
off, as a stream that floweth and standeth not, — no less is it
true in the hardest than in the most frail and transient phenomena: "*They* are flowing, but *Thou* abidest", *Ps.* cii, 27.

In this passage, and in the other from Isaiah, on which we
have dwelt in the note, there is the same musing state of soul,
whether we may call it sentiment or philosophy, which pre-

---

* The term "*outside*", is used here in the sense of that which hath ever something still interior, to which the material, even in its most recondite departments,
still stands as outside, surface, or outward vehiculum.

With the utmost respect for the translators of our English Bible, we cannot help
regarding "fashion" here as a very poor rendering. We do not refer merely to
its present frivolous sense ; but it could never, at any time, express σχῆμα, either
in its philosophical or its more general acceptation. It is still worse in that important passage, *Philip.* ii, 8—ἐν σχήματι ὡς ἄνθρωπος—" in fashion as a man". Rather
in nature, in organization, in all that is physical, or according to the flesh,—including here, however, even the human soul.

† As it is expressly said, *John* ii, 17 : ο κόσμος, "the world itself", παράγεται,
"is passing away".

sents itself to us in the teaching of these solemn old Greeks. This latter did not take so religious a form, but it was the same ideally. The two "worlds" in the Bible, and the two forms of "being" in the other, have, to say the least, a striking resemblance. Two forms of being, we say, not strictly, but by way of accommodation, on account of the poverty of our own and most modern languages. In the Greek, with its two well-defined substantive verbs* (as we defectively call them), there was no such amphibology. If that alone which abides for evermore — if that alone is being, or differs essentially from what is called being in other things, then we want some other word for that which is ever the flowing manifestation of the law and the idea which dwelt in the higher, — this lower thing never remaining for a moment the same, — never truly a *thing*, but ever a *doing*, an e-vent, a coming out, or " becoming ". If the one was *being*, this was well named thus, " a becoming ". If the one was truly ὄν, τὰ ὄντα, then the other was γιγνόμενον; and what was γιγνόμενον was, of course, ever ἀπολλύμενον, as the Psalmist says in one of the passages we have cited: " They perish ", that is, are continually perishing, " but thou abidest " — תעמד, literally, " *Thou standest* ". It is almost the very language of the Timæus (28 B), or Plato's famous distinction of the two great worlds or states of existence, — whatever we may think of the coïncidence.

All this, however, seems very funny to Dr. Hall. Let us see how he treats it. He says :

" The Natural Realist is not troubled with difficulties like these. If his senses give to him, for the moment, an outward horse, he will take him, and use him, not questioning whether he has a horse in a " flow ", created anew and different every moment, nor whether—supposing a real horse— sense never presents him as a horse in *being*, but only as " *becoming* " a horse—a horse *about to be*. If all this be so, a flowing man will use the flowing horse, for the flowing moment,—the horse for the moment created in a flowing creation. Questions about the being and the becoming — let those who meet them solve them."

* The writer hopes he may be pardoned here if he refers the reader to the *Platonic Theology, Dissertation* XXIV, entitled, "Philosophy of the Verb To Be, or the Verbs Εἰμὶ Γίγνομαι.

Doubtless he thinks that he has met this "famous" question, as he sneeringly calls it, of the "being and the becoming". We leave the above extract to the reader, without note or comment, except to remark briefly on the very happy state of mind in which the writer appears to be. He seems to give thanks that he is not like some other men. He is not in trouble as other men. He has no such difficulties as those bilious men of ancient or modern times, the μελαγχολικοί, as Aristotle styles them*. If his senses give him, for the moment, an outward horse, he will ride him without asking whether it is a horse in a flow. Contented man! We are reminded here again of "the elephant", and "the cane", and "Nichts", and all that. "Questions about the being and the becoming" he regards as very trifling matters; "let them who meet them solve them".

Dr. Hall doubtless thinks he is doing God service in this way, and he has an unquestionable right, if he regards a thing as ridiculous, to endeavor thus to represent and expose it. But if the question is intrinsically a most serious one, then the attempt at ridicule recoils on him who would thus employ such a double-edged weapon. The highest aim of religion is to draw men to the contemplation of true being; to get them, if possible, above the sense, the temporal, the flowing, into the unseen and eternal,—to lead them from the shadow to the substance. Now, a man directly thwarts this aim, whether he mean it or not, who rejects, much more who would ridicule, that in philosophy which constitutes, or even seems to constitute, a true religious ground for such distinction. He does this who asserts, whether understandingly or not, that "that which is for the present, just as truly IS as that which is for eternity".

Is this a true way of treating such a question, a question, it cannot be repeated too often, which has come, not from any mystic or transcendental affectation, but from the purest common sense, the purest and most unaffected and most religious thinking of the human soul in all ages?

---

* *Book of Problems, Sec.* **XXIX.**

It requires no science, no schooling, no philosophy, to form the thought that nature, and the world, and all things in them, are passing away,—not merely as a sentimental Sunday evening thought about some better land of Epicurean being, where man will enjoy more happiness than here, but as a truth sure as anything in the mathematics, that all things are flowing without intermission. Matter is a stream. There is no rest ; there can be no rest in the natural ; there nothing ever stands. It is a necessary law of the material, both now and forever ; it is the condition of its finite existence ; it must be ever flowing, from the most enduring, phenomenally, to the most frail of its manifestations. There is the moon-beam playing on the rippled waters. For a moment it occupies space. For a moment it has figure and color. There would seem to be something very like a *thing* there. It is matter, too, if light be a material undulation. It is, like all other matter, and neither more nor less than any other matter, a *doing*, a doing in space ; at least, take away the doing, and nothing else, either sensible, or conceivable, or thinkable, is left. And yet even this common thinking, if it be pure, is enough to make us certain that such a moon-beam figure, or even the still fainter image-speck that has its space and time among the fluids of the eye, and which is gone the moment we attempt to look at it—that these are no more flowing than the oak of a thousand years, or the hard boulder of the Alps, — no more or less *becoming* than the solid granite of the Andes, which has seemingly "*stood*" for ages. For even that has been all this time, and is now, a flux,—a slower stream to be sure than the tree, or the human body, or the river, or the moon-beam on the water, but none the less a stream—not a particle at rest—ever dissolving and flowing off like the salt crystals in the lens of the solar microscope. Could our vision of time be enlarged with our vision of space, we would see that neither mass, nor any part or particle of the mass, had been the same for even the smallest moment (if there are degrees in moments) of ever flowing time. It has been moving, changing (for all change is motion) continually, continuously, and throughout ; so that were our time-vision thus enlarged, we would see the

age-built Chimborazo as much a stream as any of the snow-
fed rivulets that flow down its rocky hills, as much a going
and coming *event* as the falling rain, or the flashing lightning,
or the rolling thunder, of which it seems to stand the everlasting witness. There is no rest in matter. It could be shown,
mathematically, that there can be no rest in matter, whether
organic and growing, or dead and decaying. They are not
standing things, but *doings* all of them, doings of invisible
powers. They are all *events*, from the floating mote to the
rolling world; as much *events* as the shower as distinguished
from the river, or the river as distinguished from the tree, or
the tree as distinguished from the mountain. And all things
that go to make up these larger *doings*, they, too, have the
same character. We do not call events *things* when plainly
conceived as events, that is, as having no standing reality.
And when it is shown that all that are called things are strictly motions, doings, or events, as much so as any that *come out*
in history or nature, then are we prepared to see that in this
world of matter the real things that *stand* are forces, ideas,
laws, producing these out-comings or events that meet the
human sense. These are the things immovable, the " unseen things from which are made ", in God's good time and
way, the " things that do appear ", — whether in the great
creation, or in the time-pulsations that have ever since been
coming out of that originating *act*.

These unseen things not only stand above our present world,
but they are ante-mundane. *Force*, too, was there, as well as
will and *wisdom*. Dr. Hickok would, perhaps, limit this word
to what he calls the " counteraction ", or the outward doing in
space, prefering the term *activity* to denote its ante-mundane
existence in God. But for our more general, or less precise
argument, we would rather say the *force* or *forces*, regarding
them as plural, and having diversity before the creation, as
well as the νοουμένα, or ideas; so that they together would be
the ". unseen things ",* from which, as the Apostle says, were

* *Heb.* xi, 3. The translation of the Syriac, Vulgate, and Philoxenian Syriac
which represents the most ancient Greek manuscripts, requires ἐκ μη instead of μη
ἐκ, which brings out the Vulgate rendering, *ut ex invisibilibus visibilia fierent.* The

made the βλεπόμενα, the φαινόμενα, or "things that are seen ". But Dr. Hall says (p. 636) : " Nothing is hazarded in affirming that Dr. Hickok has no conception of any possible meaning in what he affirms " about spiritual activity.   The ground of this rather hazardous assertion, as stated in the same paragraph (p. 636), is, that neither he, Dr. Hall, as he seems to confess, nor any other man, as he rather hazardously implies, can conceive of *spiritual activity*, except as thought or intelligence, and then he asks : " Is it the activity of intelligence or thought pressing *physically* against another similar activity "?   These (" thought and intelligence ") he regards as the " known properties or acts of spirit".   His meaning must be, that this activity or force, in its ante-mundane state, is not a real *potentia potens*, a power *in esse*, but only a *possibilitas*, a power *in posse*, which may, indeed, be predicated of a finite being, but contradicts every thought we can have of that Being whose very " essence is energy " ἀρχὴ ἧς ἡ οὐσία ἐνέργεια ἔστιν, as Aristotle says, in perfect harmony with the Scriptures, which affirm that his very command is power (*Ps.* xxxiii, 9), not creative *of* power, for that would necessitate a prior power to create the power, and so on with a *retrogressus ad infinitum*, which is an infinite absurdity.   This is worse than pantheism.   Force has assumed the form of matter in creation ; but there is no more power in the universe, power *in esse*, than there was before " the morning stars first sang together " at the laying of earth's foundation stone.

Dr. Hall's difficulty is answered by a consideration even of the human spirit.   There is power there, power which God

common view, as given by Bloomfield, is that μὴ βλεπόμενα is equivalent to our phrase "*out of nothing*".   But there are very strong objections to this.   It seems well to us, but did not agree with ancient thinking.   It would be a strange phrase, any how, for absolute nihility, but its plural form would seem to be still more strongly against it.   τὰ μὴ ὄντα would be a mere negation, and may be allowed to be used for nothingness ; but the other, τὰ μὴ βλεπόμενα, " the things unseen ", has too much of descriptive specification.   The " unseen things are not *nothings* (if the word nothing can have a plural), since diversity, in its very essential idea, implies reality.   They are varied *generic* entities.   Such a thought, too, of nothingness is wholly at war with the high sense of τὰ μὴ βλεπόμενα, 2 *Cor.* iv, 15, and just above, *Heb.* xi, 1.

has given, an *active* spiritual energy, never *iners*, but ever *ef-ficiens*, outwardly or inwardly,—in short, a true *potentia potens* (though limited and finite), from His own infinite energy. It is true we apply the term power to the thought and the intelligence.   A strong mind, we say—" knowledge is power ", etc.   But that is only metaphorical.   There is a real *dynamical* strength in the spirit.   It as much, and as essentially, belongs to it, or is one of its "properties", as its thought or its intelligence.   The strength of Hercules was in the soul of Hercules before it was in his arms.   When a man lifts or propels a hundred pounds, it is ultimately by the soul he does it; and that, too, not simply by the soul, as determining will, using the outward means, but as *potens potentia*, or spiritually indwelling force, that is, a real spiritual thing.   It is counteracted by the immense divine force lying all around it.   The body, too, is not a means for producing, but truly a limitation to, the spiritual strength ; and that is the only reason why one man is stronger than another.   His healthier, stronger, organization is simply one that is less hindering, that is, gives a better outlet to the spiritual force within.   A man can even feel this,—let him try to will beyond his muscular strength, and he will feel the *vis obluctans* that is in the soul, even when every nerve and muscle are lying still.   And so in nature, as we have shown, the greatest power may be held in the most quiescent rest.

Let Dr. Hall, if it pleases him, make light of things that called out the deepest thoughts of Edwards or Newton.   Let him try to raise a laugh at " the flowing " and " the becoming ", but for the honor of humanity, and for the honor of Christianity, let him not style this contented hard-matter philosophy of his, and of his brother philosopher of the *Princeton Review*, the religious doctrine preëminently, whilst, at the same time, he talks of the irreligion of that view which finds some higher being than that of sense, some veritable ὄν, in distinction from the γιγνόμενον,—something, even in man, that *stands* in distinction from that which is ever flowing.

This is not merely speculative, but most practical doctrine. It has been loved by the most pious souls that have ever been nursed in the Church. The contrary view has ever tended to darkness and unbelief. Whatever truly *is*, *is* forever. Man has in him the Eternal ; therefore man *is*, and *is* forever. The world is but a manifestation,—a manifestation of the eternal, and, therefore, that which it manifests, and that alone, truly *is*. All the rest is ever passing off, and passing away, flowing, disappearing. "The things that are seen are temporal ; the things that are unseen are eternal." Πρόσκαιρα and αἰώνια, here, do not denote a present, and a future, however long, as parts of one duration, but two *opposite* states, as significant of two opposite natures or characters that belong to them. What does the Apostle mean by this ? Is his " *unseen* " here simply equivalent to *not seen*,—now out of sight? Is it simply an unseen heaven, because shut from the sense by intervening clouds or sky? Or does he mean things in their very kind and essence unseen,—now unseen—always unseen—or, to make use again of that expression at which Dr. Hall shows so much alarm, and asks, " Where, then, did he find his Bible?" — The things which alone are real, because they are " above the world of sense for evermore " ?

But still this is dangerous language, he thinks. It is the Platonic ideal world again, — at all events, looks very much like it. But what if it does? And what if there be much truth in it? What if the Bible teaches something very much resembling it, in distinction from the very modern notion of a six thousand years of hard matter, with an eternal blank of all but a lonely inconceivable divine Being, before and after it? Will it be any the less entitled to respect because the mighty mind of Plato once thought it, and the noblest souls in the Church have loved to lose themselves in its entrancing vision of reality?

Art. II.—DORNER ON THE SINLESS PERFECTION OF JESUS.

[THE following essay, by the distinguished author of the *History of the Doctrine of the Person of Christ*, was originally written for the *Revue Chrétienne*; published, with alterations and additions, in the *Jahrbücher für Deutsche Theologie*, and translated in the *British and Foreign Evangelical Review*, No. XLI. This translation is here reproduced, revised throughout.—H. B. S.]

IN discussing this subject, with a conscious though not always express reference to recent productions, we are aided by the fact that the words and narratives in the life of Jesus which bear reference to his moral character have, in point of credibility, well-nigh passed unchallenged; and we are therefore relieved from entering into preliminary questions of that nature. Apart from *à priori* grounds, the assaults on the sinlessness of Christ are in fact chiefly derived from passages of the New Testament itself, which even the opponents hold to be faithful and credible as to the moral bearing of Christ, and the impression it produced. But the following discussion will also be conducted under a further limitation. It will refrain from entering upon the question of the *possibility* of a sinless and yet true human life; and also from drawing inferences from the sinlessness of Jesus as to his origin and inner nature. We shall rather adhere strictly to this question, Whether we can hold, on good historical grounds, and with a good conscience, the *reality* of the sinless perfection of Jesus as an historical fact. We will only remark as to its possibility, that those who regard human nature as so good that they do not need to seek a Redeemer, are wont to fall into striking self-contradiction when they speak of the sinlessness of Jesus; for this, on the contrary, is doubted by them, because they hold that sin is a power which cannot be thoroughly overcome by any man in his own strength. Let a man deal in earnest with the latter experience, without playing false with conscience and its problems, and he will feel that the claims of Christianity deserve a hearing; and that just because sin is such an invincible power in us, Christ must have been sinless, in order to be able to cope with sin in us.   Were we, on the other hand, content with that power of evil over us as an inevitable destiny, it would amount to the assertion of an essential contradiction in our nature—a self-contradiction in the very idea of moral perfection, thus amounting to a dissolution of the idea itself, since it unconditionally demands the very thing which is absolutely denied by reason of its impotence in the face of what is physical.   Faith in unconditional rectitude and the unconditional goodness of moral good, implies that this is the only true reality, not to be withstood by any thing physical—not an empty, impotent *Thou shalt;* but the principle of all that truly is.[*]

I. The true humanity of Jesus in relation to his sinless perfection.

We approach every man with the assumption, which never fails, that however great the moral differences of various individuals, no one is free from sin.   This is not an experience of yesterday; to attain this presumption the high intellectual culture of a later age is not required.   It prevailed in the time of Christ, and was applied even to him.   There were not wanting some who, on this point, considered Jesus as, at best, different from others only in degree.   The Pharisees regarded him as a sinner, because he did not observe their Sabbath commandment; because he did not share their reverence for the temple; because he did not enjoin on his disciples the prescripts of purification, fasting, and much prayer, after their manner; because he did not place the claims of the external Jewish theocracy, and its independence, above that of the Roman

---

[*] Among recent writings on our subject, along with Ullman's classical work, *The Sinlessness of Jesus,* 6th ed. 1854, we may mention some writings in the English language, especially Young's, *The Christ of History;* Schaff's, *The Moral Character of Christ.*   Among French works on our subject, may be named, on the one side, Edm. de Pressensé, *Le Redempteur,* (*The Redeemer;*) on the other, the most acute hostile work, Pécaut, *Le Christ et la Conscience.*

state, whose coin they had accepted ; not to speak of his testimony that he was the Son of God.   They sought to persuade
themselves that they did God service in persecuting him.   In
like manner Judas Iscariot thought himself justified in taking
offence at the anointing of Jesus by the sister of Lazarus, and
called to interest himself in the supposed waste of what might
have been given to the poor.   To this is added his treachery,
whether it was that, before committing it, he cherished the
suspicion that Jesus wanted courage to proceed with the establishment of his Messianic kingdom, and therefore needed an
impulse by which he must be driven forward, if he was not to
fail ; or, whether he fancied that, in spite of his testimony regarding himself, he, Jesus, did not really have a divine call, as
he neglected all those appliances which, in the opinion of Judas, were needful for success.

On the other hand, his disciples, especially the eleven, spontaneously received and preserved that impression of a wonderful elevation and greatness in his person and moral character,
which even Judas Iscariot did not at first resist ; their souls
became more and more indissolubly attached to him, and more
and more filled with admiration of him, even to adoration.[*]
For they were imbued with the deepest conviction, which they
afterwards sealed with their blood, that every human standard
that could be applied to him was too narrow and too contracted.
They who enjoyed the most confidential intercourse with him,
who must have observed and known him most intimately, proclaimed to the world, that a sinless saint had arisen among
mankind ; that he is the Redeemer, the fulfilment of the law
and the prophets; and that to suffer and die for him is gain, and
only the grateful reciprocation of his love.   And this preaching of him founded the Church, gathered out a world of redeemed ones, and placed a boundary line as clear and manifest
as any event in general history between a perishing, lost world
and a world restored and becoming green again.

The eleven were not utterly inaccessible to the offence which
the Pharisees, Judas, and others took at Jesus ; for the power

[*] It is worthy of remark, that sinless holiness was not one of the features of the
then prevalent conception of the Messiah.

of moral traditions over what is good and pious, reaches to an immeasurable extent; especially if, as in Judea, they are mingled imperceptibly with national patriotism, and error has assumed an embodiment and organization, and found a system supporting itself on holy Scripture, and ruling life down to its minutest details. The more we weigh this, the higher must we rate that spiritual power, which must have influenced not only the understanding, but the conscience of him who raised his disciples high above these stumbling-blocks lying so near the national mind, and enabled them to found their souls' salvation upon him in opposition to the prevailing Judaism. If he was not pious and upright after the ideal of the Jews, there must have been something else to supply this want, something higher, the vision of an original holy purity and goodness, which attached their consciences to him, so that they were ready, in virtue of this impression, to allow themselves and their inherited moral and religious conceptions to be formed and remodelled by him, instead of seeking to measure and to judge him by them.

Even his enemies the Pharisees, however, betray their impression of an entirely original and wonderful grandeur. For though they may have regarded him as a sinner and despiser of the law, from the stand-point of their inherited moral and religious axioms, yet they could not stop short at this, and view him as an ordinary sinful man, or teacher of error. Rather, he appeared to them, in the very estrangement in which they had placed themselves towards him, so much like one who *had power* (Matt. 7 : 29 ; John 7 : 46), so wonderfully firm, strong, and great of his kind, that they were obliged to attribute to him a superhuman power of *evil*, after they had resolved not to concede to him a superhuman power of *good.*

The coat of mail, the scaffolding of those once powerful Jewish traditions about moral and religious things, has been rent asunder by Christianity. There are no longer any who share in those Jewish stumbling-blocks. On the contrary, it has become the triumphant general conviction that Jesus again evoked the real source of our original moral and religious consciousness from the rubbish of those dead forms and institutions. What were then stumbling-blocks to many, so that they only believed on him in spite of them, or were wholly baffled thereby, are now to us rather a sign how high he towered above his time in moral wisdom and virtue, a sign that has now become an argument to attract to him, and to awaken confidence. It may be that in a state of more advanced knowledge, those very stumbling-blocks or doubts (afterwards to be discussed), occasioned by other, perhaps heathen views, may have a similar effect; and that mankind may discern in just these points peculiar revelations of his moral grandeur and divine originality. At least, there will ever be the same alternative, to which suspicions against his moral purity and perfection must come, namely, that if he is a sinner at all, in spite of his testimony about himself, he surely cannot any longer be called preëminently *pious* and *pure ;* but there will remain only the dilemma which was presented to the Pharisees, when they reached the verge of the sin against the Holy Ghost, " singularly and marvellously superhuman either in evil or in good".

But, according to the Evangelists, whom we must hold to be worthy of belief *pro* and *contra* in this matter, if we would speak of it at all, does not Christ acknowledge himself to be on a perfect equality with mankind ? Does he not himself, by word and deed, as it were, repudiate for himself perfect goodness ?

Certainly his likeness to us in his ethical nature may not be abridged or curtailed. He was not merely in a physical and intellectual, but in an ethical, point of view, not absolutely complete from the first. He learned obedience. He proved and maintained his sympathy with us in its fullest power only after he was rejected by mankind. He grew in favor, not only with men, but with God. Growth points back to previous deficiency, or, what is the same thing, forwards to an absolute goal, to which the reality approaches only by degrees. Now, if deficiency in entire perfection were identical with sinfulness, then certainly all real humanity and sinfulness would be identical. But the ethical goal of perfection prescribes a gradual attainment, and excludes the finishing stroke from the beginning. Absolute normality consists well enough with the reality of progress. If the complacency of God rests on every stage of a normal progress, it surely may also be said that it rests upon it in a higher degree, the nearer it has come to the goal of perfection, because abnormal possibilities have been in the same degree overcome, and the condition of immutable confirmation, of the absolute union of ethical freedom and of the ethical necessity has already advanced so much nearer. This leads to a *second* thing which we must attribute to real humanity, the liability to temptation, the passing through conflicts and temptations.

Jesus says himself that he had been in πειρασμοῖς, not once only, in what we are accustomed to call *the temptation*, but also on other occasions, and subsequently (Luke 4 : 13 ; 22 : 28). Some, as Schleiermacher, in order to guard his sinlessness, seek to weaken the force of this, by admitting in him only conflicts with outward foes, but not internal temptations at all. Others see in this a proof that even Jesus did not continue free from sin. Both agree in this, that all internal conflict of man with the good involves an evil desire, though only in germ. Hence the petition in Gethsemane, " Father, if it be possible, let this cup pass from me", and the temptation in the wilderness, are either not historical facts, as Schleiermacher contends, or prove that even in Jesus there were stirrings of the germ of evil, though, as Menken and Irving maintain, it was always held in check, and never penetrated into the personal life which was to regenerate and transform our assumed sinful nature. This last view is so far correct, that Christ had a real moral task, not only external to himself, but in himself, which could not be solved at the beginning, if he was to be like us ; that his corporeal nature had not in and of itself spiritual impulses and discipline in subjection to the will of the spirit; that it had not by nature the same law of life with the spirit, but was first only, so to speak, loosely connected with the spirit, and its complete union with the spirit as a promptly ministering organ, consenting even to the self-sacrifice to which it was called, could only be the result of an ethical process ; that this union of the spirit with the psychical and bodily life was a real labor and might become a conflict. But the opinion is wrong, that this loose connection, which was gradually to attain perfect unity, or that the assumed bodily nature, as such, is evil in itself. That the bodily and physical nature of man shrinks from suffering and death, is not evil, but belongs to its (metaphysical) perfection. The opposition which natural inclination makes to suffering and death is perfectly innocent, and so very proper in its place, that a longing on the part of the sensitive human nature of Christ for suffering and death would rather have been unnatural, and would have deprived his self-sacrifice of its value. It would have converted it into a seeking of his own. Moreover, to this innocent conflict in Jesus were added traditions, hallowed by antiquity, and by the authority of his dearest associates, as well as by the Messianic anticipations of the whole people, above which he could not, from his birth, be exalted, but only by the severe toil of acquiring knowledge and fathoming the true will of God; and as these traditions and still more the temptations of the prince of this world might possibly have led him to flee from suffering, or to make a wrong use of that conflict, which was innocent in itself, but capable of leading to sin, we have grounds enough for discerning the necessity of a severe conflict prepared for him, while we have no warrant to infer sin from the fact of such a conflict; as, on the contrary, the cessation of this struggle would furnish a proof that the ethical process imposed on him had come to a dead lock.

It is true we have not, before his baptism, any trace of such conflicts and temptations. Though we may not question the severe internal discipline of Jesus up to the time of his baptism, his learning obedience towards his parents,* his silent

---

* His obedience to his parents is also expressly mentioned in the period after his twelfth year, Luke 2 : 51. The record of his first visit to a feast is by no means recorded as one of an act of disobedience, or of mistake on the part of the boy Jesus. Jesus knows nothing of the departure and anxiety of his parents about him; and, summary as the record is, it nevertheless shows that a child-like certainty possessed the mind of Jesus that he was not staying in the temple against the will of his parents, but that his pleasure in holy things would rejoice them, and that they would make no effort to tear him away from them until he had refreshed and satisfied himself. Only the unfounded assumption of an omniscience of the

perseverance, notwithstanding the sharp contrast between his higher self-consciousness, as it manifested itself after his twelfth year, and his lowly condition,* yet the harder struggles were spared for the last years of his life.   His earlier life of retirement bears, in comparison with this, as it seems to us, the character of an even, clear mirror, of an untroubled, quiet stream, in which was reflected man's approval of such a symmetrical youth, as well as the complacency of God, Luke 2 : 52.   It was no disorder in him, but the disorder and sin without him, which occasioned him the contests, temptations, sufferings, which filled his official life.   These later conflicts were only assigned him because he remained the pure One, had become morally harmonious in the midst of moral anarchy; but they were still inward and personal struggles;

boy Jesus, whereby he would have had knowledge of the pain of his mother, would make the matter difficult. Such, however, does not consist with his questioning the teachers.

* Forebodings of the conflicts, which the history of the temptation fully unfolds, may, under the above aspect, have occurred in the period before the baptism, when the divine seal and testimony of God's approbation was stamped on his former life. From his twelfth year he knew God to be in a special sense his Father ; and as the difference of his pure nature from that of other men could not escape him, so a wish to serve and help the world and his people would as certainly be excited in him, as his heart was full of love. Just as we cannot assume that he had a definite consciousness of his calling as Redeemer while still a boy and youth,† when his task was rather personally to be about his Father's business, and to be, both at home and in the temple, absorbed in divine things, so this, his calling, must certainly have dawned upon him before his baptism. On this occasion, however, he is said to have sought and found the divine seal to it, the Father's answer to the question awakened in the heart of the Son, regarding the work of his life. The superficial opinion of Strauss, Pécaut, and others, that this coming of Jesus to baptism proves his consciousness of sin, would then only be worthy of regard if the baptism of John, historically viewed, could be proved to have had the exclusive design of working repentance. But, according to the Gospels, it had the more comprehensive design to prepare for the dawn of the kingdom of God, and to invite men to the resolution, to which Jesus had also in his way dedicated himself, ver. 12, to subordinate and sacrifice everything to the kingdom of God. Thus Jesus apprehended his baptism, as he places it in closest connection with his submission to suffering, and with his sacrifice for the world, Luke 12 : 50; Mark 10 : 38, 39. Compare my article on the baptism of Jesus in Piper's *Evang. Kalendar*, 1860.

† Christ's own language, when a boy of twelve years (Luke 2 : 49), would seem to imply the very opposite.—ED. B. & F. E. R.

for he was to introduce the power of his harmony and his sufferings, in order to overcome the disharmony in the world.
He, the righteous one, must, as it were, in a way of suffering,
take upon himself disorder and disharmony, must live through
it, and taste it, in order to establish a power which is not only
harmonious in itself, but so potent in harmony as to take the
disharmony into itself, master .it, and transform it into harmony.

The impression that the labors and the conflicts of his *public*
life were not, in the ordinary sense, a moral conflict in Jesus
himself, but only external, because his ethical self-cultivation
had reached its goal at his baptism, has been constantly urged
from ancient times.   It is not in that case purity defending
itself against possible disharmony, and ever more and more
excluding that possibility ; but it is virtue seeking out external
disharmonies, and rectifying them by its own harmony, which
forms the character of his public life ; and to this work his entire organism, soul and body, must be devoted, in spite of the
natural and just resistance that health has to sickness, life to
death, purity to the touch of impurity.   To this promptness of
sacrifice the organism was to become accustomed, not that
Jesus might thus acquire purity and personal virtue, but that
he might approve his personal virtue in his high office by self-
sacrifice.

It is an inadequate view to make this manifestation of his
moral perfection something so different from the common duty
of all men, as is done on the theory that there was in him only
a divine fredom, bound to no law, in which also his humanity
participated.   He is, it is said, the free Son of God, whose
moral duty involved no such self-sacrifice.   He is Lord of the
law, and therefore did not need to fulfil it for himself.   Whatever moral arbitrariness appears in this phraseology is blame-
worthy.   Such a freedom from the law as would make him the
master of it, and which is said to be imparted by the *Com-
municatio idiomatum* to the humanity of Jesus, so that without detriment to the moral perfection he might have acted as
he pleased, simply according to his own choice, is a misconcep-

tion. Arbitrariness dwells not with God. Such a super-ethical elevation would rather be a falling below the ethical—because it belongs to the mere category of absolute omnipotence, nay, is subject to it; and the real humanity of Jesus, his identity of nature with us, would not be consistent with it. If he be the sinlessly Holy, he is certainly also the Free, and high above the level of the law, but only in such a way that law has become life and reality in him. He does not first become good and virtuous through his ministry, he but executes it in the power of his own virtue; yet his ministry, as is the case with every man in every normal work, is so thoroughly interwoven with his person, that he could only maintain himself in the position he assumed at his entrance on his mission by responding to his calling, and yielding to the new sacrifices which the will of God imposed upon him in it—sacrifices which, as above mentioned, touch the innermost constitution of his harmoniously-ordered personal character, imposing a certain inward experience of the disharmony without. But however unique and peculiar his mission, and however thoroughly free and devoted his love, so far forth as this, that we could have no legal claim to it, still it was not his at his mere discretion, if he were morally perfect, to be and to exercise such love. There was a higher moral necessity for him; without it he would not have been morally perfect; and however different the measure of his powers from that of others, he could satisfy that love which acted in him so divinely free and divinely wise only by placing all these powers entirely at its service—just the same as is also the case in our higher law of life.

Hence, because he was and remained genuinely human in his calling, however unique, we are not to conclude that he exhibited a different kind of morality from that which passes current among men; that he was elevated above the moral obligations of the family, the moral duty of obedience to authorities, and the moral right of property; that he could regard all these only as far as he pleased, and that he might violate general human duties in these respects in the interest of his higher calling, and in virtue of the greatness of his person.* In the moral domain the higher includes the lower, preserves and confirms it *in its place.* The opposite view would lead to

---

* My excellent friend, the late Professor Bonifas, of Montauban, whose early loss I bitterly lament for myself, and still more for science, especially in the French Church—for, after his fair first fruits, distinguished service was to be expected from him—said many beautiful things in his article in the *Espérance,* on Pécaut's writing, in which I perfectly concur. But when he explains some facts in the life of Jesus, on the supposition that the usual moral laws incumbent on us were not incumbent on him, this appears to me hazardous, and superfluous for the object in view. Hazardous, because then Christ would not have exhibited our human morality, and into it would have entered what christologically borders on Docetism, and morally borders on Antinomianism, and which would bring into question the universal, eternal, and absolute character of morality. The consequence would be the necessity of conceding a purely empirical or positivist origin to ordinary morals. But no such expedient is necessary. As to the objection that Jesus did injury to the Gadarenes, Matt. 8, it would be pertinent only in case he had either willed this injury or known it beforehand. There is no ground for the first supposition ; rather, it is certain enough that the casualty, which also by the way shut him out from the Gadarenes, happened without his will.† Certainly this issue of the affair would at once have occurred to any one, if we put the matter as is so often done : Jesus permitted the devils to go into the swine. But that is not the statement of the evangelists ; and if any one will not believe their narrative, they must not seek to derive argument from them against the sinlessness of Jesus. They record that the *demons* prayed him not to banish them back into the abyss, but to be permitted to go into the herd. Jesus does not *command* them to do that ; he only permits them, as he does not banish them, as they feared, into the abyss. Since he does not do this, they retain liberty, not immediately, it is true, but yet mediately to do damage to men. This liberty they use in such a manner, that they seek by means of it to damage the cause of Jesus. But we have no right to assert that it belonged to the official prescience of Jesus to prevent what they would do to the herd of swine, or that his power should ward off damage to property, which may come equally by storm, tempest, or pestilence. Compare Trench, Notes on the Miracles of our Lord, ed. 5, 1856, pp. 151– 180. The same thing holds good of the cursing of the fig-tree, in which it is not at all certain, that damage was really done by it, an unfruitful fig-tree being no better than barren wood. The action of Jesus, however, is no miracle of display, whose object was annihilation, but a symbolical action, the object of which was an awe-inspiring warning of the people and city of Jerusalem for their repentance unto life, a warning of impending judgment ; for Israel is the unfruitful fig-tree, which cumbers the ground, and which is cut down, because it does not improve, is rich only in leaves above others; that is, promising, pretentious, but disappointing hope (in the fig-tree, leaves certainly warrant us to look for fruit, because the fruit comes before the leaves). (Compare Luke 13 : 6–9 ; Trench, p. 439.)

† The language of Jesus, ὑπάγετε, is plainly a permissive imperative ; and it is more natural to regard the event, with Lisco, as an act of punitive discipline upon the Jewish proprietors driving a trade not in harmony with their Jewish religion.—ED. *B. & F. E. R.*

various species of moral goodness according to Roman Catholic doctrine, and would introduce inner contradictions and caprice into the moral world.   But we must emphasize *in its place.* God is the highest good ; without him or contrary to him, nothing may be loved or spared.*   Thus every thing depends

---

* When Jesus (John 2 : 4), with a severe word, directs his mother to the exercise of patience, and does not allow her to interfere with his calling (as he deals with Peter similarly, Matt 16 : 22), he gave her something which she needed, if she was to come to faith in him. He faithfully observed the duty of a son, even in his last words on the cross (John 19 : 2). But for Mary (as in a less degree for his brothers) it was, from obvious reasons, more difficult than for others to subordinate herself to him as her Redeemer, on whom she, as well as others, must believe. Hence love to her, which could not exist without truthfulness, could not otherwise evince itself than by the fact that he could concede nothing more to her than to others, when he was acting and speaking in his office. By placing her in the position becoming her, which she soon feels (John 2 : 5), he lightens and facilitates her faith as much as possible, and imparts a counterpoise to the customary intercourse of their lives. He honors her as his mother, but not at the expense of his Father, of his office, and of true love to her soul.—Things which in themselves do not possess moral necessity and utility, and belong only to conventional propriety, Jesus did not allow when he foresaw that there would grow out of them danger and violence to that salutary and decisive step in life which was just on the point of becoming ripe. Thus he addresses him who would first go bid farewell to those who were at home at his house, before he will follow him, " No man having put his hand to the plow, and looking back, is fit for the kingdom of God ". And to him who would leave him again, in order to bury his father, he said, on the one hand, that the dead body of his father would not lack burial, and that his presence was not required for the last honors to be paid to it ; and, on the other hand, he calls him away from this over-estimate of a service for the dead, which to Jesus himself is only a single symbol of the spiritual deadness of this man's life, to the divine fountain of life, to fellowship with God, to whom even the dead 'live (Luke 20 : 38), and who, little as he desires outward sacrifices and gifts from children at the expense of the necessity of parents (Matt. 15 : 4–6), will as little permit a filial love which places the soul in the background, but rather claims the heart of man, and infuses into it a still higher than natural love to parents. The hating of fathers and mothers (Luke 14 : 26) is manifestly to be understood *cum grano salis*, and cannot be taken in any other sense than the hating of our own life, demanded in the same place. Everywhere is zeal and conflict with natural affection demanded, when it idolatrously and self-contentedly interferes with the higher love ; but the self-denial and the struggle against such ungodly love which is here demanded is itself again only a condition of true life and of the resurrection of true love (Luke 17 : 23 ; Matt. 19 : 29 ; Luke 14 : 26).—With regard to the decisive step which Christ demands, namely, to seek first the kingdom of God, and leave all other goods behind, and to count as gain all loss in money, property, honor among men, the reference is, of course, to the period of Jesus' sojourn on earth, the outward disruption of previous employ-

on understanding what is truly, that is, divinely good ; not what
is conventionally moral, or that certain moral notions prevalent in a particular age or nation are, without examination, to
be made a rule by which to measure Jesus, instead of first
rectifying our own views of the moral, as we have seen above
in relation to the Pharisees. But a word about this below.

But does not Jesus himself say to the young man : " Why
callest thou me good ? No one is good save God alone."
(Matt. 19 : 16, and following verses.) Some have interpreted
this as a reproof to the youth for regarding him as a good
human master, instead of the Son of God. Certainly Jesus
did not mean to point him away from himself to God—to a
God who had nothing to do with the sending of Jesus—as if
the youth had no need of Jesus. It is true he does not say to
him, Thou hast not kept the commandments, as thou thinkest,
from youth up ; but tells him that he is not perfect, and invites
him to follow him, which would reveal to him still more. Nor
are the words of Jesus to be understood as implying that voluntary poverty would make him perfect, for the demand to renounce his goods is only the negative side of the summons to

ments and relationships being then a condition of following Jesus, such as is no
more the case. Jesus, in whom the kingdom of God was embraced, could only be
in one place at one time ; and, consequently, all who sought the kingdom of God
must also join his train, and break with old relationships. After his exaltation, the
gospel of the kingdom had more and more omnipresence—nay, it worked as a
leaven on earthly relationships. Hence, in order to draw near to Christ, it usually
requires only the separation of times for retirement and self-recollection, rather
than a change of place or calling. The exposition just given explains a series of
passages which on a superficial consideration have given offence, or which do not
seem to harmonize with pure moral conceptions, because many have found in them
the implication that the true following of Christ is inconsistent with the pursuit of
an ordinary calling, with riches, or the administration of property, or even with
entrance into the marriage relationship. (Compare Matt. 9 : 9, 5, 29, and following verses ; 6 : 25, and following verses ; 10 : 37–39 ; 12 : 48, and following
verses ; 16 : 24–26 ; 19 : 21 ; Luke 6 : 24 ; 16 : 1, 19 ; 18 : 23 ; 12 : 33.) Connected with this, it is also worthy of observation, that the first limitation of the
kingdom of God to local boundaries, just because it involved the necessity of separation from house and home to follow Christ, won for itself the means of over-
coming those limits by introducing numerous laborers into the mission service, and
thus procuring room and material for a second stage of the kingdom of God, the
systematic, ethical elevation of earthly relationships.

follow Jesus, which he would no longer need, if he had already kept the law from his youth up, or if he could have earned for himself a supererogatory perfection by his voluntary poverty. Verse 23 shows plainly that in the eyes of Jesus the youth was outside the kingdom of God, to which he was only approaching by the inquiries made of Jesus. Thus there is no doubt that the design of Jesus was to keep him near himself, not to send him away to God without Christ; and equally certain is it that he would have led him to the true knowledge of Jesus himself in due time. But the first thing needful for him, as Jesus perceived from his light and liberal use of the word " good", was self-knowledge, not the preaching of Christ's mission and dignity, for the comprehension of which the pre-requisites were still lacking; and upon these, according to the method which he evidently followed in other cases, Jesus was silent. The youth thought that he was done with the task of the law, and inquired after a new one, since the law gave, indeed, temporal promises, but not the promise of eternal life. To attain self-knowledge, he required to be awakened to a sense of God as holy, as alone good; to discern the difference or contrast between God and the world, which he, in relation to goodness, was disposed to place so near to God, that there would be no absolute necessity for either a perfecting or a redeeming revelation of God. The intention of the passage, therefore, is not to deny the goodness of Christ's person, or positively to declare what he is, but to reprove the thoughtless ascription of goodness to a master at the expense of the fear of God, the source of good, and to tell the youth in one striking sentence, fitted to win on his heart from its very humility, his fundamental error—namely, that he was dealing too lightly with goodness. That Jesus meant to assert sinfulness of himself is impossible; for with this his other declarations concerning himself and his office as the Redeemer contained in the synoptical gospels, as well as in John, and the position which he assigns himself in reference to the kingdom of God, would not harmonize. The evangelists, as well as the primitive church, never understood the word in that sense. But certainly Jesus could hardly say, There is none good save God only, if he had not distinguished himself, the man, with the goodness belonging to him, from the divine Being himself, and that, too, not only so far as God is the original source of all goodness, (for the perfect cause might also have a perfect effect), but because all earthly creature-goodness cannot be called perfectly good, as it is not yet perfected or raised above temptations and mutability. Hence the passage bears testimony anew to the complete real manhood of Christ in his ethical character, but not to any participation on his part, even the least, in human sinfulness. For his participation in the misery of human sin, there is place, according to the evangelists, only in the sense that his love permitted the disharmony without him to exercise an influence on his susceptibilities (see above). Hence the Christian mind will ever view it only as a profanation of his love, when his soul-agony in Gethsemane, and his sufferings on the cross, even to desertion by God—suffering which his own self-forgetting love brought upon him, and which is the brightest manifestation of his pure divine soul—are explained as a confession, an admission of his sinfulness.

He was perfect man in growth and progress, in his temptations and conflicts, but without any historical trace of a flaw or blemish in his life. He was in all points made like to us, without being necessitated to become like us as sinners. For sin is the negation of the truly human. He laid claim to no exceptional law for himself, as a privileged individual, but subjected himself to the universal human moral law. With this he was satisfied, but this, in its purity, depth, and fulness, he fulfilled. He knew nothing of, and would have nothing to do with, a super-moral religious genius. His religion is moral, his morality religious.

It is true, in one respect, it may seem that he lacked that which all other men have—namely, the peculiar *individuality* of virtuous character. His moral character, as it addresses us in the gospels, bears not the impress of any particular time or nationality, but reveals the eternal beauty of universal morality, of generic humanity in the deepest sense, refreshing, humbling, and yet elevating the inmost heart of every age, and race, of every century, to which his image is unveiled. It is a prerogative of all that is classic, and even of the classic in .ethics, that there breathes in it an air of the eternal—an air of unfading ideality. His portrait, as the evangelists sketch it for us, with the emphasis of artless simplicity, the strength of which lies in its truth, places before every susceptible mind a historical personage irradiated by moral ideas and moral truth in all the loveliness and power of reality. In the contemplation of him, the seeker after a living knowledge of human good stops to breathe again ; here he rests, for every one's conscience shouts, as it were, exultingly to him, as if at last THE MAN had appeared, or as if the conscience of mankind had now become an objective and living reality. Moreover, what he carried on as his *calling* did not lie, as with us, in a single region of human existence, but it is directed to what is central, to the setting of mankind right in their relation to God, and to the truly universal and human in every man, whence the renewing life-blood is to flow into all the spheres of human existence. In this, too, lies the marvel of his character, that his acting and discourse do not run into the vague and the abstract ; his character does not leave the impression of the flat, the feeble, the tame, the monotonous. Rather, we must say, so far as one understands by individuality, the opposite to the undefined and undeveloped, that he exhibits the most definite and clearly marked character. His peculiar distinguishing individuality just lies in this, that he exhibits in his own person what is essentially and truly human, and, that, too, in a manner fraught with saving power. The delusion is common that the good in itself would be monotonous and tame, and that it is indebted for its loveliness and color, not to its creative power and originality, but to the evil, its opposite. The picture of this life-full finished character is the triumph over this dead opinion, which makes good the eternal debtor of evil, and evil and death the dispenser of life.

Thus he lived as an individual, just like others, and along with them ; but there was in him the power of the universal. He was THE MAN absolutely, for whom the enlightened part of mankind waited, a Plato as well as the prophets. And hence his calling is "the calling of callings", the central calling, touching the principle of life in humanity, on which depends the power and the imperishableness of all individualities. For they win eternal life only as they incorporate into their individuality that essential excellence, which is at once divine and human, and became real in his individual person. He is the Son of Man.

II. How Christ's Sinless Holiness can be historically known.
If the holy, sinless character of Jesus is perfectly human, it is then also *knowable,* a revelation of the idea of what is truly human, not in doctrine only, but in fact. It is not a mere mystery, believed on foreign authority ; but a historical certainty of his sinlessness and moral perfection is attainable. There are, we conceive, many errors abroad in this respect. Too much is usually conceded to those who deny that Christ's moral perfection can be historically evinced ; and it is forgotten withal that a revelation which does not really reveal, and cannot give a certainty regarding itself, would be no revelation, but a mere secret, the purport of which men perchance take for granted according to some agreement.

Yet let us hear the objections to this knowableness. It is said, we lack sources of information as to the early years of Jesus' life. The early life of Jesus, therefore, cannot with certainty be pronounced sinless. We reply, the credibly reported purity of his later life guarantees the earlier. All the errors of earlier life leave scars in us, of which in Jesus we observe none. And if those who associated with him from youth up, as Mary and even his at first obstinate brothers, subsequently became, as no one denies, sincere believers in him as their Redeemer, have we not in this a weighty testimony that sin was never detected in him, and that they received from him a deep impression of a holy life ? From this point of view, the passage in Luke 2 : 51, 52, which without doubt goes back to the source of the holy family itself, like the entire narrative of the first visit to the temple, receives a high significance. What his relatives perceived was obedience to his parents, growth in wisdom and in favor with God and man.

Further, it is said the sources of information for the time of his public life are imperfect. We have indeed the words and deeds of Jesus ; but important as are these for forming a judgment as to his moral character, still we see not his demeanor and bearing, the glance of the eye, the tone of the voice ; all this is wanting to us, so that a sure judgment is not possible. To this finally it is added, that in morals everything depends on the heart, which always remains hidden from human gaze. With regard to the first of these statements, we certainly have not that visible presence which the disciples had ; but we know from them what impression his character produced. We hear them speak of the gracious words which proceeded from his mouth ; of the eye which lingered lovingly on the rich young man, which shed tears at the grave of Lazarus, and as he gazed on Jerusalem ; of the heart-piercing glance which revealed to Peter the pain of denied love, and with irresistible power filled him with bitter repentance. On the other hand, we hear of the power of his discourse, and of the dignity and majesty of his appearance. "We saw his glory, a glory as of the only begotten of the Father, full of grace and truth." We have thus enough in this respect to know that demeanor, gesture, tone, were not in contradiction, but in perfect harmony, with the divine nobility which beamed from his speech and action.* With respect, however, to the alleged necessary se-

* Even in the purification of the temple, at which Pécaut takes great offence, the result cannot be understood by a passionate, uncontrolled vehemence on the part of Jesus, but only from the awe-inspiring, majestic impression made by his person, for which the uncultivated and rough showed more susceptibility than highly-cultivated but spiritually-blunted minds (John 7 : 32, 45, 46). When Pécaut presumes to censure the purification of the temple, whether as to its form or substance, it is surprising that he combats the authority of Jesus, which those whom it concerned did not dare to do. For certainly they would willingly have punished him ; but they must have had good ground to let the matter drop, after a feeble protest, in which their conscience must have convinced them of a gross neglect of duty. How important was this act of Jesus when taken in connection with the current accusation against him on account of the temple! He performs it as a token how deeply he loved the people of God and his sanctuary, and how truly conservative his action was! Just before it he had wept over Jerusalem, while he was flooded round with Hosanna-cries, and knew beforehand the ruin of the temple. But he works while it is day ; he gathers and warns as long as possible. The desecration of the temple is the precursor of the profane treatment

crecy of his feelings of love, it is forgotten that the ethical, the more inward it is, has an essential and intimate relation to actual life; and will reveal itself actively and passively therein; and that it would be tantamount to asserting the impotency of the ethical idea, and of ethical power, if it were said that, to manifest one's self, to let the heart, as it were, be gazed into, is indeed the highest necessity of love, but cannot be effected on account of the invisible character of the ethical; or, what amounts to the same thing, by the incapacity of the material, corporeal world to express and exhibit the truly moral.*

The opponents of miracles in former days often appealed to their lack of adequate evidence, and thus sought to make them worthless. The sinless perfection of Jesus would be equally in vain—nay, would not have been perfectly real—if it could not be made historically evident. Of the miracles this much is to be said, that their opponents, in seeking to ground their impossibility on their contradiction to all the known laws of nature, do thus just assert, that they are easily distinguished from ordinary events, and also that they receive their light in connection with their cause and their divine end, thus confirming their connection with the higher world. Still closer is the connection between the sinless perfection of Jesus and the possibility of knowing it. For that love is not love which remains shut up in itself, and which has nothing for others. If it is the essential predicate of light that it is for the eye, and will illuminate not only itself but all things else; or of mind, that it is for mind; it is still much more the essence of mind in its reality, that is, as a loving personality, to aim to be for others, that a fellowship of love may be formed. Redeeming love cannot perfectly satisfy itself without this real self-revelation of its inmost heart, as all our salvation is based upon the

---

which they would inflict on him, the antitype of the temple. He reproves that desecration, because whoever approves it would much more easily misunderstand his holiness and sin against him.

* Compare the profound word of the mystic master (Suso): "To whomsoever inwardness grows into outwardness, to him inwardness becomes more inward; for to him inwardness grows in inwardness".

knowledge of being loved by the prevenient love of God in Christ.

Earthly material is not so intractable as to be incapable of expressing the ideal. Falsehood, it is true, can attempt to speak the language of love and truth; selfishness can, for its purpose, borrow or purloin the expression of the heart, or its noble sign-language. But that only proves, that we must inquire whether the language of love is borrowed, but not that there is no language or expression of love; for, were there none, it would occur to no one to borrow it from love.

The assertion that the holiness of Jesus can be historically evinced certainly implies the acknowledgment of the possibility of deciding with historical certainty (not indeed with mathematical certainty, the acknowledgment of which can be wrung from the most morally insensible, provided only he has understanding) whether the deeds and words of Jesus were really the expression and revelation of his heart, or hypocrisy and dissimulation.

We mean not to waste a word on the question, whether Jesus was a hypocrite and liar. Even Pécaut, the acutest and most open opponent of the sinlessness of Jesus in modern times, readily concedes to Jesus a high degree of moral perfection. But he should see that he has thereby given up the right to appeal from the manifest moral character of Jesus to the fact that the feelings of the heart cannot be discerned, in support of his theory, that we cannot surely know the sinlessness of Christ; for the picture of high moral perfection which he himself sees in Jesus does not permit the assumption that Jesus sought to reveal one thing in word and deed, while another, a worse, was in his heart. For if Jesus was as sincere and pure as Pécaut will have it, then hypocrisy was far from him, as it was his deepest abomination;* and then we have the revelations of his heart in all the manifestations of his life.

We, however, arrive at the same result, from another consideration. Where falsehood and hypocrisy assume the ap-

* Compare, for instance, Matt. 23 : 6, 2, 5, 16; 7 : 5; 15 : 7; 16 : 3; 21 : 18; 24 : 51; Mark 7 : 6; Luke 12 : 1; 13 : 15.

pearance of goodness, it always happens that, being inexperienced in the region of love and truth, it attaches itself
involuntarily to custom, mimics what is in some circle regarded
as exquisitely pious or strictly moral, be it even in the inventing of new artistic or striking forms, which suit the prevailing
moral tone on the one hand, and excite astonishment on the
other, but has neither courage nor strength for the simplicity
of moral originality. For where would be the intended success
of the deception if one did not, even in an exaggerated way,
use, and pay his way with, the sign-language or coin which was
already current? But now it is evident that, in this very sphere,
Jesus broke with the traditional views and expectations as to
what is to be esteemed just, and pious, and good, and with their
representatives; that he came into violent collision with them;
and that he, with creative originality, set forth in his teaching,
life, and sufferings, an example of moral excellence, directly
opposed to the prevailing one, appealing to the primitive moral
sense in man, commending itself to susceptible minds (much
like a genuine work of art), and over-mastering them. This
was only possible so far as he himself was possessed and filled
by the glory of the truly and essentially good, which he knew
and brough to light, seeking nothing but its victory and prevalence.

We say then, far from love being powerless to reveal itself
in this earthly world, amid its chaotic and distracted relations,
that this world is the very place where its glory may manifest
itself most brilliantly. The earth, with its frailty and sin, is in
such a state, that the external majesty and power of the Son of
God must necessarily be concealed and abide in mystery, and
could not be revealed, at least in all their fulness; while, on
the contrary, his sinless, holy love could nowhere more clearly
manifest itself than just in conflict with the world's sin in behalf of righteousness. We add, it *has* revealed itself, but *only*
to *susceptible* minds. There were and are blind persons who
do not see this glory, much like as harmonies pass over the
unmusical unheard, or like a disconnected volume of sound.

Christ's sinless perfection can be objectively known. It had
the will and power to make itself known or manifest, as that

which it really was in its essence. He who calls it unknowable, lays the blame, as usually happens, on optical delusions, on the object, and not on himself. In opposition to coarse empiricism of every form we take for granted, that truth is not found merely in the sensible and palpable, but rather that the palpable itself cannot be apprehended and understood without mind, spirit, and spiritual principles; that, on the other hand, we are not limited in our knowing to the naked intellectual forms of logical or mathematical principles, and so shut up in thought within ourselves. But as it is given to the will, without losing itself, to have a being beyond itself in love, so is it given to knowledge; more precisely, it is given to the spirit of love to be self-conscious in itself, and yet, at the same time, to have a being in its object. True knowledge or wisdom is the love of thought, love incorporated with *thought;* as the ethical and the good is love incorporated with the *will.* As in contemplating a work of art, we seize the idea of beauty itself, but *in* the reality, so we maintain that in *that* life which stands before us as the highest ethical work of art, that is, in the life-portrait of Jesus, the idea of the good is capable of being apprehended by every one, as it is presented to every one, though not every one can appreciate it without some preparation; and it is-presented there life-like, not as mere thought, but as reality. As we have this life before us only in written documents, it may indeed be asked, Is it reality or is it fiction? That we here find an exhibition of the very ethical idea in its glory is perhaps conceded. But is this representation only the moral idea made objective in the guise of reality, a mere poetic legend, whether intentional or unintentional; or is it the historical record of a real life lived upon earth? To this the simple counter question might suffice, where, in all history, is there a historical personage that has drawn such deep furrows in the inmost nature of mankind, as Jesus of Nazareth, whose historical existence no one doubts? But, still more directly, the historical evidence can strictly evince that the moral phenomenon of Jesus is historical reality, not fiction.

As we have already seen that the doubt whether Jesus's representation of himself may not have exhibited something better than perhaps was personally in him, or that the mistrust about his inner truthfulness can only be proved or refuted by seeing what he himself really was by the actual facts of his life ; so too the sum of his life and character can alone furnish a decision on the point whether his character is a myth or historic reality.

In next proceeding to address ourselves to the consideration of these activities of his life, we believe we may safely make the assertion, that the contemplation of the living character of Jesus awakes in every true conscience the lively concrete idea of absolute purity and sinless perfection. We believe, too, that it can be proved on historical grounds that Jesus awakens this idea by his life recorded in the Gospel, and not merely by his words and deeds ; and further, that his followers did not invent his portraiture, but found it and looked upon it ; that they did not create it, but described it as well as they could. But yet we are far from the assumption, that real faith in the union of the ideal and the historical can be attained by demonstration. On the contrary, we reckon it as a reserved right of the Head of the Church and of his majesty, that it perpetually evinces itself as creative, and that he commits it to none but himself to reveal himself to his own, and to give them the assurance that he knows and loves them. To know him is in fact due to his perpetual self-manifestation, a power and virtue essentially inherent in himself, without which he would not be the Redeemer ; just as the holy Scripture could no more hold its normal position, if we ceded its *perpicuitas* or *semet ipsam interpretandi facultas* to any other court.

[TO BE CONTINUED.]

Art. III.—BULGARIAN POPULAR SONGS.

By ELIAS RIGGS, D.D., Missionary of the A.B.C.F.M., at Constantinople.

[THE following communication from Dr. Riggs was read before the American Oriental Society at its recent semi-annual meeting in Princeton, N. J. To Professor W. D. Whitney, the Secretary of that Society, we are indebted for the permission to publish these admirable translations in the pages of this REVIEW.—EDS.]

THE following pieces are selected from a collection of Bulgarian popular songs recently published, *Bulgarski Narodni Pesni*, collected by Demetrius and Constantine Miladinov, Agram 1861, pp. 542, 8vo. I have rendered them in the measure of the original and very literally. The reader will be struck with the resemblance of these compositions to the song of Hiawatha, in which, if Mr. Longfellow has given us, as I suppose, a fair specimen of the style and composition of Indian Songs, the coïncidence is truly remarkable. The measure, the absence of rhyme, the repetition of words from the close of one line in the beginning of the next, and the repetition of entire lines in a question and its answer, or in a promise and the story of its fulfilment, appear alike in both.

This collection consists of more than six hundred pieces, large and small, all professedly taken from the mouths of illiterate common people, and is one of the largest volumes yet printed in the Bulgarian language.

The measure of which the first two pieces are specimens is the one most used. Other songs exhibit lines of various lengths, from five to seventeen syllables. The themes too are various. Some are heroic, some erotic. Some exhibit religious legends, fables of the doings of fairies or dragons, or the contests of saints with monsters inhabiting pools or fountains. The whole present an interesting picture of the traditions and fancies prevailing among the mass of the Bulgarian people.

CONSTANTINOPLE, June, 1862.   ELIAS RIGGS.

5

IVAN POPOFF AND THE FAIRY.

Our he started, Ivan Popoff,
To go off on Easter Sunday,
Easter Sunday, to his ploughing;
He had gotten about half way
When there issued out a fairy,
A wild fairy of the mountain,
And she stopped the way before him.
" Turn you, turn you, Ivan Popoff,
Don't go out on Easter Sunday,
Easter Sunday to your ploughing."
Ivan handsomely her answered :
" Get away, away, you fairy,
Or I'll down from off my courser,
By your flaxen hair I'll catch you,
And I'll tie you to my courser,
To the tail of my swift courser,
And I'll drag you like a harrow."
Then the fairy she was angry,
And her flaxen hair she loosened,
And she tripped up his swift courser,
Longing his black eyes to swallow.
Then was angry Ivan Popoff,
And he caught the wily fairy,
By her flaxen hair he caught her,
And he tied her to his courser,
To the tail of his swift courser,
And he dragged her like a harrow.
Swiftly to his home he took her.
From afar he calls his mother :
" Oh! come out, my dearest mother,
For a bride to you I'm bringing,
For a bride I bring a fairy,
To relieve you, dearest mother,
Wash the linen for my father,
Comb the hair of little brother,
Plait the tresses of my sister."
Then he locked up her right pinion
In a parti-colored casket,
And three years this bride lived with him,
And a little son she bore him.
Then she called a worthy sponsor,
And her little son they christened ;
Then came in the sponsor's lady,

Thus accosted she the fairy :
"Fairy bride, now dance a little,
Let us see a fairy dancer."
    Thus replied to her the fairy :
"Listen to me, worthy sponsors,
Let but Ivan Popoff give me,
Let him give me my right pinion,
Then I'll dance for you with pleasure."
    "Ah ! but fairy bride, we doubt you,
You'll escape, for you are faithless."
    "If you doubt me, Ivan Popoff,
If you fear that I'll escape you,
Then the door securely fasten,
Fasten too the gate securely,
Then I'll dance for you with pleasure."
    So the door secure they fastened,
Fastened too the gate securely.
But as she began her dancing,
Quick she flew from out the chimney.
    Then her mother-in-law called her :
"Fairy bride, but baby's crying,
Crying to be rocked and suckled."
    Thus to her the fairy answered :
"When for me my baby's crying,
Baby's crying to be suckled,
Tuck him close under the rafters,
And a gentle dew I'll shed there,
And I'll nurse my little baby.
When for me my baby's crying,
Baby to be rocked is crying,
There upon the bed you lay him,
And a gentle breeze I'll blow there,
And I'll rock my little baby."
    So her mother-in-law cheated,
When she heard the baby crying,
Baby crying to be rocked,
Then upon the bed she laid him,
But no breeze the fairy blew him,
But she came herself, the fairy,
Came and took away the baby,
And she thus accosted Ivan :
"Ah ! but look here, Ivan Popoff,
Did you think that you could hold me,
Think that you could hold a fairy,
Have a fairy for a mistress ?"

ANNA THE CUCKOO.

SOMETHING white and something waving,
On white Belashetzar's summit,
Can it be the drifted snow-banks?
Can it be the swan's white plumage?
No 'tis not the drifted snow-banks,
No 'tis not the swan's white plumage,
But 'tis only one white tent there,
Under which the youthful Stoyan,
Youthful Stoyan sick is lying.
Thus did he accost his sister:
"Hark, my sister dear, fair Anna,
Go, dear Anna, bring me water
From the cool and foaming Danube."
Anna thus her brother answered:
"Ah! my brother, youthful Stoyan,
But I do not know the way there,
Know the way to foaming Danube,
Either going or returning."
Stoyan spoke and thus he answered:
"Listen, sister, my poor Anna,
Cut a gash upon your finger,
Cut and let the crimson blood run,
Then as you go down the mountain,
Mark the trees and rocks in passing;
When you reach the foaming Danube,
Fill your jug with its cool water,
Then return as you descended,
By the marks your way discerning."
Anna listened to her brother,
Cut a gash upon her finger,
Then she started down the mountain,
Marked the trees and rocks in passing;
When she reached the foaming Danube,
Filled her jug with its cool water,
Then on her return she started.
But alas! alas! poor Anna,
Is it that the fine dew falling
Has erased the marks you made there,
All the marks of bloody crimson,
Made on trees and rocks in passing?
So she lost her way, poor Anna,
And she wandered down the mountain:
With three days of weary walking,

Not a trace could she discover
Of the way back to her brother,
Back to her sick brother Stoyan.
Then she turned to Heaven, poor Anna,
Sadly prayed: " O God of mercy !
To a little bird now change me,
Change me to a sky-blue cuckoo,
Let me fly among the beeches,
To my brother let me hasten,
To my poor sick brother Stoyan."
And the Lord her prayer accepted ;
To a sky-blue bird he changed her,
To a sky-blue bird, a cuckoo,
And she still is singing: " *Cuckoo*."

KING IVAN SHISHMAN.*

In the dawning, listen to me, mother dear, dawning of the morning,
Then it was that, listen to me, mother dear, there advanced an army,
Ranks of horsemen, listen to me, mother dear, ranks of daring yeomen,
And their sabres, listen to me, mother dear, like the sun in brightness;
Fire gleams from them, listen to me, mother dear, through the verdant
      forest ;
And their leader, listen to me, mother dear, is King Ivan Shishman ;
Thus he speaketh, listen to me, mother dear, he, King Ivan Shishman;
God of forces, listen to me, mother dear, God, the great Creator,
Kindly grant us, listen to me, mother dear, strength and noble daring,
We shall battle, listen to me, mother dear, on the plain of Sofi,
Shed our blood there, listen to me, mother dear, for the name of Christian,
And will honor, listen to me, mother dear, there the faith of Christians.

* The last King of the Bulgarians—slain in battle with the Turks in 1395.

ART. IV.— LABOULAYE ON THE UNITED STATES OF AMERICA.

ÉTUDES MORALES ET POLITIQUES, par ÉDOUARD LABOULAYE, Membre de l'Institut, Avocat à la Cour Impériale de Paris, Professeur au Collége de France. 8vo. Paris. 1862. Pp. 889. Ibid. LES ETATS UNIS ET LA FRANCE. 8vo, pp. 72.

GERMANS discuss political affairs from the point of view of universal history; Englishmen from the standpoint of the British Isles; Frenchmen under the aspect of general culture and civilisation. In relation to our present national crisis, this difference between the French and the English has been displayed in a most marked manner, of course with exceptions on both sides. The cultivated mind of Great Britain, as a whole, has been inimical to the cause represented by the United States; the severance of this mighty Republic has been looked upon as a foregone conclusion. French writers, on the contrary, as a general rule, have stood fire in the belief that this country ought not to be dismembered—that the interests of humanity and the progress of mankind demand the continued union of these States. Even the recent bold proposition of the French government for an armistice is not advocated on the ground of a disruption; for France must naturally desire that this country remain one and powerful, as a counterpoise to England's naval supremacy. But, excepting this chimerical and unfriendly proposal, the voice of France, like that of Russia, like that of Germany, has been, on the whole, favorable to our continued unity.

The contrast is still more marked when we turn from the political to the moral bearings and sense of our conflict. On the high ground of moral progress and culture, the two ablest defenders of this country, in the time of its death-struggle with the domineering and barbarizing slave-power, have been the two Frenchmen, De Gasparin and Laboulaye. Of the works of the former we have already given an account in the previous numbers of this REVIEW. Laboulaye is equally deserving of grateful recognition for the breadth of view, the manliness, and the humanity of his utterances, for a long series of years, in our behalf. And his words, being those of an eminent publicist, who writes with an almost judicial impartiality, if less impassioned than those of De Gasparin, may carry greater weight with many a candid thinker. And he is no novice in his utterances and predictions. For years, like De Tocqueville, he has carefully studied our history and institutions. For years he has been an eloquent and able defender, under even the imperial *régime*, of freedom of conscience, freedom of speech, freedom for all mankind. His varied learning, his professional reputation, his general philosophical and political views, as well as his mastery of the case, and his clear exposition of facts and principles, give him a rightful claim to be heard, as one speaking with authority on the momentous principles and issues involved in the conflict between freedom and slavery.

M. Laboulaye was born in Paris in 1811. Educated for the legal profession, he early obtained fame by a work on the *History of the Law of Real Estate, from Constantine to the Present Times,* published in 1839, and crowned by the Academy of Inscriptions and Belles Lettres. This was followed in 1840 by a life of the great German jurist, Savigny; in 1843 by an account of the *Civil and Political Condition of Woman in Ancient and Modern Times*—crowned by the Academy of Moral and Political Science; in 1845 by *Essays on the Criminal Law of the Romans, respecting the Responsibility of Magistrates.* In 1845 he was chosen a member of the Academy of Inscriptions; in 1849 he became Professor of Comparative Legislation in the Collége de France, of which he is one of the most illustrious members, his lectures being eagerly attended. He published *Contemporary Studies on Germany and the Slavic Nations* in 1855; on *Religious Liberty,* made up of eloquent and learned discussions, in 1858; on

Literary Property in France and England, 1858; an Introduction to the French translation of Channing's Works, discussing the question of *Slavery*, 1855; an edition of *Fleury's
Institutes of French Law*, 2 vols., 1858. In the same year
appeared the first volume of his *History of Political Institutions in the United States*, A.D. 1620—1783. Besides all this,
he has contributed largely to periodical literature in the
monthly reviews, and in the *Journal des Débats*. Some of
these essays were collected in the works, above named, on
Germany and on Religious Liberty. The volume referred to
at the head of this article, *Moral and Political Studies*, is
another collection, which, altogether apart from its bearing on
our country, is worthy of being read by all students of philosophy and lovers of human culture and progress.

Of the seventeen papers which make up this volume, six
are devoted to the United States, occupying about a third of
the entire volume. The others are on the Divine Personality,
Devotion, Mademoiselle de la Vallière, Christian Rationalism,
the Western Monks, Philip II, the Near Horizons, the Letters
of Everard, the Lottery, Bibliomania, and About a Catalogue.
In these essays he shows an intimate acquaintaince with the
English and German literature, and a deep sympathy with all
that concerns the relgious, moral, and political benefit and
progress of mankind. Modern infidelity, especially in its
pantheistic form, he opposes with a keen logic and an elevated moral sense. He shows himself throughout a firm believer
in God, freedom and righteousness. Of pantheism he discourses thus :

"The divine personality involves also our own ; and here it is that this
question touches the depths of our souls. If God has neither will, nor
liberty, nor consciousness ; if, in a word, he is not personal, we are indeed
nothing. If there is in the world only one universal being of which we
make a part ; if rock, plant, animal, man, are but different manifestations
of this blind force, which does not know itself, what are we then but
a drop of water in a torrent that rushes ever onward and never stops ?
Talk to us of liberty, of virtue, of immortality! all this may be our heritage,
if we are dependent upon an intelligent and supreme goodness ; but all this
is but an illusion, if we are an imperceptible atom in that Leviathan,

which we call the universe. In the midst of these phenomena, which pass in a flow, we no longer know where and what we are; as says the poet:

> ' We are such stuff
> As dreams are made of, and our little life
> Is rounded with a sleep.' "

He then proceeds to discuss the various systems of atheism and pantheism—Comte, Spinoza, Hegel, and others, and displays a competent familiarity with the works bearing on this theme. Of Sir William Hamilton, he says that his system is in reality one " of philosophical scepticism ", since he makes God to be an object not of knowledge (science), but only of faith. "Without knowing it, Mr. Hamilton gives the hand to the school of sensualism, as well as to the pantheism of Hegel. . . . The only difference is, that in leaving us faith, he at the same time leaves us hope ; he at least does not take from us the God whom our hearts need ". His critical examination of the system of Hegel we cannot follow in detail, but add a few of the closing sentences :

" After eighteen centuries, the wisdom of the day transports us back to the doubts of an expiring world. After eighteen centuries Christ speaks to us of God, of our souls, of salvation, of liberty, of duty, of justice, of truth, as if he were hearing our troubled voice, as if he responded to the cry of our troubled hearts. See what Hegel has brought forth in painful travail after a life of meditation and of research ; study these tormenting constructions ; follow his subtle reasonings, where words take the place of things ; and now, take up the Gospel and read perchance a discourse of Christ ; seek therein, not a dogma, but a philosophy ; put fearlessly by the side of Spinoza and of Hegel the mild and serene person of Jesus. Where is the ideal of the true, the beautiful and the good ? Where is the doctrine that can charm the greatest minds, and console the least ? Where do you find the rule of life for man, the rule of duty, and of justice for the citizen ? Where is life, where is hope ? "

But in the midst of all the errors of speculation, M. Laboulaye preserves a profound and noble faith in the intimate union and alliance of philosophy and faith :

" In my view, Christians and philosophers are not sufficiently aware that the spiritual philosophy springs from the Gospel, and leads back to it those souls who feel the need of loving, as well as of knowing. Spiritual philosophers need Christianity ; Christians need a spiritual philosophy. This

assertion may surprise these tranquil souls, who enjoy the peace of God
and the Gospel, and fear tumult and discussion.   But let them take heed;
faith that does not reason and that disdains philosophy, is a faith insecure-
ly poised, and exposed to more than one peril. . . . .   Bossuet and Fénelon were sufficiently Christian to have no fear of looking their faith in the
face; sufficiently philosophic to see in the Gospel the highest and soundest
of philosophies; the only system in which love and reason unite to lead us
to God."

In illustration of his positions about the rights of conscience,
and the relation of Church and State, we can only cite one or
two passages from a lecture given at the Collége de France,
February 5th, 1861:

"The Gospel, from its first days, has been propagated by raising up and
quickening the human conscience.   It is sometimes imagined that Europe
was christianized as if by an overwhelming invasion of miraculous grace,
without bringing the individual forces of the human spirit into action.
This is a great mistake.   The Gospel made its way, as all great political
and religious convictions have done, by conquering to itself a free adhesion.
It spread by gaining souls, one by one.   Christ did not impose any merely
external authority.   He did not say, *be* my disciple, but, *will* you be my
disciple?   It was not outside of ancient society that Christianity developed
itself, spreading itself alongside of it without touching it.   We generally
separate the first Christians too much from the world in the midst of which
they lived.   They were mixed up with it, and thus alone were they able to
act upon it.   In every society a strong conviction necessarily makes its influence felt.   There are always a great number of people who have need
of support, and who, by degrees, gather round a man of faith.   In a free
country this influence is not dangerous, for controversy despoils each opinion of the falsehood it contains, and truth alone abides.   It is only under
despotism that any opinion is certain to triumph, irrespective of its truth.
Christianity triumphed, not simply because of the enlightenment it
brought, for at the time in which it appeared, the Roman world was as enlightened as the world is now.   Its philosophies were not defective in this
respect, for the boasted scepticism and pantheism of our day are only the
rejuvenescence of the religious faiths of that age of decadence.   The souls
of men wanted liberty, and the Gospel gave it.   By freeing man from the
dominion of the temporal, it restored his dignity, it formed his conscience,
it taught him to die rather than renounce his faith.   That was its glory."

"A return to the close alliance of the Church with the State has led, in
France, to the persecutions of the Protestants.   The eighteenth century,
with its infidelity, grew out of that alliance, and in its turn the Church was
oppressed.   Finally, in our days, the great principle has been proclaimed

of the separation of the temporal and the spiritual, and we see churches founded upon this principle which ever abound and flourish increasingly."

But it is time for us to come to his writings upon the United States of America. In the preface to his last volume, he says:

"One of the greatest evils of our epoch is, that the Catholic Church, troubled as to its temporal interests, or menaced in its political institutions, distrusts modern ideas, and has only anathemas for those principles of 1789, from which our safety will one day come. This is a baleful misapprehension, from which religion is suffering no less than society. Nothing in the Gospel justifies this vain panic. Christianity is at once religion and the philosophy of liberty. It is in order to combat this error, and to annul this fatal divorce, that I have so often recurred to the institution of the United States. America, so badly judged in France, gives us the spectacle of a fruitful democracy that holds fast to the Gospel, and makes Christianity the essential condition of liberty. A people risking its fortunes upon the exorcism of slavery is the grandest sight that this nineteenth century has seen. Here is an example which ought not to be lost, and which I signalize for all pious souls, for all generous hearts, that do not despair of God or of the future."

The first of the six essays on our country is a general sketch, reviewing the works of Miss Bremer and of Pastor Grandpierre (1854); the second is on Education in America, noticing Everett's *Oration*, and Wimmer's *Church and School in North America*, published in 1853; the third grapples with the question of Slavery, *àpropos* of Channing's works; the fourth is on the Presidential Message of 1856, and reviews the Kansas imbroglio; the fifth is on the Civil War in the United States, reviewing De Gasparin's first book, and Eyma's *American Republic;* the sixth on America and the French Revolution, is a discourse delivered at the Collége de France.

From these papers we select a few paragraphs giving M. Laboulaye's general views about our country, its institutions, and its prospects:

"A century hence, when the immense and fertile valleys of the United States shall contain a population of more than two hundred millions of men of the same language and race, secure upon a territory twelve times the extent of France, and twenty-five times as great as England, what will become of Europe, with its national divisions and jealousies, confronted with this people, master of two oceans, and all-powerful in numbers and in union ?"

" The nearer we come together the better shall we comprehend the solidarity of the two continents, and what I will call the European part played by America. While we attract this new society by the brilliancy of our civilisation, it draws us to itself by the spectacle of its youth, its audacity and its success. This reciprocal action is visible in the sphere of industry ; there is no invention which does not at once pass beyond the seas and become a common benefit ; it is the same, though less noted, in all that concerns science, letters, morals, politics, and religion ; everywhere men try to march to the same step."

" From the political separation of Church and State, and the entire internal liberty of the churches, singular effects have resulted, setting at naught all previous calculations. As soon as believers alone were charged with the duty of supporting their own worship and propagating their faith, each one began to take a more lively interest in his own communion ; each one made himself an apostle of his faith, and, at the same time, as a natural consequence of liberty wisely understood, each one has better respected the rights of others in proportion as he was jealous for his own rights. Hence the remarkable spectacle in each church of extreme ardor and infinite tolerance."

" Europe is not effete ; it is in transformation ; and in this difficult trial it may take example from the United States. The American people is not a new race ; it is our own society upon a new theatre, in different circumstances. It is the same civilisation ; but perhaps there they better understand the conditions under which liberty may be fruitful, and all that is still to be derived from Christianity and education."

" I do not believe that there is in history anything comparable with the prodigious growth of the United States ; and in truth there is no spectacle which gives rise to more earnest reflections." After considering various theories propounded to explain this growth, namely, the democratic character of our institutions, the breadth of territory, the paucity of population, and finding them all insufficient, M. Laboulaye proceeds : "The Americans have for a long time known the secret of their greatness, for they brought it with them from England. For two centuries, while seeking for the most simple and the most popular political institutions, they still attached to these only a secondary significance, knowing that liberty depends rather upon the spirit of citizens than upon the frame of government. From the times of Louis XIV they have clearly seen, what we are beginning to suspect, that liberty is a force and nothing more, a force indifferent in its nature, and which may lead either to evil or to good. Compressed, it shines ; left to itself, it ravages or fructifies, according to the hand which directs or uses it. The direction to be given to it was found by Americans on the day when they learned that the problem to be resolved is the same in the case of a nation as in that of each individual, and that political liberty must be treated just like natural liberty, since it is the same liberty. Moral law, if we wish to live honorably, must not be put in an external observance or in a book, but in the heart of man. So political rules are not to be found in the mechanism of government, but in the soul of the citizen. It is only an internal guide that can prevent us from abusing liberty and destroying ourselves by that which ought to save us. This internal guide was found by the first colonists of America in their religion. . . . Those two sisters, religion and education, are the guardians of freedom in America. . . . The first axiom of politics is, that no liberty is possible without religion and without education."

But the most important part of Laboulaye's work is in the essays upon slavery and our present civil conflict. He has reviewed, with a clear knowledge of the facts, the whole history of slavery in this country; the efforts of reformers, giving special prominence to the works of Channing; the history of the later struggles, including the mortal strike in Kansas; the circumstances and results of our last Presidential election; the causes and varying aspects of the war, and its probable issue. In all. he sees only one probable result — the triumph of freedom and the continuance of the Union.

"Let us", he says, "again recall the subject of the conflict that divides North and South. In the midst of the smoke and the tumult of battle, we are too ready to forget the right; we think ourselves wise and politic in recommending all parties to yield. By such counsel prudence is easily deceived. 'Justice and peace have kissed each other', says the Scripture; but the kiss of injustice is the kiss of Judas. It does not give peace; it gives birth to violence and death. Attempt to trace the condition of a treaty between the North and the South; I defy any one to come to an acceptable solution. It is because the question at issue is quite another thing than a question of justice. The South is not defending its independence, for this was not menaced. What it wants is domination. Who would then advise the North to abdicate? . . . What is at the bottom of this fratricidal war? It is slavery. On this point Europe, all the world, is agreed. Every body denounces that execrable institution; but after blaming it, they begin to talk very fast about the interests of commerce and of industry; they no longer speak of servitude, but of the free exchange of cotton."

"For forty years the South, faithless to its grand ancestral traditions, pursued, as they say in the United States, a *sectional* policy. It sacrificed everything to one interest; it plotted to raise slavery to the rank of a federal institution, to force the free States to respect, maintain, and propagate slavery for its own advantage. The election of Mr. Lincoln was a protest against this invasion upon the North, and nothing more; but in this resistance the South read its arrest in the future. From the day when it could no longer command, it ceased to obey."

"War, without doubt, is a terrible scourge; let it fall in malediction on those who have unchained it. But it is also true that it is a noble and holy thing to fight in defence of country, justice, and humanity. This the North is doing. This war could be arrested by the South with a single word; let it but be content to be sovereign in its internal affairs, as it has been for eighty years; no one will outrage, no one will menace it. All that is asked of it is, not to dismember the country by a sacrilegious ambition, but to yield—the North cannot do this without dishonor. It is imagined in Europe that interest will be stronger than honor, and that the power they call King Cotton will prevail over the claims of humanity; but I dare assert that such prophets are deceived. The sons of the Puritans are slow to move; but once enlisted in a cause, when the right is at stake, they will not recede. To believe that the first defeats will break them down, is not to know them; in all things they are patient, and go right through to the end."

Besides the essays contained in his volume of *Moral and Political Studies*, M. Laboulaye has also collected a series of papers on the *United States and France*, published originally in the *Journal des Débats*, reviewing in part the last work of De Gasparin, and Fisch's account of this country. In the introduction he sums up the case in three positions: 1st. That slavery, or rather the desire to perpetuate and propagate slavery, is the real cause of the rebellion. 2d. That the South had no right, constitutionally, to secede from the Union. 3d. That the political interests of France require her to remain faithful to the traditions of Louis XVI and of Napoleon; and the unity and independence of America are, for all Europe, the only guarantee of the liberty of the seas and of the peace of the world.

"In writing these pages", adds M. Laboulaye, "I have not once forgotten that I am a Frenchman, and not an American; though, to tell the truth, that is making a needless distinction. Until very recently, until we were acute enough to invent a new political theory, it was a maxim received on both sides of the Atlantic, almost an article of faith, that America and France were two sisters, united by a community of interests and by glorious memories. The North remains faithful to this friendship, and can it be that for the love of slavery we shall, after eighty years of mutual regard, break the only alliance which has never imposed upon us a sacrifice, or caused us a regret?"

He argues the question with reference to the point of intervention, or recognition of the South, opposing most vigorously any such policy.   His hopes, as to the course of the French government, have been disappointed by the recent proposition of the Emperor, recommending to the chief European Courts, that they persuade this country to agree to an armistice of six months — so that the South may replenish its exhausted resources, and the North be arrested at the moment when its ample preparations are completed for assailing the rebellion at all exposed points.   This modest proposal, wisely rejected, for the present, by England, will doubtless be renewed, unless our army and navy are vigorously pushed onward. Only our success can avert it.   But, meanwhile, both the astute Emperor and the United States have before them a vigorous campaign; and if both are successful, their outposts may meet on the Mexican frontier.   And then it may have to be decided whether Paris or Washington is to be most potent on this continent.   The future alone can determine whether the Emperor of the French has not made a venture that will be equally hazardous to him at home and abroad.   The arguments of M. Laboulaye against intervention show the light in which such a project is viewed by an enlightened and liberal publicist :

"This wise neutrality, which is imposed on us by our precedents, displeases a school which wishes France to have a hand in everything, at the risk of wearing and exhausting its country.   These are the uneasy and restless men who propose to us not to intervene, but to recognise the South. Would this recognition procure us cotton ?   No ; it would not give us a right to dispute the blockade, and it would not end the war.   What would we gain by it ?   Nothing; except to lose the attitude of mediators and friends, which, at the proper time, would permit us to terminate the conflict. To recognise the South is to give it our moral support; it is to declare, in advance, that its pretensions are legitimate ; it is to take sides and renounce being arbiters.   What will avail us this measure, which will wound the North and compromise the future ?   'Recognition', it is said, does not bind us to make war.   This is a mistake.   A great country like France makes no useless movement.   The sequel of the recognition of the South is war with our ancient allies.   The North will see in it a menace.   For a long time already it has been troubled at this tempest pointed out to it on the horizon.   'Every nation rent by civil war', says Mr. Lincoln, 'must expect to be treated without consideration by foreign powers'. Let us add, however, that, right or wrong, it is from England that the North fears intervention ; it still counts on the old and constant friendship of France."

"If the North does not yield to the first summons of England and France, will we go further ? Have we calculated what the most successful war would cost, carried on at such a distance, in a vast country, with a brave and industrious people, who would defend their hearths with the energy of despair ? What will be the losses and sufferings of the cotton manufacture, compared with the evils and burdens that will be incurred by an enterprise longer and more difficult than the Crimean war ? If the honor of France were at stake, indeed, we should not hesitate ; but the Americans have done us no harm ; they have always been our friends. At this very moment it is in us that they place their hope. The neutrality of France is their salvation. In such conditions the war would never be popular ; it would be in contradiction to the interests, ideas, and feelings of the country."

"Suppose that the North yields to the first menace ; suppose that, through fatigue, it bows before an armed mediation ; suppose that it does not take vengeance forever on the party calling itself a foreign power ; suppose it suffers us to regulate the dismemberment of America—all impossible suppositions when we think that a youthful, patriotic, and ardent people are in question, which for a year past has been living under arms — when we have succeeded in this gigantic work, what shall we have done ? We shall have given the lie to all our political traditions, weakened France and strengthened England, by crushing our most useful and faithful allies."

"There is a political interest involved here which is greater than that of our manufacturers, and which seems to be forgotten or designedly lost sight of."

The bearings of a dismemberment of our Union upon the relations of France and England, are also truthfully set forth in the following paragraph :

"England holds the maxim that its navy must always be twice as strong as ours ; which is equivalent to saying that the English wish always to be in a condition to brave Europe united. Take away America, which holds England in check, and forces her to respect the rights of neutrals, and be sure that the first continental war will witness the reäppearance of the ambition of former days, and of a prepotence from which we should be the first to suffer. The dismemberment of America is the restoration of the empire of the seas to our rivals, as the unity of America is the liberty of oceans and the peace of the world. This is what we must not weary of repeating to those who, for the sake of applying a more than doubtful remedy to the sufferings of a moment, would condemn us to begin anew the terrible trials of the past. If the United States, with their thirty million men, had existed in 1810, does any one believe that the continental blockade would have been possible ?   If to-morrow they are crushed, does any one believe that this blockade would never be renewed, if, which God forbid ! we should experience a disaster on the ocean ?"

The arguments in this pamphlet against the pretended right of secession are put with great force, and a thorough knowledge of our constitutional history. Not less able is the advocacy of the position, that slavery is the real cause of the Southern secession and rebellion. That the North is fighting the battle, substantially for freedom, is also shown by incontrovertible evidence — the logic of facts, the necessity of the case. Then in burning and eloquent words, the true position of the South in relation to the public conscience of mankind, is thus depicted :

"While the North so proudly flung out its flag, what did the South ? What hindered it from rivalling its enemies, in order to dispute with them the sympathy of Europe ?   Where are the measures taken in favor of the negroes ? Where are the pledges of a speedy emancipation ? For, in short, if the tariff is the true motive of the war, if the supremacy of the North is the only fear of the planters, a fine occasion is offered to throw overboard the fatal dead-weight of slavery. Show us, then, the programme and pledges of the South ; these alone can give it the support of public opinion. The North acts ; why does the South preserve a silence, the danger of which cannot be disguised ?"

"Let not the South deceive itself. Its soldiers are brave, its politicians skilful ; it holds back the cotton which Europe so imperiously needs ; it flatters certain European jealousies and fears, by holding out the coming dismemberment of the United States ; but in spite of all these favorable chances, the South will be deceived in its ambition. The new Roman empire which was to extend as far as Mexico ; that new civilization, based on slavery, which they have promised us, is but a vanishing dream, a bubble which the wind will burst. To succeed, the South will require the aid of Europe ; this aid it shall never have. Whatever may be the sufferings of commerce, whatever may be the calculations of diplomatists, there is one fact which overweighs all, and that is *slavery*. The victory of the North is the redemption of four millions of men ; the triumph of the South is the perpetuation, the extension of slavery, with all its miseries and all its crimes. It is this consideration which causes more than one government to pause. The masses, whom great politicians despise, but whom they dare not brave ; those fanatics who believe in the Gospel ; those narrow minds who understand nothing but liberty ; those simpletons who are moved at the sufferings of an unknown negro ; that sentimental mob

6

which throws into the scales its love of right and of humanity — always carry the day at last. The world belongs to these simple ones, who, refusing to listen to the cunning combinations of politics, consider justice and charity above their own interests. *Public conscience* is the rock on which the South will be wrecked.

"Among us, in France, can the cause of slavery ever become popular? Our fathers went to America with Lafayette and Rochambeau to uphold liberty. It is one of our national glories; for this service rendered to the United States we are there considered as brethren and friends. Shall we blot out this glorious past? Shall the name of France be associated with the triumph of the South, that is to say, with the perpetuity of slavery? This cannot be. France, it is said, never fights for interest, but for ideas. I adopt the proud saying, and I ask: What ideas should we be fighting for in helping the South?"

"Whatever may be the course of events, there is a duty for the friends of liberty and French greatness to fulfil at this moment. It is necessary to speak, it is necessary to enlighten the country, it is necessary to show it the abyss toward which it is urged by those fair-spoken politicians who, through love of peace, would force us to war, and in the name of independence would enlist us under the banner of servitude. Christians, who believe in the Gospel and the rights of an immortal soul, even though clothed in a black skin; patriots, whose hearts beat for democracy and liberty; statesmen, who do not wish the return of the colonial policy which for two centuries stained the seas with blood; Frenchmen, who have neither forgotten Lafayette, nor the glorious memories which we left behind in the New World, it is your cause that is being resolved in the United States. This cause M. de Gasparin has defended for a year past with as much courage as talent; it is our duty to range ourselves around him, and to hold with a firm hand the old French banner on which is written *Liberty!*"

This is noble and eloquent language. It may well inspire us with a firmer faith, not in our righteous cause, but in the welcome we shall receive if we but succeed in this deadly struggle, from the friends of liberty and justice all over the world. And we rejoice that now, as in the times of our Revolution, such words of counsel and of cheer come to us from the land of Lafayette. And these words have about them a Christian spirit and a moral tone higher than was reached by any of the political writers of France in the period immediately preceding its Revolution. And thus they indicate, not merely the progress of liberty, but progress in right views of liberty—that it can be secure and permanent only as founded in Christianity, and pervaded by the Christian spirit and Christian ideas.

And thus is our conflict itself illumined by a higher light than that of mere natural reason. It is a part of the historic process by which the kingdoms of this world are to become the kingdoms of our Lord. The victories of truth and righteousness, of liberty and law, are the victories of an everlasting kingdom.

Art. V.—BAPTISM FOR THE DEAD. 1 Cor. xv, 29.

By Rev. HERVEY D. GANSE, New York.

THE true interpretation of any passage, whether difficult or easy, must be consistent with its grammar and with its context. The natural method is to consider the context first; for, in reading, we come to the passage through the expressions which have preceded it, and if it do not readily yield a sense, we instinctively glance down to the next plain sentence, in hope that it will throw its light back upon the obscure one. Yet, so soon as a passage gets a reputation for difficulty, especially if it be brief and easily remembered, there is a temptation to pluck it out of its connection, and to manipulate its mere terms into some possible meaning. Let us be careful to avoid this mistake, and make our approach to this difficult verse through its context.

The particular discussion, to which the text belongs, begins at the 12th verse: "Now, if Christ be preached that he rose from the dead, *how say some among you that there is no resurrection of the dead?*" The following verses, down to the twenty-fourth, are a direct assault upon that bold and dangerous assertion. But for whose advantage? Is the Apostle's audience made up of the deniers of the resurrection themselves, or of those who are in danger of being misled by them, or of both? The following indications will decide this ques-

tion. St. Paul cannot have had the unbelievers exclusively
in his mind, since he carefully discriminates between them
and others whom he, at least, addresses equally. The sceptics
are at most "*certain* among *you*". That is, the Church is addressed in the second person, while he describes the doubters
in the third. The same he does at the end of the discussion,
in the thirty-third and thirty-fourth verses—"Be not deceived.
Evil communications corrupt good manners". "For some
have not the knowledge of God." Unquestionably the τινες of
his last assertion were the τινες of the twelfth verse, and the
persons addressed in the second person in both these verses,
and all through the intermediate discussion, were not those
very unbelievers. Nay, there is proof that the discrimination
of these verses was kept up throughout, and that the false
teachers were not directly addressed at all. Twice the Apostle speaks of "your faith", and once of "your rejoicing, which
I have in Christ Jesus". Whatever may be the meaning of
that last somewhat obscure expression, it must imply the true
piety of those whom it concerns. But the deniers of the resurrection had neither faith nor piety ; for it is to be observed
that Paul treats their denial of the resurrection as though it
were a denial of all immortality. "Then they that are fallen
asleep in Christ are perished." "If in this life only we have
hope in Christ", etc. But how had the denial of the resurrection of the body limited their hope to "this life only", unless
it followed upon that denial that there was to be no future
life? The same estimate of their doctrine appears in the
closing appeal : "Why stand we in jeopardy every hour? If
I have fought with beasts at Ephesus, what advantageth it
me?" "Very much", might the doubter reply, if his doubt
concerned only the resurrection; "you shall live for ever in
spiritual happiness". The Apostle could not have failed to see
so great a flaw in his argument. It follows clearly that the
"some among them" who denied the resurrection—whose
"evil communications" were to be shunned—who "had not
the knowledge of God", were outright infidels, whether Sadducees or Pagans — wolves in sheep's clothing, who aimed to

destroy the flock. To these men St. Paul did not speak of their "faith" and Christian "rejoicing".

But the scope of the reasoning itself makes it most evident that it was addressed, not at all to those who denied the resurrection, but to the pious Corinthians, who were in danger from their reasonings. If we leave our obscure text aside for a moment, there is not an argument adduced in the whole discussion that a radical doubter concerning the resurrection, would not have laughed to scorn. Paul reasons to the consequences of the denial, and his opponents would have consented to them all. "Our preaching is vain"; "Your faith is vain"; "We are false witnesses of God"; "Ye are yet in your sins"; "They that are fallen asleep in Christ are perished"; "We are of all men most miserable"; "Why stand we in jeopardy every hour?" These are not the weapons of mere logic with which to confound an adversary. Unless those, to whom they were addressed, had a pious sympathy with the reasoner, the words were wasted. So, too, of that grand picture of the great consummation, which begins at the twentieth verse, and reaches down to our text. "But now is Christ risen from the dead, and become the first fruits of them that slept." To an outright denier of the resurrection that is mere assertion. Only to a true believer is it the sublime and most persuasive announcement of Christ's apostle. To such a believer every stroke of the glowing pencil brings out the vivid future more distinctly, till he sees Christ in the midst of his risen people, all enemies beneath his feet, death destroyed, and the consummated kingdom given to God and the Father. The scope of the Apostle's reasoning, then, is very plain. He is counteracting in the minds of the Corinthian Christians the influence of a most mischievous infidel error, and that by an appeal not to mere intellect, but to the most exalted sympathies of Christian faith.

It is in the midst of this appeal that the text occurs. Now, if every manuscript had shown a hiatus at this point, we might still have assured ourselves of one thing; namely, that when the text was complete, that verse was in sympathy with all the rest, and, like them, appealed to the highest Christian consciousness of those who first read it. But the manuscripts are complete, and so well agreed in their reading, that any material departure from the accepted text is sheer conjecture. We pass then at once from that graphic description of the final glory of Christ and his people, which reaches from the twentieth verse to the twenty-eighth, to this question: "Otherwise, what shall they gain who are baptized for the sake of the dead? If the dead rise not at all, why are they even baptized for their sake? And why", he proceeds, with questioning evidently intended to be of the same general spirit, "and why stand we in jeopardy every hour?"

Now the favorite interpretation, especially of the German commentators, fastens at once upon the grammar of the text, and insists that ὑπὲρ τῶν νεκρῶν " for the sake of the dead", must be "*for the advantage* of the dead", since such is the natural and ordinary force of the preposition. We answer confidently, it cannot be. The kind of feeling that prompted and responded to the whole strain of argument, both before and after this verse, has nothing in common with the idea of any human act done *for the advantage* of those already dead. Masses for the advantage of the dead, said by the Papists now, are just as good a proof of the resurrection, as baptism for the advantage of the dead could have been in Paul's day. Imagine, then, a modern writer, who might be capable of rising to any such strain of sincere and grandest argument, marshalling into the midst of his thrilling appeals the question: "What shall they gain who say masses for the dead, if the dead rise not at all?" To say that there were Papists in the community to which he wrote, would only double the impossibility of such reasoning. His cause could gain nothing from such halting evidence. Would he then gratuitously put that monstrous practice upon a footing with the most genuine and exalted exercises of piety?

It is claimed, indeed, that the text is an *argumentum ad hominem,* or *argumentum ex concessis.* But the passage is not in the vein of these logical devices. Those who might have made such admissions were in no way before the Apostle's mind. His work was not the confounding of an adversary, but the building up of saints, and he needed no such stubble to eke out his broad and firm foundation.

Yet, it is not strange that exact commentators should be drawn to this interpretation; for if it does not consist with the scope of the argument, scarcely any of the interpretations, which attempt to displace it, meet the grammatical demands of the text half so well; and those demands are very distinct:

First of all, the passage is complete in its parts. There is no appearance of an ellipsis, and it is therefore a grave objection to any interpretation that it supposes one. Βαπτιζόμενοι ὑπὲρ τῶν νεκρῶν may mean "baptized for the dead", or "baptized in place of the dead"; but it cannot mean "baptized for *the resurrection of* the dead", or "for *the kingdom of* the dead", nor "baptized *in order to take* the place of the dead". To make any such addition to Paul's words, is to confess that we can make nothing of them as they stand. If we hold ourselves, then, to the precise terms of the text, we find that they are, all of them, words in ordinary use and of well settled meaning. And therefore, the farther we warp them from that meaning, the more improbable our interpretation becomes.

1. Βαπτιζόμενοι and βαπτίζονται naturally indicate ordinary Christian baptism. The radical idea of the word, of course, only covers the outward rite. But unvarying usage makes the word itself cover more. So 'crowning' a man is literally setting a crown upon him; but, according to all usage, the word includes both the act and its significance. The 'enlisting' of a soldier is strictly the writing his name in a list; but usage makes it that writing which devotes him to a soldier's life. So the 'baptizing' of Christians is the washing that devotes them to a Christian life. Out of more than thirty instances in the New Testament where Christian baptism is spoken of, there is not one in which the word has any lower sense. At this point, then, the notion of a vicarious baptism offers violence to the text itself, as we have seen it does to the context; for it supposes a second application of the rite in *form* under circumstances that could leave no room for its *essence*. As if such an expression as enlisting ὑπὲρ τῶν νεκρῶν

should be claimed to indicate the mere show of enlisting made by living men in the name of dead men. Now, a qualifying phrase might be used that should be unequivocal enough to lower βαπτιζόμενοι to such a meaning. But until the phrase is clearly proved to have that power, the assumption of such a meaning does violence to the word.

2. Ὑπὲρ, with a genitive, occurs in the New Testament one hundred and thirty-four times. Setting aside our own obscure passage, there are only three instances among all these where it does not need to be translated by some such phrase as "on the part of", or "in behalf of", or "on account of". That is, it indicates not the mere circumstances of an act, but the interest in which the act is performed. The three exceptional cases referred to constitute a class by themselves, and can shed no light upon our text. They are, Romans ix, 27 ; 2 Cor. i, 8, and viii, 23 ; in each of which passages ὑπὲρ is construed with a verb of knowing or speaking, and is therefore thought to stand for περί, and to mean "of" or "concerning". A study of these several passages, we think, will not sustain this representation, but will show that, in these cases too, ὑπὲρ was used instead of περί, just because it included the idea of interest "in behalf of" the object of knowledge or speech. But even if this be not so, and if classical usage be summoned to prove that ὑπὲρ, with such verbs, is used in the loose sense referred to, still it needs some such a verb, in each instance, so to lower the sense of the preposition ; and with any other verbs it must bear its ordinary meaning. So in English, such a preposition as "about" or "concerning" may be definite enough to describe the relation of thought or speech to its subject; but it would be very loose to speak of rendering a service "concerning" a friend, or of being baptized "concerning" the dead.

Βαπτιζόμενοι ὑπὲρ τῶν νεκρῶν, then, according to all New Testament usage, must mean "baptized for the sake of the dead". But in what sense "for their sake"? The notion of a vicarious baptism assumes that the meaning must be "for the advantage of" the dead ; and it is very clear that such is the most common sense of ὑπὲρ with a genitive. Thus, in the writings of

Paul, this construction occurs nearly a hundred times, and about seventy times it clearly indicates the advantage of the object for which the action is had.

But in many, even of these instances, a secondary sense of the word comes in. Since what one does for another's advantage, he commonly does from love to him, ὑπὲρ is made to cover the love of the actor as much as the advantage of the object. Thus, when Peter says, "I will lay down my life ὑπὲρ σου", he means two things, "for thy advantage" and "for love of thee". If the first meaning were excluded, the other would remain. So in all those passages of Paul which describe sufferings endured for "Christ's sake", or for his "name's sake", there is at least as distinct a regard of the affection which welcomes and sustains the suffering, as there is of the service which it may render to Christ. But leaving aside all instances in which ὑπὲρ may be thought to have this pregnant meaning, there remain in the writings of Paul, at least, twenty instances in which it indicates only the motive of the actor, and not at all the advantage of the object. That is, the object of the preposition is regarded as *prompting* the action, but not as *being served* by it. Thus Paul says: "For this thing (the thorn in the flesh) I besought the Lord thrice", 2 Cor. xii, 8, which surely does not mean "for the advantage of" the thorn, but "on account of" it. In nearly every other instance, the motive is identified with love or gratitude. "That the Gentiles might glorify God *for* his mercy"—Rom. xv, 9. "I beseech you *by* the coming of the Lord"—2 Thess. ii, 1. "I thank God *for* you all that your faith is spoken of", etc.—Rom. i, 8.

This last form of expression is often used. Now, if certain of those Christians, on whose account Paul gave thanks, had been known to have died, it would have been as good Greek, and as good piety, to say εὐχαριστῶ ὑπὲρ τῶν νεκρῶν, as to say εὐχαριστῶ ὑπὲρ ὑμῶν. And, in either case, the preposition would have meant "on account of" or "for the sake of", but but by no means "for the advantage of". Just so Naomi, in the Septuagint, speaking to her daughters-in-law, says: "My heart is grieved ὑπὲρ ὑμῶν—on your account".

New Testament usage, then, gives us a choice between two

well-settled meanings of ὑπέρ with a genitive, namely, the commoner sense of "for the advantage of", and the less common sense of "on account of". If we consult Paul's use of the word, it gives us, irrespective of the scope of the verse, about one chance out of four, that he used it in the latter sense. The scope of the verse, of course, might easily raise this chance to a certainty.

This second sense of ὑπέρ is assumed by Diestelmann, in the *Jahrbücher f. deutsche Theologie*, and he explains "on account of the dead" to mean, on account of the kingdom and glory of Christ who is dead, and of all those who have died or shall die in him. If the supposition of so considerable ellipsis be no objection to this interpretation, the usage of ὑπέρ surely will warrant it.

There is also warrant enough, as we think, for translating ὑπέρ, "in place of". But we will need to remember what that expression means. Careful investigation of all those passages in the New Testament which are thought to demand such a sense of the preposition, will show that it never indicates mere substitution, but only substitution for the advantage or credit of the party whose place is taken. "Baptism *in place of* the dead," then, would be vicarious baptism; and "baptism *in order to take the place of* the dead" would be baptism in order to vicarious duty; a sense which, if possible, is more objectionable still.

The notion of a baptism "*over* the dead" cannot be reconciled with the New Testament usage of ὑπέρ with a genitive.

We cannot but count the interesting and elaborate exposition of Professor Kendrick in the *Christian Review* as offering equal violence to Paul's words. For even if ὑπὲρ τῶν νεκρῶν could mean "in reference to the dead", that expression would fall far short of meaning, as Professor Kendrick claims, "baptized into relation to the dead, baptized so as to be allied to the dead, reckoned among the dead rather than among the living". He refers to no usage of ὑπέρ in the sense of "in relation to" except that by which it describes "the relation" of speech or thought to a subject; and the New Testament at least furnishes no other. But even in that case the relation is between the speech and its topic. So far as the speaker is concerned, the ὑπὲρ *establishes* no relation whatever; it only grows out of the fact that he is already, as Professor Kendrick justly represents, " an interested party". It does not appear then that " the fundamental idea in all such cases of ὑπὲρ is that it brings the parties into close relation with its object". To say that a man speaks in relation to the dead is far from saying that he speaks himself *into* a relation to the dead. And so to say that a man was baptized in relation to the dead, whatever that expression might mean, would be very far from saying that he was baptized *into* relation to the dead.

But there is no usage of the New Testament that will suffer βαπτιζόμενοι ὑπὲρ τῶν νεκρῶν to mean anything less than "baptized for the sake of the dead", in some sense or another. The whole drift of the question, besides, shows that the baptized set out voluntarily to *gain* something; for τι ποιήσουσιν, in the 29th verse, means far more than the bare τι of the 30th; and the phrase "for the dead" in the Greek, as in our version, unequivocally marks the *motive* to that voluntary act, and not an *obstacle* in the way of it.

3. The adjective νεκρῶν and νεκροί occurring three times in the passage, must cover the same idea each time, except so far as the presence or absence of the article defines that idea. Τῶν νεκρῶν will naturally cover the special dead, in whom the baptized are interested. Νεκροί, without the article, are all the dead whose resurrection the false teachers sweepingly denied; ὅλως οὐκ ἐγείρονται. St. Paul assails that denial by claiming the resurrection of those special dead baptized for. According to the natural import of his words, "the dead" of the first member of the passage are thought to have a prospect of rising, so that those who are baptized for their sake cannot admit that no dead rise. As though we should say, why procure medicine (or do whatever else) for the sake of the sick, if sick men never get well? In any such question the sick are persons, the distinct hope of whose recovery prompts the care bestowed on them. So in the text the dead are persons, whose rising among the other dead is to reward those who shall have been baptized for their sake. This meaning at least lies on the

face of the passage, and any other meaning is elaborated and unnatural.

Now this condition of the text is fully met by the theory of a vicarious baptism. The dead who omitted to be baptized, have the omission supplied by friends, who in the resurrection rejoice in the results of their kindness. But no accidental correspondence with inspired language can sustain such a monstrous idea. And yet its friends may fairly demand that the interpretation which claims to be the true one shall come as near to the Apostle's words as their false one does.

There arises thus another decisive reason for rejecting the interpretation "baptized in reference to the dead" or "in anticipation of death". For in the view of that interpretation the dead of the first clause, so far from being definite persons, are as nearly as possible an abstraction. And since the νεκροὶ of the second clause are surely persons, the same adjective in a sentence of twenty words passes from abstract (with the article) to concrete (without it), and then back to abstract again ; unless, indeed, with many critics we read αὐτῶν in the last clause, which would summarily prevent such an inconsistency.

The interpretation "baptized for the resurrection of the dead" confessedly dispenses with the idea of any special dead whose resurrection is anticipated in the baptism, and as Professor Kendrick has well shown, reduces what Paul put in the tone of a thrilling appeal into the bald truism, that those who were baptized because they expected a resurrection, will be disappointed if there shall be no resurrection.

If the Apostle could have had reference to a baptism intended to furnish substitutes who should merit a reward for the dead, such a baptism, surely, would anticipate a resurrection of those departed friends, and so far conform to the text. But if in spite of the settled sense of ὑπὲρ the reference could have been to mere substitutes, who in no way should serve the dead, such substitution would involve no hope of seeing those dead again. According to that interpretation, the hope of the baptized would concern their own resurrection, and thus leave the repeated question, "why are they then baptized for the dead?" almost pointless.

4. But one of the clearest requirements of the text remains to be noticed. Baptism for the sake of the dead, whatever it may have been, could not have been practised by all Christians. Paul speaks of the subjects of it in the third person, as οἱ βαπτιζόμενοι, and again he asks : τί καὶ βαπτίζονται; why are they even baptized for the sake of the dead? The emphasis of καὶ in this last expression is very marked, and it indicates clearly that the baptism in question was singular enough to be a matter of remark. Indeed in some degree it must have borne comparison with Paul's own exposure of himself to martyrdom; although that comparison did not need to hold in the abstract danger or self-sacrifice of the two acts as some argue, but only in their notoriety and in their power to appeal to universal Christian feeling in proof of the resurrection. No interpretation that fails to recognise the exceptional character of this baptism, can claim to consist with the natural import of the verse. Here again, as we cannot but see, the theory of vicarious baptism fits the text.

But the other most popular interpretations are quite at war with it. "Baptism in anticipation of death" is common to all Christians, and Prof. Kendrick in candor admits that his interpretation labors at this point. The same is manifestly true of "baptism in hope of the resurrection of the dead", and of "baptism on account of the kingdom of the dead". "Baptism in order to take the place of the dead" will not be open to this objection, if "the dead" be supposed to be certain near friends or eminent martyrs, and the substitutes the special witnesses who have been won to duty by the sight of their constancy. But this interpretation of ὑπέρ, as we have seen, enlists the substitutes not only in the place of the dead, but in their behalf.

Let us now put the grammar and the context together, and see how many elements must enter into an interpretation of this passage, that shall do no violence to either.

The baptism in question must have all the ordinary significance of Christian baptism, and also an additional element, by which it may be said to be distinctively "for the sake of the dead". It must anticipate the resurrection of those dead for whom it is had, and that so confidently and so justly, that a mere allusion to the act will thrill all Christian hearts with a sympathetic conviction that there must be a resurrection; just as Paul's after allusion to his own steadfastness under persecution awakened an instinctive sympathy with his hope of rising again.

Our own attempt to meet these demands of the text we make with interest rather than with confidence. Let us suppose then that there was in St. Paul's day, as there has not failed to be at any time since, a considerable class of Christians who, assuming the vows of baptism with true evangelic feeling, were known to be moved to that act in a large degree by their affectionate regard of Christians recently departed, whether relatives or martyrs or both; and so to have been "baptized for the sake of the dead". Then three things need to be considered:

1. That the deference which might have been shown by any to such an appeal, would have been in full accordance with the highest motives that ever lead to baptism. A loving regard of the pious dead is one of the most marked products of evangelical religion. In this very chapter Paul proves the resurrection to a Christian heart, by showing that according to any other doctrine " they that are fallen asleep in Christ are perished ". The same Apostle was careful to say to the Thessalonians: " I would not have you to be ignorant, brethren, concerning them which are asleep, that ye sorrow not even as others which have no hope. For if we believe that Jesus died and rose again, even so them also which sleep in Jesus will God bring with him ". The rest of the glowing passage, 1 Thess. iv, 13–18, which is too long to quote, carefully provides for the reünion of the parted friends who " together " are to "meet the Lord in the air ". Nor was the recollection of such departed saints intended to be a mere sentiment. "That ye be followers of them who through faith and patience inherit the promises ", Heb. vi, 12. " Whose faith follow, considering the termination of their lives " (ἔκβασιν τῆς ἀναστροφῆς),

Heb. xiii, 7. Indeed if grace in Christian life and speech is meant to have persuasive power with men, can that power ever be greater then it is in recent recollections of the faith and triumphs of our pious dead? There is nothing excellent in our nature that does not kindle under such an appeal when God's grace points it; and there is nothing excellent in the Gospel that does not find freer access to a heart so moved. We need not say how well adapted the persecutions of that age must have been to give unusual impressiveness to such appeals. Let us conceive of the faith of a beloved parent uttering itself in songs from the stocks or the stake; when the last note of triumph should have been hushed, would it leave his children believers or unbelievers, timid or decided? Nay why should the effects of such spectacles be limited to the kindred or near friends of the martyr? The very constancy of the sufferer creates a regard of him in the heart of a stranger, and every such death is the increase of the Church. It is very safe to assume then that in Paul's day new converts as well as old may have been drawn to Christian duty in part, at least, by a regard of the pious dead.

2. If this were the meaning of the text it would perfectly serve the purpose of the Apostle's argument. Let us remember his appeal is made, not to cold intellect, but to the intelligence of a Christian *heart*. " Men tell you ", he says, " that there is no resurrection of the dead. Then Christ is not risen; your faith is vain; we are false witnesses; your dead are perished, and you are losing all the comfort of this life, in the hope of another which you will never reach ". This exhausts the appeal to their pious sympathies, and he rises to a higher level: " But Christ is risen, his kingdom is prepared, and shall, by and by, be complete; the saints shall rise at his coming; all enemies shall be destroyed, and Christ's whole work being done, the Father shall resume his delegated authority, and fill all the redeemed with his own glory." Now this grand delineation does not fail to take hold of Paul's inmost feeling, and he will have it do as much for his readers. But he has gone over all the ground of Christian consciousness already. What shall he do? In effect, he repeats himself—

that is, he drops the general and didactic language which he has used before, and by two vivid questions launches the eternal truth into their very souls : " If there be no such king- dom of Christ and his people, what a folly is theirs who suffer the love of the faithful dead to win them to Christian vows and duty ! If there be no resurrection, why are men even baptized for the sake of the dead ? " This is the very thought of the 18th verse, " Then are they that are fallen asleep in Christ perished". It is only put into keener words. Just as the argument of the 19th verse — "we are of all men most miserable"—bursts out in the second question : " And why do I expose myself to danger of daily death, if I am not to live again ? " The two connected verses are two glances into the future glory ; the one through our attested affection for those who have already died in the faith, the other through the con- fident hope which we nourish for ourselves. In all Christian consciousness these two emotions belong together ; and the one serves the argument as well as the other. Even if it were certain that Paul did not choose to appeal to such an emotion, the yearning of an affectionate heart after the parent or friend whose faith it is seeking to follow, is an instinctive assertion of a future life too strong for mere reasoning either to confirm or to disturb.

3. But now we have to meet the question, does the expres- sion, βαπτιζόμενοι ὑπὲρ τῶν νεκρῶν,—" Baptized for the sake of the dead"—fairly cover the act and motive which we have suggested ? After the experience of eighteen centuries it will be safe to confess that the expression is compact and obscure. Its fundamental difficulty lies in the fact that Christian bap- tism, which has its own distinctive motive in faith in Christ, is here referred to some contingent motive covered by the phrase, ὑπὲρ τῶν νεκρῶν. That difficulty increases in propor- tion as we hold baptism to its narrowest idea of a mere *rite :* and diminishes in proportion as we include in baptism the idea of a *profession.* To say that a man receives the sacred washing itself for the sake of the dead, amounts to vicarious baptism, and confuses all our notions of that holy sacrament. But to say that a man assumes the duties and dangers of a

Christian life for the sake of the dead may be only to bring a real though subordinate motive of Christian action into unusual prominence. Now let us suppose for a moment that the knotty phrase, ὑπὲρ τῶν νεκρῶν, had never been written in the text, and that Paul had spoken absolutely of οἱ βαπτιζόμενοι. It is safe to say that in that case every reader, whether Jew, Gentile, or Christian, would have understood by "the baptized" just what we now understand by "church members". So Paul elsewhere speaks of "one Lord, one faith, one baptism", Eph. iv, 5, where the thought of the rite is quite subordinate to that of the practical Christian life to which it was the introduction. The rite was the door of the church; "the baptized" were those who had passed through the door and were within. Thus we meet the solecism, "baptized *into* a baptism", Acts xix, 3; an expression which sets the rite and the profession almost in contrast. We only claim that the baptism of the text shall cover both ideas, giving to the latter just so much prominence as the argument and the circumstances assign to it.

We must remember then that the persecutions of those times could not but connect with the act of baptism the most serious regard of its external relations. It was a matter of outward danger as really as of inward faith. Then if there was any special consideration that was known to overbear that thought of danger, and to fire a courage that rejoiced to meet it, it was according to all the laws of speech to assign that consideration as a motive to the baptism. How prominent that motive would be made by any writer would depend upon the part it was to bear in his discussion. If St. Paul were expounding the *nature of baptism*, he might not allude to such a motive, nor think of it. If, on the other hand, he were proving that Christian instinct looks for a resurrection, his mind might most naturally fasten, first on the living sympathy which surviving Christians have with the departed, and next upon the readiest and most striking proof of that sympathy, whatever it might be. It might be the assumption by some survivors of all the duties and dangers of the piety that had so impressed them; and in that case his argu-

7

ment would require him to claim that some men are even baptized (καὶ βαπτίζονται) for the sake of the dead. There are hundreds of men in our churches to-day who are ready to use this very language, with the sole difference already insisted upon, that where New Testament usage spoke of " being baptized ", we now speak of "joining the Church ".

Should a youth, for example, who had listened in silence to infidel flings at the hopes of the pious dead, at length break forth, " It was for the sake of my dead mother that I joined the church, and you will not convince me that there is no resurrection ", would the words shock us or thrill us ? Or if a Christian minister, in impassioned appeal, should say : " Have not some of you become Christians for the sake of the Christian dead, and will you give up your hope of meeting them ?" who would think of technical criticism where the sense is so plain and so honest ? Add, then, that material element of persecution which in our day is quite wanting. Make Paul the preacher, and let him say to his Corinthian hearers : " You have taken this step of greatest danger, you have even been baptized for the sake of your dead, and what will you gain if your dead never rise ?" Would such an appeal have degraded baptism ?

But our interpretation assumes that the taking of such a step for such a motive was a thing so common and well known, that the briefest allusion to it would appeal to all hearts with a thrilling power. This assumption we do make, and if it be too great, we have lost our cause.

How very soon persecutions and martyrdom began in the Church, no one knew better than Paul. Stephen's death followed close upon that of his Master. Nor was his case a solitary one, for " a persecution arose " at that time, and Paul, speaking of " many of the saints ", says, " when they were condemned to death I gave my voice against them ". But Paul's conversion did not relieve the Church of danger. The martyrdom of James followed that of Stephen, and nothing short of a miracle saved the life of Peter. What dangers beset Paul himself, after his conversion, we know not only from the Acts, but from his epistles. Such words as " I die daily ", " in deaths oft ", " daily delivered unto death ", " we are killed all the day long ", could be written by no candid man except in the view of perpetual peril of life. And these words were all written either in this epistle, or within a year of its date.

Now we have no reason to believe that every case of early Christian suffering and martyrdom has found a record in the Acts. We catch but a glimpse of the "many" whose death Paul compassed. There may well have been many others of whom we do not see even so much. Timothy was exposed to peril of which the only hint is in Paul's declaration that he had been "set at liberty", Heb. xiii, 23. And the martyrdom of James the Less, though occurring within the period covered by the Acts, is narrated by Josephus, but not by Luke.

Moreover, we have distinct reason for believing that such scenes had no more been excluded from Corinth than from other cities. When Paul first appeared there, Gallio alone saved him from injury and possible death. That the enraged Jews, doubly excited by the circumstance of that failure, and spurred on as we know they everywhere were by the Sanhedrim at Jerusalem, would always find an equal check upon their fury, is by no means to be assumed. Upon the other hand, Paul in this very argument ascribes the preëminent temporal "misery" of the early Christians as much to the Corinthians as to himself. Within the five or six years of their Church's existence, there might well have been not only sufferers but martyrs among themselves — their "sleepers in Christ" having "fallen asleep" as Stephen did.

But at the very least they knew of such deaths and of their fruits. For it is not too much to say that no feature of that ancient piety was more striking than the zeal that flamed up under persecution. Men soon came to pant for martyrdom. By the boldest assaults upon the prevailing paganism, they challenged the violence of their enemies. They became their own accusers, and courted their fate with an eagerness that confounded their heathen observers. Early in the second century a Roman proconsul needed to drive the self-accusers from him, exclaiming : " If you wish to die, cannot you find

precipices and ropes?"   (See Tertullian, quoted in Mosheim's
Commentaries, p. 235.)   This surely was the frenzy of piety;
and Christian zeal must have grown into that excess.   And
yet Ignatius, who was living when our text was written, as he
approached his martyrdom about fifty years later, betrayed an
almost equal eagerness to reach his "crown of glory".   It
was a contagion, and men felt it from the first.   The death of
Stephen was shortly followed by the conversion of a "great
number".   Paul's "bonds" made Christians "bolder", and
Peter's death "glorified God".   The persecutors soon came
to understand this, and therefore, as the Acts of the Martyrdom of Ignatius inform us, Trajan was unwilling that he
should suffer at Antioch, lest the sight of his fortitude might
increase the number of Christians.   Gibbon, with whatever
motive, describes only fairly the effect of every such spectacle
when he says: "On these melancholy occasions there were
many among the Gentiles who pitied, who admired, and who
were converted.   The generous enthusiasm was commmuni-
cated from the sufferer to the spectators; and the blood of the
martyrs, according to a well-known observation, became the
seed of the Church".   (*Decline and Fall.* ch. xvi.)   "Nothing",
says Maitland,* "could have been devised better adapted to
display the power of the new faith than submitting its professors to martyrdom. . . . The executioner often caught the
flame, gazed upon the dangerous spectacle of the power of
true religion till his heart burnt within him, and fairly overwhelmed by the triumph of faith and hope, hastened to un-
dergo the death which his hands had inflicted on another".
"Crucify us, torture us", exclaimed Tertullian, in his Apology,
"when you mow us down, we increase as in a harvest.   The
blood of Christians is their seed".

Now we are careful to admit that these delineations belong
especially to the age which followed that of Paul.   We must
therefore lower the coloring till the picture shall suit the very
times of the text.   The number of the martyrs will be less,
and the zeal of their sympathizers will be calmer.   But the
power of Christian piety in a steadfast sufferer, whose face

* *Church in the Catacombs*, p. 100.

men see "like the face of an angel", belongs to the first century as much as to the second.

Let us conceive, then, of converts nerved to duty by such a sight, and seeking at the hands of the Christian teachers the baptism that should expose them to equal dangers. If they were asked to explain the choice which they had made, would it not be most natural for them to refer it to the influence of "the dead"? A child or near friend of the departed could by no means fail to do this. Then, if those who had witnessed their profession should afterwards find a class of Christians described as οἱ βαπτιζόμενοι ὑπὲρ τῶν νεκρῶν would they not have before them an act and a motive which those words would exactly cover? We venture to believe that if two classes of men could have been equally distinct in the view of the Corinthian church; namely, a class which in fact, but without warrant, received the mere *form* of baptism in the name of the dead, and another class who had been led to baptism itself by their regard for the dead, the expression of the text in its place in Paul's argument, would have indicated the latter class rather than the former. One has only to throw into the words the fervor that pervades all the passage, and they describe that class in the most natural sense of every syllable. The "baptism" is real; "the dead" are real, and the one is "for" the other. Nay, this baptism of sympathy and affection is tenfold more truly "for the advantage of the dead" than any vicarious baptism. It does not indeed contribute to their safety — an impossible and absurd idea. But it does offer a tribute to the dear idea of the departed as it lives in the heart of the survivor; and it aims directly at that final meeting which the memory of past affection foreshadows as a joy in store for the friends that have gone, as well as for those who have set out to follow them. If a father, who had exhausted all argument upon an undecided child, should turn his last conscious look upon him, and exclaim, "ὑπὲρ ἐμοῦ", "for my sake", the expression would be good Greek and full of meaning. Whatever tender and persuasive suggestion might be embraced in such words, when taken at their most obvious sense, we find in the similar expression of the text.

But if this be the meaning of Paul's words, why did not the early Christians so understand them? We have no reason to think that they did not. The earliest historic interpretation of the text is Tertullian's, which dates about a century and a half after the writing of the epistle. He, in a single sentence, so far admitted the notion of vicarious baptism as to say that it would not conflict with his pending argument. But if he had formally adopted that view of the passage, and if half of the church of his day could be known to have gone with him, such an interpretation could not stand. Neither Paul nor his argument, nor Christian piety, has any fellowship with it. But now we find another interpretation which, if the book* containing it be Origen's, as is thought, is about as old as this allusion of Tertullian. We know that the book is ancient, and it may have been written in Origen's day, even if not written by himself. According to this interpretation the baptism was had *over* the dead. Now let us assume, for argument's sake, that the earliest and purest church held the view of the passage which we have been presenting. Then we know that the regard of martyrs soon ran to excess; that their graves became places of superstitious resort, and that baptism and other acts of worship were performed over them. We know, besides, that the phrase ὑπὲρ τῶν νεκρῶν, while according to New Testament usage, it excluded the idea of a local relation — "*over* the dead", according to classical and conversational usage admitted that idea. Under these circumstances it would be most natural that the very affections which, in Paul's day, might have welcomed the risks of baptism for the sake of the dead, should come to seek the consecrating sacrament over the very graves of the martyrs, and that the meaning of the text should be warped to suit such a practice. If we relieve that interpretation of what is clearly a superstitious gloss upon Paul's words, a living intelligible sentiment remains, namely, a regard of the pious dead which anticipated their resurrection and so prompted to baptism. This is the very sentiment which we find in the text. If it

---

* *Dialogus de Recta in Deum Fide.*

had no place in the earlier church, whence grew the later superstitious practice?

But we do not need to insist upon this coincidence. It is enough to claim that there must have been in the bosom of the most ancient Church an accepted sense of this text, which did not come out in the writings of the earliest fathers. The lapse of time and the growth of superstition might withdraw attention more and more from that real but delicate meaning of the passage, until when, in the fourth century, Chrysostom and others began fairly to study it, the equivocalness of the mere language and the prevalent perversions of it may have misled them utterly from its original sense. Indeed there must have been a meaning of the text in the earliest times of the Church, which the historic interpretations of a later day have not handed down to us. Unless this be true, alas! for the text. If that original sense shall ever be discovered, it must be through such methods of candid investigation as we have sought to employ.

We are far from feeling that this interpretation relieves so obscure and compact a passage of all difficulty; but yet we claim that it is fairly consistent with every word of the text, with all the drift and dignity of the Apostle's argument, with the known circumstances and impulses of the times, and with universal Christian feeling. It carries the argument home to the strongest and most sensitive instincts of sanctified affection, and makes the denial of the resurrection treason against human sympathy and human love. Just this it is, and an appeal to pious feeling could not place the heresy in a more odious light.

This is our view of the letter of the text, with which an interpreter has chiefly to deal. But now, if any one shall insist that here, as so often elsewhere, Paul suggests more than he says, we are glad to admit it. We will still hold the sense of the text to the exact limits of its grammar, and make "the dead" the special dead who furnished a motive to the baptized. But it is clearly impossible for any such thought to be separated from the conception of Christ's great heavenly kingdom. No surviving Christian locates his departed friend in a solitary

world.   Special affection binds the believer to a few of the
dead, but faith relates those few to all the rest, and so, in effect, affection for the dead we love most, embodies for us the
whole heavenly glory.   All this must have been in the mind
of Paul when he passed in a breath from the delineation of
that glory, to this question concerning the special dead.   He
embodied them within it, just as the faith that braved his own
dangers foresaw himself in the midst of that company.   It
was thus that either argument carried with it the hope and the
proof of the resurrection of all the saints.   And thus, too, all
those great thoughts concerning the dead and risen Saviour,
and the glorious company of his people, which other interpretations have labored to fasten upon the terms of the text are,
according to our view, awakened and defined by its affectionate spirit.

Art. VI.—CAIRNES ON THE SLAVE POWER.

The Slave Power; its Character, Career, and Probable Designs: Being
an Attempt to Explain the Real Issues involved in the American Contest.
By J. E. Cairnes, M.A., Professor of Jurisprudence and Political Econo-
my in Queen's College, Galway; and late Whately Professor of Political
Economy in the Univerity of Dublin. 2d edition. New-York: Carleton,
Publisher, 413 Broadway.

    This is by far the most able and satisfactory work on the
American contest which has yet appeared in England.   As
an exposition of the character, history, and designs of the
Slave Power, it is a master-piece of candid and thorough discussion.   The matter and the manner of it are alike admirable.   It is, indeed, a refreshing oasis in the moral desert of
British speculation and dogmatism concerning America.   Professor Cairnes enjoyed already the reputation of being one of
the first writers on Political Economy in Great Britain.   This
book will not only enhance his reputation as a political economist, but will also place him high among the best social and
political philosophers of the age.   Instead of the wretched

sciolism, ignorance, and immorality, which have characterized so large a portion of English writings and opinions about our national struggle, this treatise bears throughout the marks of careful, conscientious study and profound reflection; while the ethical tone is eminently pure and earnest. Professor Cairnes is "far from being an admirer of democracy as it exists in the Northern States", but he is evidently an ardent admirer of justice, freedom, humanity, and the other great principles of Christian civilization involved in this contest. We hail his work, therefore, with sincere thankfulness; and, although differing with him on some points, and especially as to the probable issue of the struggle, we heartily commend it to all our readers. Would that a copy could be placed in the hands of every voter in the United States who is able to read it! We are glad to see that a new edition, carefully revised by the author, is soon to appear. Let it be republished in a cheap form and sown broadcast over the land; let special pains be taken to have it read by our public men, both in civil life and in the army and navy; and also by our leading merchants. We know of no work better fitted to diffuse and to render still deeper and more vivid the conviction of the loyal American people that the cause for which they are fighting is not their own merely, but that in a preëminent sense it is also the cause of Christian progress and civilization the world over.

With these remarks we proceed to give our readers some extracts from the work, illustrative of its general aim and character. The main scope of the argument is to show that the SLAVE POWER (which Prof. C. defines as "that system of interests, industrial, social, and political, which has for the greater part of half a century directed the career of the American Union, and which now, embodied in the Southern Confederation, seeks admission as an equal member into the community of civilized nations") "*constitutes the most formidable antagonist to civilized progress which has appeared for many centuries, representing a system of society at once retrograde and aggressive, a system which, containing within it no germs from which improvement can spring, gravitates inevitably toward barbarism, while it is impelled by exigencies*

*inherent in its position and circumstances to a constant exten-
sion of its territorial domain*" (p. 26).

To establish this startling proposition the author enters at
once upon an elaborate and searching analysis of the institution of slavery, pointing out its different fortunes in the North
and South, rejecting the common explanations of this phenomenon, which attribute it to climate, race, or diversity of
character in the original settlers, and asserting the true solution of the problem to be economic. Slave labor is given
reluctantly; it is unskilful; it is wanting in versatility. These
are its defects. But slave labor is susceptible of complete
organization — it can be combined on an extensive scale and
directed by a controlling mind to a single end. This is its
merit; and this is why it has so flourished in the South in
spite of its inherent defects.

But it must not be inferred that because, under certain conditions, slavery is economically profitable it is, therefore, con-
ducive to at least the material well-being of countries in which
these conditions exist. This does not follow—and to show that
it does not, the author discusses at length the internal organization of slave societies and points out the varied and fatal
obstacles which it puts in the way of industrial development
and general well-being. He thus concludes the chapter: "To
sum up in a few words the general results of the foregoing
discussion: the Slave Power—that power which has long held
the helm of Government in the Union—is, under the forms of
a democracy, an uncontrolled despotism, wielded by a compact oligarchy. Supported by the labor of four millions of
slaves, it rules a population of five millions of whites—a population ignorant, averse to systematic industry, and prone to
irregular adventure. A system of society more formidable for
evil, more menacing to the best interests of the human race, it
is difficult to conceive" (p. 63).

Having examined the internal organization, the author proceeds to discuss the tendencies, internal development, and external policy of slave societies. All these points are treated
with signal ability. In considering the first-mentioned, he
notes the radical differences between American slavery and

the institution as it existed in the ancient world.　There is the vital fact of the difference in color between the American slave and his master ; a difference fraught with the most disastrous consequences.　Another difference arises from the vast growth and extension of international commerce in modern times—

"So long as each nation was in the main dependent on the industry of its own members for the supply of its wants, a strong motive would be present for the cultivation of the intelligence, and the improvement of the condition of the industrial classes.　The commodities which minister to comfort and luxury cannot be produced without skilled labor, and skilled labor implies a certain degree of mental cultivation, and a certain progress in social respect. To attain success in the more difficult industrial arts, the workman must respect his vocation, must take an interest in his task ; habits of care, deliberation, forethought, must be acquired; in short, there must be such a general awakening of the faculties, intellectual and moral, as by leading men to a knowledge of their rights and of the means of enforcing them, inevitably disqualifies them for the servile condition.　Now this was the position in which the slave-master found himself in the ancient world.　He was, in the main, dependent on the skill of his slaves for obtaining whatever he required.　He was, therefore, naturally led to cultivate the faculties of his slaves, and by consequence to promote generally the improvement of their condition.　His progress in the enjoyment of the material advantages of civilisation depended directly upon *their* progress in knowledge and social consideration.　Accordingly, the education of slaves was never prohibited in the ancient Roman world, and, in point of fact, no small number of them enjoyed the advantage of a high cultivation. 'The youths of promising genius', says Gibbon, 'were instructed in the arts and sciences, and almost every profession, liberal and mechanical, might be found in the household of an opulent Senator'.　Modern slaveholders, on the contrary, are independent of the skill, and therefore of the intelligence and social improvement of their slave population.　They have only need to find a commodity which is capable of being produced by crude labor, and at the same time in large demand in the markets of the world ; and by applying their slaves to the production of this, they may, through an exchange with other countries, make it the means of procuring for themselves whatever they require. Cotton and sugar, for example, are commodities which fulfil these conditions ; they may be raised by crude labor, and they are in large demand throughout the world.　Accordingly, Alabama and Louisiana have only to employ their slaves in raising these products, and they are enabled through their means to command the industrial resources of all commercial nations. Without cultivating one of the arts or refinements of civilisation, they can possess themselves of all its material comforts.　Without employing an artisan, a manufacturer, a skilled laborer of any sort, they can secure the products of the highest manufacturing and mechanical skill" (pp. 68, 69).

Then there is the difference of the slave-trade :

"Trading in slaves was doubtless practised by the ancients, and with sufficient barbarity. But we look in vain in the records of antiquity for a traffic which, in extent, in systematic character, and above all, in the function discharged by it as the common support of countries breeding and consuming human labor, can with justice be regarded as the analogue of the modern slave-trade — of that organized system which has been carried on between Guinea and the coast of America, and of that between Virginia, the Guinea of the New World, and the slave-consuming States of the South and West" (p. 71).

The chapter on the internal development of slave societies is exceedingly impressive. The rude industrial state of *the mean whites,* and the absurdity of looking to *them* for social amelioration, are vividly set forth. Can we look to the slaves or their masters? It were equally absurd. The condition of the slaves, as such, is utterly hopeless: it contains no germ of promise. And as to their masters, what prospect is there of emancipation in a government based upon slavery as its "corner-stone"? Ultimate barbarism—not freedom and civilisation—is the inevitable goal of Southern slave society.

The chapter on the external policy of slave societies is full of power. We give a portion of it :

"In free societies, the paths to eminence are various. Successful trade, the professions, science and literature, social reform, philanthropy, furnish employment for the redundant activity of the people, and open so many avenues to distinction. But for slaveholders these means of advancement do not exist. Commerce and manufactures are excluded by the necessities of the case. The professions, which are the result of much subdivision of employment where population is rich and dense, can have no place in a poor and thinly peopled country. Science and literature are left without the principal inducements for their cultivation, where there is no field for their most important practical applications. Social reform and philanthropy would be out of place in a country where human chattels are the principal property. Practically, but one career lies open to the Southerner desirous of advancement — agriculture carried on by slaves. To this, therefore, he turns. In the management of his plantation, in the breeding, buying, and selling of slaves, his life is passed. Amid the moral atmosphere which this mode of life engenders, his ideas and tastes are formed. He has no notion of ease, independence, happiness, where slavery is not found. Is it strange, then, that his ambition should connect itself with the institution around which are entwined his domestic associations, which is identified with all his plans in life, and which offers him the sole chance of emerging from obscurity ?

"But the aspirations of the slaveholder are not confined within the limits of his own community. He is also a citizen of the United States. In the former, he naturally and easily takes the leading place ; but, as a member of the larger society in which he is called upon to act in combination with men who have been brought up under free institutions, the position which he is destined to fill is not so clearly indicated. It is plain, however, that he cannot become blended in the general mass of the population of the Union. His character, habits, and aims are not those of the Northern people, nor are theirs his. The Northerner is a merchant, a manufacturer, a lawyer, a literary man, an artisan, a shopkeeper, a schoolmaster, a peasant farmer ; he is engaged in commercial speculation, or in promoting social or political reform ; perhaps he is a philanthropist, and includes slavery-abolition in his programme. Between such men and the slaveholder of the South there is no common basis for political action. There are no objects in promoting which he can combine with them in good faith and upon public grounds. There lies before him, therefore, but one alternative: he must stand by his fellows, and become powerful as the asserter and propagandist of slavery ; or, failing this, he must submit to be of no account in the politics of the Union. Here then again the slaveholder is thrown back upon his peculiar system as the sole means of satisfying the master passion of his life. In the society of the Union, no less than in that of the State, he finds that his single path to power lies through the maintenance and extension of this institution. Accordingly, to uphold it, to strengthen it, to provide for its future growth and indefinite expansion, becomes the dream of his life—the one great object of his existence. But this is not all ; this same institution, which is the beginning and end of the slaveholder's being, places between him and the citizens of free societies a broad and impassable gulf. The system which is the foundation of his present existence and future hopes, is by them denounced as sinful and inhuman ; and he is himself held up to the reprobation of mankind. The tongues and hands of all freemen are instinctively raised against him. A consciousness is thus awakened in the minds of the community of slaveholders that they are a proscribed class, that their position is one of antagonism to the whole civilized world; and the feeling binds them together in the fastest concord. Their pride is aroused ; and all the energy of their nature is exerted to make good their position against those who would assail it. In this manner the instinct of self-defence and the sentiment of pride come to aid the passion of ambition, and all tend to fix in the minds of the slaveholders the resolution to maintain at all hazards the keystone of their social order.   To establish their scheme of society on such broad and firm foundations that they may set at defiance the public opinion of free nations, and, in the last resort, resist the combined efforts of their physical power, becomes at length the settled purpose and clearly conceived design of the whole body.   To this they devote themselves with the zeal of fanatics, with the persistency and secrecy of conspirators.

" The position of slaveholders thus naturally fosters the passion of ambition, and that passion inevitably connects itself with the maintenance and extension of slavery " (pp. 97, 98).

The career and designs of the slave power form the subject of the two following chapters.   They are written with great force, and evince an extraordinary familiarity with our political history during the last thirty years.

In his concluding chapter the author shows the impolicy of European intervention, the duty of neutrality and the obligation to render us moral support.   He also considers the possible modes of settlement, and suggests one of his own, which he thinks would involve an ultimate victory over slavery. His plan is to recognise the Confederacy with the Mississippi for its western boundary.   We trust and believe that a much better plan — even that of a regenerated, free, and unbroken Union — is in the decree of Almighty Providence.

G. L. P.

ART. VII.—BELIEF OF THE INDIANS IN INFERIOR SPIRITS.

By J. A. VAN HEUVEL, Esq., Ogdensburgh, N. Y.

THE Indian nations of America, besides acknowledging a Supreme Being, believe also in good spirits subordinate to Him to whom they offer prayers and supplications.

"The Indians", says Lafitan, "believe not only in a Supreme Being, but also in spirits inferior to him. Their number is not fixed. Their imagination sees them in all things in nature; but especially in all such as are wonderful, whose origin is not known and have the character of novelty".*

"To all their inferior deities", says Charleroix, "the Hurons, Iroquois, and Algonquins, make various kinds of offerings. To propitiate the god of the waters, they cast into the streams and lakes tobacco and birds that have been killed by them. In honor of the sun, and also of inferior spirits, they consume in the fire a part of everything they eat. Strings of wampum, ears of corn, the skins, and often the whole carcases, of animals are seen along difficult and dangerous rocks, and on the shores of rapids, as so many offerings made to the presiding genius of the place ".†

Mr. Bancroft, in his *History of the United States*, thus remarks on this part of the Indian belief: "The red man sees a divinity in every power. Every hidden agency, every mysterious influence is personified. A god dwells in the sun and in the moon, and in the firmament; a god reddens in the eastern sky; a deity is present on the ocean and in the fire; the crag that overhangs the river has its genius; there is a spirit in the waterfall; a household god makes his abode in the

* *Mœurs des Sauvages*, vol. i, p. 153.   † *Travels in Canada*.

Indian's wigwam, and consecrates his home. So the savage deity, broken as it were into an infinite number of fragments, fills all place and all being. . . . Hennepin found a beaver-robe hung on an oak as an oblation to the spirit that dwells on the Falls of St. Anthony. The guides of Jontel, in the southwest, on killing a buffalo, offered several slices of the meat as a sacrifice to the unknown spirit of that wilderness. As they passed the Ohio, its beautiful stream was propitiated by gifts of tobacco and dried meat, and worship was paid to the rock just above the Missouri ".*

Tobacco is an offering especially made to the inferior spirits. "There is", says an early traveller, " an herb in Virginia called uppowee, which is tobacco and is held in such estimation that they think their gods are extremely delighted with it, for which reason they make hallowed fires, and cast some of the powder therein for a sacrifice. Being in a storm upon the waters, they cast some up into the air ; all done with strange gestures, stamping, and sometimes dancing, clapping of hands, holding them up, looking to the heavens, and uttering strange words and noises ".†

The adoration of these inferior deities is the ordinary worship of the American Indians. To the Great Spirit or Supreme Being their addresses are made only on particular great occasions.

Harmon, in his Journal, says of the Indians generally, offerings are sometimes made to the Supreme Being, but rarely. They occasionally supplicate of him success in their important undertakings.

Lederer observes of the Indians of Virginia: " Okee is their name for the Creator of all things. To him the high priest offers sacrifices ; but their ordinary devotion is to lesser divinities, to whom they suppose sublunary affairs are committed".

It is, perhaps, from this that the early French Catholic missionaries who, Lafitan complains, did not make themselves

* *History of the United States*, chap. xxii.   † *Purchas' Collection.*

sufficiently acquainted with the religion of the American Indians, have expressed an opinion that they had no belief in God, and paid no worship to him, of which Mr. Bancroft gives several instances. "As to the knowledge of God", says Jontel of the southwest, " it did not seem to me that they had any notion. True we found upon our route some who, as far as we could judge, believed that there was something exalted which is above all; but they have neither temples nor ceremonies nor prayers marking a divine worship". Le Jeune says : "There is among them very little superstition ; they think only of living and revenge ; they are not attached to the worship of any divinity".

But these accounts of the Jesuits are certainly without foundation, and could have arisen only from a very imperfect examination. It is true the American Indians have no temples or religious ceremonies for the worship of the Great Spirit or Supreme Being ; but that they acknowledge him and make " prayers to him, marking a divine worship", which Jontel denies, has been most abundantly shown. The contradiction of the statements of the Jesuits, by Lafitan, who had most thoroughly inquired into the religion of the Indians, is indeed, of itself, a sufficient refutation of them.

The American Indians have images or idols of their inferior spirits. "The Iroquois", says Charleroix, " make *Manitous*, or carved images, of their good spirits which they carried with them wherever they went. Kitchi-Manitou is their name for the Great Spirit. There is a Manitou of the rivers, the lakes, etc. To these manitous they have recourse when they are in any danger, when they go on any enterprise, and when they would obtain any extraordinary favor".*

" I have seen", says Heckewelder, " the Chippewas on the lakes pray to the Manitou of the Waters that he might prevent the swells from rising too high while they were passing over them. In both cases they threw tobacco in the air or strewed it on the water".†

" The Hurons and Iroquois", says the Bishop of Meaux, "in

---

* *Travels in Canada.*   † *History of the Delawares.*

their march, encamp a long time before sunset, and commonly leave before the camp a large space surrounded by palissadoes, or rather a sort of lattice, in which they place their manitous facing toward the spot to which they are going. They invoke them for an hour, and the same time when they decamp. After this they think they have nothing to fear ; they suppose that the spirits take upon themselves to be sentinels, and all the family sleep quiet under their supposed influence ".*

In this worship, of the American Indians, of inferior deities, we see an idolatry of the heathens of the old world. Dr. Leland observes : " The belief that God did not concern himself with mankind in their affairs, but committed the arrangement of them to inferior deities, obtained among many of those pagan nations who retained the idea of a Supreme Being, which was the source of the prevailing polytheism. As men fell from the worship of the One True God, the providence they acknowledged was the providence of the deities they adored. It was parcelled out among a multitude of gods and goddesses, among whom they think the administration of things to be distributed. To them, therefore, they offered up prayers and sacrifices for obtaining the good things they stood in need of, and averting the calamities they feared ".†

Dr. Hinds, in his *Early History of Christianity*, thus explains the origin of this idolatry : " That the Israelites did not consider polytheism as implying a disbelief in the unity of God, will hardly be denied. That the heathen originally adopted it under the same impression, is also highly probable. But what, it may be asked, could have suggested to the early world a system so strange, and apparently incongruous, as polytheism ? . . . A doctrine in the Bible, we think, gave rise to it. A belief in angels and ministering spirits appears in the earliest records of God's dispensations ; nor can there be any difficulty in fixing on this article of belief as the point from which religion first began to diverge into error and superstition and impiety. Men, for instance, attributing whatever

* *Origin of the American Indians.* By John McIntosh, M.D.   Quebec.
† *Necessity of Revelation.*

blessings they received from God to the intermediate agency of his good angels, would (if neglectful of the appointed preservatives against error) fall into an undue regard and reverence for these ministers of good. A kindly season, the rains which caused their crops to grow, the sun which ripened it, would become associated in their effects with sòme invisible superintendent, the agent and the creature".

It is doubtful whether in ancient idolatry, in which the whole world was divided among a multitude of gods and goddesses, absolute independent power was given to each in his particular sphere, or that every one was considered only the minister of the Sovereign Power through whose mediation and intercession gifts and favors were obtained from him. But in regard to the American Indians, it appears from several authorities that the latter is the idea entertained by them of their inferior spirits.

" To the inferior spirits", says Harmon in his Journal, " the offerings of the Indians are commonly made ; and to injure anything wantonly is considered highly insulting to the Great Master of Life, *who is the secret object of their adorations*".

Of the Delawares or Lenni Lenape, Loskiel says they sacrifice to a hare because, according to report, their first ancestor was a hare ; to Indian corn they sacrifice bear-flesh, etc. ; but they positively deny that they pay any adoration to the good spirits, and affirm that they only worship the true God *through them.**

In a very distant quarter we find the same idea among the American Indians. Martyr, the contemporary of Columbus, in his very authentic work on the New World, says : " The Indians of Hispaniola had hung about their necks little idols called Zemis, which they reverenced as intercessors for them with the Great Spirit ".

No one of the writers from whom these extracts are taken appears to have considered the conformity of this belief of the American Indians with the doctrine of Mediation, the foundation of the Christian religion.

* *History of the Missouris.*

In ancient times the existence of two principles, Good and Evil, producing the varied character of human affairs, prevailed extensively in the Old World.

" Men", says Dr. Leland, "unable to account for the evil in the world under the administration of a Good Being, believed that there was an evil and opposing principle continually endeavoring to thwart his designs. Plutarch, who gives his assent to this doctrine, says it was the general sentiment of the most famous and ancient nations, and of the wisest and gravest persons among them; that it obtained among the Persians, and that it may be traced in the astrology of the Chaldæans, in the mysterious and sacred rites of the Egyptians, and even among the Greeks. This belief found its way, in early times, into the Christian church and gave rise to the sect of Manichæists".*

The same mythology exists universally among the American Indians.

Of this belief among the tribes of North America we omit any account as it appears in their manner of curing the sick by expelling the evil spirit, which is well known, being related by all travellers, and will be tedious to repeat.

A few instances in nations south of them will be mentioned.

The Caribees of the West India Islands, Rochefort says, believed in an evil spirit whom they called Maboya, and said that he often appeared to them in hideous shapes, and they showed marks on their bodies of the bruises he had given them.†

Of the Indian tribes on the Orinoco, Gamilla says there is not one that does not believe in an evil spirit, to whom they attribute all the calamities that occur to them.‡

The Galibis of Cayenne call the evil spirit Iroucan (the Caribees of British Guiana above them call it Hyorocan). They ascend at break of day a high mountain, turn to the east, and invoke Tamouzi, their name for the Supreme Being, then to the west, and pray with fervor to Iroucan; but they

* *Necessity of Revelation.*
† Rochefort, *Histoire des Antilles,* book ii, chap. 10.
‡ *History of the Orinoco,* chap. 28.

said to the missionaries, that they did not pray to Iroucan with a good heart, but because he is powerful and wicked.*

"The Brazilians", says De Lery, "believe in a devil, not thát they worship him, but are tormented by him. Even in speaking of him they tremble. Sometimes in the form of a bird, in another in that of a beast, they grievously torment them".†

It is chiefly in diseases that the power of the evil spirit is endeavored to be counteracted. Among all the American Indians is an order of priests who unite in their office the practice of the medical art, and are believed to have intercourse with the Good Spirit, and in curing the sick call in their aid his influence to expel the evil spirit, who is supposed to have taken possession of the patient. They have in their hands a rattle, called by the Algonquins Chichikoné, by the Brazilians and other Southern nations Maracca. The chichikoné is made of a gourd with a handle fixed to it; the maracca of the Southern Indians is formed of the calabash, a fruit of the shape of a melon, with a stick thrust through it, the upper part of which is decorated with feathers. In both cases, the contents are removed, and seeds or pebbles placed in to make a rattling sound when shaken. The ceremonies of the priest when called to cure the sick are very similar among all the Indians of North and South America, and substantially the following : With the rattle in his hand he moves about the patient, who is lying on a bed or hammock, leaping and dancing with a variety of motions, shaking the rattle and uttering some unintelligible words to induce the Good Spirit to expel the evil spirit from him, employing meanwhile, doubtless secretly, medical remedies which he carries with him. Then drawing from his mouth a thorn, a bone or splinter of wood, exhibits it and declares it was the cause of the sickness which is now removed.

The ceremonies of the Caribees of the West India Islands have something peculiar, as particularly related by Rochefort in his account of them. When a person is taken sick, and all the remedies used for his recovery are unavailing, he sends for

* Barrere, *Histoire de la France Equinoctiale.*
† Purchas' Collection.

a boyer or priest, who first endeavors to procure the appearance of the chemin or Good Spirit of the patient; for which purpose he makes an altar in a corner of the cabin of three of their small tables called matoutons, one laid above the other, on which he places an offering to the chemin 'of cassava, the bread of the Caribees, and a bowl of ovicon, their favorite drink. The fires have been all put out and the lights extinguished, so that there is perfect darkness in the cabin. The boyer then enters and vociferating some uncouth words, stamps on the ground and smokes a roll of tobacco, blowing the smoke upwards, then rubs the tobacco in his hands and scatters it in the air. On this a dreadful sound is heard, supposed to come from the chemin, and he is believed to be entering the cabin through the roof. Perfect darkness being in the cabin, those in it do not perceive the deception practised. The boyer then inquires of the chemin the cause of the illness of the patient, whose answer gives hopes of his recovery, which is doubtless made by the boyer with a counterfeited voice. This he announces to the patient, and then passes his hand over the part of his body where the pain is felt, rubs it and pretends to extract from it a thorn or bone, etc., which he says was the cause of his illness. If the patient does not recover, he has various reasons at hand to account for it. He says that the evil spirit had taken such firm hold of his body that it was not possible to expel it, or that there was another boyer who was unfriendly to him (the patient), or that sufficient gifts had not been made to the chemin. If he is restored, as an acknowledgment to the boyer, he prepares a feast, at which the first place is given to him, and an offering of cassava and ovicon is provided for the chemin.*

In the smoking of tobacco, in this ceremony, to call down the chemin, we have another instance of its being an offering made by the American Indians to inferior spirits. But the calumet was not used, which is exclusively an instrument of the North American Indians. Instead of it, it is seen that a roll of tobacco was employed.

---

* Rochefort, *Histoire des Antilles*, book ii.

The chichikoné or maracca appears to be of a sacred character, and an instrument through which the answers of the Good Spirit are given.

In the ceremony of the Brazilians for infusing the spirit of courage, those assembled formed themselves into three rings, in each of which were three or four Caribees, who were their priests, each having a maracca in his hand, which he continually shook, from which they said the spirit would speak. De Lery, from whom we take this account, says, Toupan, their name for the Supreme Being, goeth about to reveal secrets to these Caribees, who possess the interpretation of dreams, and are also esteemed as wizards that confer with spirits. They say that a spirit came from the remotest parts of the world who gave the maracca power to make answers to questions.* Stade, who was taken prisoner by the Brazilians, and ascribes his captivity to the prediction of the maracca,† thus relates the manner in which it was consecrated : " After the ceremony for infusing the spirit of courage, the paygi or priests order every one to carry his tamaraka to the house where it was to receive the spirit of speech, who sticks its stem (or handle) in the ground, and all offer to the chief paygi arrows, feathers, and earrings, who then blows petum (tobacco) on it, puts it to his mouth and says, Nee Kora, speak if thou art within ; and follows a squeaking voice, which I, says Stade, thought the wizard did, but the people ascribed it to the tamaraka. Then the paygi persuade them to make war, saying that those spirits long to feed on the flesh of captives. This done, every one takes his rattle and builds a house to keep it, and places meat and drink before it, which the Indians believe they eat, and ask of it such things as they need, and these he says are their gods".‡

The Indians about Auzerma in New Grenada, called the Spaniards, when they first saw them, Tamaraka, as if it signified a superior being.§

* Purchas.
† *Southey's History of Brazil*, vol. i, p. 187.
‡ *Purchas' Pilgrimage*, p. 1038.
§ *Southey's History of Brazil*, vol. i, note 44.

Narvaez, one of the earliest navigators to Florida, says, in some places, as we passed, we saw the physicians or magicians with rattles of gourds which they suppose to have come from heaven, and to have great virtue in them.*

From the view which has been given of the religion of the American Indians, two conclusions may be drawn.

First, that they were derived from the old world. This might à priori be admitted, as the Scriptures inform us that all mankind are sprung from one pair, and that the only survivors of the deluge which destroyed the world were Noah and his three sons, who, with their immediate descendants, having collected on the plain of Shinar, in Central Asia, on their attempt to build a tower " whose top should reach unto the heavens", were by a divine command frustrated in their attempt and their language confounded, on which they dispersed in different directions over the earth. It is pleasing, however, to find the derivation of the people of the American continent from the other hemisphere shown by the similarity of religious ideas in both sections of the globe, confirming the Scripture account of the Human Species.

Second. We learn from the same view what was the first religion of the world. Dr. Hinds remarks, that two Greek historians observe that it is from uncivilized barbarous nations that this knowledge can be best obtained. " Can we do otherwise", exclaims Ælian (Book ii, chap. 31), than commend the wisdom of the barbarians? Among them no one followed atheism. With them there are no controversies about the gods, nor questioning whether there are such things or not". " The barbarians", says Diodorus Siculus, "go on in one course, firm to their principles; but the Greeks, who consider philosophy a gainful profession, are for setting up new sects and opposing things to theory on the most important subjects, so that the people only acquire the habit of doubting".

The American Indians acquaint us with what was the primitive religion of mankind in these respects.

1. They worship only one God, whom they term the Good

---

* *Purchas*, vol. i, book viii, chap. 7.

Spirit, who governs all things. Among nations of the old world, when idolatry was introduced among them, gods and goddesses were multiplied without number. Hence the first commandment in the Decalogue, "I am the Lord thy God, thou shalt have no other gods before me".

2. The American Indians have no statues or images or any representation whatever of the Supreme Being. Such was the case at first in the ancient world; but when religion became corrupted, there was this other prohibition in the Decalogue, "not to make any graven image, nor to bow down to them nor serve them".

3. The American Indians have no temples or altars for the worship of the Supreme Being. They worship him in the open air under the canopy of heaven. They ascend to the tops of high mountains to pray to the Great Spirit.

In all these particulars there is a resemblance between them and the ancient Persians. "The Persians", says Herodotus (Book i, sect. 151), reject the use of temples, of altars, and of statues. The tops of the highest mountains are the places chosen for sacrifice. The Supreme Being who fills the wide circuit of heaven is the object to which their addresses are made.

Art. VIII.—POLITICS AND THE PULPIT.

By Rev. William Adams, D.D., New York.

Public attention has been frequently directed of late to what is generally understood by "*preaching politics*". We propose to state a few principles, of permanent use, pertaining to this subject. Confused and inconsistent notions concerning it are entertained by many. Some are very jealous of any allusions from the pulpit to matters affecting the state. Others insist that the pulpit shall be out-spoken and explicit in the advocacy of their own favorite policy. So long as the ministry is a power in the world, its influence will be deprecated or invoked in aid of all objects where power is coveted. Few men have objections to the preaching of politics, so long as it is their own politics which are preached.

A clergyman preaches a discourse which he thinks is demanded by the perils of the country. The doctrine he advocates is distasteful to certain conductors of the political press, who forthwith censure him for transcending his proper vocation. He is accused of meddling with subjects which do not belong to his profession. He is distinctly informed that if he ventures to intrude into such an arena, his high and holy calling will be disgraced, and the white robes of his office will be sullied by the missiles with which he will certainly be pelted by excited men. Ere long the pulpit speaks again, from another quarter and in another tone. It promulgates doctrines now which happen to be agreeable to the very men who before censured the clergy for presuming to speak at all on such subjects, but who now congratulate themselves, the country, and religion itself for such wise, wholesome, and timely counsels. 'Now the ministry is doing its proper work. It does not stand aloof from those practical concerns which affect the well-being of society, but as God's most beneficent agent, it is shedding the light and authority of heaven on the interests of time'.

Herein is a manifest inconsistency. Silence and speech at the same time, and in regard to the same subject, cannot both be right. That is no pendulum which swings only on one side. Surely there must be some fixed principle pertaining to the subject which ought to be ascertained, otherwise the Christian pulpit is destitute of all dignity, exposed by turns to flattery or contempt.

As to the *chief and distinctive object* of the Christian ministry there can be no diversity of opinion. It is to announce those truths which affect man in his highest relations—to God and immortality. Unlike other teachers who, beginning with the lower ascend to the higher, the Christian ministry are appointed to proclaim those truths which relate to the *supreme* interests of our race. In the act of doing this, irrespective of all earthly distinctions, ignoring all those strata and conditions of society which the Apostle intends by " knowing man after the flesh", the teachers of religion are by an insensible and indirect process contributing most to that secular prosperity which others make their direct and exclusive endeavor. Elevating man in the scale of character, by introducing him to an immediate fellowship with his Maker, you are sure to confer importance on all which concerns his relations to his fellow-men and this present life. We need not expand this thought, that intelligence, freedom, law, order, enterprise, commerce, arts, industry, wealth, follow in the train of the Christian religion. Any tyro in history and geography will admit as much. He who preaches then, as he is bidden, repentance toward God and faith toward our Lord Jesus Christ, employing himself with those distinctive and germinant truths which are his peculiar themes, is contributing more than he knows to the welfare of states, and the true prosperity of nations. In this sense, political reforms are embosomed in the doctrine of justification by faith and national progress is insured by Christian devotion.

True religion should pervade the whole of man's being.

The Sabbath, the closet, the church, are not its exclusive sphere; his business and his politics belong to it as well. By politics we understand his relations to the state. It cannot be admitted that these and other secular interests, as they are called, are too common and unclean for contact with religion, since the broad requirement of the Scripture is that whether we eat or drink, or whatever we do, we should do all to the glory of God : and if political duties and relations are not to be pervaded by the spirit of religion, then are we involved in the practical solecism, that there is a large part of our existence which is necessarily irreligious ; and still farther the necessity is entailed of a sufficient number being detached, even in the millennium, to rig and work the ship of state, an ungodly crew, beyond the suspicion of all sanctity and piety. This common distinction between the secular and the religious is a convenience of speech for certain purposes, but it conveys a falsity, since in the better generalization of the New Testament religion covers the whole extent of our being, the countless variety of our interests and relations ; just as the sea fills all the bays and inlets and creeks with its in-flowing waters.

From these general principles, in this form, there can be no dissent. The difficulty is in the application of the latter principle on the part of the ministry, in an official capacity, to *specific cases*.

Perhaps it will help us in reaching the truth on this subject, if we refresh our memories with a few historical facts. The time was, in our ancestral land, when, Church and State being combined in one organism, the clergy with few exceptions were little more than the tools of the throne. "Tuning the pulpits" was a very significant expression, as used by Queen Elizabeth, to describe the subserviency of courtly chaplains in advocating the royal will. We are conscious of pitiful regret for the times and the men, when it was not uncommon, if a preacher expatiated with anything of freedom, for a gruff Tudor voice from the royal pew to bid him return from his " ungodly digression and keep himself to his text".

Life cannot always be cramped and fettered, and at length there arose an order of men who claimed the right to declare the truth of God, in utmost freedom, accountable only to its divine Author.* The assertion of religious liberty necessarily prepared the way for personal and political liberty, and Hume himself, tory and sceptic as he was, was compelled to admit that English Puritanism was the root and life of all true English freedom.

The colonization of New England was a *religious* movement; and to subtract from it the direct and positive influence of church and ministry, would be like taking out the bones and soul from the human body. Those colonists have been often censured and ridiculed for the ecclesiastical requirements which they exacted in political relations and magistracies. The truth is, that at that time every nation in Christendom required religious conformities of those who officiated in affairs of state. That which was peculiar and novel on the part of the Puritan colonists was that their ideas of the church and of religion went beyond the outward form, to a heart-renovation;—a new test which repelled and disgusted the adventurers who had no sympathy with spiritual religion.

So the foundations of our national life were laid. There are two distinct periods in our national history, when the agency of the clergy was very conspicuous, the object of reprehension or encomium by different parties. The first of these was at and during the Revolutionary war, and the formation of a new government, independent of Great Britain. The second was from the change of politics under President Jefferson, culminating in the war of 1812, and extending down, with a gradual diminution of prejudice and violence, to a time within the memory of most of our readers. Consulting these several periods we shall find much to admire, and much to censure; many mistakes, many fidelities and proofs of wisdom.

When troubles arose between the American Colonies and the British Government the whole structure of society was shaken, and men of all professions and pursuits were com-

* What Jeremy Taylor has called the "liberty of prophesying" in his famous θεολογία εκλεκτικη.

pelled to avow their sentiments and choose their position. At this distance of time it is common to suppose that the action of the American people was unanimous in advocating independence from the British throne. This was far from being true. The people were divided among themselves. The crown officers and many of the leading and opulent citizens were opposed to separation from Great Britain. The result was invective, reproach, and violence — distracted counties, towns and parishes. The idea of multitudes was to resist what they held to be unjust and oppressive on the part of the British Crown ; to demand the sanctity of charters— the right of representation ; but not to sever themselves as integral parts of the British realm. In this assertion of colonial right and justice, the clergy with wonderful unanimity sympathized ; but God intended more than they at first foresaw. The rock once loosened from its bed was destined to roll on notwithstanding all obstructions. The idea of national independence gained familiarity and force ; and at length the struggle began. There was a necessity that the clergy, in common with all other citizens, should adopt one side or the other. Some for a while hesitated to commit themselves to what appeared to be *irreligious* rebellion. Their scruples were founded on religious grounds. The Episcopal Church, with some notable exceptions, was particularly conspicuous in this position ; indeed, some of the early pamphlets relating to the Revolution inform us that the hostility to Great Britain cherished by the Congregational and Presbyterian ministers was imputed to a sectarian origin, as being moved by the fact that the Episcopal Church was sustained and established by the parent country. The precise state of many among the American people, in the incipient stages of the Revolution, will better appear from a few examples.

Dr. Jonathan Mayhew, one of the best names of New England, at that time the pastor of the West Church, in Boston, published a thanksgiving sermon in May, 1766, on the occasion of the repeal of the Stamp Act, from the text : " Our soul is escaped as a bird from the snare of the fowlers, the snare is broken and we are escaped ". This discourse, full of patriotism, is pervaded with the idea that justice had been done, the wrong redressed, and the difficulty adjusted. It was dedicated to William Pitt. On the 22d of June, 1775, Dr. William Smith, Provost of the University of Pennsylvania, preached a sermon in Christ Church, Philadelphia, in which he "pants for the return of those halcyon days of harmony during which the two countries flourished together as the glory and wonder of the world"—and while demanding that Britain should do justly with her colonies, he affirms that the idea of independence from the parent country is "utterly foreign to their thoughts, and that our rightful sovereign has nowhere more loyal subjects, or more zealously attached to those principles of government under which he inherited his throne". Another instance yet more to the point. Dr. Duché, of Philadelphia, is known as the divine who opened the Continental Congress, in 1774, with prayer. In 1776 he was appointed Chaplain to the Congress, but at an early stage of the war he manifested a decided opposition to independence, and in a long letter to General Washington endeavored to dissuade him from the cause to which he was pledged. Dr. Zubly, of Savannah, in 1775 a member of the first Provincial Congress of Georgia, preached a sermon in that year at the opening of that body, impregnated with the spirit of patriotism and liberty, but strongly discountenancing the independence of the colonies. These examples will suffice to show how great was the hesitation on the part of many, and this on ethical and religious grounds, to a severance of the body politic. As Christian men they dreaded schisms in church and state. The discourses from which we have drawn our illustrations were delivered in the *beginning* of the war, when ethics were not yet classified and adjusted by facts. With a very few and notable exceptions—such as the witty and eccentric Dr. Byles of Boston, whose connection with his congregation was dissolved in 1776 because of his toryism—who was denounced in town meeting as an enemy to his country, and afterwards tried before a special court on the charge of praying for the King; receiving visits from British officers, and remaining in the town during the siege—who, in his own words, was "guarded, re-guarded and disregarded" — the vast body of the unprelatical ministry of the country advocated the Revolution, in public and private, on Christian principles. They justified the war on religious grounds. They believed that human rights and liberties would gain by its success. They had the sagacity to foresee its issue. Among the most faithful of religious men, modest and pains-taking in their parishes, there was no concealment of their sympathies. Many of them went as chaplains into the army; among them Dwight — *clarum et venerabile nomen* — and he retains in his lyrical collections that paraphrase of the Psalms which is now dropped out of our books, as judged to be obsolete:

> " Lord, hast thou cast the nation off,
>   Must we forever mourn;
> Will thou indulge immortal wrath,
>   Shall mercy ne'er return?   .
> Lift up a banner in the field
>   For those that fear thy name,
> Save thy beloved with thy shield,
>   And put our foes to shame.
> Go with our armies to the fight
>   Like a confed'rate God,
> In vain confed'rate foes unite
>   Against thy lifted rod.
> Our troops shall gain a wide renown
>   By thine assisting hand,
> 'Tis God that treads the mighty down
>   And makes the feeble stand."

Scarcely was there a battle-field in the Revolutionary war, where the clergy were not present, as chaplains or surgeons, to cheer and bless. Their patriotism was a thing of general admiration. They reasoned themselves and the country out of all hesitancy and scruples, as they knew how to reason. They abounded in what Sir John Hawkins calls "precatory eloquence"; calling down the blessings of the Almighty upon the country; and the depth and sway of their influence in achieving the independence of the colonies cannot be too highly extolled. Withal, it was with them a time of great personal privation and hardship. They shared in the largest measure the calamities of the country. They practised the extremes of frugality to eke out their scanty subsistence. They were exposed to violent opposition in their distracted parishes. But they were, as a body, brave, patient, meek, pious, patriotic, and learned — an honor to any land. Under God, we owe it to the ministry of that day that the morals of the country were not hopelessly wrecked in the convulsions of the Revolution. The profession emerged from the war with increased credit and honor, and with the confidence, respect, and gratitude of the people. The war over, they led the nation in song and thanksgiving on the shores of the sea they had crossed, and forthwith addressed themselves to their appropriate work, in conservation of the liberties which the Revolution had helped to secure. A few here and there were left in a most pitiful predicament. In tacking ship they had missed stays, and were stranded on a lee shore. In proof that no human ministry is infallible, some had misjudged the case, and were forced to suffer the consequences. What was the state of feeling in those parishes, where the minister retained either loyalty to the British crown or a professed neutrality, may be inferred from a single incident. Rev. Dr. Burnet, of the Presbytery of New York, was settled in Jamaica, L. I., and at the return of peace felt himself obliged to resign his charge. At the close of his farewell service, he gave out the 120th Psalm. Whether the muscles of the choir were equal to its musical intonation, or the minds of the people to its devout response, tradition does not inform us :

> " Hard lot of mine, my days are cast
>   Among the sons of strife,
> Whose never-ceasing quarrels waste
>   My golden hours of life.
>
> " Oh ! might I fly to change my place,
>   How would I choose to dwell
> In some wide, lonesome wilderness,
>   And leave these gates of hell.
>
> " Peace is the blessing that I seek :
>   How lovely are its charms ! .

9

- I am for peace ; but when I speak
  They all declare for arms."

We come now to the second period referred to, when the
preaching of some of the clergy on political affairs was of a
most notorious character. A change had taken place in political parties, and it was so marked that the clergy could not
conceal their sentiments. With few exceptions, they had been
on the side of Washington, and bore the name of Federalists.
When this unanimity was disturbed by the election of Mr.
Jefferson to the Presidency, they inveighed against it in some
instances with a tremendous emphasis. It must be borne in
mind that party spirit was then at fever-heat. Families and
neighborhoods were set at variance—church-members of different parties refused to pray together, and young people
from families of different political preferences would not dance
at the same assemblies. Never before or since did the spirit
of party prove itself so ardent and violent. It was a new experience for the country. The clergy thought that it portended worse than it proved. The people of New England
especially looked with horror upon French infidelity—French
revolutions—which they had associated with the new party in
in our own land. The French Republic had just before de-
creed the abolition of all religion, and the enthronement of
Human Reason. All Christendom was convulsed with terror.
In 1798 President Adams appointed a day of national fasting.
Doubtless this association was in part the cause of the hostility
which they manifested towards Mr. Jefferson and his party.
The clergy stood aghast, thinking that the country was ruined.
They thought that they would be unfaithful to a solemn trust,
if they did not lift up their voice in testimony. It amuses us,
at this distance of time, to read what they said and did. Some
of the sermons of that day have a historic renown. Such, for
example, as what is known as the Jeroboam Sermon of Dr.
Emmons. It was on the day preceding the annual Fast-day
in Massachusetts, in the year 1801, that the acute metaphysician of Franklin sat in his study, greatly perplexed what to
preach on the ensuing day. What he did preach was never
forgotten. It was just after the inauguration of Mr. Jeffer-

son, and Jeroboam was made that day to play a parallelism which would have astonished himself. The curious analogy is a rare specimen of long-drawn, solemn and withering rebuke. After it had been extended through nearly two hours, it hardly needed at its close what, according to the phraseology of the day, was called an "improvement", which was given in these words : " It is more than possible that our nation may find themselves in the hand of a Jeroboam who will drive them from following the Lord, and whenever they do, they will rue the day and detest the folly, delusion, and intrigue which raised him to the head of the United States".

We are referring now to facts which need some explanation ; for which much may be said in apology, but nothing in justi- fication as a model of duty for ourselves. The mistake was that in the intensity of feeling which then prevailed there was no discrimination between what was ethical and what was partisan. Opposing the new administration on one point, be- cause of its supposed affinity with French Atheism, some fought it at every point, *pugnis et calcibus*—embargo, gun- boats, alien and sedition laws, no matter what—wherever it showed its hand or head.

These political antipathies were long-lived. They culminat- ed during the war with England, in 1812. But they cropped out long after whenever they could claim a show of decency. Some of the sermons preached during that period were of a most extraordinary character. No physical appliances of dried orange-peel or caraway-seed were necessary to keep audiences awake, under those pulpit deliverances. One denounces Na- poleon Bonaparte as the "first-born of the devil", and Thomas Jefferson and James Madison his twin brothers. Another takes for his text the 8th verse of the 109th Psalm : " Let his days be few ; and let another take his office". The " Bramble " sermon of Dr. Osgood, of Medford, (founded on the parable of Jotham, Judges ix, 14 : " Then said all the trees unto the bramble, Come thou, and reign over us "), is as famous as the Jeroboam sermon of Dr. Emmons. There was no circum- locutory preaching in those days. Velvet phrases and uncer- tain inferences were alike discarded. It is reported of one minister, that for a considerable time he was accustomed to pray for the Chief Magistrate that God would "gently and easily remove his servant by death". It will be remembered by many of our readers that on a certain year a worthy gentleman in Massachusetts, after being a candidate of the Democratic party for Governer for twenty years, was finally elected to the office by a majority of one vote. It will also be recollected by all whose early life was passed in that State, that the custom prevailed, whenever the Governor issued his annual proclamation for thanksgiving, of sending. by the sheriff of the county a copy of the same, on a large hand-bill, to be read from every pulpit, which document invariably closed, after the signature of the Governor, with the pious exclamation, "God save the Commonwealth of Massachusetts!" On the year referred to the newly-elected magistrate issued his proclamation in the usual form. It is said that a venerable clergyman, of the old party, laid the broad sheet over his reading-board, and after performing the professional duty of reciting it, with an ill-disguised aversion, actually announced the official signature with this significant intonation: "Marcus Morton, Governor? God save the Commonwealth of Massachusetts"! It is for an important purpose that we have referred to a few of those notorious incidents which belong to the history of the American pulpit.

Admit that such acts and expressions on the part of the ministry were mistakes, never to be imitated; much should be said for their exculpation. In the first place, the instances of such distinctively political preaching were comparatively few. The very notoriety which these have attained is in proof that the great body of the ministry, whatever may have been their private sentiments, addicted themselves faithfully to the great concerns of their office. In many instances, those who had practised this method of political preaching lived to express their personal regret for the same. The late Rev. Dr. Lyman, of Hatfield, at the installation of his successor, used language truly pathetic in the acknowledgment of what he regarded as a great mistake in his own ministry. Another thing to be said in their vindication is, that such utterances were not on the Sabbath-day, but perhaps without exception, on Fast-days, or Thanksgiving-days, or what was always celebrated in New-England by a sermon—Election-day. Still another thing should be said. The clergy of that period had been educated to regard themselves as the "moral police and constabulary of the country", and silence, sudden and complete, was more than could be expected of mortal man, when on the losing side, after a lifetime of explicit and applauded testimony. Nor must we forget to add that, in times of high political excitement, the words of a minister, in prayer or sermon, receive a construction from interested and jealous parties which they were never intended to bear. Minds surcharged with political partisanship will pervert, and exaggerate, and apply the simple utterances of a minister, in a way which might well astonish him. Rev. Dr. David Ely, of Huntington, Connecticut, is described as one of the most prudent, faithful, spiritual pastors of his times. In a season of great political excitement, it was reported by persons hostile to him that he had preached on political subjects in a neighboring parish. It was thought proper to trace the report to its source. The neighboring parish was visited and the inquiry made: "Did Dr. Ely preach politics when here? Yes. What did he say? Well sir, if he did not preach politics, he prayed politics. What did he say? *Say?* he said, 'Though hand join in hand, yet the wicked shall not go unpunished'." Seasons there are when auditors are so magnetized with partisan passion, that they put their own sense on the language of a preacher, exaggerating or misapplying it, so that in the presence of such a suspicious and watchful jealousy he stands no chance at all, unless he adopt the resolution of the Psalmist on a certain occasion: "I will keep my mouth with a bridle, while the wicked is before me".

This rapid survey of a very extended historic period, with its motley assemblage of incidents, may help us in our undertaking to state some of the principles which should govern the Christian ministry in their official relations to political concerns. Starting from that which we hold to be the grand design of the Gospel and its appointed heralds — to save the souls of men — whatever their nationality or their politics, we hold that everything pertaining to the sphere of *morals* belongs to the province of the Christian theologian and

preacher.   We emphasize the word which helps us to discri-
minate between what has been right and what wrong in the
practice of the pulpit.   What is distinctively *ethical* may be
discussed in its proper time and place on Christian principles.   There are ethical principles which should govern our
conduct in political relations.   There are many things pertaining to what are called politics which involve no special relation to morals, concerning which a minister may have his
personal preference, but which it would be highly indecorous
for him to introduce and urge officially.   The relations of
morality and immorality to political economy are many ; but
we would hardly judge that theories of free trade, and taxa-
tion, and naval architecture, and embargoes, were the proper
material for pulpit instruction.   Are we required to give the
rule which should govern a minister in his treatment of those
political questions which are directly related to morals?
None can be given, beyond this — they should be presented
according to the *proportion of faith;* in the right season ; and
in the right manner.   The whole gradation must be left to
the GOOD SENSE and ENLIGHTENED JUDGMENT of the preacher
himself.   If he is lacking in these qualities, no number of
specific directions would be of any avail.   Topics in the
whole range of moral relations from the highest to the lowest,
belong to his sphere—but the order, frequency and emphasis
of their discussion must depend on seasons and necessities,
which cannot be defined in advance.

Some things, however, may be made more specific.   Happily we live in a country where there is no alliance between
church and state.   No political power, organized or unorgan-
ized may prescribe and dictate what a minister shall preach.
This freedom, however, has two sides or aspects ; for neither
may a preacher prescribe or dictate to his hearers what they
shall think or do, except in those cases where he has the authority of the Supreme.   We touch at once the secret of popular jealousy in regard to pulpit utterances.   These have been
made, sometimes, with arrogance and assumed authority.
There was a time when the clergy wore big wigs and an imposing official dress ; and it was expected that their opinions
would be received with deference by a reverential parish.

"For still they gazed and still the wonder grew
That one small head could carry all he knew."

The time has come when opinions do not prevail because uttered *ex cathedra*.   If an incumbent of the pulpit indulges in crude thoughts, immature judgments, ebullitions of feeling, and false reasoning, he must expect animadversion, correction, and refutation.   Another cometh after him and searcheth him.   No one would curtail the freedom of the ministry, but the ministry must remember that there is a freedom and right of judgment for the pews as well as the pulpit.   We should not for a moment hold controversy with a man whether he ought or ought not to assert and promulgate the will of God, when *he knows it*—and to challenge the obedience of all men to that supreme authority.   But when he assumes the same tone and manner of authority in reference to matters unwritten, involved and debatable, we may surely ask him to exhibit his credentials.   We will be the first to submit to his dictation when we have actually seen the seal of heaven in his hand, and are satisfied on the capital point of his divine legation.*   The occult principle which has occasioned all the rancor and hostility excited by the interference of the pulpit is this assumption of divine authority in behalf of what is nothing but an individual opinion.   If the man who derives his opinion, simply, by his own confession, from the personal study of the Scriptures and who has enjoyed none but ordinary aids, who can advance no pretensions which others may not also challenge, is entitled to speak in the tone and to exercise the authority of a prophet or apostle, then what was the necessity of the extraordinary powers wherewith prophets and apostles were endowed?   A vast distiction is there between the prodigious pretensions of the zealot demagogue and the modest expression of an individual judgment.

Every minister of the Gospel is entitled to the same freedom of opinion and preference on all subjects as other men. Paraphrasing the language of Shylock, he may say: " I am a minister: hath not a minister eyes ? hath he not hands, organs,

* Isaac Taylor.

dimensions, senses, affections, passions? fed with the same
food, hurt with the same weapons, subject to the same diseases, healed by the same means, warmed and cooled by the
same winter and summer as other men? if you prick us, do
we not bleed? if you tickle us, do we not laugh? if you
poison us, do we not die? and if you wrong us"—we will not
add with the Jew "shall we not revenge", but we will say,
"shall we not show you how to bear it"? This freedom of
judgment allowed him, no minister has the right to protrude
officially his private opinions and preferences in regard to
matters which do not affect the sublime moralities of his vocation. Especially to indulge in personalities, in partisan
advocacy or military criticisms in the pulpit, whatever right
or liberty he may claim elsewhere, is a public scandal and
wrong. It would seem to be the doctrine of some preachers,
because *they* had certain opinions in regard to men and measures, therefore, they are bound on all occasions to avow them,
going through the world, like the iron man Talus in the
drama, with his iron flail battering down whatever opposes
their private sentiments. The meanest thing which crawls
on the earth is a man who, for his private advantage, will
follow and cringe and swallow his own opinions; but the
noblest form of manhood is he who holds his personal opinions
on things indifferent in reserve for the sublime end of another's advantage—as the Apostle himself has expressed it: "I
become all things to all men, if by any means. I might SAVE
SOME"; that nobility and grandeur of Christian motives imparting versatility of address, and deportment in the use of
his varied faculties and opinions, lest he should frustrate that
object—the salvation of the soul, which was his disinterested
and lofty intention.

It is time that we cease from general rules and proceed to
what is more specific and practical to our own affairs. Never
was there an occasion when the counsels of religion were more
needed, and the clear strong voice of Christian faith and courage more essential in the vanguard of the nation. A fortunate thing it is for our country, in this solemn crisis, that its
clergy of all denominations, unlike the clerical party of Continental Europe, regarded with suspicion as enemies to liberty and

progress, are known to be eminently patriotic, and as a body are
possessed of the confidence and respect of the people.   If the
great events of our time, absorbing thought, and eliciting national energy ; events which are rapidly consuming hecatombs
of lives and millions of treasure, and threatening to involve
the peace of the world, do not afford an occasion for the teachers of religion to lift up their voice in the name of God and
humanity, then must we confess ourselves utterly unable to
conceive of any conjunction of earthly interests to which Christian truth and motive are applicable.

If war, considered as an act of lawful magistracy, employed in defence of national rights and national existence be not justifiable on *religious* grounds, then our wisdom and duty are to oppose it and denounce it as utterly reprehensible.   "It is certain that two sections cannot
engage in hostilities but one party must be guilty of injustice ; and if the magnitude of crimes is to be estimated by a regard to their consequences, it is difficult to
conceive an action of equal guilt with a wanton violation of
peace.   Though something must generally be allowed for the
complexity and intricacy of national claims, and the consequent
liability to deception, yet when the guilt of a gratuitous and
unjust war is clear and manifest, it sinks every other crime
into insignificance.   If the existence of war always implies
injustice, in one at least of the parties concerned, it is also the
fruitful parent of crimes.   It reverses, in regard to its objects,
all the rules of morality.   It is nothing else than a temporary
repeal of the principles of virtue.   It is a system out of which
almost all the virtues are excluded and in which nearly all the
vices are incorporated.   Whatever renders human nature
amiable or respectable, whatever engages love and confidence
is sacrificed at its shrine.   In instructing us to consider a portion of our fellow-creatures as the proper objects of enmity, it
removes, as far as they are concerned, the basis of all society,
of all civilization and virtue ; for the basis of these is the good
will due to every individual of the species as being a part of
ourselves.   From this principle all the rules of social virtue
emanate.   Justice and humanity, in their utmost extent, are
nothing more than the practical application of this great law.

The sword, and that alone, cuts asunder the bond of consanguinity which unites man to man. As it immediately aims at the extinction of life, it is next to impossible, upon the principle that every thing may be lawfully done to him whom we have a right to kill, to set limits to military license; for when men pass from the dominion of reason to that of force, whatever restraints are attempted to be laid on the passions will be feeble and fluctuating".* All this is to demonstrate the tremendous crime which attaches to those who inaugurate war gratuitously, and in the absence of such an absolute necessity as is imposed by real benevolence. This admitted, there are wars which are justifiable to Christian ethics. "The magistrate", says the Word of God, " beareth not the sword in vain". It is to be wielded in defence of what is good,—for the conservation of a well-ordered society. It is not an inference, but the explicit assertion of Scripture, that government is God's ordinance, and as such *must* be obeyed, and those who do it violence, putting in jeopardy the dearest interests of society, must be punished. Evil doers must be smitten, not with a feather, but with the sword, otherwise vaster mischief will ensue to the many, in the total overthrow of society, than by the extinction of the few. An army is only the instrument of magistracy, the reduplication of official weapons.

We are engaged in a contest, not as some abroad suppose for the holding of so much territory, but for the conservation of our national existence, and in such a cause we may appeal to something higher than honor, the aid and blessing of that religion which has given its sanction to lawful magistrates and constituted governments. So long as this one object is kept in mind, distinct and unalloyed by malignant passions, we may leave our appeal with the Almighty, going forth to battle, with faith and prayer, for justice and humanity. What greater evil could befall—we will not say our own land, but all lands—than the success of ambitious and wicked men, misleading communities, dragging States into the vortex of war at their own passionate will, without rebuke or punishment? Let us stand, therefore,

---

* Robert Hall.

in the evil day the more steadfast, because calm in the confidence of what is right.

It has been objected, and that by two different classes of men, that the sacred Scriptures fail to inculcate patriotism : the one sceptical as to the Christian morality, the other seeking an excuse for inaction or indecision in national concerns. By the latter it is alleged that inspiration does not insist on this sentiment, because it is a *natural* sentiment like that of the affection between parents and children. To which the reply is, that the Scriptures do inculcate emphatically on parents and children to love each other most earnestly ; and he must be a poor interpreter of the Old Testament who does not detect love of country in the most inspiring odes which have been given to the Church for its use to the end of time. "The duties which result from the relation in which a people stand to their rulers are prescribed in the New Testament with great perspicuity, and enforced by very solemn sanctions ; and when these duties are faithfully discharged by each party, the benefits derived from the social compact are so justly appreciated, and so deeply felt, that the love of country is less liable to defect than to excess. In all well-ordered polities, if we may judge from the experience of past ages, the attachment of men to their country is in danger of becoming an absorbing principle, inducing, not merely a forgetfulness of private interest, but of the immutable claims of humanity and justice. In the eyes of an enlightened philanthropy, patriotism, pampered to such an excess, loses the name of virtue— it is the bond and cement of a guilty confederation. It was worthy the wisdom of our great Legislator to decline the express inculcation of a principle so liable to degenerate into excess, and to content himself with prescribing the virtues which are sure to develope it, as far as is consistent with the dictates of universal benevolence".*

In exhorting, in the name of religion, to love of country, the Christian ministry would give the instruction not in the form of the popular expression, "Our country, right or wrong"— for that is the very blossom and consummation of

---

* Sermon on Death of Dr. Ryland, by Robert Hall.

the blind and excessive passion of which we have spoken;
but our country to be loved always out of a pure heart fervently, and, because of that love, avoid and correct what is
wrong, lest wrong lead to ruin.   Our country, be it remembered, stands not in the rear but in the van of the grand army
of nations.   Behind us are great historic forces; before us
are great duties, great hopes, great destinies.   The drama of
History is not complete.   We have our own peculiar work to
achieve, and that work is related alike to the past and the
future of the world.   We are acting now, not merely for ourselves and our children, but in the interest of all contemporary nations, and in behalf of all the nations that ever shall be
organized on the earth.   The question now to be decided
is — and there is not an aspirant for freedom, nor an agent of
despotic and irresponsible power in any part of the world,
who does not watch the issue on the very tiptoe of expectation — whether any people are capable of self-government;
whether the passions of men can be so curbed and moderated
that of their own accord free citizens will subject their private will to the public welfare, preferring the order and sanctity of law and government to personal ambition and private
resentments; whether a free, equitable, and benignant government shall spread its protection over all classes alike, or
whether it shall be stricken, stabbed, revolutionized and overthrown for the pleasure and promotion of a few.   This is the
core and heart of our crisis.   Others may misinterpret it,
misunderstand it; but we should all comprehend it, intelligently and calmly, pledging ourselves heartily to its issue.

Nor can we, if we would, blink the fact that we carry ex-
plosive problems in our own bosom, especially related to that
unhappy race on whose ebon faces the sad experience of centuries has sculptured the cast of patient subjection.   We
know not a subject which has more points of contact and relationship with the proper province of the Christian ministry
than the existing condition and prospects of the African race.
First of all, he who questions the unity of the human race,
by denying those bronzed in hue a place in the common
brotherhood, aims a blow higher than he knows, at the very

structure of Christianity. That there is one parentage, one race, one historic necessity, one and only one Redeemer for all mankind, is the very alphabet of our creed. Then again comes in the doctrine of the New Testament, that while there is something better than liberty, even a relationship to Christ which lifts a human soul so high that it may be oblivious to the ordinary distinctions of earthly condition, yet on the same authority we learn that freedom is better than slavery, and so is, if it may be, to be preferred and used. These things we should say are axioms in social and theological science. If it were our object to express ourselves in strongest terms on this subject, we would agree to confine ourselves to the language used by the fathers of the Republic, especially those who were personally related by birth and inheritance to a system which they pronounced and reprobated as a tremendous evil, social, political and moral.*

We see not that it would conduce to any advantage just now to attempt any explanation of the causes which have led

---

* Henry Laurens, for two years President of the Continental Congress, and afterward appointed Minister to Holland, wrote to his son from Charleston, S. C., 14th August, 1776 : "You know, my dear son, I abhor slavery. I was born in a country where slavery had been established by British kings and parliaments, as well as by the laws of that country ages before my existence. I found the Christian religion and slavery growing under the same authority and cultivation. I nevertheless disliked it. In former days there was no combating the prejudices of men supported by interest: the day, I hope, is approaching, when, from principles of gratitude as well as justice, every man will strive to be foremost in showing his readiness to comply with the golden rule."—*Collection of the Zenger Club*, p. 20.

Mr. Jefferson, when in France in 1786, in a note to M. Demeunier, whom he had furnished with copious materials for his article on the United States, about to appear in the great *Encyclopédie Méthodique*, uses this language : "What a stupendous, what an incomprehensible machine is man, who can endure toil, famine, stripes, imprisonment, and death itself, in vindication of his own liberty, and the next moment be deaf to all those motives whose power supported him through his trial, and inflict on his fellow-men a bondage one hour of which is fraught with more misery than ages of that which he rose in rebellion to oppose ! But we must await with patience the workings of an overruling Providence and hope that that is preparing the deliverance of these our suffering brethren. When the measure of their tears shall be full ; when their groans shall have involved heaven itself in darkness,—doubtless a God of justice will awaken to their distress, and, by diffusing light and liberality among their oppressors, or, at length, by *his exterminating thunder*, manifest his attention to the things of this world, and that they are not left to the guidance of a blind fatality."—*Jefferson's Writings*, vol. ix, pp. 278, 279.

to a very different theory; or to hurl recriminations to and
fro at those who were responsible for the change. We must
look at facts as they are. Whether the conservation and extension of slavery be merely the pretext or the cause of the
war; whether any who enlisted in the war can plead provocation in the form of fanatical acerbities, is not now the question in debate, though we cannot but regret that the temper
which governed our fathers, regarding this as a common concern, to be tolerated as a necessity for a season and removed
as soon as it could be — a temper which was merged and
blended in a blessed patriotism—was not continued and perpetuated; though we often frame to ourselves a picture of
what this country might and would have been if all its different sections could have looked and acted on this subject in
the charitable spirit of a family community of interest and
honor, and a small portion of the immense treasures now
expended in war could have been fairly appropriated for
the removal of the mischief. So it was not to be. Our
regrets cannot recall the past, and the issue is made and
joined. This war is not in our interpretation and intention
for the abolition of slavery, though that event seems to be
involved in its issue. The responsibility of such an issue is
with those who inaugurated the war, not unwarned of its inevitable consequences. The contest on our part is for the
conservation of the national life, and the preservation of that
constitutional government which, under God, is the only
barrier between us and universal chaos. We know of nothing
between us and that object which should obstruct our end.
We intend to love nothing, conserve nothing, consult nothing,
occupying intermediate ground between us and the life, honor
and constitution of the country. Whatever interposes itself
between us and that grand and sacred end which religion
sanctions, must take care of itself. So clear is our conviction on this point that if our voice could claim any regard,
we would say to government and to the people: Avoid
all collateral issues; let alone debatable questions; abstain
from everything which leads to partisan distinctions. Leave
all that you can to be reformed and settled by legal and prescribed processes. Be cautious not to divide the country by

needless debates. The grandest opportunity which ever a nation had has been passing over us for burying out of sight the petty names and partialities of party in a noble, magnanimous and Christian patriotism. Whatever lawful magistracy may pronounce essential to success in the execution of its beneficent work, let it be *done*, wisely, promptly, thoroughly, but save us from endless and unavailing theorizing and resolving and speculating and debating.

Lift high the bright banner which symbolizes Unity, Constitutional law, National honor and integrity, dearer to us now that the blood of our citizenship has sanctified every fold and star. Avoid every suspicion of political jealousy and ambition. Weaken not the "red right arm" of magistracy by suffering party rivalries to invade our armies. The very animals in the time of a deluge, seeking refuge in the same caves, forget their ancient antipathies. Common dangers, common sufferings, common necessities, ought to unite us at that point where unity is essential to the preservation of life.

Well may we be jealous of all encroachments on constitutional liberty. If perils and evils there are in connection with liberty, the cure of them is more liberty. Powder is consumed harmlessly on the surface of the ground which accumulates tremendous power when driven into the chamber of a gun under superincumbent wads. Above all things, whatever comes to pass, let us hold ourselves firm in the faith that there is an essential difference between what is right and what is wrong, between good government and wild revolutions, and as God lives, that which is right will ultimately prosper. We do not flatter ourselves and our readers with the promise of a speedy or immediate issue of the strife. The future is hid from our inspection. No words of empty boast or defiance have we in regard to menaces from across the sea. We are neither over-sensitive nor indifferent. Willing or unwilling, all nations are related by manifold bonds which mountains and oceans cannot destroy. What is of real and permanent value to us as a nation, will prove the same to all other nations in the end. We are very calm and confident as to the *final* issue. Intermediate suffering there may be, perhaps beyond all which we have ever imagined. The fires may wax hotter which heaven shall see to be needful to burn up our dross and weld us into a purer and firmer nationality. Thus far the suffering, it would seem, in largest measure has fallen on those who inaugurated the war. Wonderful indeed is the prosperity of these Northern States. We are startled into fear and trembling when we think of it. Drained and depleted, but instead of fainting in prostration, producing and exporting enough to feed the world! Let us not be high-minded, but fear. Let us improve the time of trial for the cultivation of all that is honorable, heroic, charitable, patient, and good. It has been the theory of many that the effect of these distresses through which we are passing must be to elevate our aims, make us less selfish, increase our patriotism, and make us more thankful for our blessings. God grant that it may be so! Whether the trial shall develop these results is not yet decided, nor the perfect result brought out. It is the effect of affliction on thoughtful natures to enrich and mellow the heart; and now is the time for us all to lay up treasure in heaven by acts of sympathy and charity and sacrifice and fellowship of suffering.

Hilarity is not becoming this hour of suffering, but cheerfulness is, and patriotism, and hope and love and faith in God. What a day will that be, when prejudice, passion, and falsehood shall all disappear; when there shall be no more occasion for war, because there is no more of lawlessness and crime; when there shall be no breaking in nor going out; when there shall be no more complaining in the streets; when that deepest of all questions, underlying the relations of employers and employees, the question of races, shall be solved in the harmony and love of the latter day; when all the cities which gem the shores of the sea, and all the valleys and cottages which brighten the landscape of our beautiful country, shall be cheerful with the music of industrial freedom; when confidence and goodly fellowship shall displace suspicion, rivalry and jealousy; when Peace, with her olive boughs and dove-like tones, shall bless the land, and all the people shall go up to the temples of religion with their songs of melody, thanksgiving, and praise. The Lord grant it in his own time!

Theological and Literary Intelligence.

ANTIQUARIAN RESEARCHES. *Jerusalem Underground.*—An account of Signor Pierotti's discoveries in the subterranean topography of Jerusalem has been published. Employed by the Pasha as an engineer, he has discovered that the modern city of Jerusalem stands on several layers of ruined masonry, the undermost of which, composed of deeply bevelled and enormous stones, he attributes to the age of Solomon, the next to that of Zorababel, the next to that of Herod, the next to that of Justinian, and so on till the times of the Saracens and Crusaders. He has traced a series of conduits and sewers leading from the "dome of the rock", a mosque standing on the very site of the altar of sacrifice in the Temple, to the Valley of Jehoshaphat, by means of which the priests were enabled to flush the whole temple area with water, and thus to carry off the blood and offal of the sacrifices to the brook Kedron. The manner of his explorations was very interesting. He got an Arab to walk up through these immense sewers, ringing a bell and blowing a trumpet, while he himself by following the sound was able to trace the exact course they took. About two years ago he accidentally discovered a fountain at the pool of Bethesda, and, on his opening it, a copious stream of water immediately began to flow, and has flowed ever since. No one knows from whence it comes or whither it goes. This caused the greatest excitement amongst the Jews, who flocked in crowds to drink and bathe themselves in it. They fancied it was one of the signs of Messiah's coming, and portended the speedy restoration of their commonwealth. This fountain, which has a peculiar taste, like that of milk and water, is identified by Signor Pierotti with the fountain which Hezekiah built, and which is described by Josephus. The measurements and position of most of these remains accord exactly with the Jewish historian's descriptions. Some of the Signor's conclusions are disputed, but no one has succeeded in so disinterring the relics of the Holy City.

CODEX SINAITICUS.—The most remarkable literary novelty of the day is the claim of the notorious Constantine Simonides that he himself wrote this famous codex, in 1839, at the solicitation of "the venerable Benedict", his worthy "uncle". Simonides, as usual, gives names, dates, facts in abundance. It was copied by him, he says, to be presented to the Emperor Nicholar I, together with remains of the Apostolic Fathers. His letter is given in full in the *Journal of Sacred Literature*, for October. It seems strange that he should have kept so entirely silent about it for three years, and until Tischendorf had published the main facts respecting the manuscript, on the basis of which some acquaintance with the MS. might be claimed.

Man and the Gorilla.—In the Zoological Section of the British Association at its late meeting, Professors Owen and Huxley had a lively debate on the relations of man to the lower order of animals; Mr. Owen taking the ground that man should be placed in a distinct sub-kingdom by himself, and Mr. Huxley flatly replying that Mr. Owen in no way represented the real nature of the problem under discussion. This personal controversy attracted a great deal of attention. Mr. Huxley claimed that in the course of former controversies with Mr. Owen he had exposed the mistakes of the latter, and had established the fact that the structural differences between man and the highest ape are of the same order, and only slightly different in degree from those which separate the apes one from another. In conclusion he expressed his opinion of the futility of discussions like this. In his opinion, the differences between man and the lower animals are not to be expressed by his toes or his brain, but are moral and intellectual. No definite result ensued from the controversy. Gardner Wilkinson writes to the *Athenæum* (Oct. 11): "Resemblance of form has evidently little to do with resemblance of intelligence; for though the head and hair of the canine species are so unlike those of man, no chimpanzee, gorilla, or other ape, is to be compared in point of intelligence with the dog".

Nullification.—Professor De Morgan in the *Notes and Queries* says, that the first use of the word nullify was by the English clergy, about 1621, in application to the mathematician Harriot, who rejected the Old Testament; they said he *nullified* the Word of God. This was evidently in allusion to the phrase—Math. xv, 6—making the word of God *of none effect.*

The *"Essays and Reviews" in Court.*—The controversy raised by this noted book is still going on—some two hundred books, pamphlets, and articles having already appeared. Several cases connected with it have been, or soon will be, decided in the ecclesiastical courts of England. The first, already decided by the Judicial Committee of the Privy Council, is that of the Bishop of Winchester against Rev. D. I. Heath, since 1846 Vicar of Brading, Isle of Wight. The judgment runs thus:

"Reviewing, therefore, the whole case, their lordships decide that Mr. Heath has maintained and affirmed doctrines directly contrary and repugnant to the Articles.

"He hath done so: First, by maintaining that justification by faith is the putting every one in his right place by our Saviour's trust in the future, and that the faith by which man is justified is not his faith in Christ, but the faith of Christ himself. Secondly, by maintaining that Christ's blood was not poured out to propitiate his kind and benevolent Father. Thirdly, by maintaining that forgiveness of sins has nothing at all to do with the Gospel; and fourthly, by maintaining that the ideas and phrases, 'guilt of sin', 'satisfaction', 'merit', 'necessary to salvation', have been foisted into modern theology without sanction from Scripture, and do darken and confuse the clearest of the otherwise most intelligible and comforting statements of Holy Writ."

But the chief cases, not yet finally adjudicated, are those of the Bishop of Salisbury *vs.* Williams, and of Fendall *vs.* Wilson, on which Dr. Lushington rendered a judgment (allowing an appeal to the Privy Council) on June 25th. The following is the substance of Dr. Lushington's judgment:

I. In ecclesiastical prosecutions in England, the court will not determine whether litigated opinions are *in contravention of God's Word*, but only whether they are *in contravention of the Articles of the Church of England.*

II. The decision in the Gorham case is reäffirmed, that *in all matters not settled by the standards of the Church of England, liberty of expression is allowed.*

III. In reference to the articles of the Church of England, the following positions taken in the *Essays and Reviews*, are declared to be heretical, and subject to ecclesiastical censure :

1st. To say that the Bible is *"an expression of devout reason"*, which is declared inconsistent with the Sixth Article.

2d. To deny a *particular, vicarious Atonement*, and to make "propitiation " to consist in a mere "recovery of peace".

3d. To describe the Articles in a *non-natural* sense, though, oddly enough, not to advise others to do so.

4th. To deny that every person brought into the world deserves God's wrath and damnation, and that there is no distinction between covenanted and uncovenanted mercies.

5th. To assert that, after an intermediate state of discipline, all will be saved.

IV. On the other hand, it is declared *not* to contravene the Articles to hold—

1st. That the moral element in the prophecies predominates over the literal prognostications.

2d. That the greater part of the alleged Messianic prophecies do not apply to the Messiah.

3d. To deny that the Book of Daniel was written by Daniel, but not that it is canonical.

4th. To declare that the fourth Gospel was the latest of all the genuine books.

5th. To speak of the Apocalypse as " a series of poetical visions", which is declared not to deny the Apocalypse to be a part of Scripture.

6th. To deny the Pauline origin of the Epistle to the Hebrews.

7th. To state that the Biblical account of the deluge is "figurative".

In addition to these positive points, several litigated expressions are passed over by the judge with the comment, that though he thought their *tendency* heterodox, yet he could not, on account of their obscurity, declare them, in a criminal case, in contravention of the Articles.

In concluding, the Judge said: " I cannot leave these two cases without adding a few words in conclusion.   I have discharged my duty to the best of my ability.   I am aware that these judgments will be severely canvassed by the clergy and by others.   Be it so; thereby it may be ascertained whether they are in accordance with law ; and accordance with law ought to be the sole object of a court of justice.   It may be, that on the present occasion some may think that, so far from having gone too far, I have taken too limited a view of powers entrusted to me, and consequently have failed to apply a remedy where a remedy might seem to be wanted.   I can only say that I have shaped my course according to the authority I am bound to follow—the authority of the Privy Council."

In reference to this judgment, Dr. Rowland Williams writes :

" The position involved in all my writings, and illustrated in my essay, is, that an ingenuous freedom from disguise, in respect of views of the Bible accredited amongst scholars, may be permitted without violence to the theology of the Church of England, though softening modifications of that theology may ultimately result.   The counter-position of our Episcopate is, that all possible statements in the domain of Biblical criticism must be fashioned with a view to the safety or convenience of formal theology ; and that every scholar who refuses to be corrupted as a critic, may be calumniated as a clergyman.   Upon this antagonism of principles, the interlocutory judgment of the Court of Arches pronounces that the clergy are not obliged to falsify the evidence for the canon, or the origin or meaning of Holy Writ, so long as they respect the landmarks of those doctrines which I have taught with a fidelity and clearness unsurpassed by living man.   The practical result is that no clergyman will again be prosecuted in England for refusing to misrepresent the origin of the Book of Daniel and of the Psalms, for abstaining from distortion of Hebrew Prophecy, and from calumny of the Hebrew race.   Hence, literary misrepresentation is so far checked that, although Bishops will still make it a passport to their favor, they can no longer enforce it by law.   Glory be to God, who brings strength out of weakness, and that to the least worthy of his servants, if we have thus far broken the rod of falsehood, brandished in right reverend hands ! ”

Dr. Lushington's judgment has been published in full ; and also the very able argument of Mr. Stephen, in favor of Dr. Williams ; the latter makes a volume of 355 pages.   Professor John Grote, of the University of Cambridge, has also published an Examination of the Judgment.

One striking point in this decision is, that Dr. Lushington ruled that neither the Bible nor the opinions of the Bishops had any place in court in such a question of doctrine.   Only the Articles and formularies, in their plain, grammatical sense, were admitted.   So that, after all, a lawyer with no theological training, might decide in the first instance what is the doctrine of the Church of England.

SWITZERLAND.

Prof. C. J. Riggenbach has published in a separate form his Report to the Evangelical Alliance on *Rationalism, especially in German Switzerland* — a candid review of present movements.

M. Ernest Naville has published an article in the *Bibliothèque Universelle* of Geneva, to show that Rousseau did not commit suicide ; but that in the latter part of his life he became a believer in a positive revelation. In proof he cites from a fragment of Rousseau, recently published, called *An Allegory.*

A new translation of the Scriptures into French is in the course of publication at Lausanne, by a Society : a large portion of the Old Testament has appeared.

M. Bungener, of Geneva, has published a work on *Calvin, sa Vie, ses Oeuvres et Ecrits*, which is highly eulogized.   Dr. Merle D'Aubigné's last volumes are devoted to Calvin and his Reformation.

ITALY.

Archbishop Liverani, well known as an opponent of the temporal sovereignty of the Pope, is publishing a collection from mss. called *Spicilegium Liberianum.* Among these are 12 Sermons of Jerome and Ambrose ; 37 Homilies of Bede ; a Homily by Leo the Great, etc.   Of special interest to English readers is a narrative of the trials of Thomas à Becket, from unpublished letters ; also a petition of Henry II to Alexander III for the canonization of King Edward.   This last was vainly sought for by Baronius, for his Annals.   The collection embraces documents prior to A.D. 1208.

The directors of the National Museum of Naples have resumed the publication of the deciphered papyri of Herculaneum, in a volume entitled *Herculanensium Voluminum quae supersunt Collectio Altera.* They are not of much value, consisting chiefly of fragments of Epicurean writers one Philodemus being the most voluminous.

The Royal University of Naples was opened for students, Nov. 18, 1861. It consists of five Faculties — Philosophy and Literature, Jurisprudence, Medicine, Natural Science, Mathematics.   The professors number 56; among them are Cavalier Sacchi, Professor of Mineralogy, Guiscardi of Geology, Spaventa of Law, Scubriani of Philosophy, Seticulbrini of Italian Literature.   The last three have been for years in exile.

Count Carlo Arribavene, exiled from Venetia by the Austrians, has published, in London, a work entitled *Italy under Victor Emmanuel.* It contains a narrative, mainly from the Count's personal knowledge, of the circumstances of war and peace attending the formation of the new kingdom of Italy, up to the fall of Gaeta.

There are twelve daily papers in Turin, a city of not more than 160,000 inhabitants.   At Naples, Milan and Florence the same mania for newspapers is exhibited.   Parma, a town of 40,000 inhabitants, has three dailies, and Modena four.

In the Ambrosian Library at Milan there is a MS. referred to by Mai, in *Spicilegium Romanum* (vol. iv, p. 247), as containing an account of Constantine, and of the acts of the Councils of Nice, Ephesus and Constantinople.   The late Prof. Robiati had in view the editing of it.   Prof. Oehler obtained a list of the contents of a portion, the heads of chapters, etc., which he published in the late number of the *Zeitschrift f. wiss. Theologie.*   It is believed to be the third book of the History of the Council by Gelasius, supposed to be lost.

Dr. Chiesi, editor of the *Buona Novella*, is preparing an Italian Hexapla of the New Testament, consisting of the versions of Diodati, Brucioli, Malermi, Pagnini and Vatablo.   He has also written a useful book, with the title *Who has falsified the Bible, the Protestants or the Catholics.*

The Pope has commissioned the celebrated German priest, Augustin Theiner, member of the Congregation of the Oratory, and Prefect of the Secret Archives of the Vatican, to draw up a report on the work of Dr. Döllinger, Canon of Munich, entitled *Church and Churches.*

The extracts made from Savonarola's marginal notes to the Bible, found in the Magliabecchian Library of Florence, are to be published, in part, by Villari, the biographer of Savonarola.   A transcript was made by request of Mr. Charles Topling.

GERMANY.

The Zeitschrift f. die historische Theologie, Heft 4, 1862, continues Rippold's exhaustive sketch of the life and opinions of Henry Nicholas, founder of the so-called Family of Love.   Dr. Ebrard, of Erlangen, begins a thorough reëxamination of the History of the Culdees, from the sixth to the eighth centuries, devoting this article chiefly to an account of their practice in the celebration of Easter, coming to the conclusion that we find among the Culdees the last appearance of the time and mode of celebration prevalent in the earliest church, in the East to A.D. 380, and in the West to A.D. 450.   Dr. Baumgarten, of Rostock, gives two documents upon his noted controversy.

In the *Theologische Zeitschrift*, Lutheran, edited by Dieckhoff and Kliefoth, May to August, Kliefoth continues his investigations upon the symbolism of numbers in the Scriptures, criticising, especially, the views of Bähr.   G. W. Brandt, in an account of the life and labors of Eric Jansson, presents interesting sketches of the later ecclesiastical movements in Sweden ; the Consistorial Councillor, Münchmeyer, contests· Kraussold's position, that the ecclesiastical· regimen of princes is *jure divino ;* J. E. Huther contributes exegetical illustrations of the epistle to the Philippians; Prof. Bachmann praises Keil and Delitzsch's new work on the Pentateuch as learned, orthodox and timely.

The *Zeitschrift f. Lutherische Theologie* is henceforth to be edited by Guericke and Delitzsch. The 3d and 4th parts, 1862, contain the following articles : Rudelbach's Confessions, embracing his school-years, 1805–10, giving interesting details about the course of study in the Danish schools. K. Ströbel on the Revision of the Lutheran Bible, criticising the Cansteen translation and Stier. L. de Marées, Preaching in the Old Testament. J. R. Linder, Interpretation of difficult Passages in the Old and New Testament; among them the contested passage on the Baptism for the Dead, 1 Cor. xv, 29. His interpretation is : "If the dead do not rise, how useless it is to be baptized ; if this baptism is after all only for the good of the dead, who can derive no benefit from it." Dr. Laurent, on Queen Candace (Acts viii, 27) : his conclusion, based on Æthiopic researches, is that Candace ruled in a district north of Meroe ; that Napata, not Meroe, was her chief city : that the name of the eunuch was not Indich or Judich, but is lost : and that Candace was not Queen of Æthiopia, but a queen in Æthiopia. A queen of that name is also spoken of as ruling in Alexander's times, and another B.C. 22. E. Engelhardt gives a valuable account of the witnesses for the Reformation in Bavarian Suabia.

Theologische Quartalschrift. 3d Heft. 1862. (Roman Catholic.) 1. Hefele on the peace between Frederick Barbarossa and Pope Alexander III, Venice, 1177. 2. Welte, the Apology of Melito of Sardes—translated from Cureton's *Spicilegium Syriacum,* 1855. The Apology is addressed to Antoninus, and contains valuable illustrations of Christian opinion. Cureton and Welte accept it as genuine ; but this is contested by Jacobi, in his edition of Neander's Lectures on the history of Christian Dogmas. Renan has also published this Apology, with a Latin version, in the *Spicilegium Solesmense.* 3. Langen on the Jewish Sanhedrim and the Roman procurators, contending that the Jewish court lost the power of life and death in religious matters under the Roman rule. 4. Nolte, Extracts from an unpublished Chronicle of George Harmatolus.

Zeitschrift f. Wissenschaftliche Theologie. Tübingen, 3d Heft, 1862. Hilgenfeld on the Epistles to the Thessalonians contends, against Baur, for the Pauline origin of the First Epistle. Baur allowed only four Epistles, viz. Galatians, I, II Corinthians and Romans (excepting the last two chapters), to be genuine. M. Uhlemann on Gog and Magog, a learned and able dissertation, which will be translated for a future number of our RE-VIEW. Egli, Criticism of the Text of the Septuagint. L. Paul, the Doctrine of the Trinity in the writings of Theophilus· of Antioch. With all the obscurity of his views, it is shown that Theophilus in several passages distinctly recognized the personal character of the Logos. Paul shows incidentally that the Gospel of John is cited by Theophilus (who wrote about A.D. 175), as an undisputed work. The 4th *Heft* contains only two articles. K. Furrer, a sketch of the life of Rudolf Collin, a Zurich reformer and classical teacher, born 1499, died 1578 ; and Hilgenfeld on Gnosticism and the Philosophoumena (ascribed to Hippolytus), reviewing the works of Möller and Lipsius, of which an account was given in the last number of the AMERICAN THEOLOGICAL REVIEW. Hilgenfeld gives up the position, which he with Baur once defended, that Cajus, the Roman presbyter, was the author of the Philosophoumena. Gnosticism as there portrayed, he views as freed from the elements of dualism and emanationism, which characterized its oriental forms.

The Journal of National Psychology and Philology, edited by Lazarus and Steinthal, has completed its second volume. Among the papers of general interest are Steinthal on the Saga of Prometheus, on Superstition, on the Characteristics of Languages, and on Greek Individuality ; Lazarus on the relation of the Individual to the Generic ; Lübke, the Gothic style and the Nationalities ; Tobler, the Poetic Treatment of the animal world.

The third *Heft* of the *Jahrbücher für Deutsche Theologie*, 1861. Dr. Burk on the terms, Wisdom and Knowledge ($\gamma\nu\tilde{\omega}\sigma\iota\varsigma$) in the Scriptures. Ehrenfeuchter, The Stages of Church Instruction. Hasse, The Pathology of the Christian Hope. Schultz, The Doctrine of Justification by Faith, in the Old and New Covenant. The first article makes an ingenious distinction between wisdom and knowledge—the former term signifying the direct act of the mind in relation to the object, the latter, an indirect or reflexive act, as determined by the object—and applies this to what the Scriptures say about both the divine and the human intelligence. Ehrenfeuchter's catechetical essay is excellent. Hasse gives a sketch of all the abnormal forms of Hope, which are grounded on unscriptural ideas of human nature and destiny.

Luther's Opera Latina, now republishing at Frankfort, edited by Irmischer and others, are offered at a very low price—for the first twenty volumes, five thalers ; for the next six, three thalers ; twelve more will complete the work, at one half thaler per volume.

The first important German work on natural history, called the *Book of Nature*, by Konrad von Megenberg, which was reprinted seven times in the course of the fifteenth century, has been newly edited by Franz Pfeiffer, in Vienna, in the original Bavarian idiom of the author.

In Germany, the Protestants have 1500 bookstores, the Catholics only 24 of any account; the former have over 200 journals, the latter only 30. Among the latter are the *Zion*, founded in 1832 ; *Wiener Kirchenzeitung*, 1848 ; *Tübinger Quartalschrift* (the ablest) 1819 ; *Katholik*, 1821 ; *Archiv für Kirchenrecht*, 1857. The *Historisch-politischen Blätter*, of Munich, edited by Jörg, aided by Döllinger and Binder, have wide influence. Michelis has begun a monthly called *Natur und Offenbarung*, against the materialists.

Austria, with a population of 35,795,000, has only 472 booksellers. Its journals number 130 political and 281 of all other kinds, in 14 languages.

In Germany, were published in 1861, 9,398 works, (9,496 in 1860): Theology 1,394, carries the palm in numbers ; Jurisprudence 936, etc. Of Sclavonic and Hungarian works there are 152, (in 1860, 116).

University Students : Vienna, 2,250 ; Berlin, 1,542 ; Munich, 1,280 ; Leipsic, 887 ; Breslau, 850 ; Bonn, 836 ; Göttingen, 751 ; Halle, 720 ; Tübingen, 719 ; Wurzburg, 651 ; Heidelberg, 588 ; Erlangen, 583 ; Jena, 454 ; Königsberg, 419 ; Giessen, 335 ; Friburg, 318 ; Greifswald, 293 ; Marburg, 254, and Kiel, 178.

One of the most important measures for which Austrian Protestants are indebted to their government is the reörganization of the Protestant Theological Seminary, or, as it is called, the *Protestant Theological Faculty of Vienna*. Until the reign of the present Emperor, it seems to have been the design of the Austrian government to exclude from it every eminent scholar. Recently, the Theological Faculty and the Protestant churches in general have applied to the government to incorporate the Faculty with the University of Vienna. This petition, as was to be expected, has met with the most violent opposition on the part of the Catholic bishops and the Ultramontane party, and the Archbishop of Vienna has even threatened to prohibit all students of Catholic theology from attending the lectures of the University in case the Protestant Theological Faculty should be recognized as a part of the University. But his threats and opposition have had little effect. The most numerous of the Faculties of the University, that of Philosophy, at its last meeting, voted with an immense majority in favor of admitting the Protestants—and little doubt is felt that the Government will soon pronounce the incorporation.

The Old Lutherans, who have been so violent against the Union, are becoming divided among themselves on doctrinal points and on union with Rome. One of their leading periodicals, the *Monatsschrift für die Evangelische Kirche Preussens*, edited by Wangamann, complains of the sluggishness and divisions of the party. The Romanizing tendency is represented by the *Hallisches Volksblatt* and the *Neue Preussische Zeitung;* the opposite by the *Nues Zeitblatte für die Angelegenheiten der Lutherischen Kirche*, edited by Dr. Münkel in Oiste, near Verden, and by the bi-monthly periodical, *Theologische Zeitschrift*, edited by Kliefoth and Dieckhoff. Dr. Kahnis, who has been recognised hitherto as one of the leaders of the Old Lutherans, in his recent Dogmatics has avowed such unorthodox views on the canon, inspiration, Trinity, etc., that Dieckhoff is out against him in a series of severe articles in the *Theologische Zeitschrift*.

A full collection of the Acts and Documents in the controversy between the Greek and Latin churches at the period of their separation in the 11th century, is given for the first time by Cornelius Will, in his Acta et Scripta, etc., published at Leipsic, in an elegant 4to volume of 272 pages.

D. F. Strauss, the author of the life of Jesus, has published a work on Reimarus, probably the real author of the *Wolfenbüttel Fragments*, which were edited by Lessing. In it he eulogizes the rationalistic tendencies, but criticises Reimarus for still retaining belief in Christ and the immortality of the soul. A volume of Strauss's miscellaneous essays and reviews has also been recently published.

The 157th part of Herzog's Real-Encyclopädie, comes down to Ubiquity. Piper contributes an exceedingly valuable article on what he calls Monumental Theology, that is, theology as set forth and illustrated in monuments and works of Christian art, inscriptions, etc. Prof. Landerer has a very able essay on Aquinas and his theology. Peip on the Trinity is also a thorough and speculative discussion.

Johann Ludwig Uhland, one of the foremost of the lyric poets of Germany, died recently at Tübingen, where he was born on the 20th of April, 1787. In 1815 he published the first collection of his poems; some of which, on political topics, had already had a great influence on public sentiment in Germany. He gave up legal practice in 1830, and became extraordinary professor of the German language and literature in the University of Tübingen. Several of Uhland's songs have been translated into English by Professor Longfellow; and in 1848 a translation of other of his poems, with a memoir, was published in London. Since 1848 the poet had lived in retirement.

FRANCE.

M. Renan has published a pamphlet upon his suspension from teaching, entitled *The Chair of Hebrew in the College of France: Explanations with my Colleagues.* He arraigns the action of the Government, and then proceeds to expound his views—denying the supernatural and miracles. "He offers us," says the *Revue Chrétienne*, "faith in our father, the abyss." He says: "The historical sciences presuppose that no supernatural agent has ever troubled the march of humanity; that there is no free being, superior to man, to whom may be ascribed an appreciable part in the moral guidance, any more than in the material ordering of the universe". He has drawn down upon himself the opposition of the deists (Simon, Saisset and Larroque), by his declaration, that "there has not been established any fact, either in nature or history, manifestly proving the existence of a will higher than that of man". *A Life of Jesus*, by Renan, forming the first part of a work on the *Origin of Christianity*, is also announced as soon to appear.

Pastor George Fisch has republished his articles on the United States in a volume, with large additions on our political history. Laboulaye says of the work in the *Journal des Débats:* "These solid pages, *breves quidem sed succiplenae*, give the secret of the American life and greatness". Fisch says: "There are happily in the North millions of men who believe that God governs in the affairs of the world, and who, at every new reverse, ask what is the lesson to be drawn from it. Since the Richmond battles they hear more distinctly the cries and groans of the poor negroes".

The *Revue Chrétienne*, in its recent numbers, has four excellent articles by B. Pozzy, on the Unity of the Race, on the basis of the work of Quatrefages; two articles on the Lyric Poetry of France by Rosseeuw Saint-Hilaire; a sketch of the Life and Last Days of Francesco Spiera, who became a Protestant in the early Italian reforms, recanted, and afterwards suffered dreadful torments of conscience; an able criticism of Hugo's Les Misérables by Secrétan, and an account of the Last Days of Lefèvre d'Étaples, by Jules Bonnet. On the attitude of England in respect to this country, the editor, De Pressensé, says: "The book of De Gasparin has aroused great wrath in England, expressed without bounds, in journals which profess to be Christian, and yet are enlisted in a revolting campaign in favor of the South, thus serving the worst passions of their country. . . . We are compelled to say, without holding the majority of English Christians to be responsible for these outrages, that their position on this great question is lacking in firmness and clearness. It is high time for these Christians to protest energetically against the sophisms, which have falsified public conscience, and which are only in place in the mouth of the foes of all right and of all progress". In the October number the editor hails the President's Emancipation Proclamation as the best omen of the war.

The Basque language has always been a puzzle to philologists—as to where it should be classed. William von Humboldt thought he detected affinities with some idioms of South America. Prince Louis Lucien Bonaparte has recently published at Paris, a work, showing its relation to the Finnish. And from M. Hyacinthe de Charency, a volume is announced, with the title *De la Langue Basque et de ses Affinités avec les Idiomes d'Oural.*

New Edition of Calvin's Works.—A critical and complete edition of all the works of Calvin is at last projected. Three Professors of Theology at Strasburg, Reuss, Kunitz and Baum have undertaken it, and they are now at Geneva examining all the manuscripts of Calvin in the library of the city. This edition will comprise much material never before published. It is supposed that it will extend to thirty or thirty-five volumes, 4to, in double columns. The beginning is to be made with the Institutes, in three texts, viz. the original edition, in Latin, Basle, 1536—most rare ; the folio edition of Strasburg, 1539, in which the work received its definitive form ; and the French translation by Calvin, about 1560. These will all be annotated by the editors, and subsequent variations noted.

The *Bulletin* of the French Protestant Historical Society for August gives indisputable evidence, from the parish registers of Caen, that the father of the French poet Malherbe was a member of the Reformed Church. It has hitherto been disputed.

At the last examination for the baccalaureate in the Faculty of Letters, Paris, out of 465 candidates, 260 were refused ; 170 were marked *passable; * 13 *assez bien; * 2 *bien; * and only one *très-bien* — *Corresp. Littéraire.*

A Paris letter says : " It is curious to see the heterogeneous elements of which the papal army of *littérateurs* is made up. M. Proudhon does not profess Christianity. M. Drouyn de L'Huys believes in transmigration of souls, and other theories held by French dreamers, which are in direct opposition to all the Catholic dogmas. The majority who rejected Jules Favre's motion for the evacuation of Rome are Voltaireans. M. Guizot, who represents the temporal power of the Institute, is a Protestant of the Evangelical school. M. Cohen, late the principal editor of *La France*, is a Jew, and although he declared in the columns of that journal that the Papacy is the great conservative principle of modern society—goes every Saturday to the synagogue, and is a scrupulous observer of the law of Moses and the ordinances of the rabbis."

An important collection of documents, relating to the Seven Years' War and the military events of the last years of Louis XV's reign, has lately been received by the Dépôt de la Guerre, and is now being classified for consultation. They were formerly in the possession of Bernadotte, and have been given up to France by the Swedish government.

It is proposed to publish a nineteenth-century " Encyclopédie," to renew the famous undertaking of the eighteenth. The project has been taken up by a capitalist, a political economist and a projector—namely, M. Isaac Péreira, M. Michel Chevalier and M. Duveyrier, so that it looks like business. These gentlemen, who began life with St. Simonianism, still retain its bold spirit. One feature in the " Encyclopédie " will be that, instead of an alphabetical arrangement, its subjects will be placed in a continuous order, according to their rational connection.

Two translations of Shakspeare are now appearing in Paris : one, a revision of Guizot's, first published in 1821 ; another by a son of Victor Hugo. French critics are comparing the two, and award the praise of greater fidelity to the latter ; e. g. the line " Chewing the cud of sweet and bitter fancies," reads in Guizot " Se nourrissant de pensées tantôt douces, tantôt améres ;" in Hugo, " Mâchant l'aliment doux et amer de la rêverie."

Charles Jourdain is publishing an extensive work on the *History of the University of Paris* in the seventeenth and eighteenth centuries. It will be in four parts, folio, costing seventy-two francs : the first part is out.

A new edition of E. Haag's *History of Christian Dogmas*, in two volumes, is announced. The author is one of the editors of *La France Protestante.* It is said to be a careful and conscientious collection of the main facts, with a somewhat rationalistic bias.

Abbé Glaire is publishing a new French version of the Bible. The New Testament has appeared. It is the first French translation authorized by the Church of Rome. De Sacy's is the one in common use. There is also one by De Genoude. Abbé Glaire is Dean of the Theological Faculty of Paris, and has written an *Introduction to the Bible*, 1843, a *Hebrew and Chaldee Lexicon*, an *Arabic Grammar*, and a *Vindication of the Scriptures*.

A bibliographical work is announced at Paris, which, if well executed, must be of great value to the student, viz. A. Potthast, *Bibliotheca Historica Medii Aevi*—a bibliographical guide for the history of Europe, from A.D. 375 to 1500. The first part is out—price 10 francs; the second is promised soon. It gives a full Index to the *Acta Sanctorum* of the Bollandists, and an account of all the sources for European history.

Theology.—Abbé Jager, *History of the Catholic Church in France, from its Origin to the Concordat of Pius VII.* Vol. 1. The work is to be in eighteen volumes. A new *History of the Jesuits* by Daurignac, in two volumes—the first is out. G. F. Astié, *The Two New Theologies in the Midst of French Protestantism.* Cardinal Gousset, on the *Temporal Sovereignty.* Nourrisson, *The Sources of the Philosophy of Bossuet.* B. Poujoulat, *History of the Popes, and Account of the Roman Question.* 2 volumes. Athanase Coquerel, *History of the Reformed Church of Paris,* from inedited documents. First Part. 1512–1594. Waddington, *History of Protestantism in Normandy,* 1685–1797. Adolphe d'Avril, *Documents on the Eastern Churches in Relation to the Holy See.* It is proposed to republish the *Acta Sanctorum* of the Bollandists, in fifty-four folio volumes, 1200 pp. double columns, at twenty-five francs the volume.

The Secretary of Prince Napoleon, M. Hilbaine, has just published a work entitled *The Pontifical Government judged by French Diplomacy.* It is divided into three parts: I. Diplomatic despatches from the time of Louis XIV to that of the French Revolution; II. Documents of the period of Napoleon I; III. Documents of the Governments of Louis XVIII and Charles X. The tenor of this diplomatic correspondence is summed up by M. Hilbaine as follows: "The judgments given at all these different periods, as to the temporal power of the Pope, is *unanimous.* On that point the representatives of France at Rome are of the same mind in the seventeenth century as in the eighteenth, and in the eighteenth as in the nineteenth. The statesmen of the ancient monarchy; those of the First Empire, which had revived the altars of the Church; and those even of the Restoration, whom no one will accuse of irreligion— all declare that such a *régime* cannot endure, and that it is a danger for Catholicism."

GREAT BRITAIN.

The British and Foreign Evangelical Review, October, contains: 1. Jeremy Taylor, from the *Presbyterian Quarterly;* 2. Guizot on the Signs of the Times; 3. Hengstenberg on Sacrifices, sharply criticising his views; 4. Stendel on the Inspiration of the Apostles—an excellent article, transferred from the *Christian Review*; 5. Modern Humanitarianism; 6. The Pharisaism and Sadduceeism of Modern and Primitive Christianity; 7. Astié on the Two Theologies; 8. The Controversy on the alleged Platonism of the Fathers, translated from the German *Journal of Historical Theology,* a very valuable article; 9. The Three Generations of Puritanism—a good account of the works of many eminent Puritans.

The British Quarterly Review, October.—1. Muir's Life of Mahomet— an excellent account, on the basis of this best of the biographies of the founder of Islam. 2. The Letters of Mendelssohn. 3. Arndt and his Sacred Poetry. 4. Gibraltar and Spain. 5. French Protestantism—a good historical summary. 6. Mediæval Preaching—with copious extracts

from English metrical Homilies of the Fourteenth Century, edited from
MSS. by John Small, of Edinburgh.   8. Hallucinations and Illusions—on
the basis of De Boismont's treatise.   9. The Church of England in 1862
—What next?   This article shows the position into which the Church is
thrown by Dr. Lushington's decision in the cases of the Bishop of Salisbury v. Williams, and of Fendall v. Wilson, and gives an account of the
state of parties.   The conclusion reached is : " That such is the condition
of the law in our Established Church, that men in that communion may
rationalize so far, on the one hand, as to become little better than deists ;
or may Romanize so far, on the other hand, as to become little better than
Papists, and still be accounted good Churchmen".   In his Epilogue, the
editor, Dr. Vaughan, again discourses of American affairs.   He thinks our
war is the greatest blow that the friends of human progress have received
in modern times.   "The most self-governed people of modern times has
become the most ill-governed".   He ascribes our evils to the "want of
moral and religious culture".   We are suffering for "worshipping the
dexterous man".   And this same Review, which finds no sense in our conflicts, in speaking of Gibraltar, says: "If Marshal O'Donnell seriously
asks Lord Palmerston or Lord John Russell for a surrender of the rock
fortress, both will respond with a will : ' Take it if you can.'   The old
rule practised in the past will be practised in the future,

> 'That they should take who have the power,
> And they should keep who can.' "

The Quarterly Review, London, November, on the Confederate Struggle
and Recognition, is steeped in the old, stupid tory prejudices against all
democracy.   Prophesying our inevitable failure, it ascribes it to the inherent inefficacy of a democracy to meet a great national crisis.   The assumed superiority and success of the South is explained on the theory,
that slavery tends to cultivate some of the aristocratic virtues.   The *North
British Review* continues its tirades against the North, in a somewhat less
florid vein, but still ignoring the vital elements and issues of our strife
with the slave power.   Even the Emancipation Proclamation fails to convince these reviewers that the North is contending in the interest of human
justice and freedom.   Nothing will convince them but success.   Even the
London Quarterly Review (Wesleyan), in its last number, under its new
administration, has turned against us.

Mr. Thomas Duffus Hardy, Deputy Keeper of the Public Records, and
member of the late Record Commission, has published, in two volumes, a
*Descriptive Catalogue of Materials relating to the History of Great
Britain and Ireland, to the end of the Reign of Henry VII*—a work of
great labor and invaluable, giving an account of all the materials, printed
and manuscript, pertaining to any man or period, with a critical estimate
of the value of each, and an account of the writers.   It is the first work
of the kind, aiming at completeness, and gives the results of forty years
of painstaking research.

Journal of Sacred Literature, October, 1862.—Nature of Prophecy ;
Ernest Renan, a eulogistic sketch ; Dean Ellicott on the Destiny of the Creature—opposing the Dean's position that "the creature" means all animate
and inanimate creation related to the saints ; The Atonement in relation to
Heb. ix, 16–18, by Wratislaw—taking the ground, that Christ's death
symbolized the death of both *God* and man, in behalf of the New Covenant ; The Tree of Life—historical notices ; Syriac Literature ; Life and
Miracles of Apollonius of Tyana, on the basis of Chassang's recent work ;

Biblical Canon; Marcus Antoninus, a Persecutor—a reprint of an old English tract, by Moyle; The Resurrection—a sermon, by Luis de Granada, translated.

The old *Sarum Missal*, the national liturgy of England, is at last to appear in a superior edition.   It is sent out from the Pitsligo press, by Mr. Forbes, all of the printing being done by women, "mostly converts from Presbyterianism".   The first volume, comprising the *Temporale*, is out; the second, the *Sanctorale*, will soon follow.   The title is Missale ad Usum insignis et præclaræ Ecclesiæ Sarum.   C. J. Stewart is the London publisher.   Some of the earlier editions were 1492, 1510–11, 1534; Paris, 1527; two editions by Prevost and Regnault, Antwerp, 1527.   The Sarum Missal prevailed in the south of England; was used in Scotland and Ireland, and in Portugal and Gallicia.   It was moulded on the missal of the church of Rouen.   The present volume is sold for seven shillings; previously it cost three or four pounds.   Within a few years, says the *Christian Remembrancer*, the way to liturgical studies has been made easy and cheap by the reprints of the Sarum Breviary, the Aberdeen Breviary, the primitive liturgies, and the English church services—so that the student can obtain for fifteen shillings what not long since cost as many pounds.

Rev. A. R. Roberts, in his discussions on the Gospels, has revived the theory that Greek was the language spoken by Christ.   From the fact that the New Testament was written in Greek, he concludes that this was the language of the Apostles and those to whom they wrote, and also of Christ.

Two new works on the Hindu Religion and Philosophy have recently been published by native converts.   One is entitled *Dialogues on the Hindu Philosophy*, by Rev. K. M. Banerjea, Professor of Bishop's College, Calcutta.   The other, by Nehemiah Nilakantha Sâstrî Gore, was written in Hindu, and translated by Fitz-Edward Hale, of Oxford.   The former is said to be written by the author, in admirable English, and shows remarkable refinement in speculation.   Mr. Gore's work, *A Rational Refutation of the Hindu Philosophical System*, has a more direct practical value for the training of Hindu scholars.

A Church Congress, presided over by the Bishop of Oxford, was held at Oxford, July 8–10.   Many topics of general interest were fully debated, but that of ministerial education took the lead.   The deplorable defects of the present English system were fully brought out.   Professor Harold Browne complained of "a gradual dearth of men for the clerical office, at least of the intellectual and academic mark to which bishops' chaplains (the examiners) had heretofore been accustomed".   Dean Ellicott suggested cutting down the academic course to two years, and then to devote a third year to theology.   Bishop Wilberforce was in favor of instituting a theological tripos, and of having a kind of apprenticeship to a parish priest. No conclusions were reached.   As to the present state of things at Oxford, the *Christian Remembrancer* says, that at Oxford they have "nearly let go" theological teaching, and at Cambridge it "holds only by the slender thread of 'voluntary' examinations'".   It adds that the disputations for the bachelor's degree of divinity "are to a dry humorist the funniest yet dreariest thing at Oxford".   As to the decrease in the number of ministerial candidates, the following statement was made by the Bishop of Winchester, in a recent charge, "that the number of candidates for Orders, which in 1841 was 606, in 1851 was 614, was in 1861 only 510.   The population of England has doubled in thirty years, while the clergy have increased by only one fifth.   He stated at the same time that the proportion of University graduates among those who are ordained is steadily diminishing, especially with Oxford men; and that the proportion of *literates* (*not* University men) is as steadily on the *increase*".

Newsapers published in Great Britain in 1861, 1,165, viz. 845 in England, 139 in Scotland, 33 in Wales, 134 in Ireland, 14 in the British Isles. The number in 1851 was 563.

A report that requires confirmation, is, that 1,300 new letters of John Knox have been discovered. Mr. Laing is now carrying through the press the 6th and last volume of Knox's writings.

The Most Rev. John Bird Sumner, D.D., late Archbishop of Canterbury, was born in 1780, and was educated at Eton and King's College, Cambridge, where he graduated, 1803; was appointed a Canon of Durham, 1820. He was consecrated Bishop of Chester in 1828, and translated to the See of Canterbury in 1848. Dr. Sumner was a prolific theological writer, having published besides other works, "Evidences of Christianity," "Expository Lectures" on the whole of the New Testament except the Apocalypse, in nine separate volumes, and several volumes of sermons. The vacant Primacy has been offered to, and accepted by, the Archbishop of York, Dr. Longley. Dr. Longley was born 1794; educated at Westminster School and Christchurch, Oxford, being first-class in classics. He was public examiner in 1825. In 1829 he was elected to the head-mastership of Harrow School. In 1836 the See of Ripon was founded, and Dr. Longley was appointed the first Bishop.

The Right Rev. William Thomson, D.D., nominated to the Archbishopric of York, was born on the 11th of February, 1819; entered at Queen's College, Oxford, where he became scholar, fellow and tutor, and provost; graduated in 1840, when he took a third class in classics. In 1853 he was chosen to preach the Bampton Lectures at Oxford, his subject being "The Atoning Work of Christ". In 1858 he was elected preacher of Lincoln's-inn; in 1859 made one of Her Majesty's chaplains; and in 1861, nominated Bishop of Gloucester and Bristol. The new Archbishop is well known by his work entitled, *An Outline of the Laws of Thought*, and by his preface to the work called *Aids to Faith*, which was intended to be a contractive to the *Essays and Reviews*. A curious precedent is quoted from ante-Reformation times, in the case of Cardinal Baynbrigg, who, like Dr. Thomson, was born in the Northern Province, raised himself by his own ability, was educated at Queen's College, Oxford, of which he became Provost, and after being Bishop one year (of Durham, however, not Gloucester and Bristol), was translated to York.

Albert Durer, the celebrated German artist, engraved about A.D. 1508 or 1509, a series of thirty-seven wood-cuts, which were published with a text, under the name of *The Passion of Christ*. Thirty-five of the original wood-cuts were by some singular piece of good fortune preserved, and are now in the British Museum, having been obtained by the trustees in 1839 An edition of these cuts, with the missing ones supplied as well as possible, was printed in 1844 at the Chiswick press.

Mr. Lovell Reeve, who has recently published, in *fac-simile*, by the new process of photo-zincography, Shakspeare's *Sonnets* and *Lover's Complaint*, will follow it up with the *Venus and Adonis*, *Lucrece*, the rare quarto plays published before the collected edition of 1623; and lastly, the famous folio itself. *Much Ado about Nothing* is already in hand.

Sir George Cornewall Lewis has in the press a new edition of *An Essay on the Origin and Formation of the Romance Languages; containing an Examination of M. Raynouard's Theory on the Relation of the Italian, Spanish, Provençal, and French to the Latin.*

Mr. Nichol, of Edinburgh, proposes a reïssue of the following commentaries, edited by Rev. Jas. Sherman—subscription price 25s. 6d.—formerly published at £8 5s., viz. Rev. Thos. Adams on Peter's Second Epistle, (1663); Hosea, by Burroughs, (1643); Jude, by Wm. Jenkyn, (1653); and Daillé's Philippians and Colossians (1639), translated by Sherman.

Dr. Robert Vaughan's bicentenary memorial volume on English Nonconformity is announced. In three Books it gives an account of the Religious Life in England before 1660; the Confessors of 1662; and English Nonconformity since 1662.

The *Home and Foreign Review*, the new Roman Catholic Quarterly, succeeding the *Rambler*, has already been denounced by Cardinal Wiseman, Bishop Ullathorne, and other prelates.

The Gospel according to St. John has been translated from the eleven oldest versions, except the Latin, by Rev. S. C. Malan, with Notes. 4to, 50 pp. 36s. The translations are from the Syriac, Æthiopic, Armenian, Georgian, Slavonic, Sahidic, Memphitic, Gothic, Anglo-Saxon, Arabic and Persian.

A literary triplet has just been published in London—*Specimens of Ancient Gaelic Poetry.* It was collected between 1512 and 1589 by the Rev. James McGregor, Dean of Lismore, and is translated and edited by the Rev. Thomas McLaughlin; with an Introduction and Additional Notes by Mr. William F. Skene.

The British government has granted a pension of £100 to Mr. Isaac Taylor, as an acknowledgment of his eminent services to literature, especially in the departments of history and philosophy.

Professor A. De Morgan has been long employed upon a work examining the Logic of Sir William Hamilton. He has repeatedly called upon the Hamiltonians to answer him some questions about the logic, and repeats them in a still more urgent style in the *Athenæum*, thus:

"What was the meaning of the word '*some*' in the system of the quantified predicate, which Hamilton taught from his chair 'to place the keystone in the Aristotelic arch'? When he enunciated—'Some A is B'—'Some men are wise'—or the like, did his nomenclature imply 'and the rest as may be,' or did it imply 'and the rest are *not*'?'"

Rev. John Keble is writing a Life of Thos. Wilson, Bishop of Sodor and Man.

Among the new books announced are—Lyell on the *Antiquity of Man;* Rawlinson, *The Five Great Monarchies;* a new edition of Dean Milman's *History of the Jews;* Stanley, *Lectures on the Jewish Church;* A. S. Farrar, *History of Free Thought;* Horner's translation of *Villari's Savonarola;* R. W. Mackey, *The Tübingen School and its Antecedents;* Prof. Huxley, *Man's Place in Nature; Book of Job,* by Geo. Croly; *Revised Translation of New Testament,* by Highton; a translation by Wm. Alexander of *Saisset on Modern Pantheism*—an acute work; *Historical Theology,* by the late Principal Cunningham, of Edinburgh; *Hymnologia Christiana,* by Dr. Kennedy—full and valuable; a translation of Wieseler's *Chronological Synopsis of the Gospels;* a third edition of Fairbairn's *Ezekiel; Beza's Codex,* edited by Scrivener; *Leo's Sermons on the Incarnation,* translated by Bright; C. J. Vaughan on the *Epistle to the Philippians;* Theodore Parker's Works, in 12 vols.; Ed. Churton on the *Latitudinarians;* Alford's *New Testament for English Readers,* 2 vols.

UNITED STATES OF AMERICA.

The Census of 1860 *on Periodicals in the United States.*—In 1850 their number was 1,630. In 1860 it was 3,242, being an increase of nearly 100 per cent. In 1850 the number of religious papers and periodicals was 191. In 1860 it was stated at 277, being an increase of 45 per cent. In 1850 the number of papers and periodicals of every class in the United States was 2,526. In 1860 the aggregate under this head reaches, as before stated, 4,051, showing a rate of increase of 60.37. The total circulation of all kinds amounted in 1850 to 426,409,978 copies. In 1860 the annual circulation is stated at 927,951,548 copies, showing a ratio of increase of 117.61. In 1850 the annual circulation of all kinds afforded 21.81 copies to each white person in the Union. In 1860 the total circulation was at the rate 34.36 per person. Of the total circulation in the country, three States, New York, Pennsylvania, and Massachusetts, furnish 539,026,124 copies, or considerably more than half of the aggregate amount. Of 4,051 papers and periodicals published in the United States, at the date of the census of 1860, 3,242, or 80.02 per cent, were political in their character; 298, or 7.38 per cent are devoted to literature. Religion and theology compose the province of 277, or 6.83 per cent, while 234, or 5.77 per cent, are classed as miscellaneous.

In New England, the Middle and Western States, the value of book, job, and newspaper printing is returned as $38,428,043, of which eleven millions' worth consisted of books, the value of the latter being nearly equal to the whole product of the same branch in 1850, which was returned at $11,586,549. The manufacture of paper, especially of printing paper, has increased in an equal ratio, the State of Massachusetts alone producing paper of the value of $5,968,469, being over fifty-eight per cent of the product of the Union in 1850. New York returned paper of the value of $3,516,276; Connecticut, $2,528,758, and Pennsylvania, $1,785,900.

The Evangelical Quarterly Review, Gettysburgh began a new volume in October (the 14th), under the able editorship of Prof. M. L. Stoever. The articles are. The Book of Job, from the German of Schlottmann, by Dr. Schaeffer; Martin Luther, from Köstlin, by Dr. Diehl; Spener, from Tholuck, by Prof. Muhlenberg; Our General Synod; The Crusades, by Dr. Lintner; The Great Commandment, by Dr. Lintner; Remarks on Romans vi, 3, 4, by Dr. Greenwald.

A tract of Franklin's, long supposed to be lost, is soon to be republished, viz. *Discourse on Liberty and Necessity, Pleasure and Pain, in a Letter to a Friend.* He wrote it in London, when first there, in reply to Wollaston's *Religion of Nature,* the types of which he was setting up. His main position was, that nothing could be wrong in the world, since God was infinitely good and wise—that virtue and vice were empty distinctions. Becoming dissatisfied with it, he burned all but a few copies. Of one of these there is an account by James Crossley, in the *Notes and Queries,* 1852. Mr. Stevens has a copy dated 1725, 8vo, pp. 32.

Mr. Tibbals, New York, is bringing out a compact and cheap edition of Stier's *Words of the Lord Jesus,* in 2 vols., revised by Dr. Strong. The Edinburgh edition has had a large sale in this country.

Chronicles of the Franciscans in Brazil, vol. 2, Rio Janeiro, 1861. The first volume was issued just a century ago.

An English translation of *Graul's Distinctive Doctrines,* by the Rev. D. M. Martens, of Ohio, is published by Rev. J. A. Schulze, Columbus, Ohio. It is a valuable work.

Mr. Fletcher Harper, in a letter to the *Athenæum*, says, that the Harpers have paid more money to British authors than all the other publishers in America; and, in the past five years, have paid more to British authors for early sheets than British publishers have paid to American authors since the first book was printed in this country.

Prof. I. D. Rupp, well known as editor of a *History of Denominations*, is preparing a *History of the Germans in Pennsylvania*, giving, also, an account of various sects. *The Lutheran and Missionary*—an excellent and well-conducted newspaper, furnishes extracts, which show that it will be a work of decided value.

Mr. Charles Perkins, of Boston, who has been for some time residing in Florence, has recently finished a work on sculpture, which has been accepted by the Longmans, of London, and will be shortly published there. It is profusely illustrated with outlines of sculpture, drawn by Mr. Perkins, and will bear much the same relation to the plastic art that Mrs. Jameson's works do to painting.

The Theological writings of Archbishop Whately are to be republished in this country, under the direct editorship of the author, by Draper, of Andover, who will put to press, at an early day, *Essays on some of the Difficulties in the Writings of the Apostle Paul*, to be followed by *Essays on some of the Peculiarities of the Christian Religion*, etc.

The *American Bible Society* is now publishing, besides the English Scriptures—1. The Armeno-Turkish translation of the whole Bible, by the Rev. Dr. Goodell, of Constantinople—the work of a long and devoted missionary life. 2. The continued translation of the Bulgarian Scriptures, by Dr. Riggs. 3. The Arabo-Turkish translation of the New Testament, by Dr. Riggs—nearly completed and in press. 4. The completion of the revised edition of the Bible in Chinese, by Rev. Dr. Culbertson and his coadjutors—a work of years, and of vast importance. 5. The Arabic Bible, begun by the late Dr. Eli Smith, and completed by Dr. Van Dyck; now ready for the press—will be in great demand. 6. Added to the above is the interesting fact, that a native of Syria has cut a complete set of matrices and punches for the type of a Syriac New Testament, soon to be printed at the Bible House. 7. Within three years we have printed, says the *Record*, 14,000 copies of the Scriptures for Turkey. Of the Armenian Scriptures six editions have been issued from the Bible House, from three sets of electrotype plates, of three different sizes. This is a most beautiful specimen of Oriental typography; and is very popular among the Armenians. 8. A new Spanish edition of the Bible is now in process of revision and of electrotyping. To this work Dr. Brigham gave many laborious hours, down to the close of his life.

Skedaddle. Etymological speculations are still rife as to the origin of this word. Some prefer the Greek. A writer in the *Historical Magazine* says that "it is of both Swedish and Danish origin, and has been in common use for several years through the Northwest, in the vicinity of immigrants from those nations. It is Americanized only in orthography; the Swedes spelling it '*skuddadahl*,' while the Danes spell '*skyededehl*,' both having precisely the same signification. This phrase is also becoming Indianized, at least among the Sioux, who frequently use it in place of their word '*poch-a-chee*,' which signifies 'clear out,' 'go off,' etc. I will also add that the Swedes use the word *skudda*, and the Danes the word *skyede*, in the same sense as we do the word 'scud'". Lord Hill writes to *The Times* (London) October 13th, that "skeddaddle is commonly used in Dumfriesshire, my native home. To *skeddadle* means to spill in small quantities any liquids. The Americans totally misapply the word".

11

Literary and Critical Notices of Books.

BIBLICAL LITERATURE.

The Pentateuch and Book of Joshua Critically Examined. By the Right Rev. JOHN WILLIAM COLENSO, D.D., Bishop of Natal. New York: Appleton & Co. 1863. 12mo, pp. 226. If it be not praise, then it must be terrible satire, to say of a new work like this that it is "a remarkable book by a remarkable man". So have many critics pronounced it. So we think it. And yet, in our judgment, there is nothing very remarkable about either the book or the man, separately considered. The remarkableness is all in the conjunction of the two. A stranger phenomenon certainly has not occurred of late in the literary world. That an English bishop — who has been for nine years amongst the Zulus of South-Eastern Africa, trying to convert them to Christianity — should thus have struck his flag in the face of heathendom, abjuring his life-long faith, not only in the Divine inspiration, but even in the historic truth of the Pentateuch, and other, if not all the other Scriptures, is, to say the least of it, something to be stared at. Had this book been written by a heathen Zulu, or had the Natal Bishop written quite another sort of book, in defence of the Pentateuch as inspired and credible, no great stir would probably have come of it. In the one case, we might have had to pity and pray for the poor Zulu ; or, in the other case, we might have had to thank the worthy Bishop for good intentions not very vigorously realised ! But now we have to do with a Zulu book from an English bishop ! The conjunction staggers us.

The champions of orthodoxy, it is often said, are apt to enter the lists against a heretic by denouncing him as a bad man. We shall indulge ourselves in no such charge, in no such suspicion even. We believe the Bishop to be a very good man. His book certainly is pious ; altogether too pious for the common run of infidel readers. The tone of it is not defiant, but deprecatory. Evidently it pains him to march out of the old camp, and range himself upon the other side. He pleads for charitable judgment on the part of his former comrades, with the pathos of one who really values the sympathy of Christian men. He prints his book, as he embraced his new opinions, not in wrath, but in righteousness of purpose ; not in obedience to any lust of reputation, place, or power, but simply because he felt constrained thereto by the instincts of an honest mind. He *ceased* to believe, and therefore speaks. Cost what it may, he cannot be silent even, seeming to hold opinions which have departed from him. Having discarded alike, and equally, the Divine inspiration, the Mosaic authorship, and the historic truth, of the Pentateuch, he must make a clean breast of it in the face of Natal, England, and the world. He may cease to be a bishop, but he cannot consent to be a hypocrite. And so he disrobes himself like a martyr for the stake. Yet not quite, for "the decision of the Court of Arches" holds out some promise that one may hereafter be a bishop without believing. And to make a sure thing of it — that there may be neither martyrdom, nor wear and tear of conscience, in the future as in the past— he importunes the English laity to let their Bible slide. Not without interest shall we await their answer to this appeal. We are curious to know whether, in the land of Wycliffe and Latimer, the Bible, the Koran, the Vedas, the Zend-Avesta, and the nine Classics of China, are all to go upon the same shelf.

But if not a bad man, how could Bishop Colenso have been left to write such a book? The secret is an open one. It comes of a meagre professional discipline. In the University, probably, he studied Thucydides and Æschylus more than he studied Moses and Isaiah. And from the University, like the majority of English clergymen, he went probably to his parish without anything like a proper theological training. The way in which he speaks of such writers as Bleek, Ewald, Kurtz, Hävernick, and Hengstenberg, shows plainly enough that he has not been familiar with the higher literature of his profession. In *Allibone's Dictionary* he is named as Rector of Forncett St. Mary, Norfolk, and author of works on arithmetic, algebra, and plane trigonometry for schools. In Africa, he had to study the Bible in order to translate it into Zulu; and, in attempting it, his faith went to wreck against difficulties, which he ought long ago to have encountered and escaped. He deprecates in advance the imputation of having borrowed his infidelity from Germany. For those who know anything of German infidelity, there was no need of this. His infidelity is all his own, of English seed on heathen soil.

Doubtless the book may work some mischief as coming from a bishop's pen. There are those who will be imposed upon by his sweeping assertions of absurdity and contradiction, launched against the Mosaic records. There are those who have not the perspicacity to detect the exaggeration with which he states a difficulty, nor the skill to turn its edge. There are those who do not know why an *argumentum ad ignorantiam* is not as cogent as any other. And there are those who have not been taught to read the Scriptures in the light of the well-established principles of modern science. All such persons are likely to suffer harm. But the mischief wrought will soon be redressed. Those whose business it is to expound the Scriptures will be driven to a more critical and deeper study of them, and compelled to give a better account, than they are now able to do, of the faith once delivered to the saints.

This is not the place to notice in detail the points chosen for assault by the Bishop. There are some eighteen or twenty of them in all. So far as we have observed, none of them are new, and, to judge from the few that we have carefully examined, none of them are formidable. To make difficulties where there are none, by holding the writer of the Pentateuch to a strictness of construction not at all required by the context, and then to exaggerate ingeniously existing difficulties, such as are always to be expected in rapid and concise narration, is not quite so fair as it is easy. A faith which can be overwhelmed by such tactics, deserves to be overwhelmed. That the Bishop of Natal should have frittered away his own faith by a process so utterly at war with the very rudiments of criticism, though painful enough, cannot be surprising to such as have noticed his previous vagaries. An interpreter of Scripture who can plead for the permission of polygamy to heathen converts amongst the Zulus, and teach for doctrine that Christ has not only made an atonement for the sins of men, but actually redeemed the race by his sufferings, is an interpreter whose final landing-place may be guessed but never calculated.   R. D. H.

THEOLOGY AND CHURCH HISTORY.

Die göttliche Offenbarung, von Dr. E. A. AUBERLEN. Bd. I. Basel. 1859. Prof. Auberlen is well known to English readers by the translation of his work on Daniel and the Apocalypse. He belongs to that school of German theologians, who have revolted against the abstractions of philosophy, and insist upon historical facts, as containing the reality of the Christian revelation. This new work on Divine Revelation is a defence of the Christian system against rationalism, in a method conformed to this view. The first part gives the evidence, on historical ground, that a supernatural revelation is found in Christianity, attested by miracles, proved by all proper historical tests. The second part recounts the history of rationalism—a very able review. The third part, not yet published, will discuss the underlying metaphysical questions, as to the possibility of miracles, etc., on the basis of the true idea of God and his workings, vindicating the necessity of a revelation. The principles and arguments of all the later German schools of philosophy are ably reviewed, as well as all the main modern theological systems. In the historical proof of the reality of a supernatural revelation, he begins with Christ and the Apostles, starting with only those epistles which even the school of Baur acknowledge to be genuine, Romans, Corinthians, and Galatians. Then in a regressive method, he goes to the Old Testament, and examines particularly its prophecies, as well as the evidence of a divine economy running through the elder dispensation. "The last alternative", he says, reviewing the whole, "is, that the world is a mad-house, or the temple of the living God".

S. Bonaventurae Opuscula duo praestantissima, Breviloquium et Itine-rarium Mentis ad Deum. Ed. C. J. HEFELE. Editio tertia. Tubing. 1861. 18mo, pp. 356. This beautiful, correct and cheap edition of two of the best treatises of John of Fidanza, to whom St. Francis gave the name Bonaventura, and whom the Greeks, for his pacific counsels, called Eutychius, —is a boon to the scholar. Baumgarten Crusius said that the Breviloquium is the best dogmatic work of the mediæval period. It goes over all the main topics of theology in a natural method, and gives clear doctrinal statements. The Itinerarium is a manual of practical divinity, in the best spirit of the mystics of the middle ages. Chancellor Gerson said of these two works: "Bonaventurae opuscula duo tanta sunt arte compendii divinitus composita, ut supra ipsa nihil". The volume can be had for about 75 cents.—Bonaventura became Prof. of Theology in Paris, in 1253; and was at the Council of Lyons in 1274. A Protestant German theologian, Hollenberg, has just published *Studies on Bonaventura*, giving an account of his theology and of his mystical writings.

Preuves que Thos. à Kempis n'a pas composé l'Imitation de N. S. Jésus Christ. Par P. TAMIZEY DE LARROQUE. Paris. 1862. No country has honored the immortal Imitation of Jesus Christ with more profound devotion than France. De Larroque states the number of translations at more than a hundred; the editions are countless. It is no wonder, then, that an effort should be made to disprove its foreign origin, even if a French authorship cannot be proved. This was the object of M. de Larroque in his elaborate articles in the *Annales de Philosophie Chrétiénne*, now collected in a small volume. His object is to prove from internal evidences that à Kempis cannot have composed this work. Germany, Italy, and France have contended for the authorship; Germany for à Kempis; Italy for Gersen and Jean de Cabanaco; France for Gerson. Ullman, Liebner, Gieseler,

Delprat, Scholz, Clarisse, Quérard, Lalanne, and Malon of Belgium, advocate the claims of the first; the work of Malon, 1848, new edition' 1858, gives all the arguments in a complete form.   The claims of Gerson are defended by Cajetan, Guerini, De Gregory (2 vols. 1842), Renan, Chateaubriand, and Rohrbacher.   Many French writers have favored Gerson;. M. Gence wrote 21 works in his favor; with him agree Berbier, Vert, and Villemain.   Some enthusiastic Frenchmen have even said, the Imitation is "the work of France itself".   The contest has also been carried on between the monastic orders; the regular canons of St. Augustine and the Jesuits contending always for à Kempis (as Amort, Molinet, Géry, Bellarmine, etc.); and the Benedictines for Gersen.   What Gregory the Great said of the Book of Job has also been applied to the Imitation, that "the only thing that seemed certain was, that the Holy Ghost was its author".   And it is reported of de Merillac, that after hearing Malon's prolix arguments for à Kempis, he remarked, "that God had granted to the saintly author the honor of being forgotten".   But M. Tamizey de Larroque reöpens the question with great zeal.   His work is devoted to a comparison of the Imitation with the acknowledged writings of à Kempis.   He certainly shows marked differences in style; e. g., *abnegation* and *resignation* constantly recur in the Imitation — the former in à Kempis rarely, the latter not at all; the adverbs of the latter end usually in *ter*, of the former seldom; allegory and antithesis abound in à Kempis, and not in the Imitation; citations of holy books are frequent in the former, and not in the latter, which however has several from classical authors, in which à Kempis was not versed.   The devil is introduced into the Imitation only seven times, he appears on every page of à Kempis; the former rarely speaks of hell, and of heaven only in general terms, while the latter describes both minutely.   In the Imitation there is only one narrative, but stories abound in à Kempis.   The latter has many artificial metaphors; the former abounds in simpler tropes.   A multitude of special and characteristic terms are found in the Imitation, and not in à Kempis; e. g, absorption in God; the abyss of deity (abyssalis deitas); the aliment of immortality (immortalitatis alimonium); ambulare; tuba for buccina; contradicere, contradictiones; conditor mundi; genera and species, etc.   And so in à Kempis are many phrases never occurring in the Imitation : carnis aestus, carnis lascivia; frequent diminutions, similes on all fours, etc.   The meditations on death in the Imitation are simple and profound; in à Kempis descriptive and imaginative.   The Imitation has no preface; even the minor works of à Kempis have long introductions.   One of the most remarkable facts however is, that in the Imitation the Virgin Mary is spoken of only three or four times, and then quite incidentally, without any special homage; while à Kempis prayed every day an hour to the Mother of God, and introduced her with rapture and veneration into almost every discourse.   De Larroque thinks that à Kempis may have received the credit of writing the Imitation, because, being a caligraphist, he wrote it out in a fair hand, adding the equivocal formula : "*Finitus et completus anno Domini MCCCCXLI, per manus fratris Thomae à Kempis*".   There are mss., however, older than this of Antwerp (now at Brussels).   He also thinks that the testimony to à Kempis of Buschius, a cotemporary, is interpolated.   He also tries to show that the author must have been a Frenchman, but is not able to decide for Gerson.   *Adhuc sub judice lis est.*

Bibliotheca Patrum Selectissima.   Ed. G. B. LINDNER.   Fasciculi i-iv.   Lips.   1857–61.   This *Bibliotheca* is intended to give some of the minor treatises of the Fathers of the Church, unabridged, at a very moderate cost. Four fasciculi have been published : the first contains the Epistle to Diognetus—one of the very best of the post-apostolic writings in the second century ; and the Martyrdom of Polycarp. The second gives in full the text of Tertullian on the Resurrection ; the third, Clement of Alexandria's treatise, entitled, Quis Dives Salvetur ; the fourth, Tertullian De Anima. The cost of the four is about one dollar.

Les deux Theologies nouvelles dans le Sein du Protestantisme Français. Etude historico-dogmatique par J.-F. ASTIÉ. Paris. 1862. Pp. 344. Professor Astié, of Lausanne, in this interesting and well-written work, reviews the conflicts and progress of opinion among the Protestants in France and Switzerland, for the past twenty years. A devoted admirer of Vinet, whose system he has presented, with pertinent extracts, in another work,—he is radically opposed to the rationalism of Scherer, Colani, and Pécaut, and to the attempt to carry theology back to the scholastic formulas of the *Consensus Helveticus.* While pleading for liberty of thought, and the freedom of the Church, he is reverential to the Divine Word, and opposed to the license of unillumined reason. The work is divided into three parts. 1. The Past. 2. The Crisis — a full account of the controversies with Scherer, Colani, Réville, Pécaut, and Renan. 3. The Future—a eulogium of the theology of Vinet, as the theology of conscience.

Lange's Bibel-Werk. 1862. IX. Theil. The ninth part of this valuable commentary contains Schenkel on the Epistles to the Ephesians, Philippians, and Colossians. He defends against Baur the genuineness of these Epistles, and gives a lucid and condensed commentary, under the three heads of exegetical, doctrinal, and homiletic. Though Schenkel is not as thoroughly orthodox as some of the writers of this Bible-Work, he is always suggestive, and he has the gift of clear statement and arrangement.

BIOGRAPHY.

Johannes Brenz. Von JULIUS HARTMANN. Elberfeld. 1862. 8vo, pp. 838. This life of the distinguished Suabian reformer forms the sixth volume of the *Lives and Selected Writings of the Fathers of the Lutheran Church,* now in progress. Hartmann published in 1840–2, a larger work on the same subject, very much of it from unpublished sources. This new work will be of more interest to the general reader. Brenz was born in 1499, and died in 1570. Luther won him to the reformation at Heidelberg in 1518. He was a man of great learning, eminent as a divine and preacher, the author of numerous commentaries, and also the chief instrument for organizing the Church in Würtemberg. Of his works, 8 vols. folio appeared, 1576–90, not comprising the whole. The Syngramma Suevicum, 1525, on the Lord's Supper, is from his pen ; the Würtemberg Confession was also drawn up by him. He wrote against the Münster Anabaptists. This new life will commend him anew, as a faithful, earnest and able reformer and divine, to the gratitude and favor, not only of the Lutheran church, which he so faithfully served, but also of many in other communions.

Joannes Saresberiensis, nach Leben und Studien, etc. Von Dr. C. SCHAAR-SCHMIDT. Leipzig. 1862. 8vo, pp. 359. Another example of those excellent monographs for which the German literature, especially in church history , has become so noted.   John of Salisbury was born in England "not before 1110 nor after 1120 "; studied in France, returned to England, and was involved in the controversies about Thos. à Becket, 1163–1170; became Bishop of Chartres 1176; died 1182.   His chief works are the Policraticus, addressed to Becket; the Entheticus; the Metalogicus; biographies of Anselm and Becket; Epistles.   Some of his commentaries are lost.   Dr. Schaarschmidt goes over all the ground of his life, writings, influence, and of the times in which he lived, with full research.   The second part of the work, on the Teachers and Studies of John, is particularly interesting, giving accounts of the state of classical and patristic learning in the 12th century in the most famous schools.   His relation to the realistic and nominalistic controversy is also fully discussed.   Usually accused of being indifferent or negative in his philosophical views, Dr. Schaarschmidt tries to show that he was rather discreet than undecided; too wise to be a partisan of any extreme speculations.

Memoirs of the Rev. Nicholas Murray, D.D.   By SAMUEL IRENÆUS PRIME. New York: Harper & Brothers.   1862.   12mo, pp. 438.   Dr. Prime has here given to the public a truthful and interesting biography of an honored minister, a laborious pastor, and a popular writer.   We might not fully agree in the very high estimate put upon Dr. Murray's ministerial ability by his friend, still we willingly concede to him many admirable qualities of mind and heart; and we believe he was a conscientious, earnest, and faithful preacher and pastor.   That he was industrious and methodical beyond most men, genial and warm-hearted, is known to all who enjoyed his acquaintance.   His "Kirwan" letters were an extraordinary success, making him favorably known abroad as well as at home, and were blessed to the conversion of many from Romanism.   We confess that the reading of this Memoir has not a little increased our respect and admiration for Dr. Murray.   It is well adapted to quicken the zeal of his brethren, and stimulate them to work while it is day.   A very speaking likeness accompanies the volume.

The Life of Edward Irving, Minister of the National Scotch Church, London.   Illustrated by his Journals and Correspondence.   By Mrs. OLIPHANT.   New York: Harpers.   1862.   8vo, pp. 627.   With a portrait. This biography is of absorbing interest.   It is the only full record of the dazzling career of one who, with all his faults and errors, will ever be regarded as a man of extraordinary genius.   Only a great nature could have fallen into such great errors.   There is a strange fascination about such a life.   And what a wonderful conjunction there is in the three Scotch names: Chalmers, Carlyle, and Edward Irving!   And in magnificence of native genius, the last was the most regally endowed.   But he was always soaring and visionary; and the dizzy height at last bewildered his senses.   As Carlyle so nobly says of him: "Irving clave to his Belief, as to his soul's soul; followed it whithersoever, through earth or air, it might lead him; toiling as never man toiled to spread it, to gain the world's ear for it — in vain. Ever wilder waxed the confusion without and within.   The misguided, noble-minded, had now nothing left but to die." "Adieu, thou first Friend; adieu, while this confused Twilight of Existence lasts!   Might we meet where Twilight has become day."   Coleridge, too, said of him (*Church and State*, p. 153): "Edward Irving possesses more of the spirit and purposes of the first Reformer, he has more of the head and heart, the life, the unction and the genial power of Martin Luther than any man now alive, yea, than any man of this and the last century ".

This volume, too, is most instructive as well as intensely interesting. It lets us into the inner religious history of a great soul struggling with great problems. Irving, like few men, tried to make the facts of religion living realities. The truths of his creed were not mere propositions, but solemn, awe-inspiring facts. He dwelt in the most mysterious of them, remote from common thought and ways. Prophecy and the millennium, heaven and hell, the sacred Person of our Lord and his coming, the reality of the Divine promises and of spiritual gifts—these themes absorbed his soul. And nature at last gave way—and there is only a sound as of Babel left behind.

The chief doctrinal and ecclesiastical points, by which he became suspected, were: that Christ assumed our fallen, sinful humanity (but by assuming also sanctified it) ; that Christ made atonement for all ; baptismal regeneration ; the gift of tongues, and the apostolate revived. As to the Person of Christ, his own statement (p. 301) of the point at issue, is, " whether Christ's flesh had the grace of sinlessness and incorruption from its proper nature, or from the indwelling of the Holy Ghost; I say the latter ". He quotes on his side the old Scotch Confession, which he preferred to the Westminster.

The author of *Margaret Maitland*, in this, to her, new field of literature, has achieved a marked success.

PRACTICAL RELIGION.

A Catechism for Sunday-Schools and Families. By PHILIP SCHAFF, D.D. 18mo, pp. 167. Philadelphia : Lindsay & Blakiston. 1862. The plan of this Catechism is excellent. After sundry Introductory Lessons, Part First is on the Lord's Prayer ; Part Second, on the Apostles' Creed ; Part Third, on the Commandments. It happily blends the historical and doctrinal elements. In doctrine it is most nearly conformed to the Heidelberg Catechism. While we might except to, here and there, a form of statement, or a somewhat un-English idiom, yet, as a whole, we heartily commend its method and execution. With slight modifications, it would be an invaluable help in Sunday-school and Family instruction.

The *American Tract Society*, New York, has published several excellent volumes for the young in an attractive style : *Illustrations of the Ten Commandments*, pp. 172, full of illustrative anecdotes ; Dr. E. P. ROGERS, *The Prodigal Son*, pp. 151, a series of pertinent and impressive sketches ; *Harry the Sailor Boy*, pp. 119 ; *My Brother Ben*, pp. 142 ; *The Naughty Girl Won*, pp. 185 ; *The Woodman's Nannette*, pp. 110, an affecting narrative ; *Cheerily, Cheerily*, pp. 205, an interesting story ; *My Picture-Book*, pp. 64, beautifully illustrated.

American History. By JACOB ABBOTT. Vol. iv. *Northern Colonies.* New York : Sheldon & Co. In a perspicuous and simple narrative, adapted to interest the young, the settlement of the Northern Colonies of this country is here described. This volume is one of a series, to be completed in 12 volumes. It is well illustrated with maps and engravings. To recommend Mr. Abbott's works is quite superfluous.

A New Memoir of Hannah More ; or, Life in Hall and Cottage. By Mrs. HELEN C. KNIGHT. Am. Tract Soc., New York. 12mo, pp. 282. This excellent biography, revised from a previous edition, has already made its way to many hearts, and is destined to do still greater good, wherever female excellence of the highest type is known and honored.

PHILOSOPHY.

Lectures on Moral Science, delivered before the Lowell Institute, Boston. By. MARK HOPKINS, D.D., LL.D., President of Williams College.   Boston: Gould & Lincoln. 1862. Pp. 304. These Lectures will deservedly increase the high reputation of President Hopkins as a thinker and author. He shows himself capable of dealing with some of the highest problems of thought in a style at once perspicuous, and affluent, not only throwing new light upon old truths, but also advancing aspects of the science not so fully discussed in previous treatises.   While conservative in his general spirit, he does not hesitate to give and receive new light.   Reverential to the Divine Revelation, he allows to reason an adequate scope; and has it for one of his main objects to show that the analysis of the mind and its functions in relation to ethical truth not only harmonises, but is identical with the declarations of the Divine Word.   While we might differ with him here and there on some points of theory or of statement, yet we concur in the general aim and spirit of this able treatise.

One of the excellencies of this system is the mode in which profound speculations are made level to the understanding of almost all intelligent students.   The simplicity of the style, the pertinent use of words, the ease and fitness of the illustrations must strike the most casual reader.   This is a great gift and a rare attainment.   There is nothing obscure or mystical; no affectation of originality in speech, though there is real originality in thought.

Another advantage of the treatise is found in its conciliatory spirit in respect to theories, which the author is compelled to reject.   He is just to all, acknowledging the relative truth of those views, which he cannot accept as final.   His aim seems to be so to embrace whatever is true in other theories, as to put each partial speculation in its proper post of subordination.   Thus in respect to self-love, and the various forms of the utilitarian scheme, and the relation of virtue to the Divine will.   Adopting what is true in them, he also shows their metes and limits.

For use as a text-book, too, this volume keeps up a just proportion between the theoretical and the practical part of ethics.   The discussion of principles predominates.   The student is made a thinker.   And he is made a thinker in the best way — being guided by a superior and candid mind.

The peculiarity of the work as a scientific treatise consists in its formal adoption of the doctrine of "ends", in distinction from that of "ultimate right" as the constructive idea of the system.   This harmonises with the Aristotelian definitions.   Dr. Hopkins says, that in this respect the Lectures as they are now re-written differ from the form in which he had generally given them to his classes.   Moral philosophy is defined as "the science which teaches man the end for which he was made, why he should attain that end, and how to attain it".   Ends are divided as subordinate, ultimate and supreme.   The supreme end, or the highest good, is found "in the activity of the highest powers in a right relation to their highest objects".   This end is not holiness alone, nor happiness alone, but "holy happiness", "blessedness".   While this seems to us to be giving too large a place to the element of happiness in the construction of the ethical system, yet it is also carefully guarded by a discrimination of the different kinds of happiness.   But still happiness is so vague a term, and it has been so much abused in ethics, that it seems desirable to leave no room, in the statement of the theory, for any possible unwarrantable inferences.   And happiness, as Dr. Hopkins repeatedly in substance states, is in fact only the psychological condition of the exercise of all our powers — of all the capacities of sentient agents. In and of itself it has, and can have no moral character. The ethical element must be found in something else, that is, in the holiness and not in the happiness. Only thus can ethics be sharply distinguished as a distinct science.

Of the relation of virtue to the will of God some subtle suggestions, of a profound speculative import, are made on p. 239. "It may be that what we must reach in our ultimate analysis is a free personality, — a Person with no nature, or fate, or fitnesses of things back of him or above him; who is himself, by his own free choice, the originator of everything that may properly be called nature, and of all fitnesses of things." "It may be that the nature of God is nothing distinct from his personality, and that so he is wholly supernatural." We wish that Dr. Hopkins might develope this view still further in its bearings on pantheism.

Zeitschrift für Philosophie und philosophische Kritik, Neue Folge, Bde. 40–41, 1862. This Philosophical Journal, edited by Fichte, Ulrici, Wirth, still maintains the highest rank among periodicals devoted to speculative research, opposing pantheism and the excesses of idealism. Among the essays in the last two volumes are, F. Hoffman on the Dualism of Anaxagoras and the monotheism of Socrates and Plato; J. G. von Hahn and Carrière on the Formation of Myths; Lütterbeck on Baader's Philosophy, three articles; Sengler on the Theory of Knowing; Sträter on Aristotle's Poetics, two articles; Hoffman on Ulrici's God and Nature, (a very able work), with Ulrici's reply, etc. Reviews of the most important recent works on philosophy are also given, and a full philosophical bibliography. Ulrici reviews M'Cosh's late writings in a candid way, though taking exception to some of his indeterminate positions and lack of thorough method.

Zeitschrift für exacte Philosophie. Bde. 2, 3, 1861-2. This periodical represents the school of Herbart, and is ably edited by Allihn and Ziller, opposing all the various forms of the recent idealism, and claiming to be the true representative of the Kantian system. In the first volume a full bibliography of the school of Herbart was given. Besides reviews of recent works, the 2d vol., and vol. 3, parts 1 and 2, contain Drobisch on Locke as the Forerunner of Kant; Thilo on Happiness in Aristotle's system; Cornelius on Matter and the Theory of Vision; Volkmann, the Principles and Methods of Psychology; Zimmermann, the Reform of Æsthetics as an exact Science; Allihn, Herbart's Reform of Ethics, Hegel's Logic in Paris, and Philosophical Propædeutics; Thilo on the Religious Philosophy of Descartes; Ratkowsky, the Principle of Legitimacy and Nationality; Nahlowsky, on Beneke's Psychology, etc.

PHILOSOPHY OF HISTORY.

An Inquiry into the Philosophy of History, with Special Reference to the Principles of the Positive Philosophy. London, 1862. Pp. 461. The anonymous author of this able work, investigates three theories, viz. that of Chance, that of Law, and that of Will, or divine Providence. The method and principles of the Positive Philosophy of Comte are subjected to a searching criticism. Two other volumes are to follow, one on the Elements and Ideas of History, and another on the Laws of History. The general spirit of the work may be seen from the following extract: "Philosophy will fail to fulfil its mission, and must renounce the high character which it claims as the eye of Science and the hand of Art, the proper basis of society, and the true frame-work of history, until it places itself in intimate accord with

that theism which it sometimes repudiates and contemns. The union of
both makes science religious and religion scientific, philosophy devout and
piety philosophical, because in that union law is conceived as interpenetrated,
informed, and directed by the infinite mind, the eternal thought, the omnipotent and beneficent will of that of which it is the grand and sublime expression,
and whose faintest whisperings it is the highest glory of man to interpret
and obey."   After examining the theories of Chance and Law at length,
the final conclusion is thus stated, that the desideratum of a correct theory
"is supplied by the theory of Will, a Supreme Will, of which all phenomena
and laws are the expression, and of which, under different but accordant
aspects we may conceive as a primary cause, the source of all being, and as
a presence, a power, a providence informing all nature, energizing all life,
exercising a just and wise and beneficent moral government over rational
creatures, and guiding all events to their destined ends".   The criticism of
Comte, and incidentally of Mill, is searching, and opens many new veins of
reflection. The argument in support of the existence of a supreme will seems
to us to be much less ably conducted — being resolved in fact into an analysis of the process of thought in forming the idea of God.   The logical steps
and the ontological ideas involved in this process are not very thoroughly or
adequately analyzed.   The second chapter of the book considers three objections to the theory of will, viz. the objections to a primary cause, to a
providence, and to final causes.   The vindication of final causes is able and
ample — one of the best parts of the book.   On Providence, many just remarks are made, though it is pretty nearly identified with the chain or
series of regular causes, and the existence of free will is hardly recognized
with sufficient definiteness.   Of the problem of evil and sin, in relation to
Providence, little or no account is taken ; and it is difficult to see how miracles and a supernatural revelation would be consistent with the general
theory. Yet there are also noble vindications of essential points in the theistic belief. "Divine knowledge involves divine providence, divine providence involves divine government, and divine government is the true philosophy of life, of society, of history (p. 234)."
  The third chapter examines with philosophic calmness, the Positive
Method in the use of hypotheses against the Theory of Will, viz. the hypotheses of the perpetuity of Matter, of Spontaneity, and of Spontaneity and
Necessity combined.   An appendix discusses more fully and acutely than
any previous work, an underlying question of the whole theistic argument,
on the doctrine and Law of Causal Resemblance, how far, and in what cases,
the cause may and may not resemble the effect.
  The whole work is rather an argument for Theism, as against the principles of the Positive Philosophy, than a theory of history itself.   It is able,
acute and comprehensive on many of the questions raised.   It amply vindicates the necessity of a supreme, intelligent Will to account for phenomena.
It makes law to be the expression of such a Will ; but it subjects Will to
Law, rather than Law to Will, and leaves little basis for a specific and positive Revelation above and beyond the course of Nature.

The Divine Footsteps in Human History. Blackwood & Sons, Edinburgh.
1862. 8vo, pp. 445. The author of this curious volume has made a discovery, that is, that in Ezekiel's description (ch. xl sq.) of the city which he
saw in vision, its gates, chambers, courts, porches, we have an exact measurement and outline of human history, the cubits of measurement standing for years ; prophecy and fact fitting each other most accurately.   The
great factors and movements in history are developed under the form of
"chambers".   The four powers now in contest, are Romanism, Mohammedanism, Imperialism and Protestantism.   The whole tendency of history is

to the separation of Church and State, in order to the final triumph of Christ's Kingdom here on earth. This has been carried forward most completely, and is now peculiarly represented in the "United Presbyterian church of Scotland". The author, for example, has "one double and six single chambers, explanatory of the position occupied by the United Presbyterian church of Scotland, in the revelation of Christian history, and demonstrative of the grand result of the Roman church's claim, based on its spurious Christian unity and enforced ecclesiastical obedience". This United Presbyterian church of Scotland is, undoubtedly, a most excellent body of Christians; but we had not supposed that they occupied such a preëminent position as Ezekiel's prophecy is here made to give them. He also finds confirmation of his view in our present American crisis, it being all foreshadowed, and there being no possibility of a reünion (p. 246). Some of his interminglings of distant parallelisms are quite remarkable, e. g.: "Six chambers, having each two periods of equal duration, connecting historically the Jewish church with English and Scotch church secessions, and the Romish church with the Scotch church secession". While there are many fanciful and some ingenious combinations of facts, and parallelisms of dates, yet the whole scheme of the work is so intricate and involved, that neither prophecy nor history receives much elucidation.

GENERAL LITERATURE.

Sermons. Preached and revised by Rev. C. H. Spurgeon. Seventh series. New York: Sheldon & Co. 1862. 12mo, pp. 378. The sermons of this remarkable man improve. This volume has less of his faults and more of his excellencies on the whole than any volume which has preceded it. We rejoice that such sermons are preached to thousands, and then published and read by hundreds of thousands more. There are few preachers who would not be benefited by reading and studying such specimens of homiletics.

Lessons for the Little Ones is an excellent little book, which our Publication Committee have added to their list. It is specially adapted to Infant-schools and the younger classes in Sabbath-schools.

Ernest. A True Story. New York: Anson D. F. Randolph. 1862. An excellent book for children,—natural, truthful and scriptural in its teachings. We heartily commend it as worthy a place in every family and in every Sunday-school library. We assure our readers, from a personal knowledge of many of the facts stated, that it is a true story. The persons and scenes described are familiar to us; and the scene referred to on p. 131 will never fade from our memory.

Lyra Cœlestis. Hymns on Heaven. Selected by A. C. Thompson, D.D., author of the "Better Land", "Hours at Patmos", etc. Boston: Gould & Lincoln. 12mo, pp. 383. 1863. This work contains a choice selection of Hymns on Heaven, many of which, the author, in his preface, says are not accessible to the majority of readers; that, besides those originally English, there will be found translations from the Syriac, Latin, Russian, German, French, Italian, Spanish, and Portuguese, etc., including a great variety of topics; the productions of a large number of the very best poets. The general subjects are as follows: I. Where is Heaven? II. What is Heaven? III. Who are in Heaven? IV. What are they doing in Heaven? V. What is the Way to Heaven? VI. How soon in Heaven? VIII. How long in Heaven? Thousands will thank Dr. Thompson for this labor of love. Many of the hymns are exceedingly beautiful. The arrangement is happy, and the style of the book is tasteful and appropriate.

ECCLESIASTICAL RECORD.

---◆◆◆---

[UNDER this head it is proposed to give, in each number of this REVIEW, full lists of all appointments to the ministerial office, and of all changes in the same, in our branch of the Presbyterian Church. This record will be furnished by E. F. HATFIELD, D.D., Stated Clerk of the General Assembly.—EDS.]

LICENSED TO PREACH.

Mr. D. Henry Palmer,	June 11th, 1862, by the Presb. of Rochester.
" Edmund P. Hammond,	Oct. 6th, " " " N. York, 3d.
" John L. Landis,	" 15th " " " Harrisburgh.

ORDINATIONS.

Mr. James B. Beaumont,	June 5th, 1862, by the Presb. of Genesee Valley, Pastor, Olean, N. Y
" Horace Allen,	" 19th, " " " Rochester, Evangelist.
" Alva Allen,	" 19th, " " " " "
" John P. Watson,	" 22d, " " " N. York, 3d, "
" Lyman Dwight Chapin,	July 6th, " " " " " " For. Missionary.
" Samuel P. Halsey,	" 8th, " " " Rockaway, Pastor, Rockaway, N. J.
" Anthony Simpson,	Aug. 14th, " " " Philadelphia, 3d, Evangelist.
" John D. McCord,	Sept. 16th, " " " Huron, Pastor, Peru, O.
" A. H. Fullerton,	" 19th, " " " Chenango, Evangelist.
" Albert Erdman,	" 29th, " " " Philadelphia, 4th, Evangelist.
" Whiting C. Birchard,	" 29th, " " " Meadville, "
" G. N. Mackie,	Oct. 1st, " " " Watertown, Pastor, Adams, N. Y.
" Marcus N. Preston,	" 2d, " " " Cayuga, Pastor, Skaneateles, N. Y.
" Lewis M. Birge,	" 5th, " " " N. York, 3d, Evangelist.
" Albert G. Rulifson,	" 12th, " " " " 4th, "
" William R. Eastman,	" 12th, " " " " " "
" John L. French,	" " " " Madison, "
" Aurelian H. Post,	Nov. 18th, " " " Chicago, "

INSTALLATIONS.

Rev. James Donaldson,	June 3d, 1862, by the Presb. of N. River, Pleasant Valley, West. N. Y.
" Frederick Starr, Jr.,	" 12th, " " " Geneva, Penn Yan, N. Y.
" Job Pierson,	" 19th, " " " Rochester, Victor, N. Y.
" Stephen Bush,	July " " " Albany, Greenbush, N. Y.
" Charles B. Dye,	" 1st, " " " Geneva, Romulus, N. Y.
" John McLean,	" 6th, " " " St. Louis, St. Louis, North, Mo.
" Albert Mandell,	Oct. 1st, " " " Newark, Madison, N. J.
" Lewis Kellogg,	" 12th, " " " Troy, Whitehall, N. Y.
" Dwight Scovel,	" 12th, " " " Ontario, Geneseo, First, N. Y.
" Samuel W. Boardman,	" 14th, " " " Cayuga, Auburn, Second, N. Y.
" James Y. Mitchell,	" 26th, " " " Phila. 4th, Phila., N. L., Central, Pa.
" Erskine N. White,	Dec. 3d, " " " New-York, 4th, New-Rochelle, N. Y.

DISSOLUTION OF PASTORAL RELATION.

Rev. Alex. S. Twombly, May 31st, 1862, by the Presb. of Otsego, Cherry Valley, N. Y.
"   Asahel Bronson,   June 10th, "   "   "   "   Fly Creek, N. Y.
"   Samuel W. Bush,   July 1st,   "   "   "   "   Cooperstown, N. Y.
"   George M. Maxwell,   "   "   "   "   Cincinnati, Cincinnati, 8th, O.
"   James W. Wood,   Sept. 17th, "   "   "   Hudson, Chester, N. Y.
"   Gustavus L. Foster,   "   25th, "   "   "   Washtenaw, Ypsilanti, Mich.
"   Ebenezer Cheever,   Oct. 1st,   "   "   "   Newark, Paterson, N. J.
"   William H. McGiffert, "   15th, "   "   "   Utica, Booneville, N. Y.
"   Benjamin Judkins, Jr., "   15th, "   "   "   Phila. 4th, Allentown, First, Pa.
"   Herrick Johnston,   "   "   "   "   Troy, Troy, First, N. Y.
"   Joseph B. Bittinger,   "   "   "   "   Cleveland, Cleveland, Euclid st., O.

CHANGE OF RESIDENCE.

Rev. Edward Anderson,   from Chicago, Ill.,   to Michigan City, Ind.
Mr. Whiting C. Birchard,   "   Cambridge, Pa.,   " Cherry Tree, Pa.
Rev. Samuel W. Bush,   "   Binghamton, N. Y.,   " Greenbush, N. Y.
"   Isaac E. Carey,   "   Keokuk, Ill.,   " Freeport, Ill.
"   Henry C. Cheadles,   "   Niconza, Ind.,   " Tupper's Plains, O.
"   Jacob E. Conrad,   "   Liberty, Minn.,   " Mapleton, Minn.
"   Samuel W. Crittenden, "   Philadelphia, Pa.,   " Kingsessing, Pa.
"   Rufus R. Deming,   "   Ellenburgh, N. Y.,   " Laurenceville, N. Y.
"   Ansel D. Eddy, D.D.,   "   Wilmington, Ill.,   " Seneca Falls, N. Y.
"   William J. Essick,   "   New-Richmond, O.,   " Wabash, Ind.
"   John Glass,   "   Ypsilanti, Mich.,   " Janesville, Iowa.
"   George W. Goodale,   "   Vandalia, Ill.,   " Granville, Ill.
"   Philander Griffin,   "   Buffalo, N. Y.,   " Carlton, N. Y.
"   James Harrison,   "   Waterloo, Iowa,   " Cedar Valley, Iowa.
"   Marcus Hicks,   "   St. Cloud, Minn.,   " Manketo, Minn.
"   Horace C. Hovey,   "   Coldwater, Mich.,   " New-Haven, Ct.
"   Thomas B. Hudson,   "   Union Springs, N.Y.,   " Auburn, N. Y.
"   A. Alexander Jamison, "   Greenville, O.,   " Connersville, Ind.
"   William J. Johnston,   "   Lena, Ill.,   " Freeport, Ill.
"   Lewis Kellogg,   "   Trumansburgh, N.Y.,   " Whitehall, N. Y.
"   William Kendrick,   "   High Point, Iowa,   " Leon, Iowa.
"   Peleg R. Kinney,   "   Webster, N. Y.,   " Virgil, N. Y.
"   James Knox,   "   Sturgis, Mich.   " Clinton, Iowa.
"   George E. W. Leonard, "   Cedar Rapids, Iowa,   " Pleasant Prairie, Iowa.
"   Wilbur McKaig,   "   Peoria, Ill.   " Cincinnati, Ohio.
"   Albert Mancell,   "   Newark, N. J.,   " Madison, N. J.
"   John Martin,   "   Galena, O ,   " Sunbury, O.
"   Edwin G. Moore,   "   Chilicothe, O.,   " Wilmington, Ill.
"   Aurelian H. Post,   "   Walnut Hills, O.,   " Lake Forest, Ill.
"   James F. Read, D.D.,   "   Buchanan, Pa.,   " Birmingham, Pa.
"   Rollin A. Sawyer,   "   Yonkers, N. Y.,   " Newark, O.
"   Samuel Sawyer,   "   Marion, Ind.,   " Memphis, Tenn.
"   Hannibal L. Stanley,   "   Jonesville, Mich.,   " Lyons, Io.
"   Townsend E. Taylor,   "   Columbia, Cal ,   " Petaluma, Cal.
"   William S. Taylor,   "   Munson, Mich.   " Petersburgh, Mich.
"   Samuel L. Tuttle,   "   Madison, N. J.,   " Rochester, N. Y.
"   Daniel C. Tyler,   "   Litchfield, N. Y.,   " South-Trenton, N. Y.
"   William P. Wastell,   "   White Lake, Mich.,   " Holly, Mich.
"   Ira M. Weed,   "   Waukegan, Ill.,   " Granville, Ill.
"   Lemuel P. Webber,   "   Franklin, Ind.,   " Indianapolis, Ind.
"   Benj. F. Willoughby,   "   Parishville, N. Y.,   " Verona, N. Y.

DEATHS.

Rev. Ashbel Parmelee, D.D., May 24th, 1862, of the Presb. of Champlain, Malon , N. Y., 77.
" Hiram Gregg,   June 20th,   "   "   "   Dayton, Dayton, O.
" Josiah Hopkins, D.D.,   " 27th,   "   "   "   Cayuga, Geneva, N. Y., 76.
" John B. Hoyt,   July 4th,   "   "   "   Chenango, Coventry, N. Y., 68.
" John Dyke,   " 5th,   "   "   "   Kansas, Albany, Mo., 62.
" Benj. J. Wallace, D.D.,   " 25th,   "   "   "   Phila. 3d, Philadelphia, Pa., 52.
" Hugh Barr,   Aug. 1st,   "   "   "   Illinos, Jacksonville, Ill., 72.
" Amos C. Tuttle,   Sept. 24th, "   "   "   "   Kalamazoo, Lapeer, Mich., 60.
" William H. Corning,   Oct. 8th,   "   "   "   Troy, Saratoga Springs, N. Y., 41.
" Erastus Cole,   " 18th,   "   "   "   Elyria, Litchfield, O.
" Andrew G. Carothers,   " 20th,   "   "   "   D. of Colum., St. Pierre, Martinique.
" R. Richard Kirk,   Nov. 15th, "   "   "   St. Lawrence, New-York City.
" Tim. Woodbridge, D.D., Dec. 7th,   " .   "   "   Columbia, Spencertown, N. Y., 78.

THEOLOGICAL STUDENTS.

THE INCREASE OF THE MINISTRY.

All the Catalogues for the current year not being issued, we are unable to give the exact number of students in our Theological Institutions ; but we are credibly assured that in the Union, Auburn, and Lane Seminaries, there are not far from 185 ; Union has 89 ; Lane, 27.

The General Assembly's Permanent Committee on Education are assisting students for the ministry as follows :

In Auburn Theological Seminary,	22
Lane " "	14
Union " "	22
Private study,	1
Hamilton College,	8
Union "	8
Yale "	1
Marietta "	0
Western Reserve College,	4
Wabash, "	5
Knox, "	2
Michigan University,	2
New-York Free Academy,	1
	94

In addition to the above, there must be over fifty more who are aided by private benevolence and by foundations in different institutions.

The number of students has been diminished by the embarrassments consequent on the war. Some have been prevented from commencing study, some have temporarily suspended their studies, some have enlisted in the army, and some of them have been broken down in their health, and some fill soldiers' graves.

PRESBYTERIAN BODIES.

The following summary from Wilson's Presbyterian Almanac for 1862, shows the numbers belonging to the various Presbyterian bodies in the world, as reported that year. In some cases the statistics are estimated. For some of the churches we have added later reports.

❋ United States.	Ministers.	Churches.	Com'cts.
Presbyterian Church in United States, (N. S.,)	1,555	1,466	135,454
Presbyterian Church in United States, (O. S.,)....................	2,859	8,686	308,289
United Presbyterian Church of North America,..................	444	669	57,567
Reformed Presbyterian Church, (General Synod,)...............	56	116	10,000
Reformed Presbyterian Church, (Synod,).......................	59	78	6,650
Cumberland Presbyterian Church,...........................	1,150	1,250	103,000
United Synod of the Presbyterian Church, ...	116	198	12,934
Reformed Protestant Dutch Church,...........................	411	422	50,295
Associated Reformed Synod of the South ; of New York ; Associate Synod, etc.,..	148	165	14,500

British Provinces of North America.

Canada Presbyterian Church, ...	226	386	34,000
Church of Scotland in Canada,..............................	109	126	18,500
Church of Lower Provinces,.................................	75	95	9,617
Church of Scotland in Nova-Scotia and Prince Edward Island,....	21	26	2,100
Church of New Brunswick,..................................	21	27	1,600
Church of Scotland in New Brunswick,.......................	14	16	1,500

Great Britain.

Church of Scotland,..	1,185	1,208	......
Free Churches of Scotland,.................................	790	875	......
United Presbyterian Church of Scotland,.....................	586	540	163,554
Reformed Presbyterian Church of Scotland, etc.,..............	87	90	10,000
Presbyterian Church of Ireland,............................	560	530	57,000
Reformed Presbyterian Church in Ireland, (E. Syn. and S. Syn.,)..	45	55	4,000
Presbyterian Church in England, ...	91	108	10,000
Presbyterian Church of Victoria,...........................	187	150	15,600
Total,.......................................	10,746	12,232	1,022,460

OTHER EVANGELICAL DENOMINATIONS.

Associations, Conferences, Synods, etc.

Congregationalists' Associations,.......................... 24	2,592	2,856	259,110
Baptists' Associations, ...588	8,018	12,648	1,037,576
Methodists, (North,) Conferences,.......................... 51	6,987	....	988,888
Methodists, (South,) Conferences,.......................... 24	2,494	....	721,028
Lutheran Synods,... 40	1,805	2,487	260,185
German Reformed Classes,................................ 24	407	1,054	92,938
Protestant Episcopal Dioceses,............................ 83	2,045	2,045	149,57

THE

AMERICAN

PRESBYTERIAN AND THEOLOGICAL

REVIEW.

NEW SERIES, No. II.—APRIL, 1863.

Art. I.—MIRACLES THE PROOF OF CHRISTIANITY.

By Thomas H. Skinner, D.D., Prof. in Union Theological Seminary, New York.

1. Side by side with the recent naturalistic ideas of Christianity, have come, as might have been expected, objections to miracles as proof of it. There is a reason why the objections and the ideas should be found together: the natural in the religion can have no need of, or affinity with, the supernatural or miraculous in the evidence. Hume opposed miracles because he thought, that admitting them, they proved Christianity; our naturalists oppose them because, as they allege, they are unnecessary, if not a hindrance, to its proof. The difference is only in appearance: the naturalists agree with Hume in opposing miracles; they do not really disagree with him as to the bearing of miracles on the proof of Christianity. What the naturalists call Christianity did not in Hume's time pass under that name; it would not, in itself, have been unacceptable to him, only he would have thought it a misnomer to call it Christianity.

2. To determine whether miracles are necessary to the proof of Christianity—our present undertaking—the meaning of the terms must be fixed. Understanding by Christianity, a revelation distinctively and directly from God; and by miracles,

12

direct works of God, wrought in attestation of it, our inquiry is : Are the latter the proper proof of the former? Or, may Christianity be adequately proved without miracles? A miracle, according to its etymology, sometimes signifies what is simply wonderful or marvellous ; sometimes it is what is supposed to be *superhuman ;* sometimes it is something *supernatural,* or out of the order, if not an arrest and inversion of the order of nature, and unexplainable by any law, at least any known law of nature. In our use of the word, a miracle is a direct work of God, performed in nature and under the notice of the senses, but of divine, in contradistinction to natural or finite force. God, indeed, is in a true sense the force of nature's forces ; still there are works which God does not, and works which he does, directly and personally perform; and miracles, as we take the term, are divine works of the latter class. We assume, as out of question, that the testimonial miracles of Christianity are DIRECT OR PERSONAL WORKS OF GOD.

We would state more precisely what we take to be the true idea of revelation as actualized in Christianity. According to Westcott,* the objects of revelation are " things essentially existing beneath the suffering, sin, and disorder, which are spread over the world within us and without "; and revelation itself is " the removal of the dark veil from the face of these things": that is to say, if we understand him, revelation acquaints us with nothing extra-natural or out of the sphere of nature ; it only removes a veil from what exists essentially in " man and nature"—the world within us and without. We do not accept this view of the objects, or the office of revelation. The Scripture revelation does more than remove a veil from things essentially existing in the world ; it acquaints us, by direct communication from God, with things not existing in the world ; even the deep, the infinite things of God, of which independently of this revelation, no one would have had an idea, though all the secrets of nature had been disclosed to him. There are things, indeed, presupposed and embodied in those of revelation, doctrines and precepts of natural religion, facts of history, which are not peculiar to it ; these things do not

* *Introduction to the Study of the Gospels,* p. 34.

individuate the revelation, or distinguish it as such; some of the distinctive things are : the Trinity of Persons in the unity Divine Essence; the Divine-human character of Jesus of Nazareth; the salvation of mankind by the blood and intercession of the Lord Jesus; the resurrection of the same body; these are peculiarities of revealed religion; they are not things lying under a dark veil spread over the face of the world, but things altogether *extra-mundane*, having no place in man or nature, the world within us or without. The idea of revelation, according to which nothing is revealed except what previously existed in the world under a veil, seems to Westcott "to be peculiarly Christian"; we reject it, as identifying substantive Christianity with natural religion.

3. Our limits allow us but a word on the arguments against miracles. Hume contented himself with assailing their *reality* or trying to make out the impossibility of *proving* them. Miracles, he insisted, are contrary "to firm and unalterable experience"; which, surely, he was safe enough in saying no testimony can countervail.* But how did he know what he asserts as a fact ? Whether miracles are against all experience, is the point in question. His task was not to assert, but to prove the affirmative; a task he has evaded. A host of unimpeachable witnesses has affirmed the occurrence of miracles as a matter of their own experience. Hume has not discredited their testimony,† which, if it cannot be discredited, disproves his assumption; he is mistaken as to the reality of the ground of his argument.—Recently it has been alleged in the interest of Hume's attempt, that the testimony for miracles can be no other than testimony to sensible events seemingly miraculous; that they were really miracles, could have been to the spectators only a matter of belief, not of experience. But the witnesses of miracles were not the spectators of them only : the prime witnesses

---

* "A miracle is a violation of the laws of nature ; and as a firm and unalterable experience has established these laws, the proof against a miracle, from the very nature of the fact, is as entire as any argument from experience can possibly be imagined."—*Essay on Miracles*, p. 160.

† He has said, indeed, that there is not to be found in all history any trustworthy testimony to miracles, but he has *said* it merely. (See *Essay on Miracles*, p. 163.)

were the performers of them, who wrought them, as they declared, in the name, and simply as instruments in the hand of God. Theirs, chiefly, is the testimony to be discredited. "If St. Paul did not work actual, sensible, public miracles, he has knowingly in these letters", says Paley, " borne his testimony to a falsehood." Did St. Paul, with his fellow-apostles and others, bear such testimony in fact?

Modern naturalists, going further than Hume, deny not the reality or demonstrableness only, but the *possibility* of miracles. Science, they say, has discovered that order in the world is a pure necessity, and absolutely inviolable; but science can have made no such discovery as this, unless it has further discovered that the world is not the creature of God, or is independent of him; or, in a word, that there is no God distinct from the world. If the world with its order be the creature of God, the order in it may be necessary and inviolable in respect of creatures, but surely not in respect of God himself, who is no longer God if he cannot destroy or change as well as establish a certain order. If it be said that he is, by nature, the God of order, this, though doubtless true in the highest sense of the term order, does not imply that miracles are against order in that sense. For aught we know they may not be, and the assertion that they are, is an assertion merely. "Once believe that there is a God", says Paley, " and miracles are not incredible".

4. But now to our question. Assuming that miracles are both possible and real, may Christianity be adequately proved without them? We take Christianity as a revelation in the sense already expressed. In any other view of it, miracles, among proofs of Christianity, would, as we have already intimated, be superfluous if not obtrusive. "Those", says Mansell, " who deny the existence of any special revelation of religious truths distinct from that general sense in which mere reason itself, and all that it can discover, are the gifts of Him from whom every good thing comes, are only consistent when they deny that miracles have any value as evidences of religious truth; and are still more consistent when they deny that such works have been wrought". How gratuitous, and therefore how improper to work miracles in attestation of things essen-

tially existing in the world ! To remove the veil, to show the things, would be to prove them : if they and Christianity were identical, the latter would doubtless be self-demonstrative apart from all external evidence. The truth, revealed through Christ, would have, as Coleridge affirms it has, its evidence in itself. Infinitely different is Christianity, according to the meaning in which our question takes the term. It uses the term in its own signification when it asks whether Christianity can be adequately attested without miracles.

5. And now, first of all, let us understand what is an *adequate* attestation, a sufficient proof of Christianity? This, if we mistake not, is determinative of the main question. Whatever the requisite proof may be, one thing is certain, that Christianity is not sufficiently attested if its evidence do not justify and demand, not a persuasion of the possibility or probability, but a full undoubting assurance of the absolute verity of its averments. Christianity itself makes this demand of mankind : Wherever it comes it holds itself entitled to immediate acceptance as true and as divine ; it proclaims a fearful menace to unbelief, the menace of eternal death; it imputes to unbelief the highest criminality, even that of making God himself a false witness ; it connects this infinite guilt with every degree of unbelief, so that he who believes with an incomplete faith is ready, with a penitence proportional to his shortcoming in faith, to cry out, with the father of the lunatic child: "Lord, I believe, help thou mine unbelief". It has been said* that the assent to which Christianity is entitled is not equal to that which we owe to the discoveries of science; that a sense of probability is the utmost the former can legitimately include, while the latter must extend to a sense of certainty. But how inadvertent or disloyal to the interest of Christianity is this remark ! Well has Stillingfleet said that "an assent no stronger than to a thing merely probable, which is that it may or may not be true, is not properly assent at all, but a suspension of our judgment till some convincing argument be produced on either side".† But confront this remark with the peremptory

* In *Aids to Faith*, Essay II.   † *Origines Sacræ*, vol. i, p. 222.

claim of Christianity to our absolute assent. According to
this claim, what is there that ought to be more certain to me
than the truth of Christianity ?   Not the existence of God, or
the existence of the world, or my own existence.   " He who
believeth not is condemned already, because he hath not believed" ; " he hath made God a liar".   This fact it is that gives
the answer to the question, as to the nature of the proof, that
adequately authenticates Christianity.   The assent required
surely is not out of proportion to the proof.   The measure of
the first is not greater than the measure of the second.   The
contrary supposition charges the highest injustice on Him who
only is just and good.   " If there be no evidence given sufficient to carry the minds of men beyond mere probability,
what sin can it be in those who cannot be obliged to believe
as true what is only discovered as probable ?"* On the ground
of this postulate, then, let our inquiry proceed.   Abstract the
miracles, and will there be adequate proof of Christianity ?

6. But before advancing let us name one preliminary more,
and one bearing with decisive force on the decision of our
question.   The miracles are in fact innumerable, and they
have never been separated from Christianity.   Whether the
proof of our religion required miracles or not there has been
no experiment to determine.   Christianity has never existed
except, as we may say with emphasis, in the blaze of miracles.
Revealed religion, itself a miracle, was accompanied at its beginning with testimonial miracles, to which others were added,
from time to time throughout the whole history of its progress.
What a brilliant galaxy of miracles in days of old before the
advent of Christ ! How full of splendid miracles the life-history
of our Lord ! How is the record of the beginning and planting
of Christianity studded with miracles as the firmament with
stars !   But more, much more, than this: miracles are not only
accompaniments of Christianity, they are inwrought and con-
substantial with it.   " Miracles and prophecy", says Rothe,
" are not adjuncts appended from without to a revelation independent of them, but are constitutive elements of the revelation itself".   " The miracles in the Bible", Bolingbroke has

* *Stillingfleet*, vol. ii, p. 222.

said, " are not like those in Livy, detached pieces that do not disturb the civil history, which goes on very well without them.   But the whole history is founded on them ; it consists of little else, and if it were not a history of them it would be a history of nothing".   " Miracles", says Mansell, " are part of the *moral* as well as sensible evidences, and cannot be denied without destroying both kinds of evidence alike.   ' That ye may know that the Son of Man hath power on earth to forgive sins, I say unto thee arise and take up thy couch and go into thine house.'   ' If I with the finger of God cast out devils, no doubt the kingdom of God is come among you.'   ' By the name of Jesus Christ of Nazareth, even by him, doth this man stand before you whole :'   Let us imagine, for an instant, such words as these to have been uttered by one who was merely employing a superior knowledge of natural laws to produce a false appearance of supernatural power ; by an astronomer, for instance, who had predicted an eclipse to a crowd of savages ; or by a chemist availing himself of his science to exhibit *relative* miracles to an ignorant people, and we shall feel at once how even the most natural explanation of miraculous phenomena deals the death-blow to the *moral character* of the teacher no less than to the sensible evidence of his mission."   We see then how the miraculous enters essentially into the very constitution and structure of Christianity.   In fact, it can no more be separated from either the intrinsic or the testimonial, the moral or sensible evidence of Christianity, than color from the rainbow, or light from the rays of the sun.   Whether, then, miracles were or were not necessary, they have never been wanting.   In number, almost without number, they do, in fact, attest Christianity.   And this decides one thing, and it is the only thing needed to justify the high claim of our religion, this, namely, that, taking the evidence of Christianity as it in reality is, there can be no question as to its sufficiency ; *with* its miracles it is sufficient, whether it would or would not be *without* them.   There is no ground of certainty if there be none in this evidence : it is no less infallible than the character of God.   The presence of miracles is the presence of God himself as a Deponent.   Unbelief in Christianity does, indeed, make God a false witness : there is no deeper criminality. "When He is come, he will reprove the world of sin, because they believe not on me."

7. But though miracles are in fact inseparable from the evidences of Christianity, their absence may be imagined ; and there are those who, as apologists for Christianity, say they would prefer their absence, and would fain eliminate them, if they could ; and groundless and purposeless as our question may now seem, the cause of Christianity, as claiming to be a revelation directly from God, is staked on the decision of it. The answer to this question tests the character of the naturalistic view of revealed religion. If there is no necessity for the miraculous in the evidence, it is because there is nothing miraculous in the religion : in our sense of the term it is not a revelation. Away with miracles, means, away with a so-called miraculous revelation. The inquiry whether Christianity may not be proved without miracles, is virtually the inquiry whether essential Christianity may not be resolved into naturalism. Let us then proceed.

8. If Christianity can be proved apart from testimonial miracles, it must be either by the self-evident truthfulness of its substantive or constitutive elements; or by its moral evidence; or by its proper effects; or lastly, its collateral evidences, so called, in counter-distinction to miracles, will suffice to prove it. We are to inquire whether, *without any presupposition or aid of the miraculous*, sufficient evidence may be derived from these sources.

Is Christianity its own witness through its individuality as a revelation, or its constitutive elements ? "Evidences of Christianity !" says Coleridge, "I am weary of the word". "The truth revealed through Christ has its evidence in itself." Let us patiently inquire as to the fact concerning this : Has Christianity *its evidence in itself ?* We have distinguished, in Christianity, between what it has in common with natural religion, and what is distinctively its own. The present question has no reference to the former ; so far as that is concerned, the evidence is in itself ; but it is no part of the evidence of Christianity, as such, being no part, distinctively, of Christianity itself.   It is in respect to the latter that we ask, does it, apart from miracles, or by *mere self-evidence*, assert its own truth?   The things concerning which we inquire, whether they are self-evident or not, are of the class including the following: That the Eternal Word was made flesh in the person of Jesus; that the death of Jesus was the redemption of the world; that Jesus is the Almighty Ruler and Judge of the world; that the dead will be raised by him at the last day: are these things, independently of testimony, true to the reason of mankind?   The question gives its own answer.   "Nothing", says Dr. Hodge, "in the apprehension of rationalists, can be more absurd than that the blood of the cross can remove sin". "We preach Christ crucified", said Paul, "to the Jews a stumbling-block, and to the Greeks foolishness".   The Gospel certainly never made its way by recommending itself to the intuitive consciousness, or the natural reason, of man, apart from external evidences of its truth.   No more palpably untrue assertion could be made than that Christianity, in its supernatural peculiarities, has its evidence in itself, meaning thereby that it has no need of external proof.   "There is nothing", says Calvin, "that is more at variance with human reason than this article of our faith (the resurrection of the body).   For who but God alone could persuade us that bodies which are now liable to corruption, will, after having rotted away, or after they have been consumed by fire, or torn in pieces by wild beasts, not only be restored entire, but in a greatly better condition?   Do not all our apprehensions of things reject this as a thing fabulous, nay, the greatest absurdity in the world?"   Truly, only God himself, bearing witness directly to the truth of Christianity, could justify or warrant belief in it.   Reason, nature itself, demands that God himself, by supernatural works, or some equivalent means, attest a supernatural revelation, such as Christianity claims to be.   They are its natural and proper proofs.   "I should not be a Christian", said St. Augustine, "but for miracles".   Except for miracles, there would not have been sin in not believing on Jesus Christ.   "If I had not done among them the works which none other man did, they had not had sin."   Claiming to be the Messiah, it behooved our Lord to authenticate his claim by miracles—preännounced notes of Messiahship—which, if he had not wrought, the Jews, in reverence of the prophetic Scriptures, ought to have rejected him.   Let us inquire, then, of those who say Christianity has its evidence in itself, what they mean by this language. Taking Christianity, with its concreted testimonial miracles, it has its evidence in itself, and witnesses in its own behalf, as the sun does for himself, by the light and heat which he sheds through the world ; but apart from the evidence of miracles, ought it not to be discredited ?

9. It is demonstrated it has been said, by its moral evidence, or ethical excellency.   Is this so ?   We have seen that the moral in the evidence is, in fact, interblended and consubstantiated with the miraculous ; but still it is urged that the moral, of itself, and without need of the miraculous, demonstrates the truth of Christianity.   The ethics of Christianity stamp it, beyond all question, as divine.   And as a general fact, is it not the ethical influence, or the moral evidence of Christianity, that, as the objective cause, actually produces faith in men ?—Be it so—we assent not only, but affirm and insist.   It cannot be denied that Christianity, to one susceptible of the specific impressions from it, does witness for itself, does demonstratively assert its divinity, by its ethical peculiarity. In such a type, and with such resplendence, has the ethical element been developed in Christianity, as to make it an absolute Unique in the earth ; and challenge for it, wherever it is known, the assent of the world, as a miraculous revelation. And this evidence it truly is, that in every case prevails, in actually gaining men's assent to Christianity, so far as it is gained in truth.   None, at least, become true believers while they are insensible to the moral evidence, the ethical or spiritual excellency of the Gospel.   All the evidences pour their force into the moral, or become *moralized*, so to speak, when that impress is given to the susceptible heart, which is the just counterpart, in man, of objective Christianity.   To that spiritual discernment, in which faith has its upspring and being, all the things of the Spirit of God are, preëminently, ethical things ;—permeated and filled with the fulness of ethical

power and excellency.   Well does Edwards resolve "a spiritual and saving conviction of the truth and reality of the things
revealed in the word of God " into "a sense of the divine excellency (the moral glory) of these things".   Nevertheless
the evangelical morality, that form of morality which constitutes the moral evidence and asserts the truth of Christianity,
so far from being without the miraculous, has the miraculous
in fact, as its suppositum and ground.   It is a form or type of
morality, taken altogether from the contact and intercourse of
the principle of morality, with the miraculously attested wonders of redemption.   The moral evidence of Christianity, distinctively, is not its embodiment of morality in the abstract,
or of morality in so far as it is common between Christianity
and natural religion, but that peculiar and ineffably glorious
type of morality, which consists in the concretion of the ethical
element in the miraculous facts of the great mystery of Godliness : God manifest in the flesh, justified in the spirit, seen of
angels, preached unto the nations, believed on in the world, received up into glory.   It could not be known that Christianity
is divine or truthful in its claims to divinity from morality unmodified by influences from its own facts and doctrines: no
such exhibition or enforcement of morality could avail in any
degree, to prove the Trinity in God, or the incarnation of the
Word, or the atonement, or the resurrection.   In order to be
demonstrative by its moral evidence, Christianity with its supernatural wonders, must come itself into the sphere of morality, and take a form of morality from itself, and express
itself in that form ; that is to say, produce a morality distinctively *Christian ;* or such as has Christianity, with its miracles,
for its origin and base.   It is divinely revealed and attested
Christian truth, that entering into the ethical sphere, makes
all things there new, giving every principle a new illustration,
and every precept a new exposition and a new motive, and
making every man who becomes an example of it, a new
creature — this is the moral evidence which demonstrates
Christianity.   It has its breath and being in the miracles;
take them away, and the evidence goes with them.   Apart
from these, the ethical superiority of Christianity is, so far, to

its praise, but does not demonstrate its claims to a divine origin.

10. Next, is there proof of Christianity from its effects, or actual efficiency on mankind, apart from miracles? We do not ask whether this evidence is demonstrative, but whether the influence of miracles is to be excluded from it. The evidence is demonstrative : the tree is known by its fruits—Christianity meets the infinite wants of man ; it recovers him from the dominion of sin ; it creates him anew in the image of God; it is the power of God unto salvation to every one who believes in it. Here truly is the crowning evidence of the truth of Christianity, and it is evidence which Christianity will always be multiplying to itself. But the present question is, Does this evidence imply that miracles may be dispensed with? And the answer to it is, that the evidence is the very fruitage of miracles. Whence that efficacy of Christianity which supplies this evidence? What is this efficacy but that of a wondrous miracle, or collection of miracles, enshrined in countless witnessing miracles? Would a Christianity, so called, denuded of the miraculous, have had the same efficacy? Take away this element from the Gospel, and would it still be the perfect satisfaction of human need, the power of God unto salvation?

11. As yet, then, we have no proof of Christianity, apart from miracles. May it not, nevertheless, be sufficiently proved without them, by its collateral evidence? We have already answered this question. Christianity has evidence of this kind of an immense amount, in which apparently or distinctively, there is nothing of the miraculous. "It has pleased the Divine Author of our religion", says Mansell, "to fortify his revelation with evidence of various kinds, appealing with different degrees of force to various minds, and to the same mind at different times". In the words of Butler, "the evidence of Christianity is a long series of things reaching as it seems from the beginning of the world to the present time, of great variety and compass ". Is there not in this series of things evidence enough to prove Christianity independently of the miraculous portion of it? Butler, who ascribes great weight to this evi-

dence, " consisting of things not reducible to the heads, either of miracles or the completion of prophecy ", still, while making these two the direct and fundamental proofs, adds that "those others (the collateral proofs), however considerable they are, ought *never to be urged apart from the direct proofs, but to be always joined with them*". Why should the collateral proofs never be urged apart from the direct ones, but always be joined with them ? For two palpable reasons : first because, if the collateral proofs could exist, apart from the direct, they would not be in themselves or in their influence, equivalent to the direct. They would not be, as God himself directly deposing to the truth of Christianity, so as to make unbelief an impeachment of the veracity of God : the evidence of Christianity must be this, or equivalent to this ; miracles are the thing itself, the collateral proofs are neither the thing nor its equivalent. What they would amount to by themselves as demanding assent, what measure of assent they would call for, or justify, if perfectly appreciated, we cannot determine ; but the very fact, if it were a fact, that such miraculous matters as those of substantive Christianity had no miraculous attestation, would, as we have seen, apart from posterior requisitions, be such a presumption against its truth, as no evidence could overcome. Reason—nature itself, would, to the last, require that attestation. Christianity, without it, would be incredible. But secondly, the collateral evidences should not be urged apart from the direct or miraculous, because separate from the latter they have, and can have, in fact, no existence. The collateral evidences, like every thing in Christianity, had their origin and source in the miraculous, are an outflow from it, and can in reality be no more separated from it, or used in proof against its necessity, than beams of sunlight be separated from, and then made an argument against, the necessity of the body of the sun. It is owing to miracles originally and determinantly, that the collateral evidences are what they are. We know not what would have been the course of things in the history of Christianity, had it not originated and started in miracles : enough that we know what was the fact : the success of Christianity, the conversion of the Roman empire, the lives of the saints, the testimony of the noble army of martyrs, the progress of civilization and the arts under Christian institutions and society, the whole of that long series of things reaching from the beginning of the world to the present time, which comprehends all the collateral proofs of Christianity,— instead of implying that miracles are not necessary as direct proofs of it, infer the reality, if not the necessity also of miracles, as certainly as the fruit and foliage of a tree infer the reality of the tree.   Well, therefore, has Butler said, the collateral should never be urged apart from the direct proofs of Christianity, but be always joined with them.   Most fitly and undeniably has this other important word been spoken by the same great author: "Revelation itself is miraculous, and miracles are the proof of it".   The collateral evidences, apart from miracles, are not the proof of it, and as such should never be urged or relied on.

12. But after all, how are miracles the supreme, ultimate, decisive Test of the truthfulness of Christianity, since miracles themselves are amenable to a test?   Be it that they are decisive, that they give absolute certainty, when once their genuineness is beyond doubt : still if there are true miracles, there are also false ones ; and there is evidence which, if it be against a miracle, no miracle can countervail ; that, namely, of self-evident truth and goodness. We know from Scripture itself (see Deut. xiii, 1–11) that if the object or purpose of a miracle be wrong, the testimony of the purpose against the miracle is stronger than the testimony of the miracle, or any miracle can be, in the interest of the purpose.   And does it not hence follow that miracles, instead of proving Christianity, are dependent on Christianity for their own proof? That if we know the miracles to be true, we know this, because we know by antecedent and higher evidence, the religion to be true? This argument seems to have convinced some persons that the defence of Christianity is complete, independent of the testimony of miracles, and is rather impeded than facilitated by it.

13. But the argument is a fallacy. It assumes as true in an absolute sense, what is true only in a certain case.   Because a miracle, so called, wrought for a bad purpose, is already con-

demned by its purpose, it concludes that every miracle depends for its credibility on knowledge of its purpose; or, in ignorance of its purpose, is necessarily undeterminative as to its own genuineness. It cannot assert its own reality as a miracle, a personal or direct work of God, unless it is known to what intent it is wrought. The argument is, that since a bad purpose condemns an alleged miracle performed in its favor, no miracle, irrespective of acquaintance with its purpose, can, as a miracle, authenticate itself. The sophistry is manifest. It is a mere truism, that no miracle can countervail the contradictory testimony of a *bad* purpose or object; it is simply asserting that a true miracle cannot be wrought in attestation of a *bad* purpose; that God cannot act, cannot exert his power in the interest of moral evil; that is to say, cannot deny or undeify himself. But does this imply that he can never act and authenticate the act as his own, unless it is already known why or to what intent the act is performed? Must we know what God intends by his works, before we can be certain that the works are indeed his? Can he do no works capable of differencing themselves absolutely from the works of his creatures? We know that he can have no bad design; we know that he must have some design, not unworthy of himself; but must he acquaint us with his designs, before he can perform works which shall be able to assert themselves as distinctively his own? It is true that we know not the limit of finite power; but cannot infinite power go beyond that limit, and there put itself forth in works after its own kind, which no finite power shall be able to equal, or successfully counterfeit? And by such self-authenticated works, cannot God authenticate a revelation which, as such, could not otherwise be adequately attested? What if we knew no more as to the purpose of Christianity than that it is not a bad one, or one unworthy of the Deity? might not God, without acquainting us further with its object, seal it as a revelation, by incontestable miracles? May this be denied, without limiting the Holy One of Israel?

14. But we have been putting the matter at its greatest disadvantage. Our knowledge is not altogether negative as to

the purpose of Christianity ; its purpose is worthy of its mira
cles, and required them for its fulfilment ; and whatever may
be said of a supposed necessity or duty of testing or proving
miracles, here are miracles which are their own proof.   Admitting that the Scripture miracles were really wrought, we
may as well deny that God made the world, as deny that he
was their author.   If the genuineness of some of them, apart
from the rest, and from the system to which they all belong,
might seem to be questionable, yet, as a whole, once admit
their reality, and the possibility of reasonable doubt as to their
authorship is excluded.   If the plagues of Egypt, the giving
of the manna, the crossing of the Jordan, the regression of the
sun, the swimming of the iron, the walking on the sea, the
resurrection of Lazarus, the resurrection of our Lord—if these,
with the rest of the Scripture miracles, were matters of fact,
he who, admitting them as such, does not believe in the religion which they attest, does indeed charge God himself with
bearing false witness.   It is not because these miracles do not
assert themselves to be miracles indeed, that there is held to
be a necessity for superior or antecedent proof.   The Creation
itself is not more self-evidently of God, than the testimonial
miracles of Christianity.

15. Miracles, then—untestable, because there is nothing to
test them by—miracles wrought, it is certain, for no unworthy
purpose, but not dependent on a knowledge of their purpose
for proof of their reality, are the direct, fundamental, indispensable proofs of Christianity.   Whatever is peculiar in Christianity, would never have been known had it not been revealed,
and for evidence of its truth, or its demonstrative certitude,
rests at last on testimonial miracles.   Except as ultimately assured by these divine vouchers, I have no sufficient ground
for rational belief as to any thing distinctively or peculiarly
Christian.   I do not know that there are more Persons than one
to whom Deity belongs, or that Jesus was God, or that his
death was an atonement for the sins of mankind, or that the
dead will be raised by him ; I do not know these things by
intuition, or because, independently of external proofs, they
are true to my reason ; I know them because God, having re-

vealed them by his Holy Spirit, has sealed that revelation by evidence either in itself directly miraculous, or having the miraculous, first, last, and midst, as its ground.

16. After all, however, it may be objected that if Christianity behooved to certify itself by miracles, it behooved to continue miracles. To the masses of mankind, for whom Christianity was chiefly intended, historical miracles, so far as their ability to verify them is concerned, are as nothing. What, to the common people, as to power of verifying them to themselves, are events of the far distant past? Moreover, as a general fact, it is notorious that men do not become Christians from personal examination of the testimony of miracles, or the historical evidences of Christianity.—This objection is virtually answered already. The miracles, though performed ages ago, are present, and live in all the ages, and even to the unlearned and children, witness for Christianity to-day, not less decisively and strongly than they did at first. The Scripture miracles are not as other events of the past, in respect of the antiquating influence of time; on the contrary, they and those events, are in this respect a contrast to one another. The miracles were not left, like common occurrences, to the accidents of tradition, or chance, or human history; they were not detached, isolated, inorganic things; they all pertained to one whole, with every part of which, as with the whole, they were coörganized, interconnected, and, as it were, interfused. The miracles of Christianity are, in fact, as we have already said, among its integrant, constitutive elements; they live in its life; they live in the Scriptures, in the Church, and in the holy examples and confessions of members of the Church: in preaching, in the sacraments, in all the memorials and ordinances of Christianity, their witnessing presence and power are conserved and felt. Besides, the miracles of power which attest Christianity, are like Christianity itself, and whatever essentially belongs to it, perpetually quickened and rejuvenated by another species of miracles, comprised in the completion of the prophecies—miracles of knowledge, which are continually being accomplished, as time advances in its course. These direct and fundamental proofs of Christianity, in their

13

demonstrative force, enter into every part and fibre of the great organism which they authenticate as divine, and at once verify and are verified by it.   In this sense, it is true that the religion asserts the miracles, as well as the miracles the religion.   The proofs of Christianity, direct and collateral, "make up", to use the admirable words of Butler, "all of them together, one argument, the conviction arising from which kind of proof may be compared to what they call *the effect* in architecture, or other works of art—a result from a number of things so and so disposed, and taken into one view ".   The miracles are in the view with all the rest, attesting all, and in and through all, attesting and asserting themselves ; and in their proper influence, no less, perhaps even more effective, on the whole, at this day, than they were to many who saw them performed.   There is no need of new miracles ; indeed, they might be a disadvantage, and, after a short time, would, in effect, cease to be miracles.   If the old miracles, certified as they are to all, do not convince men, new ones doubtless would also fail to do it.   " If they hear not Moses and the prophets "— if Moses and the prophets, with the miracles which attested and still attest their mission, are disregarded by them—" neither would they be persuaded though one rose from the dead ".   Greater, doubtless, to us, the advantage from the Scripture miracles, greater as they lie together in the one view of which we have spoken ; more decisive as evidencing the truth of revealed religion, than would be the repetition of fresh miracles every day.   Miracles prove Christianity, but they may fail to make converts to it.   Referring to the too common results of miracles, Pascal has said, " the purpose of miracles is not to convert, but to condemn ".

17. The objection owes what of force it may seem to have, to great indiscrimination ; it does not distinguish between what the evidence of Christianity behoves to be in itself, and the way and the degree in which it becomes effective in individual converts—between the necessity of its having a sufficient ground for its authoritative demand for faith, and the measures and workings of faith, on the part of those in whom the demand is met. To make the former complete, the specific

testimony of miracles is necessary ; the latter, though the influence of miracles, as before explained, is never wanting in
it, vary indefinitely with different persons.   In no one is faith
commensurate with the objective demand for it; nor is it
alike as to its origin and advances in all.   St. Augustine, but
for miracles historically verified, to and by himself, could not
have been a Christian ; the generality do not distinctively feel
the necessity of miracles, or formally recognize their specific
influence and function as the supreme Test and proof of Christianity.   They also, in a true sense, would not believe but for
miracles, but it is the miraculous, as integrant and interfused
in the whole of the evidence, and pervading the essence of
Christianity, that their faith apprehends and rests in.   It is
the " one argument " of which Butler speaks, " made up of all
the proofs taken together ", the conviction arising from which
he compares to what they call *the effect* in architecture, or
other works of art.   This it is that generally produces faith,
when it becomes a personal reality.   Different minds may be
variously affected by it ; some more by one part, some more
by another ; some in a larger, some in a smaller measure ; but
in every case, the efficiency of the whole, as such, is felt, and
the result is the product of the whole.   It is so from the fact
that Christianity, with its proofs, is a single, living organism,
each part of which interconnects itself with every other, giving every other part an influential, life-producing, if not a
distinctly recognized presence.

18. This distinction between the fundamental necessity of
miracles, as outward proofs or seals of testimony, and the influence of these and the other evidences in the genesis of faith,
or in producing faith, in different persons, solves at once the
objection before us.   It was needful that the demonstration of
Christianity should be absolute, irrespective of men's belief or
disbelief; thus only could be justified its absolute claim to belief, and its denunciation of all unbelief.   How it was to fare in
the world, what fruit its evidence was to produce in the minds
of men, or which part of the evidence was to be first or most
effective, or what in the beginning and progress of a life of
faith was to have ascendant power, depended on the different

individualities of men, and the contingencies of time and circumstances.

19. On this point, it is to be further and distinctly remembered, and strongly accented, that in every case of the subjective demonstration of Christianity, there is another agency concerned besides that of the outward evidence. It is not of themselves alone that men believe; faith is the gift of God. It is the inward demonstration of the Spirit and of power, that makes the external demonstration fruitful. Amidst the full effulgence of outward evidence, "if thine eye be evil, thy whole body will be full of darkness". Without the subjective prerequisites, to use the words of Coleridge, without "that predisposing warmth, which renders the understanding susceptible of the specific impressions from the history, and from all other outward seals of testimony", the whole of the evidence, collateral and miraculous, internal and external, will be without avail, except to condemn, as Pascal said of the miracles, in particular. And it is also certain, and equally essential as bearing on the topic before us, that where the inward witnessing of the Spirit has place; where, to adopt Coleridge's language again, there is "a true efficient conviction of a moral truth—*the creation of a new heart*, which collects the energies of a man's whole being in the focus of the conscience", where there "is emphatically, that leading of the Father, without which no man can come to Christ", there the dominion of the entire external evidence is actualized. Christianity, now, has all its evidences at command, and they do their work. The miracles, whether distinctively verified or not, work together with all the rest. There is nothing now that does not bear witness to Christianity. Nature itself, under the power of this inward demonstration, this "one essential miracle", asserts the supernatural :

> "Nature is Christian; preaches to mankind,
> And bids dead matter aid us in our creed."

20. On the whole, we are brought by the discussion we have been engaged in, to the conclusion that objections to miracles as proof of Christianity, presuppose and in fact have, as their ground objections to veritable Christianity itself. As

naturalism cannot but make objections to miracles `as the proper proof of religion, so reciprocally, when there are these objections, the religion adhered to, if any, is that of natural- ism.   An objector to miracles as proof of doctrine, cannot be an intelligent believer in such a doctrine as that of a plurality of persons in the God-head, or of the two natures in Christ, or of the resurrection of the dead.   He ought not to call himself a Christian; not even a *neo*-christian, unless he intend by the prefix to deny that he is a real Christian at all.   The only religion which, after discarding miracles as proofs, has any ground of credibility in it, is that which, in the words of the *Westminster Review*, has its attestation " in the essential uni- ty and self-consistency of our moral and spiritual nature, open- ing more and more with the progressive education of the race, to a consciousness of the fundamental laws on which it rests, and which we learn partly through mutual intercourse and sympathy, partly through the awakening influence of superior minds, on those that are less developed and advanced ".   We would not press the inexorable consequences of a theory on those who shrink from them; all who disparage miracles, are not, we must hope, absolute naturalists, yet we cannot but stand in doubt, if not of the substantial loyalty to the cause of Christian truth, at least of the logical consistency, of those who say they would rather have Christianity without than with the miracles, or that the credibility of miracles depends on doctrine, rather than the credibility of doctrine on miracles. Nor can we adopt the formula, as applicable to a supernatural revelation, that, " the miracle must witness for itself and the doctrine must witness for itself, and then the first is capable of witnessing for the second ". *   We take Butler as complete; *Revelation itself is miraculous and miracles are its proof.*   If miracles do indeed witness for themselves, that is to say, assert themselves, demonstratively, to be direct works of God, they can witness for that which to us, through our ignorance, does not witness for itself, if by the will of God, they are wrought for that end.   Revelation, apart from testimonial miracles, does not witness for itself to us : in this isolation it would not be

* Trench.

true to human reason. The proper statement is: " the miracle must witness for itself; the doctrine, apart from the miracle, does not witness for itself; the first, by itself, must witness for the second". In the evidence of miracles all other evidence has its ground and its beginning. Without miracles Christianity is indemonstrable.

22. Before dismissing the subject we would reproduce, for the purpose of emphasizing with a specific reference, what has already been expressed with some particularity as to the measure or fulness of the assent demanded by Christianity. What we would further say on this point is, that, while this assent indicates the nature of the proof of Christianity, it indicates at the same time the proper task of a Christian apologist. Whatever may be the measure or form of men's belief or disbelief of Christianity, there can, as we have urged, be no question that the assent which with infinite authority it challenges of all, is that of unqualified, absolute, prompt assurance. Most assuredly therefore he who sets himself to defend Christianity, undertakes, if he knows what he is about, to make out a sufficiency in its evidences to produce, not a conviction of the probability or bare credibility, but a conviction of the absolute certainty of its truth. He must present evidence proportional to the assent required. If he does not do this, his attempt is a failure. If he only gives reason for a preponderant conviction, a balance of probability, in favor of Christianity, or for an assent short of a full sense of the certainty of its truth, he has not defended Christianity; he has at best only approximated a defence of it. Without controversy Christianity cannot be defended, if its evidence be not in itself and to a just appreciation of it, absolutely demonstrative. The claims of Christianity to positive, undoubting belief, cannot be otherwise justified. " If", says Stillingfleet, " there be no evidences given sufficient to carry the minds of men beyond mere probability, what sin can it be in them to disbelieve who cannot be obliged to believe as true what is only discovered as probable?" Yet a recent writer* on the study of the evidences has said that to require certainty as the just

*Aids to Faith.

result of the evidence of Christianity, is to require an assent out of proportion to the evidence : as if there might be evidence greater than the direct testimony of God. And have not defences of Christianity, so called, works on the evidences, too often contented themselves with this idea as the utmost which the evidence can extend to? And why, but from not thinking with Butler, or forgetting what he has said, that the collateral evidences, ought never to be urged apart from the direct, the miraculous ones, but to be always joined with them? The collateral evidences, by themselves, would not warrant the assent demanded by Christianity; but keep the two kinds of evidence always united, let the witnessing virtue of miracles be as it is in truth retained in every part of the evidence; let all the evidence involve and rest upon miracles as its substratum, what then, as to the nature, the measure of the assent demanded by it? Does the evidence then come short of substantiating its claim to a sense of certainty, absolute certainty, as its proper counterpart in man? Let men apprehend this as the fact respecting the evidence, and ought they to be less certain of the truth of Christianity than of that of natural science, or of the existence of the world, or of their own existence? In the words of Stillingfleet, we ask, " can there be greater evidence that a testimony is infallible, than that it is the testimony of God himself?" Let us not disparage the books on the evidences; there are among books few of greater power; they triumphantly refute all objections; they are victorious in all controversies; they do completely what they undertake to do; they overwhelm infidelity with its logical inconsistencies and absurdities; but after all, what for the most part have they achieved or aimed at in the battle of the evidences, but just to make out the bare credibility of the religion attested by them? When a spiritual man, after pondering, doubtless not without edification and delight, the profound and masterly treatises of the apologists, comes into the presence of the great Object itself, in whose interest they labor so well, and looks directly upon the miracle Christianity, encompassed by countless testimonial miracles, how feeble is language to express the difference of which he now becomes conscious, be-

tween the title of Christianity to assent, and the measure of
assent which these works contend for? And whence the difference, if not from inappreciation of the place and position of
miracles in the evidence? It is in two respects with the evidence of Christianity, as with that of the being of God, both
are alike demonstrative in asserting the reality of their objects, and both alike unheeded or rejected, or dimly seen, even
by the princes of human wisdom.

23. We add one remark. Is not a reässertion of the miraculous in the evidence of revealed religion an especial desideratum of the times? If it be possible should not the Scripture
miracles be made to reäppear as living realities, before the
eyes of this generation? Otherwise where before long will
be faith in revelation? Natural religion, even, seems to be
standing " a tiptoe", ready to forsake the sphere of religious
philosophy. What more notorious, than that the religious
philosophy of the day is mainly pantheistic? "It is an admitted fact", said Isaac Taylor some years since, "that already
all, or nearly all, educated men from end to end of continental Europe, those of the Anglo-Saxon race alone excepted, are
either open pantheists, or are kept from avowing themselves
to be so, by motives of conventional propriety, or of policy".
The Anglo-Saxons themselves are becoming unsteadfast in belief in a personal God. Men of high culture, English and
American, are coming to the conclusion that there is no Divine
Being different from the world, and nothing in a proper sense
supernatural. Not many of these as yet profess themselves
pantheists, but leading minds among them, employ reasonings and forms of expression, which involve pantheism inevitably, and not obscurely or indirectly. It may be traced too
perceptibly, in some of the recent review articles. Professor Powell tells us that "to attempt to reason from
law to volition, from order to active power, from universal
reason to *distinct personality*, from design to self-existence,
from intelligence to infinite perfection, is in reality to adopt
grounds of argument and speculation entirely beyond those
of strict philosophic inference". Pantheism on a large and
increasing scale is the manifest goal to which modern think-

ing on religion is tending. The fact is on all sides seen and confessed. It is beginning to be felt beyond the educated classes; the people at large are becoming more or less acquainted and pleased with pantheistic speculations. What is to be done? Something surely besides what has been or what is being done. The means now and hitherto used have failed even to check the progress of the deadly error; it was never more triumphant than at the present moment. To what other means may we look? Shall we expect new theophanies, new manifestations of the supernatural and the miraculous, to confound the naturalism on all sides so predominant? What were this but to make incomplete or transitory the original attestation of Christianity; to make obsolete or invalid all the miracles both of the Old and New Testaments? What were it moreover but to make void our own highest responsibility and privilege; to cease from personal dignity and worth; to distrust and count as nothing the indwelling power and grace of the Holy Spirit; in short, to require *unnecessary* miracles; that is, in principle, to put miracles among common things; to make them indeed miracles no longer? This were virtually to become pantheists ourselves. Still the living reality, the influential presence of the miraculous in the evidence of Christianity, the just antitheton of naturalistic tendencies and successes,—this is clearly indicated and imperatively demanded, as their proper remedy. Never more than in this our day, has the "City of our God" behooved to be known and read of men by its name: JEHOVAH-SHAMMAH, THE LORD IS THERE. It will not be so known and read without direct, infallible revelations of the Divine Presence. "Out of Zion the perfection of beauty", the excellent glory itself must shine, and it will not shine thence, except in its own proper manifestations; the natural, simply, does not directly reveal, does not attest the infinite or divine. Naturalism will be efficiently confuted by nothing but an actual exhibition and perception of the miraculous, the proper seal of God. It is far from being certain that the presence of the miraculous would impart that perception of it; but its presence, its essential or influential presence, is necessary. All just religious conviction, all true piety, consists essentially in a sense of divinity or the miraculous as at once inhering in and attesting revelation; the central miracle Christianity, authenticated as directly of God by its accompanying testimonial miracles. And may this sense be produced in the absence of its objective cause, the miraculously attested miracle itself? Must not that miracle by some means display itself anew? And by what other means, since new miracles are not to be looked for but by reässerting, producing anew, the testimony of the ancient miracles? But how is this to be done? Is it a possibility? Can Christianity, after eighteen centuries, reproduce its miraculous attestations as at first? The question has been answered. Christianity, in itself, or as an objective reality, has its first life always; its facts, its doctrines, its testimony, all live in, perpetuate, and are perpetuated by that life: therefore nothing in substantive Christianity can become stale or obsolete; by its constitutive elements, it is like its Author, in respect of time, the same yesterday, to-day, and forever: so it is in itself, and so it seems to be to every one whose understanding has been opened to understand it. To the eye of faith, Christianity is as novel, as wonderful now as it was to the disciples on the day of Pentecost. If in the primitive vigor and fruitfulness of faith Christianity should reäppear in the life of the Church, would there be any decrepitude, any wrinkle or infirmity of age, any trace of the wear or waste of time in its aspect? The doctrines, the examples, and with all the rest the miracles, would they not live again, as before the very eyes of men?* Would not this

---

* "Methought I saw, with great evidence, from the four evangelists, the wonderful works of God in giving Jesus Christ to save us, from his conception and birth even to his second coming to judgment; *methought I was as if I had seen him born, as if I had seen him grow up, as if I had seen him walk through this world from the cradle to the cross.* . . . When I have considered also the truth of his resurrection, and have remembered that word, 'Touch me not, Mary,' etc., *I have seen as if he had leaped out of the grave's mouth,*'" etc. (*Bunyan's Life.*) See also Chrysostom on Gal. iii, 1 : "It was not in the country of the Galatians, but in Jerusalem, that He was crucified: how then does he (Paul) say *among you?* To demonstrate the power of faith, which is able to see even distant objects. And he does not say, 'was crucified', but 'was painted crucified', showing that by the eyes of faith they beheld more distinctly than some who were present and saw the transactions".

be the certain, the necessary consèquence, even if to the miracles distinctively no special attention were drawn? But as the times call with such emphasis for the specific witness of miracles, as it is specially characteristic of the times to disown and deny God's direct testimony to his revelation, so abundantly given, and this for the reason that his revelation itself is disbelieved — this fact would make it impossible to the revived Church not to have a very prominent reference in all the workings of her life, inward and outward, in her thoughts, her prayers, her discourses, her books, the labors of her ministry, to the reproduction of the miraculous testimony, the sign-manual of God himself. And the result would be sure: with corresponding prominence, the miracles would return and take their proper position among the evidences. The constancy of nature is not less to be doubted than that rejuvenated Christianity, novel and fresh as at first, with the advantage of an experience as old as time and not older than opulent in teachings of divine wisdom and prudence, would renew its pristine demonstrativeness and power ; and if still confronted by adversaries, of whatever number or whatever name, — neo - christians, naturalists, pantheists, atheists, — would by their opposition, however maintained, be no more retarded, in its triumphant advances, than the sun is retarded in his circuit in the heavens by the mists and vapors of the atmosphere. " Woe unto him that striveth with his Maker. Let the potsherds strive with the potsherds of the earth."

Art. II.—PHILOSOPHY AND THEOLOGY IN CONFLICT.

By Rev. L. P. Hickok, D.D., Acting President of Union College.

In the last July Number of this Review, Art. "Psychology and Skepticism", the leading mistakes of some of the preceding reviews of Hickok's Rational Psychology were fully and fairly exposed. In the cotemporary Number of the *Princeton Review*, and also in the October Number of this Review, the criticism of the Psychology has been further pursued; and while some of the same mistakes are reïterated, some new ones are also presented. The old mistakes already exposed will need no further notice.

There is also a prevalent religious skepticism growing more and more inveterate and obtrusive, which has its sole ground in the false philosophy that the Rational Psychology was designed to correct. This religious skepticism will find its overthrow only in an exposition of the delusions in which it originates.

Sometimes it happens that two crows are killed at one shot; and it is here practicable to put the lesser and the larger mistakes in the same range, and make the dispatch of the false criticism a preliminary to the annihilation of the religious skepticism. The mistakes of the criticism will be given in direct statement without quotation or reference, careful only that the statement be plainly and fairly made; and the successive exposure of those mistakes will naturally introduce the prevalent skepticism and its refutation, thus giving method and unity to the whole article.

Among the additional false issues made in the aforesaid reviews are the following:

1. It is alleged against the Psychology that it distrusts the validity of consciousness, and holds that consciousness and reason are sometimes contradictory; and that, therefore, it

becomes a necessity for the Psychology to first prove a valid faculty for knowing, before it can be competent for it to bring any proof for the validity of any thing known.   It should first prove its very faculty for proving, and must thus stultify itself in attempting to take a *second* before it has attained a *first.* This is supported by assuming that all our cognitive faculties, normally acting, give truth, and in doubting these we can know nothing.   If consciousness is fallible, reason also may just as readily be doubted; and both alike need proving, and yet the one cannot be proved except by first proving the other.

This charge, that the Psychology supposes consciousness and reason sometimes to stand in contradiction, is but the old blunder, before exposed, of imputing to the Psychology itself that which the Psychology only affirmed of the skeptic.   The true position of the Psychology, and the necessity for it, may be seen as follows: The skeptic finds from observation that the senses often deceive.   The same things appear differently at different times; differently at the same time to different persons; and especially different as given through different senses.   The same stick plunged in water is straight to the touch and bent to the sight, and the consciousness for each equally clear.   And, further, there are all the illusions of double-vision, jugglery, clairvoyance, and dreaming, where the consciousness is not trustworthy.   Moreover, the prevalent philosophy taught from reason that distant objects could not be immediately known, though the common consciousness assumed that they were, and therefore one must be false. The skeptic, thus, was no dogmatist; he had a logical basis for his doubting.   This logical ground for skepticism may also be carried into the field for judging, and give occasion for doubting the validity of substance and cause; and also into the region of the supernatural, and sustain the skepticism for miracles, inspiration, and even the being of a personal Deity.   These skeptical arguments cannot be met by experiment and deductions drawn from observation, for they call in question the validity of experience itself.   Hence the demand for an *à priori* proof—a Rational Psychology.

And now the human mind is capable of apprehending some truths in the necessity and universality of their being. Such truths determine experience and are not conditioned by experience, and are hence known as *à priori* truths, and are of wide extent in all the fields of mathematics, physics, and ethics. They compel conviction and expel doubting. If there is any ground for skepticism through the illusions of sense and conflicting judgments, yet there can be no ground for it in the axioms of mathematics and the demonstrations of geometry. The method of the Psychology, then, is to meet skepticism with this light of *à priori* truth, and carry all along with it the conviction of necessity and universality. It will, therefore, be a legitimate criticism to show that all or some part fails in such *à priori* illumination ; but it is wholly impertinent to assume that the Psychology needs the help of logic for sustaining *à priori* truth. All logic is itself vain till it can in some way rest upon necessary and universal principle. If any one will arbitrarily deny or doubt necessary truth, the Psychology proposes no remedy. Sufficient is it for its philosophy, and it has done all it proposed or promised, when it has put the varied functions for knowing within the comprehension of an *à priori* Idea and an actual Law.

It is shown that what is given to the sense must be *distinguished* as to quality and *defined* as to quantity, and that qualitative and quantitative objects are the only ones that the functions of sense can know. In the understanding, a promiscuous coming and going of sense-objects in and out of the consciousness is shown can be no orderly experience, but that each phenomenon must have its place and period determined relatively to one common space and one common time, and that this can be effected only as the sense-phenomena stand connected in their permanent substances and successive causes. Herein is the science of the *possible ;* so a function of sense and of understanding may be, and if at all, so they must be. Then the facts of perceiving and judging are separately and extensively examined and found to have each their Law, in full accordance with the *à priori* Idea, and in this is the science of the *actual.* Thus consciousness and reason are shown not to be contradictory, for the sense-object in consciousness is the phenomenal, and the reason-object given to the understanding is the substantial; and one may be immediately known, and the other not, without contradiction.

But thus far, it is not the sense and the understanding which have been looking over and through themselves, and philosophically determining their own functions. Another faculty than either has been engaged in this *à priori* investigation, and has carried the conviction of necessity and universality all along with it. This separate faculty needs then to be specifically subjected to an *à priori* examination, and thus be philosophically "found", both in its Idea and Law, and which is thoroughly accomplished and distinctively known as the Reason. We perceive by the Sense and judge by the Understanding and comprehend by the Reason prior to any philosophical "finding" of either function, but we know them distinctively in their idea and law only as thus philosophically "found". All functions for knowing are thus brought within the light of *à priori* truth, and known in their determinate laws, and no critic can know what he is about who assumes that necessary truths must be fortified by logic before they can avail to demolish the positions of skepticism.

2. It is objected that the Psychology denies or ignores the distinction between the primary and secondary qualities of matter. The doctrine held by the reviewers seems to be, that the primary qualities are known immediately in the bodies themselves, and that the secondary qualities are admitted by them to be known only as affections in our organs. The primary qualities are extension and solidity, and the secondary qualities are the odorous, audible, sapid, and, within certain limits, the visible phenomena; the first inhere in the body, the second are occult as to the body, and known only as subjective to the percipient. Matter in its primary qualities must be known immediately by sense, and cannot otherwise be known at all. All confounding of primary and secondary qualities, as it is alleged the philosophy in the Rational Psychology does, leads to skepticism, idealism, and materialism.

It might be a sufficient answer to this criticism to say that it is wholly gratuitous, for the Psychology, so far from either denying or ignoring the distinction, expressly makes it. It does not, however, put primary qualities, as immediately inhering in matter, to the direct knowledge of the senses. They are *à priori* necessary to all body and not merely perceived in some bodies. Body *must* have extension and impenetrability, but all that sense could affirm, even with immediate perception, would be that in some bodies primary qualities *are*. In the last Number of this REVIEW, Dr. Lewis has ably and keenly exposed the shallowness of that philosophy which adopts the sense theory of "hard matter", and ridicules rational "ideas" and spiritual "forces", but it is enough for the present purpose to show that on its own ground the criticism could never determine the distinction between primary and secondary qualities, the first inhering in matter and the last existing only as subjective affections.

Thus, one is conscious that there is a color and a sound; but colors and sounds are admitted to be secondary qualities, and that in knowing them body is not immediately known. One is conscious that the color is extended and has shape, and is not conscious that the sound has spacial extension and shape. But, in vision, one cannot know that body is extended, except as it is known that color is extended, and this is knowing a primary quality only through a secondary. The eye gives nothing in consciousness why extension should be a primary quality, and inherent in body, any more than color or sound. So in comparatively few instances we get extension also from the touch, and likewise hardness. The touch of the whole hand may give a hand's-breadth extension, and the moving of the finger over a surface may give indefinite extension, and the muscular pressure may give hardness as the index of impenetrability. But though the touch be in contact with the body, as the organ of vision was not, and though for the present it be admitted that the extension and the hardness were immediately cognized, yet could not such consciousness of extension and hardness determine them to inhere in body as primary qualities. One touches a body and feels cold, and the coldness by contact is as immediate as extension and hardness, but coldness is only a secondary quality.   Should it be replied to this that the coldness is not always the same, and sometimes not at all, in the same body, and thus known not to be primary ; but that will be knowing the distinction inductively, and not immediately ; or, will it be said, that to a man who should never touch any thing that was not in temperature below blood-heat, coldness would be a primary quality of body ?   We cannot any way make the distinctions of primary and secondary qualities, in the right place, by any immediate consciousness in sensation.   If we do not use reason beyond consciousness, this alleged very important distinction will be without a difference.   The sense cannot know any quality as primary, and he who would insist on the distinction as so important must leave the empirical and come on to the transcendental ground.   The Psychology both recognizes the distinction, and in the only way that it can be made.

3. It is objected to the philosophy of the Rational Psychology that, in denying the immediate knowledge of matter and mind in themselves, it pretends to prove the existence of an outer world by the differences in certain appearances.   Some the mind can make to come and go at pleasure, and these can have only subjective being ; others the mind cannot make nor modify, but they come and go wholly independent of its pleasure, and such necessary and independent appearances are, in their circumstances, to be taken as having real outer being separate from the subjective percipient.   And that it may show the inconclusiveness of such alleged method of proof, the criticism adduces the aches and pains and pleasures resulting from a sickly or healthy body; the alternate heat and cold of a fever, and the uncontrollable anguish of morbid nerves, all of which come and go independently of the mind, but are no evidence of an outer world.

This whole dealing manifests a very perverse apprehension of the entire method of the philosophy and its results.   The argument from dependent and independent modifications of phenomena is only for the purpose of proving a real impression on the organ, and not a mere organic affection, and for which it is sufficient, but is not at all used for proving the va-

14

lidity of an outer world known in common by all. The proof
for this last is so different from the above, so peculiar in itself
from all others, and at the same time so conclusive, that an
outline of it is here given.

When I make a diagram in subjective construction, as a
mathematical line, circle, or other figure, I have a product as
pure object in my own consciousness. This pure object I know
as occupying a place in a space, and yet that the object and
space are within and not external to me. Still they so condition my own agency that I have in the same light of consciousness the constructing act and the constructed product, and thus
an *ego* describing and a *non-ego* described. I cannot make the
radii of the circle unequal to each other, nor the diameter and
the circumference equal. I can move two such mathematical
circles further from or nearer to each other, and unlike two
material rings, I can put one in the same place as the other,
and in such identification in place I can no longer know them
as two circles. I am in so many ways conditioned by them,
that I know them as objective to me and not identical with
me, and yet as object within my subjective being.

Again, I have in the organ of the eye floating colored spots
more or less defined, and I am conscious that they appear and
perhaps move quite independently of my pleasure, and are
not, as the other, products of my agency. They are in a
space, and they and their space are out of my inner consciousness, as clearly as the pure objects and their space were within. Still, I also know them as only organic in this, that direct
the organ as I may, and perhaps close or open it, they are
there and the different ordering of the organ does not modify
their appearing. There is an *ego* and a *non-ego*, and yet the
non-ego is only so far objective as to be but an organic affection.

Once more, I am conscious of appearances which I neither
produce nor order, and which will not come within consciousness except as my eye is open and in a specific direction, and
I know them as affecting the organ from without and not in it.
But now, in all the above cases of pure object, false vision,
and true phenomenon, they are wholly subjective so far, that

they are *my* objects only, and have significance and pertinence only for myself. No other can commune with me in reference to them. Their places and periods, and changes, and relations among themselves, are in *my* consciousness alone, and their world, whether within or without, are *my* worlds, and as such they are no worlds for any other percipient. I have not in this any proof of an outer world common to me and other percipients.

But lastly, instead of fugitive and transient phenomena passing promiscuously in and out of the consciousness, each in its own space and period, I have the phenomena in an ordered and determinate experience; the phenomenal qualities determined in permanent places relatively to each other in one whole space, and the phenomenal events determined in successive and contemporaneous periods relatively to each other in one whole time, and thus have my own well-ordered experience of a world of phenomena as a connected nature of things. And not myself only, I know that all others have their phenomenal qualities and events in the same ordered experience, and that all together have them in one common space and one common time. And now it is *à priori* impossible for varied subjective experiences to connect their phenomena in a common space and time, but each must have them in his own separate space and time as in our dreams, if each be not ordered from the same space-filling substances and timefilling causes. That there is then this common space and time in all men's experience is proof irrefragable that they have one and the same objective world of realities. No possible egoistic Idealism nor organic Sensationalism could put their phenomena together in one common space and time.

4. If the Rational Psychology was designed to overthrow skepticism, especially in the form of Pantheism, yet, it is objected, the design has wholly failed of its end, and has even terminated itself in Pantheism. This is sustained by affirming that it holds God to be the immediate author and upholder of the forces which compose matter, and thus makes the force or matter to be God; and also, that it teaches matter to have been a necessary product of the creating Deity.

In reference to this first charge, it is admitted that the philosophy of both the Psychology and the Cosmology holds that matter is an immediate product from God, and also that without his immediate support it would cease to exist. A created creator of the material universe, or a created upholder of the material worlds, must shut out all manifestation of the great Creator and leave only the creature to be known and worshipped, to say nothing of any higher absurdity. Any other medium between God and his creating work must be both independent and eternal, and this must so condition the Creator that he can be no absolute God. Any philosophy that shall teach the existence of the universe in any way as only mediately dependent upon God, either in its origin or continuance, must be an Atheistic philosophy. Instead of an objection, it is the necessary postulate of a Theistic philosophy, that it should teach matter to have immediately originated from God and perpetually to be sustained by God. The Bible doctrine of the Logos-creation is wholly consistent with this, for the Logos-creator was with God and was God in the beginning.

The other objection would be fatal to the philosophy, if it were truly directed against it. That there was some necessity in the nature of the case, as in the nature of the sun to produce light, or other than a moral reason that God should create matter, would subject God himself to nature, and leave no other God in reality but Nature. God would then himself be nature, and matter naturally evolved from him. It will subsequently appear that this is really the philosophy of the critics and not of the Psychology.

The Psychology carefully and completely attains the conception of spiritual being as that which is rational and free, and of God as Absolute Spirit, governing himself by what he knows is due to himself, or worthy of himself, or for his glory. He should take the best plan in creating and governing, and that is the best which will most honor himself, and there can be but one best plan. The best is also the right, for it is his right that he work for his highest honor. This moves as a claim, as something due to himself, and not as a want or sentient craving. It was best and right, therefore God creates;

not that God created, and therefore what he creates is best and right.   An ethical behest and not a natural necessity directs the ways of God.   Thus, from himself alone he creates substantial force which takes position and holds place, and in this material being begins, and nothing but God has any thing to do with it.   It is origination from nothing except its Author. Such force might have been many separately balanced molecules, and these put together individually, as we heap up grains of sand, but such world-building must follow some outer model and not an inner law.   The forces also might have lines of antagonism such as would bring masses together in any possible forms of crystallization, or of chemical cohesion, and the inner determining law would bring out the specific polyhedron for the world's form.   But the simplest possible process resulting in the most complicated but orderly product would the most likely be taken as wisest and best, giving most honor and glory to the Maker; and when we carefully follow out such process of generation in a perpetually augmenting creation of force at a centre, growing and crowding out the old from the central point in the determinate order of the law for the composition and resolution of forces, we find a cosmology thoroughly conformed to the facts and movements of the actual universe of matter about us.   God could arbitrarily at any step have broken in upon this orderly and determinate movement, but the highest wisdom demanded the persistent following of the law of forces, and the orderly and beautiful systems of worlds come from it.   Here is no necessitating nature, but a free personal Creator producing nature from himself in the wisest way and for the highest good.   He begins and consummates in absolute reason.   Here is neither Atheism nor Pantheism, but pure and positive Theism.

Atheism has worlds with no *à priori* laws.   All things are with no reason why they are.   Pantheism has worlds evolved from some efficient source, but that source already has in it all that may ever come out, and what comes out follows the already constituted arrangement in the rudimental source.   All is nature developing itself after its already possessed intrinsic law, and has no law-giver nor primal originator.   Theism has a personal absolute spirit, originating and guiding action according to what is a self-demand, and he makes and manages nature in his eternal reason and wisdom.

So much, in answer to the criticisms of the Psychology, and which brings us to a more important and interesting investigation.

5. The extended religious skepticism of the day. The fact of a wide-spread and persistent skepticism, coming out in varied periodicals and essays in foreign lands and in our own, needs no proof. That it is so extensive and persistent evinces that it is not an obstinate and arbitrary doubting, merely because doubt is wished for and has no reasons. So also, if it is the result of delusion, the same facts prove the delusive mistake to lie deep down in the current thinking of the age, and that its exposure and cure may not be hoped for as the result of any superficial examination. The truth really is, that the skepticism grows logically out of the prevalent philosophy which has been put beneath our theology, and to which the skepticism is indigenous while the theology is blighted by it. The religious world has its philosophy, and in some forms of controversy uses it extravagantly and unmercifully, but when applied to the recognition of a personal God, it directly impugns the conviction and sustains a pantheistic conclusion. The whole cannot adequately be exposed within the compass of the present article, and yet it may so far be indicated that observing minds shall apprehend it, and the method of cure be so intimated that thinking minds will be ready to catch and finish it, though at the shortest the statement must still be somewhat extended.

We will first give the facts of the philosophy in its varieties, and then show the general mistake in which the illusions of the skepticism arise, and which will be dissipated wholly and the skepticism vanish when the mistake has been corrected.

There is a form of philosophy, which indeed is the denial of all philosophy, that restricts itself wholly within the phenomenal. Colors, sounds, etc., as qualities given in sense may be known, and thoughts, emotions, etc., as exercises within may also be known, and as coming within consciousness these can

be compared and classified according to their perceived relations.   They have their places and periods and uniformities in
coming and departing, and we may call such as group themselves in the same place, substance; and such as come and go,
cause; and the uniformities in coming and going, laws; and
thus talk of a nature, but which nature has nothing in it that
one can know, save that appearances arise and depart in such
and such sequences and concurrences.   So appearances *are*,
we have no data nor capacity for philosophizing as to *why*
they are.   What *makes* them at all, or what makes them *so*, is
an illegitimate speculation.   We have no faculties for attain-
ing such cognitions.   We may talk of forces moving the inert
objects, but the conception of force is only a generalization of
motion and uniform sequence, and we know nothing of powers
but only antecedent and consequent.

A man who so philosophizes may have a Theology, but his
theology will be independent of his philosophy.   He may put
his theology to the help of his philosophy, and make God the
immediate connection for the separate qualities and exercises,
and thus say that phenomenal nature has its direct constitution in God; but on the other side, he cannot put his philosophy to the help of his theology, for his philosophy teaches that
he cannot conceive even of God's agency as any thing other
than simple separate exercises.   The philosopher, who is true
to his philosophy, can have no theology.   All phenomena and
their observed relations and uniformities are positive, and he
can positively affirm and deny concerning them, but all metaphysical speculations of physical forces and spiritual agencies
controlling the material and mental phenomena, are for this
philosophy wholly beyond the reach of our faculties, and, especially, all theological notions of a Maker and Governor of
the phenomenal world are wholly empty of all evidence, and
can come only from a superstitious fancy.

With this positive philosophy, the emptiness of all metaphysical and theological speculations, is still more abundantly
manifest from the necessary contradictions and absurdities
which they involve.   The positive philosopher can speculate,
but the inevitable contradictions induced warn him that he

has got beyond his depth, and that the topics he is considering are in an abyss, to the human mind wholly unfathomable. Space and time seem to have attributes beyond nature, and to open a way to the absolute, and speculation may here enter and investigate her metaphysical and theological questions, but she is brought up at once by endless absurdities. What is limited we can know, what is infinite runs at once into contradictions. The limited can never be carried so far that there will not be occasion to go farther. We can expand in space beyond any limits yet reached, and divide beyond any point yet taken. The smallest circle is still as infinitely divisible as the largest, and from the centre the smallest circle is no more infinitely expansible than the largest. Infinites are themselves infinitely different among themselves, and an absolute which should embrace any or all in a whole, is an absurdity. So of time as of space, its infinites have infinite contradictions. And so also of motion and rest ; a rapid motion cannot be but it must have gone through all the intervening degrees of motion, and these degrees are infinite and each must have had its time, and the present rate of motion could not have been reached but in the lapse of an infinite time ; and so for rest, the diminution of motion must pass all the intervening degrees, and the point of rest from motion must be attained only through infinite degrees and an infinite time. And then, suppose the absolute whole of space and of time to be attained, they are two absolutes, separate and independent of each other, and if they give any thing, it is the absurdity of two independent, absolute Deities ; and still further, the absurdity of two Deities, neither of which can be conceived as any thing but empty capacities, which cannot fill themselves. Positive philosophy thus positively proves the human incapacity to recognize any absolute Deity. All theology is a delusion and a contradiction, and the world is fast becoming wise enough to leave its worn-out dogmas and ritual duties to the credulous and the superstitious. Let now the religious man and the skeptic alike embrace this philosophy, as they often do, and how is the theologian to convince and cure the skeptic ?

Again, there is a philosophy that rises out of the phenomenal in sense, and recognizes a capacity for judging and know-ing by the notions in an understanding.   It admits a function other than that which can *construct* in space and time, and assumes a function that can take the phenomena of sense and *connect* them discursively into substantial things and causal series of events.   All phenomena have their substantial ground, and all passing events have their causal sources, and in these notions of substance and cause are connected all phenomenal qualities and events, so that they are known to be bound to-gether as a whole, and all make one universe.   The substances condition their qualities, and the causes condition their events, so that a nature of things is admitted, and there are inherent efficiencies working after laws which make the uniformities. They do not know what substance and cause are ; they have no knowledge or conception of their intrinsic being ; they cannot philosophize about them, but only connect and judge by them.   With them they can conceive of a connected and continuous process of nature, and know nature as an orderly and beautiful whole—a cosmos.

Now such a philosophy may have a theology, but its theol-ogy is wholly extraneous and independent.   It may use its theology to account for the origin and stability of its sub-stances and the efficiency and regularity of its causes, but it cannot employ its philosophy in expounding or defending its theology.   Its philosophy knows how to expound nature in its connections, but it denies to the human mind all knowledge and conception beyond nature.   That substances should have qualities, and like substances like qualities, and also that causes should produce events, and like causes like events, this can be conceived and known ; but that substance and cause should have an origin from that which is not still substance and cause, or that qualities and events should have an appear-ance and succession not conditioned by their substances and causes, cannot be conceived.   The philosophy can recognize no supernatural, and its votary can, consistently with it, acknowledge no personal absolute Deity.

There may still be much speculation in the attempt to find an absolute substance and a first cause, but the contradictions and absurdities here evince the weakness of the human mind, and that it has gone beyond its legitimate limits when it would enforce the doctrines of a spiritual theology. The law of thought is to connect in a judgment the present conditioned to a former conditioning, and when the former is reached, that also becomes a condition demanding a former conditioning, and a first or absolute conditioning cannot be thought. It demands a cause which is not caused, or which has no constitutional efficiency and order of development, and would be the absurdity of putting uniformly out when it had nothing rudimentally and regularly within. An original conditioning of all conditions cannot be approached, for at any assumed cause as the first, there must still be that within it which demands the recognition of a previous conditioning that it might be what it is. The very conception of cause is that of an already conditioned, and an absolute cause is the absurdity of a conditioned absolved from all conditions. The philosophy is thus truly Atheistic, inasmuch as to it a supernatural, personal cause in liberty is an absurdity, but the speculation naturally and necessarily terminates in Pantheism. This assumed first cause, which has already its conditions within, and above which it is impossible for speculation to reach, evolves itself successively and interminably in the phenomenal flow of universal nature. Our philosophy cannot transcend this primal conditioning, and that cannot deviate from its conditioned evolving. In the One is already the All, and the primal efficiency goes down into and through every link of the series. To say that all our knowledge is of the conditioned and the relative, is to affirm that all theology, except as Pantheistic, is to the human mind necessarily a contradiction and an absurdity. With this philosophy, limiting all knowledge and conception to the conditioned, alike embraced by the theologic believer and the skeptic, as is extensively done, how shall the believer convince the skeptic, or even interpret to himself or others his own creed ?

That there may be an escape from the physical necessities in the connections of nature, this philosophy is modified by adding to it a sentient nature, as a counterpart to the material substances and mechanical efficiencies of the outer world.   A source for feeling is recognized as originally in man, and its susceptibility to gratification, as sentient, is conformed to the objective appliances in the world without.   Some objects without are congenial, and some repulsive to the sensory, and the impulse to get and enjoy is according to the intensity with which the objective motive pleases the sentient craving.   The condition of the executive impulse is the longing desire, or the converse repulsive loathing, and the action is determined in what it is deemed will give the highest gratification.   There may be from experience a judgment in general consequences overbearing present appetite, but the last dictate of highest gratification must determine the stronger motive and the executive act.   The man can do as he pleases ; and what pleases, and how much it pleases, is grounded in the constitutional sensory and its adaptation to outward nature.   The sentient nature is in fact one, though having many channels for outward application, and the ultimate alternative is always that of different degrees in gratification.   This impulse from the sentient nature is known as will, and can go out as best pleases, but cannot go against the pleasing, and cannot turn upon itself and change or modify the pleasing, but can go unhindered in the direction of the pleasing.   In this is freedom, and this free agency is the only one conceivable.   It is conditioned in the constitutional being of the sensory, and such constitution is conditional for such and only such pleasing, and in the circumstances such pleasing is conditional for such and only such execution.   Outer nature and inner sentient nature conform, and what the material and the sentient conspire to make pleasing, is the end which will be sought and, if practicable, gained.

And now this modified philosophy may be held in connection with a theology, and it may be attempted to use it in support of the theology.   Its disciples will admit that with nothing but the mechanism of material working, no theology can be reached except pantheism, and that there can from it be no conception of origination or miraculous intervention.   But with the conception of free-will, they affirm, there comes in the consistent doctrine of creation and miracles. Even man, it is affirmed, can interfere in nature, and though he does not destroy, yet he often contravenes nature's laws. He throws a pebble from him, and contravenes gravity and interferes with the law and order of nature, and certainly it may then be readily conceivable that a free Omnipotence may execute his pleasing, and make worlds and modify them when they are made. When, however, they apply this philosophy to man, they teach him by it his helplessness and shut him up, in all inability to change his heart and life, to an outer sovereign interposition. But if they so apply it to God, as is logically demanded, they necessarily exclude all spiritual theology and all conception of sovereignity, and nothing but pantheism is possible. The highest sentient nature has its constituted pleasing, and which is as helpless of change as the human, and God finds himself impelled by his pleasing which he cannot modify but only execute. His sentient craving as naturally and necessarily develops itself under interminable conditions as the unfolding of vegetation. All is still nature, and matter, animal, and man run on their conditioned changes, and all are determined in and a development of the sentient nature of the Deity.

But again, this philosophy of condition and conditioning has its modification in a more imposing, profound, and masterly method. It rejects the mechanics of matter, and the impulses of the sentient, and employs the living activities of the intellectual agency only. It goes back through the phenomenal to the logical laws of thinking, and follows carefully and keenly the living movement through its consecutive logical process and statement. In the opening limit for this living thinking-movement, the thinking-process is as zero. There is yet no movement, and thus no statement; no process, and thus no product. In this point, absolved from all phenomenal positing, being is as naught, for it is a living-process which yet has no movement, and a living-law which yet has not guided. Here, to all thought, being and naught are identical. But the living-movement once away from the limit, and there is immediate occasion for denying that it is naught, and also for a counter-denying that naught is being. In such logical process of counter-negations, being is no longer abstract, but positively a distinct *standing out* from naught, and has thus become *existence*. But the living movement cannot rest in existence, it goes out from it and denies all limitation in advance and thereby states the infinite, but it also has the counter-denial that *it* is infinite, and therein states the finite, and in this counter-negation there is the limiting of existence; and thus the stating it as a positive thing *per se*. In such logical process of negation and counter-negation, and of each term positing a new state, the living-movement *throws out and retains* (" suppresses") one cognition after another, till it has posited or stated all of nature, all of mind, and come to self-consciousness, recognizing itself as the producer of all that is known and the knower of all that is produced, and having thus within itself omnipotence and omniscience it is complete Deity, the absolute subject and object of all Intelligence. And as the absolute sensory could satisfy itself only by perpetually supplying according to its cravings, so the absolute thought-process can complete itself only by interminably " suppressing" according to the law of its counter-negation.

And now this logical egoism may have its right and left sides, and one side may use the philosophy to sustain its theology, and call the absolute thought process the world-spirit and take it as a true Deity ; but the other side will inevitably force the conviction that the living-movement can never rise above its logical law, and must from first to last be conditioned by it. It is still an absolute in its highest abstraction which cannot absolve itself from its imposed conditions. Whether the positing be assumed as a real or an ideal knowledge, the primal logical being and law holds within itself the whole series, and develops itself with no alternative, and neither has nor acquires any proper personality. In any method of interpretation its only theology must be pantheistic.

Since and beside Platonism, here are the outlines of the world's philosophy. It is wholly restricted in all its modifications within the limited and conditioned, and affirms for itself that it cannot go out to the unlimited and the absolute. It immediately runs into insoluble contradictions and absurdities with

every such attempt.   However much it may be used for humbling man, it can never be used for exalting God.   It may
press upon man a spurious imbecility and helplessness, but it
cannot give to God any dignity and independence.   According
to it, in any of its forms, God is only the highest point of efficiency *in* nature, and we can conceive of nothing *beyond* nature
without a contradiction.   If man may be said to contravene
nature when he works against and overcomes some of nature's
laws, so the animal does this in the same way when he carries
himself up-hill or draws a load from place to place.   But the
motive in both the man and the animal is conditioned in the
sentient nature and its objects of gratification, and the conditions of nature determine the awakened impulse and the consequent execution.   So any assumed contraventions of nature
on a larger scale, as if they were miraculous interpositions of
the Deity, must in the same way be held to have been already
conditioned in previous constitutional arrangement, either of
sentient pleasing or logical law of thinking.   All must philosophically be held as within nature, and the supernatural is beyond the legitimate limits of thought, and cannot be approached
without self-contradiction.

And now the skeptic does not review this philosophy, but
takes it as he finds it.   He adopts it just as the religious believer himself affirms it to be, and then carries it logically out
to its conclusions, and he cannot avoid his skepticism.   The
religious believer cannot help him, but in his philosophy must
confirm his skepticism.   That very philosophy, which the believer uses so confidently for other religious doctrines, must
here establish pantheism.   Any other conception of God is admitted on both sides to induce contradiction and absurdity, and
the difference between them is that one believes notwithstanding the absurdity, and the other doubts because of the absurdity.   The believer essays to rise to a spiritual theology by a
ladder, the rounds of which his own philosophy is perpetually
pulling out beneath him.   His very faith, as well as knowledge,
has nothing on which to stand, that his philosophy does not
present openly to his conviction as self-contradictory.   No alternative is left to his faith but to discard philosophy.   Much

as he may use it in other places, and by it press heresy hard upon his opponent, here, in reference to the being of a personal God, the same philosophy must be decried as an impertinent and arrogant intruder.   His position here virtually is, that all religion is from God and all reason is of the devil ; one you must credulously take, the other you must arbitrarily reject, and then so stand before the world and vindicate your religion and " the ways of God to man" as you may.   The teacher of the coming preachers of the Gospel must have a theology rendered just so contradictory and absurd by his philosophy, and yet say that in this very way he " prefers to approach any man that lives with the sword of the Spirit which is the word of God".   The teacher and the preacher may still not see the inconsistency of their theologic and philosophic doctrines, but while the skeptic clearly does see, will the preaching be very likely to convince and convert him ?   The Bible is not answerable for such inconsistency.   Its theology is not what this philosophy would make it to be, and the theology assumed may truly be a Bible theology, only the philosophy that both hold in common fights against the believer and for the skeptic, and most pityingly does the theologian need a safer stand-point.

And here we turn to the sole purpose of showing how all these absurdities of conflicting infinites and contradictory absolutes are occasioned by a very delusive mistake, but which when fully exposed will at once do away forever the apparently insoluble antinomies perpetually coming up between the reason and the sense, and the reason and the understanding. The sense and the understanding respectively are set to the work of the reason, and from the necessity in the different laws of their working, there must come from such mistaken action, contradictions and absurdities, but which are wholly eliminated when each function is kept to the proper task of doing its own work and executing its own problems.   The whole see-saw between Atheism and Pantheism, and both equally excluding Theism, is made a direct movement to a spiritual theology, when this illusive interposition of the lower function is carefully kept from all intrusion into the field of the higher.   Many good men, yea all really Christian men, will keep their theolo-

gy in spite of their conflicting philosophy, but their erroneous
philosophy is often a great burden to themselves, and a dangerous stumbling-block to their brethren, and a direct shelter
and support to the skeptic, so that on all accounts it is most
desirable that the delusions in which it arises should be dissipated, and that the mistake wholly and intelligibly be corrected.   A few items in the working of the problems of the
reason by the sense, and then again by the understanding, will
give opportunity for showing plainly how the mistake comes
in, and the delusion spreads abroad, and once plainly to see is
forever to remove the difficulty and the danger.

We first take the illusions of the sense in throwing contradictions and absurdities over the working of the problems of
reason.   The function of the sense, so far as we now need to
notice, is a faculty for *conjoining* or constructing within limits
—i. e. for defining—whatever may be given in an organ of
sense.   When color or solidity is given, the intellect must
spread over it, or stretch its agency all around it, and thus attend to it, or it cannot perceive the definite figure or shape of
the quality as lying in space.   And so also it must spread itself
from instant to instant over the successive changes that may
occur, or it cannot perceive the definite period of the quality
as enduring in time.   The sense, thus, can perceive nothing
definitely, i. e. can completely know no object, except as it
has constructed it by carrying its intellectual agency all around
it.   There can, therefore, be nothing for the sense which has
not thus been wholly limited and therein bounded by its own
action.   Thus, to sense, a central point can be no object except as it can be defined by carrying an agency all around it ;
and so, to it, a surface can be no object in depth except as it
can give limit to the surface on both sides.   Every object of
sense in space must have an outer and inner, and an upper and
lower, and every object of sense in time must have a beginning and ending, a before and after.   The sense can definitely
cognize nothing that it does not wholly construct, and thus to
it a mathematical point is no object ; the mathematical line
and the mathematical surface are no objects.   But to the reason, a limit is an object as truly as a limited ; the centre of the

circle as fully an object as its area, its diameter as fully an ob·
ject as a plane, and its circumference as fully an object as a
circular ring.   The reason, thus, has objects for itself which
can be no objects for the sense, and hence, when it has any
problem to be executed by its own peculiar objects, there can
be anticipated nothing but confusion and absurdity if it allow
the sense-objects to be mistaken for its own objects.   And
just from such a mistake, do all the contradictions of conflicting infinites take their rise.

Thus, the reason may affirm that there is an axle in the revolving cylinder which does not turn, and it may state it as its
problem to find such axle.   If now it call in the help of the
constructing faculty, and allow the sense to illude through the
mistake of interposing its object, then at once comes in contradiction and absurdity.   The sense-object as axle to the cylinder must have outer and inner, upper and lower, be a constructed thing which has been defined by an agency all around
it.   Hence the sense-axle must itself be a cylinder; a bounded
object; and which can itself revolve and make it necessary
that you get still an inner axle which does not revolve.   But
any axle to the sense will still be a constructed total, and hence
the necessity for infinite diminutions of the axle, and all the
absurdity of unequal and contrary infinites.   But, if we will
exclude all such mistaking by the sense, and let the reason
alone work its own problem, there can be no contradictions
nor absurdities.   Every diameter of every circular plane in
the revolving cylinder revolves about its mid-point, and on opposite sides of that point, the movements of the two portions
of all the diameters are in opposite directions.   This mid-point
is a limit between opposite movements, and can itself have no
movement, and as being the same for all the diameters of any
one circular plane it becomes a limit at which all the radii of
that circular plane meet together.   So the contiguous points,
limiting all the radii of all the circular planes in the cylinder,
become a central line as axle to the cylinder, and which in no
part can have any revolution.   Now this axle to the cylinder
is, as object for the reason, a mathematical line, a limit and
not a limited; it demands no diminution and can have none, nor

15

give any occasion for conflicting infinites. The antinomy comes from the contradictory laws of the function of sense and that of the reason, one of which must have a limited and the other only a limit, and when the function of the reason executes its own problem there is no antinomy and therefore no absurdities. And just so with all the contradictory infinites in space, time, motion and rest. They can never arise except as there is a mistaking of a sense-limited for a reason-limit. .

So is it with contradictions when we approach the infinite by *diminishing*; the contradictions come from a mistake in a different way when we go out after the infinite by *expanding*.

The line extended or the circle enlarged never reaches a limit that may not be surpassed; but as, to the sense, there is no definite object in space except as its construction has been completed, so the longest line and the largest circle are yet finite, and the largest may yet as infinitely be augmented as the least. The point is thus as near infinity as the longest line or the largest circle. The reason can however say that there must be a whole of space which includes all its parts, and it may propose its problem to attain a cognition of infinite space. If, then, it allow the constructing function, as the sense, to come in here and delude by mistaking the sense-object for the reason-object, there must arise the perpetual absurdities of contradictory infinites. The sense-object must be constructed, and to sense there can be no object and no known space but as the constructing act has gone all around and limited it. To the reason there is the infinite as space without limit, to the sense there can never be an infinite, and thus mistaking the one for the other there must be antinomy and absurdity.

But let the reason clearly apprehend and do its own work, rigidly excluding all mistaking of sense-objects for her own, and all contradiction and absurdity will be wholly avoided. While space, as an object in sense, comes and goes with every sense-construction in and out of consciousness, and no space is known save as some space is conjoined within limits, to the reason, space itself becomes object without any construction or conjoining of limits within it. The reason cognizes space itself as a concrete, every part adhering to its contiguous parts

and no part movable from where it is and transferable to any
other place.   Every portion of space holds its own place and
there can be no putting more in nor taking any out, and therefore no void of space either within or out of any part of space.
To the reason, then, space is already a unit prior to any sense-
constructions in space, and there can be no *extra* space which
is not already concrete with all space.   Here is a true infinite
with nothing finite.   Just so soon as we construct a limited
within space we spoil the infinite by putting a finite over
against it and then have only two finites, one within and one
without the limit.   Exclude all sense-object, and space is to
the reason a one concrete object changeless in its infinity with
no contradiction nor absurdity.   Herbert Spencer notices,
"that when we imagine a limit, there simultaneously arises
the consciousness of a space existing beyond the limit", and
this nascent consciousness of space outside the bounds he affirms "though not definite, is real".   "So when we think of
any definite cause there arises a nascent consciousness of a
cause behind it."   But of this outer space or higher cause, he
says, "duty requires us neither to deny nor affirm personality".
Still, he answers to Mansel's and Hamilton's contradictory absolutes, "let those who can, believe that there is eternal war
set between our intellectual faculties and our moral obligations.   I for one, admit no such radical vice in the constitution
of things".   But exclude all sense-limit in space, and space is
to the reason a concrete infinite.   The finite is as irrelevant to
the reason-object as the infinite is to the sense-object.   There
is contradiction only in the confounding of the cognized objects of the two distinct functions for knowing.

But after all, the cognition of Infinite space and Eternal
time would help us but little in our spiritual theology.   We
may remove the reproach and annoyance of perpetual contradiction, but infinite space and eternal time can never have any
efficiency nor ever become personality.   There would be nothing in such infinites to trust, to love, or to adore.   If we thus
relieve philosophy from absurdity, we still do not attain a
spiritual theology.   Religious skepticism for any personal
Deity may be held as pertinaciously as ever.

But we will now pass from all speculation about pure space and time, to the qualities and events which occur in space and time. While we restrict our knowledge to experience, we have the sense-phenomena as qualities connected in their substances and the events with their causes, and all the passing changes in experience are judged to be the orderly development of nature, but this inner working of nature is a mystery wholly beyond all comprehension or conception, and the static substances and dynamic causes are wholly inscrutable beyond what the phenomena reveal. No phenomenon, and then no substance nor cause. Power is wholly inconceivable except as working in and through some inert matter as apprehended in sense. Substance and cause are no objects but as appearing in the standing or changing qualities. When, then, we follow successive events backward to find a First Cause, we run at once upon our old solecisms and absurdities. The first quality would be an event needing a prior quality as its cause, and we are thrown directly amid all the contradictions and conflicting infinities of an eternal series. A sense-quality must always be if a cause is, and as no quality can be thought as coming from nothing, so quality and event must eternally have been coming and departing. The sense-object is phenomenon as thing in itself, and all changes in the phenomena are induced by some powers working in and on them beyond our perceiving and thus impossible to become objects for our cognition. The experience-objects are the phenomena in their sequences, and they must have first been for the powers to work in them.

But to the reason, power itself is an object. The forces which constitute the substantial matter and the causal changes are themselves the ground and source for all qualities and events, and must have been prior to them and determined the whole order of their coming and going. The experience-object in the passing phenomena is as nothing separate from the reason-object in the essential force. Let there be space-filling forces, and these are to the reason substantial space-filling matter, and the phenomena are the modes of its expression through the senses. These substantial forces changing their internal working, the phenomenal expression through the senses must correspondingly vary. Let force work on and in force in accordance with the mechanical laws of the composition and resolution of forces, and the substantial matter has its determined laws of change, and the sense-phenomena their determined order of succession. When, then, the reason works its own problem of a first substance and cause, and excludes sense-phenomenal objects, the substantial space-filling force is its object, and it knows that phenomenal qualities and events can begin in that and go on their interminable successions. An acting force already is, and it may be holding itself in balanced rest, or be in loco-motion from unbalanced antagonism, or be working intrinsic changes from its inner unequal energies. The series begins in it, and the absurdity of eternal successions is excluded by the existence of a substantial force, in which all phenomenal being and succession, and thus all sense spaces and times, have their beginning.

This again only removes absurdities, but does not help to a spiritual theology. The reason-object as efficient may be the physical force, the sentient nature, or the living thought-movement, and in either case will hold within itself the conditions of all phenomenal events that shall come after. Of itself, this solution of the problem would establish Pantheism, for it makes the All that shall be, already to be in the existing One, and the development of the One into the manifold can have no alternative of either fact or order. In this way, neither creation, nor miracle, nor liberty, can be possible conceptions. We have eliminated all contradictions but the last and greatest contradiction, namely, an endless flow of conditions and conditioned, with no originating nor directing author. We need an unconditioned source, and have not found it. Our first cause has already a constitutional nature, and can evolve itself only in a particular way, and the determination of that way is already given rudimentally within it. "The philosophy of the conditioned", which can know only through "plurality and difference", can reach to this pantheistic position logically, and may intelligibly remove all contradictions, but it can mount no higher. With Baden Powell, we have to say, that our admission of miracles must " depend upon the *nature* and *degree* of our Theism, which may vary through many shades of opinion ". A personal God can work miracles, for he is supernatural ; a pantheistic Deity can work no miracles, for this is nature itself, and must express in the development only that which is within, and just as it is already conditioned. And this philosophy can in no form admit the conception of a supernatural. It denies knowledge ; it also really though not confessedly destroys faith. The very object of the faith is a necessary contradiction in the philosophy, and the two cannot stand together. The process and result, the steps and the landing-stair, are thorough absurdities, and the faith can only be arbitrary credulity. There needs an exposure yet of one more fundamental mistake.

The highest object for an understanding, and one which the reason gives to it as its medium for connecting in judgments, is that of force, which as statically balanced is substance, and as working changes is cause. The understanding conception of cause is always that of an already conditioned efficiency, working out only what has been put in, and just as put in. An assumed first cause is still a conditioned efficiency, and working out an already constituted nature.

But the object of reason, for its own work of comprehending, is another and higher kind of cause, namely, a cause in liberty. Not that which can merely *grow* as a development of what rudimentally now is, but that which can *originate* the rudiments that subsequently are to grow, and determine their conditions of growth. And such object it gets in knowing itself. As rational spirit, reason knows itself to possess an intrinsic excellency, and not that it is a mere commodity. It is itself an end of action, and not a means to some further end. It knows its debasement when put to serve any animal want, and if it has itself consented to any such service, it knows its guilt. The reason can act from what it knows is due to itself, and can thus originate and guide action from a law within, and not wait for a law imposed. When law is imposed from higher authority, i. e. higher reason, it still obeys from what it knows is due to itself, and that it would debase itself and incur guilt in not obeying.   Such self-action and self-law is person, and not thing, an agent who can use and refuse to be used.   Here is a cause that can originate and direct action without being bound in the conditions of nature's causes, and is thus thoroughly a supernatural cause.

Such personality may have within him the ideals of all possible being, and the capability outwardly to express them, and the self-claim that what shall be so put out shall be worthy of himself, or to his glory, and then such person will stand independent of nature and absolved from all possible conditions that are not self-imposed in his own right, and he will in this be absolute Person, with all the attributes and perfections of Deity.   He can be known perfectly only to himself, but may also be known to beings of finite reason, so far as he shall show himself in his works or communicate himself in revelation. He can, however, be known only in the reason, and be no object as phenomenon in sense, nor as substance or conditioned cause in the understanding.   Such an absolute personal Agent can be Creator, and the Governor of what he creates to its consummation.

Let, then, the Reason keep such Object of absolute personality in view, and exclude the conditioned causes which are object in the understanding, and work its problems of creation and moral government by its own objects solely, and there will arise no contradictions nor absurdities.   Such a Creator and Governor acts from his own worthiness' sake, and not mechanically, nor from a craving appetite, nor from the logical law of the thinking-process ; and as the fountain of all being, he originates from himself all substantial forces, and sentient natures, and thinking-processes, after the determinate counsels of his own wisdom.   This reason-object is conditional for all understanding-objects and sense-objects ; the Person is conditional for the substance and cause, and all their changing phenomena.   As clearly as the reason sees space and time to be necessarily implied in all sense-defining, and substance and cause in all understanding-connection, so clearly does it also see an absolute Person to be necessarily implied in all reason-comprehending.   The phenomena cannot be defined but in their spaces and times, nor connected but in their substances and causes, nor comprehended but in a personal Creator, who has put into nature's causes all the conditions of nature's changes.

Not only does all contradiction and absurdity cease, but all skepticism and Pantheism are excluded, when in our philosophy and psychology we know the sense and the understanding and the reason as the different functions of the one Intellect, and rigidly keep them at work, each in its own province, and using only its own objects for solving its own problems. Philosophy has deluded and wearied herself long, and given her aid in the service of skepticism, and perplexed the thinking world with seeming inexplicable anomalies and antinomies, simply by mistaking the functions and the objects of the sense and the understanding for those of the reason, and setting the former to do the work of the latter. Philosophy is to-day strong and in large masses denying all knowledge to the human mind as possible, beyond what the sense can construct and the understanding can connect, and wholly ignoring the function and the objects of Reason, except as men ignorantly employ them spontaneously and unconsciously. The mistake is fatal to a spiritual theology, and no matter whether prejudice or negligence conserve the false philosophy, the skeptic will take the advantage of it. The logical understanding cannot be a substitute for the comprehending reason, any more than the dead can do the work of the living. It is as philosophically as it is theologically true, that "the natural man receiveth not the things of the spirit, for they are foolishness to him; neither can he know them, for they are spiritually discerned ".

Art. III.—FREEDOM BETRAYED BY THE EVANGELICAL ALLI-
ANCE OF ENGLAND.

EVANGELICAL CHRISTENDOM, JAN.–DEC. 1862.—ARCHBISHOP WHATELY'S LETTER TO
MRS. STOWE.

THE *Evangelical Christendom* is a monthly periodical conducted by members of the Evangelical Alliance in London,
and its design is to advocate and promote the interests for
which the Alliance was formed.   In the formation of the Alliance in 1846, the subject of American Slavery was the one
grand obstacle to carrying out the objects of the organization,
and so strong and intense were the anti-slavery feelings of the
British members, that the effort to form an Alliance nearly
failed, because the American members would not admit the
principle that no slaveholder, under any circumstances whatever, should be admitted, while no other sin but slavery was
honored with any special reference.

The *Evangelical Christendom* was pledged to freedom from
its birth ; not to any political doctrines, or political organizations, but to the highest Christian principles of freedom.   The
Christendom and the Alliance have freely and uniformly expressed their sympathy for suffering humanity in all parts of
the world—in Italy, in Spain, in Africa, in Turkey, in Sweden,
in Austria, and in *Dahomey.*   From all its antecedents, we
had a right to expect its fullest and warmest sympathy with
the North in its mighty struggles against the great sla: ehold-
ers' rebellion.   But we have searched in vain for one such
expression of sympathy.   Each number has a *Monthly Retrospect,* designed to sum up the matters of chief moral and religious interest which had occurred during the month reviewed.
In these " Retrospects," there is an occasional reference to
slavery which, taken by itself, would indicate anti-slavery sentiments ; but there is constantly exhibited an unfair, and we
are compelled to say also, an untruthful tone of criticism upon

the North, and in no instance is there distinctively expressed any condemnation of the character and aims of the rebellion.

In the number for January, 1862 (p. 51), President Lincoln's proposal to employ negro labor is represented as a "step in measured though intelligible language towards *raising a servile war*". His proposal to establish a plan of colonization for the freed blacks willing to remove from the country, is represented as a design to transport the whole negro population, North and South, free and emancipated, to some genial clime. An act of deliberate, designed inhumanity, and an act of the most absurd folly, are here charged upon the President, who had exhibited the most unexampled forbearance towards the basest of rebellions. But not a word of abhorrence is spoken, not a whisper of disapprobation, for the bloody crime which had inaugurated the war.

In the March number, after implying that the American Government has not sufficient credit to obtain supplies from its own contractors, it remarks : "The only redeeming feature in this calamitous strife, is that the slave influence can never be so powerful again " (p. 168). There is, then, no patriotism, no love of freedom, no hatred of slavery and oppression, in the strife. Its only redeeming feature is the incidental result that slavery will be weakened. American Christians have given themselves and their sons, and their wealth, to what they believed to be the holiest war freedom ever waged, and their brethren of the Evangelical Alliance deny that there is one redeeming feature, one right or noble motive, in their struggle. The only thing it does not strongly condemn, is an incidental result.

We regard the libels of the political newspapers, malicious and insolent as they are, as far less significant of the wonderful change of sentiment upon slavery and America, than this almost incredible course of the Alliance. If there is any thing in Great Britain which we had a right to rely upon as true to our cause, it was the Alliance. The grand deception which has been practised upon us will not be repeated.

In the April issue, the war is characterized as "a suicidal conflict ", and yet it is regarded as important that the President " recognizes the slave question as at the bottom of the whole difficulty " (p. 216).　Does the *Christendom* intend to teach the Christian world that a Christian nation ought to submit to the dictation of a slaveholding minority, and that to resist is *suicide?*　Has slavery suddenly become such a social institution in the view of British Christians, that it ought of right to override all other institutions, even to the dismemberment of a nation, and that whatever its claims, resistance to it is to be denounced as suicide?　It will doubtless disavow any such intention, but this is the logical result and natural influence of its teaching.

In the number for May, " The war is carried on with increased bitterness, rapine, and slaughter.　There is an increase of ferocity and savage hatred on both sides " (p. 270).　There never was a war conducted with the forbearance which the United States have shown towards the rebels, under provocations which no other government ever so patiently endured. Of the people of the United States, no class has entered into the war with such steady and persevering zeal as the evangelical Christians of all the free States.　When they are denounced by British Christians as ferocious savages, and especially when they are so denounced by the Evangelical Alliance, is it the surest way to promote brotherly love?　Is this keeping the unity of the Spirit in the bonds of peace?　Or has the Alliance *faced about*, and does it now intend to throw overboard the American Branch, because of the national resistance to the slaveholders' rebellion?

In this same number, without expressing the least sympathy with American Christians, black or white, suffering in Southern prisons, without a word for those who have been tortured unto death for merely refusing to join in this bloody rebellion, the two or three Spanish prisoners are spoken of in the following truly Christian and refreshing manner : " We regret we are not able to report any improvement in the condition of our persecuted Spanish brother, Metomoros, and his companions. Notwithstanding the promises of O'Donnell to the deputation that waited upon him, these persecuted men are still undergoing the penalty for their fidelity to conscience and to God's

Word.   There is no present hope of their punishment being mitigated.   But our trust is that a higher than earthly power will interpose on their behalf.   At the request of the Evangelical Alliance, simultaneous prayer was offered for these confessors in most of the gatherings for prayer that were held on Monday, the twenty-first ult."

In the June number, we have the astonishing announcement that the negro population do not hail the Federalists as their deliverers ! ! (p. 320).   We could pardon this in a political newspaper, sold to Southern interests.   It would well become the *Times*, but we did not suppose a Christian editor, a member of the Evangelical Alliance, capable of such perverseness.

The steady flow of victory for the North is acknowledged, and then haste is made to show that it will accomplish little. It is all characterized as "miserable fighting", from which "a few good results have already been obtained".   These few good results, thus slightingly mentioned, and slipped over as hardly worthy of mention, are, slavery abolished in the District of Columbia and in the Territories—in all the regions of America, in fact, where the Federal government has jurisdiction (p. 320).   This is all the notice which the *Evangelical Christendom* deigns to take of this grand stride in the moral progress of the nineteenth century.

A few lines below, the modification of our treaty with Great Britain in regard to the slave trade, is pronounced "an ample compensation for all the evils of the war".   The treaty was the natural result of the predominance of the Republican party, and had no connection with the war.   But the moment Great Britain becomes a party to a measure, how its magnitude expands and fills the entire field of an Englishman's vision !

In the July number, we have " the deplorable war in America ", " the most malignant passions of our nature more fully developed, mad shouts for victory, conquest, subjugation, and blood ", drown every feeble cry for peace (p. 360).   This is plainly intended for the North.   Such language would not surprise us in the *Richmond Inquirer*.   It has always accused the North of blindly and madly shouting for conquest and sub-

jugation.   But when our brethren in England, our brethren,
too, of the Evangelical Alliance, join with the South in this
cry against us, is it possible to regard it as any thing less than
the intentional sundering of every tie which binds English and
American Christians together?   It is vain to reply that the
Evangelical Christendom repeatedly and distinctly avows its
opposition to slavery.   Of what value is this avowal, while on
the same page it pours contempt upon those whose efforts and
sacrifices are the only hope of the termination of slavery? of
what value while it holds up to the world as *ferocious savages*,
all who resist the slaveholders' rebellion ?

In the August number, the successes of the great slaveocracy
are painted in glowing colors.   " In Tennessee, the Confederates are overpowering their opponents, and threaten Nashville,
where *the Protestant clergy* were lately sent to jail because
they refused to take the *new oath of allegiance to the North*"
(p. 417).   Does the *Evangelical Christendom* mean to teach
that *Protestant clergymen* are privileged to be traitors if they
are only slaveholders and Southerners?   Was the threatened
disaster to the Northern arms a Divine retribution for the crime
of *imprisoning Protestant* clerical traitors? The oath required
of them was the ordinary oath of allegiance to the United
States.   Why is it here called the new oath of allegiance to
the North?   Does the Evangelical Alliance of England decide
that no such government as that of the *United States* exists,
and that in resisting slavery we have become a horde of Northern barbarians, fighting for the conquest of foreign States?   If
this be the view of the Alliance, American Christians are
thrust out of the pale of the Christianity represented by the
Alliance, and both we and they must take the consequences.

But while " the Protestant clergy " who were imprisoned for
being traitors—and traitors for the blackest and direst purpose
of keeping four millions of their fellow-men and fellow-Christ-
ians in the most accursed bondage—have thus a word of sympathy and the shield of a Divine providence held before them,
what of those faithful ministers of the Gospel, few but noble
men, who, in Tennessee, in Texas, and in other places, have
been tortured, shot, or hung, for simply refusing to join the

slaveholders' rebellion ? Their sufferings and martyrdom have not been considered worthy of a mention in any number of the *Evangelical Christendom* for the year 1862.

It joins, however, the Southern howl about General Butler. American Christians understand that howl perfectly well. It is the cry of the slave-fiend, who is *hurt*, and who begins to fear that his time is short. They can also understand, though not without a blush for human nature, why the British Parliament should degrade itself by joining in with the slaveholders' cry. But that the Evangelical Alliance should do so is humiliating, and a disgrace to our common Christianity.

In the September number, " the civil war ever darkens down into more savage ferocity ". " The thoughtful observer cannot fail to be struck with the insignificance of the causes that are producing these mighty events. So far as America is concerned, there are hardly two men who can agree upon the questions the North and South are fighting about " (p. 470). This is the deliberate moral estimate of the *Evangelical Christendom* in regard to this gigantic war, in which the liberties of four millions of slaves are involved, and the ulterior and greater question to be decided is slavery or freedom for an entire continent. Indeed, in the next number (p. 515), it is coolly announced, without an expression of regret, that " as matters stand at present, it seems more likely that slavery will be spread over the North than exterminated at the South ". Still the cause of the war, which it has repeatedly confessed to be slavery, is *insignificant*. A few millions of slaves to be freed or continued in hopeless and cruel bondage ! Slavery or freedom for the whole United States, north and south, that is all ! It is nothing which British Christians feel any interest in, or regard as of the slightest importance !

When we see such moral monstrosities put forth in a calm, sedate, religious publication, representing the religious sentiments and principles of England's most Christian men, it requires a large faith to believe that her Christianity has not become corrupt and worldly and the slave of political opinions. The *Evangelical Christendom* itself is a periodical of little influence and but little known in this country. We give it this prominence simply because it represents the opinions and feelings of men widely known and of great influence in Great Britain.

What is *omitted* inthese Monthly Retrospects is quite as remarkable as what is inserted, and quite as significant of the feelings of the Alliance class of Christians in Great Britain towards us.

Most of the great moral triumphs which have already accompanied the struggle, are passed over in absolute silence. When the Southern army, flushed with victory, rushed into Maryland, a slave State, with the most undoubting confidence that the State would rise in mass and welcome them, the volunteers hardly balanced the deserters. This remarkable change in the views and feelings of the people of a slave State with regard to the slaveholders' rebellion, was not considered worthy of notice in the *Christendom.* The advance of the Southern army into Maryland was announced, but its retreat was never noticed, and it seems to suppose the army still there !

The emancipation spirit of Western Virginia is nowhere noticed. The remarkable change of sentiment in Missouri is nowhere referred to. The Union demonstrations in New Orleans have not a line. The fearful sufferings of Union men in Tennessee, Kentucky, and Texas, the cool-blooded murders of men and women for not falling down and worshipping the slave-power, are nowhere referred to! The honor of the South is kept immaculate !

The December number closes the year by leaving the North in " a storm-whirl of passion". It expresses an apparently innocent surprise at the irritation of the religious papers of New York towards England, and wishes they could see their own faults as others see them, and at the charges of jealousy, envy, hatred, and ill-will bandied across the Atlantic by sections both of the English and American press. It stands in the temple of God in the pride of its own purity, waiting to see others strike upon their breasts and cry : " God be merciful to me a sinner !"

The Evangelical Alliance closes the year with a cool, rigid, and severe indifference and consistency. With a spirit akin to Papal supremacy, it has presumed to exclude America, in the agony and bloody sweat of her fearful struggle with slavery, from the sympathies and prayers of the Christian world. This supreme hour of slavery and freedom on the American continent, this nation clothed in mourning, are not to be referred to in the week of prayer which the Alliance organizes for the Christian world. If any defence is attempted it must be from the subjects assigned to Saturday, which read thus: "Thanksgiving for our numerous temporal blessings and spiritual privileges; prayer for kings and for all in authority, for all who are suffering from war or necessity or any other affliction, for all sorts and conditions of men". There is no reference here to the four millions of slaves any more than to the nobility and Queen of England; there is no reference to America more than to the Montenegrins, the Circassians, and the Chinese; in a word, distinctive and special prayer must not be offered for her in her hour of trial. If God shall send her salvation it will certainly not be in answer to the prayers of those British Christians who represent the Alliance.

This course has not been pursued by the Alliance without warning and remonstrance. The General Conference, which met at Geneva in 1861, passed resolutions strongly favoring our country's righteous cause. The Paris branch, partly in view of the Anglican neutrality and indifference, issued, Oct. 25th, 1862, an address to *all the members of the different evangelical denominations in the United States,* in which they bore true and unflinching testimony to the real character of the conflict going on in our country. We cite a few passages:

"It is true the Evangelical Alliance is bound to raise itself above all differences which separate religious or political parties. But here it is not a question of one of those accessory points of doctrine, of discipline, or of organization, which here divide evangelical Christians. It is a question of those great ideas of justice and injustice, and of the supreme law of charity, in the name of which our Alliance was formed. It would be a lie if it interdicted itself from protesting against those great social iniquities which dishonor the Gospel under which it is attempted to shelter them.

"It cannot remain indifferent while in an age when the conscience of the world condemns slavery, and all the countries of Europe, except Spain, have abolished it at the cost of great sacrifices, and when Russia has just, by an admirable effort, emancipated thirty-five millions of serfs, Protestant theologians are seen attempting to justify that institution by the Bible, and men inspired with their doctrines excite an atrocious war to maintain the enslavement of an unfortunate race.   The Alliance feels itself directly wounded in the faith which it professes, when it assists at so monstrous a spectacle as that of a Confederation which boasts of being Evangelical, (evangélique), yet at the same time is founded (as one of its principal magistrates has said) on slavery, as 'the stone refused by the builders', but which is precious in the sight of God.   The Evangelical Alliance would no longer be the great association of fraternal love that it is, if it forgets those hundreds of thousands of brethren in Jesus Christ, who are now sold in the South like wretched cattle, marked with a redhot iron, and who often perish under the lash of pitiless drivers.   Nor should we be less wanting to our duty towards those of our brethren in the South, who have voluntarily associated themselves with a colossal enterprise formed to perpetuate and to extend slavery, if we did not declare to them the profound sorrow which we feel at that spectacle, the fearful scandal which results from it, and the immense damage which they are causing to the interests of our Divine Master."

This document was signed by Guillaume Monod and Georges Fisch in behalf of the Paris Committee, and Oct. 29th approved by the General Conference of the French-speaking branch of the Alliance assembled at Geneva.

Strongly contrasted with this is the action of the British branch in its Sixteenth Annual Conference at London, Oct. 14. The Paris branch had addressed to them a special communication, which elicited a warm discussion.   Rev. W. Arthur nobly advocated our cause with his accustomed fervor.   In general terms opposition to slavery was expressed.   But there was a very careful avoiding any statement which might imply that the cause of the North was the cause of freedom ; or that the North should be sustained ; or that the Union might be restored ; or that the rebellion was unjustifiable.   The most that could be gained was the passing of the following "compromise" resolution :

"That the fraternal communication received from the Paris branch be affectionately acknowledged ; that the best thanks of the Conference be conveyed to our French brethren, for their expressions of warm interest in the operations and success of our branch of the Alliance, with the assurance that we participate in their deep sympathy with our common brethren in America in the fearful calamities which have sprung from the war now rag-

16

ing. That this Conference desire to express their deep sorrow for the continuance of the civil war, and the fearful amount of bloodshed and suffering to which it has led. Believing that sin is the cause of God's sore judgments, and that the evils connected with the maintenance of slavery in the South, and complicity with those evils in the North, are one great cause of this solemn visitation, they renew their expression of the earnest prayer that peace may be restored, that these evils, and all others which have led to these calamities, may be removed, and the immense resources and energies of the American churches be set free to promote the cause of the Gospel of peace and love. They desire further to record their conviction, as British Christians, that the duty of our country is to read in this war not a warrant for self-righteous pride, but a loud call to humiliation, prayer, and repentance, lest our own many national sins should draw down upon us in turn the judgments of God. That considering further the distress thus occasioned to large classes in our country, they recommend that November 9th be made an occasion for public and private confession of sin, and special prayer on these grave subjects, so far as practicable, in all the churches of Christ and Christian families throughout the land."

This, then, is all that the most "evangelical" of British Christians can say to us in the midst of our intense conflicts for the maintenance of the Constitution and laws, and after Congress and the President, the whole legislative and executive power of the country, by a series of the most solemn and momentous acts, have deliberately put themselves upon the ground of freedom. This Alliance knew well the whole series of acts by which the Government has been purging itself of complicity with slavery, and yet they still taunt the North with "complicity with its evils", as if the history of the past two years had no being or meaning; they imply that the North is still criminal as well as the South. They know that the rebellion was fostered, and the Confederacy established, in the interest of the slave-power, and yet have no testimony to bear against it. With a fearful unconcern they plant themselves in the centre of indifference between the free Republic of the North and the slaveholding Confederacy of the South, and preach the Gospel of peace, which, in their view, can only mean that we shall let the South be consolidated as an independent power.

One of the most remarkable parts of this debate is found in the reported speech of the President of the British Alliance,

Sir Culling Eardley. In this country, where the real sentiments of the "Southern brethren" upon the matter of slavery
are well understood, such appeals afford matter for merriment
at the simplicity of the noble speaker, rather than of sympathy
with his Christian wisdom. " Southern brethren", he says,
" you are free-traders, and therefore know what the word
competition means. Now I should like to whisper in your
ears, or rather, if you would not think it unkind or un-Christian, to thunder in your ears, Competition. Compete with
President Lincoln! Take the wind out of his sails! (*sic*.) He
is emancipating, some say, your slaves badly; do you do it
well. He is doing it as an act of war; do you do it as an act
of peace. He is doing it instantly; do you do it safely and
gradually. . . . Do you give every negro the right of buying
his freedom at a price fixed by law. You want troops: do you
declare that every negro who will serve in your army shall
instantly be a free man." Now, why won't you? Do! What
a charming simplicity! What ineffable confidence in the
power of evangelical exhortations! We have not yet heard
of any response from " the Southern brethren".

We are profoundly grieved at this attitude of the Evangelical Alliance. Formed for the promotion of Christian union,
it has proved faithless to its own mission and betrayed the
cause of the slave under circumstances that will never be forgotten in America, and will never perish out of the records of
history. The suffering operatives of Lancashire have proved
themselves nobly faithful to the interests of humanity, truth,
and freedom. Men like Newman Hall, one of whose admirable lectures lies before us, and Wm. Arthur, and Spurgeon,
(not to speak of Mill, Cairnes, and Newman), have done much
to place this great rebellion in its true light before the British
mind. All honor to those who have " faithful stood among
the faithless". Their labors have been in vain among the
titled, wealthy, and influential Christians of Great Britain.

We care comparatively little for the *Times*, the *Post*, the
Saturday Review. Let the dead bury their dead. It is the
Christianity of Great Britain in its high places that has be-
trayed our hopes and our confidence.

We append a singular contrast to the course of the *Evangelical Christendom*. The extract below is from the Annual Retrospect of 1862, found not in any Protestant periodical of England or Europe, but in the *Anatolikos Aster* (the Oriental Star), the official organ of the Patriarchate of the Greek Church in Constantinople — a source to which we could not look for sympathy, hardly for justice. We give a faithful rendering of the original :

"The United States of America, after many years of union and peace, after gigantic material and moral development, are separated into two hostile camps. The Northern States, guided by true reason and evangelical principles, persistently seek the abolition of the slavery of the blacks. The Southern States, blinded by a badly understood material interest, obstinately and anti-Christianly seek the perpetuation of slavery. This war of ideas and physical interests is prosecuted to desperation. Bloody battles are delivered, but victory until the present is doubtful, and the return of peace does not seem near. But if we cast a careful eye upon the wonderful events of this age, we shall be inclined to believe that those who contend so nobly for the most unquestionable and humane rights will, God helping them, reach the object of their desires."

We cannot refrain, in conclusion, from adding another instance illustrating the tone of British sentiment in high places towards this country, though it is not directly connected with the doings of the Evangelical Alliance. We refer to the letter addressed to Mrs. H. B. Stowe by the Archbishop of Dublin, bearing date, Palace, Dublin, January 6, 1863. It may be taken as indicating, with an almost judicial impartiality, not to say indifference, the state of opinion prevailing among even the most thoughtful and charitable representatives of the ruling class in church and state in Great Britain. And it shows how little they are aware of the real nature and magnitude of the issues involved in this war. Consciously or unconsciously, they ignore the vital elements. The object of Dr. Whately's letter is to exhibit "the prevailing sentiments here on American affairs". He says :

"Of course there is a great variety of opinion, as may be expected in a country like ours. Some few sympathize with the Northerns and some with the Southerns ; but far the greater portion sympathize with neither completely, but lament that each party should be making so much greater an expenditure of life and property than can be compensated for by any advantage they can dream of obtaining.

"Those who are the least favorable to the Northerns are not so from any approbation of slavery, but from not understanding that the war is waged in the cause of abolition. It was waged, they say, ostensibly for the restoration of the Union, and, in attestation of this, they refer to the proclamation which announced the confiscation of slaves that were the property of secessionists, while those who adhered to the Federal cause should be exempt from such confiscation; which, they say, did not savor much of zeal for abolition.

"Many, who have a great dislike for slavery, yet hold that the Southerns had at least as much right to secede as the Americans had originally to revolt from Great Britain. And there are many who think that, considering the dreadful distress we have suffered from the cotton famine, we have shown great forbearance in withstanding the temptation to recognize the Southern States and break the blockade. Then, again, there are some who are provoked at the incessant railing at England, and threats of an invasion of Canada, which are poured forth in some of the American papers.

"There are many, also, who consider that the present state of things cannot continue much longer, if the Confederates continue to hold their own as they have done hitherto, and that a people who shall have maintained their independence for two or three years will be recognized by the principal European powers."

He then states that this is the ordinary procedure, with some illustrations.

"Moreover, there are many who say that the negroes and people of color are far from being kindly or justly treated in the Northern States. An emancipated slave, at any rate, has not received good training for earning his bread by the wages of labor; and if, in addition to this and his being treated as an outcast, he is excluded, as it is said, from many employments by the refusal of the white laborers to work along with him, he will have gained little by taking refuge in the Northern States."

The letter concludes with the statement of the plan of Bishop Hinds for gradual, compensated emancipation. Though Dr. Whately says that he is not himself "responsible" for the above views, yet they plainly show all that he knows, or thinks best to say, in favor of the United States and against the Confederacy. The omissions are as significant as the positive statements. No allusion is made to any of the acts of our Government for the past two years, which relieve us of responsibility in the matter of slavery in the District of Columbia and in the Territories. Not a word is said of the army orders forbidding the return of fugitive bondsmen, freeing all who aid our cause, and confiscating and freeing slaves held by rebellious masters. There is not an allusion to the President's proclamation of September last, announcing his emancipation order to be issued the first of January, 1863. Of these things, it seems, they do not talk in the cultivated and godly circles of England and Ireland. Can it be, that they have never heard of them? Nor is there any reference to the causes of the war, or to slavery as one of these. That, too, they willingly are ignorant of. Nor is the question raised as to the ultimate destiny and welfare of the black race, so long and cruelly oppressed, and of which the English people have been the special advocates and champions for at least a quarter of a century. They have ceased to speak of this, even in connection with a war of which it is the central problem. Whether the South will emancipate, and whether emancipation would be more sure under the triumph of the North, or with the independence of the South, is not a debated point.

But what they do think and say is, (1) that the war cannot yield any adequate "compensation" for the "expenditure of life and property". But why not, if this Republic can thereby be made a united, powerful, and free Protestant community, stretching from the Atlantic to the Pacific, from the lakes to the Gulf? Why not, if the spirit of secession, the foe of all true national life, can thereby be extirpated? Why not, if our broad Western lands can be opened to free settlers from all the countries of Europe, where no poor man can get an inch of soil, he may call his own? Why not if this country can become a first-rate power among the nations of the earth, with an army and navy equal to that of any European monarchy, and able to resist further European encroachments upon our continent? Why not, if thereby the curse of slavery can at length be eradicated, and all men enjoy their actual rights? Would not this, if practicable, be some "compensation" even for the loss of so many lives and the expenditure of so much money?

But it seems (2) that this war is not waged for "abolition", but for the Union. If it were waged for "abolition", would that insure us the Archbishop's sympathies? His significant silence on all the measures that imply emancipation is still more puzzling, if this be the fact. And it is also clearly implied, that if it be a war for the Union, that is reason enough for England to be indifferent to the issue. But now just suppose, that it is a war for the Union, and that the success of this Union would probably give the death-blow to slavery, might not this be a fair statement of the case? But it seems that Dr. Whately's well known logical skill did not suggest to him this combination. Might we not hope, that, under that aspect, he would see some cause for throwing a heavy weight into the Northern scale? And with this in view, the difficulty he suggests about exempting the slaves of loyal men is no real difficulty. It is not formally a war for abolition, but a war against treason. Hence we cannot punish the loyal by confiscating their property. But, if we punish the disloyal by such confiscation, the doom of slavery is well nigh insured. And besides, the President's proclamation does announce freedom to all in the rebellious States, with compensation to the loyal. Is not that quite enough? Ought not this to satisfy even an English abolitionist?

(3.) "The Southerns had at least as much right to secede as the Americans had originally to revolt from Great Britain". But the cases are far from being parallel. Were the colonies living under the same Constitution with Great Britain, and had they ratified this by a solemn compact? Were they represented at all in the Parliament which taxed them? Did the revolted States complain, as did the Colonies, of an infraction of their chartered rights, and could they point to a single case of wrong and oppression by the General Government? On the contrary, had not the Government really done their bidding for half a century? Was there any constitutional way in which the Colonies could obtain redress for their grievances? And has a part of a State a right to revolt at pleasure? Would England allow Ireland to do so, because her Colonies once revolted?

(4) As to the "forbearance" of England in not breaking our blockade—our only wonder is, that Dr. Whately could speak of it without rebuking the unrighteous and illegal suggestion. How could such a violation of all international right be tolerated by a Christian bishop? The "threats of invading Canada" in "the newspapers" of course do not implicate our Government. And it is long since even our newspapers have alluded to the matter, and then, under the prospect of collision with Great Britain. .

(5) The Archbishop's statement of international law on the question of recognition is very loose, and against all English precedent. To "maintain independence for two or three years" he seems to think quite enough. In the debate in the English Parliament in 1824 on the recognition of the South American Republics, Lord Lansdowne, in an elaborate speech, maintained the position, that, in order to such recognition, it must be established "that the contest was substantially at an end", and that this was a question, not of mere "policy", but also of "right". The question of the recognition of Peru was at first not entertained on the express ground that "the contest still subsisted". This general ground was also maintained by the leading statesmen of both parties. In 1778, the Marquis de Noailles communicated to the English Government, a treaty of commerce made between the Court of Versailles and the American States. This was referred to in the King's message as an "offensive communication", and orders were sent to the British Ambassador to withdraw from the French Court. The message adds that "his Majesty trusts he shall not stand responsible for the violation of public tranquillity, if he should feel himself called upon to resent so unprovoked and so unjust an aggression on the honor of his crown and the essential interests of his kingdom, contrary to the most solemn assurances, *subversive of the law of nations*, and injurious to the rights of every foreign Power in Europe".*

(6) The last point made in this Letter is, that the negroes are said not to be well treated in the Northern States, and hence

* See an article, signed Historian, in *The Times* newspaper, London, January 28, 1863.

will gain little by "taking refuge" there. He is "excluded from many employments by the refusal of the white laborers to work along with him". Does the Archbishop happen to know who these "white laborers" are, that refuse to work with the blacks? that they are chiefly his own compatriots, the immigrant Irish? All this is, we confess, very unjust and cruel; but it can be righted only by the progress of emancipation. The fact, that the blacks are generally held as slaves has fostered this prejudice. It can only be eradicated, when the laws fully recognize their manhood. And the sympathies of the Englishman, who rebukes all such prejudices, ought to be with that part of the nation, whose policy favors emancipation.

Such in substance are the reasons, which one of the most distinguished and able prelates of the Anglican church gives for being indifferent to the issue of our great contest: and this indifference favors the South. The epistle may not be profound or sagacious, but it certainly is full of meaning. It has a suggestive force. It indicates that the ruling class in Great Britain do not desire the success of our free institutions: that they would rather tolerate the existence of slavery in a separate Confederacy than have us again united under one flag, even though it be the banner of impartial freedom. They know full well, that the essence of our conflict is found in its testing the strength of Republican institutions; and that, if the United States are now successful, the problem is solved. They also know, that the war was fomented in the interests of slavery, and have come to be willing that the Confederacy should succeed, not for the sake of its slavery, but for the sake of its aristocratic element, and because this great Republic will then be rent in twain, and can be dealt with more easily by the powers on the other side of the Atlantic. But, happily, there is another power in England besides that of the aristocracy; it is the power of the people, who are fast coming to understand, that our victory is their victory, and our defeat their defeat. A few more such gatherings as those of last month at Exeter Hall, and in the chief towns of Great Britain, will give vent to the long pent-up fire; and then, let those of England's statesmen who will, talk of breaking our blockade. The masses may for a time be drugged with base fallacies and decoyed by false lights, and for a time seem indifferent where freedom is at stake ; but let them once be informed and aroused, and no power on earth can resist their influence or stay their course.

And the resistless course of events, the ordering of divine Providence, is fast bringing out into clear light the substantial forms of the conflict, and dispersing the mist of partial and selfish theories. The question is, Shall there be on this earth a great and free Republic, where man as man is honored, and labor has its rights and its reward ? The question is, Shall a caste govern the people, or, can a people govern itself ? The question is, Can a whole nation be educated into the dignity and consciousness of freedom ? The question is, Shall a slave republic be permanently organized upon this American continent ? No sophistry, no prejudices, no arts of politicians, can long blink these inquiries. They look us full in the face. They have laid firm hold upon the conscience and reason of all the thinking men of this land. And, in spite of apparent checks and delays, the full power of the United States has never yet been concentrated, with so full a purpose, upon pressing these questions to their solution, as it is now. The conviction is deepening, that, whatever be the cost, this nation must be one and indivisible. It is slavery that stands in the way of our union and triumph. Then let slavery die, that the Republic may live.

Art IV.—DORNER ON THE SINLESS PERFECTION OF JESUS.

[CONTINUED FROM PAGE 64.]

III. The Moral Unity and Harmony of the Life of Jesus.

In proceeding, now to cast a glance at the moral activities that fill up the life of Jesus, it is not our intention to make a catalogue of virtues,* and in this way prove, as by a sum in addition, his moral perfection. In this way we should not arrive at any living idea of his moral character, nor have any guarantee for his perfection. For all virtues attain their perfection only by unity and harmonious symphony, and this exists only when they all proceed from the totality and fulness of the one principle of virtue. This unity of his virtue, by means of which all his virtues are harmoniously bound together, cannot, it is true, be brought into full view without the concrete and the details. But the main point is to combine in one view the most contrasted elements, united in his moral character, and to show in the concrete that one spirit harmoniously regulates and orders all according to one great law of life. Therefore, we shall not dwell on those points in which other distinguished characters approximate to a high standard of moral excellence, or on what is willingly conceded to Jesus by those who regard him as a man of extraordinary virtue (which none without profanity can deny), while they do not concede his sinless perfection. Let our view be specially directed to this point. What is there in his moral character which tells of an unexampled uniqueness, distinguishing him from all the great moral characters whom we know, and to be understood only on the supposition of his inward sinless perfection?

Painting is, in certain respects, better for this than words; for it places the figure before the eye in its unity and totality,

---

* Schmid Bibl. Theol. N. T., A. 2, S. 80.

while human speech struggles to bring it into full view in separate sentences, parted from each other. The verbal representation demands the power of mental combination. The reader or hearer must in this case put all together by an exercise of mind, while in the other case it is presented to the view without effort. On the other hand, language has the advantage of precision and clearness; for much that language easily expresses can only be slightly hinted by a picture without words. For it is especially by the words of holy Scripture and the word in the church that Christ's portrait is most vividly and clearly preserved in the hearts of men.

The church has nourished itself for many centuries on the life-portrait which the gospels have drawn of Jesus; but long as she has already explained this life in her literature and in her life, every age beholds new sides, new nuggets of gold, in the simple and chaste gospel narratives. She is ever discovering new beauties in Christ's character the further she advances; and after so long a time she feels as little need as primitive Christianity to look about for another model than that which has appeared in him. On the contrary, the more it is understood, the more unconditionally, and from all sides, does the living image of Jesus lay claim to a regulating power with the growing consent of conscience. For whatever unveils itself to view as having been realized in Jesus, has also the power of testifying to its inner truth and excellence in every human breast. Hence we must say that the work of no one individual can supply an exhibition of the character of Jesus in its totality and purity; and that it is the business of the whole church, the business of her contemplation and life, in a course of growing imitation, to make him ever more and more fully understood. On the other hand, this great common work of the church can only progress by every age doing what it can to bring out the pure figure of Jesus with greater precision and all-sidedness. The evangelists themselves have each exhibited an individual portrait of Jesus; hence the necessity of a merely individual, nay more, of a limited apprehension of it, which our nature imposes upon us, must not deter us from the task. For the individual apprehension, if it is only not erroneous, will fit into the whole that stands before our eyes, and lives in the heart of Christendom.

The evangelists, instead of supplying a complete picture of Jesus' character, or an enumeration of his virtues, rather give us histories of the doings, the sayings, and the sufferings of Jesus; and in doing so, refrain almost from all reflections of their own, only narrating, objectively and chastely, what they learned or saw. But still, now and then, feeling overmasters them, and they break out into words in which they strive to give expression to the combined impression made by his person. So John i, 14; xiii, 1, and fol. ver.; xii, 44–50; 1 John i, 1 and fol. ver.; Matt. xi, 27–30; xii, 18–21. The great difference of their narratives—which, however, so marvellously harmonize for the purpose we speak of—is a guarantee for the historical reality of the original character. It could not have become so by collusion,—that is proved by its diversity; while the inner harmony of the features shows that this portrait has not flowed from the invention of the individual evangelists as its source. That it owes its origin not to poetry, but to historical reality, we trust, will be more definitely established in the course of our discussion.

The selection of the historical materials is different according to the aim, design, and angle of vision selected by each, particularly by Matthew, Luke, John. But so far as Jesus showed himself to be a morally perfect character in small things as well as great, there lives in all the details the unity and totality of his character, and hence all that was needed was a true report; and the harmony with which the gospels supplement each other is self-supplied. On this impossibility of inventing the character of Jesus, Channing (*The Evidences of Revealed Religion*, p. 78) has spoken beautifully;—a Unitarian, it is true, but one who, by the love and devotion with which he sounds the character of Jesus, surpasses many a more orthodox delineation, and leaves them far behind. We will consider then, first of all, the different ways in which the image of Jesus is reflected in each of the four evangelists, that we may add some things which may show how the details which they narrate, and which they divide among them, supplement each other, so as to form a complete historical unity; more particularly, so as to place in their true light some sides of what is characteristic and unique in the character of Jesus.

MARK gives least of what is peculiar. In him, the miraculous deeds and displays of power on the part of Jesus preponderate over discourse and over the record of his conflicts; he comes, therefore, only more indirectly into our present consideration, viz. so far as the words, and deeds, and sufferings of Jesus come into a new light, when seen elevated on the background of this consciousness of power and ἐξουσία; for lowliness and condescension have their full moral value only as voluntary self-abasement. With this are connected, in Mark, several additional features, important for the true humanity of Jesus,—e. g. xi, 13; xiii, 32.

To MATTHEW, Jesus is the fulfilment of prophecy—the promised king of Israel, and hence destined to be the light and king of the Gentiles. He sketches the portraiture of Jesus (xi, 27 and fol. ver., xii, 18 and fol. ver. in connection with Isa, xlii, 1 and fol. ver.) in the following way. He states that he represented himself as the servant of God, the righteous one, fulfilling obediently the will of God, the law; as the promised crown of the Old Testament, the beloved Son, in whom God is well pleased; that he should not strive nor cry; that he would rather be quiet, meek, and lowly in his dignity, full of sympathy for the bruised reed and the smoking flax, bearing on his own heart the griefs and sorrows of mankind before he healed them. His scope and object are silent, deep influence on the heart; not public display, nor authoritative dominion. But this quietness, calmness, and patience, and condescension, in his mode of working, are not weakness. The spirit of the Lord is upon him. He brings the crisis upon nations. Conscious of victory and assured, he perseveres in seeking the lost in this silent lowly way, till he brings forth "judgment" to victory. It is just this course that ushers in the sure decision in a spiritual way—that ripeness for judgment which is his victory in relation to foes and friends.—Matthew next exhibits the courage and the divine self-forgetting zeal of the Son. As the truth of Israel, he comes into the strongest conflict with

the falsehood, deterioration, and corruption of Israel, and tes-
tifies against those who established themselves in false ceremonies and ideas, traditions and manners, with all faithfulness,
and with terrible earnestness (*e. g.* Matt. xi, 21 and fol. ver.,
chap. i, 23); for the most part in vain, especially among the
rulers, but saving what was to be saved.   He has no recourse
to measures of authority or violence against his enemies, and
desists not from his work, but patiently suffers the people
whom he loved to reject him and deliver him to the Gentiles.
But it is just by such humiliation that his judgment is " taken
away".   He permits, in his person, sin to execute its judgment on itself, and conducts his work to victory through the
most manifest and deepest endurance of wrong.

In Luke, the physician and helper of the apostle of the Gentiles, we find in an especial manner traits of the tender and
pure humanity of Jesus far above all Jewish narrowness.   He
mentions the gracious discourse in Nazareth (iv, 22); the re-
past in the house of Simon (vii, 36–50); and in the house
of Mary and Martha (x, 38-42).   He records the raising of the
youth at Nain (vii, 11); the healing of Malchus (xxii, 51);
and of the ten lepers (xvii, 11–17).   He narrates those words
of Jesus after his rejection by the Samaritan village (ix, 52–
56), in which he contrasts the spirit of the New Testament
with the spirit of Elias, and impresses on his disciples that he
did not come to destroy, but to save.   Luke mentions the tears
of Jesus over Jerusalem (xix, 42, xiii, 34), and his words to
the daughters of Jerusalem on the way to his death : " Weep
not for me, but weep for yourselves and your children" (xxiii,
28).   He mentions the look of Jesus which he cast on Peter
(xxii, 61).   He communicates the parables of the prodigal son
(ch. xv), of the rich man and Lazarus (ch. xvi), and of the
good Samaritan (x, 30–37), just as he also specially notices,
too, the love of Jesus for publicans and sinners (xv, 1, and fol.
ver. ; xviii, 9–14; xix, 2–10), (Zaccheus).   Luke mentions
with particular frequency the prayers of Jesus, and that he
spent nights in prayer (iii, 21, iv, 42, v, 16, vi, 12, ix, 18–28,
xi, 1); that he prayed for his disciples without their knowing
it (xxii, 32); that he prayed on the cross for his enemies

(xxiii, 34–46). Luke has the sweet exhortation to prayer, (xviii, 1, and following verses). He mentions the word of promise to the malefactor (xxiii, 43), and his walking and talking with the mourning disciples on the way to Emmaus (xxiv, 13–45).

In JOHN there is vouchsafed to us a deeper insight into the *inner life of Jesus.* Jesus knows his oneness with the Father as his constant possession. Thus his consciousness is eternal, elevated above time. Resting in a calm, clear, in-dwelling in God, he looks out from the world's true centre into its complications, and conflicts, and darkness, with an unshaken spiritual clearness. But not only does he *look* into the unhappiness and unquiet of the world, he allows himself to be put in contact with it on every side ; he enters into the unhappiness of the world with the feeling heart of a most sympathetic love, ever promptly following the Father's voice, which he hears within, ever doing what he sees the Father about to do. He does not stand above the world, in the cold abstraction of a merely negative liberty, whether it be in resignation or in indifference and estrangement, nor with that sadness which is powerless to lend a helping hand, nor with that irony which attempts nothing, which leaves what is perverse to its own self-destructive contradictions ; but his inner dignity of nature is united with the tendency to enter fully into men's real position, to penetrate into "the deepest sense of every moment", to bring out its everlasting side, and not only in a contemplative way to place every thing in the divine light, the light of eternity, but to live through every moment in the fulness of spiritual power, and in view of its connection with all the phases of life. And yet, in thus entering into the world and time, he remains himself,—entire master of himself. Hence the infinitely rich applicability of what he says and does. In the details, when rightly apprehended, there always appears again the *ensemble* of his power and nature, and thus every detail wins a more general and typical significancy, appropriate to all times, to the individual and to the church.

In attempting to place before our view, at least in some of its features, what is peculiarly great and unique in Christ's character, according to the gospel narratives, we will not dwell upon the breadth of his views or the depth of his mind, nor the proofs which he gave of fidelity to his friends,* of his truthfulness, even when confession surrendered him to persecution,† of his mildness,‡ and justice;§ nor shall we speak of his other single virtues which come to light in every page of the sacred memorabilia.   We shall only dwell on three characteristic features, all intimately connected, and indicating a soul of peculiar constitution.   The first is the PERFECT HARMONY of his whole being.   The second, his FREEDOM, whereby he knew himself to be in this universe a Son in the Father's house.   The third is his SPIRIT OF SACRIFICE, or his love.

The harmony in Christ's nature is not evinced in such a way that every thing energetic and strong in feeling and mood, in words or deeds, was toned down to mediocrity, feebly and monotonously avoiding the impression of disharmony only by the fact that there is no decisive character or well-defined individuality.   On the contrary, the harmony which we here perceive is the most life-like and active, appearing not as a laborious product, wrung from a conflicting mass of thoughts, feelings, and desires, but as the natural expression of an inner harmony, ever conscious of itself, and maintained by a vigorous will; that is, it is the expression of a harmoniously balanced, holy, spiritual personality.

Let us pursue this point in some of its aspects.   The life of Jesus, considered as a whole, makes on every one the impression of calm greatness (see Matthew, as cited above), which bears a truly marvellous stamp when we reflect that this calm greatness has entered more deeply into general history, and there wrought greater and more lasting effects than that of any one of the heroes of humanity.   His heroism is not a mere natural courage, which has as its auxiliary material power, or the world of resources outside itself, by which its ends are to be realized.   He is solitary, without connection and without outward rank and position, nay, born in mean condition, a

---

* *E. g.* John xviii, 8 ; xix, 25, 26 ; Luke xxii, 32, 48, 61.
† John vi, 15, and 27–66 ; Matt. viii, 20 ; xxvi, 64.
‡ John viii, 1–11 ; Matt. xi, 19–28.   § Luke xii, 13 ; John xviii, 36.

member of a nation despised and hated by the Gentiles, of a
decayed family, yet laying claims to be the King of a kingdom, the Saviour of the world, the Ruler of hearts and minds.
With the consciousness of this aim he was constantly possessed. But even the outward power which he had or might
have he does not use for outward ends.* As his designs were
of an ethical kind, he knew well that no bare power could
achieve any decisive result, and he will not have it, nor rely
on it. His heroism was consecrated to a work which was first
of all purely spiritual, and which could not be accomplished
by man's coöperation. He takes it entirely on himself, with
the clear foreknowledge of the contradiction and hatred of the
whole world,† and conscious only that he is not alone, for the
Father is with him.‡ Great projects are made and executed
by great men. God has given to mankind many heroic spirits who were benefactors, as princes, lawgivers, patriots, and
sages. But there is none who even conceived the thought of
the great work which Jesus proposed to himself and executed.
The salvation, the redemption of a world, which he proposed
as his life's task, as it is the most necessary and daring, so is it
the most undemonstrative and noiseless work, the ἔργον absolutely, the work of works. It is the fundamental work, the necessity
of which the heroes of mankind have not often recognized, not
to mention that they would never dare think of realizing it.
It is a work, accomplished in the deepest silence, covered by
the hatred and murderous hostility of the world; and only after it was finished by Jesus, and by him alone, did it enter
into men's consciousness as an unveiled mystery of a new and
heavenly world of love, which now became the loud and triumphant message of the gospel. Only after it was finished
did the world learn how it had to help on this work by its
hatred and oppression of innocence, and how the triumphant
power of sacrificing love had, in its calm heroism, converted
evil into an instrument for the accomplishment of its work.
For herein is the power of Christ's calm greatness that it combined majesty of character with humility, in an absolute internal confidence and self-repose. Even in the most dazzling

* John vi, 15.   † Luke iv, 23; John ii, 19.   ‡ John xvi, 32.

times of his ministry he is fully aware of the necessity of passing through suffering, and even in his sufferings he holds fast
the assurance of victory ; and as to the future, he is as certain
of glory and of the perfecting of himself and his kingdom
through the depths of his sufferings, as of being despised and
rejected.   That is not heroism, which in this world still hopes
for victory, or makes sacrifices for the sake of personal glory,
or dreads death as an enemy of its work.   Forgetting himself
and undaunted, he offers his life to his work and calling.   It
is a heroism of faith.*   Other heroes manifest their power in
action, or, though more rarely, in suffering.   We must call
him, in virtue of his invincible power of will, truly manly in
the full sense of the word, but we must not on that account
place his characteristic peculiarity in manliness, so far as this
is opposed to the feminine, for he evinces also the entire softness, tenderness, and purity (we may add, too, the power of
suffering and patience) of woman's nature.   This *force of will*
and purity is also accompanied by high *mental endowments ;*
but it would be absurd to designate him on that account as
predominantly subtle or profound, ingenious or imaginative,
for he exhibits all these gifts, but none of them alone.   We
observe in him, besides, various *moods* of mind, cheerfulness
without care, pensiveness and a melancholy mood, exquisite
sensibility, and perfect equanimity, painful sorrow again, and
then joyous elevation.   But we should consider it unsuitable
to ascribe to him, on this account, a temperament in the ordinary sense of the word, for all that is handed down to us concerning him makes the impression of a thoroughly healthy,
harmonious blending of spiritual qualities and a natural succession of mental moods.†

This succession is of such a sort that it, on the one side, presupposes the purity of his nature, the healthy blending of his
capacities, and, on the other side, maintains and verifies his
strength of character and force in will, by bringing the most

---

* Heb. xii, 2.
† Comp. Ullmann, p. 68, Martensen's Dogmatik, § 141, and his sermons
Comp. Schaff's Moral Character of Jesus, Chambersburg, 1861

opposite sides or tones into living, harmonious expression. This we must dwell on somewhat further.

Luke and John in particular show us, that there was in him the most tender sensibility, a susceptibility for the emotions of joy and grief, vivacity and strength of affection, and ever with full self-possession. We can perceive how the affections of joy and sorrow were sanctified in him, and were ever kept in such a pure equilibrium that, far from clouding his mental clearness or weakening his self-control, they only revealed in full measure the power of his inner harmony. This lofty harmony, or rather this strongly-marked power of harmony, evinces itself most strikingly in this, that he always interweaves with his affections of joy and transport a consciousness of the solemnity of his work, and conversely with the affections of sadness and pain, the joy and the sure consciousness of his union with God, and of the glorification to be realized by his sufferings. There is no monotonous, stiff immobility of inner life, no dead insensibility, no stoic apathy; but, far from pride and severity, he is humanly moved by every thing human. And there is also never a one-sided prominence of one side of his moral nature, isolated from the *ensemble ;* but before a vital movement terminates, or is rung out, it is always made apparent that, to the more momentary and single mood of mind, there is not wanting the full complement of all the rest, but that they are inwardly present, coöperating and preserving each movement in its equilibrium, and he thus preserves the unity and totality of the character which unites these contrasts in itself. Let us consider this in some examples.

In the frame of joyful elevation we always find interwoven the consciousness of the solemnity of his career, from which he must not deviate even in thought. When the Nazarenes are full of joy at the gracious words which proceed out of his mouth (Luke iv, 22), he adds immediately, as it were to arm them and himself, "Ye will surely say unto me this proverb—Physician heal thyself". (Luke xxiii, 35, John ii, 19)* In his

---

* If Keim ("The Human Development of Jesus Christ," 1861,) had considered this passage, which carries us back to the beginning of his Galilean ministry, he

joy at the faith of the Samaritan woman he at once thinks of his end (John iv, 35–38). When the multitude will make him king (John vi, 15), he points immediately, in a lengthened discourse, to his death. The joy at the first fruits of confession, on the part of Peter, passes at once into the thought of Judas' menacing treachery, and into the warning on account of it (vi, 70–71); nay, he takes occasion from it to announce his own rejection by Israel as the Christ now recognized by the apostles, and summons them to prepare themselves to deny themselves, and to take up their cross and follow him. They recognized his dignity in the spirit, and this is to him only a token that his disciples are now ripe to be spoken with freely on the subject of his rejection, and to be prepared for it (Luke ix, 20–23, Matt. xvi, 20 and fol. ver.). The first thing which he sought to impress upon his disciples after his transfiguration on the mount was, that he must suffer many things and be rejected (Matt. xvii, 12, Luke ix, 31–44). The honor of anointing him reminds him of his burial (John xii, 7, 8). The arrival of the Greeks who desired to see him was a token to him of the diffusion of the gospel beyond Judea. He celebrates and he signalizes this prospect by the allusion to the corn of wheat which must fall into the earth and die that it may bring forth much fruit (John xii, 20–24). With the full consciousness of his origin and destiny as portrayed in John xiii, 1–3, and which on that evening so filled him that his appearance in word and look was indelibly impressed on his disciple, he proceeded to the ministering office of washing the feet of the disciples, which was to be to them a pattern and symbolical pledge that his near-approaching shame and humiliation were a voluntary self-abasement, a service of love for them (John xiii, 4–19).

could not have placed the expectation of his suffering so far down in Jesus' life, with which there is much else, too, that will not harmonize, even if one permits himself to arrange and order the sources according to *à priori* grounds, the historic evidence of which is disputed. That Jesus expected and desired a kingdom of suffering before the kingdom of glory is plainly shown by the sermon on the mount (Matt. v, 10–12, vii, 22, viii, 11, ix, 18, x, 25–38); that belongs to the elements of his Messianic calling and his knowledge of mankind—above all, to his knowledge of the nature of sin and divine holiness, by which there was imposed upon him the calling to become, through suffering, the atoning "high priest before God".

The reverse of this does not less regularly occur. The woe pronounced on Chorazin, Bethsaida, Capernaum (which is not a curse, but as in Luke vi, 25 and fol. ver., and Matt. xxiii, 13 –16, 23–39, an expression of righteous sorrow, pain, and sadness, and warning), passes into a joyous thanksgiving (Matt. xi, 25–27) for the babes whom the Father had given him, nay, even of contentment that such things must remain hid from the wise and prudent of this world, from the intellectually cultivated, for the pearl of the gospel is too good for all those who will not give their all, give their heart for it. The abasement of Jesus, the consciousness of worldly contempt and rejection, awakens in him the consciousness of his dignity (John viii, 28, compare xii, 32, iii, 14, viii, 40, and xlii, 52 and 58). While at Mary's anointing of him he regarded himself as already dead, and permitted his body to be treated as a dead body, he speaks in the assured tone of one who has power to assign immortality by name to whom he will, and he utters the great word so consolatory to Mary, yet expressive of his confidence that his work would outlast him : " Verily, I say unto you, that wheresoever this gospel shall be preached in the whole world, there shall also this, that this woman hath done, be told for a memorial of her " (Matt. xxvi, 13). And thus, too, to those solemn words, touching his approaching fate, to Peter the confessor (Matt. xvi, 22, 27, 28), he immediately subjoins the majestic words : " The Son of Man shall come in the glory of his Father, and then he shall reward every man according to his works". In like manner, after it was clear to him, at the coming of the Greeks, that before the gospel came to the heathen, he must be rejected by the theocracy and be delivered to the Gentiles (John xii, 27), he is seized indeed with a deep anguish and agitation of mind at the ingratitude of his people, but he closes thus (ver. 28–31, fol. ver.): " Now is the judgment of this world ; and I, if I be lifted up, will draw all men (Jews and Gentiles) unto me ". Splendid results thus did not dislodge in him thoughts of his death ; these again, and his sufferings, did not shake in him the assurance of his victory. Standing as prisoner before Pilate, he says : "Thou sayest it ; I am a king : to this end was I born, and for this cause came I

into the world, that I should bear witness unto the truth"
(John xviii, 37, and fol. ver.). And when he was judged, and
stood as the accused before the high priests, he speaks with the
authority and dignity of a judge to them (Matt. xxvi, 64); nay,
when he hung on the accursed tree itself, ostensibly forsaken
of God, he adjudges paradise and his own fellowship to the
malefactor (Luke xxiii, 43).

The same confidence and harmony, the same symmetry of
character, may still farther be traced on many other sides; in
holy anger against sin along with sympathy toward sinners,
which are both perfectly united in him (John ii, 13, Matt. viii,
23–27); in courage, action, and energy, along with endurance
and patience. All his public acting is attended with suffering
(Matt. viii, 17), and all his suffering is also action, the revelation of a higher power, or, to speak with John, the revelation
of his δόξα. His greatness does not lie merely in the sphere
of susceptibility to God and the world, nor in the sphere of action alone; rather, both are united in him. He is neither a
predominantly moral, nor a predominantly religious character,
for he is perfectly imbued with both; and thus, to employ
Ullman's happy expression, he sets forth a perfect holiness;
for in his hands and in the breath of his mouth every thing is
consecrated to be the symbol of the spiritual and divine; nay,
to be the initial, typical, or prophetic expression of it. The
harmony of his mind—one with nature, with history, and
with the laws of life which regulate it—saw everywhere what
was cognate or prefigurative or preparatory to the kingdom
which he was to found, however conscious he was, on the other
side, of the newness of the gospel which he had to bring.
With nature and its kingdoms, that of the plants and the animals, etc., with home and family—with the state and the history of mankind—with all he is in harmony. What he wishes
is, to be in every thing at unity with the divine law of life,
and the inexorable foe only of that which disfigures, and per-
verts, and desolates creation.

This leads us to the *second* of the points indicated. What is
the root of this marvellous yet living symmetry, which does not
shun to go into the most stirring agitations on both sides, and

yet remains so sure of returning to a pure and perfect moral harmony within ?   What is the root of this calmness in the highest excitement, this mental serenity that enters into the complication of finite and sinful affairs, yet contracts no stain, but, as it were, moves above it like its mistress?   It is perfect *self-possession* and *liberty*.   By means of these he stands forth, perfectly unique and incomparable.   Here lies the historical guarantee for his sinless perfection.

The men around him were either slaves of lust and sin, or self-righteous servants of the law.   The most advanced had a knowledge of the universal bondage to sin, a sense of their separation from God, a longing after liberty, but scarcely a presentiment of their true state.   Thus their life was one of fear and hiding from the nearness of the Holy God, for they lacked the reconciliation, peace with God.*   What an impression then must have been made upon the disciples by Jesus, whose spirit was full of peace and serene cheerfulness, never exhibiting a trace of having achieved this inward peace by a laborious effort or a conflict with sin !   Here is a man in whom there is no trace of remorse, regret, or repentance, a man without care about his soul's salvation, for he stands already in eternal life, he lives as in heaven.   There is no prayer for forgiveness of sin for himself, no shrinking from going into the society of publicans and sinners.   It is clear, in the most decided moments of his life, that he is conscious of no sin.   That his self-consciousness was really of such a sort that his conscience never accused him of any fault or error, is the firmest and most indisputable historical fact, explain it as we may.   That he imposed upon himself as his life-task, the salvation and reconciliation of the world ; that he was conscious, too, of being occupied with the solution of this problem, in suffering even to the cross; and that he died in the full consciousness of having solved the problem, as well as of unbroken communion with God, is just as undeniable as that it would have been an insane and absurd thought to wish to redeem and reconcile others, if he had himself been conscious of needing redemp-

* Comp. *ex. gr.* Luke v, 8, the words of Peter: " Depart from me, for I am a sinful man, O Lord."

tion himself. Now, however (to speak with *The German The-ology*), it is only God and the devil that have no (accusing) conscience. Men in whom the Satanic wickedness does not yet reign, have the consciousness of sin. Jesus evinces, in his entire life and character, the deepest aversion to evil, and especially of hypocrisy, in which pride and falsehood are mated, just as he passed judgment, more severely on the Pharisaic spirit than on publicans and sinners. How then can the phenomenon be explained that He, to whom even skeptics do not deny the rarest measure of purity and clearness of mind, stands before us without being conscious of a single sin, or of the necessity of conversion and amendment which he requires of all others; if not in this way, that he was *conscious* of no sin because he *was not* a sinner. He was, though completely man, like God in sinless perfection ; and though not, like God, incapable of being tempted, nor perfect (in degree) from his birth, and therefore not holy in that sense, yet holy in the preservation of an innate purity and holiness, and by a fully normal development, in which the idea of pure humanity is finally realized in order that the ultimate end of the world might not be unfulfilled. Yes, the impression which he gives us is that of a being *free*, the true Son of Mankind. He needs no regeneration, but is by nature the new-born Man; he needs no remedy, and is conscious to himself of having power to be the Physician of sick humanity. But let us enter somewhat into detail.

How does he feel and conduct himself toward nature as a Son in the Father's house, lingering in it with a free and open sense for nature ; beholding there the laws of the great house of this world, unveiled in their concord and harmony with his work ; or when he stands intrepid amid the storm of the sea, amid his trembling disciples, well knowing that God has his hand upon him even while he slumbers. As his free Son he stands before us in his self-possession, freely ruling his own nature and its powers, using every thing just as a performer strikes the strings of his instrument, with a mastery over himself, and an adaptation to the higher end and mission of his life. He stands before us free, and independent of the world's means and possessions. He seeks no outward possession in it, even when it might serve his objects, but without being careful for the morrow, rests contented with what is before him, knowing that he who feeds the fowls of heaven does not forget the children of men. "The Son of Man hath not where to lay his head." He is homeless and poor, for his mission is not to be the founder of a family, or to use earthly goods, though he highly commends a faithful steward, and never designates the casting away of property as a merit or as any thing good in itself. He can be rich and can be poor (John xix, 23, xii, 3 ; Matt. xxvi, 2–14). There is nothing there of ascetic, spiritualistic virtue (Matt. xi, 9). But yet is to be an example of what is the main condition of all fidelity in earthly things, and also in a stewardship, viz. the weaning of the heart from all vain possessions, which rather makes us bondsmen in mind and body, which enslaves us instead of enriching us, which is not worthy of being called ours because it affords an illusory satisfaction, and cannot truly be assimilated to our true nature, or be imperishable and forever our own. He seeks to sever us from what is foreign that we may be capable of inheriting that which alone can be ours, and which corresponds to the idea of real wealth. He renounces outward property to realize the idea of property such as is befitting the Son (Luke xvi, 12.) He who has been made free, severed from the illusion of earthly possession or the desire of it, carries within him the eternal treasure, he only will be able to become a true administrator of the riches that fall to his lot without necessarily being seduced by deceitful riches. Jesus walks about, as it were, in paradisaic freedom from care, at once poor and rich, not careful for the morrow, not longing after outward glory, and also not rejecting any thing which is the expression and sign-language of love, when a superfluity exceeding the measure of necessity is offered to him (John xix, 23, xii, 1, and following verses). While he has nothing, he can yet call all his own, for the Father gives him what he needs, and disposes and regulates all so as to lead to the central point of his purposes, which govern all. Now this centre is the work of the redemption and perfection of humanity in Christ. Hence Jesus stands before us as the *Free One* in the presence of human powers, a faithful Son of his people, obedient to the law, honoring its authorities and right, typically to prepare the way for his kingdom; honoring, too, the heathen magistrates, and their demands for service; yet in heart far beyond the typical economy, knowing himself to be personally free from the obligation of the temple service, and from care on its account. For he had nothing to receive from it, and could not, without untruth, recognize in the temple and its economy the ideal to which he had to give tithes. (Comp. Heb. vii, 4, and following verses; Matt. xii, 6; ὅτι τοῦ ἱεροῦ μείζων ἐστίν ῶδε, 4–5).* And yet he presently adds, after he had spoken of the temple tax, "Nevertheless, lest we should offend them, go thou, and pay for me and thee" (Matt. xvii, 27).

This unique position of perfect liberty becomes more manifest when we compare him with John the Baptist, and consider the relation of Jesus to the law and to the Old Testament in general. His doctrine about the law corresponds entirely to his own self-consciousness in reference to the law; his teaching is thus but an expression of his own individual self-conscious life, as on the other hand his life is doctrine so far as it reveals the principles of his life.

Jesus felt that he was inwardly at one with the Old Testament. That is actually attested by his entire relation to the Baptist, in whom he sees the greatest of all the prophets, and the summary of the Old Testament, of the law and the prophets. He comes to him for baptism, that the New Testament may, as it were, receive its sanction from the Old, and be ushered in by it (Matt. xi, 10, and fol. verses; iii, 13, and following verses).

* To his disciples he here gives a hint which they, without doubt, understood at a later time. When that is brought to light which is still only inward and hid beneath the veil of the legal economy, they will also be discharged and set free from the temple and its service. For by the plural and by the communicative tone of the entire address (οἱ υἱοὶ ἵνα μὴ σκανδαλίσωμεν αὐτοὺς ἀντὶ ἐμοῦ καί σοῦ), Jesus represents this free position towards the sanctuary as one that would belong also to his disciples. This passage, with others, having reference to the temple (Matt. xii, 6; John ii, 19), proves, therefore, that we are not to conclude, from his silence regarding the abandonment of the temple service and the synagogue, or from Matt. v, 24, xxiii, 19, that the spirit of Jesus was not elevated above the Jewish economy. But more concerning this presently.

Jesus takes up John's preaching of repentance, and of the nearness of the kingdom of heaven (iv, 17 ; compare iii, 2). He finds already in the law the ἐντολὴ μεγάλη, in which all the commandments are comprehended (Matt. xxii, 36–40 ; and he who has the knowledge of this ἐντολὴ is not far from the kingdom of God (Mark xii, 34). The substance of the law remains inviolable in the new covenant (Matt. v, 17 ; Luke xvi, 17). It is easier for heaven and earth to pass away, than for one tittle of the law to pass away. Whosoever shall break one of the least of these commandments, shall be called the least in the kingdom of heaven (Matt. v, 18 ; compare Matt. xxiii, 2, 3). Hence it is manifest that all precipitate breaking with the Old Testament, all reform from without, and not from within, is repudiated ; with which we must connect the fact that he nowhere gives his disciples a commandment to forsake the sacrifices and temple-service, or even to separate from the synagogue, or to drop the sabbath-law. Hence several representatives of the recent Tübingen school have believed that their hypothesis of the Ebionitism or Judaism of primitive Christianity could be historically established by the gospels.

But to the passages which prove that Jesus was conscious of being at one with the Old Testament, there are opposed a multitude of others, which so strongly declare the *newness* of the gospel, that Marcion, on the contrary, thought he could maintain that, according to primitive Christianity, the gospel entirely broke with the law.

These two opposite extremes are indeed at one in this, that they explain a whole series of sayings and narratives as the interpolations of a later time, and hold as non-authentic what the other side regards as genuine, and *vice versa*, without reflecting that this makes them guilty of historical caprice. Rather, as it belongs to the privileges of intellectual greatness to unite the remote, the peculiar spiritual elevation of Jesus is the only satisfactory explanation of the seemingly opposite statements as to the Old Testament.

The newness of the gospel in relation to the Old Testament is as strongly expressed by Jesus as we find it any where in Paul. Unity with the Old Testament is not identity. The

Baptist is not Christ; he baptizes with water, but not with
the Holy Ghost (Matt. iii, 11 ; Acts i, 5). He came ἐν ὀδῷ
δικαιοσύνης (Matt. xxi–xxii, 3, 1), neither eating nor drinking;
he fasted much, and so too did his disciples ; he lived according
to a rigid asceticism (Matt. xi, 18). Jesus came eating and
drinking ; he did not shun the society of sinners ; he demanded
no outward asceticism, but left fasting to be only the natural
expression of the state of mind, but not a prescript. The law
and the prophets reach down to the Baptist ; with him as the
last and greatest of a series or grade, one period of universal
history closes ; with Jesus a new one begins (Matt. xi, 11 ;
Luke xvi, 15), that of the gospel (vs. 16). The least in the
kingdom of heaven is greater than the greatest of the pre-
Christian age (Matt. xi, 14). As to the law itself, Jesus ascribes to himself divine authority to determine what is the
will of God. Such is the scope of this—the six times repeated
ἐγὼ λέγω ὑμῖν (Matt. v), with which he plainly enough places
himself formally far above Moses, who does not thus speak in
his own name. On the other hand, Jesus regards what he
gives, not as something foreign or contradictory to the Old
Testament, but as the development of its pith and marrow, or
as the fulfilment of its promises and shadows. With a view
to delineate the true righteousness of the kingdom of heaven,
he goes back to the essence of it in such sort that he forbids
many things hitherto tolerated by the law, if not commanded,
as an oath, divorce, the right of retaliation,* and he forbids
them, in virtue of what is already demanded in the Old Testament, the principles of truth and love. Of special importance
is his position towards the laws of purification, of sacrifice, and
of the Sabbath. The Old Testament still considers man indefinitely as a unity, without expressly distinguishing between
outward and inward *purity*. It is true it says, " Ye shall be
holy, for I am holy ". But the laws of purification refer only
to the holiness of the body. Jesus (Matt. xv, 11–15 ; Mark
vii, 15–23) lays down the principle, that it is the impurity of

* Personal retaliation, with the implied revenge (Matt. v, 39, and following
verses). He does not thereby dispute the right and duty of the state in this matter
(Matt. xxii, 15–22 ; John xviii, 13–38 ; vi, 15 ; Matt. xxvi, 52).

the heart which defiles the man in soul and body; and that outward (ceremonial) impurity, unconnected with that of the heart, defiles no man. The body and its impurity, it is true, were by no means treated as something indifferent. Jesus himself calls his body a temple: it should be sanctified by us, but from within outwardly. Hence, of course, the Levitical ordinances of the Old Testament, as means of keeping man holy, fall to the ground as a secondary, powerless attempt to exhibit the idea of the undivided holiness of the entire man. But this idea itself remains; nay, is now only to be realized. It is similar in regard to the *sacrifices* to be offered to God. Jesus did not forbid these outward gifts; but in themselves they have no value. Love, mercy, and obedience are better than sacrifice; i. e. the sacrifice of our own will and heart, the sacrifice which is the man himself, is the true sacrifice (Matt. xii, 7; xv, 1, and following verses). Finally, his freedom and his position, elevated above the legal stand-point, evinces itself particularly in relation to the *Sabbath-law*, in his doctrine and in his practical conduct. " The Son of Man is Lord also of the Sabbath." " The Sabbath is made for man, not man for the Sabbath " (Mark ii, 27; Matt. xii, 1–13; Luke vi, 1). God does not need on his own account that men should offer to him a portion of time for himself, to honor him thereby. The Sabbath is instituted for man, for his spiritual and physical nature, as a gift and a blessing, in which Jesus himself rejoiced, though personally Lord of the Sabbath. But it would be selfishness, nay, hypocrisy, to use a blessing given us for the promotion of goodness, as an occasion to abstain from good works.· There is nothing more frequent in the gospels than the collisions into which Jesus is brought with the Jews on account of the cures wrought on Sabbath, which he might have avoided could he have prevailed upon himself to omit any thing good in itself, on account of an offence which was to be foreseen. Whoever considers the power exercised by the traditions respecting the Sabbath, and that the observance of them was regarded as a pillar of piety, will wholly dismiss the thought that Jesus aimed at a show of peculiar piety among his countrymen; for then he must have acted quite differently as to fasting, asceticism, the Sabbath, and prayer. Rather we discern in him the courage which acts out among men what he knows to be good and true, in a firm and self-consistent, free and intrepid way, unconcerned about good report or bad report in the world.

Yes, Jesus exhibited both in doctrine and life a connected and entirely new mode of understanding the law, and man's relation to God. They who regard the law of God as only an external thing, and not within them, never escape, as repeated experience shows, the apparent collision of duties, and a morbid scrupulous conscience, because it is but formally bound by the revealed will of God, but has not come to a free knowledge of its own as to what is the real good (John viii, 32), and falls into an endless casuistry; thus one commandment is turned against another, till every thing dissolves into moral scepticism or probabilism which puts outside itself the knowledge of what is good, and permits a foreign conscience to be implanted in it, if it does not fall into entire indifferentism. Now the characteristic trait of Jesus is, that *he is quite above the legal stage* on which every one stands and must stand, where conscience is awakened without reconciliation to God, peace and an immediate living communion with God. Now, it does not suffice to say, Jesus is the first man truly reconciled to God. For where is there a trace of his needing conversion or reconciliation to God? Rather the breath of an unearthly peace breathes through his whole life; nay, there was in him the power of communicating this peace to those around him. This peace he could have, however, only because he was the free man, free from the curse of the sense of guilt and of sin, free in reference to the law, inasmuch as by the fulfilment of the law he trod and lived and walked above the law on the ground of the liberty of the children of God. He had in himself a knowledge of what is good, and of the will of God, while the servant knoweth not what his Lord doeth. Standing in the law, and the law or the will of God having become a living reality in his knowledge and will, he had that open, direct look of a child or son, which leads back the mind to the simple, to that which " is from the beginning", and takes it away from the tendency to divide the one principle of good·

ness into a distracting multiplicity, the parts of which are in-dependent of each other, and also away from the confusion of Jewish casuistry and its moral collisions. Now since he does not stand before us as a servant subject to the law (though he was conscious that he fulfilled the prophecy about the servant of God, Luke v, 18), but as the Son of the house standing *in* the law, so too is he *the* man who has open access to God, and cultivates free and uninterrupted fellowship with God. Therefore he, the free Son, always calls God Father and not merely Lord; nay, "his Father", as if unconsciously describing his unique relation to God. And because he lives entirely in the law, the law as it were revives in him, he him-self becomes the exhibitor of it, the living law, according to which all shall be judged (John v, 27, Matt. xxv, 31–41). Hence, too, judgment upon all belongs to the Son's rights, of which he is conscious. On the other hand, he will share his Son's rights with those who through the Son have God as their Father, and are made sons of God through the first-born brother. Here again his peculiar dignity and freedom evince themselves. To the Father indeed he desires to lead back all fallen brethren, to himself he will draw all (John ii, 32). But he alone is the bridegroom (Matt. ix, 15), mankind is the bride; he is at the right hand of the Father (Matt. xxii, 44), and as the Son glorifies the Father by the work of man's re-demption, so the Father glorifies the Son, for he is not a mere *means* of redemption, but also has his own proper object, and it is the Father who prepares the marriage for the Son (Matt. xxii, 2; xxv, 1). And so it ever continues to be his joy to make his disciples partakers of his peace and joy.

In the nature of the case those who neither anticipate nor seek this peace, cannot rightly know what is meant by the fact that Jesus, by the fulfilling of the law and prophets, brought peace and a new stage of life, nay, a new era to mankind. They can speak perhaps of the peace of a landscape, of music, of sentimental or æsthetic feeling, which they confound with the peace which passes all understanding, and which is not of an æsthetic but of an ethical and religious nature. They must, if they think logically, regard the stage of legal life as the highest stage of humanity, and as one that is not to be surmounted, and assign to Jesus his place within this platform ; and just because they have no need of a higher, they cannot see why Christ is to be thought sinless, why a high degree of moral excellence may not suffice.   But we have shown that we cannot stop short at this.   Either they must permit this phenomenon to awaken their moral sense, and to awaken the necessity of atonement, in order to find, by means of faith in him, a peace which is neither transitory nor delusive, and new substance for all their life ; or Jesus must become to them less than he was.   They must regard him, in contradiction with their own conscience, and with the impression which he cannot fail to make even on them, as a profaner of holy things, and a fool blinded as to his sin by unprecedented spiritual pride.   But the church of the Lord, because some justify the Jews in condemning Jesus, will not cease to receive from his person the impression of unparalleled innocence and purity— a phenomenon not of this world ; full of a different, new, and holy spirit; so unique and lofty, and towering above all others, that it would involve new self-delusion not to recognize it.   He who has any moral sense knows by experience that the archetype of moral good is presented to us in Jesus. This archetype, where it is known, commends itself by its excellence, and attests its own proper truth in every human breast.   But it is not true that this archetype is in the heart of every man ; it lives only in Christendom, in which the historical portrait of Jesus lives and reproduces itself, but nowhere beyond it.

This obviates, too, the opinion that this personage is a creation of the apostles' mind.   It is certain and beyond doubt that their wonted Jewish mode of thought and feeling was wholly different from that of Jesus, into whose views they could enter only with difficulty and by degrees.   How they reached their subsequent moral and religious elevation fashioned after him is absolutely inexplicable, if we take away the only natural ground of explanation, which lies in his sacred and marvellously attractive person.   We only surround ourselves with a world of enigmas if we despise the only solu-

18

tion of the enigma. We must still further maintain that the conception of such a new and free humanity within the old could not have arisen of itself, without a divine communication of the Spirit, as indeed the essential idea here is just the union of man with God, the real and perpetual fellowship with God. None can speak, as is done in the gospels, of God as the Father but he who has experience of it, whether immediately as the Son, or mediately as those who, through faith in him and not otherwise, are reconciled to God, and made partakers of his peace. Hence, in every instance of transmuting the person of Christ into a myth there is a great *petitio principii*, if not a denial of the new element that is found in the gospel, and which to the church of the Lord is certain and inalienable. There lies in it this opinion, that there cannot be any thing higher than what the gospel terms the platform of the law, and that this cannot be surmounted; in short, that the absolute religion is Judaism, after divesting it, perhaps, of the national and the particular, but also of the promises. That, however, cannot be the absolute religion which leaves room for conceiving the possibility of a higher and more perfect one; which leaves unfulfilled, or suffers to be extinguished, not only among the Jews but also among the Gentiles, the holiest aspirations of the human heart, as well as their most glorious anticipations and promises.

If we have hitherto considered the Son of Man as a unique phenomenon, since he alone stands before us as the Free One, as contrasted with sin and law, and in his relation to God and the world, to nature and the human race, as well as in relation to himself; we must now look still further at the *ground* and *source of this liberty*. Thus only will the contrast between him and all his contemporaries—not excepting the disciples—fully appear, and the impossibility of inventing his character will be manifest. It is holy love; it is, to express it in the language of a well-known English theologian, the *great law of sacrifice*, consciously and energetically carried out to the end—which distinguishes his entire life in the most peculiar, strange-looking, yet world-subduing way.

Christ's character is purely incomprehensible on the principles of ordinary human nature, or from the modes of thought, motives, and impulses of his nation and age. It has its origin in a higher region; in true humanity united to God. All other men we see moulded, in a certain measure, by the spirit of their age and nation. Even in him we do not deny all influence of companions and of history; but the inner nature of Christ, and his moral life, do not bear the impress of the period in which he lived, or of any particular age in general; it has an everlasting tone. He is in this sense, too, the free one. He belongs to no particular age, and yet to all ages at once; for he is the expression of the everlasting life. His appearance is the direct opposite of that which even the pious Israelites had hoped and pictured to themselves: to destroy the myth of the Messianic advent which they had sketched for themselves was his hard task; and just because he would not, and could not, realize this eschatological myth, he earned hatred and rejection on the part of his carnally-minded contemporaries. On his disciples, after he had drawn them to him, we see him unweariedly laboring, with calm wisdom and patience indeed, as they were able to bear it, but also with an equal and constant clearness, fearlessness, and confidence; first to destroy their dearest Messianic hopes, that he might thus make room for what was brought right before them, namely, that which himself he had directly to demand and to give. The same reason which forbade him to oppose directly at the outset their wishes and expectations—expectations of the still unbroken natural heart, trained though it had been in the discipline and order of the theocracy—had also not permitted the Spirit of God in the prophets to communicate more than they could bear. But Jesus had from the beginning unveiled, in his life, and progressively too in his doctrine, love, as the great law of sacrifice—to him his life's law of liberty, and to his disciples the fundamental condition of their regeneration from the death of natural life into that which is spiritual, and of their share in his liberty and blessedness.

We can only indicate, by a few traits, what we mean by this; for the theme is too rich and too deep to be exhausted.

Jesus did not first wish to bring in or gain a worldly reform and a worldly kingdom.*   Moreover, he did not in the beginning count on a general, religious, and moral revolution in the people of Israel.†   He knew his people and the human heart too well, and had too early experience of obstinate resistance,‡ to yield to the illusion that the mere power of his doctrine, or the impression of his deeds, would at once effect that reform, even the new birth, of men's hearts, at which he aimed. From the beginning, his work was planned with more depth, grandeur, and daring ; that is, in such a way that he should not give up his people and mankind, though they should reject him, as he foresaw they would (Mark xii, 32); that he should never cease to love them ; and that his very sufferings at their hands, and for their sakes, should only be turned into the clearest proof of his disinterested love, which sought not himself, but their good.   The purity of his self-forgetting, self-sacrificing love was to kindle up the last spark of human feeling which still glimmers in the hardest sinner's heart, and by awakening contrition and shame, to make room for his spirit of love.

Human defiance may defy all external might and power, or bend before it only outwardly and reluctantly.   To the doctrine of divine wisdom, man may oppose his own wisdom, may arm himself against its assaults ; the example of a blameless life before one's eyes may leave entire the self-righteousness of the human heart, nay, provoke it to maintain a good opinion of its own excellence by suspicious and uncharitable falsehood ; condemning words, however just they may be, might darken still more a heart alienated from God.   Jesus did not think that his deeds of power, or the wisdom of his doctrine, or his blameless life would bring the decision and crisis for hard hearts.   He knew, on the contrary, that, though all this might not pierce the heart, he was in possession of another power, which could operate only after his death, that is, the power of

* Matt. iv, 9, 11 ; Luke iv, 19, etc. ; Matt. xi, 4–7 ; v, 3, 4, 11, and following verses ; x, 16 ; John ii, 19 ; iii, 3.

† Compare the sermon on the Mount ; Luke iv, 24 ; John iv, 44.

‡ John ii, 19–24 ; iv, 1, comp. 3 ; Luke iv, 29.

his death itself, as a sacrifice of love to a world rejecting him. That he fully gave himself up as a voluntary, defenceless, and disarmed victim, only not giving up the love which embraced his people and mankind, and which, when dying, prayed for his enemies—this disarmed the enmity, the pride, the falsehood, and the resistance of the insolent, complacently-wise, and self-righteous heart in a far other way than even reproof and condemnation could do.

How absurdly he seems to act, and contrary to all the usual rules of life! He is full of the kingly spirit; he wishes to become a king, as he is, the Lord of minds, the King of souls; but only by entire self-renunciation, by giving himself up, only not giving up love, and not giving up faith in the power of suffering, dying, disinterested love.

He wishes to win the victory over all enemies, visible and invisible. He wishes the dominion which, he knows, is foreordained for him. But he will have this by subjecting himself to the shame, nay, to the death, of a malefactor, and he consciously and voluntarily gives his enemies their will, to which he falls a victim. From the curse, and what is worthy of the curse, he will draw the blessing, and from death life. It is a thought so grand and bold,—a faith full of marvellous divine originality, in all the calmness of power, a patience and moderation without enthusiasm, purely formed in free obedience to the Father's known will, and carried out to the last breath of life—that nothing but stupidity can deny the impossibility of such a character being invented by his disciples. The disciples themselves, though belonging to "the poor in spirit", and not indifferent "to righteousness", had, without him, no idea of the law of sacrifice, of the spirit and power of suffering love. They clung to the hopes of an outward Messianic glory with a tenacity of self-will which caused Jesus the hardest toil, and more than once extorted sighs. True, they knew that the Messianic kingdom was to be a kingdom of righteousness, but they will have that so mated to their darling hopes that, averse as they were to sacrifice, they expected moral reform, so far as they acknowledged its necessity, on the easier path of the alluring and terrifying, judicial and dividing power of the Messianic glory. , Sacrifice, the cross, and self-denial were to them nothing else than images of terror, against which they shielded themselves with might and main. How should they, how could they, have invented or created the character of Jesus?

But how did this very thing, so thoroughly repugnant and offensive to the apostles, and which seemed a sufficient warrant for rejecting him, how did this divine foolishness of self-sacrificing love approve itself as divine wisdom, as an unveiling of the mystery which contains the unique and conquering power—the power of dissolving all the world's disharmony into harmony, nay, the power of uniting the countless, often self-conflicting powers of the world into the unity of the kingdom of God! All the strife and discord in the world springs from nothing but the spirit which flees from sacrifice, the happy death of the selfish nature. The solution of the deepest enigma of the human breast includes in it the mystery of a spotless sacrifice, which unfolded itself in the whole life of Jesus in an increasing measure till he came to Golgotha.

The entire life of Jesus was a *sacrifice of love;* he regarded true greatness as consisting in self-abasement for men's good ; serving them, but with a high sense of liberty, which can be all things in itself, high and low, poor and rich, nay, which is inwardly of the royal sort, but accepts and uses every thing just as the spirit of sacrifice or of love demands. Requiting hatred with love, far from a feeling of revenge and condemnation, seeking enemies as lost brothers, and consuming himself in such love, he verified that divine self-forgetfulness, from which nothing can be taken, because it seeks and retains nothing for itself, and to which, for this reason, every thing belongs, and hearts must yield. Such loving, in truth, is the emanation of the eternal divine life. It proves itself an absolutely immortal inextinguishable flame, by its power converting what opposes it into what feeds the flame, so that its fire burns the brighter. This view breaks even a rocky heart in two with shame, contrition, and penitence ; melts the ice of the natural heart, which only sought itself and loved itself in poor delusive pride; and displays in the love which " has nothing " the having of all things, the true wealth, the abiding riches, the liberty which none can take away. This love is the power that can move the world, raise it from its entanglements and fetters, heal its distractions, and thus implant it anew in its divine centre. Not of this world, it yet enters into the world, rejoicing with the joyful, weeping with those who weep, in order to serve it, and by serving to conquer it, and by conquering to vivify and glorify it.*

This love, this spirit of sacrifice, cannot, indeed, be in us, in the copy, *without our being first reconciled* and knowing the peace of God. And, as we need expiation above all things, burdened as we are with sin and guilt, therefore the pure love of Jesus, bearing mankind upon his heart, with the fullest sense of the justice of the divine curse, and of the displeasure which lay heavy upon us, must needs make our cause his own by sympathy. His love must, according to his office, take the direction of bearing our weaknesses and diseases on his priestly heart (Matt. viii, 17; ix, 36; xiv, 14; xv, 32; xxiii, 37; xx, 28), and thereby be made a surety for us to the satisfied justice of God, so that God can regard the world as reconciled in him, the righteous one. But though he stands before us unique in his calling, in virtue of his sinless holiness, yet our entire life may be, and ought to be, a sacrifice on the ground of atonement, a priestly service in which we sacrifice to God every thing impure to which our heart clings, self-will and all self-seeking, and dedicate and devote ourselves to him without reserve in the sacrifice of faith, and thank and praise him in the sacrifice of love, which at one time streams forth in child-like words of prayer to the Father, and at another occupies

* From this point, a number of features in the life-picture of Jesus come into the light of a great connection. We name them, but refrain from carrying them out. So Matt. v, 3–7, 9–12, 12–25, 38–48, 29, 30; vi, 24; viii, 21; ix, 11–13, 15–17; x, 16–28, 32–39, particularly 38, 39; xi, 25, 26, 28–30; xii, 7, 8; xii, 16–21; xiii, 4–8, 11–16, 45, 46; xv, 11–20; xvi, 21–25; xvii, 24–27; xviii, 1–5, 8–11, 15–17, 21–35; xix, 14, 21; xx, 20–28; xxii, 2–10; xxiii, 5, 10–12, 23, 26–28, 34, 37; xxiv, 9–13; xxv, 29; and the parallels, Luke xxiii, 34; John i, 14; iii, 3–6, 16, 17–19; iv, 22, 32–38, 48; v, 17–20, 30, 35, 38–47; vi, 27, 45–47; vii, 17–19; viii, 32, 42–50, 54; ix, 39–41; x, 11–18; xi, 9, and following verses, 35, 51–52; xii, 22–26, 32, comp. 8–28, 37, and following verses; xiii, 1, 4–17, 31, 32, 34, 35; xiv, 31; xv, 16; xvii, 19–25; xviii, 30, 37; xx, 29; xxi, 15–19.

itself, with all its powers, in self-forgetfulness for the good of the brethren, simply seeking another's good, and thus dying the progressive death of love, which is ever a self-renewing life.

Jesus, as he is historically attested, stands before us in the world as a *miracle;* not as a miracle deranging the orderly connection of the world, but a miracle raising aloft the true image of humanity, which is the end of creation, and restoring the world, that had become a moral chaos, to the κόσμος, everywhere dispelling its moral discord, where room is given him, by the power and example of his sacrifice. As to the eternal higher life of the Son of Man, John specially instructs us. It is his being one with the Father, whose voice and will he constantly heard, whom he always saw working, and whose face he beheld. Standing constantly, and without intermission, in this oneness, perfectly united to the Father in love, he becomes himself the revelation of the Father and of his love. It is the absolute moral communion with the Father, and, by consequence, also the ontological, or essential communion with the Father, in virtue of which he is what he is, and lives as he does. How such a personage would arise in a sinful race, how his first earthly origin is to be understood, are considerations that lie beyond the limits of this inquiry. It is enough for our purpose if we have succeeded in proving that the sinless perfection of Jesus is an historical fact, which sober history has to accept as certainly as any other historical fact, and if we have been able to exhibit it in some of its aspects of entire originality.

[CONCLUDED IN THE NEXT NUMBER.]

ART. V.—THE ZOROASTRIAN RELIGION.

By ROSWELL D. HITCHCOCK, D.D., New York.

ESSAYS ON THE SACRED LANGUAGE, WRITINGS AND RELIGION OF THE PARSEES. By MARTIN HAUG, Dr. Phil., late of the Universities of Tübingen, Göttingen and Bonn; Superintendent of Sanscrit Studies, and Professor of Sanscrit, in the Poona College, etc., etc. Bombay. 1862. Pp. 268.

THE first attempt to expound to modern Europe the ancient Zoroastrian religion, was made by Thomas Hyde, of Oxford, in his celebrated work on *The Religion of the Ancient Persians, Parthians and Medes*, the first edition of which appeared in the year 1700. This work is one of great learning, drawn from Greek, Latin, Arabic and Persian sources; but the author's ignorance of the Zend language, and consequent inability to make use of the Zend manuscripts which were in his possession, prevented him from giving his readers a real insight into the subject of which he treated. In 1762 the entire Zend-Avesta, the Bible of the Zoroastrians, or what was then supposed to be the entire work, was brought from India to Europe by Anquetil du Perron, who published a French translation of it in 1771. In 1776-7 this French translation was in turn translated by Kleuker into German. These publications produced a profound sensation amongst the scholars of Europe. Such a sudden unveiling of a famous ancient and almost extinct religion, at once opened up questions of the greatest interest, alike to theologians, philosophers and linguists. Kant expressed disappointment in regard to the contents of the Zend-Avesta, but German divines eagerly made use of it in their interpretation of the Old Testament. The chief controversy, however, was with respect to the authenticity of the book. Sir William Jones at first thought it a forgery, imposed upon Anquetil by the Parsee priests; and was followed in this opinion by most English scholars. But in

France the authenticity of the book was not doubted. And in Germany the doubts for a time entertained by not a few, gradually gave way before the arguments of Kleuker.

The authenticity of the Zend-Avesta having been thus established, the correctness of Anquetil's translation of it was the only point remaining to be considered. Of this there was at first no question. But since his day scholars have arisen, whose knowledge of the Zend language goes far beyond that of Anquetil; such as Rask and Westergaard of Denmark, Bournouf of France, and in Germany Justus Olshausen, Bopp, Brockhaus, and Haug, whose recently issued work is now before us. The result is, that while Anquetil retains his place of honor as the first great leader in this branch of Oriental study, he has lost his authority as an interpreter of the Zend-Avesta. His mistakes in rendering are numberless, and some of these mistakes involve a radical misrepresentation of the Zoroastrian system. Of living Zend scholars, Haug is now undoubtedly one of the most exact and thorough. Since 1852, with all the help afforded by the labors of his learned predecessors, he has been devoting himself to the study of the Zend and Pehlevi languages and literature; and with such success, that the Parsees of western India have lately importuned him to take the presidency of their ecclesiastical seminary at Bombay. The ripe fruits of this decennium of ardent study, are now before us in this volume from the Bombay press.

Four essays make up the volume. The first is a history of the researches into the Sacred Writings and Religion of the Parsees, from the earliest times down to the present. The second is an outline of the Zend grammar. The third gives a brief statement of the contents of the whole of the Zend-Avesta, with translations of the more important parts of it. And the fourth expounds, with admirable precision, the origin, development and genius of the Zoroastrian religion. Few books have ever been published containing so much within so small a compass.

The Zend language, now dead, was of the Arian family, and an elder sister of the Sanscrit. In the Zend-Avesta two dialects of it are found, an earlier and a later, both of which appear to have been dying out in the third century before Christ, leaving no daughters behind them. The general character of the language in both its dialects, as shown by Haug, is that of a highly developed idiom, quite equal, if not superior, to the Sanscrit, inferior only to the Greek. It is rich in inflexions and in compound words. Its verbs have three voices; its nouns, three numbers and eight cases. The Pehlevi, into which the chief parts of the Zend-Avesta were translated in the time of the Sassannides (235*–640 A.D.), is also an Arian language, much like the modern Persian, but containing many Chaldee, though no Arabic, words. This Pehlevi translation ought of course to be highly serviceable to an interpreter of the Zend-Avesta.

So nearly was the Zoroastrian religion annihilated by the Mohammedans in the seventh century, that there are now only two remnants of this ancient communion; the Guebres, or "infidels", of south-eastern Persia, and the Parsees of western India, each numbering about a hundred thousand. The Guebres are compelled by their Mohammedan masters to occupy one of the least fertile provinces of Persia, and are exceedingly ignorant, although on the whole more virtuous than the majority of their countrymen. But the Parsees of India, so called from the country out of which they were driven twelve hundred years ago (Persia), are remarkably intelligent and interesting. They are amongst the wealthiest and most respected and influential of the native citizens of Bombay. In 1852 they organized a society for their own social improvement, and especially for the revival of the pure old Zoroastrian faith. It is amongst these Parsees, that Haug is now pursuing his studies with such brilliant success.

In regard to the date of Zoroaster's appearance in history, three leading opinions have hitherto prevailed: (1.) The earliest date is that of the Persian writers, who make him contemporary with Abraham, about 2000 B.C. Gibbon (chap. viii) accepts this date. (2.) Heeren and Guizot assign him to the reign of the Median Cyaxares, 633 ?–593 B.C. (3.) Hyde,

---

* The date commonly given is 226 A.D. Haug, for reasons not named, but probably sufficient, says 235.

Anquetil and Kleuker put him down still lower, into the reign of Darius Hystaspes, 521–485 B.C. This last differs but little from the opinion of the modern Parsees, who say he lived at the time of Hystaspes, the *father* of Darius, about 550 B.C. This, however, is not the opinion of Haug, who finds indications of a much higher antiquity, both in the earlier portions of the Vedas of India, and in the Zend-Avesta itself. Under no circumstances, he says, can he assign to Zoroaster a later date than 1000 B.C., and he is not disinclined to regard him as contemporary with Moses.

As to the origin of the Zoroastrian religion, having pointed out the close relationship existing between the Brahmanism of the Vedas and the system taught in the Zend-Avesta, Haug takes the ground that Zoroastrianism was a schism, brought about by those Iranians who had migrated and become agricultural, in order to widen the breach between themselves and their nomadic brothers, who soon began to make predatory excursions amongst them. Hence the Ahura religion of these agricultural Iranians, who had previously been addicted to the Deva worship of the Brahmanic Vedas. The shaping of this schismatic faith was not, probably, the work of a single man' but of several men in succession, who, perhaps, were priests ; and yet much was due, no doubt, to the influence of one great personage, whose name was *Zarathustra Spitama*, known to us as Zoroaster. The date of this schism was probably as far back as 1200 B.C., or farther still, and the theatre of it the high lands of Bactria.

The Zend-Avesta (or Avesta-Zend, as Haug says it ought to be written, and which means "Text" and "Commentary"), in which is embodied the religion thus established, is a comparatively small book ; large portions of the original work having perished under the hostile influence of the Greek civilization introduced into Persia by the conquest of Alexander, 335 B.C. What we have now is only the fragments gathered up by the Sassannides, 235–640 A.D. And yet the names of all the books, with short summaries of their contents, are still extant. From these it appears that the whole work consisted of twenty-one parts, called *Nosks*, each composed of Avesta

and Zend, Text and Commentary.   The work in its completeness contained hymns, prayers, rules of life for all classes of
men, instructions about God, spirits, the resurrection, heaven
and hell, with much information pertaining to medicine,
botany, geography, astronomy and other sciences.   Of these
twenty-one Nosks, only the twentieth (the *Vendidâd*) remains
entire.   Of some others only fragments are extant ; and more
than half of them are wholly lost ; while parts of the Zend-
Avesta now in use amongst the Parsees, appear not to have
belonged to any of the original Nosks.   But enough remains
to indicate the character of the Zend-Avesta, as an exhibition
of the whole religious and scientific culture of the ancient
Persians.

The only complete edition of the extant portions of the
Zend-Avesta, is that of Westergaard, Copenhagen, 1852–4.   Of
these remains the most ancient are the five *Gâthas*, consisting
of metrical prayers and hymns, believed to be the work of
Zoroaster himself.   The monotheism of these *Gâthas* is distinct
and positive.   Next in rank is the *Yasna*, of later date, in
seven chapters, which consists of prose prayers, addressed,
however, not like those of the Gâthas, to the Supreme God
alone, but also to inferior spirits, to fire as the symbol of the
Supreme God, to the earth, the waters, the angel presiding
over food, to truth, speech, growth and the like.   Then follows the *Visparad*, another collection of prayers.   Then the
Vendidâd in twenty-two chapters, embracing the legislation,
religious, civil and criminal, of the ancient Iranians.   And
lastly the *Yashts* in twenty-four parts, consisting of songs,
prayers and conversations with the Supreme Spirit.   As to
dates, the *Gâthas*, Haug thinks, were written about 1200 B.C.,
the *Yashts* from 450–350 B.C., and the other portions of the
work at different times between these two extremes.   Only
the *Gâthas* are believed to be the work of Zoroaster ; the other books having come from his disciples and successors in the
priesthood, who steadily declined from the lofty and uncom-
promising monotheism of the great Iranian Reformer.

The most interesting portion of Haug's book is that in which
he gives an analysis of the Zoroastrian system, which, in its

more important features, is widely at variance with the expositions hitherto attempted, and is of course much more reliable than any thing which has yet appeared, by reason of the author's better mastery of the Zend language. The emphasis which has for so long a time, and by writers of such various prepossessions, been put upon the dualism of the system, is here shown to be unjust. Gibbon's verdict, that "the first and original Being" of the Zend-Avesta "seems rather a metaphysical abstraction of the mind, than a real object, endowed with self-consciousness, or possessed of moral perfections", must now be set aside; as also the judgment of Ritter, that "the *fundamental* doctrine of the Zend-Avesta is a distinct dualism, with monotheism in the background". On the contrary, monotheism is found to be conspicuously in the foreground, and is the fundamental principle of the system as originally taught by Zoroaster. The misconception in regard to this matter, which has been so widely prevalent, proceeds from the mistranslation by Anquetil of an important passage occurring in the *Vendidâd*. As rendered by Anquetil, the passage reads : "Ahriman, master of the bad law! the being absorbed in glory has created thee, the *boundless time* has given thee", etc. Haug's rendering is : "O evil-knowing Ahriman! the white spirit made thee *in the boundless time*". The words here rendered "boundless time", are *Zruni akaranê*, which are not, as Anquetil supposed, in the nominative, but in the locative case, whose proper force is, "in; at, or on". There is therefore no support for the assumption that the first great Original of the Zend-Avesta is a vague abstraction, which may be called "boundless time". The *Gathâs* throughout are intensely monotheistic ; but especially the second Gathâ (of twelve pages in Haug's translation), which is pervaded by the doctrine of one supreme, eternal God, Creator of all things. The name given him is *Ahuramazda*, which means "Living Creator of all". Under the Sassannides, this name was changed to *Ahurmazd ;* and in modern Persian it is *Hormazd.* According to Zoroaster, he is the light, and the source of light. He is the fountain of all good. But while he rewards good men, he likewise punishes the bad. All created things, whether good or evil, are his work. A separate evil spirit, of equal power with *Ahuramazda*, and always opposed to him, as Haug says, finds no place in the theological system of Zoroaster. This dualistic idea appears in the Vendidâd, but not in the Gathâs. Account for it as we may, whether we consider it an old tradition devoutly cherished, or a happy inspiration of genius, the fact is indisputable that the theology of Zoroaster is strictly monotheistic. He is at the farthest possible remove from teaching the doctrine of two original independent spirits, the one good and the other evil.

In his philosophy, however, though not in his theology, Zoroaster was clearly a dualist. Strongly theistic as he was in his belief, he had no other way of solving the problem of evil. In order to account for existing derangements in nature, in the individual, and in society, he had to suppose two minds in *Ahuramazda ;* a white mind, which he called *Spentomainyus*, and a dark mind, which he called *Angromainyus*. These, indeed, were both of them creative spirits, but not separate and independent beings ; they were only the two sides of the one Divine being. From the former came all that was wholesome, bright, and good ; from the latter, all that was unwholesome, dark, and bad. It was an awkward device of a baffled thinker, and yet it served to hold back Zoroaster himself from the abyss of pantheism. But in process of time, amongst the followers of Zoroaster, this decided dualism in his philosophy invaded the sphere of theology. *Angromainyus*, the modern Persian *Ahriman*, instead of being regarded as merely one side, or mind, of God, came to be regarded as entirely independent of God, and always at war with him. Hence the later doctrine of *Hormazd* and *Ahriman*, God and Devil, as rival beings, dividing between them the empire of the universe. The dualism was thus complete ; in the theological dogma, as well as in the philosophical speculation. The exact date of this apostasy cannot be determined. The Zoroastrian religion, as we know, was grossly corrupted by the Parthian Arsacidæ, who ruled Persia from 250 B.C. to 235 A.D. We also know that the Sassannides, who in 235 subverted and expelled this foreign dynasty, made a desperate and not altogether ineffectual effort to turn back the national faith from the offensive dualism into which it had developed.   Hence, in part, their persecution of the Christian Manichæans, who had borrowed their stern dualism from the corrupted Zoroastrianism of the Arsacidæ. Hence, also, the great account they made of *Zruni akaranê*, " boundless time ", as the eternal antecedent, and Creator even, both of *Hormazd* and *Ahriman.*   With whomsoever this idea originated, it was evidently an after-thought, brought in to counteract a harsh and hated dualism ; an attempt to restore the system to its original monotheism.   It is also well known, on the authority of ancient Armenian writers, that in the fifth century of our era, the Zoroastrians were split into two parties, bitterly hostile to each other, the Magi and the Zendiks, the latter being the more dualistic of the two.   The Parsees are now all dualists, as well in their theology as in their philosophy.   Such certainly is the natural drift of the system, the monothism of the theological part of it not sufficing to withstand the dualism of the philosophical part of it.   But such was not the earlier faith.   In the cuneiform inscriptions, which are thought to belong to the age of Darius, God always appears as One, just as in the Gathâs of Zoroaster.   If such was the belief of Cyrus, we can the better understand his readiness to favor the monotheistic Hebrews ; he was only befriending a kindred faith.

The Zoroastrian anthropology, as might be surmised, is dualistic.   In man also, as in God, there are two minds, distinguished as " first " and " last ".   The former is heavenly and divine ; the latter earthly and sensuous.   Evil spirits tempt man downwards and astray ; but by the fear and worship of God, and by the careful practice of virtue, he may please his Maker, and attain to eternal life.   Of redemption through atonement, no trace appears.

The ethical system of the Zend-Avesta is *triadic* in form. Duty is taught under the three categories of thought, word, and deed.   Virtue consists in pure thoughts, true words, and just actions.   Lying, theft, and even the incurring of debts, as tempting one to falsehood, are frequently denounced. Kindness towards those of the same faith, is fervently enjoined.

Suicide and adultery belong to the class of "deadly sins", which lead straight down to hell. Special stress is laid upon the duty of cultivating the earth, the products of which are represented as a triumph of good over evil. In the third chapter of the *Vendidâd*, it is written :

> " When barley there is,
> Then the devils whistle ;
> When barley is thrashed,
> Then the devils whine ;
> When barley is ground,
> Then the devils roar ;
> When flour is produced,
> Then the devils perish ".

The religious rites enjoined in the Zend-Avesta, consist of prayers, hymns, and sacrifices. Worship is rendered ultimately only to *Ahuramazda*. Sun, moon, stars, and fire are reverenced only as symbols of the pure Spirit. The sacred fire is kept always burning. In prayer, the priest holds before his face a bundle of twigs ; in sacrificing, great use is made of the juice of the *Soma* plant, obtained by bruising and pouring water over the plant. The most singular rite prescribed, is that of purification by drinking the urine of the cow, a sacred animal amongst the Iranians—a kind of purification required after the touching of a dead body, by women after child-birth, and the like. Some writers speak of a daily morning ablution in cow-urine, as practised amongst the Parsees ; but Haug says nothing of it.

The eschatology of the Zend-Avesta is especially noteworthy. The immortality of the soul is most abundantly and emphatically taught ; as also the doctrine of rewards and punishments beyond the grave. The fate of the soul immediately after death, is very minutely described in one of the *Yasht* fragments. The soul of a good man sits for three nights on the top of the head of the dead body, reciting the *Gathâ Ustavaiti*. After the third night, a soft, fragrant wind, blowing from the south, bears the soul aloft through several paradises, until it reaches the throne of *Ahuramazda*, where it enjoys the most splendid meals, shining like gold. The soul of a bad man also sits for three nights on the top of the head of the dead body,

19

reciting the prayer, " To what country shall I go, where shall I find shelter " ?   After the third night, at day-break, a badly smelling wind, blowing from the north, bears the soul along the same track taken by the good soul, but beyond the region of bliss, into " the darkness without beginning ", where *Angro-mainyus*, the Devil, dooms it to the eating of poisoned meals. The Zend name for heaven is *Garô-demâna,* " the house of hymns "; the name for hell is *Drugô-demana,* " the house of destruction ".   Between heaven and hell is " the bridge of the judge ", which only the souls of the pious can pass safely, the souls of the wicked falling down from it into the abyss.

The resurrection of the body is also a prominent doctrine ; if not very clearly taught by Zoroaster himself in the *Gathâs*, certainly developed out of his teachings very naturally, and at an early date. At the end of the world, the dead will be raised and judged, the Devil and his followers destroyed, the earth made smooth and pure, and *Ahuramazda* worshipped on it eternally.   The last great prophet, who will accomplish this triumph of good over evil, is *Sosiosh*, who is to bring to mankind a new Nosk of the Zend-Avesta.   What connection there may have been between this prophecy and the visit of the Magi to the Babe of Bethlehem, is easily imagined.

Such are the points most worthy of notice pertaining to the Zoroastrian religion, drawn chiefly from the essays of Haug. The origin of this system is a question of the greatest interest. That Zoroaster was somehow indebted to the teachings of Moses, is the opinion of many.   But Haug urges as a strong argument against this opinion, that in the Zend-Avesta there are only two words which can be traced to the Hebrew language, and these have no reference to religious subjects.

Art. VI.—LYMAN BEECHER, D.D.

By Joseph F. Tuttle, D.D., President of Wabash College, Indiana.

Few men have been fitted by nature and grace to walk a road which was " the rough one of battle, confusion and danger". In the church we have a few such as Moses and Paul, and Luther, and Calvin and Knox. But there are thousands of good men who " with faithful heroism have brought down a light from heaven into the daily life of their people ; leading them forward as under God's guidance, in the way wherein they were to go". It has been said finely that God has created only one Niagara but thousands of brooks and rills. Although the elect few were valiant for truth and for God, yet the other and larger class is made up of men as valiant, fighting as good a fight, finishing as difficult a course, and keeping as precious a faith.

Lyman Beecher was born at New Haven, October 12th, 1775, and died at Brooklyn January 10th, 1863. He was the son of David Beecher, a blacksmith noted among his neighbors for strength and originality of mind. He spent nearly eighteen years on a farm with his uncle at Guilford. At eighteen he entered Yale and was graduated in 1797. Having studied theology a year with Dr. Dwight, he was in 1798 licensed to preach by the New Haven West Association, and in 1799 was ordained and installed pastor of the Presbyterian church in East Hampton. He entered upon his work with great zeal and with such success that in eleven years three hundred converts were added to the church.. " His career to this day at East Hampton is one of the most fragrant traditionary memories."

His labors here greatly impaired his health so that he was obliged to give up his work for a time. And to this period of constrained rest belongs one of those delightful reminiscences with which he favored at least one of his classes at Lane. He had crossed the Sound and was recuperating his energies, as he told us, in the place where he had spent his boyhood. Among his old acquaintances was a *Churchman*. One day Beecher walked over to see this farmer, and found him cradling grain. And, unless the *reaping* be a more agreeable sight in agricultural life, there is no operation more admirable than when a strong man skilfully swings the cradle into the yellow wheat ripe for harvesting. The greeting was cordial, and soon the apostolic farmer complimented the young preacher on his success over on "the Island", only he regretted so much that instead of joining a sect he had not "gone into the Church", and instead of becoming an unauthorized minister he had not taken pains to get the apostolic grace from a Bishop in the Succession!

Beecher heard him patiently, and then said in his abrupt way, pointing to the scythe with which the farmer had been cutting the grain: "Fine tool, that! Cuts like a razor, don't it?" "Why, yes, to be sure it does", was the reply of the farmer, whose puzzled looks gave evidence that he was in doubt whereunto these things would lead.

"Did you ever hear that St. Thomas is the patron saint of blacksmiths?" asked Beecher with an ill-concealed mirthfulness in his eyes. "Why, no, I never heard that," said the farmer, "and if I had, I do not see what that would have to do with the point we were discussing."

"Suppose St. Thomas were the patron saint of blacksmiths, and that there was a class of consecrated blacksmiths deriving authority from him and pretending that not even a good scythe could be made except by some one of their class! And suppose one of these successors of St. Thomas should try to convince you that your scythe is good for nothing because an unconsecrated blacksmith had made it!"

"He would be a fool for his pains," said the farmer, laughing heartily at the droll illustration.

"So I thought. I never saw a tool cut better, St. Thomas to the contrary notwithstanding. Now I have a scythe of another sort. It didn't come from any succession of spiritual blacksmiths. No'Bishop made it or even whetted it. I have tried it over on the Island and it cuts as keen as a razor. What is the use then of my asking whether *Peter* had any thing to do with it? It *cuts*, and that proves that it was made by some one that knew how. My friend, I am entirely satisfied with my scythe!"

Well we remember the Doctor's face all alive with drollery and fun as he related this anecdote to his class, and finally burst into that infectious laugh, which was as merry as a boy's.

In 1810 he removed to Litchfield where he remained as pastor until 1826. His labors here were abundant and his success equal to his exertions. And here again we may refer to the notes we made at Lane for a reminiscence which we heard him relate at a Temperance meeting at Walnut-Hills in 1842. "I had long been impressed," he said, " with the growing evils of intemperance already swelling into a deluge of ruin. Excited by my observations, and feeling that something must be done, *I blocked out those six sermons, and laid them on the shelf for the moment when Providence should bid me preach them.* The tide was running with gulf-stream power in favor of intemperance, and one wanted nerve to stem it singlehanded. There was a young man living in a remote part of the parish in whom I felt an almost paternal interest. I had married him and had watched his course with pleasure. Occasionally I preached at his house and remained over night. For some time my visits were evidently pleasant to him, but at last I began to notice that as soon as meeting was over he would hurry off to bed, but I did not suspect the cause. I knew something was wrong, because his wife seemed crushed by some terrible grief. One night after meeting I drew my chair beside her and said: 'My child, tell me what it is!' For a while she hesitated, and then with a passionate outburst of grief exclaimed: 'My husband has become a drunkard!' This was a peal of thunder in a clear sky. My heart bled for her, and I heard Providence almost audibly saying: 'Go preach the preaching which I shall bid thee.' I felt the time had come to take the sermons down from the shelf, and I did so, with what result is known to the world." But he added, " it was too late to reclaim the young husband. Still, others have been saved, for which God's name be praised."

It will be observed in this statement that it is not a *father* and son, but only a son who is mentioned, and that the outline of the six sermons was sketched some time before he preached them. The statement in both particulars slightly differs from some we have seen.

In 1812 he preached a sermon at New Haven on " a Reformation of Morals Practicable and Indispensable ". The discourse abounds in passages of great power, and the keynote is the same as in the sermons on Intemperance. Of these last, preached in Litchfield near the close of his ministry, it is not necessary to speak at length. We believe they are equal to any he ever gave to the press, and perhaps to any he ever produced. There were several elements which contributed to their greatness and success. He then was at that happy age when the fervor of youth is combined with the power of a ripening manhood. Here was the glow of youth and the iron force of middle life. What fire burns and flashes through these discourses, and yet what invincible logic and strength! Then, his warmest personal sympathies were enlisted to save his friends. His mind, always practical and never working so forcefully as when it was pursuing some grand and tangible object, had one of the most terrible evils to wrestle with. And how do his metaphors—they were his favorite and natural figures of speech—cause to stand out before our eyes the very thing that was destroying fathers and sons and brothers and husbands in the town of *Litchfield!* How we almost faint as we read of the serpent of vast dimensions wreathing a child about with his cold elastic folds, tightening with every yielding breath his deadly gripe! Indeed it seems to us that there is a passionateness, a consuming vehemence, an agony of apprehension in the descriptions, the appeals, the warnings, in these sermons, which excel any thing he ever published, and which has rarely been excelled in any similar production. The nearest approach to them we can now recall are some of the descriptions and appeals in certain of Dr. Griffin's sermons, and in one or two of President Edwards'. In his fiery,

vehement, wonderfully condensed expressions, what equal has
be?. Here is a sermon in a sentence when he says of certain
evils : " They are not warts but cancers." What sentence
ever better described tippling-shops than his "breathing-holes
of hell "? What orator ever crowded more vehemence, holy
passion, lofty eloquence, into as few words as he standing by
" this commencing vortex " of intemperance? "To all who
do but heave in sight, and with voice that should rise above
the winds and the waves, I would cry, ' Stand off!! spread
the sail, ply the oar, for death is here ;' and could I command
the elements, the blackness of darkness should gather over
this gateway to hell, and loud thunders should utter their
voices, and lurid fires should blaze, and the groans of unearthly voices should be heard, inspiring consternation and
fright in all who came near "!

In 1814 his sermon on " Building the Waste Places ", was
preached, and in it we find the elements of that zeal for Home
Missions which was so conspicuous in him at a later day.

In 1826 he removed to Boston and became the pastor of the
Hanover-street congregation. At that time *orthodoxy* was
neither savory nor popular in the " Modern Athens ". The
influence of Harvard in respect to the central doctrine and
glory of Christianity had been baneful there in an eminent
degree. The wealth, the social standing, and the culture of
Boston, all gave to Unitarianism a respectability which had
hitherto been denied to orthodoxy. Park-street church,
which had rung with the pathetic appeals of Dr. Griffin, was
still sneered at as " Brimstone Corner ", so that it required almost as much moral courage to profess an Evangelical faith
in Boston as it once did in Athens. That highly cultivated
and in many respects admirable scholar and preacher, the late
Dr. Channing, was then esteemed to be the model of every
pulpit excellence, and what his influence was it is not difficult
to determine. However polished or scholarly, he spoke more
like an ancient Greek in the days of Paul than a modern Christian, when " the strange doctrines " and "fictions of the theologians ", meaning thereby Trinitarianism, were under discussion. As for revivals, he said vehemently : " We owe it to

truth and religion to maintain that fanaticism, partial insanity, sudden impressions, and ungovernable transports are any thing rather than piety ". As for the vicarious atonement, it is " a crime to lay the penalties of vice on the pure and unoffending ". As for the teachings of " this gloomy theology ", if he believed it he "should feel himself living under a legislation unspeakably dreadful, and laws written, like Draco's, in blood ". And he compares the cross of Christ to " a gallows in the centre of the universe ". In contrast with these assaults on " the glorious gospel of the blessed God " were the exquisite and well-turned phrases in which he "reverenced human nature, ... turning to it with intense sympathy and strong hope. The signatures of its origin and its end are impressed too deeply to be even wholly effaced. I bless it for its kind affections, for its strong and tender love ",—and a great deal more of a similar character, in marked contrast with the descriptions of the human heart which the Spirit of God moved Jeremiah and Paul to give.

This was the type of the theology and preaching which was popular in Boston when Dr. Beecher was called to exercise the ministry there. All the terrible and all the glorious doctrines of the Gospel had been slaughtered and offered on the altar of an extravagant, unscriptural, and untrue humanitarianism. Besides this, the few years preceding his removal from Litchfield had been remarkable for extensive revivals throughout New England, the Middle, and the Southern States. On no theme was he more jubilant than when speaking of " the revivals in the bosom of which God laid our great missionary institutions". It is not too much to say that these revivals provoked great opposition on the part of Unitarians. To meet this, a leader was needed, and found in Dr. Beecher. He was in his full power. He had been twenty-seven years in the ministry, and while not a scholar, he was a ripe thinker and an effective preacher. He was in his fifty-first year, and his tough, elastic constitution, " with only one weak place in it ", as he playfully termed it, was as vigorous as it was at thirty. His voice was yet a commanding one ; and above all, his intellect was at its zenith when he began his ministry in the metropolis of New England. He threw himself at once into his work with an almost boyish enthusiasm, and soon achieved such a reputation for genius and power in the pulpit, that Boston became proud of him as her foremost preacher. His spirit was so magnanimous, his polemics so humane, his aims so benevolent, as to commend his views of the Gospel to the favorable attention even of his opponents. His genius cast such a dazzling radiance around his ministrations, that men of the highest culture hung on his lips with admiration. We have heard him say that his mind was so fruitful during this period, "Sundays did not come often enough". He preached the doctrines in his own way, never presenting them as abstruse metaphysical subtleties or mere abstractions, but as a preacher of "*the Word*". To discuss these doctrines as mere theses was, in his opinion, like "handling the dry bones of a skeleton. Bones are necessary, but he would set them up, clothe them with flesh, cover them with skin, and pray God to breathe the breath of life into them". He was intensely practical, and gifted in the diagnosis of spiritual ailments, laying his finger on the precise spot, and fearlessly prescribing the remedy. Cursed as Boston had been by such a gospel as Dr. Channing represented, there were multitudes entangled in the net of a semi-skepticism, and struggling to free themselves from the hateful thraldom. For such cases, the preaching of Dr. Beecher was "the power of God". With as much sagacity as the hound tracks the game he would follow human depravity to all its hiding-places and "refuges of lies". We never knew his peer in meeting "difficult cases" and solving the doubts which so often amount to chronic infirmities. It was this which made his theological lectures in after days so fascinating to young men, who were thoughtful enough to anticipate the difficulties both in theology as a system and in its applications to specific cases, as they come up in an actual ministry. How often have his explanations met our own personal wants, and how often, years after we had left his class-room, have we thanked God for the help we had derived thence for our work in the ministry!

Such a ministry, in such a city, could not be otherwise than eminently productive. He used to say that there was hardly a month, for years, when his ministry in Boston was not attended with more or less signs of revival influence. His church was constantly thronged, converts were multiplied, and the pulpit he filled for six years was rated the most famous in America. Occasionally he went abroad; but whether in New York or Philadelphia, the tide of an extraordinary popularity followed him. In Boston orthodoxy received the impulse which carried it over all opposition, and it became a power in that city, the State, and the world.

In 1831, Arthur Tappan, Esq., of New York, agreed to endow a Professorship of Theology in Lane Seminary, at Cincinnati, on condition that Dr. Beecher should be the first incumbent. He was now in his full power, and in a most important post. His people were tenderly attached to him, and to die among them was his desire. But the West was coming forward with amazing strides. When he was a young man, the West was the Genesee country. Ohio became a State after he was ordained a preacher at East Hampton. He had been at Litchfield six years before Indiana was admitted into the Union, that is, in 1816, Illinois in 1818, and Missouri in 1821. Michigan, Wisconsin, Iowa, Minnesota, and Kansas were hardly possibilities when the Doctor was " blocking out his six sermons". About the time he went to Boston, the tide of emigration to the West was swelling into a flood that startled good men with the question: " What is to be the character of the Western commonwealths?"

The spiritual wants of the West early engaged the attention of the Eastern churches, and it was soon evident that to meet those wants institutions of learning must be established at the West to train the ministry at home. This widely experienced conviction gave life to Marietta and Western Reserve colleges in Ohio, Wabash college in Indiana, and Illinois college at Jacksonville. In a word, collegiate and theological education in 1832 was in its infancy, whilst the population of the West was increasing with unparalleled rapidity. Thus these two great facts pressed on Dr. Beecher's mind when he was invited to the Presidency of Lane Seminary. The letter written by the Committee of the Seminary's Board of Trust makes the wants of the West in regard to education the main reason why the Hanover church should give up its pastor to go West. "To accomplish this great work—the evangelization of the West—we want indeed hundreds and thousands of additional laborers, . . . men baptized into the spirit of revivals, ... fearless and firm in their attacks on the strongholds of infidelity and the devil." How better can this be done than to put young men in contact "with one who, without invidious comparisons, has no superior in the characteristics now mentioned in this or any other part of Christendom"?

Dr. Beecher's acceptance of this call gave great satisfaction to the friends of the West; and when he entered upon his duties, in November, 1832, he found that a large number of students had been drawn together principally by his fame. These young men greatly admired him. His simplicity and generosity, his eloquence as a preacher, his power as an analyst of difficult theological and philosophical questions and mental states, his terse style of thought and diction, his metaphors as hot as brilliant, his elevated piety, all of which qualities were rendered doubly delightful by his very eccentricities, attached his students to him in a remarkable degree. This attachment on their part reäcted on himself, bringing back to him the freshness of his earlier manhood, so that both in the pulpit and lecture-room his friends considered him as equal to his best days in New England. The large assemblies in the Second Presbyterian church of Cincinnati, especially at the Sabbath afternoon service, proved that he was meeting the most sanguine expectations of his friends. It is a fact which reflects credit on that Church that it remained firmly attached to him until his infirmities warned him to resign.

Of the difficulties which soon after arose to embarrass him in an enterprise so hopefully begun, we have not space to speak, except to remark that, had he been on the ground at the time, his common sense and his influence with all the parties concerned, might have prevented that exodus of young men from Lane which left it for a time very weak, while it added strength and *éclât* to Oberlin, then in its vigorous infancy. It was an unhappy affair, to which he was wont to refer with great sensibility.

In June, 1835, the trial of Dr. Beecher for heresy, on charges preferred by Dr. J. L. Wilson, began, and it was in some respects the severest test ever applied to him. Dr. Wilson was pastor of the First Presbyterian church in Cincinnati. In that post he wielded a powerful influence. In person and in the firmness of his will, he was said to bear a strong likeness to Andrew Jackson. He was an able and instructive preacher, and until Dr. Beecher came he was regarded by many as the first in the city. He, as a member of the Lane Board of Trust, had joined in sending the letter to the Hanover street church, assigning reasons why they should let their pastor come to Cincinnati. Perhaps the brilliant success of the new comer, overshadowing his own, may have made him seem to be a rival and an intruder. That the prosecutor had a very decided human nature, no one who knew him doubts, and yet we are slow to believe that jealous rivalry was the prominent incentive to this prosecution. The times were in a strange degree full of ecclesiastical bitterness in the Presbyterian Church. Duffield, of Carlyle, and Barnes, of Philadelphia, were made to feel this wrath of church partisanship, which good men of both parties deprecated but could not restrain. There was a wide-spread alarm, also, among the straiter sect of the Presbyterians, both at the lax church government and the unsound doctrines which were said to be prevalent in certain parts of the Church. At the West the feelings of both parties were greatly exasperated. Among these alarmists was Dr. Wilson. How strange in our day sounds the fifth charge he brought against Dr. Beecher : " I charge him with the sin of hypocrisy : I mean dissimulation in important religious matters " ! The main points of the charges pertained to the doctrine of total depravity, natural ability, etc., as involved in the controversies between the Old and New School. Dr. Wilson's speech contains painful evidence that he was in full sympathy with the heated spirit of the times. The response of Dr. Beecher is one of his most remarkable performances.

We do not wish to diminish by an iota the well-deserved honor which both Duffield and Barnes won, and the fine Christian spirit they were enabled to maintain in their trials. It is sufficient to say that Dr. Beecher was their worthy peer in similar circumstances. His opening is touching and eloquent. There are some passages which subdued his audience like a spell; and now that both these great men are gone where there are no trials for heresy, the same passages move us to tears as we read them. Whatever may have been the feelings of his hearers as to the Doctor's orthodoxy, there could have been but one feeling as to his spirit. It is singularly elevated and charitable, in marked contrast with the prevalent spirit of the times. As for his doctrinal discussions, they are in the main satisfactory, and large parts of them, with slight alterations, such as he would have declaimed in his own pulpit. Some of these discussions are magnificent, and they are free from ill-humor or even irony. And in closing his triumphant reply, aware that his prosecutor was liable to be visited with the punishment he had sought to bring on the accused, he deprecated any such infliction, exclaiming: "I am not willing to stand here and hear my church-bell ring, while his is put to silence. We are not alienated from each other. There is no personal bitterness between us. We are as ready to see eye to eye, and as ready to draw in the same harness as two men ever were, if we could but agree in our views. And although Dr. Wilson does not see his way clear to extend his hand to me, it is not certain but that after he has conned this matter over; after he has communed with his friends, and above all, after he has communed with his God, he may come to a different conclusion". Noble enthusiast! thy hope was not realized here; but can we doubt that it has been in that other state, where there are no mistakes, no estrangements between good men, and where you and "brother Wilson" see face to face, and know even as you are known!

Our first sight of Dr. Beecher was at Marietta, during commencement week of either 1838 or 1839, and as he was the most famous preacher we had ever seen, we watched him with great interest. All that day the one great thought with us was, "To-night we are to hear the great Dr. Beecher preach"!

And we did ; and we confess it was a great disappointment. Save a few sentences at the close, the discourse was very dull. But our broken idol was repaired and set up the next day in its old place, for on commencement afternoon he discoursed from sundry bits of paper, apparently strung on a pin, concerning the dangerous theme of *Eloquence*. It was racy, original, humorous, gorgeous, and at times really powerful. In 1841, we became his pupil, and in looking over the jottings in our note-book, and the more enduring records made in our memory, we find nothing recorded that we wish he had not done or said. In the class-room, at the " Wednesday evening talks ", in his pulpit, at his own cheerful fireside, and in his thoroughly up-side down study, he was a man without guile, without meanness of any sort that we ever saw, gentle and simple as a child, sympathetic, genial, godly. We loved to hear him pray, and confess that we always stared at him with our eyes wide open, simply because his face was itself a prayer, which added double emphasis to the petitions he uttered. He could no more suppress his own individuality in prayer, than he could compose himself into the stately dignity of Dr. Woods. And yet when he prayed he seemed very near to the mercy seat ; and then there were so many thrilling originalities that were constantly darting out of his inspired lips ! How simple, fitting, and original the prayer with which he began his class-lectures !

> " When one that holds communion with the skies,
> Has filled his urn where these pure waters rise,
> And once more mingles with us meaner things,
> 'Tis e'en as if an angel shook her wings ;
> Immortal fragrance fills the circuit wide,
> That tells us whence her treasures are supplied."

As a teacher of " systematic theology ", Dr. Beecher was not very systematic, but he had an amazing influence, a sort of magnetic power, over his students, teaching and compelling them to think for themselves. This was one of the chiefest benefits conferred by him. Our notes show that he began to lecture our class on the abstruse themes of Butler's Analogy. Among our most delightful hours, were those spent in listening to his illuminated lectures on Butler ; and we hope to see those lectures in print, although it is certain that some of the best parts of them were never written. Then came his lectures on Existence, Cause and Effect, and Mental Philosophy, followed by the lectures on Conscience, by far the most thrilling discourses we ever heard from him. He delivered them, out of place as to the system, to our class, and we heard them the second time in Fireman's Hall, Cincinnati, which the church, now under the care of Dr. Storrs, occupied the first winter of its organization. The Doctor delivered his lectures on Conscience at the Sabbath evening service. We regard the occasion when he spoke of the *Power of Conscience*, as among the grandest exhibitions of his pulpit power. His whole nature seemed permeated with a realizing sense of what he was saying. Although interrupted by several alarms of fire, and compelled to sit down twice, not an auditor left his seat, nor did the speaker lose a whit of the fiery vehemence with which he discoursed on his dreadful theme.

After this splendid episode of lectures on Conscience, came his course on the Will, the Affections, and Moral Government, and in the midst of a discussion of his favorite theories of Man's Free Agency, the whole course was dislocated by the introduction of his lectures on the Trinity! These were very able and practical, and brought us as a class to the mid-winter of 1842–3, when lectures and every thing else were set aside by the distressing sickness which laid twenty-five of our number on sick beds, and two in the grave.

This finished our immediate contact with Dr. Beecher in the lecture-room, and while it is evident that his course was not systematic, yet we look back to his class-room with delight that knows no abatement. He was there proved to be a man of uncommon genius, who had profoundly reflected on some of the most difficult problems of natural and revealed religion. The flashes of his mind are still shining upon us, as they did twenty years ago ; and we believe that, all things considered, his connection with the present generation of preachers at the West should be regarded as the most productive in its results, of his life, and they fully verify the anticipations of those who invited him to the West.

His Plea for the West, delivered many times in 1834, will

show that then there had been no abatement of his energy. Crowds of admiring people heard that plea at the East and at the West, and there is but one testimony rendered concerning it as a discourse to be read and especially as one to be pronounced. What finer passage can we find with which to illustrate his own glowing eloquence than this, in which he urges the necessity of the most prompt planting and sustentation of literary institutions at the West? And if his words were weighty then, when the Mississippi was the western border of civilization in the North-west, what shall we say of them now when the frontier has been pushed back to Pike's Peak to meet the retreating frontier of the Pacific civilization, not dreamed of in 1834, which, having developed two States and several territories, is breaking over the barriers of the Sierra Nevada and already washes the base of the Rocky Mountains? "But whatever we do, it must be done quickly; for there is a tide in human affairs which waits not, moments on which the destiny of a nation balances, when the light dust may turn the right way or the wrong. And such is the condition of our nation now. Mighty influences are bearing on us in high conflict, for good or for evil, for an immortality of woe or blessedness; and a slight effort now may secure what ages of repentance cannot recover when lost, and soon the moment of our practical preservation may have passed away. We must educate the whole nation while we may. All, all who would vote, must be enlightened and reached by the restraining energies of heaven. The lanes and alleys, the highways and hedges, the abodes of filth and sordid poverty, must be entered and the young immortals sought and brought up to the light of intellectual and moral daylight. This can be done, and God, if we are willing, will give us the time, but if in this our day we neglect the things which belong to our peace, we shall find no place for repentance, though we seek it carefully and with tears."

It was a noble and timely utterance. Would that we of this day would heed it as our salvation!

It is but candid to add that, personally, we have heard Dr. Beecher only a few times, when through an entire discourse he came up to the brilliant standard of his Litchfield and

Boston efforts, or even those of his first years in Cincinnati.
Once we heard him, in Wesley Chapel, deliver a speech before
the Bible Society, once on Eloquence, at Marietta, once on
the Power of Conscience, and once on a first Monday in the
year in the Seminary chapel, when as an orator he came up to
his traditional greatness. Then he was truly a Boanerges, and
his mind overcame the disabilities and languor of approaching
age. We often heard detached passages of great power, but
they were few and small compared with those which, judged
by his own standard, were inferior and weak. But it must be
remembered that he was sixty-four years old when we first
saw him, and sixty-six when we became his pupil. A very
large part of the forty previous years had been passed in a
ministry of such urgency and of mental excitement so vehement that he felt as if there were not " Sundays enough", and
it was not to be wondered at that his eye was somewhat dim-
med and his mental force abated. In fact, he was not a little
sensitive on the subject. In 1845 he attended the meeting of
the American Board during the anniversary week in New
York. Dr. Todd alluded to his presence by saying that " he
had understood that the *infirmities of age* had deprived the
audience of the privilege of hearing the venerable father from
the West". In an instant, with all the sprightliness of a boy,
the Doctor sprang to his feet and, amid explosions of laughter,
exclaimed : " It's the first time I heard of it !" When Dr. Todd
took his seat Dr. Beecher verified his own claim to youthful-
ness by a brief speech in which the fire of his early manhood
blazed and·the power of his traditional eloquence took every
heart by storm. And this was the man of whom Mr. Barnes
wrote, that " no oratory which he had ever heard equalled
Lyman Beecher's in his grand flights".

In 1852 Dr. Beecher's relations to Lane Seminary and the
West were practically ended, although his venerable name
stood as President of the Seminary until he died. In 1856 he
was present at the anniversary exercises. It was known that
he was to be there, and a large number of his pupils and
friends met to welcome him back to a spot so dear to them
and to him. The Rev. Daniel Rice, now the honored and able

20

pastor of the church in La Fayette, Ind., was appointed to speak our affectionate and tearful salutations to the instructor and friend of former years.   Very beautifully and eloquently did he do it in a strain of reminiscence and anticipation that moved the great assembly.   But when the Doctor replied we saw that "the old man eloquent" had begun to verify the saying :

"Last scene of all
That ends this strange eventful history,
Is second childishness and mere oblivion."

The manuscript he had prepared for the occasion seemed beyond his grasp, and he laid it aside to *talk* to us.   Occasionally the fires of his former genius would flicker and flash up for a moment.   As a mental effort it stood in painful contrast with others in the same place that all remembered; but the benignant spirit, the magnanimity of soul, the loving docility of his piety, the quick sympathy with all that is great in the love of God and the efforts of man for a world's salvation, were still there as apparent as at any former day—a beautiful compensation for the mental senility which was so evident.   "And now abideth faith, hope, charity, these three ; but *the greatest of these is* CHARITY."   In LOVE our instructor was, as ever before, great, and we thanked God that this divine virtue was shining about him so luminously that in spite of the mental feebleness which grieved us, the unabated force and undimmed brightness of his love to God, to Jesus, to the saints, to a world of sinners, imparted a beauty to the old man as when the shadows of the closing day are forgotten in night's holy silence, the unclouded sky in whose serene depths we behold the stars, and the untroubled sleep which predicts a morning so bright as to eclipse the stars themselves with light.

His death was peaceful as the close of day.   A few days before, he had " a vision of transfiguration" for some hours, and his exclamation, " Such scenes as I have been permitted to behold!" reminded us of his once alluding to his friend Evarts who, when dying, exclaimed: " Oh! wonderful, wonderful! praise Him in a manner ye know not of!"

We close this tribute to his memory by extracting from our

note book a reminiscence characteristic of him, and prophetic of what he is now enjoying. "But the difference between the embodied and the disembodied states can be seen more plainly in the fatigue and exhaustion which seize the body after the long and intense action of the mind. How often has the enthusiastic student, with restless ardor, driving his inquiries and researches, careering on to victory, been checked midway in his course by his jaded body, and his mind, fretting and chafing, been compelled to cease its labors? How often is the untiring nature of spirit shown in dreams when that flame, kindled by the breath of God, burns with intense brightness, whilst the senses are locked in repose, and gleams through the chinks of its material prison-house?"

His voice was now ringing like a clarion, as eloquent and emphatic to a handful of admiring disciples, as it ever was before a spell-bound multitude. At this point he suddenly closed his book and, jerking off his spectacles, he delivered these sentences: "Excepting exemption from sin, intense, vigorous, untiring action is the greatest pleasure of mind. I could hardly wish to enter heaven did I believe its inhabitants were idly to sit by purling streams, fanned by balmy airs. Heaven to be a place of happiness must be a place of activity. Has the far-reaching mind of Newton ceased its profound investigations? Has David hung up his harp as useless as the dusty arms in Westminster Abbey? Has Paul, glowing with God-like enthusiasm, ceased itinerating the universe of God? Are Peter and Cyprian and Edwards and Payson and Evarts idling away eternity in mere psalm-singing? Heaven is a place of restless activity, the abode of never-tiring thought. David and Isaiah will sweep nobler and loftier strains in eternity, and the minds of saints, unclogged by cumbersome clay, will forever feast on the banquet of rich and glorious thought. My young friends, go on then; you will never get through. An eternity of untiring action is before you, and the universe of thought is your field."

> "The good, great man—three treasures—love and light
> And calm thoughts, equable as infant's breath;
> And three fast friends, more sure than day or night—
> Himself, his Maker, and the angel Death."

Art. VII.—BISHOP COLENSO ON THE PENTATEUCH.

By Daniel R. Goodwin, D.D., Provost of the University of Pennsylvania.

The Pentateuch and Book of Joshua Critically Examined. By the Rt. Rev. John William Colenso, D.D., Bishop of Natal. Part I. pp. 229. New York, 1863.

An Answer to Bishop Colenso. By M. Mahan, D.D. Pp. 114. New York, 1863.

In undertaking to refute an argumentative work, it is important first of all to ascertain and recognize its true logical position. In the book before us, we understand Bishop Colenso's position to be, that the Pentateuch, and particularly that portion of it which contains the story from Jacob to Joshua, is "unhistorical"; that the things which it relates never took place as matters of fact. What may follow from this he does not hold himself responsible for. That it will necessitate the abandonment of certain current theories of inspiration provided we would retain the Divine authority of the Canonical Scriptures, he admits and maintains. It may involve the destruction of that authority altogether, and of Christianity with it; but this Colenso neither maintains nor admits. Rather, he foreshadows a theory of inspiration which shall be consistent with these results of his criticism; a theory, according to which inspiration is a gift far more widely bestowed, and, at the same time, far more restricted in its scope, than is commonly supposed. According to this view, inspiration is intended to convey moral and spiritual truth,—and *all* moral and spiritual truth comes by inspiration; but it furnishes no guaranty of truth or accuracy in regard to any thing else. All else is of trifling importance; the spiritual truth, the spiritual instruction, is the grand and sufficient object. Thus Colenso will undoubtedly propose to retain the profession of Christianity, as a spiritual religion, and the Pentateuch itself as a part of the inspired word of God, while insisting, nevertheless, upon its "unhistorical" character. Such we understand to be Colenso's position.

Scarcely had the Bishop's book been published in this country, when Dr. Mahan announced his intention of making a reply. That reply is before us. It is a spirited, off-hand performance, bearing evident marks of haste, as well as of great vigor, in thought and composition; we shall, therefore, enter into no criticism of its general style. In many points of detail it exhibits great adroitness and ability. But upon the main point upon which it was his business to answer Colenso, he gives up, as it seems to us, the whole field, and goes over to the adversary's side. That such was his intention we are far from imagining. We believe it to have been just the contrary. We state only what seems to us the actual result. In this we may misunderstand, but we would not misrepresent him.

His motto is: "The spiritual view, or the glass reversed", or "spiritual things are spiritually discerned". He says, "Every portion of the word, whether true or not considered in itself, is infallibly true from the spiritual point of view; that is, considered in its bearing upon the aim and purport of the Scriptures in general", p. 15. "We may have to abandon a surface sense, which is of no importance, and to take in its stead a deeper and more spiritual sense", p. 17. "A history may be quite accurate in dates and matters of fact, yet taken as a whole may convey an enormous lie", p. 20; where the connection seems to imply that the "lie" follows of course from the "accuracy"; or, at least, that an "inaccurate statement of matters of fact" may be, and indeed, is most likely to be, true history, that is to say, true in the inspired and spiritual sense. "The Bible uses facts as but secondary to truth; about 'dates' it seems indifferent and hardly conscious of their importance; and as to arithmetic, its 'rule of three' was certainly not learned in any of our common schools", p. 37. (Could Voltaire have put it better?) "The Holy Ghost did not inspire Moses to be a pedant or arithmetician. He was raised up and inspired for a holier and better work. As a historian of truth, and not a detailer of mere facts, [the "mere" has no pertinency here]—as a Prophet of the old world, and not a Gradgrind of the nineteenth century,—he concerned himself chiefly with the weightier matters of the law", p. 59. "The Hebrew writers, like all writers of antiquity, had a 'habit of not realizing to their own minds the *actual* meaning of numbers'. In fact, they knew but little of arithmetic, ... they might have been gravelled by a simple sum in the Rule of Multiplication", p. 74. The application of all this about "arithmetic" can be only to inaccurate statements, or rather, *exaggerations*—for the alleged inaccuracy is always on one side —of actual numbers; for, in general, Moses has confessedly performed his additions, subtractions and multiplications—has applied the Rule of Three,—with great accuracy. "The Prophets certainly used mystic numbers. If the historians sometimes did the same, ... it might lessen the value of their writings as far as 'statistics' are concerned; but would weigh nothing against their general historical character", p. 77. He then refers to Origen, and to "the *mystic* interpretation of Scriptural numbers so common among the Fathers", p. 81. "In the use of numerals especially, Moses wrote on some system, or in some habit of mind, unintelligible to us", p. 93. "The ancients in fact knew nothing of statistics on a large scale", (referring, in a note to Herodotus having given the army of Xerxes as more than five million men). "Their histories, therefore, are unreliable on that point. But do we conclude for such reasons that ancient histories are 'unhistorical'? Or, if we do not, why should we condemn Moses?" p. 95. May Moses, then, be supposed to have made the same sort of mistakes that Herodotus committed?

These citations will suffice to show the ground taken by Dr. Mahan. And we submit that it is substantially the same as that taken by Bishop Colenso. We apprehend that Dr. Mahan mistook entirely Bishop Colenso's position, if he supposed it to be, that, inasmuch as the Pentateuch relates things which were not matters of fact, and particularly, makes erroneous statements of numbers, therefore it is not *inspired Scripture.* We understand Colenso to stand ready to maintain—we do not mean that he will be *able* to maintain,—just the contrary proposition; and when Dr. Mahan contends that errors in regard to matters of fact, and especially in regard to numbers, are entirely consistent with inspiration, we doubt not Colenso is quite ready to say, Amen. The primary question is whether such errors have really been committed by the sacred writer. Colenso openly says, Yes; Dr. Mahan, if we understand him, says it may be so, and he is rather inclined to think so it is. Dr. Mahan admits that certain statements of the Pentateuch are not in accordance with "facts"; Colenso says they are "unhistorical". Dr. Mahan intimates that the numbers are probably "mystical", certainly not "arithmetical"; Colenso says they are "unhistorical". What is the difference? To suggest that the Pentateuch deals in symbolical representations and mystical numbers, like the prophets, or epic or dramatic poets,—what is this but to acknowledge that, in so far, it may be "unhistorical"? To say that these points of detail, these numbers and arithmetical calculations are insignificant, petty, trifling affairs, in comparison with the "weightier matters of the law", with the great themes of moral and spiritual instruction, and hardly deserve the notice of an earnest religious man, is no answer to Colenso; it is just what he will say for himself; "it is but the husk", he will say; "let the husk go". It is true, we may not charge a historian with a misstatement of facts until we have ascertained his *real meaning;* we must make all due allowances for interpolations, corruptions, or errors of transcribers, idioms of the language and of the times, etc.; but after all such allowances have been made and the true meaning of the writer ascertained, if then it appears that his true meaning is still inconsistent with facts; that he really did not intend to state facts, but to convey symbolically some spiritual truth, would it not be as fair and non-committal a word as we could use, to say, his statements are "unhistorical"; they are not intended to set forth historical fact? If, however, it had been the Doctor's object simply to correct the Bishop's language in the use of the word "unhistorical", he need not have written even a *small* volume for that purpose. Where there is substantial agreement in regard to *things,* men need not contend long about mere propriety of *words.*

As an illustration of the relative logical positions of the two critics, let us take the leading example. The Pentateuch states that there were 603,550 fighting men among the Israelites who came up out of Egypt, and that, when numbered in the plains of Moab some 39 years afterward, there were 601-730. Bishop Colenso says there were not so many; Dr. Mahan thinks there may not have been so many, as a "mere matter of fact". Bishop Colenso says therefore the statement is "unhistorical". Dr. Mahan says, no, it is simply not "arithmetical".

The manner in which Dr. Mahan endeavors to dispose of the checking of the numbers by the amount of the contribution that was made for the tabernacle of half a shekel for each man, seems to us particularly unsatisfactory and even unfair. What has "the depreciation of English money" to do with the question? It is of no consequence whether the shekels of money *weighed* more or less. It is their *number* only, and neither their weight nor value, with which we are concerned. And this will remain the same so long as it takes two half shekels to make a whole one, ten hundred shekels to make a thousand, and a certain number, say 3000, to make a talent. If Moses was the writer of the story, he must have known how much silver was used in constructing the tabernacle, and how much for each "socket"; he must have known how many shekels it took to make a talent; he mentions but *one* "thousand" shekels, and this he puts side by side' with 775, apparently recognizing the exact arithmetical ratio of the numbers. Unless Dr. Mahan will make him a "simpleton", he knew the ratio of the half shekel to the whole sum, and consequently had an exact arithmetical notion of the number of contributors; he had the pieces of money in his hands and might have counted them upon his fingers;—which number he states with precision, and it is precisely the same number that he gives when summing up the census of the several tribes.   He does not deal merely with thousands but with tens and fives; and with all these always in their exact arithmetical ratios.   He uses a "thousand" as ten hundred, a hundred as ten tens, and ten as ten units.   As to "round numbers" he certainly went as low as *ten* in numbering the people, for we have 550 in one census and 730 in the other; but it seems not unlikely that any units, in the number of each tribe, less than ten, were neglected in the report, and likewise in summing up the amount of the poll-tax.

The allusion to the extravagant computation which Herodotus gives of the army of Xerxes does not strike us as particularly happy.   To make the cases parallel : suppose Herodotus had professed that he was himself present in the army of Xerxes, and in high command ; that he and his brother had presided over a commission for ascertaining its exact numbers, and had, with that commission, checked off separately the number of every nation and tribe composing it, counting man by man; suppose that he had added up those numbers, and had added them accurately, giving the details as well as the result, and had stated the sum to be 5,283,320.   Suppose, moreover, that he had collected a tribute from the army of so much a head, had counted the money and found the sum to correspond with the census; and then suppose we were satisfied that the real number was less than one quarter of that thus given by him, and that there was no interpolation or corruption in the text, what should we say of his veracity ?   If, in the case before us, the author of the Pentateuch had really given us merely the round numbers of a gross sum, or if there were reason to suppose the text to have suffered from the meddling or the mistakes of transcribers, or if the real author were not Moses himself, but some writer of a later age who derived his information from tradition or from ancient documents of uncertain authorship, we might admit the numbers to be inaccurate to almost any degree, and yet believe the historian to be honest and trustworthy.

To suppose, as some do, that to make mistakes in regard to

mere matters of fact in consequence of imperfect information or knowledge, is consistent with a writer's being inspired, is one thing; to suppose such mistakes in an eye-witness to be consistent with inspiration, when they would not be consistent with common honesty, is quite another thing. We presume Colenso calls the Pentateuch "unhistorical", in order that he may not call it *false ;* and supposes Moses not to be its author, in order that there may be room for admitting its author's ignorance instead of impugning his veracity, and consequently room for supposing him *inspired*, in the Bishop's sense of inspiration.

We have proceeded here upon the assumption that we have the text as Moses wrote it. Indeed the *numbers* are so interwoven with the story that it is difficult to suppose them to have been interpolated or altered by copyists. But if there is any evidence or any credibility of such a tampering with the text, let it be brought forward. We shall be ready to give it its full weight. We do not take it into consideration here, because it belongs to an entirely different line of argument; and so far from tending to confirm the charge against Moses of a "strange habit about numbers", of "arithmetical negligence", or of ignorance of the "Rule of Multiplication", it would tend to relieve him from such charges altogether.

If it be said, "the Prophets use symbolical numbers", and that the apocalyptic "144000 of the 12 tribes of Israel" is symbolical; what then? Is the Pentateuch to be put upon the same level in point of *historical* character with the visions of Ezekiel and the Apocalypse? What does Colenso ask more? "The Prophets use symbolical numbers"; yes, and they employ also symbolical actions and symbolical scenes. And suppose the whole story of the sojourn in Egypt, the exodus, the wandering in the desert, and the conquest of Canaan, to be, not statements of strict historical facts, but symbolical representations of human destiny and Christian experience, conveying thus great spiritual truths and important religious instruction; might the story still be accounted inspired? Dr. Mahan's theory is broad enough to admit it. Bishop Colenso is satisfied with it. And this is what is called "answering the objections of future Colensos for many generations to come". Assuredly they will not object to the answer.

One thing more upon the grounds assumed in this answer to Bishop Colenso. It ascribes the Bishop's errors to his following "private interpretation", and not listening to the voice of the Church, "the witness and keeper of holy writ", to his being a "Bibliolater", that is, having more respect for

the authority of the Bible than for that of the Church.   But
when and where has the Church given her dogmatic decision
in regard to such points of the exegesis of the Pentateuch as
those discussed by Colenso?   Among points of this kind, that
in regard to which we have come nearest to having a dogmatic ecclesiastical decision, is, that the earth is immovable in
the centre of the universe.   Will Dr. Mahan " listen to the
voice of the Church " on this point, or follow " private interpretation "?   Will he quote the Fathers against Colenso?
But the moderns are " the Church " as much as the ancients.
Bishop Potter has as good a right officially—and except so
far as " private ", personal qualities, such as learning, intelligence and piety, may make a difference,—to speak in the
name of " the Church " as St. Augustine had.   St. Augustine's authority, such as it is, is almost entirely a " private "
and not a public, official, or ecclesiastical authority.   Colenso
himself has as good a right to speak in the Church's name as
Origen at least; and the notions of the two are probably
about equally near the truth.—Bishop Colenso writes a book
maintaining that the Scriptural account of the exodus is " unhistorical ".   Suppose Dr. Mahan were to content himself
with showing by documentary evidence—which is just what,
in consistency, he ought to have done,—that the general judgment of the Church Catholic, that is, the prevailing sentiment
in the Church in all ages, has been to the contrary; would
even high Churchmen have been satisfied with this as a refutation?   No doubt the prevailing judgment or sentiment of
the Church is against Colenso, and he knows it; but that does
not convince him, nor will it satisfy thoughtful Christians, or
even Churchmen generally, on such points as these.   The
Church herself—that is, not the Church acting in her organic
capacity, but the mass of her members and teachers,—may
become more enlightened on various points of exegesis.
Would Dr. Mahan have all questions of Scripture interpretation decided by a mere appeal to Church authorities, without
any other evidence or argument or criticism addressed to the
" private " reason?   Even his very authorities would confound
him by continually resorting to such evidence and arguments.
Nay, he himself admits that the science of interpretation is
progressive,—" the interpretation of different parts of Scripture may wonderfully develop ".   " In fact there is an essential difference between our Faith, which rests upon the sense
of Scripture as a whole, and what we properly call our 'views'
of particular passages of Scripture.   The latter may be enlarged or modified, or rendered more clear, *or may even in*

some cases be materially changed, without in the slightest degree affecting the former.   And as with our views of certain texts, *so also with our views of the nature of Inspiration*". The Italics are ours.   Surely here is room enough, after all, to furnish Colenso a way of escape from the charge of not "listening to the voice of the Church".

Bishop Colenso says the narrative of the exodus is not "historical ", i. e., is not an account of matters of fact.   The main question is, not how he came to think so, or what he will come to think next, or whether such an opinion is consistent with receiving the Canonical Scriptures as the word of God, or consistent with the received judgment and teaching of the Church.   The question is,—the first and proper question is, as to the truth of the opinion itself : *Is* the narrative of the exodus, so far as *internal* evidence goes, a statement of historical facts ? that is to say, may it be so, by its own showing ? or does it bear on the face of it, as Colenso maintains, in its own inconsistencies, contradictions, and absurdities, manifest marks of being " unhistorical "?   To the answer to this question we shall now address ourselves.

Bishop Colenso finds his first puzzle in connection with the number of the descendants of Jacob, who are related to have gone down with him into Egypt.   Among these are enumerated Hezron and Hamul grandsons of Judah, two grandsons of Asher, Dinah, Jacob's daughter, and Serah his granddaughter.

Now the grandsons of Asher may have been born in Canaan.   That Hezron and Hamul, under the peculiar circumstances narrated in the history of Judah, could not have been born then before the descent into Egypt, is no new discovery of Colenso.   But, having taken pains to establish this undisputed point by a physico-mathematical calculation, he proceeds to argue, how could Hezron and Hamul, then, have gone down with Jacob into Egypt?   Yet, he adds, the text declares, " ' All the souls that came with Jacob into Egypt which came out of his loins, besides Jacob's sons' wives, were three score and six ', (Gen. 46. 26)—which they would not be without Hezron and Hamul ".

The text introduces Hezron and Hamul thus :   " And the sons of Judah, Er and Onan, and Shelah, and Pharez, and Zarah ; but Er and Onan died in the land of Canaan ; and the sons of Pharez, Hezron and Hamul ".

Now it seems plain to us that the sacred writer means as much as if he had said, with the careful balancing of modern historical style, " but Er and Onan having died in Canaan, instead of them are reckoned Judah's next two descendants, the sons of Pharez, Hezron and Hamul, although these were not born until after the descent into Egypt ".

It may be said, indeed, that this is acknowledging the text not to express *literally* the historical truth. But the historical veracity of an author is to be tested, not by any rigid abstract " literal " or grammatical sense of his words, but by his *probable meaning* gathered by a fair and candid criticism from the text and context interpreted according to the idioms of the author's language and his own peculiar habits of thought, style and expression. His *real meaning* is what we want to find, and by this his truthfulness must be tested.

But the sacred historian, in this same connection, tells us, " the sons of Joseph, which were born him in Egypt, were two souls : all the souls of the house of Jacob, which *came into Egypt* were three score and ten ",—which they would not be without the two sons of Joseph. And again, " all the souls that came out of the loins of Jacob were seventy souls ; for Joseph was in Egypt already ". Now here it is said, taking the historian *literally*, that Ephraim and Mannasseh, the sons of Joseph, *came into Egypt,* and at the same time it is said they were born there ; and so, according to Colenso's style of argument, the sacred historian contradicts himself upon the spot. Also it is said that the souls " that came out of Jacob's loins " were seventy ;—which they would not be without including Jacob himself in the number. This may be called a loose style of historical narrative, if you will, but is it to be charged as contradictious and untruthful? Does not every candid reader see that the narrator *meant* to include Jacob himself in the number 70, and Ephraim and Mannasseh among them who " came into Egypt"; although it certainly is no more " *literally* " true that Jacob came out of his own loins, or that Ephraim and Mannasseh came with him into Egypt, than it is that Hezron and Hamul were born in Canaan, and so came with the rest of the 66 souls into Egypt. The Hebrew language and the current historical style of some three or four thousand years ago may not have been as exact as later chronicles; but Moses, or whoever Colenso may suppose to have been the author of the Pentateuch, is not to be presumed a fool.

As for the two females enumerated, we know that there had been something peculiar in the history of Dinah, which has led to her being particularly mentioned in the preceding story, and may be the reason why her name is recalled in this enumeration. There may have been equally strong special reasons for the mention of Serah, which we do not know. It is well known that the usual custom of Hebrew genealogies is, to omit the names of females, except in extraordinary cases. For ourselves we see no reason to doubt that Jacob had other daughters and granddaughters besides these two; it would have been almost miraculous, certainly a very strange case, if he had not; but these two only are mentioned, and mentioned for some special reasons.

When, therefore, it is said, Gen. xlvi, 15, "All the souls of his sons and his daughters were thirty and three", *daughters* is manifestly put in because Dinah had been mentioned as one of the thirty-three.   But when it said, "all the souls that came with Jacob into Egypt, which came out of his loins, besides Jacob's sons' wives, all the souls were three score and six", it is certainly fair to suppose the historian to mean, "all the souls thus reckoned, according to the usual method of reckoning genealogies".   While in the statement which has been made at v. 7: "His sons and his sons' sons with him, his daughters and his sons' daughters, and all his seed brought he with him into Egypt", it may be presumed, as this precedes the genealogical enumeration, that the meaning is, according to the literal expression, that he took with him his daughters and granddaughters, of whom there were probably several, as well as his sons and grandsons.

It may be added that, if it be supposed to be the object of the sacred writer to set forth how *small* was the number who went down into Egypt contrasted with the great multitude of the children of Israel at the exodus, and if it was contrary to modern notions to have omitted the enumeration of the females with the rest, *that* was, on the other hand, in perfect accordance with the style and usages of the times; while the two females who *are* mentioned, and Hezron and Hamul who are added, are in fact four more than that style and these usages would have required the author to have included in his small number.

As to the difficulties, so elaborately set forth by Bp. Colenso, in regard to the size of the Court of the Tabernacle compared with the number of the congregation summoned to assemble unto its door; and in regard to Moses and Joshua addressing *all Israel;* they are almost too puerile to be seriously noticed.   They are such difficulties as a Sunday-school teacher might be reasonably called upon to remove for a class of quite young but inquisitive pupils.   It would be very natural for young children, in reading these statements in the Bible, to imagine that all the Israelites were assembled in a mass within a few rods of the door of the tabernacle, and that they

all listened at once to the voice of Moses and Joshua. But to
the mind of men of growth and reflection such imaginations
have ceased to present themselves. Either Colenso has not
yet put away childish things, or he has intentionally made it
his business to puzzle and if possible to mislead the young and
the illiterate.

We must suppose the children of Israel in the wilderness to
have been ordinarily very much scattered from day to day, in
their different encampments, and far beyond, in the care of their
flocks and herds and in various avocations. On such an occasion as the consecration of Aaron and his sons, it is not unnatural that there should have been issued to them a general invitation to come together; and a very large part of them may
have actually congregated towards the door of the tabernacle
as the central point of interest. Colenso admits that absolutely every individual could not have been there. It was
not necessary that they should all see what was going on within, any more than the whole multitude of the people who
waited without while Zacharias was offering incense. It was
not necessary even that they should all be near enough to see
either the door or the tabernacle itself; Daniel, *in Babylon,*
could pray with his face towards Jerusalem. Each one would
naturally come as near the door of the tabernacle as he conveniently could; Colenso does not imagine it necessary for
each one to touch it. The thoughts, the minds, the eyes of all
were earnestly directed towards this central point during the
solemn ceremony; and though they might not see the act of
consecration or even the tabernacle door, they could all see
the pillar of the cloud which symbolized Jehovah's presence,
hovering over the spot where the tabernacle stood, and where
the sacrifices were then slain before the door. And Moses or
Joshua are properly said to have spoken or read to all Israel
when they spoke or read publicly to as many as could or
would hear; and so, that what they uttered, being in its nature
intended for all alike, might be communicated, either incidentally or by some systematic method, to all those who could
not or did not immediately hear them. Nor does it com-
plicate the matter at all to allow the women and children and
strangers to be present in the group of immediate listeners, or
among those who more indirectly heard the general announcement. But we cannot see the slightest ground for the bold
assertion of the Bishop that "the story implies" that Joshua
read all the words of the book of the law to all Israel *in one
day,* and that "in the very same day he had been engaged in
writing a copy of the law of Moses upon the stones set up in

mount Ebal". Surely if "the story implies" all this, it is to a childish imagination only.

The Bishop has another curiously childish fancy. He sees the priest, Aaron himself or one of his sons, "carrying on his back on foot" the skin of the sacrificial bullock, "and all his flesh, with his head, and with his legs, and his inwards, and his dung, even the whole bullock, forth without the camp into a clean place where the ashes are poured out", and there burning him on the wood with fire. Lev. iv, 11, 12. At least he supposes that whoever wrote the Pentateuch regarded this as a veritable part of the Priest's proper personal office. And he might have cited Lev. vi, 10, 11, as a text still more to his purpose.* But surely, it must be plain enough, on reflection, to an ordinary English reader of mature understanding, that the meaning of the text is fully met by supposing the Priest, having made the proper preparations, to send the offal or the ashes abroad from time to time by the hand of the ministering Levites, or even of inferior servants and porters. And if any one will be so puerile as to contend that, in that case, the text is admitted to be not "literally" true, we have only to appeal to the Hebrew word for "carry forth", which *literally* means "cause to go forth".

The passage in Deut. xxiii, 12, 13, is merely an injunction of cleanliness given by way of example, and implying in general that all excrements and impurities were to be carried abroad. And as regards the distance which it would be necessary for those near the centre of the camp to traverse for such purposes, "the camp" here, as in many other parts of the Pentateuch, may mean that camp to which each individual especially appertained, the camp of his tribe or of his family. For many purposes of convenience and comfort, it is natural to suppose that the multitude of the Israelites were distributed into distinct cantonments, separated by considerable intervals; and so we read of the camp of Judah, and the camp of Reuben, and the camp of Ephraim, and *the camp of the Levites,* etc.; and these camps may have been subdivided into yet smaller portions, separated by narrower intervals, each of which, for particular individuals, would be "the camp", their own camp.

That the number of those who paid the poll-tax for the tabernacle (Ex. xxxviii) should have been the same as of those whose names were recorded at the census made six months later (Num. i), is a difficulty only to a person who insists upon having a difficulty, and who will admit of no hypothetical ex-

---

* But see, on the other hand, Lev. xvi, 26–28.

planation, however probable, as well as possible—of no explanation, indeed, short of a demonstrated or directly attested fact. We think the objector, rather, is bound to prove that there *must be* a contradiction here, and not we to prove that there *can be* none, or that there *is* none. It is enough for us to make it appear on reasonable grounds that there *may be* none.

Is it not then perfectly reasonable, and indeed almost necessary, to suppose that when the poll-tax was assessed on the males of 20 years old and upward, some specific common date was assumed with respect to which the 20 years should be reckoned? And may not that date have naturally been the beginning of the next year, which would follow in less than 6 months; i. e., that all were reckoned as 20 years old who would be 20 years old on the 1st day of the next first month? If this is a credible supposition, the whole difficulty is credibly removed. Or, it may be that, in collecting the poll-tax, simply the names of the individuals paying were taken, and the gross sum ascertained; while at the subsequent numbering, they were required to "declare their pedigrees, after their families, by the honor of their fathers", and were distributed to the several tribes with reference to the order of encampment and martial array. And as, by a general law (Ex. 30), this poll-tax, or "ransom", was to be paid whenever a census was taken, and as this tax was assessed and paid in view of a formal numbering shortly to be made, it is certainly not unnatural that, when the numbering *was* made (Num. 1), only those should be included in it who by their age had been liable to pay the tax. And this seems to be intimated by the phrases which are repeated with each tribe, "according to the number of the names from 20 years old and upward, . . . *those that were* [had been ?] *numbered of them* "; where a previous record of the names seems to be referred to, which were now distributed by tribes and families. And the original direction for taking the census confirms the same view (Num. i, ii, iv). It was taken with reference to military arrangements and a tribal distribution: "from 20 years old and upward, all that are able to go forth to war in Israel: thou and Aaron shall number them *by their armies*. And with you there shall be a man of *every tribe* ".

We read in Ex. xvi, 16 : "Take ye every man for them which are in his tents ". Colenso is greatly exercised to know how the Israelites could have got, or could have carried, a supply of tents. He seems not to be aware that אֹהֶל may mean a dwelling of any kind, or whatever shelter they may have had for their households.   The word ordinarily means "tent", because a tent was the ordinary movable dwelling.   Colenso is altogether unaware that the Israelites had had some considerable time to make preparation for their desired and expected journey into the wilderness; and *that*, in perfect consistency with their starting in haste, when they *did* start.   Some of them may have had tents, larger or smaller, heavier or lighter, imperfect or entire; some may have dwelt in booths at their halting places; some may have had little or no shelter at all. It is not necessary to suppose that their three days' journey out of Egypt occupied just three days and no more, with no intervals whatever for rest.   Their cattle may have been used to help carry their burdens, whether of provisions, domestic utensils, or tent skins; but there is nothing to hinder the supposition that they may have had asses and mules beside.   They went down into Egypt with asses; is it incredible that they should have had asses when they came up?   Or is nothing to be admitted as credible or possible except what is expressly mentioned in the immediate text?   If so, any history can be proved to be "unhistorical".   If a writer were to state that a general crossed a certain river with his troops, and did not state how he crossed it, whether by ford, boat, or bridge, it would follow that, even though it could not be shown to be either impossible or difficult to cross the river in either of those or in other ways, yet the story *must* be a myth.

"The children of Israel went up *harnessed* out of the land of Egypt" (Ex. xiii, 18).   So they were *armed*, says Colenso; but where, he asks, did they get their arms? and if they were armed, how could 600,000 men have been panic-stricken at the report that the Egyptians were pursuing them?   Even Gesenius will show that the difficulty here raised is forced and imaginary.   The Hebrew word for "harnessed" may mean *harnessed* or *prepared;* or it may mean *roused, excited, eager, agile;* or it may mean *brave* and *bold;* or *by fifties*, or *fiveparted,* i. e., front and rear guard, centre, and two wings; as well as *armed.*   It often means *armed*, undoubtedly, but must a word always have exactly the same meaning, and that expressly in order that the Pentateuch may be convicted of being "unhistorical"?   The plain truth is, it is not necessary to suppose that the Israelites were either all *armed* or all *unarmed.* They went up out of Egypt with the fighting men in orderly array; some of them armed in one way, it is likely, some in another; some with proper warlike weapons, and some with no weapons at all.   And even if they had been *all armed*, it is not at all incredible or even surprising, that 600,000 men, or

21

even ten times that number—great numbers are far from being any protection against panics—who had just escaped from a state of servitude, should cry out for fear when they heard that their old masters were after them, trained warriors, with their horses and chariots.

It is a general trait of Colenso's negative exegesis, that he finds a statement incredible or contradictory by refusing to receive, in the way of explanation, any thing which is not expressly contained in the text. In undertaking to show that the account of the institution of the Passover is " unhistorical ", he goes one step farther, and positively rejects a portion of the story, for no other reason apparently than because it is inconsistent with his destructive interpretation of the rest, and, if admitted, would remove his difficulties and silence his objections. He insists, therefore, in the very face of the express statements in the beginning of the twelfth chapter of Exodus, that, according to the story, the first mention made by Moses to the Israelites of this institution of the Passover, was made on the very day on which, at evening, the Passover was killed. He then finds it easy to show how impossible it was that, in that short time, notice should have been circulated through all the tribes of Israel, whether at Rameses or scattered throughout the land of Goshen, and preparations made in every family for keeping the Passover. He regards it as decisive against the Israelites having had notice several days beforehand, that " the expression, in Ex. xii, 12, is distinctly הַזֶּה, ' this ', not הַהוּא, ' that ', as in chapter xiii, 8: ' I will pass through the land of Egypt *this* night ' ": a very nice point, certainly, on the strength of which to convict the Pentateuch of being "unhistorical ". And, unfortunately for his argument, this very point itself entirely slips away when we look at the general usage of the Hebrew language. Take, for example, Gen. vii, 11: " In the six hundredth year of Noah's life, in the second month, the seventeenth day of the month, the same day, בְּיוֹם הַזֶּה, were all the fountains of the great deep broken up ". Now, in this case, " the same day ", literally " *this* day ", does not mean " to-day ", but is perfectly equivalent to " *that very day* ". In like manner, " *this* night " need not mean " to-night ", but " *that very night* ".

For ourselves, we do not suppose that all the children of Israel were engaged in making brick. While large levies of them may have been thus employed at or near Rameses, the great mass of them were probably in the land of Goshen, with their flocks and herds, spread over a large extent of territory. But they had all been for several months, it is most likely, in close communication with Moses, and earnestly awaiting the moment when Pharaoh should let them go. At some time in the first month — the day not mentioned, probably near the beginning of the month—Moses was directed to announce to the Israelites that, on the tenth of the month, they should select and have in readiness the Paschal lamb, and, on the fourteenth, at even, should kill it. The people went away and did so. *If* any one among them had not heard of the command, or were unable either by himself or in connection with others to procure a lamb, Moses did not deem it necessary to inform us, nor would any person having tolerably enlightened views of the Divine character need to be informed, that the angel of death would as certainly pass over that ignorant or poor man's house, as if he saw the blood on the lintel and on the two side posts of the door. And as to the number of the lambs required, it would take a more potent calculus than that of Colenso, and a higher authority than that of all the sheep-masters in Natal and Australia, to convince us that it is at all incredible for the Israelites, a people of shepherds, to have had a sufficient number of male lambs of the first year to spare one for every 15 or 20 of their population, however numerous they may have been. Their great number creates no additional difficulty at all ; for the greater the number of the people, the greater the number of their sheep. And, besides, it is to be observed, the lamb might be " from the sheep or from the *goats* ".

Thus the Israelites were not all-unexpectedly roused up at midnight, to begin their march, but had received notice and minute directions before. And as to " the sick and infirm, and women in recent or imminent child-birth ", we are expressly told by the Psalmist that " there was not one feeble person among their tribes ", which plainly implies that there was something miraculous about this ; and that there should have been, is surely not inconsistent with the general drift of the story in the Pentateuch.

It is only Colenso's childish imagination which requires us to suppose that the whole congregation of the people started together and at once from Rameses, on the morning after the Passover. Moses and those who were with him at Rameses, we may suppose, set out from there, and the rest, starting from where they were, as soon as they heard the call, joined the leading body as rapidly and at such points as they conveniently could. Thus all may have begun their march out of Egypt the same day. They are said to have journeyed from Rameses to Succoth, because that was the direction and distance of the movement of their headquarters. They may have rested at Succoth a considerable time, till all were collected together and organized; and in like manner they may have rested again at Etham. Bishop Colenso says, indeed, there is nothing about this resting in the Scripture. That is true; but there is nothing against it in the Scripture, and certainly there is nothing against it in nature or in reason. And after all the Bishop's elaborate calculations of space and distances, tending to show that there was not room enough in Egypt or in the wilderness for such a multitude to subsist, or even to march in, we still see no cause to discredit the simple narrative of the Scripture. Two millions, or two and a half millions of people, could have migrated in a body from Egypt.

But how were their flocks and herds subsisted on the way out of Egypt, and during the journey through the wilderness? We answer: They may have started with a certain amount of provender, and gathered some as they passed along. They and their cattle may have suffered severely, at various times, for food and water. In the wilderness, the flocks and herds may have been greatly dispersed for subsistence, in the charge of servants and other persons, particularly of the older and the younger portion of the people,[*] while the mass of the congregation, and particularly the warriors, were generally more concentrated about the head-quarters, where Moses was, and in the vicinity of the tabernacle. Their flocks may have consisted in a large proportion of *goats*. There may have been much more verdure in the wilderness then than now. They were miraculously supplied with water, which may naturally have furnished additional verdure. How far and how copiously it flowed, we may not say. The manna itself, which lay about the camp in the morning, like coriander-seed, on the ground, may have furnished at least a portion of the food of the flocks and herds, as well as all the food for the men. The men loathed it, and murmured for flesh. The cattle were likely to be more contented, and it was no more profanation for the cattle to eat the miraculous manna than to drink the miraculous water. And, finally, there may have been something of a miraculous or specially providential character in furnishing subsistence for the cattle in the desert.

---

[*] If in scattering abroad with their cattle they were liable to be attacked, as Colenso alleges, by the tribes of the desert, it implies that either there were more powerful tribes finding subsistence in or around that "waste, howling wilderness", as Colenso delights to call it, or there was no *great* danger after all. We may well suppose that a fear of this mighty and wonderful people fell upon all the surrounding tribes, and generally kept them at an awe-struck distance. An early lesson had been given by Joshua to the Amalekites, upon their interfering with stragglers: Ex. xvii.

We have a right to appeal to miracle; and, so doing, we do not trench in the least upon the *historical* character of the narrative, or imply any acknowledgment that it cannot be defended as a relation of matters of fact. It is no more necessary to the historical character of the narrative that every thing which transpired of a miraculous nature should be expressly recorded, than that every thing else should be so recorded. The whole story, the whole scene, is impregnated with the miraculous. God is there; and his hand is visibly manifested from beginning to end. Miraculous Divine agency is the substratum and fulcrum of the whole history. Without it the story of the exodus undoubtedly becomes incredible. If this agency must be eliminated or ignored in order to establish the "historical" character of the narrative, undoubtedly that "historical" character must be given up. If what we have before us were merely an account how certain men, Moses and Aaron, led the Israelites, 2½ millions, with their flocks and herds, out of Egypt and for forty years in the wilderness, we should without hesitation pronounce it a fable. But if the account is, how Almighty God brought this people out of Egypt with a mighty hand and an out-stretched arm, and led them through the wilderness, bearing them and carrying them, guiding and sustaining them, and bringing them at length to the land he had promised to their fathers, — this is quite another thing. What Moses could not do, God could. But still it is urged that the miracle we appeal to is not recorded; and again we answer it is unnecessary that it should be. The truth is, if the objector would fairly and ingenuously admit what *is* told in the story, his difficulties would immediately vanish. If he really and honestly believed that God went before his people in a pillar of a cloud by day and a pillar of fire by night, that he led them through the Red Sea on dry land, that he fed them with manna, and gave them water out of the rock,— would he still find it impossible to explain how their flocks and herds were subsisted in the wilderness? And simply because this is not expressly explained to him, must he give up the whole narrative as " unhistorical"; while yet, if this had been explained in the text by an additional miracle, he would have admitted the historical credibility of the whole?

In the exhortations of Moses contained in Deuteronomy, he tells Israel, " Thy raiment waxed not old upon thee, neither did thy foot swell these forty years": and again, " I have led you forty years in the wilderness : your clothes are not waxen old upon you, and thy shoe is not waxen old upon thy foot". Now these things must have been the result of miraculous interposition, and Moses appeals to them as such; yet they are nowhere mentioned in the narrative proper, in Exodus, Leviticus, or Numbers; and if the book of Deuteronomy had been lost or had not been added, or if Moses had omitted these traits in his address, would such miraculous facts have been incredible and inadmissible suppositions, even though the rest of the narrative should have presumed them as necessary to its own explanation? But Colenso returns with his refrain of " that waste howling wilderness, where there was no water, and where no man dwelt", and with his flocks and herds lowing and bleating; and nothing for them to eat. He thinks that because it is called " that great and terrible wilderness which no man passed through", it must have been just as desolate and barren then as it is now; but plainly that does not follow. Colenso would exaggerate the desolation of the scene in order to show that the flocks and herds could not possibly have been subsisted in it. Moses paints it in the most vivid and terrible colours, for a very different purpose: " Who led thee", says he, "through that great and terrible wilderness, wherein were fiery serpents, and scorpions, and drought, where there was no water; *who brought thee forth water out of the rock of flint; who fed thee in the wilderness with manna*". How different the sentiment, the religious tone and character! Which is the more elevated and noble, that of the rude Hebrew some three thousand years ago, or that of the Christian Bp. of this 19th century? The Bishop imagines the people shivering and starving with cold during the winter they spent near Sinai; Moses remembers the burning and quaking mountain, the solemn Divine voice, and all the awful and glorious manifestations of the immediate presence of Almighty God. But the Bishop thinks these things could not have taken place as historical facts, because the people would have been frostbitten!

Colenso cites Ex. xxiii, 27–30 : " I will send my fear before thee, and will destroy all the people to whom thou shalt come, and I will make all thine enemies turn their backs upon thee. And I will send hornets before thee, which shall drive out the Hivite, the Canaanite, and the Hittite, from before thee. I will not drive them out from before thee in one year, lest the land become desolate, and the beast of the field multiply against thee. By little and little I will drive them out from before thee, until thou be increased and inherit the land". He then shows that the whole land which was divided among the tribes in the time of Joshua did not exceed 11,000 square miles; and thereupon triumphantly asks how there could have

been any danger that the beasts of the field should have incon-
veniently multiplied against a population of 2½ millions placed
upon such an extent of territory at once?

We answer that the original promise to Abraham was:
"Unto thy seed have I given this land, from the river of
Egypt unto the great river, the river Euphrates". And Moses
says in Deut. i, 6: "The Lord our God spake unto us in Horeb,
saying, ye have dwelt long enough in this mount: turn you
and take your journey, and go to the mount of the Amorites,
and unto all the places nigh thereunto, in the plain, in the
hills, and in the vale, and in the south, and by the sea side, to
the land of the Canaanites, and unto Lebanon, unto the great
river, the river Euphrates. Behold I have set the land before
you: go in and possess the land which the Lord sware unto
your fathers, Abraham, Isaac, and Jacob, to give unto them
and to their seed after them". And still more directly to the
purpose, Moses says, Deut. xi, 24: "Every place whereon the
soles of your feet shall tread shall be yours: from the wilderness and Lebanon, from the river, the river Euphrates, even
unto the uttermost sea shall your coast be. Then shall no man
be able to stand before you: for the Lord your God shall *lay
the fear of you and the dread of you* upon all the land that ye
shall tread upon, *as he hath said unto you*". And again the
Lord said to Joshua, Jo. i, 3: "Every place that the sole of
your foot shall tread upon, that have I given unto you, as I
said unto Moses; from the wilderness and this Lebanon, even
unto the great river, the river Euphrates, all the land of the
Hittites, and unto the great sea toward the going down of the
sun, shall be your coast". And in 1 Kings iv, 21, we are told
that Solomon actually reigned "over all kingdoms from the
river unto the land of the Philistines and unto the border of
Egypt". He had also a palace, a "house of the forest", in
Lebanon: see 1 Kings ix, 19 and 2 Chron. ix, 20.

Now the promise which Bp. Colenso cites from Exod. xxiii,
was made while the Israelites were yet about Horeb, and before the disobedience in consequence of which they were condemned to wander 40 years in the wilderness. It very naturally, therefore, referred to the promised land, in its full extent,
and according to its proper idea. And so the Bp's difficulty
on this head vanishes.

He meets with another difficulty in connection with the
number of the priests at the exodus as compared with their
duties and with the provision made for them. The laws relating to their duties and perquisites are intended by the terms of
them to be statutes forever throughout all future generations,

as Moses says again in Deuteronomy, "Behold I have taught you statutes and judgments, even as the Lord my God commanded me, *that ye should do so* in the land whither ye go to possess it". In some of these statutes the offerings of corn, wine and oil—the first fruits of the harvest—are expressly referred to, which clearly implies the presence of the people in the land of Canaan. It is true that in the same connections *the camp* is mentioned also; which shows indeed that these laws embraced the present as well the future in their purview. But whether applied to the present or the future they must of course be applied with such modifications as might be required by the law of necessity. The complete ideal of the sacrificial system is given; the extent to which, at any given time, it should be practically realized must, it was unnecessary to say, depend upon circumstances. If the animals, whether beasts or birds, required for the sacrifices, could not be had in the wilderness, of course they would not be offered in the wilderness. If the number of the priests were insufficient to offer or to eat the sacrifices brought by the people, of course those sacrifices would not be offered or eaten. The sojourn in the wilderness was an exceptional case; and if the paramount law of circumcision itself was neglected without even the plea of necessity for such neglect,—as it appears it was,—during that time; how much more may the minute complicated and burdensome regulations in regard to sacrifices have been imperfectly complied with, under circumstances rendering a perfect compliance with them impossible without constant miraculous aid. The history does not assert that they were thus complied with in the wilderness. And it is to be observed that most of these laws were either promulgated to the Israelites before they left the vicinity of Horeb, and consequently before they had been condemned, for their rebellion in the matter of the spies, to wander 40 years in the wilderness, or they were announced to them in the plains of Moab, just before they were actually about to cross the Jordan. The 13 cities assigned to Aaron's sons by Joshua may have been a prospective arrangement, providing for the future increase of the priesthood. It is evident that many of the arrangements in the division of the promised land were of a prospective character.

But it is objected that the history *does* assert that a *second Passover*, at least, was *actually* celebrated in the wilderness; and it is contended that the duties required of the priests on that occasion vastly exceed the powers of Aaron and his sons to perform.

Now it is remarkable that, while Colenso elsewhere objects

to admitting other Scripture, outside of the Pentateuch, to furnish aid in explaining its difficulties, but insists that the Pentateuch must stand upon and be interpreted by *its own data;* he yet, in this chapter, goes to the Chronicles to get a statement from which to make an inference in regard to the mode of keeping the Passover in the wilderness; although in the Pentateuch we read not a word of the kind. What is the *animus* of such a proceeding?

The mode of celebrating the Passover near Sinai is to be determined from the Pentateuch itself. The law in Lev. xvii, 2–6 applies to *other* sacrifices, not expressly to the Passover. And from a comparison of 2 Chron. xxx, 16, with 2 Chron. xxxv, 11, it would seem probable that the blood sprinkled by the priests at that time *was from the burnt offerings, and not from the Passover victims.* And besides it is by no means certain that Aaron and his sons had been consecrated before the celebration of this second Passover; for the tabernacle was not reared up until the first day of the first month of the second year; and the Lord spake to Moses out of the tabernacle announcing sundry precepts and especially those which regarded the duties and perquisites of Aaron and his sons when they should be anointed,—see the first seven chapters of Leviticus, —and then follows the account of the formal consecration of the Aaronic priesthood, Lev. viii. It is true that in Ex. xl, Moses is directed to rear up the tabernacle, and *to anoint and sanctify Aaron as priest;* but that the latter act should follow immediately upon the former does not appear; on the contrary, it appears that, having set up and arranged the tabernacle, *Moses himself* burnt incense and offered the burnt offering and the meat offering, and that *"Moses* and Aaron and his sons washed their hands and their feet at the laver, when *they* went into the tent of the congregation, and when *they came near unto the altar"*.

For the length of the sojourn in Egypt we are ready to adopt the shorter term of 215 years, on which Colenso insists, as being on the whole the most probable. While, at the time of the exodus, there may have been some of the "4th generation" from Jacob surviving, in some lines, as in the case of Moses and some others,—and thus the promise to Abraham may have been in this sense fulfilled,—it yet by no means follows that, in all the lines of descent from Jacob, the Hebrew population had reached only the 4th generation. Indeed, Colenso's own table shows that, in the line of Judah, Bezaleel was of the 7th generation from Jacob. Colenso is aware, for he expressly cites the passage, that "Joseph saw Ephraim's

children to the third generation", which would be the 5th from
Jacob; and that Joseph died about 70 years after the descent
of Jacob into Egypt,—leaving, on his own computation, yet
140 years and more, before the time of the exodus. The exodus therefore could not very well have taken place in the 4th
generation of this line. It is more likely to have been, in
general, in the 8th, 9th, 10th, or even the 11th, as the Chron-
icler places Joshua in the 11th generation from Jacob.

Supposing the exodus to have been, on the average, in the
9th generation from Jacob; that is, supposing the children of
the 9th generation to have been then, for the most part, already born, and to average say 20 years of age; we can then
easily account for the whole Hebrew population assigned to
the time of the Exodus.

Let there be 50 males, (there were 51,) and as many females (whether granddaughters of Jacob or not) of the generation of Ephraim; and let Joseph see the children of Ephraim unto the third generation, and let those of this generation, then born, be from one to four years old at the time of
Joseph's death, 71 years after Jacob's descent into Egypt.
From a comparison of Gen. xl, 46, 50, and Gen. xlv, 6, it appears that Ephraim could not have been more than 8 nor less
than 3 years old, when Jacob came into Egypt. From Ephraim's birth, therefore, to the birth of some of his descendants of the third generation, whom Joseph saw, there could
have been only from 74 to 79 years; that is to say, there are
only 25 or 26 years to be allowed to each generation. Ephraim
would be among the youngest of the 100 assigned to his generation. The length of the generations which Joseph saw,
being a part of the series of generations in question, is more
to the purpose, as a norma or guide, than the earlier and
longer generations from Abraham to Ephraim.

In the remaining 144 years to the exodus, let there be 4
more generations, allow them 30 years each, let this 4th generation average 20 years old at the time of the exodus, and let
there be children of a 5th generation from one to 3 years old.
Let the increase average fourfold at each generation; which is
less, for the males, than the increase in the families of the 12
patriarchs. Of males and females together, this would imply
an average of 8 children to each family.

Assuming Ephraim to have been 8 years old at the time of
Jacob's descent, 4 generations of 25 years each, and 4 more
of 30 years each, we have the following table:

Years.	Population.	
8		
17 100	.... Ephraim's generation.
25 .... 400	... 1st gen. Ephraim's children.
25 .... 1600	2d " " "
4 .... 6400	3d " " "
71	Joseph dies.
21	
30 .... 25600	1st gen. after death of Jos.
30 .... 102,400	2d gen. after death of Jos.
30 .... 409,600	3d " " "
30 ..... 1,638,400	4th " " "
3 .... 400,000	5th " " "
215 2,550,400	

Thus, adding the 4th generation from Joseph's death to the
two preceding, and to the children of that which followed, we
have for the number of the people at the exodus 2,550,400 of
93 years old and under. And if half of this 4th generation
were 20 years old, it would furnish 409,600 warriors; and half
the generation next preceding, being adult males from 30 to
63 years old, would furnish 204,800 more; making in all 614,-
400 of males 20 years old and upward.

We leave out of the account the question whether the
grandsons of Jacob married their cousins or got their wives
elsewhere. It is enough that they probably had wives. We
leave out of the account the effect of polygamy, which was
probably practised, especially in Joseph's lifetime. We leave
out of the account the servants and maid-servants which Jacob
probably had in his household when he went down into Egypt;
or, if *he* had not, the Israelites, by the favor of Joseph, may
have procured them afterwards. And finally, we leave out of
the account other grandchildren of Jacob, who probably were
born, like Jochebed, after the descent into Egypt, and who
may have been numbered under the other heads of families,
according to some principle of subordination or selection which
must have prevailed in Hebrew genealogies, though it has not
been fully explained to us. The sons of Jacob were yet in the
prime of life when they went into Egypt; they may afterwards,
as Levi for example, have lived ninety or a hundred years;
and it is not likely that they ceased to have children immediately upon the descent into Egypt. Nor did all their intercourse with Canaan, probably, cease immediately upon this
event. (1 Chron. vii, 20–27.) Omitting all these possibilities
and probabilities, some of which might be made to strengthen
our case very much, we let the first term, the ratio, and the
number of terms of our table, rest on given data; and the re-

sult shows that the whole number of the " armies of Israel " can be accounted for, without supposing the census " unhistorical ".

But the number of the *first born* presents peculiar difficulties. It was taken of those from one month old and upward, one year and one month after the exodus. Supposing, as is most natural, that the law of the Redemption of the first born was not retrospective, but that only those were numbered as requiring to be redeemed, who had been born within this first year, that is to say, since the destruction of the first born of the Egyptians, and the issuing of the requisition to the Israelites to redeem their first born,—for whose redemption the tribe of Levi was evidently substituted, — and the case will stand thus: Let a generation take about 30 years, as before supposed ; and as before supposed, let each generation be quadruple the preceding. Let the generation at the time of the exodus be taken as that which we have supposed the 4th from Joseph's death ; and the births, on an average, would be 204,800 in a year. Then allowing, as a somewhat exceptional case, one in every nine or ten children to be a first born male, we should have about the number given in the text, viz., about 22,000.

Let us remember, however, that " the man Moses ", as we are told, " was very great in the land of Egypt ", and that " God gave the people favour in the sight of the Egyptians ". It would not be surprising, therefore, if under these circumstances, many of the Egyptians, especially those of the lower class, seeing the Israelites manifestly objects of the Divine favor, should, during the plagues in Egypt, have fled to the Israelites for protection ; and that consequently the Israelites may have taken, just at this time, additional wives from the Egyptian women ; so that, during the following year, the number of births of first born should have been unusually great, even twice the ordinary number. We will suppose the rate of all the births increased 50 per cent. We shall then have 300,000 for the year ; and, allowing one in 14 to be a first born male, we should have about the number required.

We have to consider, it is true, that a population does not advance by the discrete steps of separate generations but by a *constant* compounding and involution. But the number of births in London, with a population nearly the same as that assigned to the Israelites, is about 100,000 annually ; and it does not exceed the bounds of possibility or even of natural probability, under the peculiar circumstances above referred to, that the number in the case before us should have been three times as great.

It is to be observed that these children were most of them in the womb before the Israelites left Egypt. It is naturally and easily understood that, afterwards, under the altered circumstances of the sojourn in the wilderness, the rate of increase was completely checked.

In general, in regard to the rate of the increase of the Israelites in Egypt,—we have supposed it to be a little more than fourfold in 30 years. Is this credible? We answer:

1. Populations are known to make their natural increase most rapidly when in a state of servitude, or of degradation and poverty; as is seen among the Chinese, or by comparing some counties with others in Ireland.

2. The population of the Free States and Territories of the American Union has more than trebled in each period of 35 years from 1790 to 1860; advancing in that time from less than 2,000,000 to more than 19,000,000. It is true that something must be allowed out of this for the effect of immigration.

3. That there was something *extraordinary* in the rapid increase of the Israelites in Egypt, is repeatedly indicated by the phrases, " The people increased and multiplied in Egypt "; and, " The children of Israel were fruitful and increased abundantly, and multiplied, and waxed exceeding mighty, and the land was filled with them "; and, " The more the Egyptians afflicted them, the more they multiplied and grew ". The extraordinary increase, therefore, of four-fold in 30 years, may not perhaps transcend the bounds of natural explanation. We have a right to take into the account, if necessary, any or all the circumstances and considerations above set aside. We have a right to take into the account also what ancient historians have told us of the wonderful fruitfulness of the Egyptian women, and what the sacred historian says of the yet greater *liveliness* of the Hebrew women. We have a right to take into the account the probability of early marriages, and the extraordinary vigor and great age of the Patriarchs and their descendants, from Abraham to Moses and Joshua. If an objector sets against us the small families assigned to some of the leading men in the history, as to Isaac, Joseph, and Moses, for example, we answer: these instances, even if we had the whole number of these families recorded, which in some cases is very doubtful, no more prove the general rapid increase of the Hebrew population to be " unhistorical ", than the small families of Washington, Hancock, Franklin, and Jefferson, will hereafter prove the rapid increase of the American population to be a myth.

4. But, finally, if the whole problem cannot be satisfactorily

explained by ordinary or extraordinary natural causes, then the sacred text would fully authorize the idea that there was something *miraculous* about it—some special blessing, in fulfilment of God's gracious promises.

Bishop Colenso raises special difficulties about the numbers of the Danites and the Levites. As to the Danites, it is true that, according to the Pentateuch, there is assigned to Dan only one son, Hushim; but then, for aught appearing in the Pentateuch, Hushim may have had as many sons as Jacob had, and his grandsons may have averaged 5 or 6 (instead of four) to each son; and so, before the exodus, the tribe of Dan may have reached the number assigned to it, as well as any other tribe. In other words, there is no special difficulty here at all; for, plainly, we have as good a right to take Jacob's family to guide us in our *average*, as to take Dan's; and it is not at all strange that any one tribe should at one time fall below, and at another rise above the general average. This belongs to the nature of averages.

In the family of Levi, the chief difficulty is found with the Amramites. To meet this the following scheme may be suggested:

```
Levi      48 yrs. old at Descent, lives to 137.
Kohath    10  "    "        "        lives to 133.
Amram born 35 yrs. after Descent, lives to 137.
      Kohath   begets Amram      at 45,
      Levi      "    Jochebed    at 96,
      Amram     "    Moses       at 100, lives to 137,
      Jochebed being then         82.
Then, Amram, born    35 yrs. after Descent,
      begets Moses at 100 years old;
      Moses at exodus 80 years old;
      ─────────────────────
      Sojourn in Egypt 215 years.
```

As to the great age assigned to Levi, Amram and Jochebed, when they had children, Colenso seems willing to admit this as possible,—the more readily it would appear, in order thus to preclude the supposition of intermediate generations, and consequently of a longer period for the sojourn in Egypt. And certainly it is credible, if the story of Abraham is credible. Abraham was a hundred and Sarah ninety years old at the birth of Isaac. Jacob was also ninety years old at the birth of Joseph; and Moses died at 120 with his "natural force" unabated. But Jochebed *may* have been merely a *descendant* of Levi; as Elizabeth, the wife of Zacharias, is said to have been " of the daughters of Aaron". And Num. xxvi, 59, may mean that " Jochebed was a descendant of Levi, whom [a woman] in

Egypt [or, an Egyptian woman] bare to him"; i. e., that she had an Egyptian mother.   Our translation of Ex. vi, 20, where Jochebed is called Amram's " father's sister " is itself based upon this passage in Numbers.   The word rendered " father's sister " probably means *one beloved, a friend, a near relative.*   In the table of affinities in Lev. xviii, this word is not used for "father's sister ", v. 12 ; but is used for the "father's brother's wife ", v. 14, and so translated " aunt ".   It need not mean precisely " father's sister ".   However this may be, it is not to be presumed without positive evidence, that Amram had no children till he was near a hundred years old.   He may have married Jochebed in his old age, and had by her Moses, Aaron, and Miriam ; and it is easy to see reasons why these alone of his children should be mentioned by name.   But he may have had other children by an earlier wife or wives ; and, *if the history implies* that he had other descendants besides those which can be traced to Moses, Aaron or Miriam, then it implies that he had other children besides those three.

If then Amram, born 35 years after the Descent into Egypt, married at 20, there would remain of the Sojourn in Egypt 160 years for, say, 5 generations of 30 years each, and ten years of a 6th generation.   Let these generations increase according to the law before supposed, and we have :

Amram	1		
1st generation	4		
2d "	16		
3d "	64		64
4th "	256	—	256
5th "	1024	—	1024
6th "	4096	$\times \frac{1}{4}$ —	1024

2370 :

Giving 2370 instead of the 2150 which would be Amram's quota of the sum of the males of the Kohathites given in the text —and it is not at all necessary to suppose that they reached this proportion.

So much for the numbers, and arithmetical calculations, whereby the Pentateuch was to be proved " unhistorical ".

In connection with the story of the war with Midian, the points objected to by Colenso are :

1. The comparative smallness of the Hebrew force, and their suffering no loss.   Ans. The transaction is expressly recognized in the text as *miraculous ;* the battle was the Lord's.

2. The great number of captives and the immense booty. Ans. There does not appear any thing impossible or incredible

in this under all the circumstances; it was an extraordinary and even a miraculous success, and is so represented.

3. The killing of the Midianites, men, women and children, charged as cruelty, butchery, massacre, &c. Ans. This was God's vengeance executed at God's express command. Is God to be charged with cruelty, butchery, murder and massacre, when by such means or instruments as he may appoint, he takes men's lives? Colenso's argument seems to be, "if men had been said to have done this of themselves, it would be credible, but that God should do it is so inconsistent with his character that it is not to be believed,—it is *unhistorical*".

4. Jehovah's tribute of slaves is regarded as a justification of slavery. Ans. The enslaving of captives taken in war was undoubtedly permitted; and these slaves especially appropriated to the Lord, were probably reserved for menial offices in connection with the service of the Sanctuary, which was, so far, an elevation and a relief to them. In general, the arrangements about slavery in the Pentateuch seem to have been among the Bishop's earliest and most provoking difficulties. He seems to forget that they were merely civil regulations at most, and probably intended to be temporary; and that severe as they were they were a vast improvement upon the system of slavery as it then existed in the world. He will not believe that any thing comes from God unless it is perfect at once; he could not therefore allow God to be the proper author of a mere civil government. He forgets the principle which our Saviour announced in regard to the law of divorce, "For the hardness of your hearts Moses wrote you this precept". He forgets his own strange views in regard to modern polygamy. The Zulus, it would seem, find that polygamy suits their natural notions better than slavery. But surely if God may have permitted to the Israelites polygamy and divorce "for the hardness of their hearts", he may have permitted slavery also, for as good a reason.

To the Bishop's final chronological objection, we reply: The war with king Arad may have been originally placed out of the historical order, or it may have been accidentally transposed subsequently, and may belong before the account of Aaron's death; or it may have taken place during the mourning for Aaron. So a month will be saved here. Then, the nine encampments may have required, for once, but nine, or say 18, days. So 10 or 20 days more will be saved here. But finally, the story of Balak and Balaam, of the abode in Shittim, of the plague, of the second numbering of the people, and of the war upon Midian,—if the 40 or 50 days above saved will not suffice, these events may come in between the third and fourth chapters of Deuteronomy. Thus Moses will have begun his address to the people (in Deut.) immediately on their arrival at the plains of Moab, near Beth-Peor or Baal-Peor, which seems to have been the headquarters of the Israelites during all or most of those events; and after those transactions, the address of Moses will have been continued in the 4th chapter. See Deut. i, 4, 5; also the last verses of ch. iii, and the opening verses of ch. iv, especially the third verse, and note their allusions. We have not space to insert the passages. It is particularly to be observed in connection with the war with Midian, that the Lord said, "Avenge the children of Israel of the Midianites: *afterward shalt thou be gathered to thy people*"; which last trait is just the point referred to at large at the close of the third chapter of Deuteronomy.

We have thus conscientiously plodded through with Bishop Colenso's historical difficulties. If we have not disposed of them all, we submit that we have shown it probable that they may all be disposed of, without giving up the historical character of the Pentateuch.

Both the tendency and the grasp of Colenso's mind may be seen in his statement in reference to the flood, that mount Ararat could not have been submerged, unless the hills of Auvergne were in due time submerged also, as the waters would necessarily seek a common level—entirely ignoring the well attested geological fact, that the relative level of the land may vary if that of the water may not, and if a continent were to sink, "the fountains of the great deep would naturally be broken up" to submerge it. The following statement gives a still more astounding view of the clearness of his physical knowledge : "The Bible says, 'the sun stood still and the moon stayed', Jo. x, 13; and the arresting of the earth's motion, while it might cause the appearance of the 'sun standing still', would not account for the moon's 'staying'". But why not? The motion of the moon in her orbit, if continued, would not much affect the result in the course of one day, and so far as it should affect it, would only exaggerate it, i. e., would make the moon seem even to go back a little in the heavens.

Whether the flood were partial or universal, and however this passage in Jo. x, 13, is to be explained,—and undoubtedly, it is susceptible of various explanations,—infidels and their abettors may as well leave off carping at these two points of the sacred history; for they will still remain perfectly credible to any man of common sense, who does not deny the possibility or the credibility of miracles altogether. If the Almighty

22

works a miracle, there are implied in it of course all those operations and conditions which are necessary to bring it into consistent connection with the ordinary course of his natural agency.   They are not additional miracles, but part and parcel of
the original miracle itself.

To Bishop Colenso's position as a moral and religious man,
it is not essential to our argument to make any allusion.   His
life as a Missionary has been so self-denying and laborious, and
he makes in his book such strong demonstrations of his devout
piety, of his deep conscientiousness, his earnest love of the
truth, and withal of his shrinking from the task which he feels
imposed upon him of undermining the simple yet cherished
faith of his brethren, that one can hardly find it in his heart to
be severe in his judgments.   But we may say that we do not
envy him his position towards the Church in which he holds
the office of Bishop, nor can we sympathize with him in his
moral attitude towards Christianity—towards the Christian faith
and the Christian religion, as they have always been understood
and received.

At one time he had written: "For myself, if I cannot find
the means of doing away with my present difficulties, I see not
how I can retain my Episcopal office, in the discharge of which
I must require from others a solemn declaration that they 'un-
feignedly believe all the Canonical Scriptures of the Old and
New Testament', which with the evidence now before me it is
impossible wholly to believe in".   But he adds, that after the
decision of the Court of Arches, his conscience is materially relieved.   That is to say, though himself under the obligation of
that "solemn declaration" so long as he remains in his present
position, he will not resign his place except to avoid being legally forced to vacate it.   Would he feel no longer obliged to
pay his debts when the Statute of Limitations would relieve him
from compulsion or punishment in case of his refusal?   Again
he says: "I implore the laity to consider the position in which
the *Clergy* will be placed, if the facts, brought forward in this
book are found to be substantially true.   Let them examine
their own hearts solemnly, in the sight of God, on these points.
Would they have the Clergy bound under pains and penalties,
to profess belief in that, which they do not themselves believe
in, to which they would not on any account commit themselves?
Are they willing that their own sons, who may feel the Divine
call to devote themselves to the ministry of souls, should be
entangled in these trammels, so galling to the conscience, so injurious to their sense of truth and honesty, so impeding to the
freedom and heartiness of their ministrations?   *We*, indeed,
who are under the yoke, may have for a time to bear it, how-

ever painful it may be, while we struggle and hope on for deliverance.   But what youth of noble mind, with a deep yearning for truth, and an ardent desire to tell out the love of God
to man, will consent to put himself voluntarily into such fetters"?   Pp. 36–37.   But if Bishop Colensoc an honestly and
conscientiously remain where he is, with his present views, for
the alleged purpose, not of retaining his dignity and emolu-
ments, but of endeavoring to "reform the system of the Church
and enlarging her boundaries", why may he not rather invite
and urge all "youth of noble mind, and deep yearning for truth,
and an ardent desire to tell out the love of God to man", to
come and help in this great work, in this mighty and glorious
reformation?   If he can conscientiously stay where he is, why
may not others conscientiously come where he is?   Does he not,
in effect, admit after all, that he voluntarily, for the sake of some
matters of personal convenience and social comfort, remains
"entangled in trammels galling to the conscience, and injurious
to his sense of truth and honesty"?

And what is his attitude towards Christianity?   He teaches
that "we are to look for the sign of God's Spirit speaking to us
in the Bible, in that of which our hearts alone can be the
judges, ... in that which speaks to the witness of
God within us, to which alone, under God himself, whose voice
it utters in the secrets of his inner being, each man is ultimately
responsible,—to the Reason and Conscience".   Is not this denying the superior authority, and even the possibility, of all
positive and distinctive Revelation?   He shows that he means
it thus, by adding "that, not in the Bible only but also out of
the Bible, not to us Christians only but to our fellow men of all
climes and countries, ages and religions, the same gracious
Teacher is revealing in different measures, according to his own
good pleasure, the hidden things of God"; and then quoting in
proof a passage from Cicero, and "the great truths of the Sikh
Gooroos", and "words which were written by one who had no
Pentateuch or Bible to teach him, but who surely learned such
living truths as these by the direct teaching of the Spirit of
God"—and the first of "these living truths, learned by *the direct teaching* of the Spirit of God", which he cites, is this:
"Whatever Ram willeth without the least difficulty shall be".
What must logically be his theory of Inspiration, his idea of
Canonical Scripture, and his notion of the character and posi-
tion of the Christian religion, one can easily conjecture, without
waiting for the next instalment of his critical examinations.

But he would not make men infidels for all the world; and
therefore, lest the faith of any should be uncomfortably shaken,
before he has an opportunity to reässure them by further
announcements of the glorious truths — or rather, *negations* —

which he has discovered, he ventures to refer them for temporary comfort and repose, to St. Paul's Epistle to the Romans? No, not exactly that, but to his, Bishop Colenso's commentary on that Epistle; in which he promulgates the doctrine of universal salvation, and travesties that of justification—the grand doctrine of Pauline instruction—into a mere make believe, a mere act of presumption; all are saved, and the use of the Gospel is to make men think so.   To think so, is, to be justified.

No wonder that such a Christian should incline to think that our Lord Jesus Christ, during his ministry on earth, was ignorant of the true character and authorship of the Pentateuch. Colenso is a wiser man.   The disciple now is above his master. He could teach his Lord and Saviour to understand the Holy Scriptures.   He clearly admits that Jesus did *not* understand them as he does.   And he triumphantly asks, "at what period of his life on earth is it to be supposed that he had granted to him, as the Son of Man, *supernaturally*, full and accurate information on these points, so that he should be expected to speak about the Pentateuch in other terms, than any other devout Jew of that day would have employed?"   The Bishop argues at large that Jesus had not such information when he said, "Moses wrote of me"; "Moses shewed at the bush"; "They have Moses and the prophets"; "If they hear not Moses and the Prophets", &c.   But we venture to ask whether Jesus had, perchance, such information, when, just before his ascension to heaven, he said to his disciples, "These are the words *which I spake unto you while I was yet with you*, that all things must be fulfilled which were written in the law of Moses, and in the prophets, and in the psalms, concerning me"?   And when "he opened their understandings that they might understand the Scriptures"?   It does not appear that he here corrected any of his former instructions; rather he expressly reïterated them. Nor does it appear that the Apostles, subsequently in their teachings, after having their understanding thus *supernaturally* opened, and receiving the Holy Ghost, the gift of Inspiration, showed any less confidence in the authenticity and Divine authority of Moses and the prophets, than, "as devout Jews", they had been accustomed to do before, but quite the contrary.

But why waste words?   Does Bishop Colenso really believe that Jesus Christ was, in any proper and peculiar sense, in any "supernatural" sense, *the Son of God*, God manifest in the flesh? Does he believe that Jesus was "very Christ", God's Anointed One, the promised *Messiah?*   Does he believe that he was conceived by the Holy Ghost and born of the Virgin Mary? Does he believe that, as an actual *historical* fact, *he was raised from the dead?*   If so, then he believes in the Christian revelation and the Christian religion as something quite peculiar in the history of the world, something quite unlike those of the Koran and the Vedas and the Shastras; then he believes in the possibility and actuality of miracles; then is it perfectly credible that our Saviour should have had supernatural knowledge, should have wrought miracles, almost incredible that it should have been otherwise; then may Moses have written of him; then may prophets have predicted him; then may the early history of the world have been arranged with reference to his coming; then may the story of the call of Abraham, and of a chosen people, be historically true; and finally the whole story of the Pentateuch, exodus and all, with its miraculous concomitants and wonderful Providential guidance, may be, not only possibly true but extremely probable, as well as highly instructive.   From the true Christian stand-point, all Colenso's petty difficulties vanish as the morning mist before the sun.

Whatever evidence there is for the truth of Christianity, is evidence for the truth of whatever else is involved in the truth of Christianity; so that, in balancing the considerations for the truth or falsity of a given point, we may allege for its truth not only all the direct evidence on the spot, but the whole weight of the Christian evidences in general.

The great question, therefore, which will come next to be settled by and with Colenso, is, How far the truth of Christianity is involved in the historical truth and Mosaic authorship of the Pentateuch.   If *salva fide*, the Pentateuch can be given up, it is no great matter, though the Pentateuch should go.   But if it will require as much pains, and as much indulgent criticism, to save the truth of Christianity, after giving up the historical truth of the Pentateuch, as it would have required before to defend the truth of the Pentateuch, considered in the abstract light of an alleged history,—of course, Bishop Colenso must either give up Christianity or abandon his present position. And the believing Christian will solve the difficulty by reflecting and concentrating upon it all the light to be derived from the whole mass of the Christian evidences.

For the Christian, there is a presumption in favor of the historical truth of the Pentateuch; and, therefore, *possible* explanations of difficulties to him become *probable*.   But Colenso, on the contrary, takes the position that no explanation of apparent difficulties or contradictions is to be received, unless whatever it suggests is *asserted* in the text, or is shown to be an actual *matter of fact*.   Even ordinary history is not subjected to so severe a test; and, indeed, difficulties that could thus be removed would hardly be difficulties at all.

For a Christian, the natural course of proceeding would apparently be—in publishing his critical thoughts to the world—*first*, to establish a theory of inspiration which would be consistent with his special interpretations, as, for example, with alleged historical errors ; and after that to set forth those errors. *For an Infidel*, the natural order is the reverse ; he will insist upon the historical errors first and at all events, and then inspiration must accommodate itself or go by the board.   He expects the latter to be the result ; but the former will suit him as well, for it will come to about the same thing.

If it is the infidel who alleges historical errors against Christianity, or if it is the doubting Christian who is troubled by them, the Christian man, not to say the Christian Bishop, would be expected to defend Christianity, not by insisting, in the spirit and style of the infidel partisan, upon the historical errors themselves, but by showing either that the errors do not exist, or that, if they do exist, they are entirely consistent with a true view of inspiration after all, *showing* this, we say, not simply suggesting that it may be so.

Whether Moses or some other man was the author of the Pentateuch, that author would seem to have been a person having a reasonable claim to a fair share of intelligence and common sense.   He may have written in the language, style, and spirit of his times ; but is not to be supposed to have written unmitigated nonsense and palpable self-contradictions, so long as any fair and reasonable interpretation can possibly avoid such a conclusion.   The presumption is in his favor.   He professes to write history, not fiction or poetry.   To an un-Christian, critical age, he may be ignorant, he may err, if you will, but he is not to be presumed a simpleton.   It were more reasonable to set him down as a thoroughgoing impostor and falsifier.

Nor is the Pentateuch to be summarily dismissed as " unhistorical ", because it is conceived according to the language and habits of the early Oriental, the Hebrew mind ; nor its statements to be pronounced not " literally " true, because they would not be true when interpreted according to the language and habits of modern times. Its real *meaning* is what we want to find ; and that meaning we hold to be neither mystical nor fabulous, but arithmetically and historically true.

The infidel method begins with discrediting the history, and then denies the miracles.   Though Colenso professes that he would have been ready to receive the miracles, had the history, in his opinion, been trustworthy, he yet apparently does not receive them.   Consequently, to him there remains no evidence of a Moses, or an exodus, or at least of any special Divine interposition in connection with them.

We shall be charged with having been obliged to resort to supposed miracles for an explanation of the text.   We maintain that we have a right, a logical and critical right, so to do. Moses does not pretend that the facts he narrates could be accounted for, or would be credible, without miracle, without constant Divine guidance and interposition. He would not go one step in his history, any more than in his leading of the Israelites, *unless God's presence went with him.* The miracle, the Divine interposition, he incorporates into his history as an integral part of it, nay, as its leading idea, its key-note, its very back-bone. That in such a story, some particular miracles should have been omitted, left untold, is no more strange or unnatural, as we have already said, than that any other particular facts, necessary to a full view and explanation of the case, should have been omitted. Yet such omissions as these are common in all histories, especially in ancient histories. What sort of critical proceeding is that, then, which begins with ignoring the miraculous element, goes on to show that, without it, the remaining story is inexplicable and must be deemed fabulous, and then turns round and says, " as the story itself is fabulous, there is no proof of the miracles ", and so the whole book is to be thrust aside as a piece of ancient mythology? Now, if the matters of fact alleged in the narrative were shown by other independent and sufficient historical or monumental evidence, to be false, the rest of such a proceeding, and its final conclusion, would be perfectly legitimate. But this is not the nature of Bishop Colenso's argument. *He does not propose to establish the " unhistorical " character of the Pentateuch by external, but by internal evidence.* He proposes to show that its statements are inconsistent with each other, impossible and absurd, and that, therefore, it is " unhistorical ". But, surely, in undertaking such a work, he was bound to take into view *all the data* the author had furnished or suggested, whether in the shape of specific facts or as general factors, agents, or causes; and therefore he was bound to recognize both the particular miracles and the pervading miraculous element, as constituent parts of the problem he had to solve. A man's testimony *may* be proved false, or judged incredible, however *consistently* given. But it cannot be shown to be *self-contradictory*, and *therefore* false, unless all its statements and assumptions are first fairly taken into view, and compared and weighed together. Bishop Colenso must give us his Second Part, at least, before he will have shown the Pentateuch to be " unhistorical ".

Since writing the above, Part II. has been published; but after all, we apprehend that if Part I. falls, Part II. will fall with it.

Art. VIII.—THEOLOGICAL AND LITERARY INTELLIGENCE.

THREE hundred copies only of Tischendorf's splendid edition of the *Codex Sinaiticus* have been struck off, and of these, one hundred have been permitted by the Emperor of Russia to go into circulation. The work is contained in four large volumes, and the price is £34 10s. The first volume contains the prolegomena, giving an account of the discovery of the manuscript, and discussing its palæographical features. The editor refers it to the age of Eusebius; that is, to the fourth century. There are twenty-one plates of lithographic and photo-lithographic fac-similes, which give the highest idea of the beauty of the original. The last two of these plates contain fac-similes of thirty-six other documents, such as the Herculaneum volumes and other ancient texts, for the purpose of comparison.

The Samaritan Pentateuch.—At a meeting of the Syro-Egyptian Society, held on the 13th of January, the Rev. J. Mills read a paper on a copy of the *Samaritan Pentateuch*, which he exhibited. He had spent some months at Nablous, and had been allowed to examine the scroll said to have been written by Abishama, the grandson of Aaron. If we mistake not, a photograph of this, taken by the photographer who accompanied the Prince of Wales to Palestine, was exhibited in Bond street not long ago. The manuscript shown by Mr. Mills is of the fourteenth century, and was lent him by a Samaritan priest. He is collating it with the Hebrew text, and with the Samaritan version as given in *Walton's Polyglot*, with a view to its publication.—*London Guardian.*

Among other curiosities lately brought to England from the East by Mr. Stuart Glennie, is a fragment of a manuscript of the *Samaritan Pentateuch*, consisting of four imperfect leaves of parchment, and containing portions of Exodus, chapter xxxii, to xxxviii. The writing is small and neat, and probably of considerable antiquity. Mr. Glennie (says the *Parthenon*) has also a portion of a paper manuscript, containing a commentary and explanation in Arabic of a part of the Samaritan text. (Genesis xxxii, 9, to Genesis xxxiv.) This fragment, which contains twenty pages, is of later date than the preceding. Both manuscripts were obtained by Mr. Glennie from the chief of the small Samaritan community at Nablous.

The *Secularists* (*i.e.* Atheists) of England now have two periodicals, the *National Reformer* and *Barker's Review*. *Barker's Review* began in 1861; the *National Reformer*, the most violent, edited by Mr. Bradlaugh, began in 1860, and at one time had a circulation of 9,800. Then there was a quarrel, and Mr. Joseph Barker started *Barker's Review* for "the unbounded license party". Another journal, recently deceased, the *Counsellor*, has been published for some 25 years under various names. Mr. G. J. Holyoake, the most noted of these infidels, is one of the editors of the *National Reformer*. Of his *Logic of Death*, it is said 40,000 copies have been circulated; he has also written *The Trial of Theism; The Last Trial for Atheism*, etc. He edited the *Reasoner* for fourteen years; its name was changed in 1861 to the *Counsellor*. He says: "God is the eternal, unanswered, Why? to which no man has replied". The *National Reformer* cites and approves some of Mansel's positions. It says: "Mansel acknowledges . . . that the true Christian philosopher must renounce all pretensions to a knowledge of the Absolute . . . that reason and religion are incompatible, that if you would believe you must not reason . . . that all you have to reason about is, whether the Bible be God's word, and then take all it says in faith, nothing doubting. And he is right". The *West-*

minster Review, from which we quote, says that "permanent organization seems impossible for Secularists". Its societies are rapidly dissolving. "A smart freethinker's all things in an hour". The *Review* pertinently asks: "Is not the true explanation of their fickleness to be found in the fact that human nature requires a religion of some kind, and withers when it is denied the nourishment of reverence and hope, and that, therefore, the Secularists, ignoring or denying God and immortality, are evermore fated to fail"! One of the most noted and successful of these Secularists, Mr. John H. Gordon, has recently renounced all connection with them, and professed the Christian faith. An exceedingly interesting account of his conversion is given in a volume published at Leeds, where Gordon was the soul of the Secular Society.

Mr. Bolton Corney has published a *Critical Disquisition on Shakespeare's Sonnets*, supporting Chasles' conjecture, that the enigmatical dedication is addressed *by*, and not *to*, W. H. He also gives a history of these Sonnets and of the criticisms upon them. D. Barnstoff's *Key to the Sonnets* has been translated by T. J. Graham; his theory is, that they are a series of soliloquies.

The Earliest Newspaper. — The late sale of Libri's MSS. and rare books produced more than $50,000. Among the curious documents was a *Newe Zeitung aus Hispanien und Italien: Mense Februario*, 1584; which Mr. Watts, of the British Museum, conjectures to be the earliest monthly journal or newspaper. It was printed at Nuremberg, and gives the earliest known account of Pizarro's expedition. It is usually stated that the *English Mercurie*, 1588, was the earliest newspaper. Another unique gazette in Libri's catalogue bears date June 7, 1475, and gives an account, in *ottava rima*, of the capture of Caffa by the Turks in 1474. A monthly publication was issued at Cologne 1596 : and one at Prague 1597. A semi-annual gazette, or compend of historical events, called *Calendarii Historici Relatio*, was began in 1590, in Frankfort, by Jacobus Francus. Other interesting details are given by Mr. Watt in the *Athenæum*, Aug. 2, 1862.

A letter from Bonn to the London *Athenæum* shows that so far back as 1529 a paper appeared at Nuremberg at intervals when news of interest came to hand, and was entitled *Newe Zeitung vom Türken, so ein gut Freund, der damit und dabei gewest ist, von Wien herausgegeben;* that is — *Newspaper about the Turks, which a good friend who was present at the affair, has forwarded from Vienna.*

HOLLAND.

The translation of the Bible in current use, called the States-Bible, was made at the suggestion of the Synod of Dort. During the last and present century there have been several other versions (Van der Palm's being the best), which have not obtained any general currency. In 1848 petitions were sent to the General Synod to take measures for a new translation, and three members were appointed to make a report upon it, Van Hengel, Wildschut and Van Sterson. Van Hengel made a final report, on the principles on which the new version should be based. Professor Doedes of Utrecht subjected this report to a sharp criticism, and the Utrecht Faculty of Theology advised against it. The poet Da Costa also attacked it, 1855, in a special work, prophesying only evil from a translation executed under rationalistic sympathies. The Synod, however, appointed a commission to carry out the project. Specimens of their version, including Ezra, Nehemiah, Jonah and Nahum, were presented to the Synod, Oct. 1861. They are still at work on it. The orientalist, Künen, author of an Introduction to the Old Testament, is the chief man for the Old Testament.   He is said to be bold in his theories.   The Walloon churches use the French translation of Martin H. Ostervald.   They have also been discussing the question of revision, at intervals, since 1832.   *Neue Evangelische Kirchenzeitung.*

The subject of Resurrection of the Body is again under discussion in Holland, having been attacked by an eminent pastor of Amsterdam, and defended by C. Leutz, a pupil of Tholuck.   Dr. Doedes, Professor in Utrecht, has written two works on this topic.

A. Reville's *Critical Studies on Matthew*, which gained the prize of the Hague Society for the defence of Christianity, have been published in a volume of 366 pages at Leyden.

BELGIUM.

QUITE a number of works have been recently published, illustrating the history of Belgium.   A new edition, in 2 vols. of Adf. Borgnet's *History of the Belgians at the Close of the 18th Century :* T. Juste, *History of the National Congress of Belgium,* new ed. 2 vols. ;   G. G. Lageman's Collection of *Treaties and ¦Conventions, from* 1815, 5 volumes ;   *Anonymous Memoirs on the Troubles,* 1565–1580, edited by J. B. Blaes ;   J. Molanus, *Fourteen Books on the History of Louvain,* ed. by de Ram ;   G. Oppelt, *General History of Belgium,* 1830–60 ;   N. Considerant, *History of the Revolution in the Low Countries in the 16th Century,* 2d ed. by Frédérix ;   J. Juste, *The Low Countries under Charles V., and Life of Mary of Hungary ;   Correspondence of Philip II. on the Affairs of the Low Countries,* 4 vols. ;   *Statistics of Belgium,* published by the Minister of Finance, 1861 ;   Amédée Adnet, *History of the Belgian Parliament,* 1847–1858 ;   J. J. Thonissen, *Belgium in the Reign of Leopold I,* 2d ed., 2 vols. ;   Ernest Van Bryssel, *History of the Belgic Commerce and Marine,* 1862.   In a population of 4,426,202, 4,339,196 are returned as Roman Catholics, 6,578 Protestants, 1,336 Jews.

A work on *The Principles of the Science of the Beautiful,* by Voituron, has been published at Brussels.   It received an " honorable mention " from the French Academy.

SPAIN.

BESIDES the Memoirs of Charles V, published by McKervyn of Le Herhove, it is said, in a bibliographical journal of Madrid, that a copy of his memoirs was recently purchased among some old papers in the shop of an antiquary.   Whether these are the same as the above is not yet known.   The Belgic government has recently bought in London 400 of his letters to his aunt, the Archduchess Marguerite.

Don Vazquez Queipo, member of the Academy of Madrid, has published in Paris, in 4 vols., an Essay on the Systems of Weights and Measures of the Ancient Nations from the earliest Period of History to the Chalifate of the East.   He traces all back to the Assyrian, Egyptian and Phenician systems.   The basis was the foot ; the cube of this was the measure for solids and liquids ; the weight of this cube, filled with water, was the talent, or the standard of weight.   The French Academy of Inscription has given the numismatic prize to the author of these elaborate volumes.

Dr. Don Manuel Rodriquez de Berlanga first made known the so-called *Tables of Malaga,* containing the municipal laws of Malaga and Salpença in the reign of Domitian.   He has now had fac-similes made of the inscriptions and sent them to various learned societies.   Doubted by some, they are received as genuine by such scholars as Mommsen and Huschke. *Corresp. littéraire.*

RUSSIA.

THE BIBLE AMONG THE TARTARS.—The Holy Synod of the Greek Church in Russia have completed a translation of the Bible in the dialect of the Morchas, who are a tribe of Tartars living in tents on the southerly ridge of the Ural mountains.   Russia is making more earnest efforts than ever to Christianize and Russianize the Asiatic tribes that are becoming subject to her rule.

At the newly-erected University of Warsaw chairs have been founded for each of the principal Slavonic idioms, especially for Russian, Polish, Czechian, Ruthenian, Slovenian and Serbian, so as to render the town the centre of literary life for all the Slavonic tribes.

The Emperor Alexander has ordered to be restored to Warsaw its library of 17,000 volumes, carried off to St. Petersburg at the time of the Polish Revolution of 1831.

An Ethnographic Description of the Different Races in Russia, to celebrate the thousandth year of the empire, by T. de Pauly ; a large folio, fully illustrated, costing $150 ;   J. Salawin, *Description of Western Siberia*, Moscow ; *Letters of Russian Emperors and other Members of the Imperial Family*, Moscow ;   *Proverbs of the Russian People* (30,000), by W. J. Dahl, Moscow ;   *On Church Service, Letters to an Orthodox Man*, by J. J. Belustin ;   *On the Russian School Books of the Sixteenth Century*, by D. Mordowtzew, Moscow ;   *Meteorological Account of Russia*, by A. Kupfer ;   *The Wolga, from the Tiver to Astrachan*, with 41 plates ;   *Remains of the Slavi on the South Side of the Baltic*, by A. Hilferding ;   *Unpublished Works of* N. Karamsin, author of a history of Russia ;   *Works* of Constantine Aksakof, Moscow, 1861 ;   *History of Russia*, by S. Solovief, Moscow, 1858 ;   *Russian People and State*, by W. Leshkof, Moscow, 1858 ;   *Provincial Institutions of Russia in the 17th Century*, by B. Chicherin, Moscow, 1858 ;   *Des Réformes en Russie*, by Prince P. Dolgorukof, 1862.   Several of the last-named works are used in an instructive article on Constitutional Government in Russia, in the *Quarterly Review*, London, Jan. 1863.   Fr. Bodenstedt's *Russian Fragments*, Leips., is a valuable addition to the history of Russia.

GERMANY.

Studien und Kritiken.   1863.   Erstes Heft.   Prof. Dr. Plitt of Bonn on the Heidelberg Catechism in the Reformed Church, exhibiting its doctrinal character and influence—a valuable account.   Eggel on Schelling's Philosophy of Revelation—a concise and careful account, the clearest yet given in the same compass ; applauding Schelling's general attitude to the Christian system, but dissenting from some of his mythologizing processes.   Nasse on Job xxviii and the knowledge of mining processes.   Bäumlein on Papias's account of Mark's Gospel.   Paret on Jas. iv, 5, and Gen. iv, 7.   A review by the late Dr. Kling of recent philosophical works by Sengler and Schmid—rather prosy.   The number ends with a delightful tribute by Ullman to the memory of Kling.

Zeitschrift f. d. lutherische Theologie.   Prof. Delitzsch takes the place of the late Dr. Rudelbach in the editing of this Review, and contributes three short articles ; one on the need of a revision of Luther's translation of the Bible : another on the time in which Arethas flourished—a Greek commentator on the Apocalypse, probably in the tenth century ; his commentary is made up chiefly of excerpts from Andreas, an earlier Greek commentator. Delitzsch's third article is on Heb. viii, as illustrated in the Rabbinic literature. Fr. Laible, on the Descent to Hades, 1 Pet. iii, 17 sq.—advocates the view that the "preaching" of Christ there spoken of was in the days of Noah. Trahndorff on Aristotle and Kant, or what is Reason? contends against the rationalistic view. Dr. Guericke prints an interesting series of letters from Rudelbach, relating to the founding of the review.—Appended to this number is a pamphlet by Delitzsch, addressed to Kahnis, in reference to his recent Dogmatics, which has shocked so many Old Lutherans. It is written with warm personal friendship, and, while just to Kahnis, dissents from his positions on the Canon, the Trinity, and the Lord's Supper.

A first attempt has just been made in Germany to naturalize the Spenserian stanza. Prof. Bodenstedt has narrated the second marriage of the Czar Ivan the Terrible in that metre; and though the quantity of double rhymes necessary in German poetry has a very different effect from the verse of *Childe Harold* or *The Faerie Queene*, the success of the experiment is said to be satisfactory.

A new German monthly, entitled *Der Ansiedler im Westen* (The Pioneer in the West), has been established at Berlin, by Pastor Eichler, in the interests of the "Berlin Society in aid of the German Mission in North America."

A posthumous work of Schiller—a dramatic joke—under the title of *I have been Shaved* (*Ich habe mich rasiren lassen*), has recently been discovered, and will be printed in exact fac-simile of the original.

The *Theologische Quartalschrift* (Rom. Cath.) ends its 44th vol. with the fourth part, 1862. The first article, by Dr. Kuhn, author of the well-known *Dogmatik* and Professor in Tübingen, is on the Relation of Philosophy to Theology, opposing Clemens and others, who allow to philosophy no independent sphere. He contends that the reception of the supernatural presupposes the natural; that theology as a science presupposes philosophy. Dr. Hefele has an instructive account of the views of Innocent III on the Relation of the Papacy to the Election of Emperors—the Pope can confirm or veto the election, and, in case of disagreement, decide in favor of one of the candidates. Nolte reviews Cruice's Paris edition of the *Philosophoumena*, criticising it sharply and thoroughly, and giving preference to the Göttingen edition. Nolte inclines to the view that Hippolytus is the author of this work.—The first number, 1863, concludes Kuhn's essay on Philosophy and Theology, and also contains various exegetical studies by Dr. Aberle, and reviews several new works.

The 4th part of the *Jahbürcher für deutsche Theologie*, 1862, has, besides its valuable account of new works, only two articles. The first, by Weizsäcker, in 90 pages, reviews Weiss's recent work on the doctrinal opinions of John, discussing the sense of the terms—life, light, knowledge of God, the truth, eternal life, being in Christ, etc. The other article, by Prof. Diestel, is a learned investigation of the Socinian views in respect to the Old Testament.

The whole of the first part of Niedner's *Zeitschrift f. die hist. Theologie*, 1863, is taken up with a thorough monograph (to be continued) by Fr. Rippold, on David Joris of Delft, an Anabaptist, expelled from Delft 1539, living in Friesland till 1544, and afterwards at Basle, where he assumed the name of John von Bruck. It is an elaborate research, and a valuable contribution to the history of the fanatical elements of those times. The account of his visions, and of his *Wonder-book* is noteworthy.

The *Theologische Zeitschrift* (Lutheran), Oct. and Dec. 1862, has a long and able article by the editor, Prof. Dieckhoff of Rostock, in reply to a work by Bishop Ketteler of Mayence, on *Freedom, Authority, and the Church,* which was the most decided manifesto of the Roman Catholics in Germany last year.   The book speedily went through three editions.   Dr. Dieckhoff thoroughly reviews its main positions—though he defends Protestantism on monarchical and high church (Lutheran) grounds.   Dr. G. Reich in an elaborate essay discusses the Ascension of Christ in its connections with the scheme of redemption.   A full account is given of the Lutheran church in Russia on the basis of Busch's recent work.   Keil reviews with considerable sharpness Kurtz's new work on the Sacrifices of the Old Testament.

Dr. Christian Gottlob von Barth, born at Stuttgart in 1799, died Nov. 12. He is known throughout the world for his zeal in promoting practical piety, missions, and the circulation of religious works.   As a preacher he was full of life and zeal.   He wrote with simplicity, force and wit.   His Bible Histories for Children have had a circulation of more than a million copies, in fifty languages.   He also wrote several other popular histories.   The Calwer Bible Society is one of the fruits of his labors.   He never asked for contributions to his charitable works, and was always well supported.   Almost all the rulers of Europe decorated him with their Orders.   Evangelical in his theology, he also adopted millenarian views, and harmonized with Menken on the doctrine of the Person of Christ.   A curious essay of his, addressed to Schelling, 1845, on the Angel of the Covenant, advocates the position that the Lord became an Angel before he became incarnate.   He belonged, in the main, to the school of Bengel.

Dr. Glückselig, under the title *Christus-Archäologie,* has produced a work, collecting all the notices about the alleged portrait of Christ.   The Edessa picture, in possession of the Pope, is reproduced in colors : and also six xylographic representations of Christ from the middle ages.   The work is beautifully got up in 4to.   3 *Thlr.*

FRANCE.

The French Academy have given a prize to M. Fréd. Godefroy's work, *Comparative Lexicon of the Language of Corneille and of the Language of the Seventeenth Century.*   2 vols.   It is of great value as illustrating the history of the French language, Corneille exemplifying a transition stage. The obsolete terms are all explained ; and many of the errors of Voltaire's commentary on Corneille are pointed out.

Victor Cousin is said to be writing a work, containing a full and final exposition of his system of philosophy, and defending it against objections.

The Duc de Luynes has presented to the Imperial Library a collection of medals and works of art valued at 1,300,000 fr.—the largest gift ever made by a Frenchman to the public collections.

The second volume of Abbe Jager's History of the Catholic Church in France has been published ; it will extend to 18 volumes.

The French Academy of Inscriptions have given a prize of 2000 francs to M. Michel Bréal for the best essay on the subject of a primitive and common religion of the Brahmanic and Iranian races : a work of Schoebel, also received " honorable mention ".

Under the title *Le Trésor des Chartes* is published, by order of the Emperor, the 1st vol. of a most important historical work, edited by A. Theulet, archivist, to contain documents, charters, treaties, laws, acts of administration, testaments, contracts etc. preserved in the archives of the

Empire, to the number of 17,000, hitherto but little used, illustrating the history of France and other lands, from A.D. 755.   The work will be in 9 volumes.   The first vol. has 1595 documents from 755 to July 1223, the date of the death of Philip Augustus.   Each volume costs about ten dollars.

In the rehabilitation of Roman Catholic history, and defence of the Papacy, the enormities of the career of Alexander VI (Borgia) have given the Catholic apologists much trouble, as they have to contend against the united testimony of Macchiavelli, Guicciardini, Paul Jove, Tomaso-Tomasi, and Burchard's Diarium.   But Rohrbacher, Tullio Dandolo, Audin, Abbé Constant (History of Popes, Lyons, 1859) have defended the pious memory of Alexander ; Abbé Jorry and Favé have written elaborate apologies ; and now Abbé Chantrel has published a work, in which he tries to prove that this infamous pontiff was " one of the most estimable and skilful of the Popes", and that Lucretia Borgia was chaste and generous.

A new edition of Bossuet by Lachat, is now in the course of publication at Paris, printed from the MSS. and "purged of interpolations".   Bossuet as we have had him, is said to be "false", "abridged", "discolored", " mutilated by an unknown Benedictine, and a Jansenist", Dom Déforis, " who suffered for his errors by losing his head on the revolutionary scaffold, in 1793".

M. Bonnetty in his *Annales de Phil. Chrét.* replies to Brownson's attacks on Traditionalism, and sums up the theories of the latter in the propositions: " The faculty of knowledge is realized by a light which is the divine Being himself : human reason is a strict participation in divine reason : the intellectual light of man is God himself : without the immediate intuition of God, man would have no capacity for receiving any intuitions ".

ENGLAND.

The Journal of Sacred Literature, January, has two articles on the Colenso controversy ; an able examination of the Egyptian Dynasties of Manetho by Dr. Hincks ; Tregelles on the Dublin Codex Rescriptus ; an account of the destitute condition of the Bohemian clergy ; exegesis of several difficult Texts ; a continuation of an article on Marcus Antoninus a Persecutor ; and the usual Correspondence and Notices of Books.

The British Quarterly Review, Jan.   1. Thiers's Romance of the Campaign of 1815.   2. The Legal Status of the Anglo-Catholics.   3. Sir Philip Sidney.   4. Mr. Herbert Spencer's First Principles — a candid and able sketch.   5. ' Les Misérables.'   6. Bishop Colenso on the Pentateuch — much more thorough than the article in the *Journal of Sacred Literature.* 7. The State of Greece.   8. Epilogue on Affairs and Books.

Christian Remembrancer, Jan.   An article on the Relation of Calvinism to Modern Doubt, tries to show, that Calvinism has given origin to the "Essays and Reviews" and like works, by abandoning the old Catholic theology, and substituting decrees, election, spiritual regeneration, and bibliolatry for the more ancient doctrines.   It says that the style of modern religious thought is Calvinistic.   The article is a queer one, and amounts to this, that if men had not abandoned Catholic theology they would not have started the modern scepticism.   A review of Saisset's Modern Pantheism shows only a secondhand acquaintance with the literature.   The writer, among other blunders, speaks of Richard Rothe as a Roman Catholic.   The American Church in Disruption is written in the interest of the Southern

Confederacy, and says there is more real Christianity at the South than at the North.   Colenso is also reviewed.

In the Church of England there are about 18,000 clergymen (20 years since there were 20,000): the number needed annually to keep up the supply is about 500 ; the Universities only supply about one half of this number : formerly they supplied the whole. *Literary Churchman.*

Several of the best ethnologists and anthropologists in England (says the *Parthenon*), actuated by the feeling that ethnology has not received in that country the attention which its importance deserves, have determined to found a new society, to be entitled, " The Anthropological Society of London ", in which the modern phases of ethnology and anthropology will be discussed.

Miss Florence Jacomb has translated, from the Sanskrit of the Hitopadesâ, the first chapter, *On the Acquisition of Friends*, and illustrated the nine fables contained in it with characteristic drawings and ornamental borders.   This, she believes, is the first time, with the exception of the translation of the *Sakuntala*, that any Sanskrit writings have been so treated, although several works have been devoted to the illustration of such stories as have been preserved in the books of the Median and Persian writers.

J. W. Etheridge has translated, for the first time, the Chaldee paraphrases on the Peutateuch into English.   His work is entitled *The Targums of Onkelos and Jonathan Ben Uzziel on the Pentateuch ; with the Fragments of the Jerusalem Targum ; from the Chaldee.*   The version is literal, and will be a help to those who do not read the original.   In the Introduction the author gives an account of the Targums, Talmud, Philo, and other subjects.   The present vol. is on Genesis and Exodus.

Scotland under her Early Kings, by E. Wm. Robertson, 2 vols., gives the history of the kingdom to the close of the 13th century, on the basis of the old chronicles.

The Shakespeare Commentaries of Prof. G. G. Gervinus of Heidelberg are translated by E. E. Bunnett.   Their aim is to give the central idea in each of the dramas.   Ulrici's valuable work on Shakespeare was translated a few years since.

Spinoza's Tractatus Theologico-Politicus ; a critical Inquiry into the Hebrew Scriptures—has been translated, with an Introduction and Notes ; Trübner publisher, London.

Mr. George Long has translated the *Thoughts* of Marcus Antoninus, Emperor.   It is the first really good English translation from the rugged Greek.   They are divided into 12 Books, and the paragraphs numbered.   Cardinal Barberini translated these lofty pagan *Thoughts* into Italian, and dedicated the book to his own soul ; in order " to make his soul redder than his purple at the sight of the virtues of this Gentile ".

Archbishop Whately has published a Charge on *Ecclesiastical Legislation*, advocating a Synod for the whole British Church, and lay delegation.

A certain Rev. G. B. Balme, who calls himself " an American clergyman", has published in Edinburgh a book on *American Churches, Slavery,* etc., the style of which may be seen in the following ludicrous passage, in which he speaks of himself as one of those " who have fought our way through the gigantic jungles of difficulty created by those pro-slavery divines and pantheistical tricksters and demagogues — leapt over their abattis — taken them by the beard and smote them under the fifth rib of their consciences, or cloven them with the scimitar of God's truth from the ' cranium to the oxcoxygus', shouting ' Jerusalem our Happy Home ' ".

Bp. Colenso's second volume on the Pentateuch is announced.   Among the replies to the first volume are Isaac Taylor, *Considerations on the Pentateuch ;* Dr. Alex. McCaul, *Examination of C.'s Difficulties,* etc. ; T. B. Marsh, *Is the Pent. Historically True ?* Chs. T. Beke, *On the Exodus and Mt. Sinai ; Colenso and the Pent.,* a *Vindication,* etc., by Alpha; G. S. Drew, *Bp. C.'s Examination Examined ; Remarks on Bp. C.'s Work, or Rationalism irrational.* The review of Colenso in the *Guardian* has been republished. Other reviews and criticisms have been published in the *British Quarterly,* the *Christian Remembrancer,* the *Westminster Review,* the *Journal of Sacred Literature,* etc. A *Refutation of Bp. C.'s Work,* by two *Working Men (a Jew and a Gentile) ;* Micaiah Hill, *Christ or Colenso* — a *full Reply ;* Dr. Cumming, *Moses Right and Bp. Colenso Wrong,* in weekly numbers ; Rev. F. W. Fowler, *Vindex Pentateuchi ;* John B. Young, *Science elucidative of Scripture,* pp. 240 — against the geological theories ; *What is this New Book of Bp. Colenso ?* Manchester ; Rev. W. F. Hoare, Letter to *Bp. Colenso,* pp. 65 ; Rev. G. E. Biber, *The Integrity of the Scriptures ;* Rev. Ed. Garbett, *The Pentateuch in its relation to other Scriptures ;* Rev. J. B. Turner, *Answer to the Difficulties of Bp. C.'s Book ;* Rev. G. V. Garland, *Plain Possible Solution of Objections,* etc. Matthew Arnold, in *Macmillan's Magazine,* shows that Spinoza is a better philosopher and critic than the Bishop. Dr. Benisch, in the *Jewish Chronicle,* is replying in detail, and exposing the Bishop's ignorance of Hebrew.

Rev. R. B. Kennard: *A Complete History of the "Essays and Reviews,"* *their Origin, History, and Character,* is announced.

Theological Works. Life and Times of St. Bernard, Abbot of Clairvaux, by James Cotter Morison. *Apocalypsis Alfordiana,* Five Letters to the Dean of Canterbury, by Rev. E. B. Elliott, in reference to the Commentary of the former. J. B. Mozley, *Review of the Baptismal Controversy,* pp. 383. Lessing's *Letters to Götze,* on the Wolfenbüttel Fragments Controversy have been translated by H. H. Bernard, under the title, *Cambridge Free Thoughts and Lessons on Bibliolatry. Sermons on Christian Doctrine,* by Dean Alford. *The Churchman and Free Thinker,* by Rev. Thos. Shore .Wm. Howitt, *History of the Supernatural in all Ages.* Dr. J. S. Howson, Hulsean Lectures on the *Character of St. Paul.*

A work in two vols. has been published in London, called *Miranda ;* in three parts, on *Souls, Numbers, Stars and the Neo-Christian Religion,* in which the author claims that he is the forty-ninth incarnation of Emmanuel.

A new edition of the *Complete Works of Bishop Butler,* edited by Joseph B. Mayor is announced by Macmillan. Tayler Lewis's admirable work on the Divine-Human in the Scriptures, has been republished by Nisbet.

In Great Britain were published, in 1862, 4828 works : 942 religious ; 387 history and biography ; 925 fiction ; 61 on art ; 278 geography and travels ; 238 law ; 129 medical ; 243 philological ; 157 current politics ; 148 scientific.

Rev. John Macnaught, who some time since wrote a work against the inspiration of the Scriptures, has, it is reported, changed his views, and is about to publish a work on *Christianity and its Evidences.*

Mazzaroth, or the Constellations. Three Parts. London. 1862. The title of this learned work is from Job xxxviii, 32 : " Canst thou bring forth *Mazzaroth* in his season ?" The object of the work is "to show, by the combined testimony of tradition and of ancient writers, and from the meaning of the yet extant names of stars and emblems, that they were invented to transmit the earliest and most important knowledge possessed by the first fathers of mankind". " The fables were invented from the constellations, and not the constellations from the fables." He refutes the theory that the signs apply to the seasons ; this explanation was first given by Macrobius, A.D. 400. The work is said to be full of minute learning.

UNITED STATES OF AMERICA.

The decease of Rev. Edward Robinson, D.D., LL.D., on Tuesday, Jan. 27, is a great loss to the Christian scholarship of our land. For forty years he has been identified with the revival of thorough exegetical studies. For more than twenty years he was a Professor in the Union Theological Seminary. His works on Biblical Geography stand, by universal consent, at the head of researches in this line. In the next number of our REVIEW we shall publish an article on his life and services, by Prof. R. D. Hitchcock, D.D.

Rev. Dr. Goodell of Constantinople has completed the revision of his translation of the Scriptures into the Armeno-Turkish — the American character and the Turkish dialect. The translation was began about forty years since ; the Old Testament was published in 1841, and the New Testament in 1844. The revision has been made with great care, with the aid of Baron Harootune.

The Ter-Centenary celebration of the adoption of the Heidelberg Catechism was celebrated in Philadelphia by the German Reformed Church, with a series of able papers by Drs. Nevin, Gerhardt, Schaff, Bomberger, Schenck, De Witt, Harbaugh, and others, besides contributions from Herzog, Hundeshagen, Ullman, and Ebrard. A volume of these papers will be published, in both German and English ; also an edition of the Catechism in German, Latin, and English. Dr. Schaff will contribute an article on the subject for the next number of our REVIEW.

Adam S. Farrar's Bampton Lectures, *A Critical History of Free Thought* are to be republished by the Appletons.

Mr. Scribner will soon send out Stanley's *Lectures on the Jewish Church.* He also has under way Dr. Shedd's *Lectures on the History of Doctrines.*

John Wiley, of New York, has in press, and will shortly publish, a volume entitled, *The Pentateuch Vindicated*, by Professor William Henry Green, of Princeton Seminary.

Messrs. Carter & Brothers announce Dr. Merle d'Aubigne's History of the Reformation in the time of Calvin. It will be in two volumes. Mr. Geo. W. Child announces the republication of Sir Charles Lyell's *Geological Evidence of the Antiquity of Man.* Ticknor & Fields announce Poems, by the author of "Patience of Hope," a new and enlarged edition of Owen Meredith's Poems, Arthur Hallam's Remains, and a new edition of Uncle Tom's Cabin.

The Congressional Library has lately been enriched by the liberal donations from the Trustees of the British Museum at London. Many of the early volumes of the *Description of Ancient Marbles*, and of the *Select Papyri*, which were destroyed by the fire which so damaged the Congressional Library in 1852, have been replaced, and the entire series of zoölogical catalogues published by the British Museum has been forwarded.

Ethnologists will be interested in the two new works announced by Mr. Shea, of 83 Centre street — the *Grammar of the Pima*, and *Rudo Ensayo.* The manuscripts of both of these were obtained in Spain by Mr. J. Buckingham Smith, by whom they were translated and prepared for the press. The Pima is the language of the West, or Sonora, which, in its different dialects, is spoken widely in Mexico, the plains, and even by the Rocky

Mountain tribes. The grammar was originally the pious labor of a Spanish missionary, who flourished about one hundred years ago. *Rudo Ensayo* is an essay on Sonora, written a century since by a Jesuit missionary, who had resided twelve years in the country, and who had prepared it from all the means of information in his power, as a report to his ecclesiastical superiors. It is written in a quaint, earnest style.

The *Southern Presbyterian Review* still lives — the only quarterly extant in the Confederacy. Among the articles in the October number are one on Puritanism, by the Rev. Joseph M. Atkinson; and another on the Life, Character, and Genius of the Rev. Dr. Thornwell, by the Rev. Dr. B. M. Palmer. From the latter article we find the following quotation, on the last moments of Dr. Thornwell:

"Upon his dying bed, the Holy Spirit placed his last seal upon his brow. Lying apparently unconscious for hours, most delightful smiles played over his countenance, like the flashings of a summer evening's cloud. His last broken words, upon which the departing soul was borne into the bosom of God, were ejaculations of wonder and of praise. 'Wonderful! beautiful! nothing but space! expanse, expanse, expanse!' And so he passed upward, and stood before the Throne."

Art. IX.—CRITICISMS ON BOOKS.

THEOLOGY.

Dr. A. Neander's *Katholicismus und Protestantismus*. Herausgegeben von Lic. Hermann Meissner. Berlin. 1863; being the fourth volume of Neander's Theological Lectures, edited from the notes of his auditors. The peculiar spirit of Neander is clearly seen in these excellent Lectures — the conscientiousness and integrity of his historical judgment, his conciliatory tendency united with firmness of personal convictions, his mastery of the points in debate, and his testing of all truth by its relation to Christ and his redemption. The First Division develops the fundamental antagonism between Catholicism and Protestantism; the former being external and Jewish, the latter referring every thing to our direct, internal relation to Christ; Catholicism substitutes the visible church for Christ the head. Lutheranism and the Reformed (Calvinistic) Church differ in this; that the former constructs the system more from the centre (Christ) to the periphery; the latter the converse, seeking more directly to reshape the whole of life and society in accordance with Christian truth; they are therefore but different aspects of the same tendency, and should be united. The Second Division exhibits "the Genetic Development of the special differences", in relation to Tradition and Scripture, the Primitive State, Sin, Justification, the Divine Law, the Doctrine of the Church, the Sacraments, and the Last Things. Constant reference is had to Möhler's Symbolism, and Baur's reply to the same. Some of the parts are unequally handled—the Doctrine of the Church having only 15 pages, and that of the Sacraments about 20. On all external matters it is much less full and complete than the recent work of Hase, but it goes more directly into the heart of the contest in its constant appeal to Christian consciousness. It ought to be translated; and would be an instructive and useful book for the laity as well as the ministry. The preparation of the matter for the press has been well done.

Der Alttestamentliche Oppercultus. (The Sacrifices of the Old Testament). By Joh. Heinr. Kurtz, Prof. at Dorpat. Also announced as the first part of an Appendix to the second volume of his History of the Old Covenant—which is to comprise the Legislation. Dr. Kurtz, twenty years ago, published a work on the Mosaic Sacrifices (1842); the present volume is, however, chiefly a new work reviewing the discussions of Hofmann, Keil, Oehler, and Delitzsch, who have all more or less opposed his views. He says that while he agrees with Gesenius, De Wette, and Knobel, in the opinion that the killing of the sacrificial animal signified a *poena vicaria*, he is obliged to defend this position against commentators reputed orthodox. His hardest polemic is against Keil (in the Archæology of the latter). He also makes constant reference to the views of Bähr.

The specialty of Dr. Kurtz's view is found in the position that *all* bloody sacrifices are expiatory, have the significance of vicarious punishment (Lev. i, 4; xvii, 11); this includes the thank-offerings, as well as the sin-offerings and burnt-offerings. The laying on of hands, he says, in all cases has the sense of transferring the sin and guilt of the offerer to the victim. This is contested by Keil and others in respect to the thank-offerings. Kurtz, however, denies (p. 73) that imputation of sin is implied in all cases of the laying on of hands: Keil and Delitzsch hold there is such imputation implied in the sin-offerings. Kurtz also holds that the expiation is not complete until the sacrifice, so to speak, is applied to the soul of him who offers it; and this is effected by the sprinkling of blood. After the sprinkling, the ritual of the sacrifice enters into another stadium, in which it comes to resemble the procedures in the unbloody sacrifices; it is no longer a merely vicarious act, but the offerer himself has direct communion with Jehovah. Here the instrument is the *flesh* (instead of the *blood*), which is not " a gift of God to man for his sanctification, but a gift of man to God, a symbol of his holy self-consecration, an expression of his obligation to such self-devotement ".

Conciliengeschichte, nach den Quellen bearbeitet. Von Dr. Carl Jos. Hefele. Vol. V. Theil I. Freiburg. 1862. Though from a Catholic source, this is the best history of Councils yet produced. The first volume was published in 1855. The present part begins with Gregory VII, and comes down to A.D. 1160, including two of the so-called General Councils of Rome, the First and Second Lateran, 1123, 1139. Besides the general history of the Councils, much light is thrown on the state and conflicts of the period. The theology of Abelard and Bernard comes into review.

BIBLICAL LITERATURE.

Bunsen's Bibelwerk. Siebenter Halbband. (The Four Gospels, edited by H. Holtzmann.) Leipzig. 1862. After an interval of two years, the publication of Bunsen's Biblework is resumed. Arrangements have been made for carrying the First Division of the work, containing the translation and commentary, to a speedy conclusion, viz. Psalms, Proverbs, Job, etc., and the remainder of the New Testament. Two sons of Bunsen will have the oversight of the publication. Lipsius and Bleek have revised the first three Gospels in the above volume, and Holtzmann the fourth: the latter will prepare the rest of the New Testament for the press. Kamphausen, of Bonn, will prepare the remaining books of the Old Testament.—The present volume contains a new translation of the Gospels, on the basis of Luther, with concise critical notes synoptical tables and summaries. The introductory matter, as to age, authenticity, and the like, is reserved for the

Second Division, of which only one volume, on the Law and Elder Prophets, has-been issued.

The Words of the Lord Jesus. By RUDOLF STIER, D.D. Translated by W. B. POPE. Revised by JAS. STRONG and HENRY B. SMITH. Part I. New York: N. Tibbals. The chief commentaries of Dr. Stier are to be published in this edition, comprising the Words of the Angels and the Words of the Apostles, as well as the Words of the Lord—which last alone are in the Edinburgh edition. The work will be published in eighteen numbers, forming three volumes, and be sold for about ten dollars. Stier's Words in the Edinburgh edition have already had a large sale in this country.

St. Paul's Epistle to the Romans: newly translated, and explained from a Missionary Point of View. By the Right Rev. J. W. COLENSO, D.D., Bishop of Natal. New York: D. Appleton & Co. 1863. Pp. 261. What Dr. Colenso means by "the missionary point of view" of the Epistle to the Romans, is not very clear. It may, however, be the position here maintained, that, by the death of Christ, all mankind, Gentiles and Jews, are *ipso facto* justified and redeemed, and that all will at last be saved. For that is the amount of this new commentary. The missionary is to go to the heathen and tell them that they are already justified in the sight of God; and that, whether they believe or not, in this life, they will probably be redeemed in the next life.—The Bishop makes no distinction between "making righteous" and "declaring righteous"; he translates *justify* from the Latin, and not from the Greek; he uniformly confounds the two senses, as if he had never heard of the controversy between the Roman Catholics and the Protestants on this central question. He says roundly (p. 115): "As all became sinners and subject to death in Adam, so shall *all be made righteous*, and be made sharers of the Life that is in Christ": "the *whole human race* are looked upon and dealt with as *righteous* creatures, in Jesus Christ their Head"; and, he adds, "the gift of life which all men possess, whether *physical* or *spiritual*, is a proof of this"! And further (p. 119), "all us of the human race, being recognized as one with our Head, are counted to be righteous as he is righteous, are made 'the righteousness of God in Him.'" In his explanation of viii, 21, he enters into an elaborate argument against eternal punishment, acknowledging a change of views since he published his Village Sermons, dedicated to Maurice, in 1853. He thinks the heathen cannot be converted by any such doctrine, forgetting that it has been preached to every heathen nation that ever has been converted.

This commentary, as a whole, is inaccurate and hastily put together, and contains no exegetical discussion of the reasons for or against the interpretations that differ from his own. Nor can we find that the new translation, as a whole, is superior to our common version. Some of the renderings are awkward, e. g., ii, 15: "Such as show the outcome of the law written in their hearts, their conscience witnessing with (it), and between one another their reasonings accusing or else excusing"; iii, 26: "For the shewing forth of this righteousness in the present season, to the effect of his being righteous, and making righteous him who is of the faith of Jesus".

Considerations on the Pentateuch. By ISAAC TAYLOR. London: Jackson, Walford & Hodder. 1863. 12mo, pp. 80. We wish that the author of *Ancient Christianity* had given us a volume rather than a *brochure* in reply to the Bishop of Natal. Not that we regard the work of Colenso as containing any thing specially new or masculine, demanding eminent talent and erudition to refute it. It is worthy of attention chiefly for two things. First, as proceeding from a prelate of the Anglican Church; second, as an idex of that coming controversy concerning the absolute authority of the sacred canon to which all things converge.   One result has been developed, incidentally of great importance on both sides of the Atlantic — to magnify the necessity of a distinct theological education.   Bishop Colenso declares that, until quite lately, he had been uninformed concerning certain grave questions bearing upon the early history of the Hebrew people !   He had known, indeed, that there were difficulties ahead in the Biblical criticism of the Pentateuch ; but he had barely known what they were, and, like the schoolboy, with his *Euclid* in hand, who has heard of the difficult theorem, he goes on in faith that when he comes up to it he shall be told how to resolve the perplexity.   But it was in conversation with an intelligent Zulu convert that a sharp point of one of these difficulties stops his way !—he is staggered ; he sends home for books, German mostly ; and now he is more and more bewildered.   He reaches the conclusion that the books attributed to the Hebrew Lawgiver, are false and spurious.   He leaves his suggestive Zulu, hastens home, and publishes a book, based, as he affirms, not on speculations or opinions, but incontestable *facts* to prove the Pentateuch no longer entitled to the place it has held in the reverent regard of the Christian church.   We venture to say that had the theological education of Colenso been as thorough as his mathematical, he never would have been startled from his faith by any of the objections which afterwards took him by surprise.   If he had given half the time to Hengstenberg in a course of theology, which he appears to have given to algebra, he would never have been overmastered by "foolish questions and genealogies and contentions and strifes about the law".   The substance of Mr. Taylor's "Considerations" is an indignant protest on the part of the Laity against *that sort* of dealing with Biblical difficulties practised by Dr. Colenso, as narrow, unscholarly, and every way unsatisfactory.   The very exceptions which the mathematician urges to the truth of the Mosaic history, to minds of more grasp and comprehension are significant evidences of its truthfulness.   So far from being ignorant of the Hebrew system, Mr. Taylor comprehends its *contemporaneousness*, and is so thoroughly acquainted with the habits and characteristics of the people whose history is called in question, that the very *incidents* which infidelity adduces against the Pentateuch are converted in an opposite sense for its defence.   Every thing that Mr. Taylor writes is worthy of study ; and our only regret in perusing this, his latest work, is that it was not largely amplified.   W. A.

The Life of Our Lord upon the Earth, Considered in its Histórical, Chronological, and Geographical Relations.   By SAMUEL J. ANDREWS. New York : Charles Scribner.   1862.   8vo, pp. 624.   It is not the design of this work to enter into any critical inquiries respecting the text of the Evangelists, nor the authorship of the Gospels, nor their inspiration, but "simply to arrange the events of the Lord's life, as given by the Evangelists, so far as possible, in a chronological order, and to state the grounds of this order ; and to consider the difficulties as to matters of fact which the several narratives, when compared together, present, or are supposed by modern criticism to present ".   "As the necessary foundation for a chronological arrangement, the dates of the Lord's birth and death, and the duration of his public ministry, are discussed in brief preliminary essays."   The author accepts "as probable conclusions, that Christ was born December, 749, U.C. ; baptized January, 780 ; crucified April 7, 783 ; length of ministry, three years and three months.   That the 25th December and 6th January were the days of the nativity and baptism, rests wholly upon tradition ".

This "Life of our Lord" is the fruit of extensive investigation, aided by all the light of modern criticism, and the labors of the older writers, from Augustine downward. Free use is made of the Commentaries of Meyer and Alford, while Strauss's "Life of Christ" is not noticed at all. The author carefully collates the various authorities, and in the spirit of candor and impartiality weighs and sifts evidence, and fairly meets and honestly seeks to solve difficulties where they really exist. While we should not agree with him on all points, we still think the work an eminently successful one. It is certainly a scholarly performance, and an honor to American literature, and no student of the Scriptures can afford to be without it. What a contrast in spirit, in scholarship, and in its conclusions, to the crude and flippant works of Colenso! "Those readers who have been accustomed to hear, through skeptical critics, of the numerous errors and mistakes of the Evangelists, will be surprised to learn how few are the points of real difficulty, and how often these are exaggerated by the misinterpretation of the critic himself."—*Preface.*

PHILOSOPHY.

Modern Pantheism. Essay of Religious Philosophy. By EMILE SAISSET. Translated with Notes, etc. 2 vols. Edinburgh. 1863. M. Saisset, well known as a prominent representative of the spiritual school of philosophy, with Cousin, Simon, and others, and also as the author of a translation and biography of Spinoza, and of various volumes of literary and philosophical criticism, in the above work traces, with historical sketches and critiques, the genesis of the ideas and principles that have culminated in Modern Pantheism. The first volume renders an account of the theological views of Descartes, Malebranche, Spinoza, Newton, Leibnitz, and Kant. In the second volume, Hegel's pantheism is sketched; and then follows a series of Nine Meditations, in which the Theism of the author is expounded in opposition to pantheism. An Essay by the Translator insists upon making God in Christ the centre of speculation, rather than the mere abstract idea of a personal Deity; for Saisset, like Simon, hardly rises in his speculations above the level of a refined and philosophical deism. Yet still, it is a volume of great interest and value, and presents, in a popular yet acute form, the various pantheistic schemes, and a refutation of the same, urged with force. It is the best book yet published in English for gathering a general account of these disastrous speculations. Some of Saisset's own views, e. g., as to the infinity of creation, would involve him in difficulties, if pressed by an acute pantheistic opponent. The volume is written with a truly French vivacity, which imparts interest to the most abstract discussions.

Geschichte der Entwickelungen der griechischen Philosophie, etc. (History of the Developments of the Greek Philosophy, and of its Influence on the Roman Empire.) By CHRISTIAN AUGUST BRANDIS. First and larger Part. Berlin. 1862. In a popular yet thoroughly digested form, this work of Brandis gives the main points and results of his larger Handbook of the Greek and Roman Philosophy. The present volume is distributed into two periods: the first comprising the history before Socrates; the second, Socrates, Plato, Aristotle, and some of the older peripatetics. In the notes, the most important passages from the original works are sparingly introduced. None who know the works of Brandis need be told that his work is well done. It is the best compendious history of these Greek systems that has yet been published. It is at once historical and philosophic, not intruding later theories to reconstruct the old speculations. This work, and that of Ritter on the History of the Christian Philosophy, make together a very complete work. The latter is in the course of translation by a competent scholar of our country ; we hope that Brandis may also be taken in hand, and that publishers may be found for this undertaking.——The section of Brandis on the Theology of Aristotle is a clear and admirable compendium of his views. The fundamental idea here, is that of movement (causal power), by means of which matter becomes form, the possible becomes actual. This causal energy also has in view ends or objects, final causes. This motion is also to be conceived as eternal—without beginning or end ; in the last analysis we must come to an unmoved cause—the primary conception of deity. Other necessary predicates of God are, necessity, immateriality, unconditioned being—subject neither to space, nor time, nor change. Such a being cannot be conceived except as having thought—he is the thought of thought. God, in short, is the eternal, perfect, living being, whose energy is eternal life, and eternal, simple blessedness. Brandis says, there is no doubt that Aristotle viewed God as self-conscious spirit, though not as the positive creator of the world. And yet he represents God as the cause of all motion, and also as the end or object of the world : the circle of the world begins and ends in him. Still further, Brandis claims that Aristotle holds that the thoughts of God enter into the world of matter, and that the essences of things are to be referred to him. Thus in one passage (Metaphysics, xii, 7) he says that "the germ is not the first, but the perfect is : as man, too, is before the germ or seed"—thus excluding the idea of a mere development. At the same time, Aristotle (like Leibnitz in respect to his *monads*) does not attempt to show *how* the divine thoughts produce, or are, infused into the essences of things.

Essays by HENRY THOMAS BUCKLE. With a Biographical Sketch of the Author. New York: Appleton. 1863. With a photographic portrait. Besides the somewhat ambitious biographic sketch, this well-printed volume contains two essays of Mr. Buckle : one on Mill on Liberty, the other on the Influence of Women on the Progress of Knowledge. We have read them with deep interest as containing indications of the author's views on points out of the range of his more elaborate work on Civilization. An episode in the first essay contains a labored argument for the immortality of the soul on the ground of the strength and permanency of our affections—affording a curious parallel with Comte's experience. Mr. Mill is lauded as combining the speculative and practical habits of mind in an eminent degree. Some of the discussions on Induction and Deduction are noteworthy, especially as indicating the insufficiency of the merely inductive method. A note gives a valuable collation of Aristotle's statements about induction.——The second essay defends woman's influence on thought, as it has never before been so defended, on the ground of her possessing, above man, the deductive, anticipatory powers in a superior degree—while man, less quick and emotional, drags along slowly in the inductive fashion. —Had Mr. Buckle but carried out some of these speculations to their logical results, he would have written his History of Civilization in quite a different spirit and method.

GENERAL LITERATURE.

The Origin and History of the English Language, and of the Early Literature it embodies. By GEORGE P. MARSH. New York: Charles Scribner, 1862. Pp. 574. This work, and the previous volume of Mr. Marsh, now in its fourth edition, are noble monuments of high scholarship and research. They place the author in the foremost rank of writers upon our mother tongue. To great fulness of learning, they add careful criticism, on the basis of a true philosophy of language. And they reveal to us the sources of the wealth and power of English speech. The hisguage is divided into three periods: First, the Early English, from 1250 to 1350, before the national literature began; the second period ends with the third quarter of the 16th century; the third comes down to the time of Milton. Ample illustrative extracts, with pertinent comments, enrich the volume. Many collateral points of great interest are incidentally discussed. Thus, he insists strongly, that in order to know a language we must study not only its lexicography and grammar, but also its literature. So, too, he refutes a current notion, that "words individually, and independently of syntactical relations and of phraseological combinations, have one or more inherent, fixed and limited meanings, which are capable of logical definition". "Words live and breathe only in mutual combination and interdependence with other words."

"The shallowness of popular English and American criticism is nowhere more glaringly manifested than in the extravagant commendations which have been bestowed on some modern dictionary-makers, as philosophical expositors and discriminators of words. Lexicographers are under a constant temptation to save themselves labor by building on the foundation of their predecessors, and to study dictionaries, not literature. Thus they acquire the habit of regarding words as completely significant individuals, and they are prone to multiply descriptions, to make distinctions where no difference exists, and especially to ascribe to single vocables meanings which belong either to entire phraseological combinations, grammatical agglutinations, so to speak, or to a different member of the phrase from that to which they assign them." "It is futile to attempt to make that absolute, which is, in its nature, relative and conditional, to formulate that which in itself does not constitute an individual and complete idea, to make technical definition a mouthpiece for words which ought to be allowed to speak for themselves by exemplification. . . . . There does not exist a dictionary of any language, living or dead, whose definitions are to be considered evidence to the exact meaning of words."

To the student of the Bible there is a rare interest in the author's admirable comments on Wycliffe's and other early versions. "Piers Ploughman and his Imitators" (Lecture vii) is full of matter of curious interest. Chaucer and Gower are admirably handled. And thus we are conducted down this living stream, until we come to the breadth and fulness, the majestic simplicity and wealth of the English tongue in the age of Elizabeth. The style is clear and sedate, yet relieved by many of the graces of literature. The volume is a treasure to the student of the English language.

Eyes and Ears. By HENRY WARD BEECHER. Boston: Ticknor and Fields. 1862. Pp. 419. The quick perceptions, felicitous illustrations, quiet humor, broad fun, and manifold sympathies of the popular Brooklyn orator are fully exemplified in this volume, made up of articles contributed to the New York *Ledger* and *Independent*. Whatever may be said about the author's theology, there is no doubt about his wide and genial humanity. No one can hear or read him, without being inspired with a deeper love for nature and for man, for human welfare and human rights. To see every day things with his eyes, and to hear every day words with his ears, is to see and hear much that would otherwise be unseen and unheard. The book will sharpen the vision and quicken the hearing of many a reader. The author has, in a liberal measure, the poet's power of—

> "Clothing the palpable and the familiar
> With golden exhalations of the dawn."

The Poems of Oliver Wendell Holmes. Boston: Ticknor & Fields, 1862. Blue and gold, pp. 410. With a full length effigy of the author. This beautiful little volume contains the poems of the most witty of our American versifiers. His recent noble patriotic songs fitly conclude the series. A graceful introduction thus concludes:

> "These are my blossoms; if they wear
> One streak of morn or evening's glow,
> Accept them; but to me more fair
> The buds of song that never blow."

Bibliotheca Ægyptiaca. Von Dr. H. JOLOWICZ. Supplement I. Leipz. 1861. This Supplement carries on this useful and carefully prepared bibliography of Egyptian matters, to No. 3,408. It contains classified lists of all the recent works and articles in reviews on Egyptian Topography, Natural History, the Coptic Language, Inscriptions, Hieroglyphics, the Religion and Mythology of the Egyptians, their Chronology, Astronomy and Mathematics, their History, Agriculture, Art, and the Arts and Sciences; also, a list of works in the Museum and Library of Alexandria. An alphabetical list is appended. A second supplement will contain a chronological and alphabetical arrangement of all the books of travels in Egypt, and of the works on the inscriptions and monuments.

Orley Farm. A Novel. By ANTHONY TROLLOPE. Illustrated by J. E. Millais. New York: Harpers. 8vo, pp. 338. Mr. Trollope's delineations of society and life are clear and impressive; his portraiture of characters is discriminating and without exaggerations. This tale is exceedingly well told, and chains the attention and sympathy of the reader through a well-drawn plot. The illustrations are natural and characteristic.

Mistress and Maid. A Household Story. By Miss MULOCH. New York: Harpers. 8vo, pp. 120. Miss Muloch writes with a truly feminine ease and simplicity, and all she writes is elevating to the moral sense and domestic virtues. This new story will take rank among her best.

The Institutes of Medicine. By MARTYN PAINE, M.D., LL.D., Professor of the Institutes of Medicine and Materia Medica in the University of the City of New York, etc. etc. Seventh edition, revised. New York. 1862. Harpers. 8vo, pp. 1130. There can be no better index of the appreciation of a work like the above named, than the rapid exhaustion of edition after edition. While the *Institutes of Medicine* is of a character to instruct rather than please, and requires close application and careful study, the continued demand for the work must be received as evidence that it is considered, by a large portion of the reading and reflecting members of the medical profession, if not as an indispensable, at least as a highly useful work. These Institutes are full of sound and practical instruction on all the main subjects of which they treat, viz. Physiology, Pathology, and Therapeutics—subjects, the understanding of which lies at the foundation of all successful practice. It is absolutely necessary for the physician to study thoroughly the system in health, then the same system in all its multifarious diseases, and finally to make himself acquainted with the various remedies which he may call to his aid in restoring the lost functions of its various organs, as well as in mitigating disease when irremediable, all of which can be profitably studied in the present work; though, on some points, a portion of the profession may differ from the author, yet no one can fail to derive instruction from a careful perusal of the work.

Poems of Religious Sorrow, Comfort, Counsel, and Aspiration. New York: Sheldon & Co. 1863. 8vo, pp. 204. This is a collection of some of the choicest gems of German and English poets who have written on these topics. The arrangement of the book is unique, the letter-press in the finest style of the "Riverside" Printing-house. Many of the pieces are abridged from the originals. The child of sorrow and faith may find in these elegant pages words of blessed consolation and hope from some of the most gifted children of song.

A History of France from the Earliest Times to the Establishment of the Second Empire in 1852. New York : Harpers. 1862. 12mo, pp. 730. An admirable edition for the student, and finely illustrated.

A System of Logic containing a Discussion of the Various Means of Acquiring and Retaining Knowledge and Avoiding Error. By P. Mc-GREGOR, A.M. Harpers. 1862. 12mo, pp. 469.

A Manual of Information and Suggestions for Object Lessons in a course of Elementary Instruction. By MARCIUS WILLSON. Harpers. 1862. 12mo, pp. 336.

WILKIE COLLINS's new tale, *No Name*, is also published by the Harpers, with spirited illustrations by J. McLenan. The tale itself is exciting, improbable, full of romance and reality, and holds the interest unflagging to the end.

Barrington. A Novel. By CHARLES LEVER. New York : Harpers. Pp. 161. Mr. Lever is unsurpassed in his delineation of Irish scenes and characters. Though his humor is less broad and overflowing than in his earlier works, yet Barrington will rank among his best novels. The plot and narrative are well conducted.

Springs of Action. By Mrs. RICHARDS. New York : Harpers. Pp. 357. This volume contains excellent precepts for young ladies upon those qualities of mind and heart, and those accomplishments which will fit them for usefulness in society. Discernment and tact mark the production.

Vesper. By Madame the COUNTESS DE GASPARIN. Translated from the third French edition by MARY L. BOOTH. New York : Carters. 1863. This work will charm many readers by the felicity of its descriptions, and the vivacity of its style. Old truths are presented in new forms. Madame de Gasparin has a high reputation among the French writers for the young, and we welcome this volume in its excellent English garb.

The Eighteenth Annual Report of the Prison Discipline Society of New York, by Dr. E. C. Wines, is a very valuable document. This Society is preparing to do a most valuable and needed work under the best auspices.

The Fourth Biennial Report of the Superintendent of Public Instruction of the State of Illinois, Newton Bateman, Esq., of Springfield, is drawn up with ability and care. It shows that, despite the war, there has been an increase of 480 schools, 42,993 scholars, and 354 school districts in 1862. The total amount received for school purposes in 1862 was $1,055,840.

PRACTICAL RELIGION.

Transition : A Remembrance of Emma Whiting. By HUGH SMITH CARPENTER. New York : Carleton. 1863. Pp. 179. There are two artists in Brooklyn by the name of Carpenter. One of them paints on canvas with a brush ; the other with tongue and pen. It is the latter—the gifted pastor of Westminster Church—who presents us with this unique biography of Emma Whiting. We know her only from these pages ; but so finely is the portrait drawn, that it lacks only voice to make her stand before us as a familiar friend. Her life was short. She was born in New York, Jan. 17, 1841, and died in Brooklyn, June 19, 1861. With a good volume of brain, well exercised by study, she had great fulness and fervor of heart, which made her, when converted, a most sensitive, engaging, and fruitful Christian. It was a church hymn which finally fixed her religious purpose; and her whole life thereafter was a charming melody. Close walking with God was her first solicitude; and this walk she maintained by a sharpness of self-scrutiny, which appears never to have become morbid. She knew how to secure soundness of spiritual health by abundant exercise in well-doing. With all her love for books, and her strong impulse towards a literary life, she appears to have been remarkably exemplary and efficient in all domestic and social relations; just the sort of daughter which a father most covets, just the sort of sister which a brother most needs. Her life was one of sweet beginnings suddenly arrested, but no failure, even in its immediate results. She labored for souls, and had them given her as seals of her eager ministry. The story of her life, so fervently told by her spiritual friend and guide, will, doubtless, prolong her ministry, and add other stars to her crown.   R. D. H.

Praying and Working; being some Account of what Men can do when in Earnest. By Rev. WILLIAM FLEMING STEVENSON, Dublin. New York: Carter & Brothers. 1863. 12mo, pp. 411. This is a book of decided interest, and we heartily recommend it as highly suggestive and stimulating to all who pray and work. It consists of sketches of five remarkable Germans whose Christian labors have been greatly blessed in Fatherland — John Falk, Immanuel Wichern, Theodore Fliedner, John Evangelist Gossner, and Louis Harms — and their work covers the most recent period of spiritual activity in that country. These sketches possess all the charms of a romance, while they bring to light a company of toiling and self-sacrificing Christian heroes, and detail some of the most extraordinary reformations and spiritual revivals of modern times. As illustrating the prayer of faith, and the connection between praying and working, we know not a more valuable work on the whole than this. The history of these German Reformatories, that especially of the "Rough House", under the guiding and moulding hand of that noble Christian philanthropist, Dr. Wichern, is full of interest; we have nothing in this country to equal it; the "Five Points Mission", of New York, is the nearest approach to it.

Just out of Hamburgh, with no means, and none but his mother and sister to aid him, young Wichern planted the first reformatory, and waited for the "juvenile rascality" of the city to come out to him. Not long did he have to wait. First three came, and soon the number increased to twelve; and with these he began his life work. A more hopeless class of boys was never gathered. But faith and love and prayer and work succeeded. The number rapidly increased. New houses were built by their own hands, till quite a village arose. Various trades were learned and practised. Schools were established, and a press. In 1848 the Reformatory was made national rather than local in its aims. The leaven spread through Germany. Similar institutions were planted, so that in 1856 the number was estimated at 260. "The old Rough House has grown to be twenty houses, and possesses property to the amount of £7,000; the old patch of garden round the fish-pond has spread out into fifty acres, the 12 boys have multiplied into 452, and 130 girls." Thousands of visitors are every year drawn to it. It has a press and book agencies by which a healthy Christian literature is diffused among the working classes. "Hundreds of helpers have been trained and distributed over the prisons and reformatories and city missions of the Continent; offshoots from this parent institution have been planted from north to south of Germany; a vast organization, called the Inner Mission [equivalent to our Home Mission] has been spread over the country, restoring the decayed forms of Christian social life, and rescuing the outcast and building up the church. And the germ of this entire work is to be found in that October evening when Wichern and his mother drew towards the little house in Horn and shut themselves in and prayed that God would build up his work on the foundation of Jesus Christ." And the secret of this wonderful success, and of the success of his co-laborers, in fields somewhat similar and related, is given in these few words : " Silver and gold I have none. But we work, and God blesses our work. And whatever else we want we pray for, and expect out of his rich hand, in certain faith that it is a faithful and true word he spoke when he pointed us to the fowls of the air and the lilies of the field. Whoever will hold this faith, and abide in it by the grace of God, will have a marvellous watch kept over him even at this day ; and what appears natural to others, will come to him as a witness of the heavenly kingdom in which he has been set and for which Christ has opened the eyes and ears and hearts of his people."

The Last Day of our Lord's Passion. By Rev. WILLIAM HANNA, LL.D. New York : Carter & Brothers. 1863. 12mo, pp. 379.

The Risen Redeemer. The Gospel History from the Resurrection to the Day of Pentecost. By F. W. KRUMMACHER, D.D. Translated from the German by JOHN T. BETTS. New York : Carter & Brothers. 1863. 12mo, pp. 298.

The Sympathy of Christ with Man : Its Teaching and its Consolation. By OCTAVIUS WINSLOW, D.D. New York: Carter & Brothers. 1863. 12mo, pp. 426. Of such books we are never weary, and the Messrs. Carter deserve praise for multiplying them. Although entirely independent, they are on related themes, and themes which will always command the attention and stir the heart of the Christian. Dr. Hanna's *Last Day of our Lord's Passion* is a most touching and beautiful delineation of a scene ever memorable and sacred. It possesses great power to awake afresh Christian feeling and confirm the faith of the believer.

Dr. Krummacher's *Risen Redeemer* glows with all the fervor and earnestness of his eloquent pen. No one can rise from a perusal of these works without a deeper fellowship with the death and the life of the Cross.

Dr. Winslow has chosen a subject of great practical interest. " The Sympathy of Christ with Man" is a glorious reality. We sometimes fear that the fact and the measure of this Divine sympathy is but dimly seen and feebly expressed even by Christ's own ministers. While Dr. Winslow's work does not fully meet the demands of this great subject, and in some parts of its arrangement is a little fanciful, still it will well repay a perusal, and carry comfort to many a sad and sorrowing heart.

Parish Papers. By NORMAN MACLEOD, D.D., one of Her Majesty Chaplains for Scotland. New York. Carter & Brothers. 1863. 12mo, pp. 328. These are brief and familiar Lectures, dedicated to the "Parishioners of Loudoun, Dalkeith, and the Barony", to whom the author has ministered as their pastor. The topics are: Thoughts on Christianity, Thoughts upon the Final Judgment, Thoughts upon Future Life, and Upon Revivals. These topics are handled with freshness and vigor, and sometimes with great beauty and felicity of expression. The "Pastor" deals kindly yet faithfully with his flock. The teaching is eminently scriptural, and is full of the evangelical spirit.

POLITICAL WRITINGS.

An Historical Research respecting the Opinions of the Founders of the Republic on Negroes as Slaves, as Citizens, and as Soldiers. By GEORGE

LIVERMORE. Boston : 1862. 8vo, pp. 215. This Research was read, in substance, before the Massachusetts Historical Society, August 14, 1862, and is now brought out in elegant style. So important and conclusive is the evidence here presented, that a cheaper edition ought to be issued, and put into wide circulation. The general facts are well known ; but they have nowhere been collected so fully and impartially. The investigation is exclusively historical. It exhibits the views of the pseudo-President Jeff Davis, and Mr. Stephens, and what Mr. Bancroft calls the " profound immorality " of Chief-Justice Taney's notorious Dred Scott decision ; and then, in startling contrast, the opinions of the Fathers of the Republic, Washington, Franklin, Jefferson, Gadsden, Laurens, King, Madison, Randolph, and a host of others. The proof that free negroes were regarded as citizens amounts to a moral demonstration. The proof of the position, " that the letter and spirit of the Constitution, fairly interpreted and faithfully applied, afforded a full guaranty of universal freedom throughout the Union at no distant day "—is sustained by an irresistible amount of evidence. Hear, for example, the almost prophetic words of Jefferson, in a note to M. Démeunier, furnishing information for an article on the United States, prepared for the *Encyclopédie Méthodique :* "When the measure of their tears shall be full ; when their groans shall have involved heaven itself in darkness,—doubtless a God of justice will awaken to their distress, and, by diffusing light and liberality among their oppressors, or, at length, by his exterminating thunder, manifest his attention to the things of this world, and that they are not left to the guidance of a blind fatality". (*Jefferson's Writings*, ix, 278–9.) The debates on the Confederation and on the Constitution, and in State Legislatures are carefully explored, and ample materials collected to illustrate the real sentiments of the Fathers of the Republic. Equally full is the evidence on the employment of negroes as soldiers. "Tacitly, or by positive law, the policy of arming the negroes and employing them as soldiers, either in separate companies, or mingled in the ranks with white citizens, almost every where prevailed." The chief exceptions were Georgia and South Carolina, which States "contained so many Tories, whose sympathies were with the enemy, that it was impossible to obtain from them enough soldiers for a 'home guard!'" (South Carolina furnished only 6,600 soldiers for the war ; only 752 more than Rhode Island ; only one half as many as New Hampshire ; the citizens of Charleston would not rally to save it. New England furnished 118,350 soldiers, more than half of the whole number placed at the service of Congress during the war.) That slaves who enlisted became free was the universal understanding. Southern delegates in Congress attempted in vain to procure the discharge of negroes from the army. The practice of British officers in respect to negroes is fully detailed. The Appendix contains accounts of Negroes in the Navy ; of Negro Regiments in the State of New York ; Jackson's Proclamation to Negroes ; Negro Soldiers under Monarchical Governments.

The Tariff Question Considered in Regard to the Policy of England and the Interests of the United States. With Statistical and Comparative Tables. By ERASTUS B. BIGELOW, Boston, 1862, 4to, pp. x. 103. Appendix, Tables, pp. 242. Boston : Little, Brown & Co. 1862. This elaborate work, prepared by one wholly familiar with the subject, presents an array of carefully digested facts, well calculated to arrest attention, and having intimate relations with our future policy and prosperity. The free-trade pretensions of England are unsparingly exposed. Her dependence upon creating a vast foreign demand for her manufactures is also clearly exhibited and proved. Incidentally, the work throws much light upon British sympathy in our present national struggle.   The author says (p. 32) : "The facts adduced clearly show how rigid and how discriminating was that protective system, under which, and by which England so increased her productive power, as at length to surpass all other countries, both in the quantity and cheapness of her manufactures.   This object accomplished, it is evident that her interests and her relations were materially changed.   By constantly stimulating the only form of industry, which, so far as we can see, lay open to her, her people had become, as it were, a vast manufacturing community.   To multiply and secure new markets abroad, and to meet a constantly increasing foreign demand by a constantly augmenting supply, was now her first necessity and her great aim.   But why, just at this crisis in her career, did the nation, which had so long been a conspicuous adherent of protective principles, become all at once the advocate of free-trade ? Her repeal of the corn-laws needs no explanation.   The removal of duty from the raw material was only another way of protecting the manufacturer. The abrogation of taxes on imported manufactures was simply nugatory, so far as the English exchequer and the English producer were affected.   Why should these simple and necessary measures, which it was so natural and so proper for England to adopt, and which, in fact, concerned England only, be held up to the world as examples of self-sacrificing yet self-rewarding virtue, that challenge universal imitation ?   For the course she has pursued in this respect, we may find, perhaps, an adequate motive, without looking very far.   Indeed, all must see how necessary to the continued prosperity of manufacturing Britain it has become, that the rest of the world should believe in free-trade."   The work is one of the first importance in relation to our future policy.   It is a manual for statesmen.   The tables are prepared with great industry and accuracy.

Camp and Outpost Duty for Infantry.   With Standing Orders, Extracts from the Revised Regulations of the Army, Rules for Health, Maxims for Soldiers, and Duties of Officers.   By DANIEL BUTTERFIELD, Brigadier-General Volunteers, U.S.A.   New York : Harper & Brothers.   1862.   18mo, pp. 124.

Thirteen Months in the Rebel Army.   By an impressed New Yorker. New York : Barnes & Burr.   1862.   The statements contained in this painfully interesting volume can be relied on as entirely authentic, and they go to prove that, in our present national conflict, we are contending against an essentially despotic and barbarizing power.   The picture of Southern society, and the account of the means used to ensure the unanimity of the South, give most useful lessons as to our duty.   Humanity itself demands that the South be delivered from this degrading bondage.   We commend Mr. Stevenson's book to a careful perusal.

Radicalism and the National Crisis.   A Sermon by SAMUEL T. SPEAR, D.D., Brooklyn.   1862.   A cogent exhibition of the causes and character of the great rebellion, and an eloquent exhortation to the duties appropriate to our present crisis.

The Union and the War.   A Sermon preached November 27th, 1862. By W. G. T. SHEDD, D.D.   New York : Scribner.   Pp. 40.   In this vigorous and lucid sermon, Dr. Shedd exhibits the occasions for thanksgiving in the midst of our civil war, in the revived feeling of nationality, in the fact that it is not a war for foreign conquest, but a righteous war against treason, and in the attitude of the Government in respect to slavery.   One of the most forcible points urged and argued is, that "the right of armed revolution does not hold good in a democracy".

God the Protector and the Hope of the Nation.   A Sermon, preached November 27th.   By Rev. W. S. LEAVITT, Pastor of the First Presbyterian

Church, Hudson, N. Y. Pp. 18. An admirable discourse, breathing a spirit of fervent patriotism and devout confidence in God, as to the final issue of our national struggle.

The True and the False. An Oration. By CHAS. TRACY, Esq. ; and *The Stars and the Stripes*, a Poem, by Rev. CHAS. D. HELMER, pronounced before the Phi Beta Kappa Society of Yale College, July 30, 1862. New Haven. 1862. Both the Oration and the Poem are well worthy of being published ; the latter, in particular, gives unmistakable evidence of poetic excellence.

The Problem of Freedom and Slavery in the United States. By Rev. CYRUS HAMLIN, D.D. Smyrna: Damiano, Printer. 1862. Pp. 28. An able lecture, delivered before the Literary and Scientific Institution of Smyrna, March 6th, comparing freedom and slavery in respect to territory, population, agriculture, commerce, the mechanic arts, general wealth, literature, and education. The skilful array of facts makes a convincing argument. The progress and aims of the slave power are clearly and rapidly sketched. "It is 'manifest destiny' that the arm of free labor shall cause the whole of the American Continent, under whatever form of government, to ring with the voices of peaceful industry and gladness. The contest into which these two great forces have, by strict necessity, culminated, is, on the part of slavery, a satanic, on the part of freedom, a holy war. Leave, then, the field to the combatants whom God has marshalled there, and, under his supreme arbitration, *let them fight it out.*"

The Sectional Controversy ; or, Passages in the Political History of the United States, including the Causes of the War between the Sections. By WM. CHAUNCEY FOWLER, LL.D. New York: Scribner. 1863. 8vo, pp. 269. Though this volume cannot be said to be written in the interest of the Southern Confederacy as an independent power, yet it certainly is written to sustain the Southern views about the nature of the Union and the sovereignty of the individual States. It has its value as a collection of materials ; though these are so arranged as to give the South the benefit of the argument. Slavery is not a creature of local law ; the United States have no right to coerce any States — these, and such like positions, show the animus of the author. How, on such a basis, the Union could either be preserved or restored, we confess that we are unable to see ; nor yet, what advantage can be derived from its publication at this juncture.

Political Fallacies: an Examination of the False Assumptions, and Refutation of the Sophistical Reasonings, which have brought on this Civil War. By GEORGE JUNKIN, D.D., LL.D. New York: Scribner. 1863. Pp. 332. With a Portrait. Dr. Junkin knows what secession is and means ; and he is able to tell others what he thinks in a lucid and logical style. His book contains able disquisitions on the nature of government, the formation and characteristics of our Union, the prolonged controversies on slavery and secession, and the political fallacies lurking under the undiscriminating usage of such words as Sovereignty, State Sovereignty, Federalism, Government, People, Allegiance, Right of Secession, and the like. He writes with ardent patriotism, and believes in the restoration of the Union under the Constitution. The chapter, proving that the Southern Rebellion is no Government, is one of the best. The work is worthy of careful study.

My Diary North and South. By WILLIAM HOWARD RUSSELL. New York: Harpers. 1863. Mr. Russell is certainly a capital narrator ; few describe passing events as well as he. While he does not enter thoroughly into the heart and sense of our struggle, he tells us, in animated style, what is going on upon the surface. His real sympathies are with Northern principles; though he does not believe that the Union can be restored. His book will be judged more wisely and charitably than his letters. If any are offended at his revelations, they must blame themselves for telling a professed letter-writer what they must have known it was his business to publish.

Modern War: its Theory and Practice. By EMERIC SABAD, Capt. U.S.A. New York: Harpers. An instructive and interesting volume, giving a concise and clear account of many of the most celebrated campaigns and battles, illustrated with maps and diagrams. Just now it will attract a large class of readers. Napoleon's campaigns receive the chief attention.

Slavery and the War. A Historical Essay. By Rev. HENRY DARLING, D.D. Philadelphia: J. B. Lippincott & Co. 1863. 8vo, pp. 48. This is an opportune and able essay. After briefly sketching the bearings of the existing war on the overthrow of slavery, the author passes to his main point — the early, persistent and resolute resistance of the Colonies to the introduction of slavery as an element of their political and social life. This vital point he establishes beyond a doubt by a mass of documentary evidence, gleaned from various authors, historians, debates in Congress, ecclesiastical judicatories, etc. etc. The policy of the mother country is shown to have been a *pro-slavery* one, early and late, discouraging and *vetoing* all colonial legislation to prevent the introduction of the system or to root it out. Virginia then took the lead in anti-slavery agitation and legislation, and her statesmen and divines gave utterance to the noblest sentiments of freedom. England "forced the institution of slavery upon this land". In her present sympathy with the slaveholding interests of the South, she is only consistent with herself. *The defenders* of slavery are shown to be *entirely of modern times.* We regret that our space prevents a fuller notice of this historical essay. Dr. Darling has done the country a good service in collecting such a mass of evidence on this all-absorbing subject and laying it before the public. We commend it to our readers as worthy of their attention.

THE

A M E R I C A N
PRESBYTERIAN AND THEOLOGICAL
REVIEW.

NEW SERIES, No. III.—JULY, 1863.

Art. I.—THE HEIDELBERG CATECHISM.

By Professor Philip Schaff, D.D.

The Heidelberg Catechism,* whose three hundredth anniversary has been so widely celebrated this year in Europe and America, was first published A.D. 1563, under the title: *Catechism, or Christian Instruction, as given in the Churches and Schools of the Palatinate*. It belongs to the Reformed, as distinguished from the Lutheran confessions, though it shows traces of the influence of Melancthon. The reformation was introduced into the Palatinate under the Elector Frederick II, in 1546, in the spirit of a moderate Lutheranism. Under Otho Henry, 1556–1559, Heidelberg was the centre of violent doctrinal controversies between the Lutherans and the Calvinists. The Elector Frederick III, surnamed the Pious, who reigned from 1559 to 1576, openly espoused the reformed confession. He was one of the most wise, earnest, and devout princes of the reformation century. Under his influence was drawn up the Heidelberg Catechism.

* The official editions bear date 1563, 1585, 1684, 1724. An American Tercentenary edition will soon be issued in three languages. The most important sources for its history are in the works of Alting, Struve, Wundt, and Planck: and in the special treatises of Van Alpen 1800, Leissen 1846, Vierordt 1847, Sudhoff 1862, Schotel 1863.

24

I. Ursinus and Olevianus.

The preparation of the Catechism was assigned by the prince to two young, and at that time as yet little known theologians, one of whom, Ursinus, was twenty-eight, the other, Olevianus, only twenty-six years of age. The selection seemed hazardous, but was fully justified by the result. The work combines the warmth of first love with the light of solid knowledge, the fresh inspiration of youth with the deep experience of riper age. The history of that period furnishes yet other spirits that had early come to maturity; as Melancthon, who in his sixteenth year wrote a Greek grammar, and in his twenty-fourth year produced the first evangelical Lutheran dogmatic (the Loci Theologici), and Calvin, who in his twenty-sixth year published his celebrated *Institutis*, which have scarcely since been excelled.

Ursinus and *Olevianus* are the authors, and the theological and ecclesiastical defenders of the Heidelberg Catechism, as Frederick III was its originator, confessor, and civil representative. Both belong to the reformers of the second generation. They were no pioneers, no creative geniuses, able to lay foundations, like Luther and Calvin; but they had power to build up and carry through what was begun. Their mission was not so much to plant as to water, and the Lord has richly blessed their faithful labors. They had this advantage, that the fundamental doctrines of the evangelical reformation had already been brought up from the mines of God's word into the clear light of day, and were able to gather in the rich harvest which had been sown during the previous forty years. Both are fathers and confessors of the German Reformed church, who, on account of their faith, suffered deposition and banishment, and at last attained a blessed death in their faith. Both were Germans by birth and education, but had at the same time, by travelling and personal observation, made themselves well acquainted with the Reformed church of France and Switzerland, and those of their leaders who were still living, and were on this account also well qualified to set forth in a formulary the doctrinal views of the German Reformed church. Besides, Ursinus was educated prevailingly under the personal lead of the German Melancthon, Olevianus under the influence of the French Calvin. They breathed into their mutual work the inwardness and geniality of the Wittenberger, and the earnestness and fire of the Genevan reformer, and avoided as well the pliability of the first as the rugged severity of the last. Ursinus was more of a theologian and professor, Olevianus more of a preacher and practical church-man ; but both were one heart and one soul, and reciprocally complemented each other.   Both exceeded themselves in the Catechism, which casts all their other works deeply into the shade.   In the preparation of it they were inspired by the spirit of the German Reformed church, and they laid into it not so much their individual views as the faith of the entire communion which they served as organs.   There is no con-tradiction here. The Catechism is a true expression of the convictions of its authors ; but it communicates only so much of these as is in harmony with the public faith of the church, and observes a certain reticence or reservation and moderation on such doctrines (as the *two-fold* predestination), which be-long rather to scientific theology and private conviction than to a public church-confession and the instruction of youth. Hence, also, the Catechism has not borrowed its name from its authors, and thousands of reformed Christians have learned it to their comfort in life and in death without knowing their names or any thing of the circumstances of their lives.

ZACHARIUS URSINUS,* the principal author and chief defend-er of the Heidelberg Catechism by word and pen, was born of poor but worthy parents in Breslau, the principal city of the Prussian province Silesia, July eighteenth, 1534.   His father, Andrew Bear, was at that time deacon in the Magdalen church, and later became professor of theology in the Eliza-bethan School in that place.   Ursinus early manifested supe-rior gifts, and was prepared in his sixteenth year to enter the University.   He studied, supported by stipends from his na-tive town, nearly seven years (from 1550 to 1557) in Witten-berg, this birthplace of the German reformation, under Me-lancthon, and became one of the most confidential pupils and friends of this reformer and " teacher of Germany".   He accompanied him to the religious conference at Worms in 1557, and from there he made with him, together with Peucer, Hubert, Languet, and other friends, an excursion to Heidel-berg, where he was later to find his sphere of activity, and supply the place of his honored teacher.   For Melancthon, as has already been remarked, had received a second call to Heidelberg as professor of theology, and felt no small inclina-tion to accept it.   " Conflicting thoughts", he wrote on the fifth of April, 1557, to the Councillor of the Elector Otto Henry,†

---

* His name originally was Bear, which, according to the custom of his time, he translated into the corresponding Latin name Ursinus.   So the name of Lupulus was originally *Wölflein ;* Œcolampadius, Hausschein ; Melancthon, Schwartzerd, etc.

† Compare Corpus Reform. vol. ix, p. 127, and Dr. Carl Schmidt's learned bio-

"enter my mind; I do not desire new, and withal strange labors; I know that in Heidelberg, where persons of all nations, French, Netherlanders, and others reside, there must reign a great variety of opinions and schemes; it is, to be sure, my fatherland, and excellent and learned men are found there, whose fellowship would be agreeable to me; but I can hardly make up my mind to emigrate. On the other hand, at Heidelberg I would have greater liberty, and could more conveniently confute the Flavians" (that is, the intolerant and exclusive ultra-Lutherans). From this letter, as well as from other documents, we may clearly see to which side of the controversy, which a few years later furnished occasion for the preparation of the Heidelberg Catechism, he inclined. The struggle of conflicting feelings and inclinations were decided by his prince, who held him firmly in Wittenberg. Instead of this, however, he paid a visit to the University of his beloved fatherland, in company with the above-named friends and pupils, during the diet at Worms, to assist in organizing it on an evangelical basis.

Those were joyful and festal days which Melancthon and his friends passed in the romantic city of Heidelberg. When he arrived there, October twenty-second, 1557, all the professors and students went out to meet him in solemn procession. Professor Posthius greeted him with an address and a Latin poem. The Elector invited him to his table in the renowned castle. On the twenty-fourth a great feast was prepared in honor of him in the Sapienz building. The venerable, modest, and retired man was overwhelmed with demonstrations of honor. But this festal joy was darkened by the intelligence of the death of his wife, who had already died on the thirteenth of October, in Wittenberg. His friend Camerarius, who was to bring him the intelligence in person, arrived in Heidelberg on the twenty-seventh, but deferred communicating the intelligence till the following day, when he opened the matter to him during a walk in the garden of the castle. Melancthon listened to the sad message with deep and painful feelings, but in pious composure raised his eyes to heaven, whither his faithful companion had preceded him, and uttered only the few but significant and touching words: "Farewell! Soon shall I follow thee!"[*]

graphy of Philip Melancthon, Elberfeld, 1861, p. 618. This work of Professor Schmidt in Strasburg ought to be translated into English, since we have as yet nothing able on Melancthon in the English language. Melancthon belongs to all churches of the reformation, and is a bond of union between them.

[*] Compare Dr. C. Schmidt, a. a. b. p. 618, *et seq.*

Ursinus, now provided by Melancthon with a very honorable Latin testimonial, in which he is represented as a "highly gifted, learned, pious, agreeable youth, endeared to all honorable men", made a learned journey to Switzerland and France. There he became personally acquainted with the leaders of the Reformed church who were still living, especially with Bullinger and Peter Martyr in Zurich, with Calvin and Beza in Geneva. Calvin (who died 1564) presented him with his writings, and recorded in them with his own hand his prayer for a blessing upon the young friend. This journey enlarged his spiritual views, and decided his preference for the Reformed church. The vacillating position of Melancthon between Lutheranism and Calvinism could thenceforward no more satisfy him, even though he was allied to his venerable teacher in mildness and love of peace, and continued to regard him with great respect and love to the end of his life.

When he, in 1556, returned to Wittenberg, he was met by a call to the office of rector in the Elizabethan Gymnasium in Breslau, which, from love and gratitude to his native city, he accepted. Yet two years afterwards, he of his own accord resigned this position from love of peace, on account of the violent sacramental controversy between the Lutherans and Philippists of that place. During the strife he wrote his first work, "Theses on the Doctrine of the Sacraments", in regard to which Melancthon, shortly before his death, expressed the judgment: "Ursinus's learning I have known, it is true; but as regards knowledge in such things, I have never before been acquainted with any thing so brilliant."

After an honorable farewell, Ursinus left the second time for Zurich in October, 1560, which now, after the death of Melancthon (April, 1560), which had meanwhile occurred, had become more endeared to him than Wittenberg itself. At that time he wrote to his uncle: "Not reluctantly do I leave my fatherland if it will not endure the truth, which I cannot with a good conscience give up. Were my best teacher, Melancthon, still alive, I would go nowhere else than to him. As he is now dead, I will go to the Zurichers. There are pious, learned, great men with whom I am firmly resolved to spend my life. God will provide for the rest." That God, to whose guidance he intrusted himself with implicit confidence, had however appointed him to a field of labor different from Switzerland.

As early as 1561, Ursinus was called from Zurich to Heidelberg. Frederick III desired to draw Peter Martyr, whom he held in high honor, from Zurich to his University ; but on account of advanced age he declined the invitation, and recommended in place of himself young Ursinus, who was admirably suited for the post, and labored with good effect. In the following year (August twenty-eighth, 1562) he was promoted to the honor of Doctor. He delivered lectures on dogmatics in the University, and was at the same time principal of the so-called Sapienz College, a preacher-seminary, founded by Otto Henry, enlarged by Frederick III so as to take in seventy pupils, and which stood in intimate connection with the University. This college, with a small salary, gave him so much labor and weariness, that he sometimes, in spells of hypochondria, called it his " tread-mill", or " martyr-chamber". He had a desire in 1571 to accept an honorable call to the theological school at Lausanne ; but the prince would not accept his resignation. He married only in 1574, in which state he lived happily, and had one son born to him. His pupils were devoted to him with much love and enthusiasm.

In this position he labored with unwearied industry, notwithstanding increasing infirmities, till the death of Frederick III, 1576, when by his Lutheran son and successor, Ludwig VI, he was, on account of his reformed faith, together with six hundred steadfast reformed ministers, deposed and directed to leave the country. Still he found a place of refuge in the small district of country belonging to the Palsgrave John Casimir, on the left bank of the Rhine. Under his auspices he, with other banished Heidelberg theologians, founded and conducted the high-school at Neustadt, on the Hardt, the so-called *Casimirianum*, which had so speedily sprung up since 1578, and continued his activity in theological teaching by word and pen to the time of his death. His last works were an explanation of the prophecy of Isaiah, and a defence of the reformed doctrine against the attacks of the Lutheran form of concord. In the full power of manhood, aged forty-eight years, he died in the triumphs of a joyful faith, March sixth, 1583—the same year in which Casimir, the younger son of Frederick III, came in possession of the government, called back the banished ministers, and restored the reformed confession in the Palatinate. His pupil and colleague, Franz Junius, delivered a Latin funeral discourse full of the warmest admiration and affection.

Ursinus was a man of thorough classical, theological, and philosophical learning, of poetic talent, distinguished teaching gifts, simple, modest, and attractive character, and deep evangelical piety. He made the best use of his time, having placed above the door of his study the inscription : "Friend when thou visitest me, be brief, or depart, or assist me in my labor".* He avoided all useless words. The excellent first question of the Catechism is characteristic of his piety, as also his declaration that he would not take a hundred thousand worlds for the blessed certainty of belonging to Jesus Christ. He exceeded the reformed theologians of his time ; and in the Heidelberg Catechism he has far exceeded himself. His other works, collected by his pupil David Pareus, at first appeared anonymously, or in the name of the faculty of Heidelberg, or as gathered after his death from notes taken by others. The most important of these is his extensive Latin commentary on the Heidelberg Catechism (Corpus Doctrinæ Orthodoxæ), of which there are also a number of English translations,† and a popular German abstract.‡ In his epitaph in the church at Neustadt he is pronounced, "a great theologian, a vanquisher of false doctrines concerning the Person of Christ and the Lord's Supper, an acute philosopher, a wise man, and a strict teacher of youth".

CASPER OLEVIANUS,§ the son of a baker, was born August 10th, 1536, in Treves, the city of "the holy coat of Christ", on the borders of France, and studied the ancient languages and law in the Universities of Paris, Bourges, and Orléans. When he, at Bourges, by a heroic venture, endeavored to save from drowning in the river Loire, or according to others in the Eure, the son of the same Frederick III who afterwards called him into his service, and thereby greatly endangered his own life, he vowed to devote himself to the Lord with all that he was and possessed. He now studied theology in Geneva under Calvin and Beza, and in Zurich under Bullinger and Peter Martyr. He enjoyed thus, like his later colleague Ursinus, the great advantage of the personal instruction and communion of the most celebrated founders and leaders of the Reformed church.

In 1559 he began his reformatory activity as a fearless preacher of the pure Gospel in his native city, Treves. On one occasion a Roman priest endeavored to interfere with his

* "Amice, quisquis huc venis, aut agita paucis, aut obi, aut me laborantem adjuva."

† The latest English edition is by Rev. W. Williard, in Columbus, Ohio, 1859, on the basis of the translation of Dr. J. Parry, with an Introduction by Dr. Nevin.

‡ Dr. Zac. Ursinus's Introduction to Christian Instruction, etc. An Abstract of his Corpus Doctrinæ Orthodoxæ. With a Preface by Lic. E. W. Krummacher. Duisburg, 1863.

§ So called from Olewig, a village near Treves, from which his father sprang. So Göbel contends, without giving any authorities.

preaching, and in so doing excited his hearers to such a degree that they were willing to lay violent hands on him; then Olevianus, with his characteristic magnanimity, took him by the hand and led him out of the church, that he might receive no injury. The half of the inhabitants had already been won over to the evangelical doctrines when he was persecuted by the Bishop, and, together with the two burgomasters of the city and nine others who shared in the same views, was cast into prison. After ten weeks, however, through the mediation of the Protestant princes, especially of Frederick III, who felt himself gratefully indebted to him, he was delivered from prison, and called by the last, in 1560 (one year before Ursinus), to the University of Heidelberg as professor, first of philosophy, and afterwards of theology. Later he resigned his professorship into the hands of Ursinus, and labored as court preacher and church counsellor.

At the accession of Ludwig VI, in 1576, Olevianus, like Ursinus, as a steadfast confessor of the reformed doctrine, was also deposed and driven away. He followed a call to Basleberg, and in 1584 went as preacher to Herborn. In his last sickness he only rightly learned to know, as he said, the greatness of sin and the greatness of the majesty of God, and often prayed: " Could I only soon return home to my Lord; I long to depart and to be with Christ". He died in Herborn, February twenty-fifth, 1587, in peace, after he had replied to the question of a friend whether he was certain of his salvation, by laying his hand upon his heart and uttering the triumphant word of faith, " Certissimus!" that is, "perfectly certain". Theodore Beza, the patriarch of the Reformed church, who outlived the rest, mourns his death in a Latin poem full of deep grief and enthusiastic praise, erecting for him thus an honorable memorial.*

Olevianus was less learned than Ursinus, and his exegetical, dogmatical, and homiletical works are not very important for scientific theology; but they are popular, true-hearted, full of energy and unction. Perhaps the best is his catechetical work on the covenant of grace. He regarded the covenant of grace as the key to the true understanding of the Bible, and thus became the precursor of Coccejus and Lampe, who further developed the federal or covenant theology. His principal

---

* The beginning of the poem is as follows:

Eheu, quibus suspiriis,
Eheu, quibus te lachrymis,
Oleviane planxero ?
Nam dotibus pases tuis,

Doloribus pares meis,
Questus modosque flebiles
Non pectus hoc siggesserit,
Non istud os effuderit.

strength, however, lay in his practical talent for the pulpit and church government, in which he exceeded Ursinus, and complemented him. In all ecclesiastical matters he was the confidential and influential counsellor of Frederick III, with whom he became associated through a singular providence.

He was unwearied in his labors to introduce into the Palatinate the Presbyterial and Synodical form of church government and a strict church discipline, after the pattern of the congregation of Geneva in its blooming period, which was also by the Scotch reformer Knox so much admired, and in accordance with the clearly expressed principles of the Heidelberg Catechism itself, Question 82–55, and for this purpose early secured the advice of Calvin. This matter, also, lay very near the heart of the prince, of Ursinus, and of all foreign Calvinists. But the practical carrying out of it succeeded only very imperfectly, and was much hindered, especially through the professor of medicine, Thomas Erastus, who was an advocate of the government of the church by the state, and an opponent of excommunication.* To this day the govment and discipline, and the self-dependence of the church therewith connected, is far less developed in the German churches than it is in other Reformed churches, especially in Holland, Scotland, and North America. The intimate union of church and state in the Palatinate, and in Germany generally, was an almost insurmountable obstacle. For the victory of strict church discipline and national presbyterial and congregational government, with lay representation, is at the same time, at least in extensive countries (the old Calvinistic Geneva forms an exception on account of its small compass), a victory of the self-dependent free-churchdom and popular churchdom over state-churchdom. In relation to self-government, the German Reformed church in the United States has a great advantage over the mother church in Germany and Switzerland, where the church is still under guardianship of the state.

II. The Preparation and Ecclesiastical Approval of the Catechism.

Intrusted with the preparation of a new Catechism, Ursinus and Olevianus first jointly collected the material from the catechetical literature of the Reformed church, especially of Swit-

---

* Hence the technical English term Erastianism, which is very much the same as Cäsaropapismus, and the teaching indicates that the political ruler of the land is at the same time the ecclesiastical ruler, or the chief Bishop of his subjects. Eras-

zerland,* which was even at that time very rich.   The mother country of the Reformed church has, therefore, at least indirectly, had share in the origination of the Heidelberg Catechism, even as both its authors also completed their education in Zurich and Geneva.   They made most use of the Catechism of Geneva by Calvin, and the Catechism of De Lasky allied to it.†   Then each one prepared a sketch or draft as preparatory work, Olevianus following the leading idea of the covenant of grace, Ursinus following the Calvinistic division of the material into five principal parts: of faith, law, prayer, word of God, and sacrament.   Ursinus wrote two catechisms in the Latin language ; a larger one (with the title, Catechesis, hoc est, Rudimenta Religionis Christianæ), and a smaller (Catechesis Minor), an abridgment of the first.

On, the basis of these careful preparations, which had been laid before the Prince and received his approval, originated the present Heidelberg Catechism.   It is however with all its affinity with its predecessors an independent creation.   This is plainly seen in the division and design of the whole, as well as in the single questions, which show a great advance on the drafts.‡   The final preparation was the work of both

tus was a Swiss by birth, and a Zwinglian as respects the doctrine of the Lord's Supper.   He died in Basel as professor of ethics in 1583.   He was a man of much spirit and learning, and one of the first among the learned who declared himself in opposition to the superstition of astrology and alchymy.

* So Olevianus wrote to Bullinger in Zurich.

† The affinity of the Heidelberg Catechism with those of Calvin and De Lasky, which, however, does not take away from the first any of its independent value, has been especially shown by Leisen and Sudhoff.   Calvin's Catechism appeared first in 1536, then entirely reconstructed and divided into questions and answers, in 1541, in French, and in 1545 in Latin, and was afterwards also translated into Spanish, Italian, English, Greek, and Hebrew.   In its improved form it is found in Calvin's works (Amsterdam edition, tom. viii, pp. 11–87), and in Niemeyer's and Böckel's collection of the Reformed Confessions.   Lasky's Catechism appeared in 1553. John Lasky (de Lasco) was a Polish nobleman who connected himself with the Swiss reformation, and labored partly in England (under Edward VI), partly in the Netherlands and Germany, and at last in Poland, where he introduced the reformation.   He died in 1560.

‡ Compare for instance the much admired first question in the Catechism with the first question in the preparatory work of Ursinus, and the great advance will at once be seen.   In the Larger Catechism-draft of Ursinus (comp. Sudhoff, Theolog. Handbook, etc., p. 477) the first question and answer are as follows :

Quam habes firmam in vita et morte consolationem ?

Quod a Deo ad imaginem ejus et vitam œternam sum conditus et postquam hanc volens in Adamo amiseram, Deus ex immensa et gratuita misericordia me recepit in fœdus gratiæ suæ, et propter obedientiam et mortem Filii sui missi in carnem donat mihi credenti justitiam et vitam æternam: atque hoc fœdus suum in corde meo per per Spiritum suum ad imaginem Dei me reformantem et clamantem in me *Abba Pater*, et per verbum suum et signa hujus fœderis visibilia obsignavit.

In the Smaller Catechism of Ursinus the first question and answer run more briefly and simplified thus:

Quae tua est consolatio qua tam in morte quam in vita cor tuum se sustentat ?

theologians under the constant coöperation of Frederick III. Ursinus has always properly been regarded as the principal author, as he was afterwards also its chief defender and interpreter. Still it would appear that the nervous German style, the division into three parts (as distinguished from the five parts in the Catechism of Calvin, and the smaller one of Ursinus) and the genial warmth and unction of the whole work, come chiefly from Olevianus.* In any case, however, as has already been remarked, the work is far better than all the private writings of both theologians. It was produced under the influence of a spirit which was higher, deeper, and more comprehensive than their own spirit.

Augusti expresses his astonishment that the Catechism should have been finished in a few months, and yet manifest in its construction " so few traces of haste, and so many perfections".† But its authors may probably have labored on it a whole year or more ; and they entered upon their work, as we have seen, with much forecast and conscientiousness. Then, also, that was a period of religious inspiration and creative activity, and very fruitful in catechetical books of instruction. The Catechisms of Luther, Brentz, Leo Judä, Bullinger, Œcolampadius, Calvin, and De Lasky had preceded, and nearly the same time the Catechism of the Roman church was also prepared. Such preparatory works served the authors a good purpose. The principal doctrines of evangelical Protestantism had been already substantially wrought out, and needed only a calm, clear presentation and combination.

When the work was finished, the Prince, in December, 1562, convened a general Synod at Heidelberg, composed of the superintendents and most prominent ministers of the Palatinate, who were conscientiously to examine and prove the Catechism according to God's word. According to Van Alpen the adoption of it was unanimous. But according to the reports of the opposite party (Baldwin, Hesshus, Flacius Illyr-

---

Quod omnia peccata mea Deus mihi propter Christum remisit, vitamque æternam donavit in qua ipsum perpetuo celebrem.

Calvin's Catechism begins with the question : What is the chief end of human life ? (" Quis humanæ vitæ præcipuus est finis ? ") from which originated the first question of the Westminster Catechism : " What is the *chief end* of man ? " The first question of the Heidelberg Catechism on the *only* comfort of man in life and in death, is, among all these preparatory attempts, by far the best.

* So think Hundeshagen and Sudhoff. The last is especially zealous for the honor of Olevianus in opposition to the frequent overestimate placed on the services of Ursinus in the preparation of the Catechism.

† A Historical and Critical Introduction to the two Principal Catechisms of the Evangelical Church, 1824, p. 100.

icus and others) there was a small minority who brought in manifold objections to it, but were outvoted. The last is more likely, and does not derogate in the least from the value of the Catechism. No good work, no new idea, no true advance can succeed without the fiery ordeal of contradiction and persecution. This belongs throughout to the militant character of the Church in this world, and to the following of Christ and his Apostles. Besides, the Catechism was required to pass through the strongest opposition after its adoption and introduction, and was bitterly persecuted from various directions, but victoriously endured the trial.

By its adoption by the representatives of the church of the Palatinate, the Catechism acquired, before its publication, a churchly character, and was thus in a position to fulfil its mission as a guide of public religious instruction in Church and school.

III. Its Publication—The Preface of the Elector—The most important Editions of the Catechism—The Eightieth Question.

After its approval by the Synod, the Catechism was for the first time printed and published, by order of the Elector in 1563, with the title: " CATECHISMUS, OR CHRISTIAN INSTRUCTION, as it is conducted in the churches and schools of the Electoral Palatinate. Printed in the Electoral city, Heidelberg, by John Mayer, 1563, 8." The preface is dated January 19, 1563. From this, however, we cannot conclude that the Catechism appeared on that day ; no doubt a few months passed before it was printed and bound, so that it was more likely published in the Spring of 1563.

The Preface is published in the name of the Elector Frederick III, and was most likely also written by him ; it speaks in an appropriate and worthy manner of the occasion and object of the Catechism. In it the Elector wishes to all " superintendents, pastors, preachers, officers in churches and schools ", grace and greeting, and makes known to them that he, by virtue of his high office, and to promote the temporal and eternal welfare of his subjects on the basis of the sincere fear of God, and knowledge of his saving word, has, " by the counsel and aid of our entire Theological Faculty here, and all superintendents and most prominent ministers, prepared summary of instruction, or Catechism of our Christian religion from the word of God, both in the German and Latin language, that hereafter not only the youth in the churches and schools may be religiously instructed in such Christian doctrine in a uniform manner, but also that the ministers and school-masters may have a sure and abiding form and measure as to the way in which they should conduct the instruction of the young, and not daily introduce changes according to their own mind, or ever deviate into perverse doctrines". Finally he exhorts and enjoins upon them gratefully to receive this catechism, to use it diligently in churches and schools, to teach and live according to it, with the firm assurance that Almighty God will also bless such good instruction from his word, to the improvement of their lives, and the promotion of their temporal and eternal welfare.

This Preface, though written in a somewhat loose, antiquated German style, breathes an excellent Christian spirit, and falls in very appropriately with the object of the work.

This first edition is now of course very rare; however, the younger Dr. Niemeyer, of Halle, in his Collection of the Symbolical Books of the Reformed Church,* has given it word for word, in the old style of writing, together with the preface of the Elector, (including the eightieth question), and thus rendered it accessible to learned readers. It has a number of peculiarities. The questions and answers are not yet separated and numbered; the division into Lord's days is wholly wanting, and the proof-texts are few in number, and the chapters only are referred to,† as the division into verses was not yet in use. Yet these are all unimportant differences, pertaining only to the form and not to the contents.

More important on the other hand is the deviation in the famous eightieth question, at the close of which the Romish Mass is called " a denial of the one sacrifice and sufferings of Jesus Christ, and an accursed idolatry".

According to the common view, which has been repeated ever since the time of Alting, the eightieth question was not contained in the first edition, but was first included in the second edition, except only the clause " and an accursed idolatry", and then introduced in full in the third edition by order of Frederick III, as a counter-blast to the anathema of the Council of Trent.‡ The same authors commonly distinguish

---

* Collectio Confessionum in Ecclesiis Reformatis publicatarum. Edidit Dr. H. A. Niemeyer: Lipsiæ, 1840, pp. 390–427. Bökel, in his edition of the Reformed Symbola, gives the Catechism in modern German. Both give the Elector's preface in full, the first in the original, the other in the modern style.

† For instance in the first question are cited: " *a*) Rom. 14.   *b*) 1 Cor. 6.   *c*) 1 Cor. 3.   *d*) 1 Pet. 1.   *e*) John 1 and 2.   *f*) 1 John 3.   *g*) John 6.   *h*) Math. 10. Luke 21.   *i*) Rom. 8.   *k*) 2 Cor. 1. Eph. 1. Rom. 8.   *l*) Rom. 8."

‡ So Alting, Struve, Van Alpen, Augusti, Nienäcker, Niemeyer (Præf. lxii. sq.), Sudhoff (who repeats this error four times), etc. The whole mistake comes from

three different editions of the whole Catechism as having appeared in the year 1563, and explain the circumstance that the first two editions are so rare, by the supposition that the Elector had called in and suppressed them.

But this view seems to rest in an error. We hold that the eightieth question was contained in the first edition with the exception of the offensive last clause, which was added by order of the Elector in part in the second printing, and entire in the third. There were therefore not three different *editions*, but merely two later *reprints of one page*, namely, folio 55, on which the eightieth question is found; so that the last reprints of the year 1563 which contain the offensive addition, and at the same time a closing remark on the last page, are in other respects precisely alike. This closing remark is as follows: "What in the first printing (not edition) was overlooked, as especially folio 55, is now added by order of his Electoral Grace, 1563".

My reasons for this view, to which Dr. Ullman* and Dr. Nevin† also incline, are the following: 1. The eightieth question, with the exception only of this last clause, is altogether inoffensive, and also complete without it; containing a worthy and calm statement of the difference between the Romish Mass and the evangelical Lord's Supper. 2. D. L. Wundt affirms on his own observation, that in existing copies of the first edition the eightieth question is found with the exception of the offensive close: "*So that the mass at bottom is nothing else than a denial of the one sacrifice and sufferings of Jesus Christ, and an accursed idolatry*".‡ 3. The still existing copies of the so-called third edition of 1563, as the reprint of Niemeyer, are not at all designated as of a third edition, and so far as I can see, differ in nothing except on folio 55, and the above quoted closing remarks referring to this page.§

Alting, who expresses himself ambiguously, and it has then without being carefully examined perpetuated itself in later works on the Catechism.

* In his contribution to the Ter-centenary Commemoration of the Heidelberg Catechism, which will appear in the memorial volume.

† In his Historical and Critical Introduction to the large Ter-centenary edition of the Catechism, which will also appear during this year. At least I have so understood Dr. Nevin in a conversation on the subject. Earlier he held the common view.

‡ Magazine for Palatinate Church History; vol. ii, p. 112, et seq.

§ Köcher even, who had before him an edition of 1563, find it remarkable, that no trace of a deviation is found anywhere else, and that no one makes mention before Alting of a *third* edition of 1563. So also Augusti, p. 115. The reprint of the edition of 1563 in Niemeyer in his Collect. Conf. Reform., which I have used as the basis of my edition, gives the eightieth question in full, and yet has exactly the same title as the other copies, without being called the second or third edition.

4. It is in itself in the highest degree improbable that a book at *that* time, when the mass of the people could not read, and consequently the reading of Bibles and catechisms was confined to a small circle, should in one year have passed through three editions. Hence also we meet with no trace of a new edition till 1571, thus eight years after the edition of 1563.

In any case it must be admitted that the *last clause* of the eightieth question, from " *So that the mass* " to " *idolatry*", is no original constituent part of the Heidelberg Catechism, and has so far no original synodical sanction. It is certainly a well-meant, but still arbitrary and unwise addition of the Elector, who in this instance suffered himself to be carried away by the intolerant spirit of the age. It was a sharp Protestant reply to the surprising anathemas of the Roman Catholic Council of Trent, which just about that time, namely, December 4th, 1563, closed its sessions; and its introduction is easily explained, and in a great measure excusable in the light of this provocation, as also by the polemical spirit of the times. But—whether true or untrue, whether righteous or unrighteous, as against the Catholics—it in either case is in disharmony with the otherwise moderate and peaceful tone of the Catechism, and has been the means of drawing upon it much unnecessary persecution from the side of the Jesuits, and even for a time placed it under the formal Electoral ban in the Palatinate. Meanwhile this polemical addition to the eightieth question has passed over into all subsequent editions of the Catechism, and must therefore also be retained in future, or at best merely be distinguished from the original text by brackets.

Cotemporaneously with the German edition of 1563, which is of course the original edition,* appeared also a Latin translation, which was prepared according to the Electoral direction, by John Lagus, a minister, and the teacher Lambert Pithopäus, who had been called from Deventer to Heidelberg as teacher in 1562.

In the same year there appeared also an order of church government and Agenda, which was however revised and improved in 1585, when the Reformed church of the Palatinate was restored under John Casimir. It is far less important than the Catechism, and has never attracted the same attention, or been so widely received.

---

* H. Alting (cited by Nienäcker) makes, in regard to this point, the important remark : " Authentica est sola editio Germanica, in qua omnia non rotundiora modo, sed etiam ἐμφατικώτερα sunt. Ei proxima est versio Latina a Josua Lago et Lamberto Pithopœo adornata publiceque approbata."

The German was again reprinted in 1571,* then anew in 1573 ; and in this third edition (according to others the fifth) the Scripture proof-texts are for the first time indicated by references to the verses.† The number of proof-texts is here also increased, and the division of the questions into fifty-two Lord's days, after the manner of Calvin's Catechism (which, however, counts fifty-eight Lord's days) is introduced, as the Catechism was to be explained to the people every Sunday, in the afternoon sermons. It were well if this venerable reformed custom of having catechetical discourses, or a catechetical exercise with the children, in connection with the afternoon or evening service, were again revived.

A larger German edition, with the proof-texts printed out in full, with a table of domestic duties, and a number of liturgical and apologetical supplements appeared in 1595 in Neustadt on the Hardt. It is regarded as the best of the older editions, and agrees in size with the Latin edition of 1585.

The so-called Small Catechism first appeared in 1585, cotemporaneously with the revised Agenda. It is an abstract of the large one, and was not designed to supersede this, but only to simplify it and render it more popular ; since, as Prince Casimir says in his preface, some questions in the large Catechism are rather long for the youth, and might also be too difficult for the common people. A beautiful edition of this small Catechism appeared in 1610 ; but it never attained the same authority as the large one. Other abstracts, which appeared in later times, have had only a local and passing significance.

The large Catechism has since then been republished unnumbered times, separately, and in connection with Reformed Church Agenda, liturgies, hymn books, and other books of devotion. S. Van Alpen, in whose work, however, are numerous errors, speaks even of half a million of *editions* which had appeared in Germany alone, previous to the year 1800.‡ This is however incredible, as at this rate there would have been over two thousand editions each year. Perhaps he may have meant that many *copies,* in which case, however, his estimate would have been too low, as there were doubtless many millions of copies published. It has been often remark-

* Niemeyer calls this edition *quarta* editio under the mistaken supposition that there were three editions of 1563. According to our view it was the second edition.

† Hence, according to the testimony of Van Alpen and Niemeyer, this edition of 1573, contains on the title page this addition : " Now newly printed *with the addition of the verses*".

‡ History, etc., p. 284.

ed, that with the exception of the Bible and the Pilgrim's Progress, no book has been so often republished as the Heidelberg Catechism. But doubtless the *Imitation of Christ*, by Thomas à Kempis, and the small Catechism of Luther, do not fall behind it in this respect.

It is remarkable that with all this there has been as yet no critical edition, unless it be that of Niemeyer, which is, however, a mere reprint of the edition of 1563.* Hence much confusion has crept into the text, and especially into the proof-texts. This want, it is hoped, will now be met by the edition for the publication of which provision has been made by the German Reformed church of America in connection with the Ter-Centenary Commemoration, and other projected editions in Germany.

IV. *Reception and Circulation.*

The Heidelberg Catechism was so true an outgrowth of the genius of the German Reformed church, and corresponded so well with the needs of this confession, that it not only found favor in the Palatinate, for which country it was originally designed, and where it was introduced by the civil authority, but also found admission, and came more or less into use in various other reformed lands in and out of Germany, especially in East Friesland, Zurich, Cleve, Berg, in Mark, in Wappenthal, in Brandenberg, in Eastern and Western Prussia, in the Electorate of Hesse, in Anhalt, and in the free imperial cities ; also in a number of Swiss cantons, where the Catechisms of Bullinger or Calvin had not already been introduced ; and finally in Poland and Hungary, in Holland and in Belgium. In the Netherlands it was early approved, recommended, and clothed with symbolical authority, by Synod of Wesel, 1568, then again by a national Synod at Dortrecht, in 1574, and finally by the great Synod of Dortrecht, 1618 ; and since at the Synod of Dortrecht, delegates were present from all the Reformed churches of the Continent, and also from England, the Heidelberg Catechism there received a kind of general authority for the entire Reformed confession.

---

* Dr. Augusti (Preface, p. viii) applies the words of St. Hieronymus spoken of the Bible, "Tot sunt exemplari, quot codices, et unisquisque pro arbitrio suo vel addidit, vel subtraxit, quod ei visum est", also to the editions of the Lutheran and Heidelberg Catechism, and adds: "The matter is of such importance that a critical edition of both Catechisms would be a very meritorious work". Some late editions, as that of Mess and Sudhoff, especially the last, lay claim, it is true, to critical care, but have many mistakes and arbitrary changes in the text, and selection of proof-texts. Sudhoff falls into an error in the very first question, in putting "Einziger Trost" for "einiger Trost."

25

It was, for the Reformed church of Holland, of far more practical significance than the more rigorous Calvinistic Dortrecht Articles, because it was taught in all the schools, and explained to the people every Sunday from the pulpits. Its use contributed no little to the world-historical significance of this remarkable country, redeemed from the sea, which not only in the history of trade, but also of civil and religious freedom, of theology, science, and art, occupies an honorable position in later history.

In France, England, and Scotland, the Heidelberg Catechism could not, it is true, supplant their own, and partly older catechisms, but it was very highly esteemed, and a number of times translated into French and English. Beside the English translation at present in use, there were many older ones ; for instance, one by Henry Parry, Bishop of Worcester, which, together with the commentary of Ursinus, appeared in Oxford, 1601, and then in London, 1633, and which has lately been republished by Dr. Steiner.* In the Reformed church of Scotland the Heidelberg Catechism appears to have been for some time in use ; for in a collection of authorized church-books, which appeared at Edinburgh, 1719–20, in two volumes ;† the Heidelberg Catechism is included with the remark, "Translated into English and printed for the use of the church of Scotland", notwithstanding the Westminster Catechisms of 1648 had at that time already been a long while in use.

From Holland and Germany the Catechism came also to America, and still continues to be the symbolical book of the Dutch and German Reformed churches in the United States. As the Dutch, as early as 1609, and hence before the Puritans (1620), Presbyterians and Lutherans, settled in the new world on the banks of the Hudson, on the island of Manhattan, where since has arisen the world-renowned city of New York, the Heidelberg Catechism, next to that of the Episcopal church (since 1607), is the oldest Catechism used in the American Protestant church. It is worthy of notice, that the German Reformed church of America, which has only during the last twenty years awoke to a powerful self-consciousness and theological life, will doubtless commemorate the three hundredth

* In the *Mercersburg Review*, and also separately printed in Chambersburgh, Pa., 1860. The English translations have been made from the Latin translation, and are therefore in many respects incorrect.

† With the title : A Collection of Confessions of Faith, Catechisms, Directions, Books of Discipline, etc., of *public authority in the Church of Scotland ;* together with all the acts of Assembly which are standing rules concerning the doctrine, worship, government and discipline of the Church of Scotland. By W. Dulop, 2 vol. 8vo., Edinburgh, 1719–20.

anniversary of the existence of the Heidelberg Catechism with more earnestness, zeal, and effect than the mother church in Europe, where, during the age of so-called illumination, it has been in many countries dislodged by modern spiritless and lifeless rationalistic catechisms.

The Heidelberg Catechism has not only been translated into all modern European languages, but also into a number of Asiatic languages and dialects (e. g., those of Arabia, Malay, Senegal), as also into Latin and Greek (into ancient Greek by Sylburg in Heidelberg, 1597, into modern Greek in Leyden, 1648), and into Hebrew. In a larger measure than any other catechism has it received the Pentecostal gift of speaking in tongues.

In like manner has it been unnumbered times explained in sermons and commentaries. Whole libraries have been written upon it, especially in Holland. The commentaries most valued are those of Zacharius Ursinus in Latin (also translated into English, French, and German), of John Coccejus, John d'Outrein, Simon Van Alpen, and Carl Sudhoff. The largest number of commentaries, sermons, and controversial writings, appeared in Holland, Heidelberg, Neustadt on the Hardt, Bremen, Herborn, Frankfort on the Main, Hanau, and Halle.

Among all catechisms there is none, even Luther's smaller catechism not excepted, which has been so widely circulated, so much used, so often translated, explained, attacked and defended, and which can show such a rich and romantic history, as the Heidelberg Catechism. The ground of all this is to be found in its inherent worth.

V. Theology of the Heidelberg Catechism.

The Heidelberg Catechism, in the very beginning, introduces us at once into the living centre of practical evangelical Christianity, teaching us the secret of all true comfort and peace, the true art of living and dying happily. Thus the first question contains the theme or fundamental thought of the whole book : Christ is mine in all that I need, and I am his in body and soul, in life and death, in time and eternity. No catechism presents such an introduction, so rich in thought, so evangelically practical, and full of comfort. By many authors has this first question been pronounced a true pearl in catechetical literature. " Never, perhaps", says Dr. Nevin, " have the substance and worth of the Christian salvation, as a whole, been more comprehensively, forcibly, and touchingly presented, in so small a compass".

The second question presents the division of the Catechism,

which consists of three parts: The *misery* of man, his *redemption*, and the *gratitude* due to God for such redemption. The first part is prevailingly negative, awakening the sense of sin by means of the sum of the law in its essence, as requiring supreme love towards God and man. The second part presents the objects of faith in the form of facts, on the basis of the Apostles' Creed, including also the doctrine of the Holy Sacraments, not as separate doctrines, but as integral parts of the system of faith. The third part is ethical, unfolding the new life of obedience, from the truly evangelical stand-point of gratitude and reciprocal love, following the decalogue, which Christ came not to destroy, but to fulfil. The third part closes with the Lord's prayer, as the expression of gratitude in the form of devotion.

The theology of the Heidelberg Catechism is, first of all, throughout, *biblical;* that is, it is based, not on the fallible traditions of men, but on the infallible word of God. Nearly every question is fortified by Scripture passages, which, as a general thing, are selected with much tact and great wisdom, although in these, from the stand-point of later exegesis, improvements might of course in some cases be made. The Heidelberg Catechism was the first which bound itself in this way to the word of God. It exhibits in this particular an important advance in catechetical literature. The smaller Lutheran and the Calvinistic catechisms are, it is true, also biblical in their contents, but not in their form, since, in the original editions, there are scarcely any Scripture passages cited. Later editions, especially of the Lutheran Catechism, have for the most part supplied this want, which, however, always necessarily involves an analysis and enlargement. At present, it is required of every good catechism, that it be at the same time a book of Scripture texts. A bare citation of Scripture passages does, of course, not answer. Many new catechisms teem with Scripture texts, and are nevertheless lean, sterile, dry, cold and dead. Every thing here depends on the selection of the proper passages, and on harmony with the spirit of the Holy Scriptures. It must be said of the Heidelberg Catechism, that it breathes throughout the spirit of the Bible, and is a stream from this pure fountain. Whoever assails it in any essential point, assails divine revelation itself. Hence also Frederick, at the German Diet, 1566, said his catechism was supported by marginal texts in such a manner that it must stand incontrovertible.

The theology of the Catechism is, further, *evangelical reformed*, that is to say, it belongs to the reformed type of doctrine, in contradistinction from the Creek Catholic, the Roman Catholic, and the evangelical Lutheran types. The reformed type is, however, not the product of a single man, but the product of the combined work of Zwingli, Œcolampadius, Calvin, Bullinger, Beza, and other reformers of the first and second generation, and hence owes something to each of them, but is at the same time independent of all. The reformed confession is the church of the pure word, of free grace, and of the free congregation; it assumes various forms under the influence of different nationalities, and in different countries in which it found a home; but its fundamental doctrines are the same in all its symbols.

In the Heidelberg Catechism the genius of the *German* branch of the Reformed church is developed and expressed. This stands mediating between the Lutheran and strictly Reformed confession, extends its hands to both, and works in upon both. It is the mildest form of Calvinism, and betrays the influence of the conciliatory Melancthonian spirit. Strictly, it is neither Zwinglian nor Calvinistic, nor yet Melancthonian, not even Ursinian or Olivianian; it rises above these human names and conceptions of doctrine, even though it has learned something from them all; and, like the bee, it has drawn honey from various flowers. It possesses Calvin's power and depth without his severity, Melancthon's inwardness and warmth without his indecision, Zwingli's simplicity and clearness without his cool considerateness and fear of the mystical.

In connection with this must be mentioned, as a still further advantage, its theological and pedagogical *wisdom* and *moderation*. Although not originally designed, like Luther's smaller Catechism, merely for the instruction of children, but also intended to hold the place of a confessional book, it nevertheless eschews all narrow-hearted confessional severity and sharp corners. Its few polemical questions* are kept within the bounds of dignity and moderation, with the single exception of the later addition to the eightieth question, directed against the Roman Mass, for which, however, Frederick III, and not its authors, is responsible. Other symbolical books of the sixteenth century contain expressions still more severe against the Roman church. In general, the Heidelberg Catechism breathes a mild, conciliatory, and friendly, in one word, a truly Christian spirit. This fact is only the more to be appre-

---

* Question 30 against the adoration of saints, question 48 against the later Lutheran doctrine of ubiquity, question 80 against the Roman mass, questions 97 and 98 against the use of images.

ciated when we remember that it was composed at a time when the " rage of the theologians", from which Melancthon so ardently longed to be relieved, had changed the entire Protestant church of Germany, and also the city and university of Heidelberg, into a battle-field, where not only Romanists and Protestants, but also Lutherans and Calvinists, contended in the most bitter and uncharitable manner.*

As regards more especially the relation of the Catechism to the peculiar doctrines of *Calvinism*, it here manifests the same moderation and pedagogical wisdom. In this respect it is more nearly allied to the Thirty-nine Articles of the Church of England than to any other reformed symbol.

In its doctrine of the *Lord's Supper*, it follows Calvin decidedly, finds, namely, as did also Melancthon, in his approved edition of the Augsburg Confession, and was still more inclined to do in his later years, a medium course between Zwingli and Luther, and seeks to unite the truth of both, whilst it sets forth the Lord's Supper as a memorial of the crucified Christ, and at the same time as a feast of living union with the exalted and invisibly present God-man, though only for the participation of believers. This doctrine is also at this day the reigning one among believing Christians of the Lutheran and Evangelical Union churches, and would be so still more largely, were it not that Luther's name and authority still attaches many pious and learned adherents to his theory that Christ's body and blood are truly present *in, with,* and *under* bread and wine, and are received with the *mouth* by *all* communicants, by the unbelieving and unworthy, as well as by the believing—although, of course, with opposite results.

---

* Even Brentz, the worthy reformer of Würtemburg, and, after the death of Melancthon, the principal representative of the Lutheran church, said, in a work against Bullinger in 1564, " The devil seeks through Calvinism nothing less than to smuggle into the church heathenism, Talmudism, and Mohammedanism". Comp. Hartmann, Johannes Brentz, p. 252. This intolerant sect spirit also early took possession of catechetical literature in the Lutheran church, even though Luther's Smaller Catechism is entirely free from polemics. Thus, there were, for instance, hyper-Lutheran catechisms at the close of the sixteenth and beginning of the seventeenth centuries, containing the following questions and answers : " What do you hold in regard to the God of the Calvinists? Ans. God protect us against such a roaring ox !" Ques. " Do you truly believe that the accursed Calvinistic heretics, instead of the living God, teach and worship the veritable devil ?" Ans, " Yes, this I believe from the bottom of my heart !" There was also a book written then, in which it is shown " clearly and solidly that the Calvinistic heretics hold 666 principles (the apocalyptic number), in common with the Turks !" I quote from memory, but have in my home (in Mercersburg) the evidence of these, and similarly curious specimens from the history of religious bigotry, the spirit of which has not yet altogether died out, although it may have changed in form.

On the other hand, in relation to Calvin's doctrine of *pre-destination*, which always found in Germany and Switzerland only isolated advocates, and which never entered into the general consciousness of the church, the Catechism manifests a wise prudence and reserve, which is the more significant, since both its authors (as in general all the reformers, even Luther and Zwingli, and at first also Melancthon) were themselves convinced of the scripturalness of this doctrine, and inclined even toward the Supralapsarian system. They were here manifestly governed by a proper tact, and felt that this mystery belongs rather to the sphere of scientific theology, and of private views, than to the religious instruction of the young, and popular instruction generally, or to the public confession of the congregation. In questions 1, 31, 53 and 54, the Catechism, it is true, takes occasion to teach the positive side of predestination, namely, *the election of the children of God to holiness and salvation in Christ*, in an uncaptious, biblical, and practical manner, as a source of comfort and ground of thankfulness; but it utters not a word of a *double* predestination, and an eternal decree of *reprobation* or *damnation*, in reference to a part of the human race; rather it teaches expressly, in question 37, the universality of the divine grace in Christ, who " sustained in body and soul the wrath of God against the sins of all mankind", which has given much trouble to the Calvinistic particularists, who hold that Christ died only for the elect. The Catechism teaches that believers are saved alone through the grace of God, whilst unbelievers are lost by their own fault. It cuts the roots of all Pelagianism and self-righteousness, without falling into the other extreme of making God responsible for evil. It holds, like the holy Scripture itself, on the one hand the unconditional sovereignty of God, which has foreseen and predetermined all things from eternity, and which works in us to will and to do, and on the other hand the responsibility of man, who is no blind machine, but an intelligent and moral, and consequently a free being. In the present state of knowledge, it is not possible fully to harmonize these apparently contradictory propositions; they are like two limbs of a large tree, whose mutual trunk stands under water, and is hidden from our view. In God, however, they are reconciled, and we shall understand this unity and harmony when once that which is in part shall cease, and we shall see face to face. The Catechism is, therefore, neither Calvinistic nor anti-Calvinistic, but leaves the conscience free in regard to this deep and difficult mystery, whilst the articles of the Dortrecht Synod and the Westminster Confession, in clear words, teach the double predestination of Calvinism, and thus place upon it the stamp of ecclesiastical authority.

This freedom of the Catechism from rigid systems and scholastic theories is a great advantage, and makes a progress in theological investigation possible without the least prejudice to faithfulness toward the ecclesiastical confession. Hence it is that the latest and most prominent German theologians of reformed origin, as Schleiermacher (the greatest theological genius since Calvin, but who stands in the transition from rationalism to the newly awakened faith), Ullman, Bähr, Hundeshagen, Schenkel, Hagenbach, Ebrard, Lange, Herzog, Krummacher, and others,* have, without any violence or inconsistency with the genius of the church of their fathers, united themselves with the positive union movement, and labor hand in hand with the moderate theologians of Lutheran origin, as Neander (who was moreover an Israelite, but baptized in the Lutheran church in Hamburg), Nitsch, Twesten, Julius Müller, Olshausen, Tholuck, Lücke, Rothe, Liebner, Dorner, etc., for the upbuilding of the later evangelical theology, who, on account of their catholic spirit and learned worth, have exerted such a mighty and steadily growing influence upon the Protestant churches of France, Holland, England, Scotland and America. The Melancthonian spirit of the Lutheran church and the German reformed spirit of the Heidelberg Catechism, as they were originally closely affiliated, have, in the nineteenth century commingled in the *evangelical union theory*, and what God has joined together let not man put asunder.

The theology of the Heidelberg Catechism is *practically edifying*. It speaks throughout the language of living experi-

---

* We must, therefore, resist as well Heppe as Sudhoff, when the first saddles upon the Catechism an anti-Calvinistic Melancthonianism, and the second, on the contrary, a rigid Calvinism. If it were *anti*-Calvinistic, the strictly Calvinistic Synod of Dortrecht would not have sanctioned it; were it rigidly *Calvinistic*, it would not have gained favor among the Melancthonians of Germany. Dr. Nevin (originally a Presbyterian, Old School) has presented the true view in regard to this point, in the following language: "The knotty points of Calvinism, as they have been called, are not brought forward as necessary objects of orthodox belief one way or the other. Only in such form could the Catechism have gained such universal credit and authority. . . . It has sometimes been made an objection to the Catechism, that it is not sufficiently definite and explicit on some of these hard points of Calvinism. But we should consider this to be rather one of its highest recommendations. For children particularly, such excursions into the territory of metaphysics, in the name of religious instruction, are ever to be deprecated and deplored. But we may go further and say that they are wholly out of character in any church confession or creed. No church has a right to incorporate them in any way into its basis of ecclesiastical communion. In any case an extensive, complicated creed must be regarded as a great evil." History and Genius of the Heidelberg Catechism, pp. 131 and 132.

ence.   It is the confession of the believing, well-grounded, graciously assured Christian, to whom nothing is holier and more precious than his Saviour.   This warm, confiding, cheerful confession, is laid into the mouth of the catechumen, that it may continuously present itself before him as ideal.   Even if he does not at first understand it, it nevertheless sinks into his heart like Scripture texts or verses of hymns, to take root and bear fruit at a later period.   Christianity is nowhere apprehended and presented merely as abstract doctrine, but, as in the New Testament itself, as fact, power, and life.   The Catechism has proceeded from deep theological study, but at the same time also from fervent prayer and living experience. It has received the baptism of spirit and fire from above.   It has the unction of the Holy Ghost.   A fresh enthusiasm of faith breathes in it, from the first question to the last.   It addresses itself not merely to the head and the memory, but also to the heart and conscience.   It is, in the best sense of the word, subjective, and brings the contents of faith into personal contact with the catechumen.   It is as edifying and consoling, as it is instructive for old and young.   It has become at once the book of devotion and prayer for the congregation.   This is well known to reformed pastors of earlier and later times.

In proof of this, I present a very striking example which has just come to my knowledge, connected with the church of the Holy Ghost in Heidelberg, where Olevianus, one of the authors of the Heidelberg Catechism, was once pastor.   Dr. Plitt, formerly pastor of that congregation, now Professor of Theology in Bonn, relates of his pastoral experience that he there met " not a few aged men and women whose eyes glistened when, in times of sickness, their thoughts were directed to the first question of the Catechism.   Most of them still knew it by heart, having committed it to memory in the years of their childhood.   Many said that as children they had never properly understood this question, and that they found great labor in learning it by heart, but now they thanked God that they knew it, and prayed it to their comfort and edification. The later generation, which had no longer been brought up under the Heidelberg Catechism, had no such an anchor in similar circumstances.   But the aged, who in their youth had become familiar with the treasures of the Heidelberg Catechism, had passed through many vicissitudes of time, without having their inward peaceful trust affected by them.   They stood on ground which could not be moved."*

* From an article on the Significance of the Heidelberg Catechism in the Reformed Church, in the *Studien und Kritiken* for 1863, No. I, pp. 24 and 25.

With the excellent contents of the Catechism corresponds finally its pithy, clear, sincere, and popular German *style*. In this particular it is, to say the least, only exceeded by the smaller Catechism of Luther, that great master of edifying popular language. Dr. Plitt calls the language of the Catechism "exceedingly beautiful", and remarks very appropriately : "The Catechism speaks the language of *faith*, even of living, personal faith. What it says comes from the heart, and therefore also reaches the heart. It speaks the language of *life*. This concrete and throughout intuitive language of life—where is it more perfectly spoken than in the Holy Scriptures ? From it has the Catechism learned it ; and hence every one finds in it what he needs—not only the child, but also the adult and the aged ; not only the uneducated and the unlearned, but also the most fully educated and learned. The Catechism speaks the language of clear *precision*." We may add : It speaks the language of *devotion* and *prayer*, or of communion with God, in language which is much less subject to change than the language of every day life, used in the intercourse of men ; and thus it speaks to us with true power and unction, as from ancient times. The verse here applies : "The mortal have many languages, the immortal only one".*

Art. II.—THE ARISTOTLIAN AND THE MODERN PLACE OF MAN IN ZOOLOGY.

By Prof. C. M. Dewey, Rochester, New York.

The rank of man in zoölogy has a higher interest as science advances, and as its moral aspects are better understood. In a previous article,† the great division of animals, by Aristotle, into *Enaima* and *Anaima*, the blooded and bloodless, the *red-blooded* and *white-blooded*, of modern times, was noticed. This corresponds to the Vertebrata and Invertebrata of Lamarck, as stated by Professor Agassiz : Essay, p. 96. But, though Aristotle followed no definite system in his excellent descriptions of animals, he saw obvious structural differences and recorded them. Thus, the division, Mammalia of Linnæus, he had named Zoötoka,‡ *viviparous*, as it actually is,

---

* Πολλαί μὲν θνητοῖς γλῶτται, μία δ' ἀθανάτοισιν.
† American Theological Review, vol. iv, p. 680.
‡ Prof. Owen on Mammalia, Sill. Jour. vol. xxv, p. 15, 1858, and Owen's Vol. on Mammalia, pp. 103, 8vo, London, 1859.

and made from it three sections : 1. *Dipoda,* bipeds (man) ; 2. *Tetrapoda,* quadrupeds, an extensive division ; and 3. *Apoda,* impeds or footless, the Cetacea or whale family.   In this actually *structural* view, man stands alone, separated from all other *mammal* forms.   So early in the history of philosophy was man seen to be distinct, though not removed by this arrangement from the animals.

The simplicity and wisdom of such a system is seen in the few and obvious characters employed, so that the man of common observation could understand it.   It required three thousand years from the day of Aristotle to that progress in science which culminated in the zoölogy of Cuvier.   Yet, in this, the characters or properties employed are so removed from common acquisitions that not one in a thousand of those who are taught the four great divisions of the system, has ever had ocular demonstration of the structure on which more than one is founded, and not even that in the nervous system of fishes and reptiles.

But Linnæus divided the same mammals into *unguiculata, ungulata* and *mutica.*   The unguiculates have *nails* on their fingers and toes ; the ungulates have *hoofs,* and the other is the *footless* of Aristotle.   Of course man is an *unguiculate,* and takes a much lower rank than that assigned him by Aristotle.   If the Stagyrite had formed a zoölogy, man would have been higher even in structural arrangement than in that of Linnæus and Cuvier, for Cuvier made the same divisions of mammals, only calling the *whale* family *mutilata* instead of *mutica.*

Aristotle, however, had other, higher, and more philosophical views of man, which place him in a rank far above and wholly distinct from that of the animal.   These are to be found in his works on Ethics, Economics, and the Soul or Spirit (psyche), and some of which are accessible to the mere English reader.   Only a brief abstract will be given.

After stating of the musician, the statuary, every artist, and all who have any work to perform, Aristotle says : " The good and excellence of each appears to consist in his peculiar work ; so would it appear to be with man, if there is any peculiar work belonging to him ".   " What, then, must this peculiar work (of man) be ?   For *life,* man appears to share in common with plants ; but his *peculiar* work is the object of our inquiry : we must, therefore, separate the *life of nutrition and growth.*   Then, a kind of *sensitive life* would next follow ; but this also he appears to enjoy in common with the horse, the ox, and every animal.   There remains, therefore, a certain practical life of a being who possesses *reason*" (logon).*

This distinguishing power, *reason*, is to be shown in an active efficient life of virtue, or, in his words, "according to the best and most perfect virtue", that is, "in a perfect (consistent) life", as he explains it. The animal in man is not the active power in this life resulting from the due action of reason.

It is obvious that Aristotle distinguishes organized bodies into *plants*, *animals*, and *man*, three kingdoms with distinct limits; and that he holds man to be separated from mere animals by his reason. It is clear also, that reason, in his works, involves the *moral sense*, or sense of right and wrong, in his definition.

This elevation of man above the highest brute, on account of a power different, in kind, from any the brute possesses, Aristotle maintained in another manner. He states, what modern science teaches, that some animals have only one of the five senses, touch or feeling; that others have more, and many have all the senses. Then he asserts that "sensation is the principle of no moral action", and gives as decisive proof, "the fact that beasts possess sensation, but do not participate in moral action".† There is great unanimity of opinion on both these points among men, except in the case of a few zoölogists and naturalists.

In his Treatise on the Soul (psyche), Aristotle maintains the same great principles, a summary of which his Ethics presents. The soul, the grand endowment of man, is composed, in his words, of three parts: 1. The *irrational*, which is "common, and belonging to plants", as well as to animals and man, and "which is the cause of nourishment and growth in all beings that are nourished", as he continues, "even in embryos, and the very same in perfect beings"; 2. The *appetitive*, or that which acts in the desires and appetites, which he also calls irrational, though it "in some sense partakes of reason, in that it is submissive and obedient to it" (reason), or "tends to opposition to it", and is the animal nature in man; and 3. The *reason* (logos), the peculiar power or endowment of man, and the high power of the soul (psyche). The reason, he says, is in part intellectual, and in part moral, and hence he speaks of "intellectual virtues", as "wisdom and prudence", and "moral", as "liberality and temperance".‡ He said also that "not one of the moral virtues springs up in us by

---

* Aristotle's Ethics, b. i, ch. 7.   † B. vi, ch. 2.
‡ Ethics b. i, ch. 13, and 2. b. ii, ch. 1.

nature", while Plato had maintained that the moral virtues " were divinely bestowed ".

These teachings of Aristotle present us with the ancient and correct notions of an intelligent and discriminating mind on the great point in which man essentially differs from even the highest animals.   Though he employed language which differs from the modern teachings, his meaning is precise enough, and easily understood.   He certainly laid the foundation for the correct classification, which places man at the head of organic life by his high rational and moral powers, of which modern zoölogists have generally lost sight.   Had this classification been adopted, and strictly followed, philosophers would have seen it to have been " instituted by the divine intelligence" as one of " the categories of his mode of thinking".

Contrasted with the system of Cuvier the vast superiority of Aristotle's basic principle is most obvious.   *Organic* is a higher state of matter than inorganic, even the tissue of a plant than a particle of sand or even a crystal ; for it has *vegetative* life.   Add to the organism *animal* life also, and great as is the advance, the animal characteristics are immeasurably inferior to the high power of ratiocination by means of language and the still superior moral sense, the *psyche* of the Stagyrite and of the world, which exalts man to a participation of the Divine image.

It is evident that if Aristotle had fully described the characters of the higher animals, the mammals, his views would have accorded with those of recent times, as the following : The higher animals are *conscious* beings, having the powers of sensation and volition, and the same five senses as man, the organs of which are equally palpable, and their voluntary actions fully manifest ; they think and feel, love and hate ; they have appetites and passions, desires and aversions, and often give proofs of anger or of kindness, as well as of some social qualities ; they remember definitely, strongly and long, and reason in some slight degree ; they contrive for protection and defence, and the good of their young ; they have varied and strong powers of instinct, as their great governing principle, evidently acting for important results without instruction or experience.   All those powers, essential to their existence and the continuance of their species, the benevolent Creator has bestowed upon them, that the object of their being may be effected.   These powers they share with man, for they constitute the animal nature in man.   Just so far as these are seen in them, the operations of animal life are decisive.   In them, instinct is far more powerful and extensive than in man, and it effects operations and results which reason could not reach. They are evidently conscious of their sensations, as of cold or hunger ; of their desires and purposes, as of providing for their young ; and of their means of communicating their thoughts or desires, or fears or joys. Such is the mere animal mind.

All these powers and actings are proofs of the *existence of mind in man*, and must be also, in the higher animals, evidence of the possession of the *same sort of mind in them*, as it understands, feels its connection with the outer world, and acts in accordance with the laws of its being. Thus far there has been a tacit agreement among all truly thinking men. .

But, man is possessed of another and superior power, unknown in the mere animal, and passing under various names. It is the sense of right and wrong, the moral sense or conscience, the feeling of moral obligation so authoritatively expressed in the term OUGHT, or the sense of religious duty to which man is bound. The explicit agreement of Aristotle, on this point also, has come down to us in his language, already quoted, that " beasts possess sensation, but do not participate in moral action".

The true system must distinguish between plants, animals, and man, as constituting three different kingdoms; for they are prominent before our eyes *by what they do*, and we cannot change the fact by refusing to notice it. The *structural* arrangement of Cuvier depends on physical (material or organic) differences, passing from the lowest or *radiate*, through the *molluscate* and *articulate*, to the highest or *vertebrate*. Thought, mind, intelligence, reason, soul and moral sense, do not appear thus far in the classification, and man is located with the beasts, and has only powers of the same mental kind with them. This is the understanding of the zoölogy of Cuvier by Agassiz, while he admits the transcendent greatness of these animal powers in man. And in Cuvier's divisions of mammals, not one of them has any reference to psychical powers, but simply relate to structure, as Agassiz also maintains. Retrograde and derogatory to the science of our age is the zoölogy of mere material form. In which of these do we see the higher thoughts of the Creator? Which approximates at all to that which is the glory of the Infinite Mind?

One of the great evils of this anatomical zoölogy is the continual controversies on the value of structural differences in determining the place of man in the system. After an extended examination of the structure of the anthropoid monkeys, the orang-outan, the chimpanzee, and the gorilla by Professor

Owen, the distinguished anatomical authority in England, he came to a decisive and full separation of man from those anthropoids.   Adopting the system of Cuvier, though he admits that only the human body is formed for a human soul, he felt obliged to depend on anatomy to support his views of the rank of man.   In an article published in 1857, by him, on the brain as decisive in the case, he formed a new primary division for man only, under the name of *archencephala* (ruling brain, or brain-ruler).   His deduction was, that there are three parts of the brain, the "posterior lobe", the "posterior corner", and the "hippocampus", which are "peculiar to and characteristic" of the human brain, and separate man by structure from the anthropoids.

This principle has been opposed on two grounds: one, is the insufficiency of any one organ to be the *characteristic* of man; and the other is the denial of the statement, and the production of proof that these parts of the brain are more prominent in some apes than in man.

It was stated at the meeting of the British Association, by Professor Huxley, another high authority, that he and others had presented this evidence in all fulness; that discussions on the minute differences in the brains or any other part, as a foot or hand, could not lead to any satisfactory result; and that the *real differences* are found in their "intellectual and moral powers".   This last declaration is the very doctrine promulgated by Aristotle so long before our era.*

Gratiolet, on the continent, has great reputation on this subject, from his examination of the brains of the *anthropoids* and *microcephals*.   The last is the class of *idiots*, from the smallness of heads or from the stinted growth of the brain.   He states that the brain of microcephals, while it is less than that of the gorilla or orang-outan, is "still the habitation of a speaking soul.   This innate, and as it were inextinguishable quality, is man's highest and most distinctive feature; and however lowered by disease or imbecility, man is still human, not an ape".   Gratiolet's important conclusion from the whole is, that "man is separated from animals as completely by his physical organism as he is by his mental phenomena".†

Another highly extolled authority on the same subject, Dr. Wagner, agrees with Gratiolet, "that there is no absolute identification of the human brain, not even of microcephals, with the quadrumane brain".   Another statement of the same author is, that "from all we know of the normal and abnormal

* *Silliman's Journal*, vol. xxxiv, pp. 440–441.   † Same vol. p. 192.

human and ape structure, the two are separated as widely as birds and mammals. . . . . All I know of zoölogy and physiology is opposed to any such transmutation as Darwin suggests".*

This history is full of interest to the inquirer after truth. The declarations of some of the learned zoölogists in this brief review, show us that they hold man to be entirely distinct from animals by his structure and by his moral and intellectual powers. The advance already made indicates the wise direction of philosophic minds towards the palpable facts of the relative and superior, but peculiar endowments of man. While this indication from the foreign authors just noticed is so grateful, the same has just appeared in the extended geology of Professor J. D. Dana. Though an adherent to the classification of Cuvier in the general, he has separated man from all the other mammals by putting him into the primary division or sub-class, under the name "*Archonts* — man (alone)," or *Rulers*, and then classing the other mammals in three separate divisions. And he maintains that the geology of that period gave, and still gives, full announcement of the high powers of the *coming* man, which separate him from the mere animals. We know that Professor Dana assigns to man all those moral powers or endowments which are here maintained to distinguish him from the brutes. For he was on earth "the *first* (being) capable of deriving happiness from beauty, truth, and goodness; of apprehending eternal right; of looking from the finite towards the Infinite, and communing with God his Maker".†

The question now occurs how, with such high and truthful views of man, an intelligent naturalist can sanction, in the general, the structural zoölogy of Cuvier? The answer is, that the system is designed to be confined to the organic characters or properties of its subjects. This is the very solution given by Professor Dana: "Science, in searching out the system in nature, leaves psychical or intellectual qualities out of view; and this is right".‡ Let the "right" pass for the present, and it is clear that the system of Cuvier may be adopted as an easy and natural classification to such a mind, even though it has the most exalted views of the moral elevation of man. Such a naturalist studies zoölogy in its mere structural relations or animal aspects, excluding mental characters from the fundamental principles of the system, if not even from the

* *Silliman's Journal*, vol. xxxiv, p. 195. † *Dana's Geology*, pp. 573–4.
‡ *Silliman's Journal*, vol. xxxv, p. 65, for 1863.

lower divisions of it.   Numbers of scientific men stand upon this ground, as they agree with Prof Dana in the statements already made.   Were these views only declared and maintained, the science would not be exposed to the general condemnation of holding to the mere animal nature of man. We should then have the full admission of the distinct and superior characters of man, while mere zoölogy would be limited to the anatomical or physical and physiological constitution.   This would be a great improvement, and would remove a great difficulty.   The actual "two-fold constitution" of man, the material and the spiritual, would find a prominent place in our philosophy.   The mental and moral powers of man would be treated of by their proper teachers, the psychologists, moralists, and theologians.   This is the first and obvious answer to the question.

This explication, let it be observed, does not accord with the views of Prof. Agassiz; for he asserts, and attempts to prove, that man and animals have the *same* intellectual and psychical qualities *in kind*, and therefore these can not be used in the systematic arrangement, as they do not distinguish, but do even unite, man and animals in the same category.* He does hold man to be only an animal.   In sorrow is it stated that he ignores the essential difference between intellectual and moral powers or characters, between brute consciousness and the sense of right and wrong, or moral obligation. This is the second general answer, and the real answer to this absurd view.

Besides the two methods, above considered, of sustaining the use of the system of Cuvier, there is only one other, and somewhat related to the first.   It is that of being a convenient system for arrangement and descriptions, whether man and animals have any psychical characters or not, for they are not even to be referred to.   This considers the system as a mere human contrivance, a natural method in the sense condemned by Prof. Agassiz†, because, though its facts are admitted, they have no reference to the wisdom of the Creator, but are merely classified for the arrangement of our knowledge, and for the more easy acquisition and expansion of it.

On these three methods some remarks are important, since in this discussion the objectists discover the Divine plan in the constitution of organized beings and the development of the highest exhibition of the Divine wisdom and benevolence. In this view, the *last* method is unworthy of reception and

---

* Agassiz' Essay on Classification, pp. 65–66, etc.
† Essay on Classification, p. 8.

26

support, as it excludes all consideration of the noblest powers of our nature. Matter and organism is the *summum bonum* of such naturalists. This is a mere *zoïc* consideration.

The *second* method, which is supported by Professor Agassiz, and may well be named the *anthropo-zoïc* system, has been considered in the previous pages, and shown to be untenable in the view of common sense, as well as condemned by many distinguished naturalists, from Aristotle to the present day. It finds, as is hoped, few advocates or defenders anywhere. Besides the distinguished European names before introduced in this paper, a great number of naturalists might be mentioned in our country besides Prof. Dana, who fill high places in our colleges and other institutions, or are educated men, well qualified for a judicious conclusion on this subject.

The *first* method depends on structure for its fundamental principle and divisions, and is thus far that of Cuvier. As now held by Professor Owen and others, it involves the principle that the distinct structure of man is significant of the high intellectual and moral powers bestowed on him by his benevolent Creator. Were these characters of the soul or the spirit only made fundamental, the system would cease to be that of Cuvier, and be assimilated to the views of Aristotle, or the system of Ehrenberg, or of St. Hilaire, and would accord with the doctrines here maintained. As it is, its supporters can adopt and maintain the strongest views of the distinct and separate moral constitution of man.

To mention no others on the "psychical or intellectual qualities", Prof. Dana* says; " these immaterial characteristics have, in all cases, a material or structural expression : and when this expression is apprehended, and its true importance fully admitted, classification will not fail of its duty in recognizing the distinctions they indicate". And again, on " *The introduction of man*—the first being of moral and intellectual qualities, and in whom the unity of nature has its full expression".† Zoölogists of this school hold that the peculiar structure of man, which separates him from the animals, is indicative of higher endowments than could be adapted to an inferior structure and organization ; or, to use the words of Prof. Dana, the intellectual and moral power " of man is thus expressed in his material structure. Man is, therefore, not one of the Primates alongside of the monkeys", as he had been ranked ; but, " he stands alone—the Archon‡ of mammals". This speculation derives the high intellectual and moral

---

* *Silliman's Journal*, Vol. 35, p. 65, 1863.
† Geology, p. 742, and ‡ p. 573.

powers from, or exhibits them through, the structural form, and from the physiology of the upper extremities as being *cephalic*, and not *locomotive*, instruments. It was of such a highly organized body, acting out such new manifestations of powers, that Prof. Owen* uttered the following in the conclusion of his work on the Vertebrata: "Such are the dominating powers with which we, and we alone are gifted! This frame is a temporary trust, for the uses of which we are responsible to the Maker. Waste not its energies; dull them not by sloth; spoil them not by pleasures! The supreme work of Creation has been accomplished that you might possess a body—the sole erect—of all animal bodies most free—and for what? For the service of the soul. Think what it may become—the temple of the Holy Spirit!"

Let it be, that the *erect* form of man is the structural expression of that Divine image in which man was created,† as uttered by a wise man of old, "Lo, this only have I found, that God hath made man *upright*", and that the abnormal action of the organs shows also that "they have sought out many inventions" or things opposed to rectitude: let it be true, that when the structural "expression is apprehended, the classification will not fail of its duty" to show the high and peculiar powers, physical and moral, which man possesses. Is this slow and obscure method, that which the Creator designs those made in his image shall pursue to a just knowledge of himself and of themselves? It can not be; it does not comport with the attributes revealed by his works. We can not say of such a system, which wholly excludes "intellectual and psychical characters"; "this is right". Especially should the moral sense, or religious principle, the highest endowment of man, and that one in which his likeness to the Divine Creator possesses the greatest importance and can be productive of the richest good, be introduced. No other basic principle is so simple, so easy, and so natural. Besides it is the most obvious way. For, the action of man immediately exhibits his moral power, and his noble and peculiar psychical characteristics. Men understood the true plan of man in the extended system of being on earth long before the Christian era,

---

* Vertebrata, p. 51.

† Since the above was written, Prof. Dana has fully presented his views of the "immeasurable" difference between man and animals, in that *spiritual element* which is "wholly distinct from any thing of a psychical or intellectual nature in the mere animal", and "through which, man bears God's image," and by which man is made "a moral being". It is the adoption of such views, long held by the great body of educated men and by most thinking minds, zoölogists or not, that *science falsely so-called* is made harmless.

and no doubt taught it also before the flood, and the first father must have shown it to his children, for it is enstamped on the very outer man and breathed forth from the inner. No parent could ever have said to his children that the young calf is your brother; and this lion is another; and that elephant is your grandfather, that horse is your uncle, and that she-bear is your aunt : and we are all of one animal race, and you possess the *same kind* of powers which distinguish us. Yes ; one exception should be made ; for *their* intimate relationship to the tribe of monkeys has always been maintained by the *Monboddites*. True, this is a modern family, and not yet extensively diffused. But it maintains very definite and dogmatic principles. Had father Monboddo met an aged orang or gorilla in the woods, he would have exclaimed with delight, " My dearly beloved and honored brother, uncle, grandsire, give me your hand ; we are of one blood." The Monboddites were unknown to the Egyptians, Hebrews, Greeks and Romans, and no Sanscrit wisdom is yet known to have spoken of them. The true system however is old as man, so prominent are its characters. But the structural system, on the other hand, has required centuries of progress to develope it, and is now passing through a fiery ordeal, by which it will probably be consumed. This result is devoutly to be desired. Then will mind and heart have their true position in philosophy, as in nature and Divine Providence.

To this the scientific world will ultimately come, as exhibiting the Divine plan in creation. No other will be admitted to be satisfactory, and accordant with the highest wisdom. Some will maintain that the zoölogist has not at present discovered an unexceptionable method of arrangement which may supersede that of Cuvier in the general ; that vertebrates, articulates, molluscates, and radiates, actually exist, and man *is a vertebrate ;* that of vertebrates, there are mammals, birds, reptiles, and fishes, and man *is a mammal ;* that of mammals, there are unguiculates, ungulates, and mutilates, and man *is an unguiculute ;* that of unguiculates, there are bimana, quadrumana, cheiroptera, &c., and man is the *only form of the bimana.* Let all this be admitted ; but is this system of Cuvier the wisest and the best ? The stamens, pistils, and seed-vessels, are the same, and as necessary and abundant as when they entered into the classification of plants and were the ground-work of the botanical system of Linnæus ; but they remain, while his beautiful and attractive artificial system belongs only to history. So it should be the effort of zoölogists to evolve the distinctions which separate man from animals ;

and they should tolerate the system of Cuvier only till a superior classification is formed, leaving that of Cuvier also to
history. Indeed, would it not be preferable to have the system
based upon broad eternal differences in fact, than upon a principle so liable to misconception and abuse, even if the latter
seemed to be more logical?   Let man fill the place required
by his distinguishing properties which separate him from all
other creatures of life, and with that great fact let the system
be made consistent.   So rational and clear is this, that opposition to it is absurdity and derogation to the Creator and his
works.

Above all, let no one be deceived by the dogma that only
the *structural* classification is *natural*, as is implied in the statement of Prof. Agassiz.   For organism is *natural* in the same
sense as is inorganic matter; the powers of animal life are
natural precisely as is vegetative life, or the mind of the animal is *natural* in the same respect as the life of the vegetable;
and, the soul, or the moral power of man, is *natural* precisely
as is the sensation and volition of the brute, or the intellect
and linguical powers of man.   It is natural for animals to act
according to their powers and instincts; and equally natural
for man to act according to his endowments.   For the horse to
neigh, the bird to sing, and for the man to reason, to feel the
approbation or condemnation of conscience, or to be sensible
to moral obligation and the duty of gratitude and praise to the
Infinite Spirit, is also natural.   Properties or powers of mind
and heart, form as definite and finely-marked distinctions as
do those of structure and organization.   In the earlier stages
of society, or before natural science can have made any considerable progress, these powers of intellect and soul must be
the ground-work of systematic divisions of men and animals.
So, *in fact*, it has been proved to be in the migrations, science,
and progress of nations.   The mere animal has held the same
rank, compared with man, it now does, namely, immeasurably
inferior to that of man.   In the history of nations, Divine
Providence has put its stamp of certainty on the correct estimate of animals by man among the civilized and uncivilized,
among the nations earliest on record and those of the latest
discovery, in the islands of the Pacific and in the midst of
Africa.

Art. III.— DORNER ON THE SINLESS PERFECTION OF JESUS.

(CONTINUED FROM PAGE 280.)

IV. The significance of the sinlessness of Jesus for Christian apologetics.

EVERY intellectually active age sees new sides in the person of Christ; sides which possess power to heal the evils recently arisen in society, and to overcome new popular errors.   These attacks must contribute to the church's own enrichment and self-confirmation. They arouse from the slumber of traditional custom, which supposes that it holds possession of that which can have a living presence only by means of constant spiritual toil, and which can be a complete, harmonious, and secure possession only as it is a living present reality. It is the privilege of the gospel that its opponents are obliged to fix intently the disciples' gaze on that by which they themselves may be overthrown, i. e., may be won.

In the earlier centuries there was among mankind a more lively sense of God, or at least a more lively craving for God, than is, in many ways, to be found at present. The old world's despair of itself was the end of its mediate or direct deification of the world. The general decay of human things, and misery, drove the heathen world to God, and to his revelation in Christ. In this revelation it was *the Divine* for which it had most directly an open eye; more precisely, it was the divine on that side which distinguishes it most from the human, in its perishableness, its chaos, and its misery; that is, it was the might and majesty, the glory and blessedness of God; and the most intensive piety of the first centuries was more a fleeing from this world as a vain show to God, than a use of the present world, animated by Christian principles.

To this characteristic trait of ancient Christianity, which had to fix its seat amid expiring nationalities, there seems to be a strong contrast made by the youthful world of the migratory northern nations, as they pressed with energy into the midst of this old world. But the latter enjoyed what I would almost call the natural blessing of a youthful age, — at least the young nations historically most important had this, — namely, a lively sense of God, and a craving for God; and entered willingly into the school and the discipline of the ancient church, according to which, men and virgins who had devoted their lives to God took rank above knights and noble matrons; nay, chivalry and imperialism became in part, even spiritually, the church's arm, by their vow of obedience. Not only was wholesome discipline established; not only were the wild shoots of these hardy children of nature pruned; but the church made an incision into the normal and divinely-constituted life of nature, as if it were theirs to annihilate the human, that nothing but the divine might be current. Not only were the earthy and moral spheres of life depreciated, and robbed of independent significance, — all worth, nay, all true reality being placed solely in the church, which sacrificed to God or transubstantiated all that is earthy; but revelation itself, and above all, its consummation in Christ, was divested of its HUMAN character; the omnipotent majesty of Christ, his legislative and judicial holiness being alone in their thoughts. The human friendship and the human tenderness of his nature were transferred to Mary and the saints.

So long as this immediate, and as it were natural, but quite indefinite sense of God, fed by the devotional life of the church, preponderated among mankind, — the feeling of general and deep reverence for God's holy, annihilating, omnipresent majesty, before which all finite being is valueless and as nothing, — there were in the prevailing mood of mankind grounds which (where Christianity must needs be proved by arguments) had a lively sense for the evidence of miracles. The mind was prepared to see miracles breaking forth at every moment and everywhere, and to see in them the omnipotence and majesty of God, and in this mood willingly believed the credibly-reported miracles of Scripture. What they proved in their own nature was, indeed, nothing but the majesty and *power of God*, exalted above the powers of mankind and of nature, but this passed for the divine κατ' ἐξοχὴν, and the deficiency perhaps felt as to the certainty of the testimonies from antiquity for miracles was richly compensated by the belief in the miracles continued in the church.*

What a wholly different turn the matter has taken in the last centuries, and how much has the feeling altered, especially in the Protestant world! How many believing Protestants

* The proof from prophecy, too, in its usual acceptation, was properly nothing but a proof of the *power* of God as opposed to accident, and revealed so little the unity and constancy of God's chief end in the world that, on the contrary, the most trivial occurrence in detail appeared to lend more stringency to this proof than what is most important and indispensable to God's chief end in the world

who hold fast the miracles of Christ have come to faith in Christ, not *by* his miracles, but, so to speak, *in spite* of them; because, the more the philosophical sense has been cultivated, the more (that is, so long as they were considered acts of omnipotence, but not equally acts of a disposing divine wisdom, and unconnected with the ultimate and absolute scope of the universe), the more did miracles stand opposed to the whole weight of the firm and regular laws of nature, nay, to the entire position of the children of this age, which sees in the visible universe a well-ordered and momentous reality, with its own life, its own meaning, and not a mere cover of a miracle-world lying behind and seeming to be a world of arbitrary will.

One has a good right to call the nearly dominant mode of contemplating the world in the physical researches of the day a dead mode, denuded of God, wanting ideality, and narrow. But it cannot be denied that, on the other hand, it has a more concrete, truer insight into the connection of the powers of the world, and of their operations and laws, than the old, and, so to speak, one-sided theological view of the universe. Whoever now stands true in the Christian faith, denies no actual fact to defend the faith. It is rather the infinite elasticity of Christianity to derive advantage from every real advance of human knowledge, and to apply it as an impulse to purify man, and to reveal new sides of the glory of the gospel. The world-despising idealism has, as Oetinger already perceived, done so much damage to true theology, and so much does it obstruct even to this day, the historical view of Christianity, that theology may well see in it a summons to give greater significance to the actual world ; and the recent mutation of idealism into materialism, which would hardly have been effected had the importance of matter and of the terrestrial world found *more* correct appreciation in theology and philosopy, points to the same task. To this we are summoned also by the undeniable fact, that the divine work of the Reformation is closely connected with that revolution, and with the advance of the physical sciences.

It is true that *Faith*, the heart's love of the Reformation, soars beyond the visible to find its rest and its life in the living God, revealed in Christ. It seeks and finds its true citizenship in heaven. But heaven is to it no longer a remote thing *in eternity*, as it was to the middle ages : it has heaven open, nay faith has heaven already *in* itself. It is only by a death that this heaven can be entered, and not by penances hostile to life, which fill up this life and a vast part of the future; but, by *Repentance* and *Faith;* and a commencement of the resurrection to a new life falls already in this life. Though faith, moreover, in this world, "possesses as though it possessed not", as far as it is directed to a future goal, the city of God, the new Jerusalem which is above, yet its whole value does not lie in eternity. Since heaven has descended into the heart, and Christ has made believers his own members, these know that something valuable is already to be found upon earth. The very personality of the man in whom Christ's Spirit dwells is already in this world something ennobled by divine love, and has thus a truly immeasurable value in the eyes of this love — a value not by transmutation into the divine and loss of personal character, but, on the very contrary, by the perfecting of the creation already begun in time. Hence it is self-evident what importance man's earthly life, or the time-side, has won in this point of view, and what importance anthropology has gained alongside of theology, which previously well nigh discerned in God nothing but the majesty of holy power. In the Reformation view of faith, there lay the germ of a new view of God; but this did not at once obtain free development. On the contrary, the human mind in the Protestant world cast itself with all its aspirations and power upon the attainment of the knowledge of man and of the salvation made for him, of mind and physical nature, and upon the investigation and mastery of the stage here given to our race as its possession.

It is true, I repeat, that the study of nature, and the entire empirico-realistic direction taken by science has in part assumed an ungodly character. Forgetting the whence and the whither, it has shut itself up in a self-created prison, and praised and extolled it as the land of liberty. It has forgotten that it is the gospel by which mankind was raised erect again in Christian nations, and the power was recovered by which even secular opinion subsists in its progressive culture. For the life-principle of human culture is worship. Still it remains true that, since the Reformation, the eyes of mankind have opened to the present world, to its history and its nature, in a measure unknown before, and that it takes possession of the world with a success never before equalled in intellectual knowledge and pratical conquest. This turn in universal history cannot be wrenched back. Our business is to adapt ourselves to it, and turn it to account as the gospel intends.

In the opinion of antiquity, the world still hovered between being and non-being.* A world not yet conscious of eternal life in itself, although having in it the breath of religion, could not yet attain to the firm persuasion that it was a real quantity having a relative independence in relation to God : men's minds could not fully. deal in earnest with the thought of a real creation, when the intensest mystic piety ever afresh substituted unconsciously annihilation in God for the world's final goal. The God of majesty, the God of absolute power, was always akin to this mode of thought, and viewed predominantly as nothing but holy power, which, as "*summum liberum arbitrium*", could any moment break, suspend, annihilate any order, any existence, any law (according to some even the moral law, which he had given to us).

Now our men of physical science, who everywhere must needs seek constancy, law, and order, and are conscious of perceiving in all this what is truly divine and worthy of God, come into keen conflict with this conception of God, with which unhappily a large section of evangelical theologians long continued satisfied. Nay, they turn away fron the living God of the gospel as a God of arbitrariness and disorder. Thus the very thing that was specially asserted as a proof of the divinity of Christianity — namely, miracles — appeared to them more and more as something unworthy of God; nay, even if the fact of miracles could be conceded, they saw therein something contrary to God, a sign of an unregulated power, of a liberty which was rather caprice, while the rising natural theology was conscious (and in one respect justly so) of possessing a higher conception of God. But yet this God of natural theology, not having any absolute historical ends, could only become either a dead iron law according to which the world-machine runs its course, or (where men will have a more living idea) the essence of the living world itself, in a pantheistic sense ; and thus men would return to the heathen doctrine of materialism. But the heathen have no hope. Were it conceivable that a people should lapse again into naturalistic pantheism, this world would again become to them a chaos, without form and void, so that the dreams of their essential divinity would perish just as in the old heathen world before Christ ; and instead of finding in themselves the true satisfying reality, they would long for nothing except death, or to throw away their existence, in order to reach the divine, just as we notice this still in millions among the Brahmanical and Buddhist heathen.

* Let the reader recall the doctrine of creation by Augustine, Anselm, and even Thomas Aquinas.

But if the Reformation emancipated men's mind, so as to view the world, and enter it as into a reality which has a value and object in itself even in time — if the Reformation has effected this, that the human mind, passing from the position of childhood and bondage, can go on its way freely, and, according to its own decision, it is particularly incumbent on the church of the Reformation to direct this decision to the right goal.   This she can only do by the unfolding more and more fully of Christian truth; and only where she neglects this, and as far as she neglects it, will the antichristian tendencies, which, under the guise of progress, are ever a falling back to pre-Christian platforms, assume an alarming compass and character.

In the treasuries of the gospel, which are the property of the Reformation faith, and of which it has the key, are contained, as we have said, the weapons of offence and defence, even for this new disposition of mind.   Had the new doctrine of God hid in the reformed principle been earlier disengaged, had the idea of man as made in the image of God been on all sides worked out agreeably to it, theology could hardly ever have seen the highest element in God's omnipotence and sovereign power; it could hardly have seen in the miracles of power as such the brightest seal of the divine; it could hardly have come into such serious collision with the powerfully-awakened philosophy, nay, with the idea of the divine order and wisdom.

The Reformation point of view places not the *miracles of power*, but the *miracles of love*, in the centre of its contemplation (not however, without giving their due place and their due elucidation to the former, as far as they are historically attested); and in these miracles of love the actual world, mankind needing redemption and called to holiness, has a direct and immediate interest.   These miracles cannot give rise even to the appearance of calling in question the reality of the world, and the good and regular order of the world; they are the affirmation and the confirmation of the position that the world of mankind is the ultimate object of God's love.

What evangelical faith teaches is this: that the power of God is not the inmost centre of his being, but that his *holy love* is a power above his omnipotence, and that it wisely employs this power for an end absolutely good — the creation of a real world of love.   To an intelligent faith, God inwardly manifests himself, not simply as he does to the heathen, as the power on whose bare will we are absolutely dependent,—nor simply as a Lord and ruler who, as a holy Lawgiver and Judge, demands our services, — but as holy self-communicating love, which proposed to itself, even at the creation of the world, something else as its end, and that is the bringing into being of loving persons made in its own image. And to realize this end, divine love entered into the world constantly and immutably, and yet with fulness of life, ordering everything to this one supreme goal, and avoiding arbitrariness, and an empty display of power without good cause. Thus no order and no law can prevent the manifestation of the inward and outward physical miracles of God's holy and wise love. Rather, every thing must ultimately minister to this one unalterable end, for the sake of which the world itself exists, and to whose power it is indebted. Everything, whether in the higher or lower order of the world's laws, must be incorporated in this world-plan. Thus evangelical faith is by no means unfriendly to miracle. It teaches us to appreciate the value of the real earthly world-order, and to engraft it into a higher order, the world of absolute aims. It thus recognises the true foundation of miracle in the absolute, i. e., the ethical world-plan. But on this account, outward physical miracles can no longer form the foundation by themselves. They await the confirmation of their own possibility from the higher, the ethical world, though the attested records of their reality serve to extend and elevate the narrow earthly sense of the natural man.

Man, however, corresponds to the end for which he was created, when, conscious of his reconciliation to God, he allows room and place within him for the spirit of love, so that he honors God not merely on account of his benefits — even the heathen honor the gods for the sake of expected benefits — but thanks and praises him as the God and Father of all ; offers himself as a means and instrument for his glory ; seeks him and his kingdom as his own end, even as God in condescension sought man's salvation and glorification. When the Christian, reconciled and saved in Christ, learns to regard himself as the personal instrument of God, nature, too, wins for him its true position: he habituates himself to view it as the instrument, his own personality as a means to the ethical world-plan of God.

When thus viewed in its organic connexions with the true view of the universe, the idea of *nature* is made available for effacing both the dread of miracles and the idolatry of miracles.*

* [Dr. Dorner's argument, at some points, seems to undervalue the real position of miracles among the Christian evidences. An able vindication of the contrasted view is given by Dr. Skinner in the last number of our REVIEW.—EDS.]

By the tendency of men's minds to Anthropology, to the actual world, and to nature, dating from the Reformation, the intensity of the natural belief in God has certainly suffered an interruption. Self-consciousness gained strength in sobriety and clearness. Reflection, the life of rational thought, began to depart from the traditional piety, and its *naïveté* was destroyed. But the loss may be, and ought to be, repaired. Self-consciousness, diving into its depths, becomes self-knowledge, in a moral and religious sense. The *consciousness* of alienation from God is a higher stage, and one more accordant with the truth than a superficial and seeming union with God; and it was superficial as long as it was predominantly nothing but a conciousness of absolute dependence on God's *power*, little mindful of the existing dissent and the ethical and religious problems. But when this universal human feeling about God's power and majesty, before which we are but dust and ashes, and without any real, firm being, is conjoined with that moral consciousness, which results only from the persuasion of an ideal personal destination, (from the 'ἐπίγνωσις νόμου), the difference between God and man, in the first place, is certainly deepened. By God's holiness we find ourselves *morally annihilated*, rejected, and unworthy of blessed union with God. But this beginning of the ethical knowledge of God, on the ground of an awakening conscience, leads further, through the operation of the Spirit of God. If the holy *law* is dividing, cold, exacting, judging, the *Gospel*, on the other hand, reveals God's ethical nature in all its fulness; and now there begins, for the first time, a deeper and more intense fellowship with God, including personal holiness, as God's end, and the outer world as its means. The most divine element in God, if we may say so, now shows itself at once as the most humanly accessible, and as the nearest; while mere holy power appears to the carnal mind as indeed the highest, but in itself it can only cast us into a fruitless feeling of impotency and distance from God.

The appearance of Christ is the divine miracle of love absolutely, but so formed that the miracle appeared as true nature, as a *human life of love*, to lead us through itself to its inner divine source. By other means, indeed, than by himself— *e. g.*, by miracles of knowledge or of action—he sought to draw us to himself; but yet he emphasizes Himself as the way absolutely, leading to Him as the truth and the life, (John xiv, 6). Hence it stands most intimately connected with the history of evangelical theology and with its deepest interests, that the later theology fixes its eye specially on this personal appearance of Christ and on his entire ethical character ; and from this point of view finds for an active conscience, a surer transition to the knowledge of his divine dignity and his office as Redeemer, than in the proof from miracles, *e. g.*, from the resurrection (the favorite mode in England), or in prophecy, and the inspiration of Scripture, or in the perfection of his doctrine.   True holiness, moral perfection, reaching to heaven in its depths, nay, into the very sphere of the divine ontology, has in it, on the other side, the charm of being the most humanly alluring, the most melodious, and the most resistlessly attractive, even for susceptible minds who are still strangers to the faith.

ART. IV.—THE CROWN OF LIFE IN JAMES I, 12.

[From the German of E. ZELLER in the Zeitschrift für wissenschaftliche Theologie, Erstes Heft, 1863.]

JAMES i, 12 : *Blessed is the man that endureth temptation ; for when he is tried, he shall receive the crown of life, which [the Lord] hath promised to them that love him.*   The inquiry of interpreters has been, *Who* promised this crown of life ? Some reply, God ; others, Christ ; and in most manuscripts ὁ χύριος, or θεός is put after ἐπηγγείλατο. One of the two must, in fact, be supplied ; but for the sense and connexion it is quite indifferent which is preferred.

Much more important, however, is the question, *where* this crown of life (στέφανος ζωῆς) is promised ? This inquiry, if I do not err, has not been started by any one of the commentators : Wiesinger alone alludes to it in passing. It seems to have been taken for granted, that the words do not refer to any definite promise, but only declare the general doctrinal belief in a future reward for Christian steadfastness. But the form of expression—*the crown of life, which he hath promised* —is quite too peculiar to be passed over so lightly. Any unprejudiced reader would at once be led to suppose that there was some definite promise, having respect, not to future blessedness or eternal life in a general sense, but in a special way to the *crown of life ;* and this all the more, since the perfect tense (ἠπήγγελται) is not used, but the aorist (ἠπηγγείλατο), the tense of narrative, referring to some definite fact. Thus in this epistle, chapter ii, verse 5, we have the same form and turn of expression—*the kingdom which he hath promised* (ἠγγείλατο) *to them that love him*—which unquestionably refers to a definite promise, viz., that in the Sermon on the Mount (as given in Matth. v, 3) : " Blessed are the poor in spirit, for theirs is the kingdom of heaven " ; nor need we here inquire, whether this was known to the writer by oral or written tradition, and, if the latter, whether from Matthew's Gospel or some other source.

Where, now, are we to look for the promise which our text has in view ?   Some passage of the Old Testament would naturally be first thought of ; but we seek here in vain for expressions which James might have had in mind.   Zechariah vi, 14, in the Septuagint version comes the nearest (on the conjectures as to the Hebrew text, see Hitzig in locum) ; it reads : *The crown shall be to the patient*, etc. ; but the resemblance is remote, for the peculiar addition—*of life*—is lacking.   Still less pertinent is the passage in the apocryphal book, the Wisdom of Solomon, v, 17 : " Therefore they [the just] shall receive the kingdom of glory and the diadem of beauty from the hand of the Lord ".

The origin of the passage may also be sought in the evangelical tradition.   Nor can it be denied that the author of the epistle may have referred to a promise of the Lord, no where else reported : as in Acts xx, 35, and in several other citations, not found in the canonical books.   But this conjecture ceases to be probable, if there be any passage in the New Testament scriptures, in which *the crown of life* is promised.   And this is in fact the case.   The words are so near at hand, that they are uniformly cited to be by all interpreters in illustration of our text ; only they have hitherto failed to note an express relation between them.

They occur in the well known passage of the Revelation ii, 10 : *Behold the devil shall cast some of you into prison, that ye may be tried ; and ye shall have tribulation ten days ; be thou faithful unto death, and I will give thee a crown of life* — τὸν στέφανον τῆς ζωῆς.   That this passage, and no other, is in the mind of the writer seems probable for more than one reason. First, it is the only declaration known to us, in which *the crown of life* is promised : and to such a promise James directly refers.   Again, it is a natural conjecture that the writer of the Apocalypse first made use of the phrase *the crown of life*, perhaps with reference to *the crown* in Zechariah ; since he brings the crown of life into most express contrast with faithfulness, even unto death, and thus gives a peculiar form of expression to the idea already expressed by Jesus Christ in Matthew, x,

39 : " He that findeth his life shall lose it ; and he that loseth his life for my sake shall find it ".   In fine, both passages also agree in what follows : James says, that the man who endureth temptation is blessed ; so, too, John speaks of those who are tried by the devil : the former promises the crown of life to him who is tried, the latter to him who is faithful unto death. The only difference is, that in the Apocalypse a definite situation is taken for granted, that is, the last conflict between Christ and Anti-Christ, and the persecutions preceding this struggle, with imprisonment and martyrdom ; in James, on the other hand, this definite historical background is wanting, and the apocalyptic exhortation, which refers to a sharply delineated issue, fades away into a general moral warning.   Hence we must not be misled by the fact that in the Apocalypse we do not find the words — *to them that love him*, by which James denotes those to whom the promise applies.   This is an addition of the writer, just like that which he makes in chapter ii, vs. 5 to the promise made in the Sermon on the Mount (Matth. v, 3) to the poor in spirit ; because he adduces the words, not in their original, concrete application, but in the most general sense, in which they are applicable, as is the case with every promise that has respect to future reward ; for every word of promise holds true of those whom God loves.

As it is thus proved, that the connection of these two passages is not accidental, so, too, it is evident, that James must have cited the Apocalypse, and not the Apocalypse James. For in the Revelation is an original freshness of expression ; it is uttered in the midst of clear, historical circumstances, by which its peculiar form and force are determined ; it gives a promise to which James refers as having been made.   Where all indications thus concur, no doubt is possible as to which is the copy, and which the original.

If the result of this investigation be confirmed, we shall have gained, not only a decisive date upon the question of the genuineness of the Epistle to James and the time when it was written, but also a valuable testimony to the Apocalypse, such as cannot be supplied by any other of equal antiquity.

Art. V.—PRAYER AND MEDIATION.

By Hon. Eleazer Lord, Piermont, N. Y.

No subject perhaps of equal concern to man, has been less satisfactorily written upon than that of Prayer ; whether considered with respect to the reasons for the exercise of it or the grounds on which the duty is acceptably performed. We propose to consider the subject only in relation to some of its primary conditions and requisites, especially those which involve the necessity and the fact of Mediation—an actual Mediator, between the infinitely holy Being to whom petitions are presented, and sinful creatures from whom and on whose behalf they are offered.

It is apparent from the nature of the case, that the chasm between the parties — the Infinite, and the finite, the holy God, and creatures polluted and guilty,—is such as to preclude the idea of any such intercourse between them, or any ground of such direct appeal of the one to the other, independently and aside from Mediation, as is implied in acceptable prayer. The creature, conscious of ignorance and guilt, naturally discerns the necessity of an intermediate helper, a Mediator. He needs an advocate, a propitiator—one acting in immediate relation to both parties, who can answer for him, expiate his guilt, adopt and present his petitions, and obviate his disabilities. But he cannot invoke the aid of such an one, and offer petitions to be presented by him, or have faith in him, unless he apprehends him as the officiating Mediator, and understands something of the nature and sufficiency of his vicarious acts. To suppose a suppliant to present his petitions—not to and through one acting in such mediatorial capacity, not in his name and by faith in his person and mediation—but directly to the offended God, would be to suppose that mediation was not indispensable to fallen man. It would be to suppose the entire theory and fabric of Christianity to have no real foundation. It is the very basis of the Christian system, that there is One Mediator between God and man, through whom alone and by faith in whom man can have access to God by prayer, and be the recipient of pardon and salvation. This must have been as true when man first fell as at any subsequent period. The Scriptures teach

27

but one way of life. The teachings of the Old Testament are consistent with those of the New. The church of the redeemed is one under all dispensations,—justified and saved through faith in the one Mediator.

In every aspect of the case the acceptableness and efficacy of prayers must depend on the qualification, disposition and official action of the Mediator; on his concurring in the petitions offered, adopting them as his own, presenting them himself at the throne of grace with his own vicarious, propitiatory, and intercessory acts and pledges proffered on behalf of the suppliant. As Mediator he takes the part of the penitent petitioner, assumes his obligation to punishment, becomes his legal substitute in the case and fulfils the terms of satisfaction; and on the other hand, takes the part of the offended Lawgiver, and of holiness and legal righteousness, against the impenitent. Of the one he is the Advocate, Intercessor, Redeemer, Saviour: of the other the final Judge. The prayers of the one are accepted solely by reason of the concurrent official vicarious action of the Mediator. The prayers of the other, wanting that concurrent Mediatorial efficiency, are vain and fruitless. The one, conscious of guilt, accepts the offered mediation, and is by faith united to him, and is heard and saved, solely through and by reason of his mediatory acts in his official and covenant relations. The other, alien to all this, continues under condemnation. But if this be a just view of the subject, and if at present such concurrent mediation is necessary to acceptable prayer, how can it be possible that the same conditions and reciprocal agencies were not equally indispensable to all who were justified under the ancient dispensations?

Here we encounter the embarrassing fact, that although the Old and New Testaments teach the same doctrine of justification and life through faith in the One Mediator, and although patriarchs and prophets were actually justified and saved through their union to the Mediator by that faith, theological writers generally teach, that the Mediator did not assume his office or act mediatorially in any respect till the introduction of the Christian dispensation; that the Second Person of the Trinity who became incarnate in man's nature then only was invested with and exercised the office of Mediator; that under the prior dispensations he was referred to only as the Messiah who was to appear at a future time; that his future coming and acting mediatorially was known simply as matter of prediction and typical representation; and that the efficacy of his mediatorial acts in respect to the justification and salvation of believers, was future and simply retrospective in relation to the Old Testament saints.

This construction, though generally acquiesced in, is, we apprehend, obnoxious to very serious objections, to some of which we purpose to refer, without pursuing the subject controversially.

In general such a construction appears to imply a far too restricted view of the nature and objects of mediation. From the relation of all the phenomena, physical and spiritual, in the sphere of the finite, to " the church " and the work of redemption, it would seem far more obviously in accordance with the Scriptures, to regard the dependent universe and all creatures, and the preservation and government of all, as due to Mediatorial agency ; as the work of the mediatorial Person, who at the appointed time assumed man's nature, than to regard it as in part his work, and in part that of the absolute Deity, as a unity, or that of the Father as a Person of the Godhead. Of the Mediator, as he appeared incarnate, it is expressly affirmed that he created all things in heaven and earth, that he preserves them all, that he is heir to all, and Head over all, the first and the last—and considering that as a Person—or as to what constituted his Personality—he was the same before as after he took man's nature into union with his Person ; that it was as a Person that he became incarnate ; and that it was the Personal Logos who was in the beginning, and was God, by whom all things were made, it is certain that there was connected with his appointment and office a qualification to act Mediatorially, a ground of relation to creatures, a ground of action on his part in finite relations and under the conditions of time and space. That the Personal Logos who was in the beginning and who made all things, was the mediatorial Person, is determined by the announcements that he became incarnate (John i.), and that at his second coming in his glorified human nature, his name is to be called " the Logos of God." If then, the mediatorial Person, under the designations which distinguish his delegated, official character, created and governs all things : then he was in a capacity as Mediator, to act as administrator and head over all things in reference to his church, and as such to be the object of faith and prayer under the ancient economy as truly as under the present.

The Greek term *Logos* is the equivalent of the Hebrew term, *Dabar*, and the English, *Word*. In the New Testament the Greek term is translated *Word*, as a personal designation of the Mediator. John i.—1 John 1 : i. 5 : 4.—Rev. xix : 13. In

Hebrew, *Dabar*, is evidently employed with a personal reference, and in connections and with reference to actions, which can point to no other than the same official Person, although our common version is not always clear to that effect. Thus, '*Dabar Jehovah came* unto Abram saying, Fear not, Abram : *I am thy shield* &c., and Abram said, O, Adonai Jehovah, what wilt thou give me' &c. Gen. xv : 1, 2. In v 5–7 it is said that " Dabar Jehovah brought Abram forth abroad, and said, Look now toward heaven, &c—and he believed in *the Jehovah*, and he counted it to him for righteousness. And he said unto him, I am the Jehovah that brought thee out of Ur of the Chaldees." Next follows the preparation of a sacrifice by the direction of the Jehovah, the utterance by him of various promises and predictions, and the ratifying of the covenant then made, by the offering of the sacrifice, on the one part, and by a customary token of acceptance on the other, the consumption of it by fire. Whatever of figure there may have been in this scene, the sense is that a Divine Person under the title of Dabar — Logos, Word,— Dabar Jehovah,— came to Abram, gave him instructions and promises, entered into covenant with him, accepted his offering, and justified him. Abram believed in *him* and *he* counted, imputed righteousness to, Abram.

When the Jehovah had called to Samuel at intervals, it is said, "And the Jehovah *came and stood and called as at other times*, Samuel, Samuel. And the Jehovah *appeared* again in Shiloh : for the Jehovah revealed himself to Samuel by *the Dabar Jehovah*." 1 Sam. iii : 10, 21. " Then *came* Dabar Jehovah unto Samuel, saying ". &c ibid xv : 10. This formula is of frequent occurrence. " Dabar Jehovah came expressly unto Ezekiel by the river Chebar ". Then follows his vision of the glory of the Jehovah, in the similitude of Man. " And he said unto me, Son of man, stand upon thy feet, and I will speak unto thee ". i : 3,—ii : 1. The same formula recurs some 50 times in the course of his prophecy.

That the personal reference of this phraseology was familiar to the Patriarchal and early Jewish church, is evinced by the Chaldee paraphrasts, who, laboring to revive that primitive faith, inserted their term *Memra*, the Chaldee equivalent for Dabar, Logos, and Word, before the name Jehovah in very numerous instances, from the beginning of Genesis onward ; that wherever any local or personal action is ascribed to the Jehovah it should be understood to be ascribed to the mediatorial Person—the mediating Jehovah—the Dabar, the Logos, the Word. Such a course on their part, and on behalf of the remnant of believing Israelites, whether considered as traditional from the time of Ezra, or as extant in writing only after the Advent, would, considering the antagonist constructions and the unbelief of the Jews in general, have been incredible and impossible, had they not believed it to be agreeable to the teachings of Moses and the prophets. It is moreover undeniable, that, to a considerable extent, the same acts which are in the Old Testament expressly ascribed to the Jehovah, are also ascribed to the mediatorial Person, as designated by the terms, Logos, Messenger, Immanuel, Messiah.

So far as the Scriptures instruct us, the Divine Being does not act externally or towards creatures, as a Unity. The Scriptures teach that there are three coequal Persons in the Godhead ; and they expressly, or by just construction, ascribe each Divine act to one or to another of those Persons. All Divine acts are personal ; they are acts of the Father, or of the Son, or of the Holy Spirit. All mediatorial acts are acts of the Second Person in his mediatorial office and character ; and since he sustained that office and character in the beginning, and in virtue of it created the worlds, and all things, we may be sure that he did not assume his office and commence his mediatorial work at the commencement of the Christian dispensation.

Again, the view in question overlooks, so far as relates to the period between the Fall of man and the Advent, a principal object of the Mediatorial appointment and agency, namely, that of thwarting and vanquishing Satan, the arch leader of rebellion. That great antagonist of the Mediatorial Person, whose final destruction is to be effected by the Logos at his second coming, (Rev. xix) commenced his career of opposition at the date of the Fall. But, according to this view, resistance to him by his eventual conqueror was deferred throughout the period of Old Testament history. His enmity and opposition were directed specially against the mediatorial Person, the second Adam. He had seduced and triumphed over the first Adam, and thenceforth it was his aim and only hope to maintain his sway over all the race of man, and to defeat and overcome the second Adam—the Jehovah from heaven (1 Cor. xv: 47.) on his advent as man. Hence the temptation of the wilderness. The facts, that it was by his direct personal agency that he wrought upon the first Adam, and that in the signal instance in the wilderness it was by the direct personal agency of the second Adam that he was resisted, sufficiently indicate the personal reference and character of the antagonism from the beginning. But if, between the Fall and the Advent the

Divine Person who at an appointed time in the progress of his work, was to assume man's nature, exerted no antagonistic agency; if, while predicted and typified as thereafter to appear incarnate, he exerted in his delegated, mediatorial character and office, no agency under his name Jehovah,—then we must conclude that the administration of Providence, the theophanies, the theocratic rule, and all the details of familiar intercourse with men during the interval, as well as all acts specially antagonist to Satan, are to be ascribed to the Deity, as a Unit, or else to the Father personally, whom we are assured no man hath seen or can see, and who is revealed and represented only by the Son, as Mediator.

From the view in question, it follows that the prayers and praises of the ancient church, were addressed directly to the Deity as a Unit, or else to the Father, without reference to any mediation, long prior to the appointment and official agency of a mediator. There could have been no personal relation, no ground of sympathy, no mutual interest, between the ancient saint, seeking life and deliverance from the power of Satan, and a Mediator not then appointed to exercise his office. How could the suppliant present his prayers through an official Person, not yet invested with his office, not yet sent to perform it, a mediator between the offended God and the guilty suppliant? How could that Person as Mediator, prior to his entering on his office, intercede for the suppliant? The necessity of mediation is immediate. The effects of it must be realized while the suppliant is alive. They are gifts conferred by virtue and in consequence of the mediation through which he seeks them, i. e. by virtue and in consequence of acts performed, and of gifts of faith, repentance and pardon, then bestowed by the Mediator; for mediation between differing agents is mediatory action. To produce present effects, the mediation, the mediatory acts necessary to those effects, must be present. There doubtless are in the absence of Divine mediation as related to the moral and redemptive system, mediatory acts ·which, like that of the incarnation, and that of the atonement, were to occur but once, which had their appointed time and place in the system, were subjects of prophetical and typical representation, and of retrospective recognition and faith. But the offering of petitions through the Mediator to be presented by him and rendered effectual by his intercession, implies at every period the present exercise of his official agency. It is inconceivable that the want of such present agency could be supplied by faith in the predictions and types of any future mediatory acts; as inconceivable as that the ancient saints could have been saved without any coincident personal action on *their* own part; or that specific effects should be produced by the concurrent action of two distinct agents, of whom one was neither present nor qualified to act.   Predictions of the future appearance of the mediatorial Person visibly in man's nature, and types of his atoning sacrifice by the shedding of his own blood, were vividly significant of those particular events; but they could no more supersede the necessity of his other mediatory agencies under the ancient dispensation, than a simple belief that at the predicted time those facts occurred, can have that effect under the present economy.

Consider the prayers and the faith of the ancient saints, in relation to the chief benefit to be attained by them, namely justification, without which acceptance and sanctification could not result.   "Justification is an act of God's free grace, wherein he pardoneth all our sins, and accepteth us as righteous in his sight, only for the righteousness of Christ imputed to us, and received by faith alone."   By faith the sinner receives and rests upon the righteousness of another Person, who, by appointment, has become his legal surety and substitute, and undertaken in his stead to obey the law which he had broken, to expiate sin by suffering its penalty, and to effect the deliverance of the guilty by the imputation to him of the righteousness thus acquired and gratuitously bestowed.   The faith embraces that Person in his mediatory offices and work, and the acquittal immediately ensues.   It is the prerogative of that Person and a part of his mediatory work, "to give repentance and forgiveness of sins."   Acts v: 31.   "He is the author and finisher of our faith."   Heb. xii : 2.   The transaction involves on both sides present personal action.   If then Abraham and the host of Old Test. saints were actually justified and therefore saved, and if the faith through which he was justified was the pattern of that through which believers now are justified, then the Mediator had entered on the execution of his office, and was entitled to perform the acts and bestow the gifts necessary to render faith in him effectual to the present justification of believers.   Hence the language of trust in the Jehovah, the prayers for pardon, and the acknowledgments of mercy, so common in the Old Test. and especially in the Psalms. "Trust in the Jehovah, for in the Jehovah is everlasting strength." Isa. xxvi : 4.   "Blessed is the man that maketh the Jehovah his trust." Ps. xl : 4.   "Bless the Jehovah, O my soul — who forgiveth all thine iniquities." Ps. ciii : 1, 3. "Have mercy upon me, O Elohim, according to thy loving kindness; according unto the multitude of thy tender mercies, blot out my transgressions." Ps. li : 1. "Out of the depths have I cried unto thee, O Jehovah. O Adonai hear my voice.— If thou Jehovah shouldst mark iniquities, O Adonai, who shall stand? But there is forgiveness with thee, that thou mayest be feared." Ps. cxxx : 12. In a word if there were *holy* men in the ancient church, they were made such through faith in the mediatorial Person as their Redeemer; and received mediatory gifts from him.

From these considerations the conclusion is just and necessary, that the Jehovah who administered the ancient economy was the Second Person of the Trinity, acting mediatorially from the beginning, and not only under that name, but also under the various appellations and titles which, interchangeably with that name, are appropriated to him, and, as designations indicate his mediatorial office, acts, or relations: as, the Logos; (Word, outward manifestation, image, representative) who was in the beginning, and made all things: the Messenger; (the Second Person of the Godhead, as Legate—the appellation indicating his local and visible appearances) the Redeemer: (Ransomer, Kinsman Redeemer, "the Jehovah thy Redeemer"—the title indicating his office under both Old and New Testaments) the Saviour; the Shepherd; the King; and others significant of his mediatorial offices. It is undeniable that under this name and its cognates, and under these titles, acts are ascribed to him in the Old Test. which are ascribed to the Messiah in the New. Compare the following passages: "In the beginning *Elohim* created the heavens and the earth." Gen. i. "Thus saith the *Jehovah* that created the heavens, *the Elohim* himself that formed the earth and made it—I am the *Jehovah* and there is none else." Isa. xlv: 18. "The *Logos* was in the beginning—all things were made by him." John i. By the *Son*, the *Messiah*, "in whom we have redemption through his blood—who is the image of the invisible God— were all things created, that are in heaven and that are in the earth—and he is before all things, and by him all things consist." Col. i. "Thou *Lord* (El, God, in the Psalm civ, quoted as spoken of the Messiah) in the beginning hast laid the foundation of the earth, and the heavens are the work of thy hands." Heb. i. According to God's eternal purpose which He purposed in Christ Jesus our Lord, He created all things by Jesus Christ: to the intent that now unto the principalities and powers in heavenly places might be known by the church the manifold wisdom of God." Eph. iii.

Now if any of these appellations distinctively designate the mediatorial Person, then it must be held that they all designate that Person; and if the acts of creation are ascribed to that Person in the character in which he appeared as the Messiah, then those acts are not intended to be ascribed to him simply as he is Divine—a Person of the Godhead—but to him as Mediator, as being mediatorial acts and part of his mediatorial work. If he was invested with his mediatorial office " before all things;" if " he created all things," and if " by him all things consist," are upheld and preserved, then it is to be believed that his mediatorial work comprised all external Divine acts in the sphere of finite existence. Hence, throughout the Old Test. he is represented as the great actor and revealer, the one manifested God, the God of providence; and in the New, as being by his original appointment, heir of all things, head over all, arbiter and judge of all, and as being in his incarnate Person, exalted to the throne of the universe, ruler over all, the first and the last. The universe is his work, his possession, his sphere of manifestation. In his relations to it he occupies the middle place between the Infinite Being and creatures. In his relations to creatures he acts mediatorially, not merely in a portion of the things which he made and upholds, but in all things, as God of providence, prophet, priest and king of his church, ruler and judge of his enemies.

This view of the universality of his mediatorial agency is illustrated in the announcements and interrogatories of the Jehovah when he appeared to Job, in " a whirlwind," a form of appearance, doubtless, like that seen by Ezekiel, of which he says: " I looked, and behold, a whirlwind came out of the north, a great cloud, and a fire unfolding itself" &c. chap. i. " The Jehovah answered Job and said: Where wast thou when I laid the foundations of the earth? Who hath prevented me, that I should repay him? Whatsoever is under the whole heaven is mine," &c. &c. Job replied: " I know that thou canst do every thing, and that no thought can be withholden from thee. I have heard of thee by the hearing of the ear; but now mine eye seeth thee." chap. xxxviii–xlii. His universal providence is often asserted in the Scriptures, as in the cxlvii Psalm; and is often celebrated, as in the cxlviii Psalm, where all creatures in heaven and earth are called on to praise him: " Let them praise the name of the Jehovah; for he commanded, and they were created. He hath also established them forever."

If it was in his official character that he created and upholds all things, then all external and visible works must be ascribed to him. If the name Jehovah signifies the second person, as legate of the Father, acting pursuant to the eternal covenant, intermediately between the invisible Deity and creatures, executing the will of the Father and in this relation subordinate to him; if in this character he exercises mediatorial offices as prophet, priest, and king, redeeming his people, erecting a kingdom, vanquishing Satan, and administering the works of Providence in their relation to these ends, then must all the works ascribed to the Jehovah in the Old Test. be ascribed to him in this official capacity, and his acts under the ancient economy will be harmonious with those under the present. On the prevalent construction, the Divine acts of local and visible appearance, of familiar intercourse with man, of personal conversation with individuals and with good men, as Abraham, Jacob, Moses, giving them minute instructions as to their personal duties, their families, their temporal affairs; with bad men, like Cain, reasoning and remonstrating with them; and even with Satan on different occasions, imposing restraints on his evil agency; these and the like Divine acts may be believed as having actually taken place, but they surely cannot be conceived of as acts of the absolute Deity, nor as acts of the Father whom no man hath seen, and whose voice except as addressed expressly to the Messiah, no man hath ever heard, nor yet of the Son considered unofficially as coequal with the Father. Such acts imply sympathies, affections, relations, conditions, which are not to be predicated of the absolute unconditioned Deity, nor of the Father personally, as he is revealed in the New Test. or as he was personated or distinctively referred to in the Old. Can any one persuade himself that the malice and opposition of Satan was aimed directly against the absolute Deity, or against the Father as head of the Triality of Persons? Was it directly against Omnipotence that he waged his spiteful and persistent war? Did he, through his rival system of idolatry, provoke that infinite, and, to him, as to all other finite agents, incomprehensible Being, *to jealousy?* Did that Being institute (otherwise than through an official mediatorial constitution) a moral system, involving the necessity of his stooping to contend immediately with this arch rebel? Was it that Being whom the factors and servants of Satan, as Sennacherib, Nebuchadnezzar, and others, openly defied? Was it that Being who, independently of all mediatory conditions and relations, led the children of Israel out of Egypt, administered a theocratic government as local chief magistrate, and directed and presided over the entire system of rites, worship, and bloody sacrifices at patriarchal altars, and in the Tabernacle and Temple? Is there, in respect to sinful man really and practically no difference, between the Divine Being as absolute and unconditioned, and that Being as he has revealed himself a Unity and Trinity in and through one mediatorial and officially subordinate Person, standing midway between the Infinite and the finite, and qualified by covenant, official appointment, and personal engagement, to act reciprocally towards both?

We proceed on this view of his relations and offices, to shew that under the ancient economy patriarchs and prophets addressed their prayers directly to the Jehovah as the mediatorial Person, in the character in which he manifested himself locally and visibly, and was recognized as the revealer, and representative of the Father. So well was this character understood by them and so familiar were the tokens of his Deity and of his official agency, that his local and visible appearances seldom occasioned surprise to the beholders. They saw the visible form, sometimes like that of a plain way-faring man, sometimes as a warrior with a drawn sword; sometimes in a radiant cloudlike envelope; sometimes as seated on a throne, above the cherubim, in the effulgence of glory and majesty. They heard his voice and witnessed the exercise of his omniscience and his power.

This Divine Person appeared to Abraham in the similitude of a man, conversed and walked with him, disclosed to him his purpose of destroying Sodom, and heard his petitions. Gen. xviii. "Abraham stood before the Jehovah and said: Wilt thou also destroy the righteous with the wicked?—that be far from thee: Shall not the Judge of all the earth do right? And the Jehovah said, If I find in Sodom fifty righteous within the city, then I will spare all the place for their sakes. And Abraham said, Oh let not the Jehovah be angry, and I will speak yet but this once: Peradventure ten shall be found there. And the Jehovah said, I will not destroy it for ten's sake. And the Jehovah went his way, as soon as he had left communing with Abraham: and Abraham returned unto his place." He thus addressed his petitions to the visible Person whom he saw, to whom he appealed as the Jehovah, the Judge of all the earth, and whose audible voice he heard in reply to his supplications. He evidently regarded that Divine Person as the ruler of the world, the administrator of providence, the revealer of the will of the invisible Father, the official mediatorial Person, to whom and through whom alone the prayers of men could be acceptably offered. He alludes to no other Mediator, or mediation. He accompanies his prayers by no sacrifices typical of the future manifestation of the Messiah; by no burning of incense; by no sacerdotal act; by no formula of faith other than that of his expressed and immediate faith in that Person whom he knew as God, the revealed God, his covenant God.

Now to suppose the Jehovah to whom he has addressed his prayers, to have been the absolute Deity without distinction of Persons, or to have been the Father,—the first Person, in distinction from the Second as his legate, is to exclude the idea of any Mediator in the case, to whom and on the ground of whose merits, intercession and official relations, his prayers were offered and accepted. There is no escape from this conclusion. Either Abraham saw and conversed with the Absolute Deity, or he saw and conversed with the Father personally, and offered his prayers directly to him without reference to a Mediator; or he saw and conversed with the official mediatorial Person; the Mediator himself who represented and officially personated the Father, so that "what he did, the Father also did"—as being one in nature and will, dwelling in each other and acting coincidently, as explained by the Jehovah incarnate as Messiah : John v : 17–38.—vi : 38–51.—viii : 26–58.—x : 19–37.—xiv : 6–20, &c. And if these prayers were addressed directly to the acting mediatorial Person, then it is just and safe to infer that all his prayers, earlier and later, were in like manner addressed to that Person; for in no instance do they refer to any other Mediator. The Jehovah " appeared " to him at different times and places. At various places where he temporarily sojourned, " he built an altar to the Jehovah who appeared unto him, and called on the name of the Jehovah."

With this agrees the testimony of the New Test. concerning him. The incarnate Jehovah himself declares in a controversy John viii concerning himself as a person : " Before Abraham was, I am", i. e. I, the person whom you reject, then existed; and by one of his apostles that Abraham believed *God* and his faith was accounted to him for righteousness; that they which are of FAITH the same are the children of Abraham, and are blessed with faithful Abraham; that the faith through which he was justified was identical with that through which Christian believers, Jewish and Gentile, are justified; that his faith in the Jehovah whom he saw, was the same as to its object and to its efficacy, as that of the Gentiles who believed in the Christ. Even in their burnt-offerings and sacrifices the ancients, so far from considering them as supplying the place or having the effect of mediation did but express in that way, their faith and their prayers by visible acts. Those offerings were made directly to the Jehovah, on altars dedicated to him. Generally and probably without exception, they were accompanied by a vocal utterance of petitions. " Abram built an

altar unto the Jehovah, and called upon the name of Jehovah."
Gen. xii.   "The Jehovah appeared unto Isaac, and he builded
an altar and called upon the name of the Jehovah." Gen. xvi.
When the continual burnt-offering morning and evening was
prescribed, it was required to be presented "at the door of the
tabernacle, before the Jehovah; where I will meet you, to
speak there unto thee.   And there I will meet with the children of Israel, and I will sanctify the tabernacle and the altar."
Exod. xxix.   When Elijah repaired the altar of the Jehovah
at Mount Carmel and offered a burnt-sacrifice, he prayed and
said, O Jehovah Elohe of Abraham, Isaac and of Israel, let it
be known this day that thou art Elohim in Israel ", &c.   2 K.
xviii.   Closely connected with the continual burnt-sacrifice,
was the burning of *incense*, in the Levitical service, symboliz-
ing the prayers offered in connection with the burnt sacrifices.
Thus Zacharias, officiating in the Temple, burnt incense.
"And the whole multitude of the people were praying without,
at the time of incense."   Luke i.   In the Apocalypse this
symbol recurs as appearing in the heavenly sanctuary.   An angel, having a golden censer, received much incense "that he
should offer it with the prayers of all saints upon the golden
altar which was before the throne."   Rev. viii.   It is thus evident that the sacrifices were not, any more than the prayers,
regarded as having any mediative character or relation.   The
efficacy of the prayers depended on actual mediation.   The
sacrifices expressed the faith of the worshipper in outward and
visible actions.

A reference to particular portions of the history, to those
portions, for example, which narrate the lives of the respective
Patriarchs, will show that, where the name Elohim is almost
exclusively employed, the name Jehovah when occasionally
interposed is connected with some act or event more or less
indicative of his mediatorial agency.   Thus, in the history of
Jacob, the names El, Elohe, Elohim occur more than sixty
times, and the name Jehovah less than a fourth part of that
number.   But the name Jehovah occurs in such connections
as the following: In Jacob's vision of a ladder whose top
reached to heaven, "Behold the Jehovah stood above it, and
said, I am the Jehovah, Elohe of Abraham,—and Jacob said,
Surely the Jehovah is in this place—this is none other but the
house of Elohim—and he called the name of that place Beth-
El."   Gen. xxviii.   In chap. xxxi : "The Jehovah said unto
Jacob, Return unto the land of thy fathers : " and "Maleach
the Elohim said unto him, I am the El of Beth-El—return unto
the land of thy kindred."   chap. xxxii, 9.   In his prayer for

deliverance from Esau, "Jacob said, O, Elohe of my father
Abraham — the Jehovah which saidst unto me, Return unto
thy country, and to thy kindred. — Deliver me I pray thee."
And, v. 24, "Jacob was left alone; and there wrestled *a man*
with him, and he said, Thy name shall be called no more Jacob, but Israel [*prevailer with God*], for as a prince hast thou
power with God and with men, and hast prevailed. And Jacob said, I have seen Elohim face to face." Hosea, chap. xii,
referring to this narrative says : "He had power with Elohim;
yea he had power over the Maleach and prevailed : he wept
and made supplication *unto him :* he found him in Beth-El,
even the Jehovah Elohe of Hosts; the [Name] Jehovah is his
memorial".

To the same effect, as in the cases of Abraham and Jacob,
is the scripture record concerning Moses. The Jehovah, in
the official character and the visible form of manifestation of
the image, representative, messenger (angel) of the invisible
Father, appeared to Moses in a shekina of flame in a bush,
and spoke to him as *the Jehovah, the Elohim,* the *Elohe* of
Abraham, of Isaac and of Jacob. It is to be observed that
throughout the writings of Moses, as in those of David and
the Prophets, these and the other Divine appellations, Jah, El,
Adonai are employed interchangeably, to designate the same
Divine Person, not only in the same connection and with reference to the same acts and events, but often in the same sentences. In the present instance "the *angel* or *messenger* Jehovah appeared unto Moses" in a flame of fire out of the
midst of a bush; Moses turned to observe the appearance;
the *Jehovah* saw that he turned aside to see — the *Elohim*
called unto him out of the midst of the bush—and he said, I
am the *Elohe* of Abraham, the Elohe of Isaac, and the Elohe
of Jacob. And Moses hid his face for he was afraid to look
upon *The Elohim.* And the *Jehovah* said I have surely seen
the affliction of my people which are in Egypt, and I am come
down to deliver them, and I will send thee unto Pharaoh, that
thou mayest bring forth my people. And Moses said unto *the
Elohim,* Who am I that I should go unto Pharaoh. And *Elohim* said unto Moses, Thus shalt thou say unto the children of
Israel, I AM hath sent me unto you—the *Jehovah Elohim* of
your fathers, the Elohe of Abraham, &c. hath sent me unto
you." Exod. iii, 6–16. It is plain that the *Messenger* who
"came down to deliver his people," and was locally present
and spoke from the midst of the bush, was personally one and
the same with the Jehovah, the Elohim, the Elohe of Abraham, the God of the patriarchal dispensation. Under these

designations he continued to converse with Moses, and to instruct and direct him, throughout the subsequent narrative: To him, Moses and Aaron addressed their petitions for the removal of some of the plagues in Egypt.   To him, as the Jehovah announced by Moses, Pharaoh repeatedly asked them to pray.   He instituted the Passover, and at midnight *went out through Egypt* and smote the first born.   When he conducted the children of Israel out of Egypt, "the *Jehovah went before them* by day in a pillar of a cloud to lead them the way; and by night in a pillar of fire."   Exod. xiii, 21—thus identifying himself with the Jehovah in the bush.   When about to pass the Red Sea, "the Messenger, *the Elohim*, which went before the camp of Israel, *removed and went behind them ;* and the pillar of the cloud went from before their face, and stood behind them : and it came between the camp of the Egyptians and the camp of Israel—and *the Jehovah looked* unto the host of the Egyptians through the pillar of fire and of the cloud, and troubled them," &c.   Exod. xiv : 19–23.

In the song of Moses "the *Jehovah*," as if recognized in the visible similitude of *Man*, is denominated " *a man of war :* Thou stretchedst out thy right hand—the earth swallowed them. Thou in thy mercy hast led forth the people which thou hast redeemed — Thou shalt bring them in, and plant them in the mountain of their inheritance, in the place O Jehovah ! which thou hast made for thee to dwell in, in the Sanctuary O Jehovah ! which thy hands have established.   The Jehovah shall reign forever and ever."   Exod. xv.   In this passage he is identified with the Jehovah who dwelt in the tabernacle and temple.

Passing by the visible appearance of the Jehovah to Moses and to the elders on Mount Sinai, to Moses at the door of the Tabernacle and on various occasions, his appearance to Balaam, and many other evidences in the Pentateuch, that the MESSENGER—the Jehovah, the Elohim—the God of the preceding and of the Levitical dispensations, was one and the same delegated, mediatorial Person, we refer briefly to some instances after the death of Moses, in which he appeared locally and visibly.   To Joshua he appeared as " a man, with his drawn sword in his hand "; and directed him how to conduct the siege of Jericho. "And the Jehovah said unto Joshua, See, I have given into thy hand Jericho " Josh. vi.   Subsequently he directed Joshua in every emergency ; and to the Jehovah, directly, Joshua addressed his prayers.   After the death of Joshua, the tribes of Israel failed to extirpate Idolatry, " and the Messenger Jehovah came up from Gilgal [the place of the tabernacle] to Bochim, and said, I made you to go up out of Egypt " &c.   The context shows that the children of Israel to whom he spoke, recognized him as *the Jehovah*, the God of Israel ; " and they sacrificed there unto the Jehovah ".   Judges ii.   At a later period Judges vi. (compared with chap. ii.), the identity of *the Messenger* with *the Jehovah* is manifested.   " And it came to pass, when the children of Israel cried unto the Jehovah because of the Midianites, that the Jehovah sent a prophet unto the children of Israel, which said unto them, Thus saith the Jehovah, the Elohe of Israel, *I brought you up out of Egypt*, &c.—and the Messenger, Jehovah, came and sat under an oak " —where Gideon was—" and the Messenger, Jehovah, appeared unto him and said unto him, The Jehovah is with thee."   A colloquy ensues between the Jehovah and Gideon.   Gideon prepares an offering.   " The Messenger, *the* Elohim " directs him how to present it.   " Then the Messenger, Jehovah, put forth the end of the staff that was in his hand, and touched the flesh and the unleavened cakes : and there rose up fire out of the rock and consumed the flesh and the unleavened cakes. Then the Messenger Jehovah, departed out of his sight.   And when Gideon perceived that he was the Messenger, the Jehovah, he said, Alas, O my Adon Jehovah ! for because I have seen the Messenger Jehovah, face to face.   And the Jehovah said unto him, Peace be unto thee !   Then Gideon built an altar unto the Jehovah."   In chapter 2d the Messenger having come up from Gilgal, affirms of himself the same personal agency, which in chap. vi. the Jehovah God of Israel affirms of himself.

To Manoah and his wife the Messenger, Jehovah, appeared repeatedly in the form of a Man.   He is called " a man *the* Elohim," and his countenance is said to be like that of the " Messenger *the* Elohim."   Manoah prayed to the *Jehovah*, that the Man *the* Elohim, might come again ; " and *the Eloheim* hearkened to the voice of Manoah ; and the Messenger *the Elohim* came again " — Manoah presented an offering " unto the Jehovah," — the Person visibly present ; and " when the flame went up toward heaven from the altar, the Messenger *Jehovah*, ascended in the flame of the altar." Manoah knew that he was the Messenger *Jehovah* and said, " We shall surely die, because we have seen *Elohim*."   His wife replied, " If the Jehovah were pleased to kill us, he would not have received a burnt offering and a meat offering at our hands, neither would he have showed us all these things ". Judges xiii.   Here the visible appearance of a Person in the form of Man ; the application to him of his name of office interchangeably with the Divine names : the recognition of him in his true character, by Manoah ; the occurrence of the *article* before the word Elohim ; and the structure and purport of the narrative, preclude all doubt as to the identity of the Person, and therefore all doubt as to his being the one only Mediatorial Person, and as to his then acting mediatorially. For if the Maleach — (angel or messenger) — who appeared locally or visibly was a Divine Person, and according to his name of office was " sent ",—a Divine Messenger,—then he was the one Mediatorial Person, for but one such Divine Person was ever " sent " to the world to represent and do the will of the Father. And if that Person was designated and identified by the name Jehovah as certainly as by the title Maleach, then the Jehovah (the Elohim, &c.) was the Mediatorial Person.

No reason can be assigned why the Divine names, Jah, Jehovah, El, Elohim, Adonai, throughout the Old Test. are, as designations, employed interchangeably, but that they were understood to be equivalent designations of one and the same Person. It may well be supposed, however, that the reason why the official title Maleach, though as a designation employed interchangeably with the Divine names, was employed only occasionally, was, that the application of it marked a local and visible appearance of the delegated Mediatorial Person, —the Jehovah, unveiling himself in the simple and irradiant, or in the glorified form of the nature he was to assume and take into permanent union with his Person. Doubtless the association of the human form, human attributes, faculties, affections, sympathies, actions, with the Mediatorial Person thus appearing locally and visibly, realized him to be objectively to the faith of the ancient church, just what he is, since the incarnation to Gentile believers.

The Hebrew word Maleach, which in our version is translated *Angel*, as if it were the name of an angelic creature, is properly but a name of office, signifying a messenger. It is translated messenger, whenever men are the subjects : but whenever the Divine messenger is referred to, it is generally rendered, *angel*. When with this reference it occurs alone, it has the article, as Gen. xlviii : 15, 16. "And Jacob said, *The* Elohim, before whom my fathers, Abraham and Isaac did walk, *the* Elohim which fed me all my life long unto this day, *the* Maleach, which redeemed me from all evil, bless the lads." Sometimes, says Gesenius (art. Maleach) the same Divine appearance, which at one time is called Mal-ach, Jehovah, is afterwards called simply Jehovah, as Gen. xvi : 7 and

28

in numerous other places.   This, he adds, "is to be so understood, that the *Angel of God* is here nothing else than the invisible deity itself, which thus unveils itself to mortal eyes."
After referring to authorities, he says : "Hence oriental translators, wherever Jehovah himself is said to appear on earth,
always put for the name of God *the angel of God.*"   The
phrase "invisible deity itself, which thus unveils itself," appears
to have no reference to Divine *Person,* as appearing;   and
apparently the orientals meant by *the angel of God,* not a
Divine Person, but merely an extraordinary impersonal appearance, or at most, a created angelic agent.   Had they believed that the Jehovah himself personally appeared on earth,
that he was locally present and visible as a Person in the likeness of a Man—(as afterwards literally in man's nature)—that
he conversed with patriarchs, and others, gave them evidences
of his omniscience and omnipotence, and was recognized by
them as a Person, the revealer, representative, messenger of the
Father, they would have seen no occasion for suppressing his
name and substituting a formula which, as a personal designation, indicates and implies only creature attributes.

When the Israelites, under the kings who succeeded David,
rejected the faith of the ancient church concerning the Jehovah and the Messiah, and turned their backs upon him as the
object of their worship and obedience, and joined themselves
to idols, they ceased, as far as possible to pronounce, write, or
otherwise to recognize and keep his name in remembrance.
For their apostacy they were subjected to captivity to idolatrous
masters ;   their temple was destroyed, and their worship discontinued ;   they had forsaken the Jehovah, and he executed upon
them the judgments which he had threatened.   They seem,
the "Remnant" of true spiritual worshippers according to the
primitive faith always excepted,—to have relapsed into practical *Theism :* and when they renounced idolatry to have renounced the doctrine and all the theories and forms of mediation.   Thenceforth the Messiah whom they expected, was to be
a merely temporal prince.   For the teachings of Moses and
the Prophets they substituted traditions and glosses by which
they made void the law, and perverted or explained away the
primitive doctrines and faith, the distinction of Persons in the
Godhead, the incarnation and divinity of the Messiah, salvation by his atonement, his mission to the Gentiles and the
spirituality of his kingdom.   It was in keeping with all this
to represent the *Maleach,* who appeared visibly, and under the
names Jehovah and Elohim performed Divine acts, was wor-

shipped by sacrifices and prayers, and exercised mediatorial offices, as one of the class of created beings called angels, who from time to time were sent on special errands to the earth. This view being adopted and followed by the *Seventy* and other early translators, was followed by the authors of the more modern versions, including our own; and the Hebrew text construed accordingly. Hence Maleach is rendered *angel;* Maleach Jehovah, *an* or *the* angel of the Lord; Maleach *the* Elohim, an angel of God,—the construction being governed by the supposed nature and character of the Maleach. Had the translators perceived that the word Maleach designated the same Divine Person as the words Jehovah and Elohim, they would no more have construed the word Jehovah, as the genitive of the word Maleach, than they would have construed the word Elohim when preceded by the word Jehovah as the genitive of the latter. It is indubitable that the words Maleach, Jehovah, and Elohim, are employed interchangeably to designate the same Divine Person; and there is nothing in the original text to forbid the first two equally with the last two of these words being construed as in apposition.

On this view the subject is relieved of difficulty. And as to the early manifestations themselves of the Jehovah, in that visible form in which he was afterwards, in the progress of his official work, to appear visibly incarnate on earth; they can hardly be thought more remarkable than that he should, while sojourning on earth as man, assume, in the presence of his apostles on the Mount, that glorified form of manifestation which was to succeed his resurrection. "He was transfigured before them: His face did shine as the sun, and his raiment was white as the light." In this form of ineffable glory, he appeared to Saul, when near Damascus; and to John in Patmos. And indeed he assumed essentially this form in some of his appearances under the Old Test. I saw, says Isaiah, the Adonai sitting upon a throne, high and lifted up, and his train filled the temple. Above it stood the seraphims — and they cried one unto another, and said, Holy, holy, holy, is the Jehovah of hosts: the whole earth is full of his glory. Then said I, Woe is me, for mine eyes have seen the King, the Jehovah of hosts; also I heard the voice of the Jehovah." Isa. vi. John referring to this scene, says it was the glory of Christ which Isaiah saw. Chap. xii. In Ezekiel's vision of the glorified appearance of the Jehovah, with its cherubic and dazzling accompaniments, there was, above the firmament, "the likeness of a throne, and upon the throne, the likeness as the appearance of *a Man* above upon it.   And I saw as the color of amber, as the appearance of fire round about within it, from the appearance of his loins even upward, and from the appearance of his loins even downward, I saw as it were the appearance of fire.   This was the appearance of the likeness of the glory of the Jehovah.   And when I saw it, I fell upon my face, and I heard a voice of one that spake.   And he said unto me, Son of man, I send thee unto the children of Israel."   Ezek. i : 2. This vision was repeated afterwards, the scene being changed to the temple at Jerusalem.   "And behold the glory of the God of Israel was there according to the vision that I saw in the plain."   After he had instructed the prophet concerning the impending destruction of Jerusalem and of the temple, and the reason for it, the God of Israel forsook and withdrew from the temple.   "The glory of the Jehovah went up from the midst of the city, and stood upon the mountain which is on the east side of the city"—that is Mount Olivet.   In a vision subsequently, of the restoration of the temple and of his return to it, it is said, chap. xliii, "The glory of the God of Israel, came from the way of the east : and his voice was like a noise of many waters : and the earth shined with his glory.   And it was according to the appearance of the vision which I saw—by the river Chebar ; and I fell upon my face.   And the glory of the Jehovah came into the house — and the glory of the Jehovah filled the house.   And I heard him speaking unto me out of the house ".   -

The vision of Daniel chap vii. resembles in the description of particulars, the instances already mentioned.   Also the descent of the Jehovah in fire on Mount Sinai.   Exod. xix.   In the earlier ages it is not unlikely that such appearances were frequent.   An impression was current at an early period, that those would not survive who saw God in a manner so visibly indicating his Divine perfections ; an impression derived, probably, from the fact that the beholders were so impressed as to fall on their faces, and sometimes to become insensible.   These glorious appearances were of various degrees of brightness. They were not always local and restricted to the view of a single beholder, or to that of a few individuals.   Sometimes the manifestation illumined the whole hemisphere.   Habbakuk says : " God came from Teman, and the Holy One from Mount Paran.   Selah.   His glory *covered the heavens*, and the earth was full of his praise, and his brightness was as the light ". Similar allusions occur in the Psalms, both retrospective and prophetic, implying that to the apprehension and faith of the ancient church, the manifestations of the Jehovah in ineffable glory as God of Providence and as King and Redeemer of his people and future conqueror of all enemies, were familiar as themes of exultation and praise.

> " O Elohim, when thou wentest forth before thy people,
> " When thou didst march through the wilderness ; selah:
> " The earth shook, the heavens also dropped
> " At the PRESENCE of the Elohim:
> "Even Sinai itself was moved
> "At the PRESENCE of the Elohim, the Elohe of Israel.

> " The chariots of the Elohim are twenty thousand,
> " Even thousands of angels :
> " The Adonai is among them,
> " As in Sinai, IN THE HOLY PLACE
> " Thou hast ascended on high,
> " Thou hast led captivity captive :
> " Thou hast received gifts for men :
> " Yea for the rebellious also,
> " That the Jah Elohim might dwell among them.　　Ps. lxviii.
> See also Ps. xviii : 8, 9.

In the New Testament, Math. xxiv : 27, the future visible appearance and coming of the Jehovah in his glorified humanity, is compared to the brightness of lightning. "And when he shall come in his glory and all the holy angels with him, then shall he sit upon the throne of his glory." "Behold he cometh with clouds and every eye shall see him."

It is in harmony with these facts that at the Incarnation, and in the transition from Judaism to Christianity, holy men addressed their prayers directly to the same Divine Person, the Jehovah then manifested in human nature, the Messiah, the Jehovah incarnate. A voice had warned them "to prepare the way of *the Jehovah*—a highway for our *God*". The glory of the Jehovah was to be revealed; the God of the former dispensation was to appear in Emmanuel. Isa. xl, &c. It was revealed to Simeon that he should not die before he had seen the Messiah, the Jehovah incarnate. An angel announced the Saviour as " Christ *the Lord* " — Messiah *the Jehovah*. Luke ii : 11. Thenceforth he is addressed by prayer and otherwise as the Jehovah, (the Lord), Jesus, the Christ; Jesus the Christ our Jehovah. Rom. iii : 11, 14.

The doctrine so evidently taught in the Scriptures, that the Jehovah acted Mediatorially under the ancient economy, that those who were justified were justified by faith in him as the one Mediator, and that their prayers were addressed to him in that character, is in keeping with every aspect and relation of the redemptive work. The church is one under all dispensations, saved in one way through faith in the Mediator. In him all who have been, and all who are to be, saved, were chosen before the foundation of the world. There is one body or church,—one Spirit, one Jehovah, one Father, one faith. Ep. iv : 4–6. Therefore the Jehovah, in whom Abraham believed and likewise all who were justified before the Advent, was the mediatorial Person; for no other is referred to in connection with his or with their faith. And those who anciently believed in him unto righteousness, must have had essentially the same apprehensions of him as a Person, and as to his offices, and the same affections towards him as those who saw him incarnate and as their successors to the present time.

Accordingly when, after the Ascension, the apostles preached the Gospel to the Jews, it was their chief endeavor to convince their hearers, that the Jehovah of the ancient Scriptures had become incarnate and was the Messiah whom they had crucified and slain, and that their relation to the incarnate Mediator was the same with that of their ancestors to the Jehovah. Hence they addressed him indifferently under the Greek appellative which replaced the name Jehovah, and the titles which belonged to him as the Messiah. Just prior to the Ascension they ask him, Acts i : 6: "Lord, wilt thou at this time restore again the kingdom to Israel?"— addressing the risen Messiah as identical with the Jehovah of the prior dispensation, the Theocratic Head of the kingdom of Israel. Wilt Thou who didst institute and rule the kingdom, now restore it and resume thy regal office? His reply signifies, that as the Legate of the Father, the revealer and executor of his will, he disclosed things future only, as he was directed. At the close of Peter's argument, Acts ii, he says: "Therefore let all the house of Israel know assuredly, that God [the Father] hath made that same Jesus, whom ye have crucified, both Lord and Christ"—the Jehovah and the Messiah: hath appointed, constituted him, to be the Mediator, as the Jehovah under the Old Test. and the Messiah, the Jehovah incarnate, under the New. On the occasion referred to, Acts iv, when the apostles had escaped the hands of persecutors, they came to their own company, who, on hearing what had happened, exultingly "lifted up their voice to God with one accord, and said, Lord, Thou art God, which hast made heaven and earth, and the sea, and all that in them is,"—meaning the same as if it had been said, that they lifted up their voice spontaneously to the mediatorial Person, the Logos who was God and made all things; the Jehovah who created the heavens and the earth; the same Person now manifested incarnate. To him directly, they addressed their prayer, v. 29, "And now Lord, behold their threatening". So Stephen prayed directly to the Jehovah incarnate as Mediator, when he said, Acts vii: 54–60, "LORD Jesus receive my spirit: LORD lay not this sin to their charge". And Saul, Acts ix: 15: "Who art thou LORD?" "LORD what wilt thou have me to do?" Ananias says, ix: 17: "The LORD, even Jesus, that appeared to thee". And, Acts ix: 27: Barnabas declared how Saul "had seen THE LORD in the way, and had preached, at Damascus, in the name of Jesus", and, v. 29, "in the name of the LORD Jesus".

The Greek word *Kurios*, translated *Lord*, in the New Test. is the equivalent of the Hebrew word *Jehovah*, rendered Lord in the Old. So also in the Septuagint. This identifies the Jehovah of the one with the Jehovah incarnate of the other, in the Person of the Messiah. John the Baptist was sent to prepare the way for the appearance of *the Jehovah* in man's nature. When he appeared, it was essential first to show and certify that he was the Jehovah incarnate. To work this conviction he, while exercising Divine attributes, called himself *the Son of man*—thereby attesting that the Divine and human natures were united in his Person. The apostles denominated the complex Person, the Jehovah, the Son of God, the Christ, the Saviour—as equivalent designations of the one mediatorial Person. Faith in that Person was essential to salvation, and as truly so under the Jewish as under the Christian dispensation. Accordingly the Jehovah says, Isaiah xlv : 22–25. "Look unto me, and be ye saved, all the ends of the earth : for I am God, and there is none else. Unto ME every knee shall bow, every tongue shall swear. Surely shall one say, in *the Jehovah* have I righteousness and strength : even to *him* shall men come. In *the Jehovah* shall all the seed of Israel be justified, and shall glory".

Acts xiii : 47 : "For so hath the LORD commanded us—(saying—) I have set thee to be a light of the Gentiles". *The Lord*, the Person whom they customarily designated by that name, who chose them to be apostles, and commanded them what to do ; viz The Jehovah now incarnate—the Jehovah of the Old Test. as Mediator who, prospectively, spoke to and of himself as the Messiah, saying Isaiah xlix : "It is a light thing that thou shouldest be my servant to raise up the tribes of Jacob. I will also give thee for a light to the Gentiles"— and xv : 16. "After this I [the Jehovah] will return, and will build again the tabernacle of David—that, (v 17,) the residue of men might seek after *the Lord*"—*the Jehovah.* See also Amos ix : 12.

Among the examples in the Old Testament of the express identification of the Jehovah of the ancient dispensations with the Messiah of the present, the 24th Psalm is referred to. Bishop Horsley, from whose version we quote, after noticing the purport of the first six verses, observes that "the song concludes with a prediction of the exaltation of the Messiah (for he is certainly the Jehovah of this Psalm) under the image of an entry of Jehovah into his temple". The Psalm opens with a chorus ascribing to the Jehovah the creation and proprietorship of the earth with its inhabitants, and all its furniture. Next, in questions and answers, sung by different voices, it describes the conditions and way of justification. Then follows the conclusion above referred to. If we conceive of the whole as being performed by choruses in the temple, at the time of the burnt offering, it proclaims the triumphant entrance of the Messiah—the incarnate Jehovah,—into the heavenly sanctuary after accomplishing his typified work of expiation. The Jehovah then present in his mediatory office in the sanctuary within the vail, is, in connection with the types of his future incarnation and vicarious work, represented as triumphant, the King of Glory, claiming admission into his tabernacle in heaven. The scene must have been most impressive, and instructive. The slaughtered lamb as a whole burnt offering vividly prefigured the atoning sacrifice of the Messiah. What should follow but that, leading captivity captive, he who had descended should also ascend "up far above all heavens that he might fill all things"? "The chariots of God are twenty thousand, even thousands of angels : the Lord is among them as in Sinai in the holy place. Thou hast ascended on high, thou hast led captivity captive : Thou hast received gifts for men". Ps. lxviii : 17. From the 24th Ps. we quote the last four verses :

Semichorus. "O ye gates lift up your heads,
          "And be ye lifted up ye everlasting doors,
          "And let the King of Glory enter.
A single voice. "Who is He, this King of Glory?
Another voice. "Jehovah Strong and Mighty,
          "Jehovah mighty in battle.
Semichorus. "O ye gates lift up your heads,
          "And be ye lifted up ye everlasting doors,
          "And let the King of Glory enter.
A single voice. "Who is He, this King of Glory ?
Grand chorus. "Jehovah of Hosts, He is the King of Glory.

"Jehovah of Hosts, i. e. He who is the principle and founda-

tion of existence to the whole assemblage of created being ".
Horsley. The Messiah whose vicarious work was typified in
the tabernacle "made with hands" and who entered "the true
tabernacle" in heaven, was personally and officially identical
with the Jehovah of Hosts, the King of Glory, the Creator and
upholder of all things.

This view of the mediatorial agency of the Jehovah throughout the ancient dispensations, is assumed and implied in the
New Testament records ; not only by evidences like those adduced, but by the teachings of the Messiah himself, to the effect
that the Father, as a Person, had not before,—(otherwise than
as anciently personated and represented by the mediating Jehovah),—been distinctively announced ; that it was by the Mediator that the Father was expressly declared : that previously
the prayers of holy men were not addressed to the Father in
the *name* of the acting mediator, but directly to the Mediator
himself as the image, legate and representative of the father.
Now, he having taught his apostles concerning the Father and
his relations to him, there was to be a change. " O righteous
Father, the world hath not known thee : but *I have known
thee*, and these have known that *thou hast sent me.* And I
have declared unto them thy name, and will declare it."
" Hitherto have ye asked nothing in my name : ask and ye
shall receive, that your joy may be full. Verily, verily, I say
unto you, whatsoever ye shall ask the Father in my name, he
will give it you. These things have I spoken to you in proverbs [figures] : but the time cometh when I shall no more
speak unto you in proverbs, but I shall show you plainly of the
Father. At that day ye shall ask in my name : and I say not
unto you, that I will pray the Father for you : [that, you, asking in my name will expect of course]—For the Father himself
loveth you, because ye have loved me, and have believed that
I came out from God. I came forth from the Father, and am
come into the world : again I leave the world and go to the
Father." John xvi : 17.

That the Christian writers immediately succeeding the
Apostolic age taught, that the Jehovah of the Old Test. was
a Divine Person distinct from God the Father, and that the
Messiah who had appeared was personally and officially the
same who was called Jehovah, Elohim, etc., is evident from
what remains of their treatises. Justin Martyr, in his Dia-
logue with Trypho, cites, in proof of this doctrine, passages
from Psalms xxiv, lv, lvii, lxxviii, xcix, and others, and from
the narrative of his visible appearances, to Abraham before
the destruction of Sodom, and to Jacob as " the messenger

and Jehovah", in his vision of the ladder, and at Luz.   His 59th Section is entitled : " The God that talked with Moses was a Person distinct from God the Father."   After stating that " this very Angel, and God, and Lord, which appeared as a Man to Abraham and Jacob, appeared to Moses in a flame of fire out of the midst of a bush, and talked with him", —he quotes from Exod. iii : 16, the declaration of the angel or messenger, that he was the Lord God, the God of Abraham, of Isaac, and of Jacob, and adds, " This Person, whom Moses calls the angel that talked with him is God, and declares to Moses that he is the God of Abraham, and of Isaac, and of Jacob".   *Theophilus*, in a note extracted, by the translator, from Bishop Bull, observes : " ' God the Almighty Father of all cannot be in place, nor is he ever found there : for there is no determinate place of his rest.' The primitive Fathers referred all those appearances of God, which were formerly exhibited to the patriarchs, to the economy of man's salvation ; which economy they supposed that the Son of God did not then first take upon him when he made his appearance in the flesh, but from the fall of our first parent : but they were fully persuaded that this economy could not possibly be performed by the Person of God the Father.   Because for the very same reason as the Catholic church of Christ always acknowledged, in opposition to the Patripassians, that God the Father could not be incarnate as the Son was, did the ancients affirm that these appearances were not made by the Father, but by the Son, as being really preludes to his incarnation." —*Bull.*

The work which, anterior to the creation the mediatorial Person undertook and covenanted to execute, comprised all that he was to do in the sphere of finite relations and events. It was one work ; and though gradually advanced in its execution from stage to stage, the execution of a part secured and gave effect to every part, and to the whole. The work of creation regarded in its relation to him, necessarily preceded the work of atonement ; but both being parts of the entire Mediatorial work, the accomplishment of the first involved and rendered as legally and immediately available the results of the second, as if the atoning Sacrifice had been slain from the foundation of the world.   Were this otherwise it would be so for reasons which would preclude the gift of pardon and justification on the ground of the atonement till all ulterior mediatorial works, a perpetual intercession and a final sentence of acquittal and glorification, were realized.

From the above considerations, and from the whole current

of scriptural doctrine, the analogy of faith, the oneness of the Church, the reality of justification as an act of God coïncidently with the exercise of faith by the sinner, and the results of this process in multitudes under the ancient economy who were justified, and who died in the faith in full anticipation of the events then predicted and typified, and which have been or are to be realized under the present and future dispensations, we conclude that there was an acting Mediator, and actual Mediation. under the ancient economy; and that the Jehovah who administered that economy acted Mediatorially under that and other names and titles, and at length as a Person, and in pursuance of his official work, became literally incarnate for the suffering of death, and destruction of the works of Satan. That those ancient believers understood the system in this light might be argued from particular facts; from the early institution of the typical sacrifices; from the translation of Enoch and Elijah; from the prophecy of Enoch as rehearsed by Jude: "Behold the Jehovah cometh with ten thousand of his saints, to execute judgment", etc.; from the miracles wrought by the Jehovah and in his name under the old dispensations; from the typical import of the judgments which he inflicted, as in the instance of Sodom and Gomorrah; from the names and designations employed in predictions of the Messiah; from the appearance and the purport of the message of Moses and Elias at the transfiguration; and from the resurrection of many of the Old Test. saints after that of the Messiah. · These and the like facts argue the sameness of the ancient with the present system, and of the way of justification and acceptance through an acting Mediator. On the other hand it may be alleged as an historical fact, that of those who like Cain rejected the revealed system, and embraced idolatry or some other false system, no one was ever justified. Their prayers and acts of homage were not offered through the Mediator, and therefore were not accepted. Their *natural religion* did not avail them.

The same conclusions might be confirmed by an examination of the terms employed as Divine names, titles, and designations, in the Old and New Testaments; the connections in which they occur, the appropriation of them interchangeably, their manifest reference and significance in particular instances, the obscurity and confusion occasioned by translating or substituting for them the secular and idolatrous nomenclature of heathens, instead of transferring those of the original text into our version of the Scriptures But our limits restrain us from further discussion.

Art. VI.—COLENSO ON THE PENTATEUCH. Part II.

By Daniel R. Goodwin, D.D., Provost of the University of Pennsylvania.

The Pentateuch and the Book of Joshua Critically Examined.   By the Rt. Rev. John William Colenso, D.D., Bishop of Natal.   Part II.   Appleton. New-York, 1863.   Pp. 303.

In the last number of this Review we ventured to predict that if Bishop Colenso's Part I should fall, his Part II must fall with it.   A more critical examination of his second part has confirmed the anticipation.   He himself admits as much. He all along assumes the results of his Part I as the necessary and sufficient basis for the argumentation of his Part II. Thus he says: " No reliance whatever can be placed on the *details* of the story of the exodus.   It will be found that *they are inextricably bound up with the numbers*" (p. 14).   " Our previous considerations have forced upon us the conviction, by reason of the impossibilities contained in it, that the account of the exodus, *generally*, is wanting in historical truth, and that, consequently, it cannot be assumed beforehand as certain, without a careful examination of each part of the narrative, that any of such ' groups of laws' as the story describes were laid down in the wilderness. . . . . The result of our inquiries, as far as we have proceeded, is that such a narrative as that which is contained in the Pentateuch, could not have been written in the age of Moses ; or for some time afterwards (175)".   (p. 71.)   After stating certain " signs of later date in the Pentateuch", he adds : " But these difficulties, after all, are by us regarded as only of secondary importance.   They are not those on which we rest the *stress* of our argument.   Being satisfied, on other sure grounds, as set forth in Part I, that the story in the Pentateuch has no claim to be regarded as historically true, etc".   (p. 92.)   " Hitherto we have been advancing upon *certain* ground.   It seems to follow as a necessary conclusion from the facts which we have already had before us in Part I, that the account of the Exodus is in very essential parts not historically true. . . . . But we are now entering upon the field of conjecture" (p. 119.)   " The above is said",—referring to the argument from the composition of names in the Pentateuch,—"assuming that it has already been sufficiently shown that there is no reason to suppose that the details of the story of the Exodus, including the lists of names, etc., are historically true. Otherwise, it might, of course, be argued that the very fact that no such Jehovistic names occur in the whole narrative is itself a strong indication of the truthfulness and historical reality of the record" (p. 129). At present, the suggestions which we have made above are only conjectural, except to this extent that (i.) we have seen reason already to conclude with certainty", —referring to a section which itself refers to Part I,—"that the main portion, at least, of the story of the Exodus must have been written long after the time of Moses and Joshua".

Thus it will be seen that his Part II is confessedly based upon Part I, and will not pretend to stand without it. Indeed he has felt obliged, in the first chapter of Part II, to review, reinforce, and defend some of the main positions of Part I, particularly that in regard to the "numbers". He makes, however, but one new point which seems to us to require attention; and that is in a note. "The *whole number* of male Kohathites, as given in Num. iii, 8,600, is more than *one fourth as large again* as that of the Merarites, 6,200; whereas the converse is the case with the *adults*, since the number of Merarite males *from thirty to fifty years old*, 3,200, is just *one sixth as large again* as that of the Kohathites, 2,750. Besides this palpable inconsistency, the Merarite males 'from thirty to fifty' are more than half the whole number of males of that family, 'from a month old and upward', contrary to all the data of modern statistical science". In reply to this, we have only to suggest the possibility that, by some accident in transcribing, either the Kohathites and Merarites, or the numbers corresponding to them respectively, have been *interchanged*, in one passage or in the other. In any event, therefore, this is not sufficient ground for declaring the Pentateuch unhistorical.

We shall take this opportunity to complete and confirm our own statements in regard to the numbers of the Israelites at the time of the exodus. We take for granted that, if it can be shown to be neither incredible nor improbable that the Israelites, in 215 years, should have increased to some two and a half million of souls, the other difficulties, about the lambs for the Passover, the departure from Egypt, the assembling at the tabernacle, the sojourn in the wilderness, the duties of the priests, etc., have been sufficiently obviated. They have all been considered, patiently in detail, in our former number,—at least, as far as our limits would admit. We have not intentionally avoided any difficulty; but have conscientiously endeavored to meet the Bishop's strongest points, and all his points of any weight in the question. As to the numbers in the Book of Chronicles, we have said nothing about them, and we shall say nothing about them here. We do not regard them as having any proper bearing upon our present discussion; and the Bishop was apparently led to refer to them only as a kind of make-weight with his other arguments. Let one thing be settled at a time; our question is now with the Pentateuch.

Is, then, the census of the Israelites when they came out of Egypt credible?

In the last number of this REVIEW we presented a hypothetical answer to this question in the form of a table. It was presumed in that table, and we supposed it would, of course, be so understood, that the number assigned to each generation was the number of *those surviving at the average age of* 30 *to* 33 *years.* And thus the surplus of the 4th generation after Joseph's death would about balance the deficit in the 3d.

To be more specific, suppose (1) this *4th* generation, being between 3 and 33 years old, and averaging 20 years, to contain, say, $\frac{1}{15}$ (or 160,000) more than would survive at the average age of 33, thus adding 40,000 to the warriors. (2) The next preceding generation, the *3d*, being from 33 to 63 years old, averaging 50, would contain, say, $\frac{1}{4}$ (or 100,000) less than survived at the average age of 33, thus diminishing the number of warriors by 50,000. (3) The other generation reckoned in the final sum, the *2nd*, being from 63 to 93 years old, averaging 80, — the generation of Moses, — may be supposed reduced to $\frac{1}{4}$ of their number at 33, thus diminishing the population by 75,000. (4) Thus the number of warriors would be reduced by 10,000, i. e., would stand at 604,400; and the whole population would be reduced by 15,000, and would stand at 2,535,400;—a result which only brings us still nearer the precise enumeration of the text.

But as various specious objections may be made to the number of generations presumed in that table, to the periods and to the rate of increase assigned to each, &c., we propose to cut the whole matter short by calling attention to the following simple facts. 1. The rate of increase of the population of the Free American States, in the last 70 years, has been more than .033 (three and three tenths per cent) per annum.[*]

[*] If the slaves in the other States have not increased, as they should have done, at a still more rapid rate, it is only so much the more to the discredit of the slave-

2. A population of 102 — the number of the Israelites of Ephraim's generation, with one wife each — would become 2½ millions in 215 years by increasing at the rate of less than .0482 (or about four and eight tenths per cent) per annum.

·Now here we have *the whole question reduced to its lowest terms.* Is this latter rate of increase, as compared with the former, absolutely incredible ; so that it would be as irrational to undertake to prove it true by testimony, as to prove, by the same means, that "three and two make seven"? Or, suppose it proved, as a matter of fact, by sufficient evidence ; would it be pronounced necessarily *miraculous ?* We think not. We are clearly of opinion that there is no need of supposing a miracle to explain such a fact if admitted ; at the same time that we are ready stoutly to maintain that *if* a miracle were necessary for the explanation, we should have a right, under the circumstances of the Mosaic history, to assume it.

But we will place the matter in yet another light.

1. Abraham, Isaac, and Jacob had an average of 2¾ wives (or concubines) each ; and each wife an average of 2¾ sons who became heads of tribes or families. Here were three successive generations.

2. Now suppose the generation of Ephraim (51 males averaging, say, 5 years old,) and the two next following generations, (all within Joseph's lifetime,) to have averaged, in like manner, 2¾ wives for each man, and each wife to have had an average of 2¾ sons surviving to be heads of families ; and assigning to these generations 25 years each, (as the text would expressly authorize us to do,) — we should then have, *without any further assumptions whatever*, the result of 2½ millions at the end of the remaining 145 years, with an annual increase at the rate of less than .029. And even if we assign to those earlier generations of Ephraim, his children, and grandchildren, the usual space of thirty years each ; the same result would be reached in the remaining 130 years, by an annual increase of considerably less than .033 ; — in either case, less than the rate of increase with which we are histori-

owners. Undoubtedly a system of slavery may be made so outrageously and abominably oppressive, or so excessively licentious, as to check the increase of population to any extent. The system of Negro Slavery is, in some places, so oppressive as to arrest that increase altogether, so that the slaves would die out were not their numbers recruited from abroad. And as to Free Negroes among us, their condition is made, *by the influence of slaveholders*, worse even, in many respects, than that of the slaves themselves. And yet it remains true that, *as a general rule*, the servile and lower castes and grades of society tend to a more rapid increase than the higher classes. Egyptian bondage was probably a light thing to negro slavery.

cally familiar. And surely it can hardly be pretended that the practice of polygamy to this extent, during the lifetime of Joseph, — which is the only extraordinary thing here assumed,—was either incredible or improbable.[*]

The attempt has been made to show that such a rapid increase of the Israelites as this, is incredible, because if the population of the United States were supposed to increase for a few hundred years at this rate, it would amount to fabulous numbers. But such an argument is a pure fallacy. If the population of the Free American States should continue to increase at the same rate as for the last 70 years, until A.D. 2000, it would amount to more than 1700 millions, i. e., to more than the present population of the globe; in A.D. 2140, to more than 154,000 millions; in A.D. 2210, to nearly 1500,-000 millions; and in A.D. 2560, it would exceed the enormous sum of 113,000 million millions, or about 100 million times the whole present population of the globe. That population is not more than 20 to the square mile of dry land; this would therefore give some 2000 million, or nearly double the present population of the globe, to be crowded or rather heaped upon every square mile of land upon the earth's surface, — or upwards of seventy persons to every square foot. Is it therefore incredible that the population of the American States has, in the last seventy years, increased at a rate which leads to such monstrous results?[†]

[*] We have given above only the arithmetical data and results; leaving the latter to be verified by our readers, who can make the calculations for themselves.

[†] In our last we made certain strictures on the Rev. Dr. Mahan's reply to Bp. Colenso. We meant and we made no personal attack. We merely stated what, in good faith, we understood to be the Doctor's logical position; and should very sincerely regret if we misrepresented it. We even expressly disclaimed—which was more than we were bound to do—any charge or insinuation that the Doctor was consciously or intentionally maintaining one of Colenso's chief positions; while we endeavored to show, what we believed to be the fact, that he was really doing it. Dr. M. has seen fit to make a rejoinder, by three successive instalments in a certain weekly sheet. The two first having been placed under our eye, we have read them; the third, which we understand to be even more acrimonious and purely personal than its predecessors, we have not read and do not think of reading. We are not disposed to indulge in personalities, or to enter into any personal controversy.

Dr. M. complains of our having published our article in this REVIEW, which he is not accustomed to see. The simple fact is, we publish our articles where we please, and shall continue to do so; and if the Doctor's theological reading is so restricted that he does not see this REVIEW, so much the worse for himself. Besides, it seems hardly consistent for him, while making this complaint, to publish his rejoinder in a sheet which we, whether as a patriot, a Christian or a Churchman, could not encourage even with the patronage of a single individual, and which we had publicly announced (see Episcopal Recorder for Nov. 8, 1862) we were not accustomed to read.

Dr. M. complains that our quotations from him were "garbled". We did not intend they should be, and we do not think they were. Meanwhile,—what is most

The additional matter of Bishop Colenso's Part II may be referred to three heads; (1) Certain signs from names, etc., of a later origin in the Pentateuch; (2) The manner in which the Divine names, Jehovah and Elohim are used in the Pentateuch; and (3) The confirmatory argument from the use of the same names in the Psalms.

Now, under this first head, we find absolutely nothing new; nothing which has not been recognized and answered over and over again. The answers are found in Theological Treatises, in ponderous Commentaries, and erudite works on Biblical Criticism, which are not familiar or attractive to the ordinary reading public; while the Bishop arrays his objections as if they were new discoveries which the friends of Christianity

material,—we do not perceive that the Doctor either disclaims or retracts the position itself which we ascribed to him; and the object of the quotations was simply to show that he held that position, — the position, we mean, in regard to the *numbers* in Exodus. We are well aware that he does not stand alone in it, — Stanley and others may be with him, — but we note that he stands in it.

Dr. M. had said that Moses was "not a detailer of mere facts"; and we had said that the "mere" had no pertinency in the case. Of this also he complains. But until it shall appear that Colenso, or some of his friends or opponents have asserted or implied that Moses "*was* a detailer of *mere* facts", we shall take the liberty to think and say that the "mere" of Dr. M. is both irrelevant and impertinent. Colenso's *proper* opponents assert that Moses was a *narrator of* FACTS; if Dr. M. means to deny this, he sides with Colenso; we are not aware that any party considers Moses a "detailer of *mere* facts";—certainly, Colenso does not, and certainly his real opponents do not.

In regard to certain hypothetical ages of Jochebed and others, which we had suggested by way of concession to Colenso or of supposing the worst, and not because we maintained or admitted them to be true or necessary,—we had observed that they were "certainly *credible*, if the story of Abraham is credible". To this Dr. M. retorts; "I cannot but think there is a vast difference between the two cases. The story of Abraham rests on the authority of the Bible. The great age of Jochebed and others rests solely on Dr. G.'s arithmetic"—as if *credibility* were necessarily proportioned to *positive evidence*. If Dr. M. really does not know the meaning of "credible", we refer him to the first definition of the word in Webster's Dictionary.

The Doctor sneers at our logic, as though we did not know the difference between *yet* and *therefore*. We would by no means presume to compete with Dr. M. either in logic or in rhetoric. But is it possible that he counts so largely upon the *ars celare artem*, as to think to make us believe, that, in his childlike simplicity, he knows nothing of such a figure as *irony*, and is too innocent even to comprehend an insinuation? If a person, referring to Dr. M., should say that a man may be very supercilious and self-confident, and may assume a very lofty and dictatorial bearing; and yet have very little real substance in him;—or that a man may abound in the expression of noble sentiments, wear an air of perfect innocence and honesty, be remarkably smooth and fair-spoken; and yet be a very Jesuit at heart;—would the Doctor not think of taking offence, considering that the "*yet*" would logically imply the inference to be still in his favor? We wish it to be observed, we are far from applying such language to Dr. M. ourselves, and use it only by way of hypothetical illustration, with a view of bringing the case within the range of his intelligence, and, thus, to use his own words, "inculcating a wholesome lesson".

29

had never thought of before, or had studiously endeavored to
conceal, and publishes them in a form and under circumstances such as will insure their being read by multitudes who
rarely if ever read a Biblical Commentary or even the Bible
itself. This is partly unfair, and partly unfortunate. The
only way fully to answer the Bishop would be to follow him
from step to step, to take up and refute his points in detail.
And this would require a work of such an extent—for it ordinarily takes many more words to answer a plausible objection
than to make it—as quite to shut it out from popular reading.
In our restricted space we can at most give but a specimen or
two of the Bishop's points, and we could heartily wish that he
or some friend of his would designate one or two of what he
regards as his strongest cases.

As to "sea-wind" [Heb.] for "west-wind" in Ex. x, 19,—
we answer that we suppose the Israelites spoke Hebrew when
they went down into Egypt, while they were in Egypt, and
when they came out of Egypt, and not the Egyptian language.
This certainly is the natural inference, we know no evidence
to the contrary, and thus we see no difficulty in the use of the
word in question.

The phrase "kings of Edom *before* there reigned any king
over the children of Israel", Gen. xxvi, 31, does not, in itself,
imply, according to Biblical usage, that there were ever any
kings over Israel, but only that it was common for considerable nations to have kings, and natural to suppose that Israel
might have them. See Matt. I. xviii, xxv, and v. 18.

The terms *Nabi* and *Roch, prophet* and *seer*, 1 Sam. ix, 9,
may very naturally be supposed to have been in use in the
earlier times, to have passed into desuetude in the period of
the Judges, and subsequently to have been restored to collo-
quial usage.

The "Book of Joshua", and the book of the "Wars of
Jehovah", may have been collections of martial odes, or poetical records contemporary with Moses and Joshua. Has any
body proved the contrary?

"The Canaanite was *then* in the land", Gen. xii, 6; this
Colenso argues must imply "but *not now*". But see Gen. iv,
26, "Then begun men to call upon the Lord"; Josh. xiv, 11,
"As my strength was then so is it now"; Job xxxviii, 21,
"Knowest thou it because thou wast then born?"

Colenso boldly says, "the Heb. אז, here translated 'then',
cannot possibly be translated 'already,' as some have supposed". And yet, curiously enough, on page 125, he himself
says: "And, generally, we are told that, *as early as* the time

of Enos, the son of Seth, ' *then* began men to call on the name of Jehovah". Is it impossible, then, that אָז, which is here translated "then", should mean "already"? — The text in Gen. xii, 6, plainly means that the same people who were in the land in the writer's time, and who were soon to be expelled, were also there in Abraham's time.

We are utterly at a loss to know how Colenso has ascertained that the appellation "Hebrew", which seems to have been familiarly applied to the Abrahamic race by strangers, generally, from the very earliest times, "did not originate till a much later age".

That בְּעֵבֶר or מֵעֵבֶר may refer to *either side* of Jordan, and need not mean *beyond* Jordan, is evident, as De Wette himself confesses, from Num. xxxii, 19, 32, and from other passages.

"Hebron," Gen. xiii, 18, was a name probably older than Kirjath-Arba, and subsequently restored. "Dan," Gen. xiv, 14, may have been Dan-Jaan; and the Salem of Melchizedek certainly need not have been Jebusi, afterwards called Jerusalem.

It is enough that the "sanctuary" was in existence before Moses died, and therefore the phrase "shekel of the sanctuary" may have been used by him in Ex. xxx, 13, etc.

The phrase "unto this day", occurs often in Joshua in a way that seems to imply a later writer; and we have supposed that the authorship of the book of Joshua, as a whole, is considered an open question by the most orthodox critics, or at least the editorship of it in its present form. Colenso has been able to find but two suspicious cases of the use of this phrase in the Pentateuch, which he has adroitly mixed up with a heap of citations from Joshua; one of these, Deut. xxxiv, 6 was plainly inserted after Moses' death; and the other, Deut. iii, 14, may be an accidental interpolation.

But we can pursue these details no farther. We must pass to his second head, viz., the manner in which the Divine names Jehovah and Elohim are used in the Pentateuch. This, he admits, is "the pivot as it were upon which the whole argument of the Part II turns". Yet, here again, he has but reproduced and set in a popular and plausible light the processes and results of German neology, which have long been familiar to theologians and scholars. Indeed the phenomena, especially in the book of Genesis, which have led to these rationalistic theories were very early observed both by the friends and by the enemies of Christianity; — in the Clementina, by Celsus, by the Gnostics and Manichæans, by Tertullian, Jerome, and Augustine, by the Rabbins Ben Jasos, and Aben Ezra. Hobbes,

Peirerius, Spinoza, and Le Clerc (who afterwards recanted), denied the Mosaic authorship of the Pentateuch. They were refuted by Heidegger, Witsius, Carpzov, and Bishop Kidder, and, with some exceptionable admissions and adjuncts, by Spencer, Warburton and Michaelis. Vitringa and Astruc broached the *Document Hypothesis*, which was more fully developed by Eichhorn who presumed *two* original documents; Ilgen supposed three, and Gramberg, two with additions by a reviser. Vater found many more, and put forth the *Fragment Hypothesis*, in which he was opposed by Van Bohlen, and followed substantially by Vatke and others. Tuch invented the *Complement Hypothesis*, in which he was followed by Stähelin and others, and to which De Wette seems, on the whole, to have given his adhesion. This is, substantially, the theory adopted by Colenso. Hupfeld defended a similar theory under the form of three documents and a reviser. Ewald drifted from one theory to another, until he finally invented what has been called the *Crystallization Hypothesis;* in which he stands alone. On the other hand the unity and Mosaic authorship of the Pentateuch have been maintained by Ranke, Drechsler, Hävernik, Keil, and Hengstenberg. De Wette admits that these theories on the Pentateuch lead necessarily to Strauss; and Davidson (Int. to O. T. p. 613) says: " It is true that various characteristic peculiarities of diction appear in common in the Elohistic and Jehovistic sections; but surely the later may have imitated the earlier writer, or the written materials whence both drew belonged to the same times "; — thus begging, or rather surrendering, the whole question at issue. Indeed a similar minute dissection and conjectural criticism applied to the works of almost any old writer would lead to similar destructive and disintegrating results. To be convinced of this, one need only consult, a somewhat rare but very interesting literary curiosity, Bentley's edition of Milton's Paradise Lost.

The case with Genesis stands thus: Jehovah-Elohim is used in 4 chapters (ii, iii, ix, and xv); Jehovah alone in nine chapters; Elohim alone in 13 chapters; Elohim *and* Jehovah in 20 chapters; and neither in 4 chapters. But these chapters are not consecutive; the succession is as follows: first we have Elohim alone; then Jehovah-Elohim; then Jehovah *and* Elohim; then Jehovah alone; then Jehovah *and* Elohim; then Jehovah alone; then Jehovah *and* Elohim; then Jehovah alone; then Jehovah *and* Elohim; then Elohim alone; then Jehovah alone; then Jehovah *and* Elohim; then Jehovah alone; then Jehovah *and* Elohim; then Elohim alone; then

Jehovah alone; then Jehovah *and* Elohim; then Elohim alone; then Jehovah *and* Elohim; then Elohim alone. Now let one read the book and note the unity and continuity of the story (for it is simply false to say that the 2nd ch. of Genesis, e. g., "contradicts the first"), and let him say which is the more probable, that we have here a confused patchwork of divers fragments,* or merely the naturally varying usage of one and the same writer?

We believe that the only text which occasions real difficulty in this part of the discussion is Exodus vi, 3; and we believe the difficulty is removed by a fair interpretation of the words, "by my name Jehovah was I not known to them". "By my name Jehovah", i. e., in my character of Jehovah, in the full significance of what I am as Jehovah, the God of revelation, the God of redemption, the God keeping his covenant and fulfilling his promises, he that was and is and is to come. Such an interpretation seems to us infinitely more reasonable than to suppose a flat and palpable contradiction between this and the preceding history, whether both were written or compiled by one author, or whether the various parts were written by several successive authors, of whom the later must of course have known what had been stated by the former. Indeed, viewed in the simple light of historical criticism, this passage presents a far greater difficulty for Colenso than for us.

We must hasten to his third head, the confirmation of his theory of the Pentateuch from the Psalms. Here he claims some originality, and perhaps justly; but his whole argument proceeds upon a most transparent begging of the question; first in regard to the historical order of the Psalms, and secondly in regard to the inference to be drawn from it.

Having first determined what are the earlier, and what the later Psalms of David, rejecting from the earlier any in which Jehovah preponderates, and from the later any in which Elohim preponderates, as in the case, for example, of Psalms xxxiv and cxlii†—he finds that Elohim is used more frequently in the earlier Psalms, and Jehovah in the later; and hence he infers that Jehovah was only gradually coming into use in the course of David's life, assuming that when it was once in use as the recognized and appropriate name of the

---

* Would Colenso, perhaps, trace to this the etymology of the word "*mosaic*"?

† "In short, the very circumstance that these two Psalms contain the name Jehovah so often, to the absolute exclusion of Elohim, is to my own mind, after what we have already seen, a clear indication that they cannot be ranked with the Psalms . . . . . which were written at an earlier period of David's life. If written by David at all, of which there is no sign whatever, (?) they must have been written *towards the close* of his life." See page 213.

true God, the God of Israel, no pious Israelite would have failed to use it most frequently in preference to the colder and more general name, Elohim. It may be interesting to compare with Colenso's tables and results Lightfoot's chronological arrangement of some 20 Psalms which he ascribes to David, assigning them to different periods of David's life, erroneously, it may be, in some cases, yet without any bias connected with the question of the Divine names:

Ps.	El.	Je.	Ps.	El.	Je.
ix,	1	9	cv,	1	6
lvi,	9	1	cvi,	4	11
xxxiv,	0	16	lx,	5	0
clxii,	0	3	cviii,	6	1
lii,	5	0	iii,	2	6
liv,	4	1	xlii,	13	1
lvii,	7	0	xliii,	8	0
lviii,	2	1	lv,	6	2
lxviii,	31	4	iv,	1	5
cxxxii,	0	6	v,	8	5

From this it would appear that Jehovah is used quite as frequently, in comparison with Elohim, in the earlier as in the later Psalms.

In regard to the 51st Ps.,—which, by the way, Davidson declares to be post-Davidic, Ewald assigns to some time after the destruction of the temple, Olshausen to the times of the Maccabees, and Hupfeld to the time after the captivity,—Colenso discourses thus : " This Psalm, we can scarcely doubt is the genuine utterance of David's ' broken spirit' when he came to repentance after his grievous sin. In this Psalm he does not once use the name Jehovah. [We might ask how this should be at so advanced a period of David's life; but Colenso proceeds.] It would seem as if in the anguish of his soul, he had recourse to the old familiar name, Elohim, as a more *real* name, a name dear to him from old associations, one which he had used all along in his childhood and youth, and in the better days of his ripened manhood, rather than the more modern name Jehovah, of new creation ". Of course, with such a style of reasoning, the Bishop can establish any conclusion he pleases, he can have no difficulties but such as he chooses to have, and must have abandoned the orthodox interpretation simply because he *preferred* to abandon it.

Psalm lx, which does not contain Jehovah once, but Elohim five times, he earnestly refers to the 45th year of David's life, though Davidson, Ewald, Olshausen, and Hupfeld concur in ascribing it to a later period.

But his argument from Ps. lxviii he claims as especially his own, and as of paramount importance.   This Psalm contains Elohim 31 times and Jehovah or Jah 4 times.   It is, according to the ordinary view, ascribed by Colenso to David, and referred to the time of bringing up the ark to mount Zion; although Hupfeld, Ewald and Olshausen assign it to a much later date.   From the coincidence of certain passages in this Psalm with parts of the Song of Deborah it is thought that the author of one must have borrowed from the other.   But to the question, which is the original, Colenso unhesitatingly answers, the Psalm; "because", he says, "the Song is thoroughly *Jehovistic* as regards the use of the Divine name (E. 2, J. 13): and it is inconceivable that, if the word Jehovah was used so freely at *that* time, David should have used it so sparingly till a late period of his life".   This is, again, a mere begging of the question.   But he instances a particular passage as his strongest argument.   While the Song of Deborah has: "Before Jehovah the Elohim of Israel", the Psalm has: "Before Elohim, the Elohim of Israel".   "Our argument", he adds, "in short, is this: Of the two phrases, 'Elohim, the Elohim of Israel', and 'Jehovah, the Elohim of Israel', it seems certain that the former was the original expression, and that the latter was derived from it".   We must confess this seems to us far from certain; for while Jehovah is the Elohim of Israel, Jehovah is also Elohim absolutely (see 1 Kings xviii, 39), and the Psalmist only rises to a still stronger expression of poetic feeling when he declares, not that *Jehovah* is the Elohim of Israel, but that *Elohim*, the universal, absolute Elohim, is the Elohim of Israel. That the Psalmist well knew and recognized that his proper name was Jehovah, is plain from the formal and solemn announcement of it in the 4th verse.   "Sing unto God (Elohim) sing praises to his name; extol him by his name JAH and rejoice before him".   Colenso also thinks, for similar reasons, that this Psalm is older than Num. x, 35; where we have: "Arise, Jehovah, and let thine enemies be scattered"; while, in the Psalm we have: "Let Elohim arise, and let his enemies be scattered."   To which we make the same answer; and add that, perhaps the reason why Elohim is, in general, so much more used in the poetical, instead of Jehovah, which prevails in the historical compositions, may be, as suggested by Tuch, that such was the received peculiarity of the poetic style.   Indeed it is not unlikely there is some reason, more or less consciously felt by the writer, and varying in strength from a *minimum* in some cases to a *maximum* in others, why either term, Elohim or Jehovah, is used from time to time in preference to the other; though we should by no means follow Hengstenberg in his fanciful attempts to trace this reason out in all cases.

But that the ground of Colenso's general inference fails entirely is evident from the following, among other, facts: (1.) In David's *last words* (2 Sam. xxiii,) we have Elohim 3 times, Jehovah but once. (2.) In David's parting address to the people (1 Chron. xxix) we have Elohim 4 times, Jehovah-Elohim once, and Jehovah once. (3.) In David's blessing of *Jehovah* (in the same chapter) we have Elohim twice, Jehovah twice, and Jehovah and Elohim three times. (4.) In Solomon's prayer (1 Kings viii) we have Jehovah 6 times, Jehovah Elohe 6 times, and Elohim twice. Also, in the prayer of Jehoshaphat, 2 Chron. xx, — and we call especial attention to this as bearing upon the present argument, — we find Elohim four times and Jehovah but once; while in the *historical* statements of the immediate context the name Jehovah is almost exclusively employed. In 2 Chron. vi, the names occur in nearly the same proportions. But in both texts, the solemn and sublime passage " Will God (Elohim) indeed dwell on the earth ?" is to be especially observed. (5.) In Daniel's prayer, ch. ix, we have Jehovah our Elohim three times, Elohim (without Jehovah) 7 times, and Jehovah alone once; and Jehovah nowhere else in the whole book out of this chapter. And that the name Jehovah was still at that time in free familiar use is plain from the names Hananiah, and Azariah side by side with Daniel and Mishael. But had all these names ended in—*el*, it would have been no proof to the contrary, for in general, we should assign but little weight to a *negative* argument from names, as the fashion of names is known to vary quite arbitrarily from age to age. (6.) Colenso admits that Deut. was written after Numb., indeed, long after, he maintains; and yet, while in Numb. we have Elohim only 34 times and Jehovah 396 times, in Deut. we have Elohim 334 times, and Jehovah 550 times.

Colenso himself seems half aware that the ground is slipping away from under him, and makes strange contortions to preserve his position.

"We find", he says, "some *very late* Psalms in which there occurs a preponderance of the name Elohim."—" This accords also with the fact that, in the book of Ezra we have Elohim 97 times, Jehovah 37 times, and in that of Nehemiah, Elohim 74 times, Jehovah 17 times, contrary to all the data of the other historical books. It is quite possible that some of these Elohistic Psalms may be Ezra's. It would almost seem as if, after their long sojourn as captives in a strange land, when Israel no longer existed as a nation, they had begun to discon-

tinue the national Name for the Divine Being.   However, if
so, it must have soon been revived after their return from the
captivity, since we find the later prophets using the term freely again,—Haggai (J. 35, E. 3), Zechariah (J. 132, E. 12), Ma-
lachi (J. 47, E. 8)."   But what then becomes of the assumption that no pious Jew, if he knew the proper name Jehovah,
and "*if the story of the giving of that name is really true*",
could possibly have failed to use it rather than Elohim?   Does
it, then, remain "impossible" that Ezra or Nehemiah, "or any
other good man", having known that Jehovah had declared,
"This is my name forever, and this is my memorial unto all
generations", should yet have habitually used Elohim instead
of it?

Colenso might have added that, during the captivity, Ezekiel uses the name Jehovah freely, in all upwards of 400 times;
while he has Elohim some 40 times, and El Shaddai once.   A
peculiarity of Ezekiel, is, that he more frequently uses Jehovah with *Adonai prefixed;* but here we find this remarkable
phenomenon, that, in the first 12 and last 6 chapters, the use
of *Jehovah* alone as compared with *Adonai Jehovi* is as 3 to
1¾, while, in the remaining portion, it is only as 3 to 4.   Were,
then, the middle chapters written by a different author from
him who wrote the first and last chapters, or must Ezekiel have
written them at a widely different period of his life?

Colenso's *positive* theory of the authorship of the Pentateuch, at least, of the "Elohistic" portion of it, is worthy of
his own character and position.   While he conceives it incredible and impossible that Almighty God should inspire a man
to utter his law at different times in a different form of words,
as in Deut. v, for example, in comparison with Ex. xx, — he
finds no difficulty in supposing that Samuel the prophet, "a
great statesman and lawgiver, imbued from his childhood with
deep religious feelings, and having early awakened in him —
we cannot doubt, by special Divine Inspiration — the strong
conviction of the distinct Personal Presence of the living God,
— anxiously striving to convey the momentous truth with
which his own spirit was quickened, to the young men of his
school", first invented and introduced the name Jehovah, and
actually wrote, at so late a day, and out of his own head,—for
surely he could not have been "specially inspired" to invent
falsehoods, — the third and the sixth chapters of Exodus, for
the purpose of bringing this new name into general and popular use;—and all this without being chargeable with impudent
deception or pious fraud, or with dealing lightly or irreverent-
ly with sacred things, although he knew perfectly that not a

syllable he was writing about the solemn revelation of this in-communicable Divine Name had the slightest foundation in truth or fact.   And then he supposes Gad, Nathan and others of Samuel's pupils and successors, to have followed with their Jehovistic revisions, interpolations, additions and continua-tions, naïvely inserting the name Jehovah throughout the ante-cedent as well as the subsequent history ; although, if they had had the modicum of common sense and simple apprehension which even persons writing in Hebrew are ordinarily supposed to have possessed,—and that irrespective of their supernatural inspiration, — they must have known, and must have known that all their contemporaries knew, that this name Jehovah was a mere modern fiction, that it had first been invented and introduced by the prophet Samuel, and of course had been neither known nor thought of, much less used, by the patri-archs.

In assuming that he knows beforehand the ways and me-thods, degrees and conditions, according to which Almighty God must make a revelation to man, if he made one at all—in prescribing to God the course which his Divine character would require him to pursue — Colenso has had many predecessors. But to suppose that the prophet Samuel, acknowledged and lauded as a pious and holy man, could pursue such a course as that above indicated, required the Bishop of Natal, required a man who insists upon retaining a Bishopric in the English Church after he has openly denied the faith which he solemn-ly vowed to hold and preach, as a condition to his being in-vested with that sacred office.

Art. VII.—EXAMINATION OF THE LATEST DEFENCES OF DR. HICKOK'S RATIONAL PSYCHOLOGY.*

By Edwin Hall, D.D., Prof. in Auburn Theological Seminary.

The writer of the present article sees no reason why it should be necessary for him to argue over again the objections already urged against the Rational Psychology. Three able and zealous advocates of the Psychology, in six labored and extended articles, have tried what can be done in its defence ; and the reviewer is quite content to leave the public to judge, whether his objections have been in any respect invalidated by any thing that has been urged in reply. It is his own unwavering conviction that they have not. The object of the present article is to show from the further development of the scheme in the recent articles of its defenders, from the false issues which they have been driven to assume, and from the evasions and representations to which they have been induced to resort, that the objections already urged are amply vindicated, and the scheme of the Psychology demonstrated to be incapable of any proper and valid defence.

The personal reflections in which four of these replies have so remarkably abounded, the reviewer has not deemed it necessary, or becoming in him, to notice. If it be true,—as Dr. Hickok charges upon him,—that his articles make it " most pitfully and painfully manifest", that he is " utterly incompetent to enter into the meaning" of the Psychology ; that his objections are " but sorry blunders of his own ignorance", that he " manifests throughout an entire want of discernment" of important philosophical distinctions ; " that if the Psychology were too obscure" for his apprehension, " he was not bound to review it until he had intelligently studied it" ; that his review was but " the foul logic of an *Argumentum*

* [We deem it but fair that Dr. Hall should have an opportunity to reply to Dr. Hickok's and Prof. Lewis's articles in former numbers ; and with this reply, in which no new points are we believe introduced, this discussion will close in this Review. Both sides have been ably presented, and our readers are competent to form their own conclusions. The pressure upon our space, if there were no other considerations, will not admit of our continuing it.—Editors.]

ad ignorantiam and of an *Argumentum ab ignorantia*", which does not " afford sufficient inducement" to answer its objections ;—or if it be true, as Prof. Lewis elegantly affirms, that the reviewer has been but " floundering" and " muddying the waters" ;—if all these, and many other allegations of the same sort be true, the public has doubtless long ere this observed it, and it would be idle for the reviewer to attempt any reply. His only consolation must be that such matters do not at all pertain to the question in debate.

It is indeed true that the present writer does believe in matter—" *Hard Matter*"—since Prof. Lewis so pleases ; matter impenetrable ; matter, so far as human experience goes, imperishable, and in its elements unchangeable ; matter, to any power below that of the Creator, indestructible ; matter that was created by God, out of nothing ; and that, when God pleases, may cease to be. He believes in both matter and Spirit, as existences, which in their essence, properties, and phenomena, are entirely distinct and inconvertible. He does not believe with Prof. Lewis that there is no substance save spirit, nor that what is called matter is only spirit, or the activity of spirit in forceful counteragency with itself. Indeed, the faith of the present writer in the existence of " hard matter" is such that the strong expressions of Prof. Lewis concerning it are not without some ground. Says Prof. Lewis (p. 16):

" Never did the poor African seem more attached to his fetish, and more determined not to let it go, than Dr. Hall clings to this hard matter".— " Ask him what is more *real* than an *idea* dwelling in the mind of God ; what is *stronger* than the power of God which *makes that idea dwell as an outward law in space.* He shakes his head. There is nothing there still he insists, unless we have something else, which is over and above the *idea,* the *law,* and the *force.*"

Truly, he does shake his head. He does not comprehend how an *idea*, now dwelling in the mind of God, can be thrust out and made to dwell as an *outward law* [outward of the mind of God] in space. He does not suppose that an *idea* is matter, nor that a *law* is matter, nor that the *power*, which thrusts that idea out and makes it dwell in space as an *outward law*, is matter. He surely thinks that matter must be " something else."

In some other representations Prof. Lewis is less accurate. Thus, p. 2, he says :

" How do we positively know that there is a real outside world ? Why, we smell it, Dr. Hall maintains ; we take cognizance of it in the spiritual olfactory; and all reasoning about it is superfluous, besides being a treasonable denial of something better and more religious. Reason and reasoning will make Pantheists, but sense is more orthodox."

Did Prof. Lewis mean to have this representation believed? " *Why, we know it by the smell, Dr. Hall maintains.*" Yet Dr. Hall expressly maintained the contrary, expressly designating the sense of smell as one which does *not* give immediate cognition of an outward material thing. And Prof. Lewis says he is not making a "caricature", but "stating Dr. Hall's position"! Nor is it true that Dr. Hall at any time decried either reason or reasoning. On the contrary he has uniformly maintained the proper functions of reason, and the validity of legitimate reasoning. He only showed that certain alleged demonstrations of reason were neither reason nor reasoning, but that in such matters reason was out of her sphere.

Of a similar character are the repeated representations of Prof. Lewis with regard to the alleged doctrine of " contact" between mind and matter. He speaks of " this language of Dr. Hall"—" this talk of soul *touching* matter" (p. 9.). He speaks of " this materialising theory of contact of which Dr. Hall is so fond", and describes it as " the dogma of *soul-contact*"—" a *touching*, (we use the language of the school) an ultimate *touching by the soul* of those primary qualities." (p. 5.). These representations Prof. Lewis repeats over and over again, dwells long upon them, and vehemently and eloquently declares the irreligious and atheistic consequences necessarily flowing from such theories and dogmas. Yet it is wholly untrue, and directly contrary to the truth in the case, that Dr. Hall any where intimates or advocates any such theory. On the contrary he expressly discarded all theories of the kind; maintaining that " *We can never tell how, at last, the connection is made between extended matter and unextended and immaterial mind.*"—"*No man can explain it. No man can conceive how any thing can be done in the premises.*" He went further, and showed that *sensation*, as well as cognition, is utterly inexplicable; and that no theory either of " *contact, combination,* or of *intercommunication,* could give the required explanation; but that all attempts, on any theory, had ended only in absurdity. And this impossibility of giving any explanation either of sensation or of cognition, he urged as fatal to Dr. Hickok's scheme of giving an *à priori* explanation of " All Intelligence."

We proceed to another representation. The reviewer had noticed how Edwards, in his youth, beginning with the assumption that, in sense, the mind has no conscious knowledge, save only of what is within, had come to the logical conclusion that there is no matter, and that the world exists only in idea : the reviewer had also noticed, that Newton on the same basis, had supposed that matter might be accounted for without the supposition of any substance, but by supposing that God simply renders a portion of space impenetrable, and gives it mobility, with other properties supposed to belong to matter.   Thereupon Prof. Lewis exultingly claims Edwards and Newton as "Spiritual Realists," holding that nothing is real but spirit ; that there is no matter, but only spaces filled with spiritual force,—the activity or "doing" of Spirit : and he thus charges Dr. Hall with perverting the words of Newton :

"All that he [Newton] could see in this matter, and all that he could say about matter, was this ; that "*God by his power renders a certain portion of space impenetrable to another portion of space rendered likewise impenetrable.*"   Thus far the sentence gives a true representation of Newton's views.   But Dr. Hall, as usual, must put in something of his own, and make nonsense of it.   *He adds, immediately after Newton's statement* the words "*both spaces continuing absolutely void as before*".   He has a "void", and not only a void, but an "absolute void" foisted upon Newton, who of all men abhorred a vacuum".—"In putting these words 'both spaces continuing absolutely void' into *Newton's terse definition*, Dr. Hall makes him not only contradict himself, but talk inconceivable nonsense" (p. 16.)

These charges are very definite, and, if true, of a very grave character.   Dr. Hall has "added—to Newton's Statement"—"put words into Newton's terse definition" and so "foisted upon Newton" a meaning which Newton "abhorred", and "made him talk inconceivable nonsense".   And this proceeding of Dr. Hall is characteristic, he has done "it" as "usual".

The public seeing these allegations under Prof. Lewis's own hand, and observing with what earnestness he reiterates them, and how long he rings the changes upon them, with such variety of holy horror and eloquent invective, would very naturally suppose them to be true.   Unless Prof. Lewis were to be regarded as entirely unworthy of confidence, it would necessarily be concluded that he had referred to the words of Newton in question, and actually found that Dr. Hall had been guilty of doing what is here charged upon him.   Yet Prof. Lewis has found no such thing.   The charges are in every respect and wholly untrue, without the slightest shadow of any ground for making them.   The words which Prof. Lewis affirms to be "Newton's Statement" and to which he pays an especial compliment as "a true representation of Newton's view", are not the words of Newton at all, but Dr. Hall's own statement of Newton's conjecture : which statement Dr. Hall is glad to find Prof. Lewis so highly approves, not only as "a true representation of Newton's view", but as a "definition" so "terse" as to be not unfitly attributed to Newton himself.

The words of Newton were referred to in Wight's Hamilton (p. 303,) and are but a statement, from memory, by *M. Coste*,—the friend of Locke and Newton—, of a *conjecture* of Newton. "The following, said *M. Coste*, is the way in which he [Newton] explained his thought :

"We may be enabled, (he said,) to form some rude conception of the creation of matter, if we suppose that God by his power *prevents the entrance of any thing into pure space ;* which is of its nature penetrable, eternal, necessary, infinite ; for from henceforward, this portion of space would be endowed with impenetrability, one of the essential qualities of matter ; and as pure space is absolutely uniform, we have only to suppose that God communicated the same impenetrability to another portion of space, and we should obtain, in a certain sort, another quality which is also essential to it."

It will be seen from this, that the charges of Prof. Lewis are wholly gratuitous and untrue, without the slightest foundation of any kind. It will be seen moreover, that Dr. Hall had accurately stated Newton's supposition, and that Prof. Lewis has "foisted upon Newton", a notion to which the words in question make no allusion, and which there is no evidence that Newton ever held :—viz., the notion that God rendered the space impenetrable by so filling it with his own Spiritual activity in forceful counteragency with itself, as to become perceptible to our senses. The conjecture of Newton was, that "God, by his power *prevents the entrance* of any thing into *pure space*". But "pure space" is void space ; and Newton's conception was, of the space *continuing pure*, while God *prevents the entrance of any thing into it*. Dr. Hall, therefore accurately stated the idea of Newton, while Prof. Lewis it is who has foisted upon Newton a notion to which, for aught that appears, Newton was an entire stranger.

The evidence on which Prof. Lewis relies to prove that Newton held the space to be so filled with a Spiritual counteragency as to be impenetrable, is contained solely in the words which he cites as "Newton's Statement" : viz., that "God, by his power renders a certain portion of space impenetrable, etc". "This", says Prof. Lewis, was "all that Newton could *see* in this matter" and "all that he could *say* about matter", and all that he could *see* in matter, or rather *think* in matter". (p. 147.)   Prof. Lewis then confesses that he has seen nothing in Newton's writings, utterances, or opinions, beyond what is expressed in these words.   Nay, he affirms that they are " a true representation of Newton's view", and all that Newton could " see", or " say" or " think" in "matter", or " about the matter".   Well, then, Prof. Lewis confesses that these words contain all the evidence in the case, that Newton, or whoever was their author, held any such view as he attributes to Newton—viz., that there is no matter, save space rendered impenetrable by filling it with a spiritual activity in counter-agency.   Then Prof. Lewis must necessarily confess further, that he has " foisted upon Newton" sentiments which New-ton never expressed, and which there is no evidence that New-ton ever held : for the words in question are not the words of Newton, but of Dr. Hall ; and Prof. Lewis has foisted upon them a meaning which Dr. Hall never conceived as belonging to them, and which he utterly abhors.

That Edwards held no such view, is evident from the fact that he discards, at last, the idea of any perception of any outward force or resistance, and concludes that matter and worlds and resistances have no existence save in idea ; creation consisting simply in God's *raising up such ideas* in finite minds.   Beginning with the assumption that we directly *cognize* nothing save what is within, he for a moment supposed the perception of an *outward resistance.*   Yet it was but a moment before he perceived that this conclusion was entirely illogical, and he at once abandoned it.   A moment's reflection showed him that the principle *that we immediately cognize only what is within, is as conclusive against an outward force or resistance, as against an outward substance :*   he in one breath changed his previous conclusion, and decided that we cognize not even an outward resistance, but only our own idea.   And to this conclusion Dr. Hickok and Prof. Lewis must come at last, or else renounce their notion, that in sense we cognize only what is within.   " *Resistance*" said Edwards, " *is but the mode of an idea*".   " How is there resistance, ex-cept it be *in some mind* "?   " The material universe *exists no where but in mind* ".   "*Place* itself is mental : and *within* and *without* are mere mental conceptions".—" The material uni-verse is absolutely dependent on the conception of the mind for its existence (Carvill's Ed. Vol. i. p. 670–1).   Edwards, therefore, utterly rejected the notion which Prof. Lewis at-tributes to him.

Prof. Lewis says that " Dr. Hall intimates that Edwards

could not see the tendency of his own reasoning". Dr. Hall certainly gave no such intimation, but on the contrary maintained that Edwards *did* see the tendency of his reasoning, and that he carried it out truly to its legitimate consequences. Even in his youth, before Kant was born, Edwards, assuming the principles afterwards assumed by Kant, and now assumed by Dr. Hickok and Prof. Lewis, carried them out, in a few brief and simple steps of the soundest logic, to nearly all the strange conclusions reached with so much labor and difficulty by three generations of German philosophers. Prof. Lewis is delighted with his fancied discovery that he has Edwards on his side in the results which he has already reached. It may do him good to see what further conclusions Edwards reached beyond. Following out the principle for which Prof. Lewis now does battle so valiantly, Edwards concluded that "*Bodies have neither substance nor property*" (p. 725.) "*Spirits are the only proper substance*" (p. 708.) "*All that is real is the First Being.*" It may be possible by subjective thought, "*from the present state of the world—to form a perfect idea of all its past changes*". "*Nothing is something*" and "*Space is God*" (p. 670.) Only one step further has been reached by the German philosophy, and that is that "*Seyn—Nichts*,"— "*Being is Nothing*," all is resolved into "a marvellous dream, without a life to dream of, and without a mind to dream". Prof. Lewis is already well advanced in this "path which philosophy has for so many ages been travelling": but go on Prof. Lewis, the logical end of your career is not yet.

There can be no doubt that Prof. Lewis says truly, when he says "There was as much light at Northampton as there is now in the chair of Theology at Auburn". Doubtless there was, and a great deal more. At Auburn, scarcely any uninspired man is held as at all comparable to Edwards. What then? Must we therefore receive these speculations as true? They form no part of the "light" of Edwards at Northampton. Not the slightest trace of them is found in any thing that he wrote after he came to years of maturity. There is no reason to suppose that he ever carried those speculations to Northampton. They were written when he was in college, a boy not seventeen years old. When he became a man, he seems wholly to have put away such childish things. And now, Prof. Lewis, having chanced to become partially informed of such speculations of Edwards, carries them in formal procession, with great proclamation and parade, challenging any one who "dares,"—"if it pleases him, to make light of things which called out the deepest thoughts of Edwards, or of

30

Newton." (p. 40.) Yet not the slightest evidence appears to show that either of them held the notion that Prof. Lewis attributes to them, viz. of space rendered impenetrable by being filled with spiritual acts in forceful counteragency.

Prof. Lewis himself for a moment supposes the possibility of preventing the entrance of any thing into a space, by another method, viz "Simply by the activity of *will*". The vehemence with which he at first maintains this position, and the equal vehemence with which he the moment after spurns it and abandons it, is very amusing. Hear him.

"Will Dr. Hall say that God cannot *simply by the activity of his will*, so make a certain space affected that he, Dr. Hall, cannot enter it without being driven back? Such a denial would surely look like running upon the thick bosses of the Almighty's buckler".

If it will calm the agitation of Prof. Lewis, in view of so great anticipated temerity on the part of Dr. Hall, let him quiet himself with the assurance that Dr. Hall feels no disposition to make such a denial, nor is he at all tempted, in that way, to rush upon the thick bosses of the Almighty's buckler. He assents to the declaration of Prof. Lewis, that "God's very *command* is power". He accepts cordially the supposition of Newton, that God may "by his power prevent the entrance of any thing into pure space". But he does not suppose that that "*command*" or "*will*" are obliged to put themselves into a forceful counteragency, and to fill the space with a spiritual —physically—resisting force, perceptible to the senses, in order to prevent the entrance of any thing into that space. Nor does he suppose that to prevent the entrance of any thing by *command* or by *will*, is necessarily the same thing as to fill it with a physically resisting force, composed of the Divine Spirit, or activity, in forceful counteragency with itself. Prof. Lewis indeed affirms the last to be "the same thing" with the first. But where did he learn that God has no other *power* of *command*, or method of executing his *will*, in such a case,— than by such a physical counteragency of his own spirit, making itself perceptible to our senses? How came Prof. Lewis to know so much about the physical force of such counteragency of the essence or the activity of the Godhead in forceful antagonism with itself? Where was he when God laid the foundations of the earth, that he should be able thus authoritatively to declare the method of doing it, and to see that no other method was possible to the Creator! And why will not Prof. Lewis explain to us what it is for the essence, or the activity, or the Spiritual acts, of such a Spirit, to come into such counteragency; and how he knows that such spiritual counter-agency becomes a space-filling force perceptible to the senses?

And here we have a little matter to settle with both Prof. Lewis and Dr. Hickok, in which, unable to answer, as it seems to us, they have evaded the true question, and substituted another issue entirely different from the question in debate. Dr. Hickok had professed to see that matter is necessarily produced by the acts of a Spiritual being in forceful counteragency with each other: and that, the counteragency continuing, the impenetrable substance so formed must necessarily grow into a world with precisely all the cosmical arrangements of this world of ours. This is the corner-stone of his philosophy. If this is not seen by the reason to be an eternal principle and necessary truth, then by the very conditions of the Rational Psychology, man has no faculty of reason, and can never know that there is an outward world or God, or any thing. Dr. Hickok's friend and pupil in the Princeton Review, p. 99. also fully maintains this. He says, " Matter may thus be the product of Spirit and cognizable by it," and thus this theory " *removes the gulf, in other systems impassable*, between the Creator and the creature, the knowing mind and the material objects of knowledge". The claim is thus very modestly made that without the reception of this all-important principle of Dr. Hickok's philosophy, the " gulf" is " impassable" between man and the knowledge of God, or of an outer world! Dr. Hickok expressly declares, that the prevalent philosophy of the Christian world can lead only to Pantheism; that his philosophy is the only remedy, and that without our reception of it, our faith in the Christian creed can be only " an unreasoning credulity". The principle in question is therefore the

" Sole prop and pillar of a sinking world".

Perhaps the reviewer was not conscious of the tremendous consequences of weakening the foundation of that pillar, when he ventured to suggest that " nothing is hazarded in affirming that Dr. Hickok has no conception of any possible meaning in what he affirms " of the acts of a Spirit in forceful counteragency with each other. To test the possibility of forming any conception of what this means, the reviewer made three suppositions which he regarded as exhaustive; no further supposition remaining possible on the subject; while each of these is palpably absurd.

(1) " Is it the activity of intelligence or thought pressing physically against a similar activity "?

(2) " Is it the essence of Spirit pressing physically against a similar essence ? "

(3) " What are these *'acts'* ?   Are they entities distinct from the spirit itself in action ?   If so, then Dr. Hickok should tell us how to create a spiritual *act*, and to throw it off as a distinct entity, and to put it into that " *push and pull* " with another act, which constitutes "*counteraction, complex action, and reaction*", (Cosmology p. 93) and so creates an " impenetrable substance."

To these inquiries Prof. Lewis replies thus :

" But Dr. Hall says, Nothing is hazarded in affirming that Dr. Hickok has no conception of any possible meaning in what he affirms about *spiritual activity*.   The ground of this rather hazardous assertion is, that neither he, Dr. Hall, as he seems to confess, nor any other man, as he rather hazardously implies, can conceive of *spiritual activity*, except as thought or intelligence ; and he asks, ' Is it the activity of intelligence or thought pressing physically against another similar activity."

It will be seen that this statement of Prof. Lewis is in all essential respects entirely diverse from the truth in the case. The question was not about *spiritual activity*, as Prof. Lewis represents, but about a Spiritual activity *in physical and forceful counteragency against another similar activity*.   Prof. Lewis has entirely misrepresented the reviewer's objection as to its matter, its ground, and its form.   He has entirely changed the issue, and wholly evaded the question in debate. Would he have done this had he seen any possibility of answering the question truly and fairly ?   But he is not content without adding another evasion.   He argues at length that " Dr. Hall is answered by a consideration of the human spirit" —" When a man lifts or propels a hundred pounds, it is ultimately by the soul he does it,"—" and that too not simply by the soul as determining will, using the outward means, but as *potentia potens*, or spiritually indwelling force, that is a really spiritual thing."

Doubtless the spirit originates or sets in motion all the force which man or beast is capable of exerting.   We need not stop to debate whether it be " *potentia potens* ", not by " using the outward means ", but by the indwelling force of spirit itself, or whether it be in some other way beyond our comprehension. Certainly, on the theory which Prof. Lewis declares, the spirit of man must have far less force than that of an ox or an ass : while in man and beast, the force is ever proportioned to the bulk and physical condition of the animal.   Sickness or age may reduce it in the strongest man to the feebleness of a child.

Be all this as it may, it is nothing at all to the question of the spiritual acts of a pure spirit *in forceful counteragency with each other:* but a simple evasion.

And now we have a similar account to settle with Dr. Hickok on the same question. In all his three replies he makes no answer to the objection contained in these inquiries. Twice expressly challenged, that he himself has no conception of any possible meaning in what he affirms in this matter, he is silent. If neither he nor any other man can form a rational conception of what such counteragency can possibly be, then neither he nor any other man can see it, as a necessary truth, that the result must be an impenetrable substance. Dr. Hickok demands that we receive it as a necessary truth without reasoning, or explanation. But a necessary truth, — a principle of rational insight, — is a truth which bears with it its own irresistible evidence to the reason of all men. If this were a necessary truth, all men would see it as clearly as Dr. Hickok: none could fail to see it: none could doubt it. Dr. Hickok indeed claims, that one in the habit of thinking, can see deeper than others. Prof. Lewis intimates the same. But while practised mathematicians and practised thinkers may make a wider application of necessary truths, they have no clearer apprehension of axioms and necessary truths themselves than the veriest child. No man sees the principle in question to be a necessary truth. We challenge Dr. Hickok, that he does not see it. Twice have we challenged him, that so far from seeing that spiritual activities in forceful counteragency necessarily produce an impenetrable substance he has no conception of any possible meaning in what he affirms of such spiritual counteragency; and consequently can have no rational insight of its necessary results. Under the strongest inducement to explain it, and to show that another conception is possible besides the three which we have set forth as exhaustive on the subject, he is silent. His whole system is at stake. His whole credit as a philosopher centres here. If such result of a spiritual counteragency be not a necessary truth, then his whole Psychology and his whole Cosmology tumble into ruins. On his own principles, if this matter of rational insight fails, then man can never know an outward world, or God, or any thing; but the skeptic remains with his "logical right to doubt whether matter or mind has any existence,".

We are now authorized to repeat the challenge with double emphasis; that Dr. Hickok has no conception of any possible meaning in what he affirms concerning spiritual counteragency; since in his last article, with the question fully before him, and endeavoring to parry its force, he has not met it, but has changed the issue, and taken refuge in a palpable evasion; a proceeding which of itself is a confession of defeat and over-throw in a point decisive of the destiny of his whole philosophy. Pressed by the objection that the supposed " acts " or " activity " of a spirit, in the supposed counteraction, can be nothing save the spirit itself in action, forcefully impinging against itself, and that on this scheme " the Creator himself in coun-teragency with himself, is himself the world he makes ", and that " so we end in pantheism," Dr. Hickok, p. 212, thus spe-cifically replies to this specific objection :

" This charge [Pantheism] is sustained by affirming that it [the Psychol-ogy] holds God to be the immediate author and upholder of the forces which compose matter, and thus makes the forces to be God : and also that it teaches matter to be the necessary product of the creating Deity ".

" In reference to this last charge, it is admitted that the philosophy, both of the Psychology and of the Cosmology, holds that matter is an immediate product from God, and also that without his immediate support it would cease to exist."—" Instead of an objection, it is the necessary postulate of a Theistic philosophy that it should teach matter to have immediately ori-ginated from God, and perpetually to be sustained by God. The Bible doc-trine of the Logos-creation is wholly consistent with this, for the Logos-Creator was with God, and was God from the beginning."

That matter was *created* immediately by God, and is per-petually upheld by God, is indeed the teaching of the Bible, and " the necessary postulate of a Theistic philosophy ". Un-less in the phrases " immediate product from God" and " imme-diately originated *from* God ", there is wrapped up a reserved meaning, like that which Prof. Lewis openly avows, viz. that matter and worlds were not " *created* " of nothing, but only "*formed* " out of " ante-mundane " and "unseen things;"— " *evolved* " out of the act or essence of the Logos, " the Great form of God," and so are not " things" but " *doings*" " *events*" " all of them from the floating mote to the rolling world "; [" *Hard Matter*", *p.* 38],— the " doing " of a spirit,—with no reality or substance distinct from spirit :—if no such meaning as this is covered up by the phrases in question, then this statement of Dr. Hickok contains nothing different from the necessary postulate of a Theistic philosophy, or from the state-ments of the Bible.

And did Dr. Hickok really suppose, that this was the ground, or any thing like the ground, on which his scheme was charged as Pantheistic ? That charge was specifically and distinctly made *as the logical result of the scheme of the supposed spirit-ual counteragency, and on no other ground.* Did Dr. Hickok

wish to make his readers understand that his scheme was
charged as Pantheistic, simply on the ground that it teaches
the Bible doctrine, and the necessary postulate of a Theistic
philosophy, viz. that God directly created and upholds the
world? One thing is clear, that Dr. Hickok has not met the
question at all, but has simply evaded it, and that, under the
strongest inducement to meet it fairly, had he seen it possible.
Are we not now authorized to consider our challenge as finally
settled, — that Dr. Hickok has no conception of any possible
meaning in what he affirms of the alleged spiritual counteragency; and consequently, that he cannot see it to be a necessary truth, that such counteragency must produce an impenetrable substance? This vital point in his philosophy failing,
the whole scheme tumbles into hopeless ruin.

Nor did the reviewer affirm,—as Dr. Hickok declares in the
extract given,—that the Psychology "*also teaches matter to be
the necessary product of the creating Deity*". The reviewer
affirmed nothing of the kind, but something far worse, viz:
that the scheme required no Deity, and left no evidence of the
existence of a Deity in the things that are made: since the
scheme required neither wisdom, nor knowledge, nor thought,
nor design, nor will, nor consciousness, in the Creator; but
only an antagonism of force; whose results must be the same
whether the Creator had any thought, or will, or consciousness,
or not.

Dr. Hickok's method is as follows: He first alleges, as the
ground of the necessity for his philosophy, such a contradiction
between reason and consciousness, as, in the existing state of
all philosophy, destroys all possibility of knowledge of an outer
world. This contradiction Dr. Hickok does not state,—as has
been affirmed — as " belonging solely to the Skeptic", but
states it *originally*, in his *own person*, in his *own behalf*, and
merely brings in the *admission* of the skeptic to corroborate
his own statement: and this, whoever takes pains to turn to
the passages in his Psychology, will find to be exactly the truth
in the case. In the present state of philosophy, then, he assumes that we know no world; nor whether experience is possible, nor whether there is, or can be any faculty of reason.
He doubts all, and undertakes to demonstrate all. But to do
this, he takes nothing from facts, since we know not that there
are any facts, or that we could know them if there were. Unless
we can *transcend* all experience, the dispute between reason and
consciousness he declares to be a "drawn battle", which can
never be ended. Using the unfound and perhaps impossible
reason to tell *à priori* all that sense and understanding can be

made to do, he comes at last to find the Reason. This he determines to be a *comprehending* agency, and assumes that if reason be possible, it must be able to comprehend the universe : and that to comprehend the universe, it must be able to tell *à priori* how it must *begin*, and what must be its *end*. But such comprehension he declares to be impossible without the compass of an Absolute. He then undertakes *à priori*, as before worlds were made, to find the Absolute, as an *à priori* position for finding the reason. Here to comprehend how the universe must *begin*, he forms the " reason conception " of two forces in counteragency—tantamount to " *the simple force of gravity* ": and professes to see *à priori* that such counteragency, or gravity, must necessarily produce an impenetrable substance: which, the counteragency continuing, must necessarily grow into just such a world as ours. So far, he supposes no Absolute, and requires no wisdom, or knowledge, or consciousness, or will, but only forces in counteragency ; and he sees by " an eternal and unmade principle " which " conditions all power, and is itself conditioned by no power," that such must be the result of such counteragency, and can be the result of nothing else.

Now to account for the force, Dr. Hickok supposes a Spirit, the Absolute : who, of thought and design, puts his activities into counteraction. But what sort of Absolute ? He can use no wisdom, nor design, in ordering the cosmical arrangements of the universe. If he puts his acts into counteragency, just such a world is made, and he cannot help it. Dr. Hickok could have told him all about it *à priori*. He needs no thought, or knowledge, or wisdom, or will, or consciousness ; for if his acts come into counteragency by *chance*, or by *necessity*, or while he is *unconscious*, the result is necessarily the same. The created universe on this scheme, can show forth the glory of no Creator, save one, who, for aught that appears, might be one destitute of thought or of consciousness.

Such was the objection of the reviewer. How entirely different from Dr. Hickok's representation, that it affirmed that the Psychology " also teaches matter to be the necessary product of the creating Deity " ! The scheme demands no Deity, and furnishes no evidence of one. It shows how the world can *begin* with no exercise of any functions of Deity, save of a blind, unconscious force. What else was to be expected of a philosophy, which, under pretence that existing worlds employ only our lower faculties, and can therefore never lead to the knowledge of God, throws away these worlds through which, God himself declares, his " Eternal power and Godhead " are " clearly seen ", and then attempts to ascend to " the Absolute "

by a " reason-conception ",—such as man can form,—of the necessary process by which God must create matter if at all; and
to tell, *à priori*, what sort of worlds such a counteragency of
spiritual acts must necessarily produce!

Prof. Lewis complains bitterly of the reviewer for getting up
" such an uproar about pantheism,—that bugbear word "; and
though he " would not be uncharitable," he can account for
the reviewer's proceeding, only by supposing that the reviewer
is intent on getting up an " unreasoning *odium theologicum* "
against Dr. Hickok!   Dr. Hickok may charge the whole
Christian world with entertaining a philosophy which can end
only in pantheism : he may affirm that "*All theology without
philosophy is a credulous superstition.*"   (Cosmology, p. 21):
he may set forth his own philosophy as the only relief from
atheism or pantheism, and declare that, without our receiving
it, our reception of the Christian creed is an " unreasoning credulity ": but if one ventures to examine that philosophy, and to
show whereunto its principles tend, Prof. Lewis regards it as
a personal outrage, a desire to raise an " *odium theologicum* ",
" against one, who though deeply philosophical, is perhaps the
least controversial—amid all the writers of the land " !   Must
there, then, be no controversy with any speculations which Dr.
Hickok may set forth ?   When he comes with such a boon to
the Christian world, has the Christian world no duty or prerogative in the case, save quietly to renounce its philosophy, lay
its hand upon its mouth, and answer not again ?

But if the objection of Prof. Lewis regards only the " uproar
about pantheism ", then we turn to the developments of the
scheme under the hand of Prof. Lewis himself, to show that
our anticipations were just, and that sooner than we expected,
the scheme has borne its fruits.

Prof. Lewis resolves all being into spirit and the doings of
spirit.   " Hard Matter ", is, with him, " an inconceivable conception ", an " idealess idea ".   (p. 6)   " It is no thing for the
sense of any sentiency; it is no thing for the reason.   To us
therefore it is *nulla res*, not a *res*, it is *unreal*, it is nothing "
(p. 22)   What is it then ?   Nothing but the " doing " of a spirit :
and what can this be, save *a spirit in the act of doing, with no
substance or thing besides himself ?*   " They are not standing
things, but *doings* all of them, doings of invisible powers.   They
are all *events* from the floating mote to the rolling world ".
(p. 38)   " The real things that stand, are *forces, ideas, laws.*"
The " *forces*, as plural, having diversity before creation ", and
the " *ideas*", (he says,) " together form the *unseen things*, from
which, the Apostle says, were made the things that are seen ".

To get this meaning out of the apostle, and to avoid the common understanding of the passage, as teaching that the worlds were made, not out of "*ante mundane*" materials, but out of nothing,—Prof. Lewis finds it necessary to alter our received text of the Scripture from μὴ ἐκ to ἐκ μὴ—φαινομένων: which he attempts to justify by the authority of some ancient translations. These "forces, ideas, and laws," he says "constitute the only real things that stand". What were these antemundane forces, "having diversity"? Were they *entities* distinct from God, so that there were *two* ante-mundane subsistences, God and his force or power? Or was there but one, the *Powerful God?* And was the "*idea*" an entity distinct from God, or was not all comprised in one,—*God thinking?* Was the "*law*" a separate entity, making two subsistences, or was all included in one,—*God willing?* Indeed, on the plan of Prof. Lewis, can there be any matter or world, save *God himself in act*, according to a certain *idea* and *law*, which are his own thought and will? The Creator himself in act thus constitutes the world he makes: the Creator himself constituted "the unseen things" out of which he made the worlds.

But Prof. Lewis does not leave us to come to this conclusion simply by logical inference, however direct and inevitable. He avows it; quotes scripture to prove it; and doubly proves it by two mathematical formulas. First, he proves it by scripture, thus:

"Ah, but the pantheism!"—"This force you talk of is God's force, and so there is not matter aside from God." [How clearly Prof. Lewis anticipates the logical conclusion of his scheme!] "We are not careful to answer Dr. Hall in this matter. By the help of scripture we cut the Gordian knot. The Bible says, "God *is* all and *in* all.'"

Where does the bible say that, in the sense intended? The passage in which are found the expressions nearest to those cited by Prof. Lewis, and the one doubtless to which he refers, is Col. 3 : 11, "Where there is neither Greek nor Jew, circumcision nor uncircumcision, Barbarian, Scythian, bond nor free, but *Christ is all and in all.*" What has this to do with proving that there is no matter nor mundane world save God?

Secondly he proves it mathematically, thus:

"Dr. Hall no more escape the conclusion of pantheism than others. He is too good a theist to maintain that his matter, be it ever so hard, could remain one moment without the imminent power of God"—"Take away then, this divine power from the space where, and the time when, this hard matter is, and immediately there is nothing left. It would seem therefore like an axiom of the mathematics, that there could have been nothing there before, besides that which is taken away, and that is *Divine, that is God.*"

So Prof. Lewis proves that the hard matter of the world is God! We do not receive such mathematics. We suppose that God may create a veritable material world, which is not himself nor spirit; that he may uphold it; and that when he withdraws his power, that world will cease to be; yet do we not regard this as proving that there can be no material world that is not God!

But to make his conclusion firm and good, Prof. Lewis gives a second mathematical demonstration: or rather an argument which seems a compound of the *argumentum ad hominem* and of mathematics, (p. 27).

> " Dr. Hall believes in an anti-mundane state when God was all. Let us repeat to him the question given a little way back: Has God ceased to be all? Then the all is more than it was, or God has become less. In either case he is comparatively finite. Now where would Dr. Hall stand, in answer *to such a perfectly clear mathematical statement?* Why, with his back to the wall, crying out Mystery, Mystery, O the depths!"—" O vain boasting reason! strive for the faith once delivered to the saints!"—" Beware lest any man spoil you with philosophy and vain deceit."

Prof. Lewis doubtless believes his own reasoning, and thinks he has mathematically, and doubly, demonstrated the impossibility that there should be either matter or worlds besides God; and that he has also proved the same from the scriptures. If he may not believe mathematical demonstration, or the word of God, what may he believe? We are loth to receive this witness of himself: we hope he may yet see some way out of this philosophical quagmire, and that, without the necessity of denying the authority of scripture or of mathematical demonstration. *As he stands at present, is he not a pantheist?* Let us call Dr. Hickok and ask him: Dr. Hickok —as Prof. Lewis now stands, is he not a Pantheist? Dr. Hickok answers; (*Cosmology, p.* 21) " *If the universe be absorbed in the Deity, it is Pantheism.*" Call another expert, (*in Krauth's Vocabulary of Philosophy*). He answers, " Pantheism supposes God and nature, or God and the whole universe, to be one and the same substance—one universal being;" Call another expert (Ibid. *citing Lacoudre, Inst. Philosoph.*) " *Pantheistae, qui contendunt unicam esse substantiam, cujus partes sunt omnia entia quae existunt.*" So Rev. Dr. James Murdock, in his work on " The Modern Philosophy," p. 185, (*citing Krug's Philosoph. Lexikon ; art. Pantheismus*") says " They expressly deny that God created or produced the world *out of nothing,* or that he gave existence to beings and things the substance or matter of which had no previous existence: they say he created or brought forth the world *from himself*"

——" thus constituting an absolute unity, as to essence or substance".

The case of Prof. Lewis, then, as represented by himself, furnishes ample evidence that the anticipations of the reviewer with regard to the tendency of Dr. Hickok's scheme, were eminently correct. Sooner than he anticipated that scheme has borne its fruits.

Prof. Lewis is, however, entirely mistaken in supposing that in view of these mathematical demonstrations, Dr. Hall must " stand with his back to the wall, crying out Mystery, Mystery, O the depths"! Dr. Hall sees neither mystery, nor mathematics, nor depths, nor reason, nor common sense, in such demonstrations. Nor is he disposed to stand with his back to the wall over such reasoning, unless it be in pity and in sorrow, that an aged man, a Christian, and a scholar, should allow himself to be so far carried away by so shallow a sophistry, as, in his old age, to avow the impossibility of believing in any other system save one which makes God and the substance of the world identical. The whole force of the sophistry lies in giving to the words " all" and " infinite" two senses, and then arguing concerning them as though each had only one exact mathematical meaning. The Christian world has long believed, that God created the world, and that, both before and after creation, God is equally infinite ; nor have they seen any mathematical or other difficulty in such a belief. If now Prof. Lewis believed the rational soul of man to be created and not eternal, then each of these arguments would prove with equal validity, the godhead of every human soul ; as it would also of the spirit of every beast. For take away the Divine power, and they cease to be. The conclusion of Prof. Lewis's argument, then, is, that there was nothing there before save what was taken away, so that the human soul or the spirit of the beast, was " Divine, *was God.*" So also of his other mathematical argument : each human soul, and the spirit of each beast, either makes the sum of existence more, or God less, so that in either case he is less than infinite, if what is created is aught else than God.

But Prof. Lewis holds that the rational part of man was not created, but partakes of the infinite and the eternal ; that it comes " from its preëxistent sphere", " truly divine", and furnished with " divine " and " eternal ideas ": that man " sees ideas and forms in nature, and (αναγινωσκει) reads them", ——" knows them *again*,"——" *remembers* them as thoughts of God given in his image", (p. 26); that whatever truly *is*, *is* forever. Man has in him the Eternal, therefore man *is*, and *is* forever.   The world is but a manifestation—a manifestation of the eternal ; and therefore that which it manifests, and that alone truly *is*" (p. 41).

If, in these respects, man is eternal and divine, then God is not his Creator, but either man is part of the Godhead, or there is another being and intelligence that is eternal and self-existent besides God.   Here is surely a basis for that principle of Moral Philosophy, which gives to man, as a *person*, an absolute *autonomy ;* he is bound to worship and serve God, not—as our Catechism says—" Because he is God and our Father", but only from what man owes to his own spirit-worthiness.

It is now thirty years, and more, since this philosophy reached its logical culmination in this country.   Rev. Dr. Murdock, in his *Sketches of Modern Philosophy, especially among the Germans*", published in 1842, shows (from the Dial, and other authentic documents) that " American transcendentalism " had already reached the conclusion, that since God is all, and our souls portions of God, whatever we do, God does : there can be no sin, but only a progressive development ; and our duty is "to foster the Divinity within",— " Holding, as they do, but one essence of all things, which essence is God, Pantheists must deny the existence of essential evil.   All evil is negative—it is imperfection, non-growth". (p. 177, and onwards.)

It is now time that we consider the importance which Prof. Lewis attaches to the distinction between the *being* and the *becoming*, " on a religious ground ".   He says, p. 36,

> " The highest aim of religion is to draw men to the contemplation of true being ; to get them, if possible, above the sense, the temporal, and the flowing, to the unseen and the eternal ".

He regards it as injurious to religion to assert that " Any thing which *is*, for the present, just as truly is, as that which is for eternity ".   He regards it as,

> " a truth sure as any thing in the mathematics, that all things are flowing without intermission.   Matter is a stream.   There is no rest, there can be no rest in the natural "—" There is the moon-beam playing on the rippled waters.   For a moment it occupies space,"—" It is like all other matter, a *doing*, a doing in space ; at least, take away the doing, and nothing else, either sensible or conceivable is left "—" and yet these are no more flowing than the oak of a thousand years, or the hard boulder of the Alps,"—" no more or less *becoming* than the solid granite of the Andes."—" It could be shown mathematically, that there can be no rest in matter ;"—" they are not standing *things*, but *doings* all of them,"—" they are *events* from the floating mote to the rolling world,"—" having no standing reality ;"—" in this world of matter the real things that *stand*, are *forces*, *ideas*, and *laws*."

Prof. Lewis regards it as essential to the interests of religion, that we adopt the philosophic notion, not merely that the granite boulder of the Alps and the solid granite of the Andes are crumbling away, and that the pyramids are wasting, and that the mummy of three thousand years is losing its substance, but that all these have no real *being*, but are only *becoming ;* the matter of the mummy and the pyramid, and the granite boulder, and the interior granite of the Andes,—is all a flowing stream of matter,—never a *real* boulder, or granite, or pyramid, or mummy, but ever one *about* to be, or *becoming* one!   And this he regards as essential to religion,— that we believe even the particles of elementary substance to be a stream of matter, never *real* matter but always *becoming* so, the *doing* of a force or spirit.   This, he thinks, can be mathematically demonstrated.   (How fond he is of the mathematics !   Would that he had favored us with the process.) Yet all our experience, science, and mathematics, are unable to show that a single particle of elementary matter has ever been in a flow, or been annihilated, or changed, or had its substance renewed, since the first creation of the world.   Prof. Lewis not only finds his notion susceptible of proof by mathematics, but he professes to find it abundantly taught in the Bible.   When Paul, 1, Cor. 7 : 29 exhorts people by the consideration that " The time is short ", and reminds them that " The fashion of this world passeth away ", Prof. Lewis will have us understand the passage, not as referring to the close of our mortal life, and to the final passing away of all earthly things, but as urging us to consider the solemn fact that " the world itself, all that is matter for sense,"—is in a *flow*, never *being*, but always *becoming*, " passing off, evermore passing off, a stream that floweth, and standeth not ".

Is this all ?   What is this to one who is himself in an equal flow with the earth ? when for aught that Paul urges here, the time of this flowing may not be " short," but continue " ever more "!   He cites also 1 : John 2 : 17.   " Ὁ Κοσμος, the world itself, παραγεται, " is passing away "; meaning that the cosmos is in a *flow*, never *being* a world but perpetually *becoming* one. Just as though the apostles were exhorting men not to love the world, because the material world is a world *in a flow ;* its matter "*flowing* "—" ever more passing away "!   In Ps. 102 : 27 where it is said of the heavens and the earth, " They shall perish but thou shalt endure."   Prof. Lewis finds instead of a final perishing of the heavens and the earth, simply such a perishing as consists in a present and continued *flowing* of the materials of the heavens and the earth.   " They perish, that is, are *continually* perishing, but Thou abidest "— They *are flowing* but Thou abidest." He says "We *must* give ראבדו here this sense to make it parallel with תצמד but Thou shalt *stand*, or standest" i. e. "through all cosmical change ". According to this the passage does not teach that God shall remain when the earth shall be no more, but only that while the earth is *flowing*, God *stands*, and stands " through all cosmical change " ! But the meaning of אבד is not *to flow*, or to be in a *constant flux*, but " to perish," " to die," " to be cut off," " to be destroyed," and in Job 6 : 18 when applied to the streams which lose themselves in the desert, it means, not that they are *flowing*, but as in our translation, " *They go to nothing and perish* ". The parallelism is quite as well preserved in our common translation, while the meaning of the word is fully preserved. The permanent being of God in distinction from the flowing of the " *gliding, slipping, flowing* world " (p. 33). Prof. Lewis supposes to be vindicated by word תעמד, " they are flowing, but *thou abidest*,"—" that which is now and constantly going on. The *flowing* and the *abiding*, or *standing*, are co-éxistent ", yet in Ps. 33 : 9 the same word is applied to the world when it is said, " He commanded, and it *stood fast* ". So also in Ps. 148 : 6 the same word is used when it is said " He also hath *established* יעמיד them forever and ever ". So also in Ps. 119 : 90 " Thou hast established the earth, and תעמד *it abideth.*" So also Eccl. 1 : 4 " One generation passeth away and another generation cometh, but the earth לעדלם עמדת *standeth forever.*"

In like manner in his article of Jan. 1862, p. 160 Prof. Lewis, in order to prove " the unsubstantiality of the phenomenal " cites the passage in Ps. 39 : 6 " Every man walketh in a vain show,". He gives to the common Hebrew word הלך " to go", " to walk," the meaning of " *he flitteth about* ". To the expressions μη βλεπομενα of 2 Cor. 4 : 18, and to ου βλεπομένων in Heb. 11 : 1 he would have us attribute the meaning of—not " unseen " in the sense of *now absent*, — oh no — they are all here present !—but they are " unseen ", as the *spiritual realities which though unseen constitute the present men and worlds !* If such criticisms were confined to the heathen classics, they might be regarded as merely pitiful; showing how far a philosophical conceit, or hobby, can unbalance the mind, and unfit it to discern the true meaning of the most ordinary language. But when one ventures to indulge himself in such criticisms on the word of God, and to corrupt that sacred fountain by foisting upon it conceits and follies to which that word is an utter stranger, then the matter becomes more serious, and

incurs for its author a responsibility which we would not bear
for worlds.

We come now to the claims of the advocates of the transcendental philosophy, that their system alone recognizes the
proper and peculiar functions of reason. Dr. Hickok charged
upon the present writer, that,

"To him all objects are just what, and just as, the senses give to us; and
all investigation of them can attain to nothing other than that which the
logical faculty can make out of them."

Yet this representation was entirely wrong; for the article
in question expressly affirmed the contrary, in these words,

"We fully admit that man is *rational*. He is able to discern in objects
of sense more than sense reveals, and what can be yielded by no analysis
of objects of sense."

The article in question then went on to specify the objects
of reason, beyond all functions of sense, and beyond all deductions of experience. When the present writer afterwards,
in the Am. Theol. Review, affirmed the same things, Prof.
Lewis scouted the whole statement as incongruous and hypo-
critical. The words of the present writer in that article were
these:

"Sense can give nothing save objects of sense. It is reason that rises to
necessary principles and truths, and that discerns in objects of sense more
than sense reveals."

Thereupon Prof. Lewis says:

"Sense can give nothing save objects of sense"!—"This admission sounds
very well indeed."—"Again, hear how men, whose vernacular is the speech
of Ashdod, can talk in the Jews' language,—"But what is meant by these
fine words? Either there is no thought in them, or they furnish an entrance large enough for the whole Rational Psychology to come in"—"A
reason, too, they would have",—"Naked materialism, besides having a
very unorthodox look, is at present philosophically vulgar. Such brave
men as Compté, to be sure, care nothing about its vulgarity; they have no
spiritism to take care of. But their orthodox co-laborers have not nerve
enough for that: they would talk a little transcendentalism now and then;
or to do them more justice, they have too much sincere religion, too much
of the spirit of the Bible to carry it out."

It is high time that such representations and innuendos should
cease: for they imply both claims and accusations that are
wholly groundless and false. It is wholly untrue that the recognition of the functions of reason, above those of sense, are
peculiar to, or a discovery of, the transcendental philosophy;

or that that philosophy has, in this respect, any mission to correct the common doctrines of our common philosophy. Reid distinctly and fully set forth the mental origin of axioms and necessary truths : perhaps no man has more justly distinguished between the province of sense and reason than he. The old treatises of Buffiér and of Beattie, fully and ably maintained the same. Edwards (*on the Will*) (*vol.* 5, *p.* 51, *Carvill's Ed.*) recognized the distinctive faculty of reason when he said, "That whatever *begins* to be, which before was not, must have a *cause* why it then begins to exist, seems to be *the first dictate of the common and natural sense which God has implanted in the minds of all mankind.*" Here is no reference to experience, like that which bewildered Hume ; but the rational origin of the doctrine of cause. Even Bacon saw the error both of the pure sensualists and of the pure rationalists ; and by a happy comparison fixed the difference between them for ever. In Book I, p. 95, he. compares the empirics to the *ant*, which only heaps up and uses what it finds. These are the philosophers who never rise above that which they receive through sense. The pure Rationalists he compares to the *spider*, which spins its web out of its own bowels. These are the *à priori* philosophers, who want no facts nor experience, but can give Rational Psychologies and Rational Cosmologies out of the pure reason alone ; they are able to tell the Lord beforehand what sort of minds and worlds he must make, if he makes any at all, giving *à priori* Ideas of All Intelligence, and *à priori* systems of all the Cosmology which the Lord can ever undertake. The true philosophers Bacon compares to the *bee*, which gathers material from all flowers, and by a power within itself converts it into honey, which before it was not. These are they who believe in soul and body both, and use both the sense and the reason which God has given them. They do not undertake to tell *à priori* whether there *are* two straight lines, but two supposed straight lines being given or conceived, they can tell, without experience, that these cannot enclose a space. They cannot *à priori* prove that there must be a God ; but given "the things that are made," they can thereupon see that these must necessarily have had a cause, who must be both designer, Creator, and moral Ruler.

Here, may the present writer be pardoned, in declaring that the distinction between the functions of sense and reason he first learned from Locke, nearly forty years ago, and before he had ever heard of the transcendental philosophy. The theory, which Locke undertook to sustain, did indeed forbid the recognition of the proper functions of reason, and could

31

be consistent with nothing save a sensuous philosophy. But
he was led into this theory by abandoning, for the moment,
the Baconian method, and by assuming, *à priori*, that the
only sources of knowledge must be sensation and reflection.
But reason, though driven out with a pitchfork, was ever returning; so that the readers of Locke were ever querying
whether, by reflection, he did not mean something more than
a mere digestion of ideas derived from sense. Reason, though
often expelled, at last returned and fully asserted her dominion, in spite of Locke's transcendental assumption. In Book
iv, ch. 17, § 14, his caption is, "*Our highest knowledge intuitive*". Under this he instances not only intuitions of sense
but of reason also; ascribing to each "*the highest certainty*".
"In this," he says, "consists the evidence of those maxims
[axioms] which nobody has any doubt about, but every one—
does not as is said *assent* to—but *knows* to be true, as soon as
they are proposed to their understanding. In the discovery
and assent to these truths, there is no need of reasoning, but
they are known by a superior and higher light".
   Now surely no one can suppose that Locke regarded these
truths as having their origin in sense, or made up of ideas derived from sense, by compounding them, or reflecting upon
them.
   In his reply to Stillingfleet, he clearly asserts this domain
of reason beyond every province of sense: "Reason, standing
for true and clear principles, I have not wholly omitted; as is
manifest from what I have said of self-evident propositions
and demonstration. They are all known by their native evidence, are wholly independent, receive no light, nor are capable of proof from another."
   Has any man more clearly defined the origin and character
of necessary truths?
   In his method of showing the existence of God, "with evidence," he says, "equal to mathematical certainty," his second proposition defines the doctrine of *cause* as an "*intuitive
certainty*".
   Had Locke held here, he would have modified his theory
by throwing away his *à priori* transcendental assumption concerning the sources of knowledge, and returning strictly to
the Baconian method, he would have struck the balance truly
between pure sensualism and pure rationalism; and then the
Skepticism of Hume, the Idealism of Kant, and the Atheism
of Hegel, would perhaps have never been.
   But Prof. Lewis holds that if we admit man to be rational,
we "open an entrance wide enough for the whole Rational

Psychology to come in"! By no means. Because reason can rise above the province of sense, does it follow that reason can tell beforehand all the means and methods by which God shall be able to make minds, through sense, cognizant of external things? Because man has reason, is he therefore able to tell beforehand how largely God may see fit to extend the powers of or faculty of reason, in any case to be bestowed on angels or men? Cannot man be rational, without being able to tell beforehand how God must create matter, and without being able to describe beforehand all the cosmical arrangements of any worlds which God may be able to make? If a man is rational, does it follow that he shall be able to tell, *à priori*, of beings to be compounded of matter and spirit, who shall be led into sin by the " colliding influence" of necessitated matter over free spirit ; and that, when such beings have sinned, God will become incarnate—" use sentient nature as a tabernacle for Divinity to set forth a propitiation"? All this the Rational Psychology demands that man shall be able to do, before he shall be able to find an Absolute ; and he must find an Absolute in order to find that man has any reason ; and he must find the reason before he can find an outer world ; while, on the same system, before the finding of the world, reason can never be found, but remains a " void conception" forever : so all this beautiful system of Psychology ends in shutting men up to the dominion of unrealities and dreams :

> " Altera, candenti perfecta nitens elephanto,
> Sed falsa ad cœlum mittunt insomnia Manes".

If we admit that man is rational, do we thereby open an entrance large enough for the whole Rational Psychology to come in ? Kant explored this field for years :—and what can he do that cometh after the King !—He explored it so thoroughly as to make it his own : and he was manifestly right when he at last declared, "*Rational Psychology*"—"*is but a pretended science*" [Meiklejohn's trans. p. 238] which "*has its origin in a mere misunderstanding*". (p. 249.)

Prof. Lewis complains that we test this philosophy by trying to show its consequences in the field of religion ; and that we do not rather leave it as a mere speculation. But it was not in the interest of mere speculation that Dr. Hickok wrote his Psychology, but expressly for its uses in the field of religion. He declares it necessary, in many cases, to prepare the way for the Bible. And when the present writer said " For ourselves, we greatly prefer to approach any man that lives, with the sword of the Spirit, which is the Word of God," Dr.

Hickok responds that with the philosophy at present prevailing in the Christian world :

" No alternative is left" to the Christian teacher's " faith, but to discard philosophy".—" His position virtually is, that all religion is of God, and all reason is of the devil". (p. 223.).

And in this connection he thus refers to the words used by the present writer :

" The teacher of the coming preachers of the Gospel must have a theology rendered just so contradictory and absurd by his philosophy, and yet say that in this very way he " prefers to approach any man that lives with the sword of the Spirit, which is the word of God".

Enough. Dr. Hickok shall not even so persuade us to approach any man that lives with his philosophy rather than with the Word of God. For ourselves, we have ever made it our rule to ask as simply as possible, What has God taught? and to be as careful as possible, that no philosophy of our own, or of any other man, should be allowed to come in to help decide that question. We hope to make this our rule till we die. Sooner than allow any philosophy to bear with the weight of an atom upon the simple and fair interpretation of the Word of God, we would burn all our books of philosophy, and renounce all philosophy forever. We have never had any care for philosophy, save only to beware lest any man spoil us by philosophy and vain deceit. The more purely we can send every man to the Word of God, the better : and if any man " seemeth," in respect of philosophy, " to be wise in this world", and therefore skeptical, we know nothing better for such a man than the scriptural advice ; " Let him become a fool, that he may be wise".

·

Art. VIII.—THE GENERAL ASSEMBLY AT PHILADELPHIA.

THE General Assembly of our branch of the Presbyterian Church met at Philadelphia, in the First Presbyterian Church, Thursday May 21, and was opened with a sermon by the late Moderator, Rev. Dr. Duffield of Detroit, from the text 2 Tim. iii, 1: "This know also that in the last days perilous times shall come". The special perils that threaten the peace and prosperity of the church were forcibly described, perhaps with less hopeful views of the future than are entertained by many. The discourse, however, breathed an ardent devotion to the church of Christ, and to our country in its present conflicts. The Rev. Henry B. Smith, D.D. of New York was chosen Moderator of the Assembly. Commissioners were present from all the presbyteries excepting one in Iowa, and those in Alta California. The whole number upon the roll was 221, the largest we believe in any of our Assemblies since the separation in 1838.

And no Assembly convened during that period has been more united and harmonious. Some questions were earnestly debated, but in the most Christian spirit. No symptoms were manifest of party spirit or of divisive counsels. The spirit of God, a spirit of concord and peace, was shed in abundant measure upon all the deliberations. The spirit of Christian union was also largely enhanced. True to its traditions, the Assembly was enthusiastically loyal and patriotic, and reiterated the testimony it has so long borne in respect to the evils of slavery, and the urgent need of emancipation. The conviction was deeply felt and often expressed, that the Providence of God was affording new and constant vindication of the principles for which we have so long contended. All the great projects of our church were fully debated, and in them in all, in spite of the evils of our civil war, progress was reported. Many of the most venerated ministers of our church were in attendance, as commissioners, or to present special reports. When shall we be likely to meet again, on the floor of the same Assembly, Drs. Cox, Skinner, Barnes, Beman, Duffield, and Brainerd? Their presence, especially at the time when the delegates of the Peoria Assembly offered their fraternal salutations, imparted a heightened interest to the whole occasion, and united the present with the past.

Our limits allow only an epitome of the proceedings, which were exceedingly well reported, in full, in the *American Presbyterian*, published daily during the sessions of the Assembly.

The Report on the *Church Erection Fund* was presented by Rev. Dr. J. W. McLane:

The whole number of grants made during the year is twenty-eight, of which eleven have been in loans, and seventeen in donations. In several instances the character of a grant has been changed at the earnest request of the parties, and with the concurrence and recommendation of the Synodical Committee, from a donation to a loan, and *vice versa*. The whole amount of grants made from the beginning is $74,006; of which $60,816 have been in loans, and $13,390 in donations. There has been returned to the treasury on loans the sum of $11,348.08, and upon donations $1,526.09, making the whole amount thus returned $12,874.17, and leaving the sum, in loans and donations now in use, of $61,044.73. The tendency for the last few years has been toward an increase in the number of donations. The Plan of the Fund allows each Synod to grant in donations a sum equal to one fourth of the amount apportioned to it by the General Assembly. In most cases that limit has not as yet been reached.

The condition of the Church Erection Fund on May 1, 1863, was as follows:

Amount of Loans to Churches, secured by bond and mortgage,	$49,464 92
Amount of Donations to Churches, secured by bond and mortgage,	11,668 16
Amount of call loans and temporary investments,	52,000 00
Interest thereon to date,	340 00
Amount of securities for original subscriptions estimated,	1,000 00
Amount of cash in bank,	4,400 96
	$118,874 04

A Committee was appointed to report to the next Assembly upon some proposed modifications of the rules, to meet the pressing wants of certain congregations in the Western States. The members of this committee are J. Few Smith, D.D., R. W. Patterson, D.D., P. H. Fowler, D.D., Hon. Wm. Strong and Oliver H. Lee.

The Report on *Education* was read by the Secretary, Rev. T. A. Mills. Its receipts showed a large increase on the amount reported last year; though the number of students is somewhat diminished by the civil war. The Philadelphia Education Society is to give place to the Permanent Committee.

"One hundred and one young men have received, directly from the treasury, assistance as follows: In Auburn Theological Seminary, 22;

Lane, 16; Union, 20.   In Hamilton College, 8; Union, 8; Yale, 1; Marietta, 12; Western Reserve, 4; Wabash, 7; Knox, 3; Michigan University, 1; New York Free Academy, 1; Olivet Academy, Mich., 1.   Nine others (six theological, and three collegiate and academic) received assistance from bodies which were in a transition state, but may now be fairly placed in connection with the Committee; making a total of 110.

"It is known to the Committee that some churches and benevolent individuals have aided directly one or more young men, and that a number have been placed on foundations in different institutions.   Perhaps it would not vary far from the truth to say, that during the year about two hundred students have been assisted, at an outlay of something over $20,000.

"The rate of appropriation to these students has been $90 per annum for the theological course, and $80 for the collegiate and academic.   The rules approved by the Assembly fix the amount at $120 for the theological course, $100 for the collegiate, and $80 for the academic; but these rates have never, with one single exception for one year, been paid.   The Committee know that their appropriation to theological students has been supplemented from other sources, so that they have received one hundred dollars each, in addition to their own earnings.

"From the Treasurer's accounts it will be seen that he has received from 311 churches, 44 individual contributors, and some other miscellaneous sources, $15,271.77, and that the expenditures of the Committee for all purposes have been $13,668.64, leaving a balance of $1603.13."

In the subsequent debate, the condition of Auburn Seminary was stated more at length by Dr. Fowler; that of Lane by Prof. Day; and that of Union by Dr. Skinner.   Deserved tributes were paid by the latter, and by Dr. Cox, to the memory of Dr. Edward Robinson.   The Assembly's Standing Committee, through its chairman, Prof. Day, urged increased attention to the whole subject of education, by ministers and presbyteries.

Home Missions.   The annual Report was read by Dr. Kendall.   It appropriately noticed the decease and services of the Associate Secretary, Rev. Benj. J. Wallace, D.D.

"The correspondence with the American Home Missionary Society was read.   It appears that more than $30,000 has been paid into the Treasury of that Society during the year, every dollar of which is withheld from the feeble Presbyterian churches in the land.

"Two hundred and fifty-six missionaries have been employed the whole or a part of the year past, performing an aggregate of 192 years' labor. The Gospel has been regularly preached in more than 360 places; 225 missionaries have forwarded statistical reports, from which it appears that there have been 843 hopeful conversions; 697 have united with the churches on profession of faith, and 668 by letter; 14 revivals are reported, 12 churches have been organized, 5 have become self sustaining, and 32 church edifices have been built, repaired or relieved of debt.

"The receipts of the year reach almost $52,000 and yet more than 800 churches of the whole number, 4,166, have contributed nothing.   But the missionaries have been paid, and no church asking aid, and well approved, has been refused."

This report shows a decided advance upon the receipts of

last year, which amounted to about $20,000. The annual sermon was preached by Rev. Z. M. Humphrey of Chicago, who exhibited the claims of our country in an able and effective manner. The Standing Committee of the Assembly, through their Chairman, the Rev. Dr. Clarke of Buffalo, presented an able document, reviewing our home missionary work, and our relations to the Home Missionary Society, and commending the whole subject anew to the prayers and zeal of the churches.

The subject of *Foreign Missions* was fully handled in the Report of our Permanent Committee, Asa D. Smith, D.D. Chairman, and W. S. Griffith, Secretary. The Assembly acts in continued harmony with the American Board, under which we have 63 missionaries and secretaries. The amount of our contributions is $69,482, in a membership of 135,454. The Report says:

" Of the 1,466 churches, only 595 contributed any thing.
" It thus appears that our rolls show an army of 135,454, bound by sacramental pledge and by every obligation of love and duty to devote their hearts and lives, every power mortal and immortal to honor the King of Zion, and to build up his kingdom ; that this great army, enjoying the Gospel themselves and living in the midst of plenty which God has showered down upon them, have actually contributed to send the Word of Life to the perishing heathen during a whole year, only the sum of $69,482.68, or an average of about 51 cents to each enrolled member, which is less than one cent per week."

The Assembly's Standing Committee responded through their Chairman, Rev. Albert Barnes, and the following among other Resolutions were unanimously adopted:

Resolved, That this General Assembly and the churches we represent are called upon to cherish and manifest the deepest interest in the work of Foreign Missions, as conducted by the American Board of Commissioners for Foreign Missions, with which we have been so long and so happily connected, and which has given us such abundant proofs of the skill and fidelity which have marked the management of its great trust, and of the entire fairness of all its arrangements relating to the location of the missionaries connected with our Presbyteries, and their freedom to act according to the dictates of their own judgment as to the formation of Presbyteries in their respective fields.

Resolved, That it be recommended to the Presbyteries that they appoint one of their ministers or elders as the Presbyterial agent for Foreign Missions, whose duty it shall be to see that the cause is presented to each church, to report at each meeting of the Presbytery, and also to report annually to the Permanent Committee of the Assembly, what each church in the Presbytery has done for the cause during the year, and that the stated clerk of each Presbytery be requested to furnish to the Permanent Committee the name of the minister or elder who shall be appointed the Presbyterial agent for Foreign Missions.

A Special Report on proposed missions in Central and South America was read by Dr. Duffield.   At present there is not much opening for such a work ; but there may be ere long ; and it is upon a field not occupied by the American Board.

The Report on *Publication* by Rev. John W. Dulles stated that the sum received from contributions during the past year was only $4,212 ; from sales $12,221.   It was felt by the Assembly that this part of our work needs to be prosecuted with much greater liberality.   A long and able Report, traversing the whole subject, was read by Dr. Beman, and resulted in passing a resolution to endeavor to raise $50,000 for this object.

One of the most interesting debates in the Assembly was called forth by the Resolutions upon the state of the country, offered by Mr. Barnes, as chairman of a Special Committee on this subject.   There was no real difference of opinion on the principles involved ; the Assembly was unanimous in its loyalty, in its unconditional support of the Government, and in the view that, as slavery is the cause of the war, so the war to be successful, must end in giving the death-blow to slavery.   Still there was some debate as to phraseology, and criticism of minor points.   Dr. Spear proposed substitutes for several of the Resolutions ; but they were passed in substance as originally reported.   We should be glad to give them in full, did our space permit.   Some of the most important are the following :

"2. That in explanation of our views, and as a further and solemn expression of the sentiments of the General Assembly of the Presbyterian Church in the United States of America in regard to the duty of those whom we represent, and of all the American people at the present time, we now declare,

" First, That civil government is ordained of God, and that submission to a lawful government, and to its acts in its proper sphere, is a duty binding on the conscience and required by all the principles of our religion, as a part of our allegiance to God.

Second, That while there is in certain respects a ground of distinction between a *government* considered as referring to the constitution of a country, and an *administration*, considered as referring to the existing agencies, through which the principles and provisions of the constitution are administered ; yet, the government of a country to which direct allegiance and loyalty are due at any time, is the administration duly placed in power.   Such an administration is the government of a nation, having a right to execute the laws and demand the entire, unqualified and prompt obedience of all who are under its authority ; and resistance to such a government is rebellion and treason.

" Third, That the present administration of the United States, duly elected under the Constitution, is the government in the land to which alone under God, all the citizens of this nation owe allegiance ; who, as such, are to be honored and obeyed ; whose efforts to defend the government against rebellion are to be sustained; and that all attempts to resist or set aside the action of the lawfully constituted authorities of the government in any way by speech or action, to oppose or embarrass the measures which it may adopt to assert its lawful authority, except in accordance with the forms prescribed by the Constitution, are to be regarded as treason against the nation—as giving aid and comfort to its enemies, and as rebellion against God.

"4. That the Government of these United States as provided for by the Constitution, is not only founded upon the great doctrine of human rights as vested by God in the individual man, but is also expressly declared to be the supreme civil authority in the land, forever excluding the modern doctrine of secession as a civil or political right; that since the existing rebellion finds no justification in the facts of the case or the Constitution of the United States—in any law human or divine—the Assembly can regard it only as treason against the nation, and a most offensive sin in the sight of God, justly exposing its authors to the retributive vengeance of earth and heaven; that this rebellion, in its origin, history, and measures, has been distinguished by those qualities which most sadly evince the depravity of our nature, especially in seeking to establish a new nationality on this continent, based on the perpetual enslavement and oppression of a weak and long-injured race; that the National forces are, in the view of this Assembly, called out not to wage war against another government, but to suppress insurrection, preserve the supremacy of law and order, and save the country from anarchy and ruin.

"6. That the system of human bondage as existing in the Slaveholding States, so palpably the root and cause of this whole insurrectionary movement, is not only a violation of the dearest rights of human nature, but essentially hostile to the letter and spirit of the Christian religion; that the evil character and demoralizing tendencies of this system so properly described and justly condemned by the General Assembly of our church, especially from 1818 to the present time, have been placed in the broad light of day by the history of this existing rebellion; that in the sacrifices and desolations, the cost of treasury and blood caused thereby, the Assembly recognize the chastening hand of God, applied to the punishment of national sins, especially the sin of slavery; that in the Proclamation of Emancipation issued by the President as a war measure, and submitted by him to the considerate judgment of mankind, the Assembly recognize with devout gratitude that wonder-working providence of God, by which military necessities become the instrument of justice in breaking the yoke of oppression and causing the oppressed to go free; and further, that the Assembly beseech Almighty God in his own time to remove the last vestige of slavery from this country, and give to the nation preserved, disciplined, and purified, a peace that shall be based on the principles of eternal righteousness."

The other resolutions expressed the duty of sustaining the government; rebuked secession, and all complicity therewith; exhibited; exhorted the church to do its whole duty; and expressed sympathy for the bereaved. The document was subsequently handed to the President of the United States by a large Committee of the Assembly, who were courteously welcomed.

The reception of delegates and commissioners from other denominations claimed a considerable share of the time, and engrossed the interest of the Assembly. Only one delegate was present from New England, the Rev. A. Hyde of Vermont, who made a fraternal address. Dr. Wylie of the Reformed Presbyterians offered the Christian salutations of his church, which were cordially reciprocated by Rev. A. Barnes. Communications were read from our delegates to other ecclesiastical bodies. But the highest interest was awakened by the initiation of a correspondence with the General Assembly in session at Peoria.

That Assembly met last year at Columbus in Ohio, and there made proposals for fraternal communion, which, however did not reach the Moderator of our Assembly, Dr. Duffield, until after its adjournment. The papers were communicated to the Assembly at Philadelphia on the first day of its session. The letter of Dr. Beatty, Moderator of the Columbus Assembly, inclosed the following minute:

" In the General Assembly of the Presbyterian Church in the United States of America, in session at Columbus, Ohio, the matter of a fraternal correspondence, by Commissioners, with the General Assembly of the Presbyterian Church (N. S.), in session at Cincinnati, Ohio, being duly considered, is decided as follows:

" This Assembly having considered several overtures sent to it by a few of the Presbyteries under its care, proposing that steps should be taken by it towards an organic union between this Church and the Church under the care of the Presbyterian General Assembly (N. S.) ; and having determined against the course proposed in said overtures, has also been informed that the other General Assembly has, about the same time, come to a similar conclusion on similar overtures laid before it by a certain number of its own Presbyteries. Of its own motion, this General Assembly, considering the time to have come for it to take the initiative in securing a better understanding of the relations which it judges are proper to be maintained between the two General Assemblies, " hereby proposes, that there shall be a stated annual and friendly interchange of Commissioners between the two General Assemblies," each body sending to the other one minister and one ruling elder, as Commissioners, year by year ; the said Commissioners to enjoy such privileges in each body to which they are sent as are common to all those now received by this body from other Christian denominations. The Moderator will communicate this deliverance to the Moderator of the other Assembly, to be laid before it, with our Christian salutations."

As soon as the documents were brought before the Assembly, a Special Committee was appointed to report upon them, consisting of Drs. Spear, Cox, Gridley, and Messrs. W. A. Booth and C. N. Olds ; and at their suggestion, the following Resolutions were unanimously adopted :

" The Committee to whom was referred a communication from the General Assembly of the Presbyterian Church of the United States, that met at Columbus, Ohio, May, 1862, addressed to this General Assembly, and proposing ' a stated, annual and friendly interchange of Commissioners between the two General Assemblies,' recommend the adoption of the following resolutions by this Assembly :

" 1. *Resolved*, That this Assembly, with heartfelt pleasure and Christian salutation, accept the proposition thus made, hoping and praying that it may result in securing a better understanding of the relations, which, in the judgment of this Assembly, are proper to be maintained between the two Assemblies.

" 2. *Resolved*, That, in accordance with the suggestion of the Moderator of the last Assembly, meeting in Columbus, that this interchange of Commissioners should commence at the earliest practicable period, Rev. R. W. Patterson, D.D., and Hon. Wm. H. Brown be appointed as Commissioners to represent this Assembly in the General Assembly now holding its session at Peoria, Illinois.

" 3. *Resolved*, That it be suggested that future Assemblies of the two branches of the Presbyterian Church in these United States, hereafter designate each other respectively by the places in which their sessions are appointed to be held.

" 4. *Resolved*, That a certified copy of this action be transmitted to the Moderator of the General Assembly now holding its sessions at Peoria, Illinois, and that the Commissioners be requested to repair to that body, and express to it the fraternal and Christian regards of this General Assembly."

The Peoria Assembly at once responded by appointing Dr. Tustin (who drew up the above minute last year) and Hon. G. Sharswood as principals, and Dr. Hall and J. W. Harper, Esq., as alternates. The time for receiving them was appointed on Tuesday afternoon, May 26, when a large and deeply moved congregation gathered together in the old and honored church, where, a quarter of a century ago, the rupture of these two denominations was effected. Many who bore a part in that momentous struggle were witnesses of this more hallowed revival of a spirit of fraternal confidence and affection. Dr. Tustin delivered a most cordial and eloquent address, touching the deepest sympathies of his eager and hushed audience, as with tremulous voice he spoke words of love and peace. The past was forgotten, and hearts were melted in unison. Nor could the applause be restrained when he announced in frank terms that " so far as we are concerned the strife is at an end ". " I come to you bearing aloft the trophies of fraternal love and affection—for love has its triumphs as well as hate—peace as well as war. I come to invite you back to confidence and esteem ". The Moderator of the Assembly, in a cordial response, reciprocated the heartfelt expressions of Christian affection ; reviewed some of the events that marked the separation ; and spoke of the long slumbering desire for such brotherly interchange of Christian feelings. Those that have the same faith, the same polity, the same aims, and the same divine Head, are separated only for a time. Both of these great branches of the Presbyterian church have the same ancestry and the same history ; they rehearse their faith in the words of the Westminster Confession and Catechisms. Both adopt the Pauline, the Augustinian and the Reformed creed, in contrast with Pelagianism, Socinianism and Arminianism. Both are devoted to our national cause with unswerving loyalty: both share in sympathies and prayers for that ill-fated race, whose oppression lies so deep among our nation's sins, and whose deliverance and elevation are necessary to secure the peace and unity of our Republic. United now in expressions of mutual confidence and love, we seek not to cast the horoscope of the future. Each branch of the church has its providential work; for a more complete reunion we await the guidance of Divine Providence. This impressive scene was concluded by the singing of the hymn " Blest be the tie that binds ", and prayer by the Rev. Dr. Cox.

The action of both Assemblies is restricted to the interchange of commissioners. No projects for organic reünion have yet been definitely discussed. Enough for the present hour, that the bitterness and controversies of the past are deplored ; and that a spirit of Christian fellowship has been poured upon the heart of our churches. The Cincinnati Assembly of last year, in reply to some overtures on this subject, " *Resolved,* That while we bear in mind the prayer of our Lord that his disciples may be one, and while we can see some special advantages to be derived from a reünion of the two branches of the Presbyterian Church, we do not perceive that, beyond the previous declaration of our views, any thing remains for us, at the present, but to await humbly and teachably the movements of Divine Providence". A premature pressure of the question would be unwise. The country is passing through great changes, the results of which no human vision can foresee, and which may settle some necessary preliminary questions. No action upon this subject was taken this year by the Philadelphia Assembly. The Peoria Assembly, in reply to several overtures, passed the following minute, to which we cordially assent :

The Committee on the union between the Old and New School Churches reported as follows :

" The Committee to whom was referred the memorial from the Presbytery of Chippewa and Overture No. 1, respecting the union of the two branches of the Presbyterian Church, called the Old and New School, report that they have endeavored to consider the subject in that careful and serious manner which its importance demands, and would submit to the Assembly for their consideration and adoption the following resolutions, viz. :

" *Resolved,* 1. That, in the judgment of this General Assembly, it is not deemed expedient to take, at this time, any decided action with reference to a reünion of the New and Old School Presbyterian churches.

"*Resolved*, 2. That in the fraternal correspondence now happily inaugurated, the General Assembly would recognize an initiative in the securing a better understanding of the relations which subsist between the two Assemblies, and the means of promoting that mutual charity and that just apprehension of the true grounds of Christian union and fellowship, which may serve to prepare the way for a union that shall be harmonious, and permanently promotive of the interests of truth and vital godliness.

"*Resolved*, 3. That as a still further preparative to such a desirable union, the General Assembly deem it important — and this in reference to both these branches of the Presbyterian Church—that the ministers and ruling elders, and such as have the care and instruction of the young, be increasingly careful to exhibit clearly the distinctive principles of Christian doctrine and sound polity as held by the Presbyterian Church ; that the ministers of these two branches of the church cultivate fraternal intercourse and interchange of views and feelings ; and in all suitable ways encourage and aid one another in the appropriate work of the ministry ; and that the members of the one or the other branch connect themselves with existing congregations of either, rather than cast in their influence and their aid with bodies whose principles and form of government are foreign to their own."

The proposed correspondence with the Reformed Dutch Church also elicited an animated debate. The General Synod of that church last year initiated this matter by the following action :

"*Whereas*, This Synod considers the interchange of Christian courtesy and kindness between ecclesiastical bodies as most desirable, wherever it can be practicable and hearty ; even where differences of doctrinal views may preclude that form of correspondence contemplated in Chap. 2, Art. 5, Sec. 2, of our Constitution.

"*Resolved*, That the Synod send to the next New School General Assembly of the Presbyterian Church, a Commissioner, whose office it shall be to assure that body of our fraternal affection and interest, and to propose to it a yearly interchange of kind expressions by letter."

The Rev. Hervey D. Ganse, of New York, the appointed delegate, in an able and eloquent speech, explained the action they had taken, to free it from technical difficulties. The allusion to "differences in doctrinal views" he interpreted as not intended to cast any reproach on our orthodoxy, but simply to indicate that we were supposed not to agree with them on all theological topics, they holding to the articles of the Synod of Dort in a more literal interpretation. The Assembly, after a long debate, adopted with amendments, the report of Dr. Cox on the subject, as follows :

"The Assembly, after considering the kind and earnest address of Rev. Mr. Ganse, and considering also the printed Minutes of the acts and proceedings of said General Synod (see pages 131 to 140, inclusive, especially the resolution and its preamble, page 140), feel with Christian and catholic regret, constrained in righteousness and truth, to decline the special overture now made to us; but we hereby cordially offer correspondence with them on the same terms on which we correspond with other ecclesiastical bodies, and we appoint ——— a commissioner to attend the next meeting of their General Synod."

Under this resolution, Dr. Skinner was appointed the delegate to the Reformed Dutch Synod.

It gives us great pleasure to add that our delegate was most cordially received by that Synod, which met at Newburgh, June 3d, and a resolution formally to inaugurate a correspondence with our Assembly, and to appoint a delegate to attend the next meeting of the body, was unanimously adopted. We cannot refrain from giving the brief report of our excellent delegate in his own words, in order to show the spirit in which the act was done:

"My cup of pleasure has been overflowing since I left the Synod. They received me as if I had been, not a delegate from our Assembly, but an angel of the Lord. Their response to my address, through their noble President, was entirely cordial and magnanimous. Very promptly and magnanimously they accepted our overtures, and resolved at once to appoint a delegate to attend our next Assembly. So far as I know, there has been no parallel to the heavenly emotion which marked this consummation of proposal for correspondence, except that ever memorable one, which occurred in Philadelphia week before last."

Various other matters of importance, to which we can only allude, were brought before the Assembly. There was only one judicial case, that of S. Edwards Todd, on appeal from the decision of the Presbytery of Cayuga. This was finally remanded to the Synod of Onondaga and the Presbytery of Cayuga for revision. Resolutions approving the work of the New York Sabbath Committee were passed, after hearing an address from Rev. R. S. Cook. The American Sunday-School Society was commended anew. On motion of Dr. Darling, the AMERICAN PRESBYTERIAN AND THEOLOGICAL REVIEW was recommended to our ministers and churches. A committee was appointed (Dr. Asa D. Smith, chairman) to report to the next Assembly on the subject of manses and parochial libraries. The whole question of Sabbath-schools, and their relation to the church, and of Sunday services, is also to be reported upon by a committee, of which Dr. Joel Parker is the chairman. It was brought up in various forms, among others by an overture from the Presbytery of Genesee, to which Dr. Skinner, in behalf of the Committee of Bills and Overtures, replied, in part, as follows:

"The Sunday-school, like all the religious institutions and agencies of each individual church, is and ought to be under the watch and care of the Session, and should be regarded not as superseding, but as coöperating with the entire system of pastoral instruction, the responsibility of which it should not in any manner diminish.

"There is nothing in our constitution which prescribes the number of public services to be held on the Lord's Day, or which restrains any church from appropriating to the Sunday-school such a portion of the day as may seem to it desirable.

"The peculiar position of baptized children as members of the church, to be as members trained in all Christian virtues and duties, is so expressly set forth in our standards, that no revision of them could present it with greater clearness, or in a more authoritative form. See Confession, chap. xxv, sec. 2 ; Larger Catechism, Question 166 ; Form of Government, chap. ii, secs. 2, 4 ; Book of Discipline, chap. i, sec. 6 ; Directory for Worship, chap. ix, sec. 1–8."

The annual Historical Discourse was delivered by Rev. Dr. Fisher, President of Hamilton College. It was an able and eloquent account of what Presbyterians have done for the promotion of education in our country.

The Narrative on the State of Religion was read by Rev. John Crowell, and showed that there has been spiritual growth in our churches, in the midst of all the calamities of our civil war. The names of the ministers deceased during the year will be given under another head.

The Assembly was dissolved on Monday evening, June 1, after uniting in the monthly concert for prayer. Appropriate resolutions and addresses testified to the large hospitality extended to the commissioners by the citizens of Philadelphia. The next meeting is to be in Dayton, Ohio. Taken as a whole, this last session of our Assembly has been most cheering and satisfactory. As Mr. Barnes so fitly said in his closing remarks : "I think there is advancement : I think there has been an intensity of interest, a depth of feeling, an attachment to the church and the great interests in which we are engaged, a devotion to our country, such as will give this Assembly a marked place in the history·of our church and of our nation."

Art. IX.—THEOLOGICAL AND LITERARY INTELLIGENCE.

Archæological Institute.—At a late meeting of this body, Mr. Birch, Keeper of Antiquities in the British Museum, gave an interesting lecture on the gold jewelled ornaments discovered in Egypt and sent by the Viceroy to the late International Exhibition, where they had been inspected with eager curiosity.   They were found near Thebes, in 1859, by M. Mariette, Director of the Viceroy's Museum, and were brought to England under his charge.   The sepulchre in which their discovery was made has been attributed to the Queen Aah Holep, mother of Amosis I, of the seventeenth dynasty—one of the most remarkable personages in early Egyptian history. After a most interesting sketch of the condition of public affairs at the period, and the determined conflicts with the Shepherds, invaders from the East, who assumed powerful hostile dominion in Egypt, Mr. Birch entered upon a minute description of the rich ornaments, aided by an exquisite series of drawings.   From the great richness of the coloring, it had been supposed that some portions of these precious relics had been enamelled, but this notion Mr. Birch believed to be erroneous ; he had seen no example of true enamelling on Egyptian works.   In conclusion, he stated that the date of these objects may be placed, at the lowest calculation, at b.c. 1500 or 1510 ; but they are possibly even of a higher antiquity.   Mr. Yates pointed out analogies presented by these insignia of an ancient Egyptian sovereign, with other ancient evidence ; and Mr. Franks stated his concurrence in the view taken by Mr. Birch regarding the lack of proof that enamel was known to the ancient Egyptians.

The *Revue de l'Instruction Publique* announces important discoveries made by Volgüé and Waddington in Syria, in a region called Safa, inhabited by fierce Bedouins, never before penetrated, excepting in part by Wetztein and Graham.   They found a large series of inscriptions, in mixed characters (Greek, Semitic, and a new alphabet), supposed to give the state of the language of the region about the time of Christ.   A temple is still standing of the time of the Agrippas with an inscription in honor of Herod.   A gap in the history of architecture is also supposed to be filled by edifices ranging from the 3d to the 6th century of the Christian era—particularly in respect to the origin of the cupola.   Round and polygonal churches were also found—resembling the mosque of St. Sophia, etc.

In speaking of the restorations now made at Rome by order of the Emperor Louis Napoleon, the *Correspondence of Rome*, referring to the Triumphal Arch of Constantine, says that " at the time it was raised Rome was not yet Christian, but that the miracle of the Labarum was so striking that the Roman Senate could only see the finger of God in the victories of the son of Helena, and caused to be engraved on the two sides of the monument that this victory was INSTINCTU DIVINITATIS".   Unfortunately, the researches of archæologists have demonstrated that these words are of later origin ; that the original inscription was the Pagan formula, NUTU. JOVIS. O. M. (nutu Jovis optimi maximi), which has been replaced by the *instinctu divinitatis,* traces of the old words, however, still remaining distinct.   This is shown by the German epigraphist, M. G. Henzen, in the supplement to *Orelli's Collection of Inscriptions ;* and it also rests on the testimony of Borghesi and other Roman archæologists, who examined it with care about forty years ago.—*La Correspondance Littéraire.*

32

The French Academy of Inscriptions has awarded to M. Alexandre Bertrand, formerly member of the French School of Athens, the prize for the best essay on the discoveries since the beginning of the present century in relation to Celtic monuments.   Four essays were sent in.   M. Bertrand shows that the monuments of this kind in France become more numerous as the northwest and west coasts are approached,   It is inferred that they are due to a littoral population which penetrated towards the interior, following the principal rivers and their affluents.   He considers that the "dolmena" are sepulchral monuments, and believes that their origin must be referred to a period anterior to the invasion of the Celts.

Mr. Henry Stevens has published, in 2 vols., $8, his *Historical Nuggets*, an account of his own collection of rare books relating to America—a very valuable work.   Only 100 copies are printed.   It comprises 3,000 titles.

The Imperial Library of St. Petersburgh has purchased the celebrated collection of Hebrew and Caraite manuscripts formed by M. Firkovitch, a Caraite himself, who is well known for his scientific zeal, and who, during thirty years in his numerous travels in Palestine, the Caucasus, and at Constantinople, had collected the memorials of Jewish antiquity wherever he could find them.   The collection consists of 47 manuscript rolls of the Pentateuch, 77 collections of the Old Testament, 23 translations in Eastern languages, 272 Caraite and 523 Rabbinist works, 550 historical letters or documents, 722 funeral inscriptions, and 300 plans of the ancient fortresses of New Russia.   It also contains 124 authentic manuscripts of the Old Testament, of which 21 are anterior to the ninth century.   According to the opinions of Tischendorf, Dora, Bekker, and others, no European library possesses Hebraic manuscripts of so early a date, and consequently cannot furnish such rich materials for the complete study of the text of the Old Testament.   A detailed history of the collection is in progress.

ITALY.

C. Cantu, so widely known by his *Universal History* (of which 18,000 copies have been sold in Italy, and three large French editions), has recently published an interesting work on *Erasmus and the Reform in Italy* : E. was in Italy for some time from 1506, and mingled with the literary men of Turin, Bologna, Padua, Venice and Rome.

Farini in 1859 appointed a commission to search out mss. of the 12th, 13th, and 14th centuries ; two volumes have been published containing a *Legend of Jean de Procida*, a *Journey to Jerusalem of Nicholas d'Este*, a *Legend of a Journey of Three Monks to the Terrestrial Paradise* — all chiefly valuable as illustrative of the language and style of the period.   The apocryphal *Correspondence of Seneca and St. Paul*, written by the Florentine Lancia is another fruit of these researches.

Sciopis has written a work on the *French Domination in Italy under Napoleon I*, which is exciting much attention.

Alois Prinzivalli, Resolutiones seu Decreta authentica sacræ Congregationis Indulgentiis sacrisque Reliquiis præpositæ ab anno 1668 ad annum 1861, accurate collecta.   Rome.   1862.   8vo, viii, 855 pp.

V. Coco, *History of the Revolution in Naples*, 1799, and a Life of the Author, by Mariano d'Ayala.   Naples.   1861.

The second and third volumes of Aug. Theiner's large work in defence of the temporal power of the Papacy have been published at Rome (*Codex diplomaticus Dominii temporalis S. Sedis*), comprising the period from 1335 to 1793 ; fol.   Each volume costs fifteen dollars.

The first volume of the Chevalier de Rossi's *Inscriptiones Christianæ Urbis Romac septimo Sæculo Antiquiores*, is published at $86. The work will contain 11,000 inscriptions with fac similes.

Two new publications have been added to the *Index Expurgatorius* by the committee at Rome.   The one is the work on Sorcery by M. Michelet, the other the newspaper published at Turin by Father Passaglia, called the *Pace*.

SWITZERLAND.

Professor Cellerier, of Geneva, died Nov. 17, aged 77 years.   He taught in the oriental languages, and the introduction to the Scriptures, on which latter subject he published a volume in 1853.

M. F. Hensler, of Basle, recently deceased, bequeathed 740,000 francs to the University, hospital, orphan-house, and various benevolent associations (35 in all) in France and Switzerland.

SPAIN.

A Church History of Spain for the first Three Centuries has been published at Ratisbon, written by Pius Bonifacius Gams, pp. 422.   It is to be continued.

Juan Manuel Orti y Lara, *El Racionalismo y la Humildad*.   Madrid, 1862.   pp. 420.   Manuel Angelon, *History of Isabella II. Queen of Spain*. 4to.   Barcelona, 1860–1.   600 pp. with 16 plates.   A. Blanch, *History of Catalonia*.   2 vols.   64 plates.   Ant. Cavanilles, *History of Spain*.   3 vols.   4to.   Madrid.   José Maria Escandon, *History of Asturia*.   4to.   Madrid, 1862.   pp. 576.   Garcia del Canto, *España en la Oceania*.   8vo.   Madrid, 1862.   De Pidal, *History of Aragon in the Reign of Philip II.* 2, 4to.   1862.

For the first time a general statistical review of the population of Spain has been published.   The number of births in the past year was 571,886 ; of deaths, 432,067 ; of marriages, 120,893.   The statistics published by the "Revista-General de Estadistica", singularly enough, fail to give the total of the population ; only recording one birth in twenty-seven inhabitants, one death in thirty-three, one marriage in 129, according to which the total of inhabitants would be 15,500,000.   The proportion of illegitimate to legitimate children in the country and smaller towns is one in twenty-seven ; in the provincial capitals one in thirty-three.

PORTUGAL.

M. Luiz Rebello da Silva, a member of the Royal Academy of Sciences at Lisbon, has written a History of Portugal in the 17th and 18th centuries, in two volumes, which is spoken of as a work of unusual merit.

HOLLAND.

The Society of the Hague for the Defence of the Christian Religion, proposes a prize for the following subject: A Criticism of all the passages of Scripture that refer to Slavery, and an examination of the question, how Slavery must be regarded from the Christian point of view.   This is to include an examination of the most important recent works on the subject, including those published in America. The prize is 400 guilders ; the time till March 15, 1864. Other subjects are : The Idea of the Messiah ; the Union of Faith in the Divine Origin of the Gospels, with the results of historical criticism.

The Teyler Society of Haarlem offers a prize of 400 guilders for the best Essay on the Influence of the Empirical Philosophy in France, Germany, and England. It may be written in Dutch, Latin, French, English or German. The limit is Jan. 1, 1864.

Heinrich Egbert Vinke died last year (Aug. 27) at Utrecht, where he had long been a distinguished Professor. His successor is Van Osterzee, one of the contributors to Lange's Bible Work, and author of a Christology. His inaugural address, Jan. 30, on Modern Scepticism, was heard with deep interest. Dr. Doedes has been appointed to the chair of Biblical Literature.

A Dutch translation of Schelling's *Philosophy of Revelation* is in progress by A. Van der Linde. The first volume is published.

J. P. N. Land has published the first volume of Anecdota Syriaca, with notes. 4to, pp. xvi, 215, 28 Tables and 77 pages of Syriac text.

A Dutch translation of a selection of Burns's poems has appeared at Brussels, under the title "De schoonste Liederen van Robert Burns uit het Schottisch vertaalt door Frans de Coort," accompanied by a sketch of the poet's life.

GERMANY.

Rudolf Stier, the author of the *Words of Christ*, which are now in the course of republication in this country, died Dec. 19, 1862. He was born at Fraustadt, Mar. 17, 1800, studied at Berlin and Halle, 1815–19. At first he was sceptically inclined ; but the study of the Bible, with the aid of Bengel's Gnomon, brought him to decisive faith. In 1821–3, on Neander's recommendation, he taught in the Preachers' Seminary at Wittenberg, in conjunction with Nitzsch and Heubner. His first wife was a sister of Nitzsch. For four years he was a professor in the missionary Seminary at Basle ; then pastor at Frankleben. He worked in unison with Tholuck, Von Gerlach, and men of kindred views, and was noted as a bold preacher. In Wichlinghausen and Skenditz he was superintendent. Among his numerous works are Biblical Preaching, 1830 ; Grammar of Hebrew, 1833 ; Seventy Select Psalms ; Need of Hymn Books ; Polyglott Bible, with Theile ; Words of the Lord Jesus ; Commentaries on the Ephesians, Jude, Proverbs, the second part of Isaiah ; Privat-Agenda ; Sermons ; Words of the Lord from Heaven ; Words of the Angels. He was preparing a work on the Prophecies of the Old Testament, and also one on Job, neither completed. He also wrote several treatises on the need of a revision of Luther's translation ; and in 1836 published a translation on the basis of Luther and von Meyer. He was a warm friend of the Union of the Confessions. He likewise zealously defended the retaining of the Apocrypha in the common versions. A volume of his poems appeared in 1825, and another in 1845.

The Jerusalem Talmud is to be published at Krotoschin in Prussia, in some 15 parts at half a dollar each. Only two complete editions have been issued : at Venice, 1523, without a commentary ; and at Cracow in 1604, incorrectly printed. A glossary will be appended.

The *Zeitschrift f. d. historische Theologie*, second number, 1863, has a continuation of Hochhuth's learned account of the Weigelians and Rosicrucians of the 17th century in the Hesse church : a History of the Moravians in Livonia by Dr. J. C. M. Laurent: and a documentary account by F. Winter, of the Church Visitation in the Wittenberg district, 1528, which did so much to establish the Reformation.

The *Studien und Kritiken*, Heft 2, 1863.   Sack, Character of the Heidelberg Catechism: an excellent comparative summary.   This is to be followed by an article of Ullmann on the same subject.   Richter, the Essence of the Lord's Supper, confined to the Biblical view, and agreeing with the Reformed positions.   Schreiber on the Gregorius of Hartmann Von Aue— a poem of the 13th century, highly praised by Gervinus.   Godet on the Depths of the Book of Job, an analysis of the argument.   Kirchner on the Eschatology of Irenaeus—a careful and useful study.   Riggenbach on the Ark of the Covenant—the main points of his recent work, noticed by himself.   Wuttke's System of Christian Ethics, reviewed by Fr. Nitzsch, and noted as a vigorous attempt to construct ethics scientifically on the basis of the Lutheran orthodoxy.

Jahrbücher für deutsche Theologie, Heft 1, 1863.   Löwe on the Results of Recent Investigations upon the Trinity: the amount is, that God is essentially *love*, and as such self-communicating; and that the eternal distinction of Father and Son is to be viewed in this aspect and relation.   Frommann on "the creature" in Rom. viii, 19–23: the creature here means the human race.   Zöckler, Unity of the Race; an able defence, coinciding with Quatrefages.   Steitz on Auricular Confession in the primitive church, showing that it was not practised.   The author has written an elaborate work on the whole Discipline of primitive times.

Deutsche Vierteljahrsschrift.   (The German *Quarterly for English Theological Research and Criticism*.)   Nos. 3 and 4.   1862.   Edited by Dr. M. Heidenheim in London.   The numbers of this new periodical appear somewhat irregularly, the 3d bearing date Jan., and the 4th Sept., 1862.   Its chief value is in giving the results of Dr. Heidenheim's Samaritan researches: the present number containing some eight articles from his pen, on different codices, inscriptions, and fragments in the British Museum. One of these is a codex of the Prophets, written between the 6th and 8th centuries.   Dr. E. Hincks contributes a valuable version of an inscription on Sennacherib and Hezekiah.   Canon Stanley's Introductory Lectures on Church History are given in a German version.   Dr. Julius Hamberger presents a concise summary of the main points in Schelling's Philosophy of Mythology and of Revelation.   Reviews of recent English theological works are also given.   Dr. Heidenheim gives a short notice of visits to the libraries in Rome.   One inscription in the Vatican, of the time of the Second Temple, he thinks he has succeeded in deciphering, though it has baffled all previous explorers.   In the Barberini library he found a ms. which he thinks the oldest extant, viz. from the year of the world 4418—it is a kabbalistic work.   He also found in the Vatican a Rabbinic Hebrew ms. of the Gospels, of which he promises further accounts.

Zeitschrift für die lutherische Theologie, No. 2, 1863.   The first short article by Delitzsch is on a certain Theodore, called Hagiopetrite, whose name is found on some seven of the minuscule manuscripts of the New Test., who has usually been supposed to be a monk of Mount Athos. Delitzsch identifies this Hagios Petros as a village in Cynuria, and Theodore as living there in the 13th or 14th century.   Delitzsch also contributes an instructive article on the doctrine of the Logos in Philo and John, which will appear in a future number of our REVIEW.   H. O. Köhler reviews Hugo Lämmer's Analecta Romana, exposing the great change which two years wrought in the opinions of Lämmer, on a great variety of historical and theological topics, after his conversion to Romanism.   The interesting series of letters from Rudelbach, chiefly relating to the Lutheran Journal, is continued.

Zeitschrift für die wissenschaftliche Theologie, 1863. *Erstes Heft.* Hilgenfeld on the Theology of the Nineteenth Century describes, sharply, the three tendencies, moral, speculative, and mystic (Schleiermacher) of the later theology—partly reviewing Baur's Church History of XIX Century. A. Merx, Critical Investigation of the Laws of Sacrifice, Levit. i–vii. D. F. Strauss (author of the Life of Christ) on Christ's lamentation over Jerusalem, and the Wisdom of God as cited in Luke xi, 49. This Wisdom he conjectures to be an apocrypal book, written about the time of the destruction of Jerusalem. Ewald puts it in the 5th century before Christ—so diverging are the results of "the higher criticism". Zeller on James i, 12. Hilgenfeld on the theology of John, with respect to Weiss's recent work.

Dr. J. Petzholdt, the bibliographer, has been preparing for seven years a *Bibliotheca Bibliographica*, with critical comments. The printing of the work is begun.

Dr. J. Kelle, of Prague, will soon publish the first volume of his *Comparative Grammar* of the German languages ; the first volume will contain the nouns.

Under the auspices of the Berlin Academy, F. Ritschelius has brought out vol. 1 of a Corpus Inscriptionum Latinorum, containing lithographs of the epigraphic remains of the old Latinity, fol. 96 plates, 137 pp. letter press; price $30.

The Canon Law of the Oriental Church is digested in Jos. Papp-Szilagyi Enchiridion Juris Ecclesiastici Orientalis Catholicæ—from the sources, pp. 656.

The last part of Brugsch's *Collection of Egyptian Monuments* has been published, containing 60 pages of text and 57 tables.

In Germany, the whole number of books (excluding pamphlets) published in 1862, was 9776 (in 1861, 9566), being about 27 a day. Theology takes the lead in 1459; history and biography, 591; jurisprudence and politics, 990; philosophy, only 94; medicine, 446; classical and oriental, 316; educational, 842; modern languages, 291; mathematics, 78; military, 207; architecture, 187; belles-lettres, 961; fine arts, 434, etc.

Wilke's well-known Clavis Novi Testamenti has been out of the market for several years; a new edition carefully revised by Prof. C. L. W. Grimm of Jena, is to be published in 4 livraisons, at 20 *groschen* each. The whole of Olshausen's Commentary on the New Test. is now offered for 14 *Thaler :* vols. 5 to 7, by Wiesinger and Ebrard for 8 *Thaler.*

Thousandth Anniversary in Moravia.—The Moravians intend during the present year to celebrate the thousandth anniversary of the introduction of Christianity into their country. Great preparations are to be made for the occasion, and visitors are expected to be present in large numbers from all the neighboring countries—Bohemia, Gallicia, Croatia, Hungary, Posen, and Russian Poland.

The private correspondence between Goethe and Karl August, never published before, will soon appear in print. The present Grand Duke of Saxe Weimar has intrusted Dr. Vogel with the arrangement and publication of this correspondence, which, it is said, comprises about six hundred letters.

FRANCE.

Annales de Philosophie Chrétienne, dirigé par A. Bonnetty. 1863. Abbé Darras on the confirmation of the Bible from the Assyrian Inscriptions, as deciphered by M. Oppert : the chief point is in reference to King Sargon, mentioned in Isaiah xx, 1, and no where else ; and the account of the captivity in 2 Kings, xviii, 9–11.   The new inscriptions show that Sargon reigned after Salmanasar V, having dethroned him.   Bonnetty continues his learned account of the knowledge which the Romans had of the Jews.   A curious pamphlet of Abbé Faydit against Malebranche (1699) is given in copious extracts.   Faydit is the author of the noted satire on Malebranche's theory :

> Lui qui voit tout en Dieu, n'y voit pas qu'il est fou.

M. B. Pautex has published a volume on the Errata in the Dictionary of the French Academy, which makes out a worse list of blunders and inconsistencies than the rival critics of Webster and Worcester were able to find in their Dictionaries.

M. Gerusez, well known by his valuable History of French Literature, has published an Abridgment, in a single volume, for the use of students, very condensed and valuable.

A new work by Abd-el-Kader is announced—*Abd-el-Kader et le Catholicisme*—to prove that Catholicism is too spiritual and Mosaism too material, and that the Islam faith reconciles matter and spirit in just proportions, and hence will prevail in history.

The *Revue Chrétienne* begins the year 1863 with authority to discuss questions bearing on politics.   The editor De Pressensé in the January number has an excellent exposition of principles.   The services of the noble Chancellor L'Hôpital for religious freedom (1550–'60) are narrated by Delaborde.   St. Hilaire commends Prof. Bost's Epoch of the Maccabees : and De Guerle has an essay on the Religious Opinions of Milton.   In the February number, Schæffer concludes an essay on the mystic and unknown philosopher Saint-Martin, who saw things "beyond the sun".   Rev. G. Fisch contributes an earnest defence of our country : Astié discourses on the Religious Awakening in Switzerland and France.   March : Lichtenberger on Uhland ; Astié on the Revival of Religion.

The Academician, M. E. Littré has published the first part of his *Dictionaire de la Langue Française*, on which he has been at work for fifteen years.   Critics give it the highest praise for its thoroughness, and its superiority to the Dictionary of the Academy.   Three paragraphs are devoted to each word, giving its definition with examples, its history, and its etymology.   A new edition of M. Littré's History of the French Language has also just been issued by Didier & Co.

GREAT BRITAIN.

The British and Foreign Evanglical Review, Jan. 1863, reprints from the Presbyterian Quarterly, Rev. A. Barnes's article on the Readjustment of Christianity, and the Matter of Prophecy from the Princeton Review.   An able article on the Philosophy of the Unconditioned opposes the views of Hamilton and Mansel.   The Theories of the Sabbath, Dominical and Sabbatarian, Hippolytus against Noctus, the Literature of Pascal's Thoughts, etc., are topics of other articles.   The number for April, reprints two articles on Dr. Hickok from the *Princeton Review ;* one on the Relation of Adam to his Posterity from the Christian Review, and Dr. Pond on the Laws of Moral Influence, from the same review.   It also gives a condensed translation of Dorner on the Immutability of God : a translation of a part of Rudelbach's article on Inspiration, published some thirty years ago in the

Lutherische Zeitschrift, valuable for the history of the doctrine. Other articles are on Priestley, the Madras Mission, Davidson and Colenso.

Journal of Sacred Literature. April, 1863. The Codex Sinaiticus—a good account and vindication. Memoirs of Bossuet—continued. Notes of a Visit to Malta. Renan—an account of his pantheistic speculations. The Importance of Linguistic Preparations for the Ministry, by Rev. Chs. H. Wright—a valuable lecture ; it gives an enumeration of the Arabic works published by our American Board. The Buddhist Scriptures, and their Language, the Pali, by Jas. Alwis, Esq. The Bible as the Word of God. Exegesis of Difficult Texts. Anecdota Syriaca, an account of the recent volume of Dr. Land of Holland, edited from the British Museum manuscripts. The Samaritan Pentateuch. Obituary of Dr. Edward Robinson. Correspondence. Notices of Books. Of all the English theological publications this Journal is the best one for our ministers. Under the editorship of Mr. Cowper it is amply sustaining its high character.

Rev. B. W. Savile's work on *Revelation and Science* is said by the Journal of Sacred Literature to be one of the best works on the recent controversies raised by Bunsen, the Essays and Reviews, and similar works.

The question of Faith and Reason is agitating the English Catholics. The new periodical *Home and Foreign Review*, the successor of the *Rambler*, is denounced as rationalistic by Bp. Ullathorne. Mr. Simpson has replied in various articles, collected from the Rambler, and published under the title Forms of Intuition. He maintains that faith is a form of reason ; and that the provinces of theology and science are entirely distinct. This is denied by Brownson, in his Quarterly Review, April, who says, that thus there is no reconciliation possible between the two, and who urges a " dialectic union and harmony of the matters of revelation with the matters of science", thus alone making one whole.

The *Anti-Colenso Literature* is still growing fast. Some sixty works have been published. Edward Greswell, *The Objections to the Historical Character of the Pentateuch.* 5s. Wm. H. Hoare, *Age and Authorship of the Pentateuch*, in reply to Colenso's Part II. Rev. Jas. R. Page, *The Pretensions of Bp. Colenso.* 5s. Robert Moon, *The Pent. and Book of Joshua.* 5s.—said to be one of the best. Prof. M'Caul's *Examination*, in a people's edition for 1s. Rev. F. Ashpitel, *The Increase of the Israelites.* John B. Marsh, *Is the Pent. Historically True ?* Rev. T. R. Birks, *The Exodus of Israel*, etc., prepared for the Tract Society, with great care. Dr. Bemish's articles in the Jewish Chronicle are republished. Rev. W. A. Scott, D.D. (late of this country), *Moses and the Pentateuch*, a vol. of 185 pp. : the *Literary Churchman* says of it : " His book has an air of Presbyterian poetry about it, which will do good to many simple hearts, but touch no one's reason who is critically disposed ". G. S. Drew's *Examination* is said to be well done. Rev. J. G. Hewlett, *Bible Difficulties explained.* 2s. 6d. Rev. G. E. Biber, Veracity and Divine Authority of the Pentateuch, deals with the 600,000 armed men.

Dean Ellicott, now Bp. of Gloucester and Bristol, was born in 1819, educated at Cambridge ; obtained Hulsean Prize, 1842, for an essay on the Obligations of the Sabbath ; wrote a treatise on Analytical Statics ; Prof. of Divinity at King's College, London, succeeding Dean Trench : 1860, Hulsean Professor of Divinity at Cambridge ; Dean of Exeter, 1861 ; has written commentaries on Galatians, Ephesians, Philip., Colos., Thessal., Philemon and the Pastoral Epistles. His last work is on the Life of our Lord, republished in Boston.

An edition of the Sinaitic Codex is to be published in London by Williams & Norgate for 18s. Some English journals continue the advocacy of the impudent claims of Simonides : as others do of the pretensions of the Southern Confederacy.

It is not often that a cabinet minister is found making a collection of Hymns ; but Sir Roundell Palmer in his *Book of Praise*, 12mo, pp. 472, has gathered together one of the choicest collections that has been made.   The book is published by Macmillan & Co.   Cambridge.

Theological Works.   Rev. Rd. Brigham has prepared a revised Prayer Book under the title *Liturgicae recusae Exemplar*, consisting of old and revised formularies.   Rev. Dr. J. M. Neale's papers on liturgical subjects have been collected from the Christian Remembrancer and other sources under the title *Essays on Liturgiology and Church History.*   The late Prof. Rask's tractates on the longevity of the patriarchs, the flood, the exodus, etc. have been translated from the Danish and published by Trübner & Co.   Rev. C. P. Shepherd, *The Argument of St. Paul in the Epistle to the Romans.* Vol. I. Pt. I. 10s.   *Lectures on Theology, Science and Revelation* by Geo. Legge, LL.D., with a Memoir.——James Gibson, D.D., of Free Church College, Glasgow, *Present Truths in Theology*——on man's inability and God's sovereignty.   2 vols. 21s.——Rev. Robt. Jamieson, Fausset and David Brown, A Commentary on Old and New Testaments, 6 vols. for £2 5s. in preparation. Dr. Lange's Life of Christ is announced by Clark, Edinb. in 6 vols. £1 15s.

The first well executed English translation of the "Thoughts" of the Emperor Marcus Antoninus, has been made by Mr. George Long, one of the editors of the *Bibliotheca Classica.*   The Emperor was born A.D. 121, and belonged to the sect of the Stoics.   His Meditations have in them much of pure and lofty morality.

Spinoza's *Tractatus Theologico-Politicus ;* a Critical Inquiry into the Hebrew Scriptures, has been translated, and is published with an Introduction and Notes, by Trübner of London.

Macmillan & Co. publish *The Missionary History of the Middle Ages*, by the Rev. George Frederick MacClear, Classical Master in King's College, London.

The second volume of Dr. William Smith's *Dictionary of the Bible*, is promised to be ready in London in the course of the present month.   Little, Brown & Co. are the American publishers.

Oliphant & Co. (Edinburgh) have commenced republishing Dr. Jacobus' excellent Notes on the New Testament.

A new volume by John Foster is soon to appear.   It will contain " An Essay on the Improvement of Time, and other Literary Remains," with a preface by one of the author's oldest surviving friends, John Sheppard, Esq., of Frome, and will be edited by Mr. J. E. Ryland.   The "Essay" has never before been given to the world, but has remained in the possession of Mr. Foster's family.   Several eminent literary persons have expressed a high opinion of its merits, and we believe it will be found quite worthy of the author's reputation.   It is to be republished by the Appletons.

ORDINATION STATISTICS.—The *Clerical Journal* publishes the ordination statistics for 1862.   It appears that there have been 68 ordinations held during the past year, at which 1082 candidates were ordained ; of these 508 were ordained deacons, and 524 were ordained priests.   This number falls short by 86 of the number ordained in the previous year.   Of the candidates ordained in 1861, there were 856 from the four Universities; whilst in 1862 there were 780, thus showing a falling off of 76 in this direction.

The average number of readers at the British Museum in 1862 was four hundred and nineteen per day, and each reader, on an average consulted ten volumes.   Deducting fifty-two for the Sundays and twenty-one days (at a guess) for holidays, we have thus a total of about a million and a quarter of volumes consulted in the course of the year.

The London *Jewish Chronicle* states that Mr. Saville Davis, of Worcester College, has recently been admitted to the degree of B.A., being the *first Jew on whom that honor has been conferred in the University.*

UNITED STATES OF AMERICA.

A new edition of Mr. Ticknor's History of Spanish Literature, revised and rewritten, is announced in three volumes. Mr. Ticknor is also preparing a life of Prescott, the historian. Alger's History of the Doctrine of a Future Life will soon be published, with a full bibliography, prepared by Ezra Abbott. The second part of Allibone's Dictionary of Authors is making as rapid progress as is possible. Edward Everett is reported to be writing a work on the Law of Nations. Draper's History of the Intellectual Development of Europe is published by the Harpers. The Appletons are to republish Mill's Political Economy and Merivale's Romans under the Empire. Gould & Lincoln announce Gillette's Life and Times of Huss—an elaborate work, and a translation by Rev. W. L. Gage of Ritter's Geographical Studies. The ninth volume of Mr. Bancroft's History of the United States is in press. Mr. Scribner will publish a translation of Laboulaye's Political Studies on the United States; Bushnell's Work and Offices of Christ; a second series of Max Müller's Lectures on Language; Maurice's History of Philosophy.

Mr. Geo. W. Childs has begun the publication of the American Publishers' Circular and Literary Gazette, in a very complete form. It will appear twice a month at $2 a year. The plan and arrangement are excellent. For libraries and literary men, as well as publishers, it will be invaluable.

The Christian Review (Baptist) for January has a translation by Dr. Arnold of Alexander de Stourdza (of Odessa) on the Greek Church—a translation of his work, *The Double Parallel*, published in French in 1848, in reply to Pope Pius IX's Encyclical, exhorting the patriarchs and bishops of the East to accept his authority. It is an interesting and valuable exposition of the differences of the Greek and Roman churches, and also of the points of division between the Greek and Protestant views. Stourdza also published at Vienna in 1816, *Considerations on the Doctrine and Spirit of the Orthodox* (Greek) *Church.*

Dr. Miron Winslow's Tamil and English Dictionary, published some months since at Madras, elicits warm encomiums. The work was begun nearly thirty years ago by Rev. J. Knight, of the English mission, assisted by a native, Tissera, and others. After Mr. Knight's death it was prosecuted at the American mission at Jaffna. Rev. Levi Spaulding brought out the Tamil Dictionary, and Rev. S. Hutchings worked on the English. Since 1842 the work has been in Mr. Winslow's hands. It is a boon to the Madras Presidency, as well as to the cause of missions.

The Arabic Bible.—The Board of Managers of the American Bible Society have made provision for printing the Beyrut translation of the Arabic Scriptures, which has been for years in progress by the late Rev. Dr. Eli Smith and Rev. Dr. C. V. Van Dyck. The whole of the New Testament is finished, and the Old Testament so far as the Book of Proverbs. Editions of the finished portions have already been printed, and are in growing circulation. There will be a great demand for this translation, which is acknowledged by the first living Arabic scholars to be the best extant. It will give the word of God to one hundred millions of people who speak the

Arabic language.   It is found that vast numbers of people in Central Africa are able to read in Arabic.

A curious contrast is afforded by the respective returns of the number of newspapers and magazines in Great Britain and the United States.   In January of this year there were but seventeen hundred and forty three (1,743) papers and magazines published in the United Kingdom, while the numbers in the United States, by the census of 1860, were four thousand and fifty one (4,051).   Out of the total of seventeen hundred and forty-three publications in Great Britain, five hundred and thirty-seven were magazines, of which no less than two hundred and seventeen were of a religious character.   The population of Great Britain and the United States is about the same (in round numbers, thirty millions).   Of the daily papers in Great Britain, forty-six are published in England, nine in Scotland, and one in Wales.

A new geographical and historical map of the Holy Land and Syria, by Lyman Coleman, D.D., and Prof. H. S. Osborn, is to be published by subscription by L. Coleman, Easton, Pa., and R. L. Barnes, of Philadelphia. Every biblical place will be represented in conspicuous characters, large in proportion to the importance of the place.   The map will contain, besides, all places alluded to by historical writers, both ancient and modern, and important missionary stations.   Great pains have been taken to insure minuteness, correctness, and elegance.   The price will be ten dollars for the map, together with Dr. Coleman's historical *Geography and Atlas* and Prof. Osborn's *Plants of the Holy Land.*

The death at Yonkers, of Rev. Dr. Baird, has removed from us one whose name has been for over a generation identified with many of our prominent religious societies.

Robert Baird was born in Fayette county, Pennsylvania, on the 6th of October, 1798, and in 1818 graduated at Jefferson College in that State. He studied theology at Princeton, New Jersey, and in 1822 was licensed to preach.   In Princeton he for five years conducted a grammar school, but in 1828 relinquished it, to form a connection with the American Bible Society as a missionary agent in the State of New Jersey.   Subsequently he travelled through all parts of the United States in behalf of the American Sunday-School Union; and in 1835 extended his travels to Europe, where he remained over eight years, preaching in behalf of temperance and Protestantism.   He has since that time been connected in different capacities with various religious organizations.

Dr. Baird has written several valuable books.   His "View of the Valley of the Mississippi" was published in 1832.   The "History of the Temperance Societies" appeared in 1836, and was translated into German, Dutch, Swedish, Finnish and Russ.   "Religion in America", printed in Glasgow in 1842, won nearly as great a popularity, and "Protestantism in Italy", published in Boston in 1845, attracted considerable attention at the time. Besides these Dr. Baird has edited several religious memoirs, and has written very largely for the periodical and newspaper press of this country and England.

Mr. Richard Grant White's Life of Shakespeare is in preparation, and will probably be published the present season.   It will complete the edition of Shakespeare's Works, in twelve volumes, published by Messrs. Little & Brown.

Art. X.—CRITICISMS ON BOOKS.

THEOLOGY.

Handbuch der Protestantischen Polemik gegen die Römisch-Katholische Kirche, von Dr. Karl Hase. Leipzig. 1862. Pp. 665. It is nearly thirty years since Möhler published his Symbolism—the most plausible and effective modern apology for Rome. It was ably encountered by Nitzsch and Baur—the work of the latter, in spite of his pantheistic tendencies, containing a thorough vindication of Protestant doctrine. Dr. Hase, as his Preface informs us, began at that time to write a reply, which, after years of elaboration, is now published. It was begun and finished at Rome. Written with a full mastery of the subject, in a style at once manly and popular, acute and concise in argument, and pregnant with wit, it cannot fail to take a high place in the literature of Protestant polemic theology. On the questions of the Church, its unity and infallibility, of the papacy and its claims, of the priesthood and celibacy, of good works, of the immaculate conception of the Virgin Mary, and of the sacraments, it defends the Protestant doctrine with skill and effect. Some of the doctrinal points, e. g., original sin and man's primitive state, are only incidentally discussed. On the doctrine of justification by faith, the semi-rationalistic position of the author renders his conduct of the argument less satisfactory. The volume is divided into three Books : 1. The Church ; 2. Salvation ; 3. Incidental Topics (*Beisachen*), such as Cultus, Art, Science and Literature, Politics and Nationality. In the present state of Europe, the chapter on the temporal power (the Pope-King) claims and merits special attention for its lucid and satisfactory exposition. The volume is not written for ministers and theologians alone ; it is such as an intelligent and thoughtful reader would thoroughly like and appreciate.

The eighth (supplementary) volume of the *Lives of the Fathers of the Lutheran Church,* contains the lives of Justus Jonas, the friend of Luther, and teacher of theology at Wittenberg ; of Caspar Cruciger, also active at Wittenberg ; of Paulus Speratus, court preacher at Königsberg, and bishop of Pomerania ; of Lazarus Spengler, the reformer of Nuremberg ; of Nicholas Van Amsdorf, Superintendent at Magdeburg, and a leader in the Majoristic and Synergistic controversies ; of Paul Eber, also Superintendent and professor of theology ; of Martin Chemnitz, the renowned author of the Examination of the Council of Trent ; and of David Chytræus, Professor at Rostock, and, with Chemnitz, active in the formation of the Formula Concordiæ. All of these biographies are by Dr. Theodore Pressel, and cast much light upon both the external and internal history of the Reformation. The lives of Luther, by Schneider, of Osiander, by Lehnerdt, and of Bugenhagen, by Vogt, are still to be issued.

Letters of the Rev. John Smith, *a Presbyterian Minister, to his Brother, the* Rev. Peter Smith, *a Methodist Preacher.* Philadelphia. Lippincott & Co. 1862. 12mo, pp. 188. The points of difference between Calvinism and Arminianism are here briefly discussed, in a good spirit and with creditable ability.

A Collection of Theological Essays from various authors. With an Introduction by George N. Noyes, D.D., Professor of Sacred Literature in Harvard University. Third Edition. Boston : Walker, Wise & Co. New

York: O. S. Felt. 12mo, pp. 512. These Essays are too well known to need a formal notice in this REVIEW. Their theological character is indicated by the fact that they are published for and in behalf of the American Unitarian Association. The represent the Broad-Church School, and receive special significance from recent developments in England and elsewhere. While we should take issue with these Essays on many of the essential points discussed in them, we still commend them as worthy the attention of all thinking men, and especially of those who are set for the defence of the faith.

BIBLICAL LITERATURE.

The Pentateuch vindicated from the Aspersions of Bishop Colenso. By WILLIAM HENRY GREEN, Professor in Princeton Theological Seminary. New York: John Wiley. 1863. The pretensions, false assumptions, contradictions and illogical reasonings of Bishop Colenso are unsparingly exposed in this acute polemic treatise. Dr. Green is at home in the literature of the subject. He takes up the objections in detail, and gives in the main satisfactory replies. The subject has been so thoroughly treated by Dr. Goodwin in this REVIEW, that we need not enter into a statement of the questions involved. We notice that Professor Green adopts the view that the abode in Egypt was 430 years. His book, sharply written, almost with the fervor of a personal discussion, takes a leading place among the sixty volumes which have been published in reply to the Bishop of Natal.

The Holy Word its own Defence: Addressed to Bishop Colenso, and all other earnest Seekers after Truth. By Rev. ABIEL SILVER. New York: Appletons. 1863. If any body takes this book in hand with the expectation of finding · in it a detailed reply to Colenso, he will be sorely disappointed. It is a work on Swedenborgianism, to show that the so-called Science of Correspondences is the only way of interpreting Scripture so as to get rid of difficulties. But we think it is easier to reply to Colenso than to defend the Swedenborgian theories. To try to do both at once is needlessly embarrassing. Alleged errors of facts and detail are not refuted by supposing that the words may have some mystic sense. When an author, for example, would explain the difficulties about Jonah and the whale, by saying that the fish means skepticism, and that Jonah's being three days in the whale's belly means that he was under the power of skepticism for a time—this is more amusing than convincing. In other respects, the work is a fair and well written account of some of the Swedenborgian doctrines and imaginations.

The Spiritual Point of View; or the Glass Reversed. An Answer to Bishop Colenso. By M. MAHAN, D.D. New York: Appletons. Dr. Mahan's method of reply has already been fully discussed in the pages of our Review. On several questions of detail his replies are sharp and pertinent.

The New Testament; with Brief Explanatory Notes (or Scholia). By HOWARD CROSBY, D.D. New York: Scribner. $1.50. These notes, prepared by a careful scholar, are based on a thorough study of the Greek, without any parade of Greek learning. They are very much to the point, correcting the translation, illustrating historic and archæological references, showing the connection of thought, etc. Of course all difficulties are not explained ; and the plan of the book prevented discussion. But they will be found very valuable. We wish that the author had also given a concise introduction to each of the books.

Bunsen's Bibelwerk.—The first half of the 5th volume is just out, containing the Psalms, with a revised translation, in parallelisms, by A. Kamphausen, teacher in Bonn. Concise exegetical notes illustrate the text. This translation will take a high rank among the modern versions of the Psalms.

The Words of the Lord Jesus. By RUDOLF STIER, D.D. Translated by W. B. Pope. Revised by Jas. Strong, D.D., and Henry B. Smith, D.D. Part 2. These Words of the Lord Jesus will be published in 12 parts, making 2 vols., and including the *Words of the Angels.* The *Words of the Apostles*, by the same author, will make another volume of 6 parts. The price is 75 cents a part. The work is issued by Mr. Tibbals for the Ministers' Library Association, 37 Park Row, and 145 Nassau st. Of Stier, recently deceased, we give a short account under another head. He was a most earnest and devoted preacher. He preached the Bible. His commentaries went through the pulpit, and so are well adapted to ministers' use. He is a very ingenious, fertile and evangelical expositor. He surveys the text in all lights, and examines diverging views. No one can read his writings without great profit. He was a Lutheran, and not a Calvinist; and some of his comments show this bias, but not in such a way as to be offensive to the reader.

The Last Times and the Great Consummation. An earnest discussion of momentous themes. By JOSEPH A. SEISS, D.D., author of "The Gospel in Leviticus", "The Parable of the Ten Virgins", "The Day of the Lord", "Lecture on the Epistle to the Hebrews", etc. Revised and enlarged edition. Philadelphia: Smith, English & Co. 1863. 12mo, pp. 438. This work is considered among the ablest of its school. Dr. Seiss is an earnest advocate of the Millenarian doctrine. He has evidently bestowed a good deal of time and thought upon the subject, and gives to the world, in this new and enlarged edition of his book, his latest and maturest views upon it. To those who desire to see the argument on which Second Advent views rest, we commend this work of Dr. Seiss: we doubt if they have found an abler or more earnest advocate. We need not say that we totally dissent from the views of this school, believing them to be unscriptural and pernicious in their tendency.

Triumphs of the Bible with the Testimony of Science to its Truth. By Rev. HENRY TULLIDGE, A.M. New York: Charles Scribner. 1863. 12mo, pp. 439. This book is timely and judicious. It attempts too much to be thorough and exhaustive; and it cannot lay claim to originality either in the way of investigation or argument, and hence has no particular scientific value; still it meets the plausible attacks of infidelity in its latest developments fairly and in a popular and satisfactory manner, and vindicates the truth of Revelation by a great variety of testimony patiently collated from many of the ablest writers and presented in a style fresh and intelligible. The portion of it which sets forth the Testimony of Science to the Bible is specially interesting and valuable. The author evinces familiarity with the entire literature of the subject, and gives good and sufficient reasons for rejecting much of the science of the day, *falsely so called.* His chapters on Geology, on the Unity of the Human Race, and on Chronology aim to defend those outposts of the Bible which modern infidelity is assaulting with such ingenuity and such persistent efforts. We cordially commend the book as a timely and judicious contribution to the great mass of Christian Evidences.

Bible Illustrations, being a Storehouse of Similes, Allegories and Anecdotes, selected from Spencer's "Things New and Old", and other sources, with an Introduction by Rev. RICHARD NEWTON, D.D., and a copious Index.

Philadelphia : Smith, English & Co. New York : Carter & Brothers. 1863.
12mo, pp. 360.   This title faithfully describes the book. The selection
strikes us as judicious.   There is nothing that we discover in these illustrations to offend good taste. They are for the most part apt and suggestive, and bear on almost every point of doctrine and morals. As a book of
reference it may often aid the preacher and the Sunday-school teacher.

HISTORY AND BIOGRAPHY.

The History of the Reformation in Europe in the Time of Calvin. By
J. H. MERLE D'AUBIGNÉ, D.D.   2 vols. New York: R. Carter. 1863.
These volumes are introduced by a special address to the American public,
avowing the author's sympathy with our national cause. They are the
first instalment of a work on the Reformation in the French speaking
countries of Europe. In Switzerland the struggle resulted in political as
well as religious freedom. A large part of the first volume is occupied
with an account of parties and conflicts in Geneva, before the coming of
Calvin.   The narrative is minute yet graphic. It is here brought down, in
both France and Switzerland to 1534. The account of the early training
and preparation of Calvin for his reforming work is admirably done.
Margaret of Navarre is also fully described, with evident partiality. We
have not in English literature any work which goes over this period so
fully and accurately ; none which describes the actors and scenes in such
dramatic style. The style strikes us as an improvement upon that in the
author's previous volumes, with less attempt at artistic effect, and a more
rigid adherence to the authentic words of the speakers and actors in this
great drama.   The book cannot fail of being a popular history, in the best
sense of the phrase. It may not have as enthusiastic a reception as the
earlier volumes on Luther, but it will give pleasure to the scholar, and
instruction to all. The union of order and liberty in the work of reform
is the main theme, reading to us most important lessons in the midst of
our present conflicts. A good likeness of Calvin is prefixed to the first
volume.

*The Invasion of the Crimea : its Origin and an Account of its Progress
down to the Death of Lord Raglan.* By ALEXANDER WILLIAM KINGLAKE.
Vol. I, New York : Harpers. 1863. pp. 750.   This history of the Crimean
campaign is an attack upon the French Emperor. Written with consummate
skill, with access to the best sources of information, and with rare descriptive talent, it enchains the attention of the reader, as if the scenes were
transpiring before his eyes. The object of the author is, not merely to
vindicate Lord Raglan but to impugn the policy of the English government,
and to cover Louis Napoleon with disgrace. It is a history, but it is also
a terrible satire. The leading idea of the book is, that Louis Napoleon,
with a band of bold and perjured conspirators, by craft and violence got
possession of France, and then, to bolster up an insecure throne, entered
into alliance with England, and forced her to follow him in making war
against Russia. England is exhibited throughout as the subservient victim
of French diplomacy and intrigues. At the same time, in the account of
the Crimean campaign, the military plans and valor of the English are
defended against the covert insinuations or open attacks of French critics.
While, now, there is no doubt that the French Emperor obtained his power
through fraud and violence, yet, it strikes us that the author is obliged to
strain many facts in order to make out his main argument. The position
of England was much more honorable, and her policy much wiser, than is

here represented. Had she not then interfered, the Russian power would have become predominant in the East. The descriptions of personal character are wrought out in sharp outlines. Nobody can begin the book without running through it. The Harpers edition is well brought out, and gives us for a dollar and a half what costs five times as much in the English copy.

Lectures on the History of the Jewish Church. Part I. Abraham to Samuel. By A. P. STANLEY, D.D. With Maps and Plans. New York: Chas. Scribner. 1863. 8vo, pp. 572. The Regius Professor of Ecclesiastical History in the University of Cambridge is bringing new life into his department of instruction. By previous studies and travels well fitted for this work, he presents a vivid picture of the ancient Jewish people, making the absent present, and giving life-like narratives of the events and characters of those early days. For such descriptions the free form of the lecture is well adapted. It allows the writer to group together whatever may heighten the effect of the picture, and to bring in illustrations from various sources. Of this privilege Dr. Stanley has made liberal use, and produced a most attractive volume. He writes, too, in sufficient sympathy-with the spirit of the men and times to enter into their circumstances and give us what they thought and felt, without intermingling the doctrines and traditions of later times. As was to be expected from the author's antecedents his criticism is free, and he remains in doubt about many questions which are now sharply debated. Evidently his leanings are very strong towards the liberal school of interpretation, and his views of the inspiration of the old records are quite vague, even if he admits any proper inspiration at all. Many of the questions raised by Colenso's arithmetic he dismisses as if they were of no sort of importance for his object. He does not know whether the Israelites were in Egypt 215 or 430 or 1000 years. He leaves the question whether the number of armed Israelites who left Egypt, was "600 or 600,000 men" to be decided by others. He implies that monotheism was unknown before Abraham, and that the name Jehovah was unknown to Abraham, Isaac, and Jacob. He cannot tell how the Israelites were supported in their journeyings. He ascribes the priesthood to an Egyptian origin. If we only admit the arithmetical errors lately pointed out, and give up the Mosaic authorship of the Pentateuch, he thinks we should "remove at one stroke some of the main difficulties of the Mosaic narrative". At a time when these questions are so fully discussed, we think that an author, writing on these subjects might well have been expected to come to some more definite conclusions, or to fortify his opinions by more thorough investigations, and we regret that Dr. Stanley has not done this. The work is not satisfactory, either in affirmation or denial, in the controverted points. And yet it is a brilliant course of lectures. New matter is furnished to the historian in the appendices on the Cave of Machpelah and the Samaritan Passover. The getting up of the book by Mr. Scribner is in every respect admirable.

The Works of Rufus Choate with a Memoir of his Life. By SAMUEL GILMAN BROWN, Prof. in Dartmouth College. 2 vols. Boston: Little, Brown & Co. Professor Brown has reared a fitting monument to the memory of one of the most gifted and fascinating of the sons of New England. Mr. Choate had an oriental imagination combined with Yankee sense. He seemed almost like an exotic in the land of his birth, and yet he thrived there. No man of his times united such apparently contradictory traits. He was impulsive yet had entire self-command; in many things simple as a child, he yet swayed masses of men with great power; the closest of students, he also courted society; the most fluent of speakers, he carefully studied his utterances; the most imaginative of lawyers, a severe and sharp logic runs through all his harangues; every thing he said seemed spontaneous, yet it was all the fruit of anxious toil. He was the most magnetic orator we ever heard; nobody within sound of his voice could get disenthralled from his spell. Yet, when he was most prodigal in his vocabulary, he was also most intent upon his main object.

His life is worthy of study. And it is here admirably depicted. Ministers should read it, if only to learn the lesson, how to make all their studies and reading bear upon the great art of public address. We have been surprised at the record of his diligence, the wide range of his studies, his careful husbandry of time. His plans for reading and writing, outside of his professional course, were carefully made, and clung to with tenacity. He always had with him some classic, Greek, Roman, or English—some work in literature—some commentary, to fill up his leisure moments. Rare specimens of his translations from Thucydides and Tacitus are given in the appendix to these volumes—not prepared for the press, yet well fitted for the eye of scholars. Large extracts from his journals give us much about his method of study and glimpses into his delightful private life. Of his religious life we have only glimpses; he was attached to the orthodox faith, yet he shrunk from speaking of his personal feelings. His career as a lawyer is fully related, and also his political course. In the latter part of his life, he left the Whig party with which he had been associated, and became a Democrat—doubtless from love to the unity to his country, yet in this clearly showing how even the most sagacious and pure-minded of men may utterly mistake the true character and bearings of the history, which they may have a part in making.

This biography will take its place among our treasured books. And long will students resort to these wonderful speeches and addresses to attempt to learn the secret of that inspiring eloquence which equally charmed people and politicians, lawyers and judges, and scholars of every profession.

Memoirs of Mrs. Joanna Bethune. By her son, the Rev. GEORGE W. BETHUNE, D.D. With an Appendix, containing extracts from the writings of MRS. BETHUNE. New York: Harper & Brothers. 1863. 12mo, pp. 250. This Memoir is the last work of the gifted BETHUNE—and it is a most touching tribute to the memory of his sainted mother. These last fruits of his pen will be read with tearful interest and cherished by his numerous friends with an almost sacred regard. The lines (66 in number) addressed some years since to his mother, are exquisitely tender and beautiful. Had we space we would give them entire. They are scarcely inferior to Cowper's celebrated lines. Few sons have had such a mother to love and to bless them; and few mothers have had such a son to appreciate and chronicle their virtues! The extracts from the writings of Mrs. Bethune, which comprise half the volume, exhibit a life of deep spiritual feeling, extraordinary activity, and strong faith in the covenant promises. She bears a striking resemblance to her mother, Mrs. Isabella Graham. These Memoirs are adapted to stimulate Christian ladies in their prayers and labors in behalf of a suffering and dying world. The life of Dr. Bethune remains to be written. We trust he will find a fitting biographer.

Triumph in Trial. A Memorial of SARAH S. MUGFORD, of Salem, Mass., by S. M. WORCESTER, D.D. Boston: Published for the author by Crocker & Brewster. 1862. 18mo, pp. 108. A precious Memorial of a character of extraordinary sweetness and purity, made perfect through a long and severe process of suffering. It is eminently adapted to comfort and strengthen those who are called to suffer.

Harper's Pictorial History of the Great Rebellion Nos. 1–4. Price 25 cents each. Among the many descriptions of the Southern secession and revolt, this work of the Harpers takes the lead, in the variety and excellence of its illustrations, the beauty of its typographical execution and the careful historical statements of its text. It is of deep interest to all classes of readers. It will be issued at the rate of one number a month until completed.   It should receive a generous support.

The Life, Writings, and Character of EDWARD ROBINSON, D.D., LL.D. This small volume, published by Randolph, is made up of Remarks by Prof. H. B. Smith at the announcement of the death of Dr. Robinson, at a meeting of the New York Historical Society, Feb. 3, 1863, and of an Address of Prof. R. D. Hitchcock before the same Society, March 24.   It is published under the auspices of the Society.   In the address of Prof. Hitchcock is a long and interesting account of the ancestors of Dr. Robinson, drawn from the biography of Rev. William Robinson, written by his son, the Professor, and printed for private distribution in 1859.   The whole address is a felicitous account of the life, works and character of our great American Christian scholar.

PHILOSOPHY.

Ad BENEDICTI DE SPINOZA *Opera quæ supersunt omnia Supplementum.* *Amstelodami,* 1862, pp. 360.   BENEDICTI DE SPINOZA *Tractatus de Deo et Homine ejusque Felicitate Lineamenta, etc., edidit* ED. BOEHMERUS.   Halæ ad Salam, 1852, 4to, pp. 63.   The second of these works contains an outline of an early treatise of Spinoza, found ten years ago appended in MS. to a copy of the Life of Spinoza, by Colerus.   Soon afterwards the whole treatise, in Belgic, was also discovered by Müller, the Amsterdam bookseller, and it is now published by Van Vloten, with a Latin version.   Boehmer's work also contains additional notes to Spinoza's Tractatus Theologico-Politicus. Van Vloten has also exhumed and published, in the above volume, Spinoza's Essay on the Rainbow, and various letters and documents relating to his life and works.   Though these various publications do not add much to our knowledge of the Spinozistic philosophy, they are all valuable in the way of elucidation and confirmation.   Van Vloten's edition is accompanied with a likeness of Spinoza, and a fac-simile of his chirography.   It is printed uniformly with Bruder's Leipsic edition of Spinoza's works.   Van Vloten has also published an elaborate work on the Life and Writings of Spinoza.

From Boehmer's work, pp. 49–50, we extract a clear statement and summary of the fundamental points in Spinoza's system. DEFINITIONES : I. Deum definio esse Ens constans infinitis attributis quorum unumquodque est infinitum sive summe perfectum in suo genere.   II. Per attributum intelligo omne id quod concipitur per se et in se adeo ut ipsius conceptus non involvat conceptum alterius rei.   Ut ex. gr. extensio per se et in se concipitur ; at motus non item.   Nam concipitur in alio et ipsius conceptus involvit extensionem.   III. Ea res dicitur in suo genere infinita quae alia ejusdem naturæ terminari nequit.   Sic corpus non terminatur cogitatione nec cogitatio corpore.   IV. Per substantiam intelligo id quod per se et in se concipitur, hoc est cujus conceptus non involvit conceptum alterius rei.   V. Per modificationem sive per accidens intelligo id quod in alio est et per id in quo est concipitur.   AXIOMATA : I. Substantia prior est natura suis accidentibus.   II. Præter substantias et accidentia nihil datur realiter sive extra intellectum.   III. Res quæ diversa habent attributa, nihil habent inter se commune.   IV. Rerum quæ nihfl commune habent inter se, una alterius causa esse non potest. PROPOSITIONES: I. In rerum natura non possunt dari duae aut plures substantiæ ejusdem attributi. II. Substantia non potest produci neque ab alia quacumque substantia, sed est de ipsius essentia existere. III. Omnis substantia debet esse infinita sive summe perfecta in suo genere." ◆

Einleitung in die Philosophie und Encyclopädie der Philosophie. Von GUSTAV THAULOW. Kiel. 1862. Pp. 144. We have previously known the author of this volume only by a sharp pamphlet addressed to Barthélemy St. Hilaire, on the way in which German Philosophy is criticised in France. He has also written a work on Hegel's views on Education, and several pamphlets and essays on philosophical subjects. He is reckoned as a Hegelian, though he also claims to be an independent thinker. The present Introduction to Philosophy is a clear and useful book, discussing in part the best mode of teaching philosophy in the University course, with many pertinent hints. A good deal of it is aphoristic and merely suggestive—hints for Lectures. The First Part examines and defines the leading philosophical terms and conceptions. The Second Part is an exposition of the principles of the most noted modern philosophers. The Third Part gives an Encyclopædia of the Philosophical Sciences. His arrangement is the following: 1. Logic and Metaphysics; 2. Philosophy of Nature; 3. Anthropology and Psychology; 4. Philosophy of Religion; 5. Æsthetics; 6. Ethics; 7. Philosophy of Right and Law; 8. Politics; 9. Pædagogics; 10. History of Philosophy; 11. Historical Philosophy of Religion; 12. History of Art; 13. Philosophical History of Religion; 14. Philosophy of History.

Dr. A. Schmid, Roman Catholic Professor at Dillingen, known by a work on the Thomist and Scotist doctrine of Certainty, has just published a volume on *Philosophical Tendencies in the Sphere of Modern Catholicism*, reviewing the theories of Hermes and Günther, Baader's theosophy, Traditionalism, and especially the Tübingen Catholic School, represented by Kuhn in its conflicts with Clemens and others—which last he terms the New Scholastic School. All of these tendencies were called forth by the endeavor to reconcile Catholic theology with modern thought—faith with philosophy. Kuhn objects to scholasticism, that it subjects philosophy to theology, denying any independent philosophy; that it allows no ground or hold for the evidences; and that it does not recognize any immediate (intuitive) knowledge. His own positions are in substance these: that philosophy and theology have of right a relative independence; that both are constructed upon an immediate basis of faith; that they are to be reconciled in and by a truly speculative theology, which, however, must not confound their respective rights; that a philosophy controlled by theology, and a theology derived solely from pure reason, are equally objectionable.

The main points of controversy between these two schools are thus summed up by Schmid: 1. On immediate and mediate knowledge. Rational truths, universal and necessary, are every where presupposed, says Kuhn. 2. Ontologism and Psychologism. Aquinas and his school represent the latter; Malebranche, Gerdil, Thomassin, Gioberti, Baader, Gratry, and the Louvain professors, are ontologists. The psychologists hold that we only know the "species", or images of things; the ontologists, that we know their real being or nature in God. The truth, says Schmid, lies between them. 3. Whether philosophy be free or bound by authority. 4. The functions of reason in respect to the Evidences; Kuhn's position is, that reason must prove the authority of a revelation, and also has a right to inquire in respect to what it says and means; yet that theology as a science is built up upon the basis of authority. 5. Whether a strictly rational knowledge comports with theological belief. 6. On Tradition. The Jesuits hold that man could have made a language without divine aid (it was not so in fact, but was possible). The professors of Louvain, De Maistre, Gratry, and others, hold that man, in order to speech, needed both external and internal solicitation, both ideas and revelation. Both contain elements of the truth; for language belongs to the human organism, and language is a gift of God.

Akademische Reden. Von KUNO FISCHER. Stuttgart. 1862. The first of the two orations which make up this elegant volume is an enthusiastic eulogy of J. G. Fichte, as exemplifying the union of the profoundest thought and most inspiring popular eloquence with the highest moral energy. The second is on the Two Kantian Schools of Jena, comprising a sketch of the problems and progress of German speculation, set forth with the author's well known acuteness and critical ability. At Jena taught Reinhold, Schiller, Fichte, Schelling, Hegel, Oken, and Fries. Reinhold first gave a popular exposition of the Kantian philosophy; Fichte developed it still further; Hegel and Schelling carried out idealism to its ulterior consequences. In opposition to the latter, Fries gave to the Critical Philosophy an anthropological character, and so he represented the second Kantian school. Herbart opposed the whole idealistic scheme. Schopenhauer made the fundamental fact and source of philosophy to be not reason, but the will. These points are developed in a concise manner in this felicitous oration. As a specimen of his style, we translate an extract on Kant's system: "Space and time are here viewed as pure intuitions (of sense), without which no representation (or image of any given object) is possible. The categories, especially that of causality, are the pure conceptions of the understanding, without which there could be no judgment, no experience, no knowledge of nature. The ideas, particularly that of freedom, give the rational ends or objects, without which there could be no moral action. All these points are carefully distinguished. Perceptions are one thing, conceptions another, ideas yet another. Perceptions are only of the sense, conceptions are only logical, ideas are only practical. With the exactitude of geometrical measurement, the sense is distinguished from the understanding, and both sense and understanding from reason, as the capacity that has respect to practical, moral ends."

But this seems to split up the mind into a variety of unreconciled powers and operations, and gives different and disconnected sciences. Is there not, after all, *one* reason, and *one* system? To this the system of Schelling answers in the affirmative: "In the one reason, the different powers are *identical. Identity* becomes the emphatic word". The same unity is sought for by Reinhold, reducing sense and understanding to one common term—viz. the power of forming conceptions or representations. Fichte found the unity in the *ego*, or self-consciousness, and in this the principle of all philosophy. The absolute unity of nature and freedom, in the highest sense, however, was in the *philosophy of identity*, as developed in Schelling's *Philosophy of Nature*, and in Hegel's *Logic.*

But still the inquiry remains in what does this identity consist—what is the one principle at the basis of all phenomena. Reason, replies the Hegelian. Not so, reason is not primitive, it is secondary and derivative; there must be some absolute, spontaneous, active principle at the basis, and to be the source of all things; that principle can only be *the will;* this is the position of Schopenhauer. He accepts identity, but puts it in the will.

On the other hand, Herbart is an opponent of identity in all its forms. He says the first duty of the philosopher is to examine the general conceptions of the mind, each by itself, to free them from contradictions, to make them harmonize with the logical laws; in other words, to make them conceivable. The doing this, gives us the system of metaphysics, as the fundamental branch of philosophy.

One other position is conceivable. It makes the following assertions. The fundamental science is not metaphysics—this is against Herbart and the identity-system, equally. This science must consist in a criticism of the reason—here it follows Kant. But this criticism is not to be metaphysical—it is not a matter of the reason. It cannot give us any system of identity as its result. This criticism must consist in a knowledge of the human mind and its capacities. This knowledge can only be derived from self-inspection — from anthropology, from empirical psychology. Hence the criticism of the reason must consist in a knowledge of the soul. "Its contents must be anthropological: its knowledge empirical." This is the standpoint of Fries. This is the essence of his *New Criticism of the Reason*.

Fries agrees with Locke and Hume in making the understanding at first empty. He agrees with Leibnitz in finding in reason primitive, obscure, undeveloped ideas, which are made clear by the reflection of the understanding. He agrees with Reid and Stewart in saying that this is a kind of common sense. By this common sense, he says, we are assured of the existence of the absolute, the perfect, the world of ideas. But this is in the form of feeling or faith. Here he is allied with Jacobi; and in this, De Wette, among the theologians, agrees with him.

The History of the Intellectual Development of Europe. By JOHN WILLIAM DRAPER, M.D., LL.D. New York: Harpers. 1863. pp. 631. Dr. Draper, in this comprehensive attempt, proposes to do, what no one has done before—to "arrange the evidence offered by the intellectual history of Europe in accordance with physiological principles, so as to illustrate the orderly progress of civilization". We do not fully understand this. If it means only, that intellectual development is controlled by law; that nations in this development pass through various stages, of youth, maturity and decline; this is doubtless true. If, however, it means, that the laws of physiology are also the laws of moral, intellectual and spiritual growth, this, we think, is plainly an inadequate view. It would make physiology to be the science of the sciences. Running through the book, too, there is the silent assumption that progress in the natural or positive sciences is the real progress of the race—akin to the speculations of Comte and Buckle. Yet the author is more deferential than either of these writers to the power and need of the Christian system as an element of modern civilization, and necessary to its growth. He is, however, no believer in metaphysics, in the received sense; and he even declares "that the advancement of metaphysics is through the study of physiology". What sort of a metaphysics would that give us? Does physiology teach universal and necessary truths? Apart from this defect in the general idea of the work, it is undoubtedly a laborious compilation, and combines in an interesting exposition most of the main facts in the progress of mankind, especially in the sphere of physical research. The history of Greece and Rome and of mediæval and modern Europe is passed in review, bringing up all the main theological and ecclesiastical controversies. In some of them, as for example, in the account of the Trinitarian disputes, the author has evidently not read the most thorough expositions. But his sympathies are in unison with what tends to the general progress of mankind in freedom and well-being. The style is clear and vigorous.

PRACTICAL RELIGION.

The Preacher's Manual; Lectures on Preaching, furnishing Rules and Examples for every Kind of Pulpit Address. By Rev. S. T. STURTEVANT. New York : James O'Kane, 126 Nassau street. 1863.   This new edition of a well known and useful homiletic work, is reprinted entire from the last London edition.   It is a comprehensive work of its class, and gives ample directions about all that pertains to the preparation of pulpit discourses. It also furnishes examples illustrative of the various rules, and of the different kinds of sermons.   These are among the most interesting parts of the work, being selected from a wide circle of pulpit orators.   It will be found a valuable manual for those who use and require such helps.

Letters on the Ministry of the Gospel.   By FRANCIS WAYLAND.   Boston : Gould & Lincoln.   These plain and forcible words are designed to recall the ministry to its simplicity, and teach it the true source of its power.   They contain valuable and needed warnings.   We think, however, that undue stress is laid on extemporaneous preaching.   All ministers need to read the book.

Patriarchal Shadows of Christ and His Church: as exhibited in passages drawn from the History of Joseph and his brethren.   By OCTAVIUS WINSLOW, D.D.   New York : Carter & Brothers.   1863.   12mo, pp. 402. Dr. Winslow is certainly a very prolific writer, and his writings are uniformly good.   A decided evangelical spirit, and a practical and experimental element pervades them all.   The present volume consists of fifteen familiar expository discourses on the life of Joseph.   The author considers Joseph as a remarkable type of Christ, and runs an interesting, and in some points we think a somewhat fanciful, parallel between them.   With the one aim of the book we heartily sympathize, viz. "to present CHRIST as the central object of the picture, grouping around him, as the Saviour ever delights to be portrayed, the Church which he has redeemed by his precious blood, and taken into personal inseparable union by the Spirit. Great and frequent stress is laid upon the fact that the believer has to do with a LIVING CHRIST—a truth but faintly received by many of the Lord's people".

Speaking to the Heart; or Sermons for the People.   By THOMAS GUTHRIE, D.D.   New York : Carter & Brothers.   1863.   18mo, pp.   These sermons are characterized by great simplicity and pungency, and they bring home the Gospel to the popular mind with clearness and impressiveness. They are in many respects model sermons.   There would be far more "speaking to the heart" than now if such a style of preaching were more common.   It is to be feared that no small part of the preaching of the times is not aimed at the "People", and is not adapted to them, but is rather directed to the select few whose superior culture or æsthetic tastes enable them to understand and appreciate what is above the popular mind.

SCIENCE.

The Geological Evidences of the Antiquity of Man, with Remarks on Theories of the Origin of Species by Variations.   By Sir CHARLES LYELL, F.R.S.   Philadelphia : G. W. Childs.   1863.   8vo, pp. 518.   All the recent investigations upon the antiquity of the race are brought together in this new work of an eminent geologist, and discussed in a dispassionate method. The author evidently withholds his final judgment.   Apart from theory, the array of facts is by no means so formidable as has often been represented. With the favorite theory of Sir Charles, that the agencies of nature have always acted uniformly and slowly, inferences might be made prejudicial to the received chronology of the race; but who can prove this theory? Of the *flint* weapons of Abbeville and various parts of England, it can hardly be said that the proof of their being fashioned by man is complete; and no human remains have yet been found in conjunction with them. That any pre-Adamite men have been really exhumed is certainly quite doubtful. Human bones might be brought into contact with those of extinct animals, without their having lived together on the earth. The Engis and Neander-thal skulls are isolated specimens, and no man can yet tell where they are to be classed. On the man of 100,000 years at Natchez, Sir Charles "sus-pends his judgment". The fossil man of Denise is hardly beyond suspicion. The bones interred in the grotto of Aurignac may have been piled up to-gether by some unknown persons. The calculation that the bits of pottery from the Nile are 13,380 years old, rests upon the supposition that the de-posits are always gradually made. From the Danish peat and shell-mounds, and from the lacustrian villages of Switzerland, it is plausibly inferred, that there were inhabitants of these countries before the present races occupied the ground; but the inferences as to their pre-Adamite antiquity are inse-cure. And then there comes the startling fact, that if these races lived so long in these regions, they have left us no monuments of their existence beyond the rudest utensils ; for thousands of years, these are all that they produced. The author advocates to some extent the theory of Darwin as to natural selection : but contends that it favors the unity of the race, and strengthens the arguments of natural theology. We have no fear of the final results of these and similar scientific investigations. They will ulti-mately help theology and the right interpretation of the Bible. But yet we think that nowadays natural philosophers are more speculative and the-oretical than theologians ; from slight facts they make enormous inferences. The American edition of this work is brought out in excellent style, and well illustrated.

The Races of the Old World : A Manual of Ethnology. By CHARLES L. BRACE. New York : Scribner. 1863. pp. 540. Such a Manual as this has been long needed, digesting multifarious researches into clear and comprehensive results. The larger works on Ethnology are too prolix and minute for the beginner and the general reader : and most of the treatises are on special races. Here the whole of the Old World is classified ethnologically, with pertinent descriptions, beginning with the earliest historical records. In this respect we know of no manual of equal excellence, so well adapted to the wants of students. The division of races is made on the basis of language. The author is judicious and correct in his statement and colligation of the main facts, though in some instances he accedes to extreme theories. In respect to Egypt, while not adopting the long chronology of Bunsen, he is induced to accept the views of Lepsius, putting the date of Menes anterior to that of the creation in the generally received chronology. No attempt is made to harmonize these views with the Biblical statements. In the chapter on the Antiquity of man, the author fairly gives in his adhesion to the existence of the *fossil or pre-Adamitic man*—in existence, it may be, "hundreds of thousand of years before any of the received dates of creation". We think that he has yielded a too ready assent to the positions of Lyell's recent work. The evidence cannot be said to warrant any such extravagant conclusions. Mr. Brace defends the unity of the race; but in order to reconcile the unity with the diversity he assumes an indefinitely long period for making the changes.   This unity, then, is not a unity in the historic Adam ; it is not the unity taught in the Scriptures, and on which the Biblical doctrines of sin and of redemption hinge.   He also has a curious theory, in conclusion, that great changes in the race will still go on, until at last we shall have a race in which truth and holiness shall be propagated, as sin is now inherited.   We doubt whether Scripture, reason or physiology can be brought to sanction such a fanciful view.   The work is admirably got up.

Manual of Scientific Discovery for 1863.   Edited by DAVID A. WELLS, M.D.   Boston : Gould & Lincoln.   1863. pp. 343.   With a portrait of Ericsson.   This Manual is prepared with great care, and presents a sufficiently full record of all discoveries in the different branches of science. It is an indispensable work for all who would keep pace with the progress of physical research.

Grape Culture, Wines and Wine-Making.   With Notes upon Agriculture and Horticulture.   By A. HARASZTHY, Commissioner to report on the improvement and culture of the vine in California.   With numerous Illustrations.   New York : Harper & Brothers.   1842. 8vo, pp. 420.   This is a very readable book, as the author, who is an Hungarian, writes in tolerable English, and gives his own personal impressions of travel, as well as full and valuable reports on the subjects of which it treats.   In the Appendix, which makes a large part of the book, the author gives a translation of Johann Carl *Weine-Rund* and numerous extracts from various authors treating on the subject.   The volume is richly embellished, and will doubtless find many interested readers.

Evidence as to Man's Place in Nature.   By THOS. H. HUXLEY.   New York : Appletons.   1863. pp. 184.   With illustrations.   Professor Huxley belongs to the school of naturalists which draws no line between animals and man.   On some of the facts of anatomical structure he is in sharp controversy with Professor Owen.   This volume is chiefly made up of three Lectures, on The Natural History of the Man-like Apes—full of curious particulars, well described : on the Relations of Man to the Lower Animals—to show that there are great differences between the animals that immediately succeed us in the scale, as between these and man.   Even " the highest faculties of feeling and of intellect begin to germinate in lower forms of life " (p. 129).   But what indications of conscience, and of a knowledge of eternal and necessary truth, can be found in apes ?   " All are co-ordinated terms of Nature's great progression, from the formless to the formed—from the inorganic to the organic—from blind force to conscious intellect and will."   And yet he concedes that this progression has gaps which science has not yet bridged.   And he does not tell us how "blind force" can produce " conscious intellect and will."   The last chapter on some Fossils Remains of Man is on the crania of Engis and Neanderthal. These, he concedes, prove nothing as to an intermediate species between the highest animals and man.   The amount of the matter is, that as far as science goes, there is no evidence of a gradual transition from apes to men : it is a pure theory of naturalism.

GENERAL LITERATURE.

The Story of my Career.   By HEINRICH STEFFENS.   Translated by WM. L. GAGE.   Boston : Gould & Lincoln.   1863. pp. 284.   Steffens was an enthusiastic naturalist, a disciple of Schelling, and in the last part of his life an earnest believer. He charmed all who knew him by the vivacity of his conversation and the warmth of his social affections. He wrote largely upon the natural sciences and the philosophy of religion. In the latter part of his life, he published the Story of his Life (*Was ich erlebte*) in ten volumes—diffuse, entertaining, full of reminiscences of his student years in Freiburg and Jena, and his career as Professor at Halle, Breslau and Berlin. Selections from these volumes are translated in this little work by Mr. Gage, and they make a most interesting volume. Göthe, Schiller, Schelling, Schleiermacher, Jacobi, Fichte, Schlegel, Novalis and Neander are portrayed as they appeared in the familiarity of personal intercourse and in their public relations. The translation is very well done; the English runs smoothly. All interested in German literature will welcome these reminiscences. The translator will soon bring out a volume of Ritter's Geographical Studies; and he has also in hand a translation of Hagenbach's valuable work on the history of theological and philosophical opinions in Germany in the eighteenth century.

Paris in America. By Dr. René Lefebvre, Parisian. [Ed. Laboulaye, Professor in the Collége de France.] Translated by MARY L. BOOTH. New York: Scribner. 1863. Of Laboulaye and his various writings, especially his defence of our country, we gave a full account in the January number of our REVIEW. This new work describes, in a vivacious and amusing style, the effect produced upon a full-blooded Parisian by living in this country and becoming acquainted with the practical working of our institutions. Our social, political and religious life puts him at first into a state of entire confusion; but he gradually works himself out into sympathy with the main ideas of our democratic government, our modes of administering justice, and our freedom in matters of religion and education. Though the descriptions are often satirical, yet they upon the whole redound to our advantage; for M. Laboulaye is "the most American of Frenchmen". The work has already had a marked success in France. It is well translated.

African Hunting from Natal to the Zambesi, including Lake Ngami, the Kalahari Desert, etc., from 1852 to 1860. By W. CHS. BALDWIN, F.R.G.S. With a map, and numerous illustrations by Wolf and Zwecker. New York: Harpers. 1863. pp. 397. An entertaining story of varied and wild adventures, somewhat clumsily narrated. The writer came in contact with various missionaries, Moffat, Livingstone, Helmore, and the colonists of pastor Harms; and he always speaks well of them. It is said, that when Darwin saw the mission stations in New Zealand, he exclaimed, "The lessons of the missionary are the enchanter's wand". No book of African adventure contains more startling descriptions or adventurous exploits.

Tales and Sketches. By HUGH MILLER. Edited, with a Preface, by Mrs. MILLER. Boston: Gould & Lincoln. For sale by Blakeman & Mason, New York. 1863. 12mo, pp. 369. Whatever comes from the pen of Hugh Miller will command numerous readers. These "Tales and Sketches" were written at an early period of the author's career, "during the first years of his married life", "composed literally over the midnight lamp, after returning late in the evening from a long day's work over the ledger and the balance-sheet. Tired though he was, his mind could not stagnate —he *must write*". The Tales and Sketches are ten in number, all of them interesting and racy, some of them quite tragical; others embody evidently not a little of his own experience, while others still are vivid pictures drawn from real life around him. His "Recollections of Ferguson" are indeed "exquisitely painful", while his "Recollections of Burns" will be read with no ordinary interest.   The Preface by Mrs. Miller is a gem in its way.   On the whole the book will not lessen our regard for the memory of this man of genius and science and moral worth rarely combined.

Woman and Her Saviour in Persia.   By a Returned Missionary.   With five Illustrations and a Map of the Nestorian Country.   Boston: Gould & Lincoln.   For sale by Carter & Brothers, New-York.   1863.   12mo.   303. This volume is a fitting counterpart to the memoir of the lamented Stoddard. In connection with Miss Fiske's fifteen years' service in the Nestorian Mission, in the Female Seminary at Oroomiah, we have a pretty full and authentic history of what has been done for woman in and by means of that Mission among that ancient sect; and the record will be read with devout gratitude to God, as well as admiration for the heroic and self-sacrificing men and women who devoted their lives to the blessed work. The illustrations, copied from sketches taken on the spot by a skilful artist, add much to the value of the book.

May Dreams.   By HENRY L. ABBEY.   New York: Abbey & Abbot.   1862. 12mo, pp. 143.   There is something *taking* in the title of these Poems. How descriptive of life's early aspirations and experiences!   May dreams are so bright, so joyful, who has not indulged them; who would spoil them? And yet we discover in these "May Dreams" a slight tinge of sadness, as if some great Sorrow had touched the young Poet's heart and inspired his lyre.   There is some genuine poetry in this little volume.   Unambitious, and chaste in thought and expression, and abounding in descriptions of natural scenery and the varied passions and experiences of life, it is really a very readable book.   May these early Spring flowers be succeeded by the golden tints and mellow fruit of a ripe and golden Autumn!

Sylvia's Lovers.   A Novel.   By MRS. GASKELL.   Harpers: New York. 1863.   An excellent novel, full of incident, of an unexceptionable moral tone.   The Northern dialect, after it is spelt out, adds new interest to the scenes and characters.   In its plot it is the most complete of Mrs. Gaskell's works.

A First Friendship.   A Tale.   New-York: Harpers.   1863.   This anonymous novel shows unmistakable marks of skill in arranging the plot, and vigor in portraying characters.   The work will be a favorite with the lover of fiction.

The Fairy Book.   By the author of "John Halifax", etc.   Children can ask for nothing better than the most popular fairy stories.   Selected and re-written by Miss Mulock.   All modern stories are excluded.

Eclectic Magazine of Foreign Literature.   New York: W. H. BIDWELL.   January to July, 1863.   This noble Magazine fully sustains its well-earned reputation.   Each number is tastefully embellished, and contains a greater variety and amount of excellent reading than can be found in any similar magazine in the country.   Our friend, Mr. Bidwell, exhibits an admirable tact and great enterprise in the conduct of it.   We have the work from the beginning in our library, and we prize it highly.   No minister, no intelligent man, ought to be without it.   The amount of literature (and of the best kind which the Old World affords) contained in it would surprise one not acquainted with it.   The *Index* to the first fifty volumes recently published will give one some idea of the extent, and richness, and variety of the mental treasure here embodied.

Theological Eclectic.   Edited by Prof. GEORGE E. DAY.   Cincinnati, May, 1863.   Wm. Scott, Publisher.   Prof. Day has long had in contemplation a work of this character.   The object of it is to furnish selections from the current Theological Literature of England, France, Germany, and Holland. It is to be issued in monthly numbers of 24 pp. each. The first number has already been issued. Prof. Day is abundantly qualified to conduct such a work, and we have no doubt he will make it a valuable one. Its low price will bring it within the reach of all. We wish it all success. Whether it can be sustained, located at Cincinnati, and in this small and cheap form, remains to be seen.

POLITICAL WRITINGS.

Mr. Randolph, 683 Broadway, is doing good service by publishing excellent pamphlets on the war. Among these are C. J. Stellé's, *How a Free People Conduct a Long War*, and *Northern Interests and Southern Independence*—both able; *English Neutrality : Is the Alabama a British Pirate ?* arguing the affirmative with strong reasons; Report by L. H. Steiner on the *Sanitary Commission ; The Army of the Potomac*, by the Prince de Joinville, one of the most valuable criticisms of the campaign of 1862 ; *The Future of the Colored Race in America*, from the *Presbyterian Quarterly*, an instructive article; *The American War*, by Newman Hall, LL.D.—a hearty word of sympathy from England; *Christian Patriotism*, by William Adams, D.D., a felicitous and patriotic discourse; Lessons of Encouragement from the Times of Washington, by George L. Prentiss, D.D.—an eloquent encouragement to present duty, derived from the lessons of the past: *The Duty of the Hour*, by S. T. Spear, D.D., in his usual vigorous and loyal style ; a *Letter to Judge Curtis* by C. P. Kirkland, reviewing with ability the pamphlet of the former in opposition to the President's Emancipation Proclamation ; *A Geographical and Statistical View of the American Slaveholders' Rebellion*, by Sydney E. Morse, A.M., illustrated with a map, to counsel the taking possession of Eastern Tennessee and the adjacent region as the surest means of ending the war.

Other pamphlets bearing on the same subject are *Historical Notes on the Employment of Negroes in the American Army of the Revolution*, by George H. Moore; *Government and Rebellion*, an able Sermon by Rev. E. E. Adams of Philadelphia ; *Negro Slavery Unjustifiable*, the 11th edition of Dr. Alex. McLeod's well known sermon preached in 1802 ; *Why the North cannot accept of Separation*, translated from Laboulaye ; *A Letter from an Elder of an Old School Presbyterian Church to his Son in College*, of which it is enough to say that the anonymous author maintains that those who defend anti-slavery sentiments are guilty of the sin of blasphemy !

Mr. Randolph also has just published *National Currency :* a Review of the National Banking Law, by ELEAZAR LORD, an able and valuable Essay from one who is master of the subject.

The Results of Emancipation ; The Results of Slavery. By AUGUSTIN COCHIN. Translated by MARY L. BOOTH. 2 vols. Walker, Wise & Co. Boston, 1863. Miss Booth is doing excellent service by her well-executed translations of French works, bearing on our present conflicts. M. Cochin, Ex-Maire and Municipal Councillor of Paris, received a prize from the French Institute for the above admirable volumes. The author is a Catholic, of the liberal French school. He is an earnest lover and advocate of liberty ; he loves liberty, because he is a Christian. His works cover the ground of both emancipation and servitude. One volume narrates the progress and triumph of emancipation in modern history : 800,000 by England, 250,000 by France, and several thousand by Denmark and Sweden. At the time when he wrote, the abolition of slavery by Holland, and of serfdom by Russia, was not yet completed.   The other volume gives a darker and sadder picture—that of slavery as it still exists—some 7,000,000 slaves in nominally Christian countries.   The larger part of this volume is devoted to our own country, and it is a truthful, candid, lucid and eloquent presentation of the history of slavery in this land, including the first year of the civil war, which this fearful system has drawn upon us.   The sympathies of M. Cochin, as of so many other noble Frenchmen, are entirely with our National Government in this intense struggle.   We owe the author a debt of gratitude for his espousal of our cause.   His work is equally important for the moralist, the statesman and the Christian philanthropist.   It is most important for the slaveholders themselves.   It will be referred to as an authority in the discussions on emancipation already begun in the Border States.   It is written in a philosophical spirit, and with true French conciseness and vivacity.   The American Bibliography of slavery might easily be enlarged.   We give these volumes a most cordial recommendation, and predict for them a wide circulation and a useful career.   It is one of the best and most conclusive arguments, based on facts, that has yet been made in favor of the practicability and safety of emancipation and against the evils of the unnatural system of human bondage.   It is handsomely brought out by the Boston publishers.

Art. XI.—ECCLESIASTICAL RECORD.

By Edwin F. Hatfield, D.D., New York.

LICENSED TO PREACH.

Mr. Llewellyn Pratt,	December	, 1862, by the Presb. of Philadelphia, Third.
" Edward Clarence Smith,	"	"	"	"	"	"
" William W. Wetmore,	January 28th, 1863,	"	"	Utica.
" Charles F. Dowd,	February 20th, "	"	"	Troy.
" Charles T. Berry,	March 16th, "	"	"	Newark.
" S. Russell Johnson,	April 2d, "	"	"	Alton.
" William H. Clark,	" 7th, "	"	"	New York, Fourth.
" John H. McVey,	" " "	"	"	"	"
" Abram J. Quick,	" " "	"	"	"	"
" Leonard E. Richards,	" " "	"	"	"	"
" Albert C. Bishop,	" 8th, "	"	"	"	Third.
" Frederick A. W. Brown,	" " "	"	"	"	"
" James B. Finch,	" " "	"	"	"	"
" Ellsworth J. Hill,	" " "	"	"	"	"
" Joel J. Hough,	" " "	"	"	"	"
" Alexander Nesbitt,	" " "	"	"	"	"
" Ezra D. Shaw,	" " "	"	"	"	"
" William White Williams,	" " "	"	"	"	"
" Henry J. Crane,	" 14th, "	"	"	Montrose.
" George M. Boynton,	" 15th, "	"	"	Brooklyn.
" William H. Clark,	" " "	"	"	"
" John H. Meacham,	" " "	"	"	"
" Alexander Lambertson,	May 8th, "	"	"	Cayuga.
" William Campbell,	" " "	"	"	"
" Theodore D. Marsh,	" " "	"	"	"
" Alexander M. Heiser,	" " "	"	"	"
" Philemon R. Day,	" " "	"	"	"
" Isaiah Reid,	" " "	"	"	"
" James S. Hanning,	" " "	"	"	"
" Frederick A. Parmenter,	" " "	"	"	"
" George White,	" " "	"	"	"
" Calvin P. Quick,	" " "	"	"	"
" John Killand,	" " "	"	"	"
" Edward Dickinson,	" " "	"	"	"
" Edwin A. Spence,	" " "	"	"	"
" Charles M. Livingston,	" " "	"	"	"

ORDINATIONS.

Mr. Alvin Baker	Sept. 3d, 1862, Evangelist,	by the Presb. of North River.
" Edward P. Roe,	" " " "	" " "
" James Robertson,	" 16th, " "	" " Newark.
" George W. Mackie,	Oct. 1st, " Pastor, Adams, N. Y. " " Watertown.

Mr. Charles D. Shaw,	Nov.	5th, 1862,	Pastor, Paterson, 2d,	by Presb. of Newark.		
" James B. Fisher,	"	16th, "	Evangelist,	"	"	Rockaway.
" Joseph Little,	"	19th, "	"	"	"	Pataskala.
" Edward Payson Hammond,	Jan.	2d, 1863,	"	"	"	New York, 8d.
" Corlis B. Gardner,	"	20th, "	"	"	"	Rochester.
" William A. Wolcott,	"	28th, "	"	"	"	Chemung.
" Ziba N. Bradbury,	"	"	"	"	"	Steuben.
" Edmund B. Miner,	Feb.	4th, "	Pastor, Baraboo, Wis.,	"	"	Columbus.
" Samuel B. Sherrill,	"	7th, "	" Cato, N. Y.	"	"	Cayuga.
" Jenkyn D. Jenkins,	"	17th, "	Evangelist,	"	"	Cleveland.
" Thomas Nichols,	Mar.	11th, "	Pastor, Chester, N. Y.,	"	"	Hudson.
" Samuel J. Mills,	"	15th, "	Evangelist,	"	"	Iowa City.
" Charles T. Berry,	"	17th, "	"	"	"	Newark.
" John P. Roe,	Apr.	8th, "	"	"	"	North River.
" John E. Werth,	"	16th, "	"	"	"	Cayuga.
" Malcolm McG. Dana,	"	19th, "	"	"	"	Brooklyn.
" George M. Tife,	May	11th, "	Pastor, Nichols, N. Y.,	"	"	Tioga.
" James B. Finch,	June	6th, "	Evangelist,	"	"	New York, 8d.

INSTALLATIONS.

Rev. Joseph M. McNulty,	Aug.	13th, 1862,	Montgomery, N. Y.,	by Presb. of Hudson.		
" William R. S. Betts,	Dec.	23d, "	Otisville, N. Y.,	"	"	"
" Rollin A. Sawyer,	Jan.	1st, 1863,	Newark, 2d, O.,	"	"	Pataskala.
" Herrick Johnson,	"	10th, "	Pittsburgh, 8d, Pa.,	"	"	Pittsburgh.
" Samuel W. Crittenden,	"	18th, "	Darby, 1st, Pa.,	"	"	Philadelphia, 3d,
" Charles H. Holloway,	Feb.	17th, "	Shelter Island, N. Y.,	"	"	Long Island.
" Tertius S. Clarke, D.D.,	Mar.	7th, "	Weedsport, N. Y.,	"	"	Cayuga.
" James M. Dickson,	"	11th, "	Newark, 6th, N. J.,	"	"	Newark.
" Jacob A. Prime,	"	23d, "	Troy, Liberty St., N. Y.,	"	"	Troy.
" Howard Crosby, D.D.,	"	25th, "	New York, 4th Av., N. Y.,	"	"	New York, 4th.
" Henry B. Holmes,	"	"	Dubuque, 2d, Io.,	"	"	Dubuque.
" Wilbur McKaig,	May	8d, "	Cincinnati, 8d, O.,	"	"	Cincinnati.
" Joel Parker, D.D.,	"	6th, "	Newark, Park, N. J.,	"	"	Newark.
" Herman C. Riggs,	"	"	Potsdam, N. Y.,	"	"	St. Lawrence.

DISSOLUTIONS OF THE PASTORAL RELATION.

Rev. Elizur N. Manley,	Dec.	1862,	Oakfield, N. Y.,	by Presb. of Genesee.		
" John R. Young,	Jan.	18th, 1868,	Plattsburgh, "	"	"	Champlain.
" William T. Doubleday,	"	"	Delhi, "	"	"	Delaware.
" David F. Judson,	"	28th, "	Addison, "	"	"	Chemung.
" John E. Baker,	Feb.	9th, "	Arkport, N. Y.	"	"	Genesee Valley.
" Joel Parker, D.D.,	"	11th, "	New York, 4th Av., N. Y.,	"	"	New York, 4th.
" Charles C. Carr,	Mar.	28th, "	Burdett, N. Y.,	"	"	Chemung.
" William Grassie,	April	14th, "	Wattsburgh, Pa.,	"	"	Erie.
" George L. Little,	"	15th, "	Waukegan, Ill.,	"	"	Chicago.
" William A. McCorkle,	"	16th, "	Marshall, Mich.,	"	"	Marshall.
" William C. Clark,	"	22d, "	Warren, O.,	"	"	Trumbull.
" Alexander Trotter,	"	29th, "	Livingstonville, N. Y.,	"	"	Catskill.
" Samuel Loomis,	"	" "	Rensselaerville, "	"	"	"
" Charles A. Smith, D.D.,	"	"	Philadelphia, Western, Pa.,	"	"	Philadelphia, 8d.
" Walter S. Drysdale,	"	"	E. Whiteland, Pa.,	"	"	" "
" James Donaldson,	"	"	Pleas't Val., Westm., N. Y.,	"	"	North River.
" John Crowell,	May,	"	Orange, 2d, N. J.,	"	"	Newark.
" Lyman Glibert, D.D.,	"	17th, "	Malden, N. Y.,	"	"	Catskill.
" Homer McVay,	"	"	Delhi, O.,	"	"	Franklin.
" William N. McHarg,	"	"	Lyons, N. Y.,	"	"	Lyons.

CHANGE OF RESIDENCE.

	from	to
Rev. John E. Baker,	Arkport, N. Y.,	Cuba, N. Y.
" William T. Bartle,	Decatur, Mich.,	Vassar, Mich.
" Oliver B. Bidwell,	Boston, Mass.,	New York City.
" Elijah Bonney,	Vernon Centre, N. Y.,	Hadley, Mass.
Mr. Ziba N. Bradbury,	New York City, N. Y.,	Howard, N. Y.
Rev. P. G. Buchanan,	Oakland, Cal.,	Watsonville, Cal.
" Charles P. Bush,	New York City, N. Y.	Rochester, N. Y.
" Samuel W. Bush,	Binghamton, "	Galesburgh, Ill.
" Thomas H. Canfield,	Kossuth, Io.,	Lucas Grove, Wis.
" Darwin Chichester,	Wolcott, N. Y.,	Burdett, N. Y.
" Calvin Clark,	Chicago, Ill.,	Detroit, Ill.
" Lemuel Clark,	Westford, N. Y.,	Lawrence, Ill.
" William W. Collins,	Starkey, N. Y.,	Maine, N. Y.
Mr. Archibald Crawford,	Smyrna, N. Y.,	Paris, N. Y.
Rev. Charles D. Curtiss,	Hocking Port, O.,	Belpre, O.
" George F. Davis,	Mt. Sterling, Ill.,	Newtown, Ill.
" Friend A. Deming,	Sand Ford, Ind.,	Mattoon, Ill.
" James M. Dickson,	Brooklyn, N. Y.,	Newark, N. J.
" John H. Dillingham,	Manitowoc, Wis.,	Berlin, Wis.
" Samuel J. Dorsey,	Ripley, N. Y.,	Millport, N. Y.
" William T. Doubleday,	Delhi, N. Y.,	Binghamton, Wis.
" John V. Downs,	Ridgefield, Ill.,	Thornton Station, Ill.
" Latten W. Dunlap,	Mt. Sterling, Ill.,	Perry, Ill.
" David R. Eddy,	Wenona, Ill.,	Belvidere, Ill.
" John H. Edwards,	Rockport, Ill.,	New Lebanon, N. H.
" Ambrose Eggleston,	Binghamton, N. Y.,	Coldwater, Mich.
" John Fairchild,	Wabash, Ind.,	Menekaunee, Wis.
" John B. Fish,	Cairo, N. Y.,	Catskill, N. Y.
Mr. Edward P. Gardner,	Buffalo, N. Y.,	Cherry Valley, N. Y.
Rev. Lorenzo M. Gates,	Hillsdale, N. Y.,	Louville, Wis.
" John Gerrish,	New Washington, Ind.,	Lapeer, Mich.
" Daniel Gibbs,	Oneida, N. Y.,	Pitcher, N. Y.
" James Gordon,	Albion, Io.,	Point Pleasant, Io.
" William Grassie,	Wattsburgh, Pa.,	Edinboro', Pa.
" Chester Holcomb,	Joy, N. Y.,	Fairville, N. Y.
" Henry B. Holmes,	Belvidere, Ill.,	Dubuque, Io.
" Homer P. Hovey,	New Haven, Ct.,	Florence, Mass.
" Joel Jewell,	Wells, N. Y.,	West Newark, N. Y.
" David F. Judson,	Addison, N. Y.,	Prattsburgh, N. Y.
" William M. Kain,	Unionville, Io.	Marengo, Io.
" John W. Lane,	Bethany, N. Y.,	East Pembroke, N. Y.
" Samuel Lee,	Hudson, O.,	Mantua Centre, O.
" Alvah Lilly,	Gorham, N. Y.,	Pewaukee, Wis.
" James A. Little,	Canastota, N. Y.,	New York City, N. Y.
" Samuel Loomis,	Rensselaerville, N. Y.,	Vineland, N. J.
" Lewis H. Loss,	Kendall, Ill.,	Marshalltown, Io.
" Hugh McBride,	Monticello, Ind.,	Reynoldsburgh, O.
" William A. McCorkle,	Marshall, Mich.,	Detroit, Mich.
" William H. McGifford,	Boonville, N. Y.,	North Adams, Mass.
" Homer McVay,	Radnor, O.,	Reynoldsburgh, O.
" Elizur N. Manley,	Oakfield, N. Y.,	Boonville, N. Y.
" Augustus Marsh,	Brooklyn, Mich.,	Grand Rapids, Mich.
Mr. John Monteith, Jr.,	Jackson, O.,	Cleveland, O.
Rev. Edward D. Neill,	Saint Paul, Mich.,	Philadelphia, Pa.
" Oliver W. Norton,	Springfield Cross Roads, Pa.,	Brooklyn, Mich.
" J. Odell,	Albion, Mich.,	East Hamburgh, Pa.
" Sjoaerd Ossinga,	Thornton, Ill.,	Gun Plain, Mich.

Rev.	William Ottinger,	from	Mount Airy, Pa.,	to	Hatborough, Pa.
"	Sefferenas Ottman,	"	Pultney, N. Y.,	"	Edwardsburgh, Mich.
"	Joel Parker, D.D.	"	New-York City, N. Y.,	"	Newark, N. J.
"	Jeremiah Petrie,	"	Westmoreland, N. Y.,	"	Herkimer, N. Y.
"	James Pierpont,	"	Healdsburgh, Cal.,	"	Murphy's, Cal.
"	William H. Rogers,	"	Mason, O.,	"	College Hill, O.
"	Alanson Scofield,	"	Fremont, Mich.,	"	Shirawasse, Mich.,
"	Ezra Scovell,	"	West Newark, N. Y.,	"	Spencer, N. Y.
"	Elisha B. Sherwood,	"	Buchanan, Mich.,	"	Cassopolis, Mich.
"	Porter H. Snow,	"	Red Wing, Minn.,	"	Madison, Wis.
"	Franklin A. Spencer,	"	New Hartford, Ct.,	"	Terryville, Ct.
"	Addison K. Strong,	"	Monroe, Mich.,	"	Galena, Ill.
"	Charles H. Thompson,	"	Brooklyn, N. Y.,	"	Newark, N. J.
"	George N. Todd,	"	Maine, N. Y.,	"	Candor, N. Y.
"	Thomas Towler,	"	Jackson, O.,	"	Breckville, O.
"	William C. Turner,	"	Fostoria, O.,	"	Newburgh, O.
"	Daniel E. Tyler,	"	South Trenton, N. Y.,	"	Hermon, N. Y.
"	Lemuel P. Webber,	"	Franklin, Ind.,	"	Nevada Ter.
"	Isaac T. Whittemore,	"	Fairburg, Ill.,	"	Rushville, Ill.
"	Stephen H. Williams,	"	St. Alban's Bay, Vt.,	"	North Hero, Vt.
"	James V. A. Woods,	"	Ohio City, Kan.,	"	Marion, Kan.
"	Albert Worthington,	"	Taberg, N. Y.,	"	Rome, N. Y.
"	Samuel Wyckoff,	"	Titusville, Pa.,	"	Peoria, Ill.

DEATHS.

Rev.	Elderkin Roger Johnson,	48,	Sept. 16th, 1862,	New Carlisle, O.,	Presb. of Dayton.
"	Harvey Curtis, D.D.,	56,	" 18th, "	Galesburgh, Ill.,	" Knox.
"	John C. Campbell,		Dec. 31st, "	Cerro Gordo, Ill.,	" Wabash.
"	Lyman Beecher, D.D.,	87,	Jan. 10th, 1863,	Brooklyn, N. Y.,	" Cincinnati.
"	Edward Robinson, D.D., LL.D.,	68,	" 27th, "	New York City, N. Y.,	" New York, 3d.
"	Warren Nichols,	58,		Lima, O.,	" Dayton.
"	Harvey Lyon,		"	Strongsville, O.,	" Cleveland.
"	John J. Slocum,	60,	Mar. 12th, "	Lansing, Mich.,	" Chicago.
"	William Bacon,	73,	Apr. 2d, "	Auburn, N. Y.,	" Cayuga.
"	James Blakeslee,		" 4th, "	Ulysses, Pa.,	" Wellsborough.
"	Charles W. Gardner,	79,	" 6th, "	Philadelphia, Pa.,	" Harrisburgh.
"	Albert Smith, D.D.,	59,	" 24th, "	Monticello, Ind.,	" Alton.
"	Ralph Robinson,	83,	May 14th, "	New Haven, N. Y.,	" Oswego.
"	Warren Isham,		" 18th, "	Marquette, L. S.,	" Lake Superior.
"	William Fraser,	70,	" 22d, "	Hamden, N. Y.,	" Delaware.

SUSPENSION.

Rev. John McLeish, New Berlin, N. Y., Oct. 1st, 1862, by the Presb. of Watertown,

DEPOSITION.

Rev. William R. Smith, Shipman, Ill., April 3d, 1863, by the Presb. of Alton.

WE regret that a few slight errors escaped our notice in Dr. Goodwin's article.

On p. 449, for Jochabed read Jochebed.
" 450, 27th line, for Matt. I xviii, xxv, read Matt. 1, 18, 25.
" " 28th " " Roch read Roeh.
" " 33d " " Joshua read Jasher.
" 451, 18th " " Ps. clxii read Ps. cxlii.

THE

AMERICAN

PRESBYTERIAN AND THEOLOGICAL

REVIEW.

NEW SERIES, No. IV.—OCTOBER, 1863.

Art. I.—PRESBYTERIANISM: — ITS AFFINITIES.*

By Rev. Albert Barnes, Philadelphia.

The occasion on which we are met is one on which we may speak freely of our own system of religion, with no violation of a proper respect for other denominations of Christians. Entertaining views as Presbyterians which we regard as of great value to ourselves, and of importance to the world, it cannot be improper to suggest the grounds on which we regard those views as of value and importance, or to endeavor to strengthen the hands of each other in our efforts to maintain them, and to commend them to the attention of our fellow-men. There are reasons why we are Presbyterians and not Prelatists or Independents; why we are Calvinists and not Arminians, Arians, or Socinians; why we are respectively attached to one or the other of the great branches of the Presbyterian family represented here, and not to the Greek church; to the Roman Catholic church; to the Episcopal church; to the Methodist or Baptist churches; to a Socinian

* Delivered as an address before the Presbyterian Historical Society in Philadelphia, May 5, 1863. On account of the length of this address, a portion of it (pp. 550–556) was omitted in the delivery. Though requested by the Society for publication, it is proper to say, that for the sentiments in that portion of the address, the Society can be considered in no way responsible. A. B.

34

organization or a Society of 'Friends'; and there can be no want of charity towards others, if, when we come together *as* Presbyterians, we suggest those reasons to each other. Among ourselves indeed there are reasons satisfactory to our own minds, why, in our respective church relations, we are attached to one or the other of the different branches of the great Presbyterian family, but this is not an occasion on which it is proper to refer to those reasons. At proper times and places we advocate and defend those particular views, each one for himself: here we meet on a common level, to consider the import of the term which binds us all together as a distinct community, divided in form but not in heart from the rest of the Christian world, and in reference also to our own particular views, to enquire whether the grounds of difference among ourselves may not be further narrowed down, or made wholly to vanish; whether there may not be in the common term under which we are assembled—*Presbyterian*—so much of dignity, value, and importance, as to make it desirable that our minor differences should disappear altogether. The privilege which we thus claim for ourselves, we do not deny to others. We do not question the right of any other Christians freely to state the reasons why they hold their peculiar views; we do not deny that they have the right to examine with the utmost freedom the reasons which we allege in behalf of our own views; we claim, in turn, the right of examining theirs.

On this occasion, with almost no reference to what has been said before, or whether what I shall say may not have been better said—and indeed without knowing *what has been said*— I shall invite your attention to some remarks on the *affinities of Presbyterianism*—or, in this general topic, PRESBYTERIAN- ISM : — ITS AFFINITIES.

In the investigations of science there are always two points before the mind of the investigator : — the intrinsic nature of the object, and its affinities. He does not feel that he understands fully the former of these without an acquaintance with the latter; the latter may be, in fact, practically of much more importance than the former. Many of the works of nature are little known except by their affinities; none of them are fully understood except by those affinities. The original element— the atom—might perhaps be taken out by itself, and examined *as* purely independent, and might be described as such, but this would give but a very imperfect knowledge of its real nature considered as an object of scientific research. Its hardness, its weight, its tenacity, its elasticity, its malleability, its shape, might be ascertained, but this knowledge would be most imperfect, and of very little practical importance in the arts of life, or in understanding the world around us.   Iron, gold, the diamond, might be thus described ; oxygen, nitrogen, hydrogen might be thus examined ; the sixty or more elementary bodies which, according to the chemists, make up in combination the whole material universe, might be thus accurately investigated, and their properties *as* independent bodies defined, but we should feel that we had scarcely entered on a knowledge of the true nature of these elementary bodies. We want to know what they are in combination; what are their affinities; with what others any one of them naturally unites; in what proportions they combine ; what is the compound body which they thus produce.   We ask with what oxygen naturally combines, and we study the results in the air, in the water ; in plants and animals ; in the varieties of the vegetable creation, and the tribes of animals that people the air, the earth, and the seas ; in acids and oxides ; in vitality, in colors, in the breath which we inhale, in the water which we drink, in the vegetable on which we feed, in the living and the moving world around us. Science is busy in finding out these affinities : — the elements which naturally combine with each other, the proportions in which they combine, and the results of the combination.   Our knowledge of nature is practically measured by our attainments in this.   These sixty or more elementary bodies make up the world ; make up, so far as we know, all the material universe. If they lay scattered around with no affinities ; if they were like separate grains of sand on the sea-shore, or pebbles strewed over a field, or boulders lying detached from each other where they were dropped by masses of floating ice and earth, or borne from some distant mountain, there could be no world — there could be no science.   The most accurate knowledge of sands and pebbles and boulders in detail, could be of no practical use ; nor could that knowledge ever be reduced to a *system* of science.   It is only as combined that we feel an interest in them ; it is only as combined that they make up the beautiful creation around us and above us.

What is thus true in regard to the elementary principles of matter, is also true of the principles of moral science and religion.   We do not know fully what they are until we understand their *affinities.*   Do the principles submitted to us combine readily with liberty ; with just views of the rights of conscience ; with a proper sense of responsibility ; with social virtues ; with the progress of the race ; with the cultivation of the arts and sciences ; with the development of the human faculties ?   Are they likely to be found where there is most intelligence, most refinement, most purity of life, most courtesy of manners, most freedom of opinion, most elevated views of the dignity of man and of the government of God? Or is there a natural affinity with despotism, with slavery, with impurity of life and morals, with scepticism, with superstition, with atheism? What were the natural affinities of the doctrines of Democritus, of Epicurus, of Zeno, of Socrates, of Plato? What were the natural affinities of the opinions of Hobbes, of Spinosa, of Mr. Hume? What were those of Fourier and of Compte? What were those of Voltaire and Volney? What were those of Calvin, of Luther, of the Wesleys, of Jonathan Edwards?

Presbyterianism, whose affinities I desire, as I may be able, to illustrate, is properly a system of *government* in the church, as distinguished from Prelacy and Independency. It has, indeed, become now so combined with a certain form of *doctrine*, from a natural affinity which I shall attempt soon to explain, that we use the term familiarly, not as referring to the form of government, but in this combination with the Calvinistic doctrine. So close is this affinity; so uniform is this connection, and so prominent is the doctrine with which it combines, that in the popular estimation the *doctrine* is the prominent or main thing, and the popular feeling against it, if there is any, is arrayed against that rather than against the system as a mode of ecclesiastical government. In fact, in its bearing on the community, and considered with reference to preaching, the mode of government is rarely adverted to, and perhaps could be made to excite little feeling in the community in any way. Considered as a mere form of government, indeed, it has so much that is in common with our civil institutions, and so much, as we shall see, in accordance with just notions of liberty and the progress of the world, that it would seem to be easy to commend it to the favorable regards of mankind, if it were not for the odium excited by a form of doctrine with which, in fact, it is now invariably combined.

Yet it is strictly, and only, in itself *a system of government;* a system which, so far as would be apparent in an abstract consideration of its principles, *might* be combined with any form of religious doctrine, or with any forms and ceremonies in the public worship of God. Nothing could be detected in it, considered abstractly as a mode of government, which would forbid the idea that it might be combined in an actual organization of the church with Arminianism, with High Arianism, with Low Arianism, with Socinianism of the lowest forms; with the worship of God by a Liturgy; with splendid vestments, with processions, with pilgrimages and with genuflexions;

with the doctrine of Baptismal Regeneration ; with the Mass, or
with the doctrine of Purgatory. We shall see, however, whether
we can explain the cause or not, that it actually *has* no affinity
for any of these views of doctrine or these ceremonies, but that
its whole career in the world has been in fact a career of steady
repellancy to them all : —as we understand the properties of
matter by their repellancies, as well as by their attractions.

Considered, therefore, properly as a system of *government*,
Presbyterianism comprises the following as cardinal principles :

1. That all power in the church belongs to Christ; or that
he is the supreme Head of the church, and that all power
which is not derived from him is an invasion of his preroga-
tives, and is in fact an usurpation.

2. That power in the church resides, under Him, with the
people, and belongs to them as a brotherhood. It is not derived from men who profess to be descendants of the Apostles,
and invested, therefore, with authority over the church ; it is
not lodged with a clergy — a class regarded as invested with
authority separate from, and independent of the church — a
class to perpetuate their own order with no reference to the
will of the church ; it is not derived from the state as having
any right to legislate for the church as such, or to prescribe in
regard to its doctrines, its ceremonies, or its mode of worship;
it is a " self-governing society, distinct from the state, having
its officers and laws, and, therefore, an administrative government of its own ". This point has been so fully and so ably
illustrated before this Society by one who has preceded me in this
service, that, as I should have no ability to add any thing material to what has been said, and as there would be no occasion
to attempt to illustrate it farther, it is not necessary to dwell
on it.*

3. A third material and essential point in regard to Presbyterianism, is the entire equality of the clergy, or the fact that
there is but one order of ministers in the church. This doctrine we hold in the most absolute sense ; on this point there is
no difference of opinion among us. We do not, indeed, claim
that the belief of this is peculiar to us. Alike in the truth and
the importance of this doctrine, we agree with a very considerable portion of the Protestant world, and in defence of the
doctrine we make common cause with them. Holding this
doctrine, we, without any inconsistency, recognize cheerfully

---

* "What is Presbyterianism ? An Address delivered before the Presbyterian
Historical Society, May 1, 1855." The main principles here referred to are illustrated at length in that address.

and fully the validity of the ordination and the ministrations
of other denominations, and regard them as wholly on a level
with us, as we regard ourselves in every sense as on a level
with them.   Neither in the theory of the doctrine, nor in fact,
is there any spirit of *exclusiveness* on our part towards other
churches as founded on this article of our belief, nor are we,
nor can we, be constrained to take a position before the world
which compels us to hold up the ministers of other denominations as having no right to minister in holy things; which would
compel us to maintain that their ordination, or that baptism
and the Lord's supper as administered by them, are invalid; or
which would make it necessary to take the position before the
world that the churches to which they minister, as well as they
who officiate in those churches, are ' left to the uncovenanted
mercies of God '—to the charitable hope that they *may be saved*
—as the hope is entertained by those who hold those views on
a scale not less large and broad, that Turks, and Jews, and
Samaritans, and heathen, *may* in like manner be saved.

This doctrine of the equality of the clergy we regard as one
of great importance.   Taking the history of the church at
large, we do not believe that its importance can be easily over-
estimated.   The effect of the opposite view — of a distinction
among the clergy—of different grades of ministers—we think
can be traced far back in the history of the church, by an
affinity which is natural, and which it would be easy to explain,
with pomp, and ceremony, and formality in religion; with a
spirit of worldly aspiring in the clergy; with despotic civil
institutions; with a want of freedom among the people; with
the various forms of corruption prevailing in the Greek and
Roman Catholic communions; and with the forms of despotism
and of darkness which spread over Europe in the middle ages.
Charles I, with more sagacity as a man than practical wisdom
as a despotic monarch when a nation was struggling for freedom; with more of truth than of prudence as one who by his
office was pledged to the support of Prelacy, uttered the
memorable maxim, " No bishop, no king:" meaning, and
stating a great truth, that " if there is no despotic power in the
church, there can be no despotic power in the state; or, if there
be liberty in the church, there will be liberty in the state". *

4. A fourth material principle in Presbyterianism is, that
there is to be *government* in the church.   This we regard as an
essential principle.   We attach great importance to the idea
of government; of a government *as such.*   We shall see, in the
course of these remarks, how this idea springs from our Calvin-

* What is Presbyterianism ?   p. 11.

istic or doctrinal view, and by what a natural affinity it becomes, as derived from that, united with the Presbyterian mode of administration; and we shall see also, how it is connected with the idea of *loyalty as such*, and what position the Presbyterian church, when true to its principles, occupies in regard to loyalty and rebellion.   It pertains to the present part of my discourse only as a principle which runs through all the arrangements in the church.   Government is " the exercise of authority "; it is " direction and restraint over the actions of men in communities, societies, or states ".   *Webster's Dic.*   It is not *advice*, however wise such advice may be ; it is not *counsel*, however valuable and important such counsel may be ; it is not a suggestion of *expediency*, however proper, in its place, such a suggestion may be ; it is not an expression of *opinion* by those who are experienced, wise, or learned, however venerable by years, or however worthy of respect from their rank or social position ; it is, as far as it is proper to be exercised, *authority.*   It is power.   It is designed to settle and determine things.   It implies, as its correlative, obedience.   The submission which it demands is not the mere submission which the mind renders to good advice, or sage counsel, or sound reason ; it is the submission due to those who are appointed to rule, and who are entrusted with authority.   Up to the point where it is legitimate, and is not an usurpation, it becomes obligatory on the conscience ; and is to be regarded as a religious duty, an act of submission to God.

We attach great importance to this in the church, as we do in the state; an importance to be measured, when properly understood, by the evils of anarchy and disorder.   We believe that the church, like the state, is to be characterized by order, and that in the one such order is not less important than in the other.   We regard it as connected with all just ideas of right ; with all ideas of propriety in a community.   Our ideas of *government* are that it is universal.   The worlds which God has made, and over which he presides, are not regulated by advice, but by law ; a family listens to the expression of the will of the parent not as good counsel but as law ; a civil ruler is not merely a wise man, a good counsellor, but is one who is to administer law ; a judge decides a case not by giving advice, however wise, but by a sentence declaring what is the law ; a community is kept in order, and made prosperous, not by good opinions, but by the steady operation of law.   We regard it, therefore, as a very important principle that God has set in the church ' helps, *governments* ', as well as ' teachers ', ' miracles ', ' gifts of healing ', and ' diversities of tongues '.   1 Cor. xii, 28.

5. A fifth material principle in Presbyterianism, is, that it is a *representative* system of government. It supposes, indeed, as has been already remarked, that the power resides with the people—the church—and is to be exercised by them, and that in no case is power to be exercised which has not been conceded by them; yet still it is power to be exercised not by them directly, and as a body, but by those who are chosen by them, and to whom that power is delegated. In this respect it is contrasted, on the one hand, with the exercise of power as derived from the apostles by those who claim to be their successors, and on the other with power exercised by the assembly itself, or the body convened for this purpose: distinguished, on the one hand, from the monarchical principle, and on the other from strict and radical democracy. In this, it accords with the best ideas of liberty in the state. All just notions of liberty have tended to the establishment of this principle, and in the best modern constitutions it is admitted as an elementary principle. It is in fact, in the state, the result of all the conflicts for freedom. The world has made the experiment of the exercise of unrepresented power and authority in the monarchical and despotic forms of government, under the claim of the 'divine right of kings' on the one hand, and of the strict demmocratic principle on the other, in the struggles for freedom, and has oscillated between one and the other in the great conflicts and throes of nations—dynasties setting up the claim to a divine authority, and swaying a sceptre of tyranny when all liberty of the people was disowned or destroyed, and then a people rising in their might, and dethroning monarchs, and taking the government into their own hands, and exercising the authority directly themselves, until disorder, anarchy, weakness, and failure, prepared the way for a new claim of despotism, by an old hereditary title, or by a military usurpation. In the history of the world no safe medium has been found— no system that would combine authority and freedom; that would constitute a government, and yet not invade the rights of the people; that would secure the best administration of *law*, except that of the principle of representation. *That* combines authority and freedom; that gives to government the sanction of law; that makes the people feel that the authority exercised is their own authority; that furnishes a security against usurped power; that gives stability as distinguished from the actings of a mob; and that principle furnishes the means of defining the power to be exercised by a government, and of committing the great interests of a people where the trust will be least likely to be abused. We are confident that

this principle has been better secured in the Presbyterian mode of administration in the church than in any other form in which Christians have been organized into communities.

6. A *sixth* principle in the Presbyterian mode of government is, that the power of government is limited and bounded by a constitution. The power exercised is not arbitrary power. It is not a mere expression of *will* on the part of the people, or on the part of those who rule. It is not even by an independent and a private interpretation of the Bible, the source of all authority indeed, and the ultimate appeal in determining the government of the church. It is, in reference to government, by authority as *agreed on ;* as defined and limited by a constitution. A constitution concedes power, and expresses the limits of power. It defines what may be done; and it prescribes what shall not be done by the very fact that the authority to do a certain thing is *not* found there. The fact that there is a constitution is of the nature of a compact between the church and all who enter the church. It is a public pledge that no power shall be exercised which is not specified in this constitution ; and that no one, in regard to his opinions, his faith, or his conduct, shall be affected in any way except under the well-considered and clearly-defined processes arranged in the constitution. An arbitrary sovereign has no limit except that of will or caprice ; a mob has no rule of action, nor can any interests intrusted to it have a basis of security. A constitution defines and limits every right ; constitutes security in regard to rights ; makes the principles already established permanent ; encourages labor, secures the avails of industry, diffuses contentment, intelligence, the just administration of law, safety, and peace. All just notions of liberty in modern times are connected with the idea of a *constitution*, and all the progress which society makes is identified with the guarantees and safeguards found under a constitutional government. As agreeing, therefore, with these notions, and as connected with all that is valuable in the state as well as in the church, we, as Presbyterians, attach great importance to the idea of a *constitution*, and have incorporated that idea into our ecclesiastical arrangements more prominently than has been done by any other denomination of Christians.

With these views of Presbyterianism in the strict sense, considered as a system of *government*, I proceed now to notice some of its *affinities*.

The first which I notice, the most remarkable, but not the most obvious, is its affinity for the Calvinistic system of doc-

trine. I notice this first, not because it is the most obvious,
but because the two, which would seem to have no natural
affinity for each other, have in fact become so combined as to
constitute one system in the general estimation of men, and
the name *Presbyterianism* is now commonly so used as to
designate the result of this amalgamation.   Whatever of
power there may be in Presbyterianism, for good or for evil,
is now understood to be the result of this combination ; whatever of confidence there is in the system by those who love
it, is connected essentially with this combination ; whatever
of hatred there is towards the system by wicked men—and
there is not a little of that—is hatred cherished not so much
against the system considered as a mode of ecclesiastical government, as against a system having in itself an element of
power combined with the Calvinistic system of doctrines.
     I said that the combination is more remarkable than it is
obvious.   There would seem, in the nature of the case, to be
no natural affinity—no perceptible reason, why this particular form of government should combine with this particular
system of doctrines ; why the Presbyterian mode of administration and discipline should not be found, in fact, combined
with Arminianism, Sabellianism, Pelagianism, Socinianism ;
or why, when either of these forms of doctrine have effected a lodgment in a Presbytery or Synod, it should not
secure a permanent hold, as they may with Prelacy or Independency.
     The facts, however, are well established, in whatever way
they may be accounted for ; and these facts, therefore, as in the
natural affinities of the gases, the acids, the metals, the alka-
lies, become one of the means of ascertaining the true nature of the system.   As a matter of fact in the history of the
church, the Presbyterian mode of government does *not* combine with Arminianism, with Sabellianism, with Pelagianism, with Socinianism, and if such a union occurs at any
time it is only a temporary, and is manifestly a forced connection.   There are no permanent Arminian, Pelagian, Socinian Presbyteries, Synods, General Assemblies on the earth.
There are no permanent instances where these forms of belief
or unbelief take on the Presbyterian form.   There are no
Presbyterian forms of ecclesiastical administration where
they would be long retained.   Arminianism combines freely
and naturally with Methodism, with Prelacy, with the Greek
church, with the Papacy ; Pelagianism, Sabellianism, Arianism, Socinianism combine freely with Independency, and
most naturally assume that form of administration.   There

was doubtless some reason why Dr. Priestley, why Mr. Bel-
sham, why Dr. Channing were *not* Presbyterians ; there
was a reason why Calvin, Knox, Chalmers, Witherspoon
were.

The causes of this, not obvious at the first view, may, perhaps, be satisfactorily stated.

(*a*) Each springs essentially from the same idea—the idea
of government, of regularity, of order ; the idea that God
rules ; that government is desirable ; that things are, and
should be, fixed and stable ; that there is, and should be, law ;
that the affairs of the universe at large, the affairs of society,
and the affairs of individuals, should be founded on settled
principles, and should not be left to chance or hap-hazard.
Calvinism, though it seem to be, and though it is often represented as a mere system of doctrine, or of abstract dogmas
having no philosophical foundation and no valuable practical
bearing, is, in fact, a system of government — a method and
form in which the Divine power is put forth in the administration of the affairs of the universe. It is based on the idea
that God rules ; that he has a plan ; that the plan is fixed and
certain ; that it does not depend on the fluctuations of the human will, on the caprice of the human heart, or on contingencies and uncertain and undetermined events in human affairs.
It supposes that God is supreme ; that he has authority ; that
he has a right to exercise dominion ; that for the good of the
universe, that right should be exercised, and that infinite power
is put forth only in accordance with a plan. Its essential idea,
therefore, is that of authority, regularity, order, law ; and
hence it naturally combines with that form of administration
where stability, regularity, order, are most recognized ; where
there *is* a government ; where the government is administered
on the fixed principles of a constitution, and is not dependent
on the changing phases of society, or the caprices of human
feeling.

(*b*) Each, as we shall soon see, naturally draws to itself the
same class of minds. What that class is, it will be most convenient to describe in another part of this address. There is
in the world, in all countries and communities, a class that
characteristically loves order, law, just government, fixed
principles; that seeks to lay the foundations of society and of
government deep and firm ; that aims to carry fixed principles
into the family administration, into the intercourse of man
with man, into civil institutions, and into the laws of a
country ; which seeks guarantees for the rights of man, and
the administration of justice ; which leaves as little as possible

to the feelings of a populace, and removes government as far as possible from the ascendency and sway of passion; which seeks to preserve and send forward to future times all that has been secured of value in the past; which has a fondness for permanent endowments in education, in colleges and universities, and in eleemosynary institutions.

Presbyterianism in its fixedness, its order, and its love of law, well represents that idea, and draws to itself that class of minds—not exclusively, I willingly admit, but naturally; Calvinism, as a system of doctrine, beginning with an eternal plan on the part of God, regarding the universe as governed by settled purpose and law, and its affairs as in no sense under the control of chance, and as, therefore, fixed and stable, draws to itself also naturally—I will not here say by any means exclusively—the same class of mind. Yet though it is not in either case so universal that we can claim that all of such classes of minds are drawn to the system, yet it is so natural an affinity, the objects dear to such minds can be so well secured by the principles of Presbyterianism as a system of government, and by Calvinism as a system of doctrine, that we are not surprised to find that there *is* a large portion of the community always that finds its views better represented in this *combined* system than could be found elsewhere, or that these views are, in fact, so often found united together.

(c) Each, therefore—Presbyterianism as a scheme of government, and Calvinism as a system of doctrine — contemplates the same *results*, and we are not surprised to find them seeking a natural alliance, and often combined. That they may exist separately, I do not deny. That the Presbyterian mode of government has been found in a few instances originally combined with other forms of doctrine, or that, in some instances, as now in Geneva, and in some of the Protestant churches in France, in England, in Ireland, the form of Presbyterian government has been retained after the churches have materially departed from the original faith which bound the two systems together, is not to be denied. Nor is it to be denied that the Calvinistic doctrine may be found under other modes of ecclesiastical government. To a certain extent it *is* found in connection with Prelacy and Independency, but still the regular historical fact is, that the two seek an alliance, and that they have such a natural affinity, and are so often found together, as to justify the popular use of the term *Presbyterianism* as denoting a peculiar mode of church government combined with Calvinistic doctrines. It is the carrying out ideas of order, authority, and law as manifested in government and in doctrine; as a statement of the way in which God controls the universe, and of the best mode of preserving order, and of securing just government on earth.

Proceeding now with this idea of Presbyterianism *as* the union of a certain mode of government with a certain form of doctrine, I shall notice some of the affinities of the system as thus understood.

The most obvious, perhaps, is its affinity for a simple mode of worship.   The facts as bearing on this point are so well understood as to demand little more than a bare suggestion that they are so.   Nothing is more certain than that history, as a general statement, records the progress and the prevalence of Presbyterianism as connected with the simplest forms of worship; nothing is clearer than that the word Presbyterianism suggests at once to the popular mind the idea of a repugnance to gorgeous forms of devotion, to imposing rites and ceremonies, to a liturgy, to splendid vestments, to worship celebrated in magnificent cathedrals, and to the idea of grace communicated by official sanctity in a priesthood.   The lofty cathedrals of the old world were built with other ideas of worship than those which are embraced by Presbyterians.   It was always difficult to adjust the old church of St. Peter's at Geneva to the worship celebrated there with Calvin as a pastor, or to keep up an idea of a correspondence between the comparatively simple worship which *he* introduced there, and the lofty edifice built with reference to the pomp of the Roman Catholic worship.   Even now, with all that there is of rites and forms in the Episcopal Church, no one can enter Westminster Abbey or York Minster without feeling a sense of incongruity and unfitness between the vast and magnificent structures where the worship is celebrated, and the mode of the worship; and nothing could adapt those structures, or St. Mark's at Venice, or the cathedrals at Cologne or Milan, or St. Peter's at Rome, to the idea of *Presbyterian* worship.   In the very form of the Gothic edifice there is a manifest incongruity between the structure and the modes of worship preferred by Presbyterians; and the idea which strikes the mind where such a structure is reared is that, as it was originally adapted to a mode of worship materially unlike the *Presbyterian* view of the design of devotion, so it will be forever impossible to combine the two.

So remarkable is this principle; so deeply is it, from some cause, imbedded in the very nature of Presbyterianism, that it has been impossible to retain in connection with it, or to revive permanently even those modified forms of devotion, and those remnants of pomp and show in the worship of God, which some of the Reformers adopted under Presbyterian organizations. It is known that some of the Reformed churches under Presbyterian organizations adopted, in a modified way, Liturgical Forms of worship; it is known also that having naturally died away, from the very nature of Presbyterianism, an attempt has been made in our times to revive them. Yet these forms cannot be revived and perpetuated under Presbyterian auspices. There is, from some cause, a repellancy between the two, and Liturgical Forms, imposing ceremonies in religion, pomp, and splendor of ritual, will seek and find their natural affinities in other denominations. They cannot be attached permanently to Presbyterianism. The history of Presbyterianism demonstrates that, for some cause, it seeks simplicity of worship, and that its true spirit flourishes only there.

It is not difficult to account for this fact. Presbyterianism, in the form in which I am now noticing it, as a combination of a particular mode of government with a certain system of doctrine, gives such a prominence to one great doctrine, and guards that doctrine with such anxious care, that it looks with a jealous eye on all those forms and ceremonies which would tend in any way to render it obscure, or to displace it in the estimation of the worshipper. That doctrine is the doctrine of justification by faith. It is in the view of all Presbyterians a great principle that the merit of our salvation is wholly in the Redeemer—in the sacrifice which he made for mankind on the cross; that that doctrine is to stand *alone* in the matter of man's salvation; that nothing else is to enter into a sinner's justification; that there is no human merit that can be urged as a ground of acceptance with God; that the single idea that the merit of Christ is the sole ground of justification is to be kept before the mind, with nothing that shall tend to obscure it in the view of the worshipper, or to turn away the mind from it.

Thus Presbyterianism as a system, and in its very nature, rejects all idea of human merit, and every thing which the mind of the worshipper might be in danger of construing *as* merit. The mind is to be held to the doctrine of justification by faith alone. *Some* forms of worship are, indeed, indispensable, from the nature of the case, but Presbyterianism insists that they shall be as simple as possible; that they shall be such that the mind shall not be in any necessary danger of mistake on the subject; that they shall not be such as shall have any natural tendency to turn away the mind from the doctrine of justification by faith; that there shall be no such view of the sacredness of the priesthood by a pretended derivation from the apostles as having authority to forgive sin; that there shall be no such view of the sacraments as having an efficacy, derived from a priesthood, to regenerate the soul; that there shall be no such view of the power of imparting grace by the imposition of sacred hands; that there shall be no such idea of sanctity or merit attached to the bowing of the head at the name of Jesus, or to genuflexions, or to any other forms and ceremonies of religion, as to *displace* in any way the doctrine of justification by faith, the idea of entire dependence on the merits of the Saviour, in the mind of the worshipper.

We think that it is not easy to separate an idea of merit from imposing and gorgeous and painful forms of religion, and that while there is no indispensable *necessary* connection between such forms and the idea of human merit, yet, as the mind of man is constituted, there is a constant danger of obscuring the doctrine of justification by faith *by* such forms. As a matter of fact in the history of the church, pompous rites and ceremonies did effectually obscure that doctrine until it was lost from human view, and the Reformation became necessary to give it the prominency which it has in the New Testament. Nor is it easy now to secure in the view of a worshipper the prominency which the New Testament gives to that doctrine, in connection with the idea that there is a sacred order of men to whom properly pertains the office of a *priesthood ;* or with the idea of grace imparted directly by the sacrament of the Lord's Supper in virtue of the official character of those by whom it is administered, or with the idea of such an efficacy in baptism as to secure regeneration. Whatever justness of view there may be in individual members in such churches, and whatever influence of evangelical doctrine there may be in such churches, yet it is rather in *spite* of such views, and of such rites and ceremonies, than by any tendency in such rites and views to secure such influences; nor are we much surprised at any defection of faith in such churches on the great cardinal doctrine of the Reformation, or with any disposition in any portions of such churches towards the views which prevailed when the doctrine of justification by faith was wholly obscured and lost amidst the imposing forms and ceremonies of the Roman Catholic communion.

The next thing which I notice in regard to this combination—this union of the principles of a certain mode of government and a certain system of doctrines which we call Presbyterianism—is its affinity for a certain class of minds, or the probability that it will draw to itself a class of minds of a peculiar order which will not be as likely to find their views represented by any other form of government and belief.

I mean by this, that there may be presumed to be in every community a class of minds which will be more likely to be Presbyterian than to be drawn to any other denomination, Protestant or Papal; that an appeal to them on the subject of religion from the Presbyterian standpoint will be more likely to reach them, and affect them, than an appeal from any other quarter; that Christianity itself will be more likely to commend itself to them when presented in the Presbyterian form than in any other form; that they will be more likely to be converts to Christ under that form than any other; that they will see fewer objections to the gospel as presented in that form than in any other form; that they will see in that form more that commends itself to their views of what true religion is, and must be, than in any other; and that, in the Presbyterian church they will be more useful as Christians than they would be in connection with any other denomination.

While I say this, however, I would say also for myself, without now claiming to represent the views of any whom I address, that I believe that the same thing might be said by those connected with other denominations, and with just as much truth and propriety. For the same reasons why I believe that there is a class in every community which will find more that accords with their views of religion, and which will be more edified and more useful in the Presbyterian church than in any other, I believe also that there is a class of minds in every community which will find more that accords with their views of religion, and with the structure of their own minds, and which will be more happy and more useful in the Episcopal church, or in the Methodist church, or in other Protestant churches, than they would in the Presbyterian church. And as, with this view, I should regard it as indicating no want of charity, and as no evidence of a narrow and illiberal spirit, for one of another denomination to *say* this, so the remark which I now make cannot be construed as indicating a narrow and illiberal spirit, or as indicating a want of charity if said by one who is a Presbyterian. No man who has any just view of the human mind can doubt that men, equally honest, from their natural temperament; from the mode of their training; from their standpoint in religion; from their habit of viewing things; from their associations in life, will take different views on a subject so important and so difficult as religion, or that they may find more that is congenial in carrying out an honest purpose to lead a religious life with one class of persons rather than with another.   Nor, understanding human nature as it is, can it be doubted that harmony and peace can be better promoted by persons entertaining peculiar views being associated in one organization than would be if the same persons were associated with those of a different temperament, and entertaining different views.   In like manner, for myself, I believe that there are not a few sincere Christians who will be more edified, and who will be more useful, in connection with the forms of religion—the Liturgical services—in the Episcopal Church than they would be in the severe and simple modes of devotion which, as Presbyterians, we regard as more in conformity with the spirit of the New Testament, and as better adapted to our comfort in devotion, to our usefulness, and to our growth in grace, and to the general interests of religion in the world.

Without, therefore, in the slightest degree desiring to interfere with other denominations in setting forth the advantages of their own modes of worship, and showing their adaptedness to promote the edification of Christians, and to extend religion in the world by such words and by such arguments as they may prefer to use, and to any extent which they may please, it is not improper for us, on an occasion like this, to state the reasons why we suppose that there is a class of minds in the community which will be more likely to be Presbyterians than to be attached to any other denomination ; and to refer to our special mission in the world in securing the proper influence of religion on that class of minds.

(a) There are men whose native characteristics of mind, or whose habits of thought as they have been cultivated, incline them to the Calvinistic views of religion.   They are men who in their philosophy look first to God; to government ; to order ; to law ; to stability :—men who naturally regard all things as the result or the carrying out of a fixed plan ; who see no evidence of permanency or security but in such a plan ; whose minds could find no security or peace in the idea of chance or contingency, or in the results which would follow from making the human will, human wisdom, or human freedom, the centre or the standpoint in the contemplation of the universe.   Such men, when their minds are turned to religion, will be Calvinists and not Arminians, and any attempt to bring them under the influence of religion from an Arminian point of view would be at a disadvantage, if not a failure altogether.   Perhaps it is not too much to say that there *are* minds which sooner than embrace the Arminian views of religion

35

with all the appeals which Christianity under that form could present to them, would rather embrace an infidel view with which their philosophy *could* be identified; or, rather perhaps, it should be said that their views of order, of law, of plan, and of the necessity of eternal counsels and purposes would be so settled that they could not embrace religion in any form if it was to be presented only with the Arminian view. Whatever may be said of John Wesley, it is certain that Jonathan Edwards could never have been any thing but a Calvinist; and when we think of the native structure of his mind, we never associate it with any other possible idea in religion than that of Calvinism.

This class of minds is largely diffused through every community; and it has characteristics of great value in regard to religion. It will be likely to be calm and sober in its views; firm in principle; not easily swayed by passion; rigid in its adherence to truth; friendly to just government, order, and law. It will be found everywhere in religion as representing the religion of *principle*, rather than the religion of *sentiment*.

(*b*) Again. There are numbers of persons who by the very manner of their conversion become Calvinists, and who can never be any thing else than Calvinists. They are spiritually-born Calvinists, and the Calvinistic idea will be incorporated into all their religious convictions, and will, under any external form of devotion, attend them through life. In their conversion their sense of sin is so deep; their conviction of the native obduracy of the heart, and the perversion of the will, is so entire; they are made so conscious of their utter helplessness; they are led by their own experience to attach so significant—almost so literal—a meaning to the statement that men are by nature ' *dead* in sin;' the manner in which their attention was arrested, and in which they were convicted of sin, was so clearly a matter of sovereignty—so entirely without any agency or purpose of their own, so clearly not the act of man, so absolutely and unequivocally the work of God; and their conversion—their change of heart—was so manifestly to their view the work of God — the result of a creative power — that they can never doubt the doctrine of the divine agency in conversion — the doctrine of the divine purposes—the doctrine of election as bearing on them—and the doctrine of the perseverance of the saints as constituting the only ground of *their* hopes that they will ever reach eternal life. Knowing as we now do, the mental process through which Dr. Thomas Scott, and Dr. Chalmers passed when they were converted, we see at once how their conversion naturally issued in Calvinism, nor can we see how, under that process of conversion, they *could* ever have glided into Arminian views.

(*c*) Again. Much of the educated mind in this country, and in other lands, will be likely to be Calvinistic. In our own country, in Scotland, in Ireland, in England, in Switzerland, in Holland, a portion of the young, not few in number and destined to exert a large influence in public affairs, receive their early training in the families of Calvinists, and under the direct teaching of the Shorter Catechism. In our own country, a majority of the colleges of the land were founded under Calvinistic influences, and have received their patronage from Calvinistic sources, and are under the instruction of men who favor the Calvinistic views. The first college in the land, and the second, and the third, and the fourth, were founded by Calvinists, and no small part of those which have been since founded were originated and are controlled by those of the same faith. These, indeed, are not sectarian institutions. They are not designed primarily or mainly to give instruction in the Calvinistic views. They are not exclusive in regard to other views. But, in the nature of the case, it is inevitable that these views will give shape and form to the philosophy which is taught in these institutions; that the first impressions in regard to religion will be derived from these views; that minds educated in these institutions will go out without prejudice against these views, and that the educated mind of the country to a large extent will identify religion with these views, and be prepared to welcome that form of doctrine when such minds are brought under the power of religion at all.

(*d*) Again. The history of our own country has been such that that class of minds may be expected to be found extensively diffused over the nation. The class of minds for which Calvinism has an affinity, or which has been trained under Calvinistic influences, has had an important agency in the affairs of the nation, and has contributed not less than any one class of minds in making us as a people what we are.

The Puritan mind, to which our country owes so much in its character, and in the form of its civil institutions, is essentially Calvinistic. The form in which Puritanism first developed itself in the mother country was essentially Calvinistic; the Pilgrims who landed on Plymouth Rock were Calvinists; the churches which they formed were Calvinistic churches; the colleges and schools which they established were based not less on the Shorter Catechism of the Westminster Assembly than on the spelling book, on Euclid, and on Homer. That mind, more than any other mind that constituted an element in our early history, has been diffused over this great land, and is found now *as* a powerful element in all our States and territories from Maine to California. It is still a leading mind in religion, in education, in civil and military matters; in all the powerful organizations that affect the destinies of our country. That mind is not Unitarian; not Arminian; not Prelatical; and though Unitarianism has sprung out of it, and though that class of minds may be found in connection with Arminian views, and in connection with the Prelatical forms of worship, yet we cannot but be sensible of an incongruity in those connections, and we attach almost instinctively to the Puritan mind found in those connections the idea which we attach to those who 'remove ancient landmarks'—the idea of apostacy from the appropriate form in which such elements should be found.

The Huguenot mind, one of the most noble, liberal, large, warm-hearted, and courteous, in all the classes of mind that have moulded our institutions, is essentially Calvinistic, and naturally developes itself in the form of Presbyterianism. Not a few of the most eminent, learned, and benevolent Christians in our country have had this origin, and such minds have shed a lustre at the same time on our common Christianity and on the Presbyterian church.

The Scotch mind is essentially Presbyterian. There was a natural affinity between Edinburgh and Geneva; between Knox and Calvin. Nowhere in the world have there been such staunch defenders of Presbyterianism as in Scotland; nowhere has there been so decided opposition to Arminianism and to Prelacy; nowhere have so many martyrs shed their blood in defence of Calvinistic and Presbyterian principles; nowhere has it been so difficult to establish Prelacy, or to institute an order of bishops as in Scotland. So natural, so deep and abiding is this affinity, that the idea of a Scotch Episcopalian, a Scotch Methodist, or a Scotch Unitarian, always strikes us as incongruous: a thing to be accounted for in a particular case, and not on any general principles, as any other anomaly is to be.

The Scotch-Irish mind, so extensively diffused in our country, is also essentially Calvinistic and Presbyterian, and when we meet this mind we anticipate of course that we have found, if it takes a religious turn, an ally for Calvinism and Presbyterianism.

These classes of mind have some peculiar characteristics. They are firm, resolute decided; they act more from principle than from impulse ;' they are friendly to order and law ; they are the friends of sound learning and science ; they will be certain to found and patronize schools and colleges ; they will be reliable in all times when great principles are at stake, and they will not be far off when the spirit of martyrdom is demanded. That class of mind *may* be harsh, rigid, possibly blunt, uncourteous, and rough, regarding great principles as more important than the manner in which they are defended ; but it will be decided.

That class of minds is scattered extensively over our country, and it is one of the missions of the Presbyterian church to which it is especially called in endeavoring to diffuse the common principles of Christianity, so to direct its efforts and its influences towards this class of minds that it shall be Christian and not infidel. The question in regard to this class of minds is not mainly whether it shall be Calvinistic *or* Arminian ; not whether it shall be Trinitarian *or* Socinian ; not whether it shall be Presbyterian *or* Prelatical, Presbyterian *or* Methodist, Episcopalian *or* Catholic, *it is whether it shall be Christian* OR *infidel :* whether it shall embrace the principles of Knox and Chalmers, *or* those of Hume and Kames and Monboddo. No men make better Christians, and no men make as dangerous sceptics, and there is no more important work to be done in our country than that which seems properly to pertain to the Presbyterian church, to see that this class of mind shall be saved from infidelity, and shall be trained to believe and embrace the Gospel.

The next thing which I notice in regard to this system of religion is its affinity for the doctrine of human rights, and the principles of liberty. It is a fundamental principle, as represented in the words adopted by each of the branches of the church represented in this Society, that " God alone is Lord of the conscience, and hath left it free from the doctrines and commandments of men which are in any thing contrary to his word, or beside it, in matters of faith and worship." Confession of Faith, ch. xx, § ii. This great principle lies at the foundation of all our notions of liberty and of the rights of man. It is nourished and sustained by all our veneration for the Bible, as a divine Revelation, as the source of law, as the fountain of doctrine, as containing a true history of man in his creation, fall, and redemption, and as an emanation of divine wisdom : — by that respect for the word of God which has always so characterized Presbyterians that the great principle enunciated by Chillingworth that " The Bible is the religion of Protestants", has been more perfectly maintained and carried

out in our denomination than in any other Protestant branch
of the church. This great principle has been incorporated into
all Presbyterian Confessions of Faith, and in no other branch
of the church, and under no other form of belief, has there
been a more stern regard for liberty and the rights of man,
and a more firm resistance of tyranny and oppression.

We may begin at Geneva—abused and slandered Geneva—
and move among the Huguenots, and pass to Holland, and
recall the scenes in England in the time of Charles and in the
Commonwealth, and retrace the bloody history of Scotland,
and bring to our recollection the history of the Presbyterian
church in our own country, and we shall trace all along a close
connection between the principles which we hold as Presbyterians and the spread of the doctrines of civil liberty, and we
may challenge the world for a record of more honorable struggles in behalf of freedom and the rights of man than have
been manifested in connection with the Presbyterian Faith.

I have not time to illustrate this point properly, or to consider the full influence of our Calvinistic views on the subject
of the rights of man, or as bearing on the subject of oppression
and slavery.

I have already referred to the principle which we hold in
regard to the right of self-government in the church, or of
power as emanating, under God, from the people—a principle
which as applied to civil affairs constitutes the foundation of
liberty in the state. I have referred to the principle of representation as recognized in our system of Government—a principle now regarded as essential to all just notions of civil liberty. I have adverted to our idea of constitutional limits and
bounds in the exercise of power — a principle so vital as a
check against arbitrary power, and so essential to the protection of vested rights, to rights of property, to freedom of
speech, to personal security, and to the protection of character.
I have incidentally adverted to the right of conscience, and to
our direct and supreme responsibility to God. As these principles are applicable in the state as well as in the church; as
they pertain to men as men, and are, therefore, in our view,
of universal applicability and importance, perhaps it might be
proper for me to close this part of the subject here as having
suggested all that is essential to the point now under consideration.

But there are a few thoughts, derived especially from Presbyterianism in its Calvinistic aspect as bearing on liberty,
which it seems necessary to suggest. Part of those views are
held also by other Christians; part are peculiar to us. They

are views which contemplate the human race as on a level, and as endowed by their Maker with equal rights — 'life, liberty, the pursuit of happiness.'

The fundamental view on this subject, which we hold in the main in common with other denominations of Christians, but which we think we have some advantage over others in presenting in its full force, is that THE RACE IS ONE. The views which we entertain on this subject, partly in common with other Christians, and partly as springing from our peculiar doctrines, make it essential, if we would be consistent, that we should maintain also a steady opposition to slavery in all its forms, and that we should be advocates of universal freedom.

(a) The race, we hold, is one. "God hath made of one blood all the nations of men, for to dwell on all the face of the earth." Acts xvii, 26. This doctrine we embrace in the strictest sense. We regard it as essential to true faith in the Bible, and as vital to all just views of religion. We could not retain our faith in the Bible for a moment if we were compelled to regard men as made up of different races of independent origin; we could not retain our views of the work of redemption except as we believe that there was one head of the race, of all human beings, as originally created; and one head of the race, of all human beings, in the work of redemption. This doctrine we maintain in opposition to all the efforts which are made to establish the idea that human beings are constituted of essentially different races, having a different origin, and having each its own peculiar ancestry or head :—that there have been separate acts of creation in reference to the Caucasian, the Mongolian, the Ethiopian, or the American races. All the differences in color, complexion, cranial bones, and facial angles in the race we hold are to be accounted for on some other supposition than that God originally created different races of men, or that men have been developed from the lower forms of the animal creation. But this idea, when properly pursued and applied, is fatal to all the conceptions of slavery; to the supposition that human beings are ever to be held as property, or to be placed on a level with chattels and things. God by creating the race "of one blood" has made an impassable barrier between man and the ape, the ourang-outang, the chimpanzee, the gorilla, the ox and the donkey, and no man can be held as property without a violation of the scriptural idea in regard to the creation of man.

(b) Again. We entertain views of the relation of man to Adam such as to suggest the idea of equal human rights, and such as to constitute an argument against slavery. We regard Adam as the head of the one race, as the one ancestor of all human beings, as sustaining a peculiar covenant relation to all his posterity ; and hence we regard all, of all colors and conditions, as having his image, and as implicated in his act.   This doctrine we hold more decidedly than it is held by any other denomination of Christians, for it is *essential* to all notions of Calvinism.   It has gone into all our Confessions of Faith ; it lies at the very foundation of all our system of doctrines.   Whether the doctrine be held that we have been affected by his fall by 'immediate' imputation or by 'mediate' imputation ; whether we regard Adam as the constituted 'federal head' of all his posterity, or as merely the 'natural' head ; whether we attempt to explain the effect of his disobedience on his posterity by a direct and special act of God constituting him a 'representative' of the race, or by natural laws—by an arrangement in fact universal in its nature, but existing in the highest form in his relation to his posterity, we are unanimous in the belief that *his* act involved the race in ruin ; that it made it certain that all his posterity would be born with a fallen nature, with corrupt hearts, with a proneness to sin ; that his fall was the source of death—the reason why *any* human being would ever die, and why *all* human beings must die ; and that thus, alike in the fact that they have derived their existence through him, and have inherited a corrupt nature from him, they are all on a level before God.

The doctrine of the unity of the race, and the equality of all men before God, is thus secured by our doctrine of the creation and fall of man.   Adam in the beginning was the head of THE RACE—Caucasians, Mongolians, Americans, *Africans ;* and, as in the creation, so in the apostacy, there is one great brotherhood.   Each one, no matter what his color or his country, is a brother to every other one in human form, alike in creation and in ruin.   As the creation made no one in the condition of a slave, so the fall has put no one necessarily in that condition, and has left to no one on any ground such superiority as to lay the foundation of a claim to be an owner or a master.

(*c*) The same thing is true in the doctrine which we hold in respect to redemption.   In the views which we entertain on that subject, partly in common with other Christians, and partly as peculiar to ourselves, we regard all the races of men as on a level ; all as ransomed by the same blood; all, so far as the work of redemption bears on them, or appertains to them, as viewed by God with the same feeling, and invested with the same privileges ; all as ransomed *men,* not one of them as a *chattel* or a *thing*. There is, indeed, as is well known, a difference of opinion among those who bear the Presbyterian name, as to the *extent* of the atonement made by Christ, whether it had reference to the whole of the race, or whether it was made only for the elect, considered as elect; but whatever difference of views may be entertained on that point, there is entire agreement on the immediate point now before us. Even where it is held that the atonement was made for only a part of mankind, still it is not maintained that the application of the atonement was determined by the question of *races*, as if one were in any respect superior to another before God. Christ, even on that theory, did not die for the Caucasian race as such, nor was the African race as such excluded in his design in making an atonement for man. In the divine purpose the line, if such a line was run, was not between the Mongolian, the Caucasian, the African, the American races as such, or indeed with any reference to such classifications of the human family, or with any idea that as connected with redemption any one division of the human family had any superiority over the others. The line was run from causes which are unexplained to us, but it was not for *this* cause, nor can any one of these classes undertake to enslave any other class without the moral certainty that he is defrauding of natural rights those for whom Christ died; that in making a slave, or reducing any one to the condition of a chattel or a thing, he is subjecting to that wrong, one who in the work of redemption is to be regarded as a brother; or one, who, so far as the idea of *race* is concerned, has been redeemed with the precious blood of the Son of God.

(*d*) The same idea is suggested by our doctrine of election. With all of us this *is* a cardinal doctrine; a doctrine to which we trace all our personal hopes of salvation, and all our expectation of the success of the Gospel in the world. In the system of truth which we hold we do not think that its importance can be over-estimated.

But the division of the human race which the doctrine of election contemplates in reference to the church on earth, and to the final condition of the race in the future world, is not a division by any imagined upper and lower *strata* in society; it is not a division by geography, by climate, by national peculiarities. The line is not run by races. Men are chosen to salvation not as Caucasians, as Mongolians, as Ethiopians, as Americans. The eternal destiny of man, according to that doctrine, is not determined by the size or shape of the cranium, by the measurement of the facial angle, by the crispiness or the straightness of the hair, by the thickness of the lips, or by the color of the skin.   What it *is*, we may not be able, with our wisdom, to determine, but we are agreed that it is not *this*.   The elect of God are found in the ' *quarters* '—the humble cottages on the ' plantation ' as well as in the homes of the masters ; and we go to Africa, to the Islands of the Sea, to the abodes of Mogul Tartars, and to the wigwam of the American savages, expecting to find the elect *there* as really as when we preach to Teutons, Gauls, Celts and Saxons.

The African is a man redeemed by the blood of Jesus. The Caucasian is a man redeemed by the blood of Jesus. When we have said this, we have said what is the most significant thing in regard to man.   We have suggested that which rises above all the distinctions of wealth, and caste, and complexion, and intellectual grade.   We have referred to man as he is regarded by the Creator on his throne ; as he was regarded by the Redeemer on the cross ; as he is regarded by the Holy Ghost in his ' office-work ' in converting and sanctifying the soul.

It follows logically from this view—a view which we all entertain, that no one should regard another as a slave — as property—as a chattel—as an article of merchandise ; that no one should rob another of the proper avails of his own industry ; that no one should deprive another of access to the word of God — the sacred record of his own redemption, his guide in duty, and the foundation of his hope of heaven ; that no one should interfere in the sacred relation of husband and wife, parent and child, and " put asunder what God hath joined together "; that no one should *make* a human being a slave—that no one should *own* or sell a redeemed brother.

It was in entire accordance with these principles that in the early periods of our Presbyterian history, when as yet we were few and feeble, and when as yet there was no General Assembly in the land, the Synod of New York and Philadelphia—the original of two of the branches of the Presbyterian family represented in this Society, in 1787 gave solemn utterance to the following sentiment : " The Synod of New York and Philadelphia do highly approve of the general principles in favor of universal liberty that prevail in America, and they recommend it to all the people under their care, to use the most prudent measures consistent with the interest and the state of civil society, in the parts where they live, to procure, eventually, the FINAL ABOLITION OF SLAVERY IN AMERICA".

And it was in accordance with these principles that the General Assembly of the Presbyterian church in 1818 uttered its memorable declaration before the world — a declaration which to this day stands on its Records unrepealed—unmodified in reference to both the branches of that church:—" We consider the voluntary enslaving of one part of the human race by another, as a gross violation of the most precious rights of human nature ; as utterly inconsistent with the law of God, which requires us to love our neighbor as ourselves ; and as totally irreconcilable with the spirit and principles of the Gospel of Christ, which enjoin that ' All things whatsoever ye would that men should do to you, do ye even so to them'.   Slavery creates a paradox in the moral system — it exhibits rational, accountable, and immortal beings, in such circumstances as scarcely to leave them the power of moral action.   It exhibits them as dependent on the will of others, whether they shall receive religious instruction ; whether they shall know and worship the true God ; whether they shall enjoy the ordinances of the Gospel ; whether they shall perform the duties, and cherish the endearments of husbands and wives, parents and children, neighbors and friends ; whether they shall preserve their chastity and purity, or regard the dictates of justice and humanity.

" From the view of the consequences resulting from the practice into which Christian people have most inconsistently fallen, of enslaving a portion of their *brethren* of mankind—for ' God hath made of one blood all nations of men to dwell on the face of the earth '—it is manifestly the duty of all Christians who enjoy the light of the present day, when the inconsistency of slavery, both with the dictates of humanity and religion has been demonstrated, and as generally seen and acknowledged, to use their honest, earnest, and unwearied endeavors, to correct the errors of former times, and as speedily as possible to efface this blot on our holy religion, and to obtain the complete abolition of slavery throughout Christendom, and if possible throughout the world ".*

I need not say to this audience that the other branches of the Presbyterian church represented in this Society fully coïncide in these sentiments.   There is no portion of the whole church of Christ on earth that has been more decided in the expression of its sentiments on the subject of slavery, and more firm and consistent in its opposition to the system, than the Scotch Presbyterian churches represented here to-night. Not a slave is owned by any of their members ; not one who is a holder of human beings as property would be tolerated in their communion.

* Minutes of the General Assembly for 1818, pp. 29, 30.

This is the spirit of true Presbyterianism. This is the proper carrying out in one direction of those grand principles which as Calvinistic Presbyterians we hold. In the noble testimony to which I have just referred, there is not one word which is inconsistent with the principles which as Presbyterians we all hold ; there is not one word which those principles do not naturally suggest ; there is not one word which could be withdrawn without a violation of those principles. First in our country, except the Society of Friends, the Presbyterian church proclaimed these views — views so much in accordance with the sentiments of the men, North and South, who fought for our Independence, and who laid the foundation of our civil institutions. Nor can those principles be abandoned without a renunciation of the great doctrines which we hold in regard to the creation of man ; the unity of the race ; the work of redemption ; and the doctrine of God's sovereignty in choosing man unto life. He who is the advocate of slavery violates each and all of those principles ; and when Presbyterians violate those principles, and the church at large becomes the defender of Slavery, it is not wonderful that God visits a people with such heavy judgments ás are now spreading over the region where slavery has been established, and where it has been defended in the pulpits of our land.

It was my purpose to have noticed the affinity of Presbyterianism for learning, and for the diffusion of knowledge among the masses of men. I should not have insisted on this as *peculiar* to Presbyterianism, but I should have shown from the principles which we hold, and from the history of Presbyterianism, how it has been, and is, the patron of schools, academies, colleges, seminaries of learning ; how those principles lead to sound views on the liberty of the press ; how they are carried out in the arrangements for the diffusion of Christian literature.

But I have already detained you too long. There remains one point, however, in reference to which at the present time, and under existing circumstances in our country, I should be recreant to my duty to you and to the cause if I did not, at least, allude to it. I refer to the affinity of the principles which we hold to loyalty—loyalty to just government—loyalty to our country.

The very foundation of our principles of Calvinism is laid in the duty of loyalty—loyalty to God and to his government. The sum of all our doctrines, and all our efforts, is to bring men back to allegiance to the laws and the government of our Maker.   There is a government over the universe, a government of law; there is a government under which, from the perfection of the Great Ruler, there is secured in his administration all which we endeavor to secure, though so imperfectly, by a *constitution*.   Beyond all the powers of any human arrangement—any wisdom or permanency in the constitutions of civil government—the constitution of the government of the universe is fixed.   The limits of power and of right are determined.   There is the utmost security against any usurpation of power; there is the most absolute security against any invasion of right; there are all the checks and safeguards appointed for securing the permanency and the wise administration of government forever.

The tendency of Presbyterianism, from the nature of the case, is to loyalty.   Presbyterianism does not, indeed, reject the principle that there *are* cases where it is right to throw off a government, and to change it by revolution; but its tendency is to loyalty—loyalty to established government as such; loyalty to a government administered in conformity to a constitution; loyalty to the principles of liberty; loyalty to a country as such; loyalty to ' the powers that be'.   Were there time, it would be easy to show how this has been illustrated in other lands than ours—but that must be now passed by.

On this subject there is time to say only that the history of our denomination, in the dark periods of our country's struggles for freedom, has been such as to fill the heart of every Presbyterian with gratitude for the past, and with a profound respect for our principles as related to human rights, to patriotism, to civil liberty.   Whoever among the clergy of the land, in the time of the Revolution, were disloyal, Presbyterians were not.   Whoever they were,—and there were many such, who embarrassed the government, who rejoiced in the reverses, the sorrows, and the defeat of our armies, or in the success of the enemy; whoever they were,—and there were many such,— who gave ' aid and comfort to the enemy'; whoever they were who refused to pray for the success of the armies of the struggling colonies, — and there were many such; — whoever they were who were found in traitorous communication with the enemy, Presbyterian clergymen were not of that number.   By prayer; by preaching; by their presence in the army as chaplains; by their zeal in encouraging their people to leave their homes in defence of their country; by correspondence; by humble and constant trust in God, the Presbyterian ministers of that day have acquired, and deserve a noble place among the Revolutionary patriots, and the true history of our country cannot be written without an honorable reference to the course of the Presbyterian Church. Some other denominations are, and must be, reluctant ever to refer to the history of their clergymen and many of their people in the time of the American Revolution; our denomination is willing that all that occurred—all that was done by us as a denomination—should be written in letters of living light to be read by all mankind. The past is fixed; and fixed as we would desire it to be. We would not wish to alter it. There are no Presbyterian names as connected with the trying periods of our Revolutionary history to which the world will attach the idea of dishonor. There is not a line on that subject which we would desire to expunge or change.

The struggle is again upon us; for the same principles; the same country; the same essential issues. Happy and honored evermore shall we be if in this struggle we are found evincing the spirit of our fathers; like them sustaining the government in the great struggle; loyal to its principles and to our own; commending our country and its cause in no ambiguous language to God in our prayers; encouraging our people to the work of patriotism; frowning on treason; rejoicing in the success of our arms; standing in our place boldly, firmly, nobly, in the support of the government, the constitution, the laws, the liberty of the nation.

Art. II.—THE SOURCES OF CRIME.

By E. C. WINES, D.D., LL.D., New York.

Annual Reports of the Prison Association of New York from 1844 to 1862.

An examination of the 18 Annual Reports of the New York Prison Association has produced in our minds a profound conviction of the excellence of this organization, and of the importance and value of its labors. These Reports not only show a vast amount of work done, and well done, but they embody many able and luminous discussions of questions connected with crimes and their punishment, with prison discipline and prison reform, and with the treatment of criminals, both while undergoing the penalty of the law and subsequently to their discharge.

Prominent among the discussions to which we refer, we place those which relate to the sources of crime. Numerous and valuable hints on this subject are scattered through these Reports; but in the fourth and tenth we find two extended and elaborate essays upon the question. They are in the form of letters, addressed to the Corresponding Secretary of the Association, by the Hon. John Stanton Gould, one of its Vice-Presidents. We propose to make these essays the basis of the present paper, condensing within the limits of a single article the great mass of facts and suggestions, which Mr. Gould has embodied in his inquiries; not, however, to the exclusion of other facts and arguments, drawn from the remaining portions of the Society's Reports, as well as from independent sources.

Before entering upon the direct inquiry into the sources of crime, we offer a preliminary explanation of the term.

Crime, then, we take to be such a violation of the rights of others, as is cognizable by human laws and punishable by human tribunals. It is any conduct, which is liable to judicial investigation and punishment at the hands of the civil authorities. It is by no means uncommon for crime, in the popular apprehension and dialect, to be confounded with vice and sin. It will make our path of inquiry clearer, and the results more valuable, if we can succeed in discriminating wisely and defining accurately the meaning of these several terms. According to the strict etymological derivation of the words, crime is that which is punishable; vice, that which ought to be avoided; sin, that which is hurtful. Crime is injurious to the rights of others, violates human enactments, and may be punished by the laws of the land. Vice is injurious to ourselves, and ought, on that account, to be avoided. Sin has its seat in the heart, violates the divine law, and, by a reflex action, is in the highest degree hurtful to ourselves. Murder is a *crime*, because it invades the rights of the murdered person, violates human laws, and may be punished by human governments. Opium-eating is a *vice*, because it is injurious to the eater, and should therefore be shunned by him. Ingratitude is a *sin*, because it has its seat in the heart, is a breach of the law of God, and hurts him who is guilty of it by drawing upon himself the divine displeasure : sin, accordingly is a generic term, embracing every form of guilt, and including, as species, both vice and crime. Every crime, every vice, is a sin; but every sin is by no means either a vice or a crime. It is the province of the theologian to investigate the nature and remedy of sin ; of the moralist, to trace out the causes and cure of vice; and of the legislator, to provide for the punishment and prevention of crime.

While, therefore, we freely admit and contend, that the purification of the heart is a work which belongs only and wholly to God, we nevertheless maintain that crime may be almost if not entirely suppressed by the conjoint efforts of government and people, wisely, vigorously, and perseveringly put forth. In making this assertion, that it is within the ability, and is the duty of the legislator, to prevent the commission of crime, we invest him with no attribute of Deity, nor any power over the hearts and consciences of men. Let it be remembered that crimes are, properly speaking, only those violations of public or private rights which are susceptible of accurate definition and of clear and undoubted proof; and all theological difficulty vanishes. We may conceive crime to have been entirely suppressed in a given community, while the aggregate of sin shall have been augmented; and, conversely, that the number of crimes may have increased, while there shall have been a general growth in holiness among the masses of the people.

Crime is one of several channels through which the sins of the heart make themselves seen and felt. Sin developes itself generally through this channel, when moved upon by certain external causes. These external causes being, to a considerable extent at least, under the control of the legislator, he may, by arresting them, prevent the crimes to which, without such arrest, they would be sure to give rise.

Having thus cleared the question of ambiguity, we proceed to inquire into the causes which move men to act out the natural and inborn depravity of their hearts by the commission of crimes.

I. Grog Shops of every description, are a prolific source of crime.—That establishments for the sale of intoxicating drinks are nurseries of crime, is now generally conceded. Even those who keep such establishments admit the fact. The only justification which they attempt, is the allegation that men are so in love with intoxicating drinks, that they will get them in some way; if not openly, then secretly; if not legally, then illegally. And they allege that, great as the mischiefs are which flow from the legalized vending of such drinks, yet, upon the whole, greater mischiefs would be caused by the illicit sale of them. Since, then, the very dealers in liquors admit the tendency of the traffic to produce crime, there need be no fear of a denial of it from any other quarter.

It is certain that the convicts in our State prisons, penitentiaries, and county jails, with singular unanimity, ascribe to the use of intoxicating drinks the crimes, of which they are there suffering the penalty. " If it had not been for the grog shops,

I should never have been here," is the stereotyped complaint (says Mr. Gould), which issues from almost every cell, and swells, in melancholy chorus, through all the corridors of our prisons.

In the year 1851, there were 756 places where liquor was sold in the city of Albany. During three months of that year the police arrested 1707 persons, of whom 433 were arrested in a state of intoxication, and 1300 were known to be of intemperate habits. In 1851 and 1852, 1125 prisoners were sentenced to the Albany penitentiary. Of these, only 112 claimed that they were temperate; the remaining 1013 were notoriously intemperate.

Mr. Gould makes a statement, from his own personal observation, most significant and astounding. He says that he has visited most of the prisons in the United States,—some of them frequently; that he has had much personal conference with the prisoners; and yet that he has not found more than 20, who did not acknowledge that they had been frequenters of dram shops and in a greater or less degree, addicted to the use of strong drink.

In 1850, there were five persons lying under sentence of death, in the prisons of Connecticut, for murders committed in a state of intoxication; and while these five were awaiting their execution, a sixth murder was committed from the same cause. In 1851, of 158 convicts confined in the Connecticut State prison, 134 were habitual drinkers of ardent spirits.

In 1856, a committee of the Senate of New York visited and examined all the county jails of the State, 63 in number. Their report throws much light on our present subject of inquiry, — intemperance as a source of crime. In regard to 11 of the jails, no statement as to the drinking habits of their inmates is made by the committee. In reference to 5 others it is stated that all the inmates were of intemperate habits. Of the remaining 47, an average of at least three fourths of the prisoners were, by their own admission, intemperate. And it would be safe to assume that a large proportion of those who claim to be temperate, are in reality intemperate; Mr. Gould thinks at least two thirds. Assuming this to be a correct estimate, the true proportion of intemperate prisoners in the jails of New York, in 1856, would be eleven twelfths, instead of three fourths, as stated by the Senatorial committee.

Of 361 persons committed in 1850 to the jail of Providence, R. I., 282 (more than three fourths) were intemperate. Of 962 prisoners received into the eastern penitentiary of Pennsylvania, 745 (still more than three fourths) were addicted to

36

intoxication. Out of 975 prisoners received at Auburn prison, 736 (over three fourths as before) were drunkards ; 219 were moderate drinkers (their own notions of moderation being the standard); and only 20 claimed to be total abstinents ; while 589 (considerably more than one half) were under the influence of strong drink at the time of committing the crimes for which they were sentenced ; and 367 had intemperate parents, one or both.

According to the police records of France, 1129 murders were committed in that country during four years ; of which 446 (more than a third) were perpetrated amidst drunken brawls at taverns.

Let us now look at the proof in another form. In 1850, there were 60,000 drunkards in the State of New York; of which number, 3912 were convicted of crime There were at the same time 2,540,000 persons in the State, who were not drunkards ; and of this number, 3690 were convicted of violating the laws. These are astonishing facts. One drunkard out of every 15 is convicted of a breach of law, while only one sober man out of every 661 is guilty of a like breach. More crimes by 222 were committed by the 60,000 intemperate than by the 2,540,000 temperate inhabitants of the State. Nothing could more clearly evince the active agency of intemperance in the production of crime.

Still another form of proof. The number of taverns and grog shops in any given territory of considerable extent will be found to be a pretty fair index of the relative amount of crime committed in that district. In the ten counties of New York, where crime most abounds, there is one grog shop to every 240 inhabitants ; whereas, in the ten counties, where the fewest crimes are committed, there is only one groggery to every 396 of the population. Again in the second ten worst counties, the grog shops are one to 292 inhabitants ; in the second ten best counties, they are one to 341. Here, then, in these four divisions of the State, the relative number of grog shops is a perfect barometer of the relative amount of crime committed in each. The results, thus indicated, are another demonstrative proof of the influence of intemperance in impelling its victims to an open violation of the laws of the land.

The proofs, thus far exhibited, show very clearly that intemperance tends to produce crime. Let us now advance a step in the argument, and inquire whether, conversely, temperance has any tendency to diminish crime.

The great Washingtonian movement for the reformation of

inebriates, which began in 1842 and continued with no little vigor for a number of years, is fresh in the recollection of the public.   A marked revolution took place about that time in the drinking usages of society.   Numbers of inebriates were reformed ; moderate drinkers became total abstinents ; intoxicating drinks were, to a considerable extent, banished from the field, the work-shop, and the drawing-room ; and the motto "touch not, taste not", was inscribed upon a large proportion of the dwellings of our land.   This revolution soon began to make itself strikingly manifest in the diminution of crime. The average number of convicts in the State prison of Maine had been, for several years previously, 80 ; the average number for several years subsequently was less than 60.   Thus it appears that the number of prisoners diminished a full fourth, while, according to the census, the population of the State had increased one fourth ; making the real diminution of crime as the result of increased temperance fifty per cent. In Vermont the effect of the revolution in diminishing commitments and convictions was still more marked.   The statistics of the eastern penitentiary at Philadelphia show a considerable falling off in the number of convicts ; there having been, for the six years preceding 1842, on an average, 387, but for the three years following, 328 ; while the population of Pennsylvania had increased, within that time, nearly one third. As early as 1831, the number of prisoners in the State prison at Sing Sing had reached 1000 and upwards ; and the inspectors estimated that thereafter it would mount up to 1200 ; instead of which, after the inauguration and vigorous prosecution of the temperance reform, and, beyond a doubt, as a consequence of that reform, the number fell to 763, notwithstanding a vast increase in the population of both the State and city of New York.   These facts show conclusively that, while intemperance is a powerful agent in producing crime, temperance tends no less powerfully to diminish it.

Results of a like character have occurred on the other side of the water.   In 1849, an act of Parliament, requiring public houses to be closed from 12 o'clock on Saturday night to 12½ o'clock on Sunday night, went into operation.   In the city of Bristol, the average annual arrests during the three years prior to that date were 4063, for the three years subsequent thereto, 2903 ; in the city of Manchester, for the three years before the act, 3609,—for the three years after the act, 1950 ; and in the city of Leeds, 423 before, and 341 after, for the same number of years.   The average diminution of crime for the three places was over 30 per cent; while, for the city of Manchester, it was nearly 50 per cent.

Under the operation of the Maine law, that is, of the principle of an absolute prohibition of the traffic in intoxicating liquors, in the few States where the authorities have been able to enforce it, scores of jails and poorhouses have been emptied of their inmates. The prohibitory law went into effect in Maine in the spring of 1851. In Portland, at the March term of the police court for 1851, 17 indictments were found; at the same term for 1852, but 1 indictment was found, and that was the result of a malicious prosecution. During the nine months prior to the date when the law went into operation, 279 persons were committed to the jail of Portland; during the nine months subsequent to that date, deducting 72 liquor dealers, there were but 63, a diminution of nearly three fourths in the short space of nine months. And everywhere similar results have occurred, under a real enforcement of the law.

But a question of no little importance is here suggested which we will briefly consider in this connection: How drunkenness when it impels to and produces a criminal act affects the responsibility of the inebriate—his responsibility to God for the sin and to society for the crime.

An impression is widely cherished, that a man, if at all, is at least not fully responsible for what he does while he is drunk. A madman is not held responsible for his actions, and the drunken man is, for the moment, mad. It is not unnatural, nor, at first blush, altogether unreasonable, to transfer to the one madman the absence of responsibility attached to the other. How far this popular impression is correct, and how far erroneous, we will presently inquire; but the fact of its prevalence is, meanwhile, indisputable; and that, in despite of copious argument and eloquent declamation by the theologian in the pulpit, the lawyer at the bar, and the judge upon the bench; who all concur in enforcing the doctrine, that madness produced by drink in no degree lessens the criminality of a breach of law, whether human or divine. Still, the doctrine of responsibility for crimes thus committed, inculcated in its naked and absolute form, does, it cannot be denied, some violence to the understanding. On the one hand, it is hard to believe that the man who kills his wife with the poker at night and weeps tears of anguish over it in the morning, is as much guilty of murder, as if he had planned and executed the deed with all his senses about him. On the other hand, it would be fraught with infinite peril to the public morals and the public weal to admit even the shadow of a doubt as to the full responsibility of the criminal. In this state of the case, the public, like the double-minded man, wavers in its judgments; neither thoroughly believing nor thoroughly disbelieving the responsibility of the drunken man for a crime done under the influence of drunkenness.

Nevertheless, a compromise here, by which something should be yielded to each opinion, is, in every view, wholly inadmissible. To conceive that a portion, but not the full measure, of responsibility attaches to the inebriate for his crime, is neither good philosophy nor sound policy. What, then, is the solution? We must find some principle, which will allow that the madness caused by strong drink removes responsibility as completely as any other madness, and which will yet hold the drunken perpetrator of crime guilty, to the full extent, for his evil deed, before God and man. And this principle, we think, is found in the fact that the dethronement of reason in the drunkard,. which is often as complete for the time as that which exists permanently in the inmates of a lunatic asylum, is voluntary in his case, caused by his own free choice and act. It is a self-created, self-imposed madness. This principle lifts the responsibility from the maniac, without removing it from the man. It carries back the guilt, till the intelligent cause of the criminal act is reached; and it leaves it there, in all its weight and all its turpitude. If the man who, in madness, has committed a crime, was once intelligent, and wilfully caused his own madness, the guilt of that crime, whatever it is, was contracted when he voluntarily and knowingly destroyed his reason. A man, under the insanity of drink, quarrels with his friend and kills him. Now, wherein lies the guilt of that homicide? Not in the act of killing, for the man was, at the moment, as mad and unintelligent as the lunatic, who is suffering under a total and permanent loss of reason; but in the fact that, being sober, intelligent, and sane, he voluntarily made himself drunk, senseless, and mad. In drinking to madness, he was not guilty of a mere indiscretion; he was guilty of his brother's blood. In the act of maddening his brain by drink, he knowingly fired a train, whose other end was dipt in murder; and, being fired, it must run its course; he had no power to extinguish it. The soundness of this principle will be the more obvious, if we suppose the man to have been deprived of reason, not by a voluntary drinking of the poison which dethroned it, by a forcible pouring of it down his throat by others, against his own will and in spite of his most earnest struggles to the contrary. Let us assume that now, as before, the murder is done.   But who, in this case, is the guilty party ?   Is it the man who, against his own remonstrance and efforts, was compelled to swallow a draught, which robbed him of his faculties, and, for the time, converted him into a maniac ?   Or is it the men who forced the draught into his stomach and brain ?   There can be but one answer to this interrogatory.   He whose reason was over-powered by the draught, thus compulsorily taken, was guilt-less of the murder, — as much so as if his reason had been removed by the direct act of God.   The guilt is theirs, who, by forcing the draught, violently took away from him, for the time being, the guiding and controlling power of reason.   But if this be so, it follows, by inevitable deduction, that the guilt of a crime committed under the influence of insanity, caused by excessive drinking, lies in that excessive drinking itself, and in nothing else.

This reasoning sets in a fearful light the sin of drunkenness, even when drunkenness is but an isolated act; much more, when it is a confirmed habit.   Murder, arson, rape, and all the crimes in the calendar are wrapped up in drinking to intoxi-cation.   They are in that act seminally and essentially, even as the oak is in the acorn, and the harvest in the seed-corn. That they do not all follow every such act is owing to the providence of God, and not to the controlling reason of the in-ebriate.   One man staggers home, and beats his wife to death; another is borne home, too drunk even to stagger ; is thrown upon the floor ; and sleeps off the drunken fit.   Has the latter committed a less sin in the sight of God than the former? Not if the logic of this argument be sound.   Though the law, while it punishes the other, allows him to go free, yet, we verily believe, in the eye of reason and the judgment of God, he is the more guilty of the two.

It is no uncommon thing for drunkenness to be treated with levity, and even with merriment.   The view here submitted, of the terrible responsibility inhering in it, takes away all lightness from the subject.   Nothing can be more serious, nothing more awful, if our reasoning be correct, than drunk-enness.   It is not only a crime itself, but the mother of crimes.   To it, in effect, belongs the guilt of all the crimes, which either do or might issue from it.   This principle, in re-spect to other matters, is recognized in the jurisprudence of all nations.   A merchant stores powder in his warehouse for a single night, and removes it safely the following morning. If prosecuted, will the plea that his act caused no injury, though true in itself, be admitted in bar of punishment ?   Certainly not. He is punished for the injury which his act might have done ; that is, for the risk to which he thereby subjected his neighbors. And this principle is, in ethics, if not in law, as sound when applied to drunkenness, as it is when applied to the storing of gunpowder, or to any other act, the doing of which involves risk to the community. A risk may be valued, and is every day valued, equally with the destruction of the property involved in it. Insurance against fire or disaster at sea is a familiar illustration. " If the risks to which drunkenness exposes men and things were accurately calculated, and the drunkards imprisoned or fined accordingly, prison-walls or empty pockets would soon compel them into sobriety."*

II. Brothels are another prolific fountain of Crime.—This (as Mr. Gould observes) is not a pleasant subject to discuss, but our survey would be essentially incomplete without it ; and we cannot decline the discussion without a conscious dereliction of duty. Too many fathers have had their gray hairs brought with sorrow to the grave through this agency, too many mothers have been subjected by it to life-long anguish, too many families have been desolated by the monster ; the evil is too widely spread, too deeply seated, too rank in its growth, and too deadly in its influence, to permit us to pass it in silence.

We find a very significant testimony as to the power of licentiousness in producing crime, in the following extract from a report of the chaplain of the Connecticut State prison, cited in the 12th Annual Report of the Boston Prison Discipline Society. " Will you please, sir, preach from this text next time ?" " What text ?" " This here in Hosea, 4th chapter and 11th verse, where it says, ' Whoredom, and wine, and new wine take away the heart.' " " Why do you wish to have that text preached from ?" " Because, sir, they are what brought me here, and I guess most all the rest of us." " This man", adds the chaplain, " guessed right. Scarcely a man can be found, who was not in the habit, when at liberty, of going to those who ' put the bottle to their neighbor's mouth', or to those ' whose feet go down to death'. Some particular places may be pointed out, where, under the blighting influence referred to, criminals are multiplied, as it were, by wholesale. In a period of about five years, some 40 colored persons have been sent to this prison, who had been convicted of crime in New Haven. Nearly all of these indi-

---

* This topic is much more largely handled in an Essay on the Criminality of Drunkenness, read by the Rev. Dr. Arnott, of Scotland, before the British Association for promoting Social Science.

viduals have referred to their nocturnal visits to a den of infamy kept in that city as being closely connected with the crimes for which they were convicted."

The following testimony from Dr. Francis Lieber, a member of the Board of Managers of the Prison Association of New York and a gentleman of large experience in prison mat-ters, is in point : "I have taken pains to ascertain the character of a number of convicts, and as far as my experience has gone, it shows me that there is, almost without exception, some unprincipled or abandoned woman, who played a prominent part in the life of every convict; be it a worthless mother, who poisons by her corrupt example the souls of her children; or a slothful, intemperate wife, who disgusts her husband with his home; or *a prostitute, whose wants must be satisfied by theft;* or a receiver of plunder; or a spy of opportunities for robbery".

Mr. Gould adds upon this subject: "We, too, are enabled to corroborate these assertions of Dr. Lieber by as extensive a range of inquiries at the cells of our State prisons as usually falls to the share of a single individual. We are satisfied that licentiousness is a mighty engine of the Devil for the production of crime. A moral instructor in the eastern penitentiary at Philadelphia investigated the cases of 962 prisoners committed to that institution, and found that 182 of them were directly caused by licentiousness. And the chaplain of the Auburn State prison found that 251 out of the 425 who were willing to answer the question were guilty of the same thing."

Mr. Gould relates the story of a fallen woman, whom he encountered in one of our penitentiary hospitals, which casts a terrific light upon the tendency of licentiousness to produce crime. She had been a woman of exquisite beauty and elegant culture. Her father, a wealthy merchant of New York, failed in business, and gave up every thing to his creditors. She was reduced to the necessity of learning the trade of a dress-maker to earn her daily bread. She became a proficient in the business, and her taste and skill commanded liberal wages, which enabled her to provide an ample wardrobe for herself. She had been intensely devoted to the glitter and gaiety of fashionable life, and hope, which " springs eternal in the human breast", whispered that a fortunate marriage might yet restore her to the charmed circles, whose delights she had once tasted, and which she longed to reënter. She used every effort, by the charms of person, dress, voice, and manners, to attract the notice and win the love of eligible young men. At length, she thought she had succeeded in her object; but

the young man, whose affections she dreamed that she had
won, proved to be a cold-hearted villain, who was in pursuit
only of amusement and gratification for the passing hour.
One evening he invited her to ride. Driving into the country, he alighted at a house of refreshment in the neighborhood
of the city. He offered her a glass of wine, which she drank.
The liquor had been drugged. A profound stupor ensued,
and she awoke the following morning to find herself ruined.

With returning consciousness, the whole magnitude of the
injury burst upon her. She instantly resolved upon revenge,
and the plan for its accomplishment flashed upon her mind
with the suddenness and rapidity of lightning. She betrayed
no emotion. She uttered no reproaches. She treated what
had happened as a harmless jest, and blandly invited a continuance of the intimacy.

The young man exulted in the ease and completeness of
his victory; but from that moment she became the evil genius
of his life. Professing the tenderest and most unselfish affection, she drew money from him continually, with which she
hired sharpers to furnish him with provocatives to drinking,
gambling, and all the forms of vice and debauchery. At
every rally of his better nature, by a skilful alternation of
persuasion, banter, and menace, she choked the rising impulse of virtue, chained him to the car of dissipation, and confirmed him in his career of vice.

Full well did she know whither all this would lead him;
nor was she disappointed in her malignant expectation.
Drunkenness clouded his understanding; debauchery ruined
his health; and gambling reduced him to poverty. Not until
this point, the goal of all her prayers and efforts, had been
reached, when poverty and disease had done their work, and
he was unable to procure a wretched bed or a scanty meal,
except through her charity, did she wreak upon him the full
measure of her vengeance. Then it was her daily delight to
visit him to load him with reproaches, and to reveal to him,
in bitter exultation, the whole scheme, so cunningly devised,
and so steadily pursued, by which she had wrought his ruin.
And when the closing scene drew near, she sat by his bed-
side, and mingled her execrations with the shrieks extorted
by his dying agonies.

Nor was her vengeance even yet satisfied. Her warfare
was against the whole sex, whom she regarded as accursed;
and her insatiate revenge cried out for still other victims.
Whenever she could fasten her fangs on a young man of
genteel family, whose unclouded prospects foretokened a

brilliant career, she never relaxed her hold.   She studied, with a keenness sharpened by experience, every point in his character,—his tastes, his passions, his hopes, his fears, whatever attracted and whatever repelled him; and then, with an almost unerring sagacity, adapting the means to the end, she seldom failed in her demoniac purpose.   She claimed in this manner to have hunted down 32 young men, involving them in disgrace, crime, and ruin.   Some of them had ended their days in prison, and others, hopelessly fallen, were on the road to the drunkard's and the felon's grave.

When asked whether all her sisters in infamy felt the same hatred to mankind, she replied that she thought the feeling to be general, if not universal, among them; adding that, when a woman had once fallen, she desired to revenge herself, not only on her seducer, but on all his sex; that no game was followed with greater relish than that of involving all who came within their toils in crime and its consequent punishment; that most of them could number at least two or three victims, whom they had ruined, and that many of these victims went to the length of the actual commission of crime.

Now, when we remember that there are, in the city of New York alone, over 20,000 prostitutes, and a proportionate number in the other cities of the State, we may arrive at a proximate idea of the amount of crime in this commonwealth, which is directly caused by the vice of licentiousness.

III. Theatres are a source of crime. — Whether theatres might be so conducted as to be places of innocent recreation, or even, as some contend, schools of refinement and morality, is a question which we will not now discuss; much less do we assume to decide it.   But we maintain that, as at present managed, they are schools of vice and nurseries of crime. They operate to the production of this result both directly and indirectly; being in themselves active causes of crime, and at the same time serving as avenues to other sources of wrong doing.

Theatres tend, directly, to produce crime, by filling the minds of youth with impure thoughts, sentiments, images, and principles; and by clothing vice in an attractive and virtue in a repulsive and often ludicrous garb.   Actors and actresses are, with a few honorable exceptions, notorious for the looseness of their lives; and, as their society is apt to be sought by the frequenters of theatres, the latter are gradually but surely corrupted.

Theatres tend, indirectly, to produce crime, by begetting in the minds of the young, a distaste for the pursuits of honest industry. The glitter, the radiance, the mimic kings, queens, and heroes of the stage dance, like phantasmagoria, before the mental vision of the votary of the theatre. He is haunted with the memory of the brilliant revels, the obscene jests, the witty *double-entendres* of the previous evening; and they disqualify him for the plodding industry required at the merchant's desk or the mechanic's bench. As the mania for the theatre grows upon its victim, he becomes neglectful of his duties, despises the homely details of every day life, loses his place or fails in business, and is cast adrift upon the world. Unable to forego his customary excitements, he still frequents the theatre, and is subject to the expenses incident upon the indulgence. But as his income has stopped, his exchequer soon becomes exhausted, and he resorts to theft, burglary, forgery, the utterance of counterfeit money, or some other unlawful means of replenishing it, until the State relieves him of the necessity by providing him quarters in a prison.

That such is the course run by numbers of those who are known as frequenters of theatres, is heard at the door of our prison cells too often to leave room for doubt upon the subject. That theatres are frequented by prostitutes, that they are supplied with bars, and that they are recognized houses of assignation, are facts which admit of no dispute. Even their apologists are obliged to admit that they are the vestibule of the grog shop and the brothel; and certainly their habitual attendants gravitate towards these places, which are but so many manufactories of crime, as naturally as the stone sinks to the bottom of the well.

IV. Gambling houses and lotteries are prolific sources of crime.—Two classes of men are found in gambling houses, sharpers and their dupes. The former, having long since cast off all the restraints of virtue, make no scruple of resorting to robbery, forgery, and even murder, to recruit their finances, when exhausted. The latter are under skilful training for these crimes, and will be fully prepared for them, when their education is complete.

As with the grog-shop and the theatre, there is an infatuation connected with gambling, which, fastening on its victim, robs him of the power to escape from the habit, however much he may desire to do so. It is not difficult to understand the way in which gambling operates to produce crime. It works, beyond perhaps all other vices, a paralysis of the moral powers, while it stimulates the selfish propensities to the highest pitch; so that the gambler will stake all he is worth rather than renounce this passion. In case of failure, he is compelled to resort to crime for his subsistence; at first, no doubt, reluctantly, and with no little violence to his better feelings. But familiarity inures him to its commission, and the ruined gamester, by an easy and natural transition, soon becomes an expert and daring criminal.

Such is the rationale of the influence of gambling in the production of crime. Do facts justify and sustain this reasoning? They do, to the fullest extent. Of 975 prisoners at Auburn, 317 were habitual gamblers. Of 962 convicts in the eastern penitentiary at Philadelphia, 19 attributed their first introduction to the paths of crime to gaming and lotteries; how many have been accelerated in their career, commenced by other causes, is not stated. Out of 156 prisoners at the State prison in Connecticut, 53 were gamblers. The chaplain of the last mentioned prison bears the following testimony on this point: "Many prisoners hasten their ruin by buying lottery tickets; but rarely is one known to commit crime, when he has money in a savings bank".

V. Our prisons themselves, especially our jails and lock-ups, all whose influences ought to be restraining and reformatory, are fruitful, as they are disgraceful nurseries of crime.—Few persons, probably, are aware that the costly structures, for whose erection they have been taxed, and which they have been wont to look upon as barriers, to beat back the rushing waves of vice and crime, are themselves active agencies in producing the very evils, which they were designed to repress and to eradicate. And yet, it is the opinion of those most competent to judge, that there are few more prolific causes of crime than the one now under consideration. How can it be otherwise under the system, if system it can be called, of non-classification and promiscuous intercourse, which prevails in these institutions? The pickpocket, the burglar, the gambler, the drunkard, the vagrant, the witness, and persons charged with various offences, some justly and others unjustly, as their future trial will show; all mix and mingle together. Many a youth, locked up for his first offence, or perhaps on the groundless suspicion of wrong doing, there meets with professional thieves, who instruct him in their diabolical arts, and who, when he comes out of prison, meet him, claim acquaintance with him, introduce him to their comrades, persuade him to join their fraternity, and initiate him into a career of wickedness and crime.

Miss Dix says: "If it were the deliberate purpose of society to establish criminals in all that is evil, and to root out the last remains of virtuous inclination, this purpose could not be more effectually accomplished than by incarceration in the county jails, as they are, with few exceptions, constructed and governed ". Of some of the jails in Pennsylvania, she thus speaks : " At York, the prisoners were promiscuously associated, men and women. At Franklin county, all ages, colors and degrees of offenders associated. At Washington county were congregated old and young, the black and the white, men, women, and babies. At Beaver county, the prisoners were together, a child, the middle aged, and the men of gray hairs. At Bucks county, two men and two women, committed for immoralities, all occupy one room by day. At Chester county, two males and a female were all together." The above description, with the exception of herding men and women together, will apply to New York, and to the other States of the Union.

The British inspectors for the home district, in their first report, among the evils arising out of the indiscriminate associations prevalent in our common jails, enumerate, " Blasphemy, obscenity, demoralizing intercourse, profane jesting, instruction in crime, boasting of criminal adventures, gambling, combinations to defeat justice, concerted efforts at escape, conspiracy to effect future depredations, and many others ". In their third report they say : " The comparatively innocent are seduced ; the unwary are entrapped ; and the tendency to crime in offenders, not entirely hardened, is confirmed by the language, the suggestions, and the example of more depraved and systematic criminals ".

The French Minister of the Interior thus spoke to the Legislature of his country in 1840 : " It is in this prison that criminals make their first appearance ; from the inexperienced youth, the child even, whom a first trivial offence, and one in which he had been a forced accomplice, brings before the tribunal of justice, to the hardened old man, who is destined, after a long series of convictions, to find a tomb in the galleys. It is in this class of prisons that is unceasingly accumulated that population of dangerous idlers, of consummate malefactors, of intrepid villains, who form the dregs of every community. They are the first and most fatal schools, whether of vice or crime ; and he who enters them, for any offence, too often goes out more depraved, to appear before his judge. Sad contradiction to the law ! The precautions of justice become a source of corruption ; the prison makes criminals ; it developes, under the very eyes of the magistrate, the germs of future crimes ".

The Inspector-General of French prisons says : " To unite

in a common inclosure all the inmates of a prison is to put into fermentation, in an impure vessel, all the bad thoughts and bad actions which are engendered by mutual corruption. In these places, crime is recruited, nourished, and multiplied. The bad man becomes worse, the honest man becomes criminal, the sceptic becomes impious, the delinquent becomes a robber, the established villain more perverse, the debauchee more shameless, the depraved more corrupted, and the scholar in crime takes a master's degree. In fine, all that a prison can beget of physical or moral degradation, of persistence in evil, of vice, of crime, of all kinds of unlawfulness, has its explanation and its cause in the melancholy signification of these words—*association in prison* ".

The Boston Prison Discipline Society say : " An acquaintance formed in prison has led many a youth to houses of ill fame ; to a familiarity with the names, places of abode, principles of trade, and language of counterfeiters ; to the arts of pickpockets and thieves ; to dangerous combinations in villainy ; and to personal degradation, which the most hardened prisoner has blushed to name ".

The Prison Association of New York, referring to the contaminating influence of promiscuous prison intercourse, says : " So injurious in its consequences is the present system of imprisonment, that, with many doubtless good men, it is a question whether the interests of society would not be equally subserved by its entire abandonment as by its continuance under its present organization ".

The Senatorial Committee, who inspected the jails of New York, in 1856, in their account of the Albany county jail, say : " There are found in the jail 37 men and 8 women ; and it was represented to the committee that prisoners awaiting trial are frequently allowed to remain in this place for months. The character of the prisoners and the effect of such associations can be judged by the commitments, which are—1 for murder, 2 for rape, 6 for grand larceny, 4 for burglary, 1 for robbery of post-office, 6 for petit larceny, 4 for misdemeanor, 3 for assault and battery, 2 for vagrancy, 1 for damages, 1 for rescuing prisoners, 7 for drunkenness, 5 for disorderly conduct, and 2 witnesses. All these had free intercourse during most of the day. It would seem that those long resident in such a place and in such company, if not lost to all hope of reformation on going in, must be ruined in morals on coming out ".

It would be easy to multiply testimonies of this kind ; but we forbear. Enough has been said to satisfy all that there are evils connected with the construction and administration of our common jails, which call loudly for a prompt and appropriate remedy.

In view of the pernicious influence of these prisons, it is painful to think on what large numbers that influence operates. Not less than 35,000, probably a much larger number, are every year locked up in our common jails. It is frightful to contemplate the germs of crime, which must in this way be planted in so many minds. And the horror is increased, when we consider how large a proportion of these persons are either absolutely or comparatively innocent. From 1500 to 2000 of them are committed, not for crime, but as witnesses against those who have, or are supposed to have, committed it. And these were confessedly innocent when committed to jail ; but numerous cases are on record, some of them of a heart-rending pathos, in which persons entered jail simply to appear as witnesses on the trial of others, and came forth, after the instructions they had there received, to pursue a career of crime and infamy. But witnesses are not the only innocent prisoners exposed to the contamination of our jails. According to the testimony of ample and unquestionable statistics, nearly or quite one half of those arrested are either discharged without trial or acquitted by the jury ; that is, they are all legally innocent of the crimes charged against them, and a large proportion no doubt really so. When we consider, in view of this statement, the thousands upon thousands of innocent persons who are every year subjected to the corrupting influence of our jails, many of whom give way under that influence, and are ruined by it, the contemplation becomes truly appalling. Surely enlightened legislators ought not, cannot, much longer overlook the crime-producing tendencies of our common jails.

VI. *Carelessness on the part of the officers of justice in making arrests is a source of crime.*—This cause is kindred to that treated under the last head, inasmuch as it operates through recklessness or abuse in the administration of the law. The criminal statistics of the country already given show that nearly fifty per cent of the persons arrested on a charge or suspicion of crime are either acquitted on trial or discharged without trial. It is easy to see how this wholesale system of false accusations is calculated to lead the persons who suffer from it to the commission of crime, independently of the exposure to corrupt and corrupting associations in the prisons, to which they are thereby subjected. Public accusation of crime and imprisonment in a jail tend to destroy, even in the innocent, that pride of character, that feeling of self-respect, which all experience shows to be one of the most efficient safeguards against crime, and one of the most powerful incentives to virtue, especially among that class of persons from whom the ranks of crime are usually recruited. Would you make a child a liar? You have only to evince habitual doubt of his veracity, or to ply him with perpetual accusations of falsehood. Would you convert an honest man into a thief? The surest way to do it is to undermine the confidence of the community in his integrity. Would you destroy the chastity of a woman? Be continually whispering slanders against her purity. Let your imputations on her virtue never cease. Finding that virtuous conduct is no shield against suspicion, and even open accusation, she ceases to preserve it. She revenges herself on society by doing that with which society had falsely and cruelly charged her.

How often do prisoners, when urged to reform on returning to the world, give back the desponding reply, " What can I do? my character is gone ". The mortification, the shame, the anguish felt by innocent persons, when arrested on suspicion of crime, and confined within the walls of a prison, are often intense and indescribable. And can we doubt that causes known to be operative in all other cases, will operate here also? Must not this great amount of false accusation produce, in the end, an immense amount of crime, by destroying that sentiment of self-respect, which springs from a fair and honorable reputation? No matter how clearly the innocence of the accused person may be established on his trial, he carries the taint of the prison wherever he goes. He is scorned, insulted, and shunned. The very boys in the street cry *"jail bird"*, as he passes along. How can a man, whose only capital is his labor, bear up under such a pressure? His only resource often is either to steal or starve; and for a crime which the law virtually compels him to commit, it punishes him by long years of confinement and labor in its prisons! What the appropriate remedy for this enormous wrong may be, we are not prepared to say; but that some remedy ought to be applied we are clear; and that the wisdom of man, when once it shall have been earnestly directed to this inquiry, is competent to devise a remedy that shall be adequate and effective, we cannot doubt.

VII. Another source of crime is bad books. — Good men have ever lamented the pernicious influence of a depraved and perverted literature; but such literature has never been so systematically and widely diffused as at the present time. This is owing to two causes, its cheapness and the facility of conveyance by steamboat and rail car. Lines of railroad radiate from all the great centres of trade, and form a network of communication over the whole surface of the country. Mr. Gould estimates that more than 26,000,000 persons are transported over the railroads of the United States a year. Multitudes of these, probably, one in twenty at least, purchase books at the depot or in the cars, to while away the time. This would give over a million of volumes circulated in this way annually; and perhaps an equal number are sold and circulated in steamboats, at watering places, at hotels, and at other places of public resort. Now a very large proportion of the works thus put in circulation are of the worst character, tending to corrupt the principles, to inflame the passions, to excite impure desire, and to spread a blight over all the powers of the soul. Brothels are recruited from this more than from any other one source. Those who search the trunks of convicted criminals are almost sure to find in them one or more of these works; and few prisoners, who can read at all, fail to enumerate, among the causes which led them into crime, the unhealthy stimulus of this depraved and pernicious literature.

VIII. Orphanage, though perhaps little thought of in this connection, is, nevertheless, an active and prevalent cause of crime. — To secure respect for the laws and for the rights of others, the discipline of restraint and of education is necessary; and this discipline can, as a general thing, be had only under the paternal roof. Here, if at all, under the training of parental love and wisdom, the child must be taught to curb his passions, to practise self-denial, to respect authority, and to render unto all their dues. Even if the orphan child falls into the hands of those who are disposed to lead him in the right way, he is restive under their restraints, and will not receive their rebukes and corrections, as he would similar discipline from the hand of parental affection. But, unhappily, the orphan child rarely falls into the hands of a truly conscientious guardian, or at least of one who takes a comprehensive and Christian view of his duty in that relation. The greater part satisfy their conscience with the care of the ward's property, leaving his moral sentiments and principles to the blind operation of chance. The majority of orphans, however, do not enjoy, even nominally, a guardian's care. Having no property, they are left to the cold charity of reluctant relatives, or the still colder charity of the almshouse, where the weeds of vice are left to grow unchecked, while the tender plants of virtue are choked beneath their shade.

Thus do we perceive that, from the nature of the case, orphanage is a preparation for crime. Facts support this view.

37

Of 11,510 convicted criminals in the State of New York, 7232
—62 per cent—were either orphans or half orphans. In Pennsylvania, 515 out of 962 prisoners—more than 50 per cent—
were virtually orphans; that is, 375 were literally so, and 140
were sent away from home in very early life and thus deprived
of all parental care, guidance, and discipline. In Maryland,
out of 537 prisoners, 260—nearly 50 per cent—were orphans.
Another fact, connected with this subject, is shown by the
statistics of our prisons, viz. that a much larger proportion of
the criminal half orphans had lost their fathers than their
mothers. This fact evinces, very clearly, how much children
and youth need restraint, and how directly and strongly the
want of it tends to crime.

Want of proper parental restraint and discipline might be
mentioned as a distinct source of crime; but, as whatever has
been said under the present head is, in the main, applicable
here also, we have not thought it necessary to give to this
topic a separate treatment.

*IX. Insanity is still another of the numerous sources of
crime.*—This subject is far from having received the attention
which it merits. Even those who have made crime their
study, are but beginning to turn their thoughts in this direction. The plea of insanity, which is often advanced by the
prisoner's counsel, is looked upon with disfavor both by juries
and the general public, being considered as almost equivalent
to a confession of guilt. One reason, and probably the principal reason, of this general disbelief in insanity as a cause of
crime is the fact that, in a large proportion of cases, the derangement of the intellect is confined to a single subject, while,
on all others, the criminal may evince a high degree of intelligence and shrewdness. It is difficult for persons unused to
watch the varying forms of insanity, to understand why a
man, who evinces the greatest ingenuity in planning the details of a murder or a robbery, should yet be wholly void of
responsibility for the murder or the robbery itself. And yet
nothing is more certain than that this is sometimes, perhaps
more frequently than is commonly supposed, the case. The
story of the British Chancellor, Lord Eldon, is well known,
who, after having for six hours examined a person with a view
to test his lunacy, without detecting any evidence of it, was
upon the point of adjudging him *compos mentis*, and therefore
competent to manage his own property, when a gentleman
whispered a suggestion that he should ask him who Jesus
Christ was? Instantly he replied, "I am he?" and went into
the wildest rhapsody concerning his celestial functions, and

the Chancellor at once issued a decree, affirming his insanity and consequent incapacity to manage his estate.

Mr. Gould tells of a man whom he personally knew, who could reason with clearness and force on the obligations of justice and humanity, and was skilful and accurate in his application of the rules of morality to the ordinary affairs of life ; yet this man, under the hallucination that he himself was God, would violate every rule of rectitude which he had so clearly laid down, and would justify the breach on the ground that, being himself the sovereign of the universe, he was not bound by the laws which it was his pleasure to impose upon others.

But let us see what the testimony of competent persons is in reference to this question. We cannot doubt that not a few crimes, i. e. acts which would be criminal if done by persons of sound minds, are committed under the influence of insanity, and that numbers of insane persons are annually committed to prison.

Miss Dix, in memorializing the Legislature of Pennsylvania on this subject, writes : "I have said that within two years, 27 insane persons have been committed to the eastern penitentiary, charged with various crimes. The history of many of these I have traced. I have resolved that no labor shall be spared on my part to bring facts to light. The testimony of medical men and the opinion of intelligent citizens throughout the State, acquainted with these cases, having had them under their care as patients, settle these cases definitely. Men, having been known to be insane for years, committing recent crimes, still under the influence of insane delusion, are, every month, tried, condemned, and sentenced, precisely as if they were in possession of a sound mind, and were responsible for their speech and deeds. The fact of their *known insanity* is often recorded in the books of the prison by the officer who brought them there."

Dr. Given, for some time assistant physician to the Lunatic Asylum at Blockley near Philadelphia, and subsequently principal physician of the eastern penitentiary, a gentleman whom Mr. Gould pronounces better fitted for a prison physician, than any man he ever met with, writes as follows : "Those who are acquainted with the protean nature of insanity, its often slow and insidious invasion, and frequent development in the passions and moral sentiments, long ere the intellectual faculties show any signs of disturbance, will readily acknowledge how difficult, nay, how impossible it is, in many cases, to pronounce, with any degree of certainty, upon the actual state of a prisoner's mind, when first admitted; for, if the incipient stages of the disease have frequently escaped for several months the detection of intelligent relations, in daily contact with the patient (the experience of physicians connected with insane hospitals furnishes many such instances), is it not possible, or indeed very probable, that acts are frequently committed under the influence of mental derangement, which is not fully developed, until the sufferer may have been long in confinement, as a punishment for his so called crime?" Upon this Mr. Gould remarks: "There are very many of the class of cases alluded to by Dr. Given, to be met with by the careful inquirer, where the insanity manifests itself, not apparently in a deranged intellect, but in an entire obliteration of the moral faculties. Sometimes this condition is congenital, and sometimes arises in after life; but, in either case, it arises from bodily disease or physical malformation. It sometimes exists in a latent state, producing copious harvests of crime, before the insanity of the intellectual faculties is clearly manifested; but this is sure to become patent sooner or later." How far men may be justly regarded as not responsible for criminal acts done under this species of insanity, while yet their intellectual faculties remain clear and vigorous, we are not prepared to express an opinion. But we have no doubt that insanity is the cause of more crimes than is commonly supposed.

X. Ignorance is a source of crime.—In Pennsylvania, of 2961 prisoners, 1620—only a little more than one half—could read and write; 632 could read but not write; and 709—nearly a fourth — could neither read nor write. Of the whole population of Pennsylvania, 97 per cent are able to read and write. Out of 491 convicts in the Massachusetts State prison, 98, or about 20 per cent were unable to read and write. Of the entire population of Massachusetts, over 97 per cent have the ability to read and write. Of 215 prisoners in the Connecticut State prison, 77, or more than one third, could not read and write; while of the whole population of the State, 98½ per cent are able to read and write. The criminal statistics of other States exhibit results altogether similar to the above.

Now, on comparing the proportion of the whole population of the State to the proportion which the prisoners who can read and write bear to the whole number of prisoners, we get a clear idea, as well as a striking illustration, of the influence of ignorance in producing crime. Thus, for example, in Pennsylvania, since 97 per cent of the population can read and write, if want of education has no tendency to produce crime, the number of prisoners who can read and write ought to be 97 per cent of the whole, and the number who do not possess that ability ought to be only 3 per cent. But how does this statement tally with the actual facts ? Not at all ; for, in reality, only 55 per cent of the prisoners can read and write, while the enormous proportion of 45 per cent are without that power. Hence it is evident that 45 per cent of the crimes in Pennsylvania are committed by 3 per cent of the inhabitants. Thus a very large proportion of the criminals come from a very small proportion of the population. The Romish church teaches that "ignorance is the mother of *devotion*". How much more true the declaration that ignorance is the mother of crime ?

It must be remarked that even the foregoing exhibition, striking as it is, fails to set forth, in its full power, the tendency of ignorance to multiply crime. A large proportion of those reported as able to read have no such mastery of that art as to be of any practical utility, either as a recreation and consequent barrier against improper and injurious amusements, or as an aid in gaining a living, or as enabling them to read the Bible and other good books and so to learn the way to holiness ; the only three ways, as observed by Mr. Gould, in which learning can operate as a preventive of crime. If a prisoner can read by spelling out the words ever so slowly and miscalling the greater part of them, he is enrolled as able to read, although for all practical purposes, he might just as well be without that ability. An illustration of the extreme ignorance of prisoners, who are classed as being able to read and write, is afforded by the following statistics : 57 prisoners were committed in one year to the State prison of Connecticut, who were classed as follows : 27 could read and write ; 16 could read, but not write ; and 14 could neither read nor write. Forty three of the number, therefore, stood on the records as being able to read. These 43 were requested to spell the words "read" and "write." Only eleven spelled them correctly, the remaining 32 being unable to do it. One of the best of the readers was not able to tell whether the book of Matthew was in the Old Testament or the New. The truth is (as Mr. Gould has remarked), that nine tenths of the prisoners in the United States are ignorant men, who, although they may be enrolled on the prison books as able to read and write, are unable to do so for any practical or useful purpose.

XI. *Want of a trade or profession is a source of crime.*— Ample and reliable statistics show that, in the State of New

York, men of no occupation, or liquor sellers, sailors, boatmen, and drivers, none of which occupations can be properly called trades, constitute 65 per cent of all the persons convicted of crime; that in Connecticut they constitute 60 per cent; in Maryland, 51 per cent; and in Pennsylvania, 45 per cent. These statements show a close relation between the want of a trade and the commission of crime.   They show that the ranks of criminals are, in great part, recruited from the idle and shiftless classes of the community.   But they do not reveal the whole truth.   As a large proportion of the persons enrolled in our prison books as able to read and write have no such mastery of those accomplishments as to be of any practical utility, so those prisoners who profess to have learned trades have, in general, acquired them so imperfectly, that they are of little avail in enabling them to earn an honest livelihood. Half learned trades, almost equally with no trades, are a cause of destitution and crime.   This is made abundantly apparent from the statistics of the eastern penitentiary at Philadelphia, which exhibit the following results.   Of 3043 convicts confined in that prison, 442 were apprenticed and served their whole time; 556 were apprenticed, but did not serve out their time; and 2045 served no apprenticeship at all.   Of the whole number apprenticed, considerably more than one half, by reason of not serving through their full time, acquired their trades imperfectly.   Of the whole number reported, 67 per cent served no apprenticeship at all; and 85 per cent either never learned trades at all, or learned them so imperfectly as to be of little use.   The following statement is no less significant: 48 prisoners of 24 years and under were received into the eastern penitentiary during the year 1853.   Of these, only *one* had served out his time; 9 had been apprenticed and had left before the expiration of their apprenticeship; and 38, more than three fourths of the whole, had never been apprenticed at all.   "It is worthy of remark", say the Inspectors in their report, " and suggests serious reflections to the inquiring mind, that of the 48 prisoners received during the year under 25 years, so few have ever been taught any useful business".

XII. *Poverty is a source of crime.*—Far be it from us to speak on this subject in a way to wound the sensibilities of the virtuous poor.   Among this class are often witnessed the brightest examples of purity, gentleness, self-denial, and uprightness; too often, indeed, to permit us to doubt that poverty is compatible with the development and exercise of all these virtues.   But we must not shut our eyes to facts, which, occurring every day, show that pauperism and crime advance in parallel lines, and with equal step. They act and reäct upon each other; and each is, in turn, both cause and effect. This may be seen both in the cities and the country; but chiefly in the former, for it is there that poverty most rapidly and certainly generates crime, and there likewise its peculiar workings can be most easily observed.

XIII. *Inefficient preventive police is a source of crime.*— This is too obvious to require argument or illustration. Within the memory of men now living, highway robbery was common on the roads leading to London. Now, however, in consequence of the increased efficiency of the police, such robberies are unknown.

But the general public has a responsibility here, as well as the police. Within the past few years, the police of New York, and some other of our large cities, have been required to enforce the law in relation to the closing of the grog shops on the Sabbath; and, wherever public opinion has been such as really to demand the measure, it has been successful. A like public sentiment, on the part of the moral and religious portion of the community, would enable the police to close up the brothels and gambling houses, which, as we have seen, cause so large an amount of crime and misery.

XIV. *Foreign immigration is, in our country, a source of crime.*—Of 14,504 convictions for crime made outside of the cities of New York and Brooklyn, 38 per cent of the persons convicted were foreigners, while only 21 per cent of the aggregate population are of foreign birth. The commitments in the city of New York for the last year (1863) were 41,299. Of the persons thus committed, only 10,477, about one fourth, were native born citizens, while all the remaining 30,822 were foreigners; and this is about the usual proportion. In view of these facts, it is evident that crime is increased by the influx of immigrants from other countries.

XV. *Proximity to great thoroughfares of trade and travel is a source of crime.*—In the 18 counties bordering upon the Erie canal, there is one crime to every 1276 of the population; while in the 17 counties, lying south of the canal, and not adjacent to it, the ratio of the convictions to the population is as one to 2876; which shows an immense preponderance of crime in the canal counties. But there are other circumstances which evince still more strikingly the crime-producing tendency of such thoroughfares as the Erie canal. Schenectady, Monroe, Niagara, and Oneida, the principal points of transhipment, are the most remarkable for crime, with the exception of Erie and Albany, the two termini of the

canal, in which the relative amount of crime is greater than
any other counties in the State, not even excepting that of
New York.   Comparing the nine counties bordering on the
Hudson river with the nine counties which lie secluded from
great thoroughfares, we find in the former one conviction in
1518 inhabitants; in the latter, one in 2864; nearly the same
proportion as before, and showing still the tendency of great
thoroughfares to generate crime.

XVI. *Density of population is a source of crime.*—This
might be argued *à priori*.   A certain amount of separation,
seclusion, and quietude seems to be essential to a healthful
development of the moral faculties.   There is a tendency to
contamination and degeneracy in the crowding of men together.
But the tendency of crowding, in itself considered, to produce
crime, is doubtless much less influential than the opportunity
it affords for the action of other causes.   Indeed, nothing can
be clearer than that all the more active causes of crime are
forced into a hot-bed fertility and productiveness by crowded
populations; as grog shops, theatres, brothels, gambling houses,
the circulation of bad books, etc., etc.

But what is the testimony of facts on this point?   The
criminal statistics of the State of New York show that crime
follows compactness of population with almost mathematical
precision, so that a statement of the ratio of crime in any two
groups of counties will be, at the same time, a statement of
the ratio of the density of population in the same groups.   In
1850, there were 59 counties in the State.   Alleghany stood
midway as respected the relative amount of crime committed
in it; there being 29 counties more criminal than it, and 29
less criminal.   In the 29 counties above it in criminality, there
were 10.7 acres to each inhabitant; in the 29 below it, there
were 16.5 acres to each inhabitant.   In the 10 most guilty
counties, there were 6 acres to each inhabitant; in the 10 least
guilty, there were 24.   In the second 10 most guilty counties,
the average number of acres to each inhabitant was 8.7; in
the second 10 least guilty ones, it was 15.   The average per
cent of convictions in the 10 worst counties, was .070; in the
10 best, .018.   It is surprising to see how exactly the ratio of
crime corresponds with the ratio of density of population.
Thus 6 : 24 :: .018 : .072, which only varies .002 from the
actual percentage, as exhibited in the criminal records of the
State.   So exact, then, in the State of New York, is the relation between density of population and crime, that, if the
density of population and the percentage of crime be given in
one district, and the density of population only be given in

another, we can at once and with scarcely less than mathematical certainty calculate the percentage of crime in the latter.

The same remarkable result is exhibited in the criminal statistics of England and Wales.

XVII. *Sabbath-breaking is a source of crime.*—This proposition is amply established by the criminal statistics of New York, as set forth in the documents of the New York Sabbath Committee. It appears that for 18 months prior to August 1st, 1859 (the date on which the Sunday liquor shops were closed by order), the excess of arrests made on Sundays over those made on Tuesdays was 1852; or about 25 per cent of the whole. The Sunday arrests since that date down to January 1st, 1863, were 27,272; the Tuesday arrests, 36,363; showing an excess of arrests on Tuesdays over those on Sundays of just 25 per cent. The relative gain on Sunday crime has, therefore, been just about one half. No wonder, then, that in a recent general order issued by the Superintendent of Police, that officer holds the following language : " The good order that has been preserved in the cities of New York and Brooklyn on the Sabbath day, since the enforcement of the forty-second section of the police law, has marked an era in the history of both these cities ". The Sabbath Committee, in giving the results of the reform aimed at by their labors, say : " A comparison of the data furnished by the police returns of arrests for crime and disorder on the Sundays and Tuesdays of successive years warrants the following generalization : 1. The enforcement of the Sunday laws has resulted in making the Sabbath day the most orderly of the days of the week, instead of the most immoral, as formerly. 2. The arrests for crime have increased or diminished in the measure of obedience to these laws, not only on the Sundays, but on all other days. 3. The two years of civil war have been the period of improved public morals in this Metropolis, as compared with any recent period of our history."

XVIII. *Privation of ministerial instruction is a source of crime.*—Dividing the counties of New York into groups of ten, as we have already in several instances done, we find that in the 10 counties where crime most prevails, there is one clergyman to every 678 inhabitants; in the 10 where crime least prevails, there is one to every 503. In the second 10 most criminal counties, the average number of inhabitants to one clergyman is 572; in the second 10 least criminal counties, the average population to one clergyman is 511. Thus it appears that crime increases as clerical force diminishes, and that the multiplication of ministers of the Gospel is a means of promoting virtue, as well as piety, and tends to the prevention of crime, no less than to the growth of holiness.

We close with the remark that, although we have enumerated, *seriatim*, eighteen distinct sources of crime, yet it is seldom that they act separately and alone in working out their deplorable results. Separate acts of drinking, gaming, and the like may not lead to the commission of crime; but one of these acts leads to another, and that to a third, and so on, till their conjoint operation is to plunge into crime and its consequent wretchedness and ruin those who practise them. Thus going to the theatre may introduce a young man to the society of prostitutes; these may incite him to drink; drink may lead him to the gaming saloon; gambling may and probably will land him in poverty; and from the pressure of poverty he may be impelled to the commission of criminal acts. Each successive step has its own corrupting power; each individual lapse leaves its sting to fester in his moral nature. And when, at length, the goadings of poverty drive him to replenish his exchequer by the robbery of others, conscience has become deadened, its voice has been silenced by vicious indulgence, the temptation meets but a feeble resistance, and the youth falls an easy prey to the enemy, who is striking at the precious life, and seeking, but too successfully, to involve virtue, honor, health, and happiness in one common ruin.

But our analysis of the sources of crime would be essentially defective without the statement, that, back of all these causes and far down in the depths of our fallen nature, is the *causa causans*, the primal source of all crime and all sin,— that inborn depravity, that universal corruption of all the elements and powers of our being, which belongs to all mankind in their lapsed estate. It is in this original corruption of nature that the Word of God places the fountain of all moral evil, the original and spring of all the vice, the crime, and the sin, which darken and deform our apostate world. In the first chapter of Romans, we have the Bible theory of crime. There we learn that as men "did not like to retain God in their knowledge, God gave them over to a reprobate mind, to do those things which are not convenient; being filled with all unrighteousness, fornication, wickedness, covetousness, maliciousness, full of envy, murder, debate, deceit, malignity; whisperers, backbiters, haters of God, despiteful, proud, boasters, inventors of evil things, disobedient to parents, without understanding, covenant breakers, without natural affection, implacable, unmerciful."

In a future number we may inquire into the means of preventing crime, and the agencies by which it may be removed, as far as possible, from the body politic.

Art. III.—FALSE TENDENCY AND RADICAL DEFECT IN EDUCATION.

By Rev. J. R. Herrick, Malone, N. Y.

Education: Intellectual, Moral and Physical, by Herbert Spencer, Author of "Social Statics," etc. New-York: D. Appleton & Co. 1861.

Twenty-five years ago the literary fame of Thomas Carlyle was attracting attention on both sides of the Atlantic. Before this he had written for Reviews, and had published some of his works. He seemed to have an utter abhorrence of the superficial in literature, in morality and in religion. He possessed a keen eye for detecting "shams", and a corresponding tact in exposing them; and the foundations of modern civilization appeared almost, through his exposures, as if built on rottenness. All saw and could not but admit the justice of many of Carlyle's sharp criticisms; and not a few were hoping his work might be the beginning of a successful attempt to clear away the rubbish and superficial foundations of the past, in order that better institutions might be reared, or at least, so that necessary institutions might be better, because more truthfully founded, and a higher state of civilization ensue. But while waiting, and waiting patiently too, to see the new foundations laid on which society should positively advance, the world — always ready to be taught, by the *men* who are capable of instructing it, if not by the *God* who can do it infinitely better—discovered that the mission of Carlyle was not to reconstruct, but only, if he had rightly apprehended it, to tear down what was already built, making his attacks at points most vulnerable. This being discovered, with how much less favor were his writings received, although no less able and vigorous than before! And the fact need occasion no surprise, for the world, bad as it is, is not pleased to find a chaos when it was looking for a cosmos.

But what appears in Carlyle as a marked example, appears in many others also, and has in fact become a prevailing tendency of our age. And this tendency — which exists in England and America, as well as in France and Germany — we ought to understand, is the disposition to overturn and destroy things most sacred and fundamental. It shows itself in efforts to subvert Christianity itself. And here, too, it works most covertly. In other words, the fundamental error towards which the tendency is very strong, is, to discard what is supernatural and superhuman as essential for raising and perfecting humanity. It disguises itself under the following forms: It is claimed that every thing in existence has developed out of an original creation : 2. An attempt is made to give a rational or philosophic development of the race : 3. Then follows the assumption that nature's laws are supreme : 4. Comes an argument against the supernatural : 5. A virtual, but not direct, denial of the validity of Revelation. By these several roads the way is direct to the same general conclusion, viz., that man, as an individual, and of course the race as a whole — or *vice versa*, the race, and of course the individual also — by a wise process of development and education, let this only be adopted, will arrive at perfection,—towards which goal, it is assumed, both race and individual are advancing, spite all the blunders of leaders in reform, and the hindrances interposed by those who preach the necessity of a supernatural interposition.

Though we must not here discuss the process, we should gain as just a conception of it as possible, and in order thereto, a more full statement of the mode in which the error works may be desirable. It may also bring us to the best point of view from which to form a just estimate of Spencer's book on Education.

The first hypothesis, then, is like that of the " Vestiges of Creation ", which declares that all the creative work ever performed by God was in the dark and far off past, and that then he simply formed original germs, capable of development into different kinds of objects, first reptile or plant, as the case might be, then animal, and lastly man. This theory, though annihilated by Hugh Miller in his " Footprints of the Creator ", and " Testimony of the Rocks ",—in which he shows to all candid minds, according to Scripture statement, that every different *kind* of existence, animate and inanimate, *must be* the result of a direct " *fiat* of the Creator " — that nothing higher can possibly be produced by any thing lower in kind ; — still, the theory is determined to live again, like the beast in the Apocalypse, wounded to death, but whose deadly wound was healed.

Closely allied to this is the philosophic development of the race. This takes man in a rude state as the undoubted type of the original genus, assuming that he had then nothing more than the crudest notions on any subject, but that from necessity and by degrees, he went on learning, and that in this development, not only is experience his teacher, but reason still more, and that he advances in perfection only in proportion as he develops and is guided by the light within. Underlying these assumptions, it is implied that there has never been a *fall* of the race, but that it is now more perfect than ever before. It is pre-supposed of course that the plausible theory will be readily admitted, for then it can easily be substantiated. And as there are facts in the growth and development of objects, that seem, to a superficial view, to favor the first theory, so there are facts in the history of the race, that can be so put together as to throw around this second theory a great show of plausibility — provided we only start by ignoring the fact of sin and an original apostacy.

The working of *natural law* comes in here as a great helper. The laws of heat, laws of electricity, laws of magnetism, laws of attraction, are fixed and certain. And are not the laws of vegetable and animal life sharply defined and invariable? And is not the same true of the laws of thinking? In short, the whole universe is pervaded by law. What place is left then, it is asked, for spiritual laws, and laws of freedom? Will it do to assume that there are such, and that they are higher than the laws of nature which are invariable and necessary?

This prepares the way for an argument—a logical argument *against* supernatural agencies. But the argument here, it should be observed, is not one framed expressly in the interest of pantheism. It aims to show directly how inconsistent it is, since the laws of nature are immutable, to hold to an agency above nature, like that of miracles, for example. It may be a direct argument, as that of Leibnitz, to prove that *no miracle can take place;* or, as that of Hume, to show that no proof from testimony, can be sufficient to warrant, against the uniformity of nature, a *belief* in miracles: or, an attempt may be made, like that of Strauss, — which virtually assumes both the above points,—to turn the narrative of each miracle into myth or fable. And if no miracle-working power is to be admitted, so neither can a direct agency of the Divine spirit or the human spirit be maintained. Thus this theory, although that is not its professed aim, would indirectly establish *pantheism.*—It also prepares the way for a *denial* of Revelation and the inspiration of the Bible. The tendency strikes obliquely here also. First some parts of this book are doubt-

ed ; next, certain doctrines ; then a comparison is made between Paul and John, on the one hand, and Plato and Socrates, on the other, as teachers ; and then Paul and John are
declared to be, like Socrates and Plato, only stepping-stones
to something higher, which is being evolved from the human
reason and being enounced by Hegel, Emerson, Parker and
others ; finally, it is assumed that the magi of the West are
wiser, in these modern times, than Inspiration itself, or, in
other words, that the Bible is nothing more than a common
book.   And if so, of course, the religion of the cross can
have no peculiar claims, and Christianity, as the hope and
salvation of the world, is a vain pretence.

Such is a more full statement of the modern tendency to
pantheism and infidelity by ignoring the supernatural.   It
should, however, be borne in mind that some of the views
connected with this tendency may be embraced without any
just conception of their bearing.   Nay, even those who, at
heart, are firm friends of Christianity, may fall into the current without being aware of it.   In many cases the ultimate,
to be sure, is not reached; but this does not alter at all the
nature of the tendency itself.

Moreover, since the mode of speculation indicated enters
into prevailing views of the development of the race, it would,
in like manner, be expected to enter into theories of *individual*
development.   Indeed, education being a drawing out of what
is in man, how, it is asked, can we claim for it any thing more
than a mere outgrowth of nature?

Herbert Spencer's book, whose title stands at the head of
this article, is a good illustration of the *manner* in which
religion and the supernatural are set aside, as well as of
the *disposition* to set them aside, in the work of education.
This we think to be one good reason for calling attention
to the author's tendency.   Another is the fact that, at the
present time, Spencer seems exerting, in certain directions,
perhaps more influence than any other writer on education.   A
third is because it is announced in the Introduction to this book
that its author proposes to give to the world soon—as would
appear from the synopsis—his views on all the leading interests of man, considered both individually and socially.   Those
in America and Great Britain who stand eminent in the
departments of literature and science give their names as
subscribers to the forthcoming work.   This, as well as Spencer's confessed ability, will help give popularity to his works.
And, now that we have the first-fruits, it might be well to form

therefrom, if possible, a just estimate of the future harvest of what his teaching is likely to be in its religious bearings.

A just criticism of the work before us would perhaps distinguish three varieties in the utterances of its author—*good things, partial truths, and defects.* It is under the 2d and 3d heads that Spencer favors the fundamental error in education, and discards, though it may be covertly, the supernatural. It may be freely admitted that the author has said many excellent things, and it may be hoped that his work, setting forth so forcibly his views on the subject, will awaken inquiry in regard to what education is, and what it demands. Only it should be added that these views leave a stronger impression and are more striking, because of the important omissions of much that belongs to a safe and symmetrical presentation of the true idea of education.

He speaks well of physical education. A proper diet, not over stimulative nor under stimulative; exercise, for females as well as males, in kind and degree adapted to the constitution of each, and so applied as to develop strength from day to day; pure air in the school-room and in the bed-room; in the house as well as out-of-doors; the laws of health known and observed by parents and teachers, and rightly applied and taught to children, that they may properly observe them. All these things have an important bearing, no doubt, on the proper development of the young. It gives satisfaction to know that this branch of education is likely to be more faithfully attended to than heretofore, in schools and colleges in our own country as well as in foreign countries. For a proper physical culture will give a generation stronger in mind as well as body.

Spencer has done well, too, in calling attention to the neglect of that kind of training which is adapted to fit the young for the positions of responsibility which they will soon be called to fill in the *family* and in the *State.* Our schools rarely indicate the fact that boys will soon be men, become voters, and that they must manage, well or ill, the affairs of the commonwealth. Certainly, very little instruction is given them in respect to the principles of government and the duties of citizenship; although free institutions can have no firm or sure basis without the intelligence any more than without the virtue of the people.

And though nine tenths of both sexes, as Spencer says, will, in all probability, sooner or later become parents, how poorly fitted, nevertheless, for the responsibilities of parents are nine tenths of both sexes! If the responsibilities of the family lie before the young, why should they not be taught something that may help fit them for an intelligent discharge of the duties of parents? Simply Youman's "Handbook of Household Science" would teach most heads of families many things of which they are ignorant.

Justly, likewise, does Spencer assail the false tendency to put the ornamental before the useful—provided he always judges rightly as to what the useful is. The popular error here is, in fact, twofold. 1. To prize the ornamental more highly than the useful: and, 2. To attempt to gain the latter before the former, and without any substantial basis for it to rest upon ; thus doing violence to nature, which puts forth her blossoms and emits her fragrance, after the root that nourishes them and the stalk that bears them are developed. "It is", says Spencer, "a vice of our educational system, that it neglects the plant for the sake of the flower ; in anxiety for elegance, it forgets substance".

No doubt, too, he is right in demanding a process of education that shall be more one of pleasure. For it is while the mind acts pleasurably that it acts healthfully and vigorously. Knowledge gained in a sour mood is no better than that gained in a singing mood. And we need not be afraid of awakening a little pleasurable emotion in the minds of children even in school. We may cultivate a better nature by so doing.

The author speaks well, also, of the importance of self-education—of such a direction and discipline of the youthful mind as will make it self-reliant. " Unfortunately, education among us", says Horace Mann, as quoted by Spencer, " consists too much of *telling*, not in *training* ".

Another point of importance is that in regard to the order of calling forth the powers of knowledge. The senses are first developed by the objects with which they come in contact. This fact suggests the propriety of giving an early attention to the development of the powers of sensation and perception, and before the reason is much cultivated. The order is, the thing before its principle ; the concrete before the abstract ; objects learned through the touch and the sight, before rational principles and ideas. Not that reason and the higher intuitions of truth can be developed *out of* the senses : rather the proper unfolding in childhood of the lower faculties forms the proper condition and preparation for the later and higher development. But since this fact is liable to abuse, we may properly pass over upon it to the *half-truths* of our author, of which we will here present some illustrations. These may be good when taken with their proper limitation, as half, and not as whole, truths.

Though Spencer is undeniably right in placing the useful before the merely ornamental, it may be, nevertheless, a query whether he gives altogether the right impression as to what constitutes the useful.   If education is only to fit us to become parents and citizens, he may be right.   What he says on this point is very forcible, if we look only to our present existence.   But if man is rational and immortal, his interest extends beyond time ; and may we not say, in a still better sense, that that study and discipline are useful which are best adapted to fit him for a higher and immortal existence ?

So in respect to the prominent study of the laws, or science, of nature, recommended by this author : certainly, these laws should be known ; natural science should be, if possible, well understood ; and if there is nothing · higher than nature for the soul of man to know, and to which it stands related, then let nature be her mistress and guide.   But if there is an Author of nature, a personal God and other laws than those of nature—laws of freedom,—then would it not be quite as proper and not less " useful", to know this Being and those spiritual laws which he has made for moral action, as to limit our study by the fixed laws of nature ?

Just here a word, too, in regard to giving up the study of *language* for the study of physical law, which Spencer advocates.   Whether it is always wise to devote so much time to the study of the languages, unless this study can be made more life-like, hence more productive, may be a question. Dead languages need to have a resurrection power put into them.   But that would not be a reason for *discarding* them, which would be a good reason for *reforming* the study of them.   While the history of the world and the life of nations, is written in language ; since theology as well as philosophy is written in language ; and since we can have no true history of philosophy or true philosophy of history, without a study of language, we cannot consent to forego such study, in order to make so prominent as this author desires, the study of mathematics and physical law.

Once more, in what Spencer calls the moral discipline of the young, he would make very prominent these fixed laws.   He would have children trained from the first to feel the ill effects of breaking them.   And this study is right.   That it is not done more may be a serious defect.   It may, moreover, be right to have the penalty such as a violation of the law naturally demands.   But after all, this is no more than a half-truth.   For children are constituted to be under authority. Moreover, by properly learning obedience to parents, they

38

are to learn obedience to God. Nor can they feel too early that they are under direct authority, both human and divine. And whatever may be said of natural penalty, when we speak of free beings, their immediate relation to personal authority, is the indispensable supplement to the side of natural consequences ; if we do not say that truly moral discipline is impossible without it.

But half-truths are defects on the one side ; and since those of this book, connect themselves with the radical defect, we will pass to this omission of the religious part of our nature in education. Nor can we help saying as we pass, that, after a careful reading of this work, it seems more remarkable for the sharp manner in which it presents half-truths than for any new matter it contains.

Some who have glanced at the work may be disposed to say that it is unjust to charge Spencer with an omission of the religious element, since he does not pretend to treat this phase of the subject. He does indeed, at the end of his chapter on Moral education, make a caveat of this kind, which, for the sake of doing justice to the author, shall here be quoted in full. " Nor have we introduced the religious element, we have confined our inquiries to a nearer and much more neglected field, though a very important one. Our readers may supplement our thoughts in any way they please : we are only concerned that they should be accepted as far as they go". (pp. 217, 218).

Now, the objection, be it distinctly observed, to Herbert Spencer, is not, that he does *not choose* to discuss the religious element in education. The objection is, that, notwithstanding his caveat, he still leaves the impression that he has covered the whole ground—the objection is, that, if we do accept him as far as he goes, and take him for our guide, we shall not be disposed to go any further—the objection to him is, that he says nothing opposed to a system of neology, pantheism and infidelity, while all he *does* say, taken in its total impression, favors a tendency in that direction, more than towards a supernatural religion and the soul of a positive Christianity. Nor would it surprise us in the least, should Spencer—when the popular mind, now left free, as he says, to form its own religious supplements, adopts what he has said as he intends it, — if he should then fill up the important blank with a direct argument in opposition to religion and Christianity, and not in their behalf. Let this, however, pass for mere opinion.

Still, the view which we feel bound to maintain—and that from the book itself,—is this, that Spencer's ideal of education does not contain properly a religious element—that he did not wish to include any other agencies than these which he so strongly advocates ;—and that thus this omission is in accordance with the fundamental error spoken of in the beginning and illustrates its introduction into this important sphere.

Surely Spencer had the ability to prepare a chapter on religious culture, had he been disposed. Although Review articles are necessarily limited, books may be enlarged at pleasure. And if the author's theory admitted a truly religious element by a divine and supernatural agency, there is no reason why he should not have spoken as boldly on this point as on any other.

Another fact is suggestive. The most enthusiastic admirers of Spencer, are those who occupy themselves most with the laws of natural science and have least to do with the study of spiritual laws. Furthermore, the first and leading part of the work, was originally published in the Westminster—a Review which is the well known advocate in England, of Neology and Infidelity. This, to be sure, may be accidental.

But can it be merely accidental that he confines his " curriculum", or round of studies, so essentially to natural science ? (p. 93, passim). Can it be accidental that he advocates so strongly the study of objects, as the fit preparation for the study of nature's laws, with no allusion to the development of spiritual ideas ? Can it be accidental that he gives the impression that children naturally grow better as they grow older, and only need the true system of education to perfect them ? (p. 206.) And is it accidental, that while he would have education imitate nature, he would also have his system so completely circumscribed *by* nature ? (pp. 122, 93 and on).

Nor can it be accidental that Spencer insists that "the education of the child must accord both in mode and arrangement with the education of mankind considered historically", and that what is true in the one case must be true also in the other (pp. 97–99 and 122). It is not, let it be observed, for the sake of opposing this affirmation, that we here present it, but to indicate that Spencer had in mind a *complete* system of education.

" How to live? that is the essential question for us", says he, " not how to live in a mere material sense only, but in the widest sense. The general problem which comprehends every special problem is—the right ruling of conduct in all directions under all circumstances.   In what way to treat the body ; in what way to treat the mind; in what way to manage our affairs; in what way to bring up a family; in what way to behave as a citizen ; in what way to utilize all those sources of happiness which nature supplies—how to use all our faculties to the greatest advantage of ourselves and others—how to live completely ?   And this being the great thing needful for us to learn, is by consequence, the great thing which education has to teach" (pp. 30, 31).

This appears very much as if the author intended to give a complete idea of education.   He furnishes us also with what he calls a "naturally arranged" classification of the "leading kinds of activity which constitute human life".   And what, in his view, are these ?   " 1. Those activities which directly minister to self-preservation ; 2. Those activities which, by securing the necessaries of life, indirectly minister to self-preservation.   3. Those activities which have for their end rearing and discipline of offspring.   4. Those activities which are involved in the maintenance of proper social and political relations.   5. Those miscellaneous activities which make up the leisure part of life, devoted to the gratification of the tastes and feelings " (p. 32).

Now, this determining the activities that constitute human life, is *in order* to know positively what things are most deserving of attention and what it most concerns us to know— this being essential, if we would attain a " rational curriculum " (p. 29, etc).   Do we not here gain the impression that Spencer intends to cover the whole ground in education ? But yet the classification gives no religious " activities "— unless perchance we are to look for them among those " which make up the leisure part of life, devoted to the gratification of the tastes and feelings " ! !   And of course, as we perceive, the " rational ", not Christian, curriculum includes nothing in regard to the religious side of our complex being.   *Nature* is to be studied that we may know how we are related to her, not *God*, that we may know how we are related to him.

In what is said of moral training, it is still more evident that Spencer's religion is only one of nature, and not one of supernatural revelation.   " Have we not here then ", says he, " the guiding principle of moral education ?   Is it not manifest that as 'ministers and interpreters of nature', it 'is the function of parents to see that their children habitually experience the true consequences of their conduct—the natural reactions; neither warding them off, nor intensifying them,

nor putting artificial consequences in their place?—and therefore they cannot too anxiously avail themselves of this discipline of rational consequences—this system of letting the
penalty be inflicted by the laws of things" (pp. 178 and
191).   And to show that he holds the process to be true universally, he adds: "Thus we see that this method of moral
culture by experience of the normal reäctions, which is the
divinely ordained method for infancy and for adult life, is
equally applicable during the intermediate childhood and
youth" (p. 191).   This is that field of moral culture which
to our author's mind lies nearer and is more neglected than
the religious!

But we find a yet clearer intimation of what Spencer's conception of religious culture was when he wrote this book, and
that his own mind did not demand any thing more than he
has given us to complete its idea of education.   If his readers
should deem it needful, they might supplement his thoughts
as they pleased.   He was only concerned that they should
accept his thoughts as far as they go!   Among other things
to justify the almost exclusive study of science, he says: "We
repeat, then, that not science, but the neglect of science, is
irreligious.   Devotion to science is a tacit worship—a tacit
recognition of worth in the things studied, and by implication in their cause".   If this is not sufficiently positive, he is
more explicit.   "Nor is it thus only that true science is essentially religious.   It is religious too, inasmuch as it creates a
profound respect for, and an implicit faith in"—this is so near
a definition of religion that we almost expect the words "a
personal God" to follow; but instead of these we have—"a
profound respect for, and implicit faith in, those uniform laws
which underlie all things". . . . "Instead of the rewards and
punishments of traditional belief, which men vaguely hope
they may gain, or escape, spite of their disobedience", the
man of science, he proceeds, "finds that there are rewards
and punishments in the ordained constitution of things.   He
sees that the laws to which we must submit are not only inexorable, but beneficent.   He sees that in virtue of these laws,
the process of things is ever towards a greater and a higher
happiness."   Here is Spencer's remedial system—not the
religion of the Bible and the grace of God, but the "process
of things" working out "a higher happiness!"   But let us
hear him still further as he commends the piety of the man of
science.   "Hence he is led constantly to insist on these laws
and is indignant when men disregard them.   And thus does
he, by asserting the eternal principles of things and the neces-

sity of conforming to them, prove himself intrinsically religious " (pp. 91, 92).

This then, in the view of Herbert Spencer, is what constitutes religion ! The exposition of his religious belief is about as evident as that of Parker or Hegel ; and the religion advocated by the three seems very much alike. Their system for the education of the race, and his for the education of the individual, well agree ! And they are not very unlike in saying many good things sharply, half-truths plausibly, and, when they prefer, in leaving others to guess at their omissions.

Thus this work of Spencer on education not only falls into the wake of the modern tendency to a pantheistic infidelity ; but is also an illlustration of the manner in which this tendency works to ignore the supernatural and to strengthen the fundamental defect in the education, as well of the individual, as of the race. This is not by directly denying revelation, but by saying very little about it. It is not by affirming that there is no need of the grace of God and a life above nature begotten by God's Spirit, to perfect and save humanity, but by insisting on the necessity of a rational, nature-development, with the implication that this is all-sufficient. Nor yet is it by omitting to mention God and religion, but by using these and other sacred terms in a new sense, of the real import of which the uninitiated are little aware. Neither is it by openly advocating pantheism, but rather a reverence for the mystery and science of nature. Nor yet is it, in fine, by saying that the Bible is not worthy of being believed and taken as an infallible guide, but by making the laws of nature supreme, and demanding that they, and not God's law, shall be our guide practically as well as intellectually.*

* If we were to compare Spencer's "Essays", we might find further intimation that he favors a pantheistic development, a deistic progress, an absolute supremacy of natural law, and that he ignores the supernatural, and hence, would disregard and set aside Revelation. "The general doctrine that all kinds of government exercised over men were at first one government—that the political, the religious, and the ceremonial forms of control, are divergent branches of a general and once indivisible control—begins to look tenable." "That law, religion, and manners are thus related—that their respective kinds of operation come under one generalization—that they have in certain contrasted characteristics of men a common support and a common danger—will, however, be most clearly seen by discovering that they have a common origin." (The conquering chief in a remote era being) "alike legislator and judge, all quarrels among his subjects are decided by him; and his words become law. Awe of him is the incipient religion, and his maxims furnish its first precepts. Submission is made to him in the forms he prescribes; and these give birth to manners. From the first, time developes political allegiance and the administration of justice ; from the second, the worship of a being whose personality becomes ever more vague, and the inculcation of precepts ever more abstract; from the third, forms of honor and the rules of etiquette." (Essays.

Whether then, notwithstanding the many forcible and valuable suggestions of this author, he is not liable to mislead, through omissions of important complementary truths, and whether the result of his teachings will not be, according to their tendency, to rationalism and pantheism, and not to religion and Christianity, are questions that ought to be well considered, before Spencer, or those who follow in his footsteps, are taken as guides in education.

We know that every system for the race that leaves no room for man's free relation to a personal God, and no room for revelation and the grace of God as a remedial system, will, and must, in the end, prove a failure. So every system of individual culture, or school education, in so far as it does not rest, and because it does not rest, on a truly religious and scriptural basis, must fail. A mere system of naturalism, whatever be its application, and however attractive in some of its phases it may be, while it disregards the world to come, cannot make men perfect either for this world. All its theories, after being tried, will be found wanting. Hegel and Carlyle and Emerson and Parker and Spencer, and so all man-devised theories of reform, may have their day. But at length an infidel system of philosophy, an infidel system of theology, and infidel systems of education, must give place to a Christian philosophy, a Christian theology, and a Christian system of education. Of this we are confident. And yet,

London Ed. '58, pp. 112, 129, 130). Man needs something done for him, it is true. "The aboriginal man, coming fresh from the killing of bears, and from lying in ambush for his enemy, has, by the necessities of his condition, a nature requiring to be curbed in its every impulse" (p. 130). Science may, indeed, do something for him: "Whenever established, a correct theory of the historical development of the sciences must have an immense effect upon education, and through education, upon civilization (p. 226, on "Genesis of Science"). But it seems desirable to get rid of the control of law, religion, and manners—the common origin of which the author so admirably sets forth—as soon as possible. "The discipline of circumstances which has already wrought out such changes in us, must go on eventually to work out yet greater ones. That daily curbing of the lower nature and curbing of the higher nature, which out of cannibals and devil-worshippers has evolved philanthropists, lovers of peace, and haters of superstition (almost equivalent, one would think in Spencer's view, to religion)! cannot fail to evolve out of these, men as much superior to them, as they are to their progenitors." "When human nature has grown into conformity with the moral law, these will need no judges and statute books; when it spontaneously (?) takes the right course in all things, as in some things it does already, prospects of future reward or punishment will not be wanting as incentives; and when fit behavior has become instinctive, these will need no code of ceremonies to say how behavior shall be regulated" (p. 137). "Simultaneously with the decline in the influence of priesthoods, and in the fear of eternal torments—simultaneously with the mitigation of political tyranny, the growth of popular power, and the amelioration of criminal codes, has taken place that diminution of formalities, and that fading of distinctive modes, now so observable" (p. 133).

however much there may be that is valuable in Spencer, his
false tendency and fundamental defect should be exposed.
For the truth's sake and the gospel's sake, it should be done.
And surely for the sake of humanity, that cannot be perfected without a supernatural agency, it should be done.   It
is demanded in behalf of our children and youth, who should
be brought under the influence of a system able to accomplish
what it undertakes, and not under one, which, after making
large promises, must at last prove a failure.

We repeat, if there is a supernatural world, and man is related to it; if there is a personal God, and man as a free
being is accountable to him; if the Bible is true, and we have
need of that Christ who is revealed in it; then any system
that sees no need of God and the religion of the Bible, is
fundamentally erroneous, whether it be one for the individual
or the race.

We do not say that the objects and laws of nature are not
to be studied.   But if there are also laws of freedom, spiritual
laws, *these* are not to be discarded.   If man has a conscience
and a will, the centre of moral action, and a God, the centre
of religious action, why should he not know moral science and
theological science, as well as the science of nature?   If there
are, indeed, moral laws distinct from nature's, then the former
ought to be known as thoroughly as the latter.   If there is a
God, there is a theology, and this heaven-descended science is
as worthy our attention, to say the least, and may as justly
claim it, as any that is earth-born.   And, in education, instead of shutting up the mind to the uniformity of nature and
her necessary laws—what is well adapted to quiet the sense of
responsibility—it should have given it a system that will
reach to the full compass and supply of its real wants.   And
why do we discard, under the term "education", the idea of
the *new-life*, which, though it cannot be educed *from* the
human, is yet to be developed *in* the human?   Let nature's
laws be studied till they show the need—and they will show
this if studied aright—of something higher than themselves to
perfect humanity; or rather, let humanity itself, in its actual
condition and capability, be studied, till "the law of the spirit
of life in Christ Jesus" is felt to be necessary, in order to its
emancipation and true freedom.   Let philosophy be studied—
if studied aright—till its weakness is thoroughly appreciated;
but how shall the inefficiency of all human wisdom be seen,
if not in the light of a Divine philosophy?

And if this Divine wisdom is for all, when shall we *begin to
learn it?*   If it is a revelation from above, and if he is the

author of it who knows truly our wants, it surely must be safe to teach it to children; and, for the same reason, it must be likewise the most valuable of all knowledge. Furthermore, that *moral discipline* is best for the young which is secured by, and in accordance with, God's truth, however some popular theories may be opposed to it. It is best for the moral and for the religious discipline of the young, for their present life as well as for the future one for which they are to prepare, that they should, from the first, feel the restraints and force of positive authority, not only that of earthly parents, but that also of their Father in heaven; and that they learn to submit to this authority, as that of a being wiser and better than they. This is needed not merely as a supplement to the discipline of natural consequences. It is needed primarily. We should begin with it.

Finally, then, let us demand, for the young, a system of education, — as we need a system of government, — based on the truth of God and conformed to the religion of Jesus Christ. Let us reject an infidel and a semi-infidel system as well, and adopt a Christian system that shall make our children more truly religious, and not tend to raise up a generation of pantheists and infidels. We are to bear in mind, that to err fundamentally, is not to succeed, but, necessarily, to fail. It avails not to affirm with Spencer that our theory is good, provided only it could be well applied. Our want of success results from not building on the right foundation, and from leaving out the corner-stone of our edifice. God has made the human mind for himself and immortality, and we must treat it accordingly. He declares it to be in need of a divine renewal: we must accept the fact. He has provided the means by which we can be formed in the divine image: we must accept of this also, as the sole effectual remedy for our ruin by sin, and not trust in that which we may draw out of, or develop in, ourselves.

The world's real progress is due to the vital power of Christianity; those nations are most prosperous that are most Christian; those parents and teachers succeed best, whose efforts are regulated by Christian principles; and those schools and colleges, other things being equal, are most successful which are most truly religious in their influence. And since these things are so, we ought to have such confidence in the Divine means and method of elevating and training the human soul, that we shall make our views and methods conform to his. If we would do this, our effort will be to give greater prominence in education, not to *nature's* laws, but to *God's* laws.

Art. IV.—AMERICAN NEW TESTAMENT COMMENTARIES.

By Howard Crosby, D.D., New York.

Notes Explanatory and Practical on the New Testament. By Albert Barnes. Notes Critical and Explanatory on the New Testament. By M. W. Jacobus, D.D. A Commentary, Critical, Expository, and Practical, on the New Testament. By J. J. Owen, D.D.

The Holy Scriptures contain a Divine light; but this light shines through the defective medium of human language. Hence, to elucidate Scripture is not an absurdity, but a religious duty. It is not enlightening a light, but removing the obstacles from the path of the light. Human language is a defective medium, both from the inadequacy of all representatives of thought, and from the diversity of language among men. The former defect belongs to language as such, and the latter to the adventitious fact that language is various. The former is remedied to some degree by iteration, parallelism, analogy, and illustration; the latter is remedied by translation.

But there is still another defective medium through which the light of Scripture has to shine if it produce an illuminating effect upon the life of man. This is the perversity of the heart, which, by the accumulations of sin, obscures or distorts the rays which seek to enter and renew it. To remove this difficulty man can make tentative efforts (made effectual by the Holy Spirit), by argument and exhortation, and so far he elucidates Scripture.

In the Commentaries which have issued from the English and American press, both the defective media are generally attacked. The commentary treats of the letter and the spirit. Linguistic difficulties are examined, discussed, and often removed, while the doctrine is developed and earnestly impressed upon the reader's mind. In the older English and the most popular American commentaries the latter elucidation is the most prominent; in the German commentaries the former. The former is most important in its position, but not in its direct effect. It holds the place of a foundation in an edifice. Without the comprehension of the letter we cannot reach the spiritual import of Scripture. And yet the analysis of the letter is a work of far lower rank than the development and inculcation of the spirit, as it only requires an intellectual apparatus, while the other requires for its proper performance both this and the far rarer preparation of an awakened and discerning heart. Indeed, we may modify our assertion regarding the criticism of the letter by saying that often the want of this spiritual experience is the cause of error in linguistic interpretation, as in cases where the laws of grammar and grammatical analogy allow an ambiguity, but where a spiritual discernment would discover none, and where, accordingly, the mere letter critic might choose the wrong interpretation. It is for this reason that we cannot be too careful when under the guidance of German Biblical criticism, which is too often tainted by neological admixture, even in men of evangelical fame, where perhaps even an evangelical spirit will not use its own discernment, but will, with untimely modesty, cleave to its rationalistic teachers.

As the danger with letter-criticism is in the want of spirituality in the guide, so, conversely, the fault frequently in spirit-criticism is the want of adequate ability to comprehend the letter, when vapid truisms or pious common-places spring from the mere surface-knowledge of the text. A Biblical commentator ought therefore to be a skilful grammarian, a scholar in Hebrew and Greek, an archæologist in matters Oriental, classical, and Rabbinical, and a man of elevated piety. These embrace both sides of his preparation. As secondary qualifications we would mention an acquaintance with the host of commentators who have preceded him, and sufficient knowledge of a dozen other modern languages to read the kindred versions. We call these secondary because a man's relation with these helps is one move from the original text, and they may sometimes darken counsel by words without knowledge. Too much stress has often been put on what some human authority has said, when the face of the original rebuked the reliance.

A letter-commentary may be addressed to any one of three classes, and will differ in its method according to the class it addresses. First, there is the uneducated mind, which must be fed with babe's food. Milk is given it in Sunday-school compilations. Secondly, there is the other extreme of the Biblical scholar, who needs the independent and profound research of erudition and genius, whose results he can compare with his own. But, thirdly, between these two is the great class of educated but not learned minds, who need strong meat, but yet, from their lack of habit, or their want of special investigation into Biblical lore, cannot bear very highly condensed food.   From this class comes the large army of Bible-class leaders and Sunday-school teachers, who have to do so largely in this age with the spiritual training of the church, and upon the faithfulness of whose efforts, therefore, depends so largely the growth of true piety.   Their weapon is the Bible.   According to their knowledge of its use will be their success against sin in the hearts of their pupils.   A certain amount of Biblical study is to them a necessity, and the same amount should be performed by every Christian parent.

It is to this class that American commentators have especially directed their efforts, as, with the practical tendencies of the American mind, it might have been expected they would, and as was most proper they should.   Men among us like Stuart and Alexander have, in fragmentary commentaries, addressed the learned, and their works are of lasting value in the apparatus of the Biblical scholar.   The former's originality and the latter's masterly discrimination equally rank their productions with older recognized standards.   But the commentators whom we have enumerated at the head of this article are more distinctively American than either Stuart or Alexander, who, appealing to the student, are necessarily more German, as the large mass of Biblical criticism comes to us from Germany.   By "American" we mean "full of practical tact" to meet the real wants of the Bible-reading community.   It is the peculiar characteristic of an American that he adapts himself to circumstances.   He has a quick perception of a want, and an equally quick invention for its supply.   It is so in trade, in social life, and in politics.   It is equally so in things moral and religious.   In the commentaries mentioned above there is just the right form of letter-criticism for the educated mass of Bible readers, learned dissertations and infant-class explanations being equally avoided.   The results of learning are seen in judicious expositions and valuable auxiliary information; but the comparison of codices and the hypercriticism of verbal forms are not found.   With this style of letter-criticism there is mingled the spirit-criticism, or practical commentary, enforcing by the methods already alluded to the great truths of which the verbal text is but the vehicle.   In this the pious heart speaks forth and performs its great work of evangelization.   Just such commentaries were needed for our nervous American people, who have not, or will not, take time to explore all the sinuosities of Biblical learning, even under the best guides, but who will eagerly seize upon and use the clear testimony which he who runs can read.

We group the three works of Barnes, Jacobus, and Owen together, as they are, we believe, the only complete New Testament commentaries from American pens. Indeed, the last two are as yet incomplete, reaching each only to the Epistles ; but their authors purpose to continue their labors until the whole New Testament is annotated.

The commentary of Mr. Barnes began to appear about twenty-five years ago. Until that time the commentaries of Matthew Henry and Thomas Scott were the principal Biblical helps of the mass of American readers. Adam Clarke, Matthew Poole, Doddridge and Whitby, were less frequently seen, while Hall, Mayer, Wells, Fawcett, and many other English commentators, were almost wholly unknown. Mr. Barnes' work has very largely superseded Henry and Scott, and by doing so has been, strange to say, the innocent cause of an evil ; for where Henry or Scott was taken as the family commentator, the Old Testament as well as the New was studied ; but where Barnes has entered (and by entering has excluded the others), the want of an Old Testament Commentary has led to the comparative neglect of that portion of the Bible.

The great want of such a commentary as that of Mr. Barnes was shown by its immense sale, and we may safely say that it had a large share in increasing the study and knowledge of the New Testament throughout the United States. Its author bestowed great pains upon its preparation, and has enjoyed the satisfaction of seeing the fruit of his labors.

Since Mr. Barnes wrote his commentary Biblical science has made rapid advances, the benefit of which has been reaped by Dr. Jacobus, and still more by Dr. Owen, whose work was last issued, if we except the fourth volume of Dr. Jacobus, on the Acts. Dr. Jacobus, occupying the chair of Biblical Literature in one of our most esteemed theological seminaries, is a diligent and methodical scholar. His careful system is seen in his Catechetical Question Books, where the questions of the Westminster Catechism are admirably interwoven with his own. In the volume on the Acts the same trait is shown in the clear divisions of the chronology, and, in the volumes on the Gospels, in the discriminating introduction of the Harmony.

Dr. Owen's volumes are especially distinguished for a clear and vigorous style, while his occupation for many years as a linguistic professor has given him great advantages in the independent examination of the text. A strong common sense, as distinguished from narrow bias, marks his treatment of the more contested subjects, and throughout his notes there is a manly avoidance of trite generalities.

A good instance of these characteristics is seen in his management of the question of demoniacal possession, as given in his note on Matt. iv, 24. This note forms a clear and condensed essay upon the subject. He first gives the six different significations of the Greek word δαίμων, and shows the method of its adoption into Biblical writing, corresponding to the adoption of θεός. He then combats the notion of the identity of demoniacal possession with ordinary disease, by asking "What kind of disease is that which cries out, 'What have we to do with thee, Jesus, thou Son of God? Art thou come hither to torment us (i. e. the sickness or disease) before the time'? Who ever heard of a disorder that begged permission to enter, and actually did enter, swine"? This leads the commentator to the positive exhibition of the doctrine of the possession by evil spirits, as clearly revealed in Scripture, and to the conjecture that the same activity of these spirits may be found at this day.

Another instance of Dr. Owen's clear and manly treatment of a difficult and contested passage is found in his notes on the twenty-fourth chapter of Matthew, where he shows the applicability of the whole prophecy (to verse 43) to the destruction of Jerusalem, where so many commentators have led their readers into a maze, mingling up the destruction of the city, the Adrianic overthrow, the second coming of Christ, the end of the world, and the individual man's death.

The fifteenth and sixteenth chapters of Luke's Gospel are admirably treated by Dr. Owen. The closely related parables of the lost sheep, the piece of silver, and the prodigal son are traced in their characteristic arrangement, the increased emphasis being vividly educed in the discussion, while the preliminary remarks to the chapter form a brief yet exhaustive review of the great doctrine of these inspired and beautiful teachings.

We cannot forbear from calling attention to Dr. Owen's rich exposition of our Lord's last prayer, in John xvii, especially to the portion beginning with the twentieth verse, where the commentator's heart, elevated by the glorious subject, is poured out in a strain of pious eloquence, perhaps not exceeded in any other part of his work. Indeed, his volume on John is his best (the volume on the Acts is not yet published), and well exhibits Dr. Owen's peculiar fitness for the task of a commentator.

We regard these commentaries as of vast importance to the future of our nation. They cultivate a taste for Bible reading, and define the truth in the minds of the readers. The Bible is the source of all true theology. Natural theology and rational theology are but hideous, distorted shadows (man being what he is) without the positive teachings of inspiration. Any thing which will encourage Bible reading will disseminate sound theology, and sound theology (in its wide sense) is the basis of sound morals, which form a nation's richest element of prosperity and worth. Blessed be God! the cry of our age is, "to the law and to the testimony"! Men are becoming Bereans both in Protestant and Romanist lands. The same fact is noticeable in the countries cursed by the Oriental churches, and even Islamism and Paganism are learning to doubt their Korans and Vedas, and seek the meaning of the Christian Bible. These commentaries are fanning the flame, and the result is clearly visible already, in the more general knowledge of those archæological and linguistic facts which make more easy the comprehension of the sacred page. These commentators stand as the middle men between the original explorers into texts and versions and the reading masses, while they are, as in Dr. Owen's case, original investigators to some extent themselves. They take the ore, laboriously dug from many a linguistic and archæologic mine, and as laboriously work it into beautiful and useful vessels of gold and silver for the service of a large multitude, to whom the mere ore would be comparatively useless. In America scholars are not properly equipped with apparatus for the former portion of this two-fold work, but the eminently clear discrimination and practical tact of the Anglo-Saxon scholar fits him in a remarkable manner for the latter portion, which is really the nobler and more important.

It is no reproach to American scholarship that it has not a Masoretic knowledge of facts. Manuscripts and time are plenty in Europe and scarce here, and we must be content to obtain most of our elementary material from beyond sea, where scholars admirably fitted for this primal work by teaching, habit, and opportunity, abound. But it is an honor to American scholarship that it makes most judicious use of this material, and therein takes rank behind none. A more comprehensive view and a sounder judgment render American scholarship in this, its higher plane, superior to that of our German cousins. To the enlarged grasp and correct discrimination of the American scholar we may add a rapidity of adaptation (tact) and clearness of definition, in both which he compares most favorably with the scholars of continental Europe, whose subjectivity (if we may use the word) makes them too often clumsy and obscure to the world without them.

We make these observations, because of the readiness which some have to denounce all domestic scholarship and to exalt the German cultivation to the prejudice of our own. This cant error is founded on a lack of discrimination between the very different fields in which German and American scholarship are engaged. If an American Hebraist does not happen to know that Pazer may be preceded by one, two, three, or four Munahhs in prose, but only by three conjunctives at farthest in poetry, his scholarship is called in question, although he may be of keenest discernment in the analysis of a Hebrew passage, and be thoroughly imbued with the spirit of the language. It is as if a drill sergeant should condemn a Napoleon as an ignoramus for a lack of acquaintance with the last edition of Hardee. Mint, anise, and cummin form the standard of a vast army of critics. It is for Americans themselves to live down these unjust criticisms, by refusing to join in the self-denunciatory cry of false modesty, and by refusing to worship foreign idols.

We are full of the appreciation of the immense benefit which we have received from German sources, but at the same time we recognize a vigor and independence of thought in the American mind which we would not have marred by a base acolytism. The commentaries of Jacobus and Owen are not servile. Their authors think for themselves. They do not bow down to Bengel or Olshausen, but greet them as co-laborers, as brethren in the same great work. They are as ready to differ from them as to agree with them; and, where they differ, Jacobus and Owen are quite as likely to be right as Bengel and Olshausen.

There is one phase of evangelism which is still to greet our eyes. It is when the clear vision and sound judgment of the Anglo-Saxon commentators send a current of orthodox teaching back over the mysticism and rationalism of Germany, paying back that land of laborious scholarship for its raw material of letter-criticism in the made-up goods of true and consistent doctrine. This reflux has already begun, but it is not yet distinctly apparent to the world. The semi-orthodoxy of prominent theologians in Germany to-day is much indebted to this source, but they are not yet released from the commingled muddy waters of wordiness and worldliness.

We wish that the authors to whom we have particularly referred in this article, or others equally well fitted for the work, would devote their energies to a clear and compendious commentary upon the Old Testament. We need such a sensible exposition as American scholarship could furnish, with an especial view to the development of the New Testament in the Old.   The want is largely felt, and constantly lamented. Why may we not expect this desideratum from the scholarly, laborious, and attractive pen of Dr. Owen?

Art. V.—MARK II, 23, AS COMPARED WITH MATTHEW XII, 1, AND LUKE VI, 1.

By Rev. C. C. Starbuck, Union Theol. Seminary, New York.

In our version there seems no special necessity for instituting a particular comparison of these three passages.   They all appear to state the same fact in nearly the same words. But recurring to the original we find that the words in Mark ii, 23 translated " as they went " are in the Greek ὁδὸν ποιεῖν. Had the middle voice been used ὁδὸν ποιεῖσθαι there could have been no difficulty in this translation. 'Οδὸν ποιεῖσθαι has the idiomatic sense : *iter facere* "to make *one's* way, to proceed".   But on the other hand the phrase with the active voice has a sense quite distinct.   'Οδὸν ποιεῖν signifies : " to make or break *a* way " *viam sternere*.   If the phrase in Mark then be translated according to its established signification, it would read, " and the disciples began to open a way by plucking up the ears".   Τίλλοντες of course lends itself equally well to the gerundive or to the circumstantial use.

If this rendering be given—and it rests upon the established signification of the phrase ὁδὸν ποιεῖν — an entirely new circumstance is introduced into Mark's narrative, and one not alluded to in either of the parallels, namely that of plucking up the ears "*to make a path*".   The same action, in the two other Evangelists appears only as a means of *satisfying hunger*.   Hence arises an apparent discrepancy, which commentators have endeavored to remove by transferring to ὁδὸν ποιεῖν the peculiar idiomatic force of ὁδὸν ποιεῖσθαι namely *iter facere*, " to proceed".

Now where the middle and active voices have a sense substantially the same, even classic Greek not unfrequently interchanges them.   And where the middle only differs from the active by expressing a reference to the subject with greater delicacy, the later Greek, and especially the N. T. Greek undoubtedly often neglects the distinction.   But whatever negli

39

gence of later and especially of Hellenistic use may be allowed, it is sufficiently established, since Winer's day, that the N. T. language is essentially correct Greek for all real distinctions of meaning. With the multiplying proofs of heaven-guided accuracy in N. T. style it is not to be assumed that it neglects to mark the difference between two phrases entirely distinct and opposite in sense. If repeated perusals of the New Testament have shown us any thing it is that the distinction of voices so vital to the Greek language is observed, if not with Attic delicacy, yet with classic accuracy. Finer shadings of use are often neglected but essential differences of signification such as between *iter facere* and *viam sternere,* never.

It is true De Wette thinks the one to be taken for the other in the passage before us. But as he brings no lexical authority, even the weight of his name cannot counterbalance the presumption against the confusion of two senses so opposite as "to proceed" and "to break a way". Dr. Robinson regards ὁδὸν ποιεῖν as a Hebraism translated from עָשָׂה דֶּרֶךְ and instances Judges xvii, 8. But though hesitating to question the authority of an eminent and esteemed instructor, we must say that we cannot see that he has established his point. The phrase in Judges xvii, 8, translated in the Septuagint ποιῆσαι ὁδὸν αὐτοῦ undoubtedly shows that Hellenistic Greeks have used the active where Attic Greeks would have used the middle.

But there is here only a difference of delicacy, not a difference of sense. Ποιεῖσθαι ὁδὸν is an idiomatic phrase: ποιῆσαι ὁδὸν αὐτοῦ is not. The difference may be defined thus: an ordinary phrase retains the distinct sense of its parts; an idiomatic phrase melts them together, so that the resulting signification is something different from that obtained by merely joining its words together. The one is a mechanical, the other a chemical union. Now in the phrase ποιεῖσθαι τήν ὁδὸν αὐτοῦ, as an Athenian would have translated the passage in Judges xvii, 8, the verb and the noun retain a perfectly distinct and separable force. And the independent strength of the noun is enhanced by the addition of its two attributives, one of which remains in the Septuagint. The genitive αὐτοῦ moreover defines ὁδὸν as referring to a definite journey, and removes all ambiguity. In this phrase then the verb is sufficiently disengaged from the noun to admit any change of voice that leaves the sense of the whole not materially affected. Neither ποιῆσαι ὁδὸν αὐτοῦ . nor ποιεῖσθαι ὁδὸν αὐτοῦ can possibly mean any thing else than " to accomplish his journey". The only difference is that the middle adds a reference to the subject as undertaking the journey *on his own account*, which the active does not express. The substantial sense with either voice is the same. But in the idiomatic phrase ποιεῖσθαι ὁδὸν in the sense of " to proceed " we submit that the case is different. Here the verb and the noun are, as we have said, melted together, so that the resulting sense of the whole strikes the mind without any distinct apprehension of the sense of the individual parts. The noun has here no attributives to keep it from this coalescence and the phrase may be regarded as naturally a single word. It is evident then that a change in either of the component parts is much less likely to occur than where the verb and the noun are still felt as distinct forces. The ordinary inflections of the verb would be felt as the inflections of the phrase. But a change in the voice would be felt as affecting the verb individually, and such a change we think unlikely when once a noun and a particular form of the verb have settled together in a specific use. Idioms we know remain in a language distinct and uncorrupted often longer than single words. There are idioms in our language still in use whose separate words have become obsolete while the combination has a yet living force. It appears therefore safe to assume that when the Greek language detached from the general ποιῆσαι ὁδὸν the more specific ποιεῖσθαι ὁδὸν, in the sense of " to make a progress", and afterwards, except where an attributive to the context preserved to the noun its distinctness, blended the two into an idiomatic unity with the simple sense " to proceed", that the phrase thus formed and crystallized, would remain in this settled sense as long as the language was spoken. To suppose then that Mark, had he wished to express the sense of. proceeding, would have left the idiom lying ready to his hand to revert to the active, from which that sense had long withdrawn and which, unless defined by attributives, had a sense entirely distinct, would seem rather to attribute a blunder to Mark than to give him credit for that essential accuracy which the lamented lexicographer would have been the first to accord except for the insensible influence of a supposed harmonistic difficulty.

Dr. Robinson cites however two passages from late writers in support of this supposed confusion in use between ὁδὸν ποιεῖν and ὁδὸν ποιεῖσθαι. One is from Xenophon Ephesius. On examining the passage we find that the editors of Teubner's edition have corrected it to the middle. If the active stood however it would read ἐποίουν τὴν ὁδὸν ἐς Μαζάκα. The attributives specify a particular journey. So with the other passage, cited from Polyænus ποιεῖν τὴν πορείαν. In neither of these is there an idiomatic fusion of verb and noun as in ποιεῖσθαι ὁδὸν.

Alexander in his commentary on Mark, it is true, disposes of the matter with a somewhat dictatorial confidence. But the venerated commentator can no longer assign the reasons which he has failed to produce and we may reasonably decline the decision of simple will.

It appears to us that the reasons adduced above for supposing that Mark has not confounded voices to the confusion of senses are, we do not say conclusive, but strong; and that the instances adduced of similar negligence are not really parallels. So much we think may be assumed with all deference to the supporters of the correctness of the English version of this passage, namely, that the evidence of negligence, amounting to confusion of sense on the part of Mark, is not sufficient to warrant us in departing from the first principle of sound interpretation which requires that we should assign to every word and phrase its established sense, unless required by the context or some other source of knowledge to depart from it. Let us inquire whether there is any such necessity here.

And first: in the relation of the circumstances of events we have a right to esteem Mark as more precise than the other two synoptics; than Matthew, because this Evangelist, full and orderly in his report of our Lord's discourses, is comparatively negligent of outward details. To have the essential point is enough for him. Luke, again, deriving his accounts more at second hand would naturally care less for minutely shading his narratives of events, though he is preëminent among all the four for his delicate shadings of parables and discourses.

Mark, on the other hand, the convert and ultimately the assistant of Peter (1 Pet. v, 13), whose gospel, according to the final concurrence of both rationalists and orthodox appears now to be ratified as approximately the gospel of Peter, as the early Fathers held it, has apparently derived wholly or in part from this apostle of government and order, this apostle of externals as contrasted with Paul the apostle of doctrine, and with John the apostle of contemplation, a peculiar love for the outward frame-work and setting of our Lord's activity. In his report of discourses, less sententious than Matthew, less delicate than Luke, and infinitely less copious than either, he is for his part as much before them in the subordinate, but by no means insignificant details which give to our Lord's life a distincter form for our human conceptions. In the narrative of an event he may commonly be presumed, therefore, where there is a difference, to have retained more completely its original shape and progress. Let us see if in the passage in question, as compared with its parallels, we can verify this peculiarity. It is of course understood that we assume for ὁδὸν ποιεῖν the ordinary sense of "to open a way".

Mark ii, 23. The disciples passing on the Sabbath through the standing corn begin to feel their course impeded by grain which here and there has overgrown the neglected path. They accordingly begin to remove the ears that thus choked up the way. Alexander objects that στάχυας means *ears* not *stalks*. But as the ear is all that makes the stalk of account it is certainly no very violent metonymy to take it as denoting the whole.

V. 23. This question might mean, Why do thy disciples on the Sabbath do that which is unlawful in itself? That is, Why do they by plucking up another man's grain commit a trespass, aggravated by being committed on the Sabbath? But the words more naturally mean simply, Why do they in this way break the Sabbath? A right of way through a field implies the right of removing obstructions, as the "village Hampdens" of England have often proved against wealthy landlords. And as our Lord's answer takes no notice of any such charge it is not probable it was implied.

V. 25. Our Lord himself (αὐτὸς) taking up the answer for his disciples asks the captious *micrologists*, if David their theocratic king had not on similar necessity violated the ceremonial law, not by inference but beyond doubt. What had evoked no disapprobation from God's ministers in one man ought not on similar necessity to be condemned in others. Neither the Pharisees' question nor the reference to David decides whether the original offence were rooting up the grain or eating it. If the lighter labor were unlawful much more the heavier, and the essential point of comparison between the disciples and David is not their both eating, but their both violating the ceremonial law, David unquestionably, the disciples according to Rabbinic scruples.

Referring now to Matthew, as usual fuller in reporting the discourse, if more meagre in detailing the event, we see that our Lord after meeting the Pharisees on their own ground now takes higher ground. Mat. xii, 5, 6. He refers to the temple Sabbath service, in which the priests while doing what no ordinary necessity even would excuse in others, by toiling at the sacrifices, while it would have been death for a layman to kill an ox on the Sabbath, not only did not break the law of God but fulfilled it. Even so the Son of God in calm majesty asserts for those who ministered to him a character which rendered every act of theirs performed in this high service not less sacred than the temple-worship. "But I say unto you in this place is one greater than the temple."

Mt. xii, 7. Then leaving the defensive, he in turn charges upon the Pharisees an ignorance of the very principles of God's own being, who has declared that mercy (which would have here been exemplified by a charitable indulgence to real necessities), is in this view so much above ceremonial observances that in comparison he rejects the latter, or at least rates the two as the infinite to the infinitesimal. Then leaving the ground of argument altogether he rises into the amplitude of divine authority, and declares (Mt. xii, 8) that as the Messiah (ὁ υἱὸς τοῦ ἀνθρώπου), one in counsel and working with the Father whom he represents on earth, he is the final judge of the nature and extent of the law of the Sabbath, which was made for man and for which man was not made (Mark ii, 27); which being like all outer observances intended as the flexible means of man's good and not as the inflexible object of man's worship, is subject to his good pleasure who is intrusted with the destiny of man.

We see thus that the three Evangelists harmonize admirably and supplement each other as to the essential fact and our Lord's divine deductions from it. There remains the less important inquiry, whether Mark relates precisely the same point of the event. We see no necessity for supposing it. Allowing that ὁδὸν ποιεῖν has its regular sense and τίλλοντες the naturally inferred gerundive sense, thus indicating a path made more open by pulling up encumbering grain, still nothing could be more natural than the rubbing out of more or less of the wheat and eating it. It is an almost instinctive action in such circumstances, as any one that has ever helped pick up apples in an orchard will know. Both actions being equally opposite to Pharisaic scrupulosity their question may easily have included both. Mark, true to his peculiarity, seizes the main circumstance of opening a path, the other two Evangelists the incidental circumstance of eating some of the ears thus plucked up, either act equally well suiting the question of the Pharisees, and the latter act remaining longer in the general memory from its correspondence in form as well as in principle with the first instance adduced by our Lord.

We do not see why we cannot thus secure a harmony between the three narratives, complete in the essential particular, that is, the relation of the disciples' act to what followed, impeaching the literal truth of no one of the three, and at the same time preserving to Matthew and Mark the appreciation of their respective excellencies, the latter as exact in details, the former as complete in records of discourse.

Art. V.—DRAPER'S INTELLECTUAL DEVELOPMENT OF EUROPE.

A HISTORY OF THE INTELLECTUAL DEVELOPMENT OF EUROPE. By JOHN WILLIAM DRAPER, M.D., LL.D. New York, Harper and Brothers. 1863. 8vo, pp. xii. 631.

THE subject of this work is of the highest importance, and beset with great difficulties. Any scholar who should give a complete account of the intellectual development of Europe would win a noble guerdon in the fame of the achievement. It demands a union of the highest intellectual powers, with a scholarship adequate to sweep the whole realm of literature and thought. Such a development must comprise at least an outline or summary of what has been accomplished by the human race in the way of grasping and solving the great problems of human destiny. Whatever science, art, religion, morals and politics have done or are doing for the race, is to be set forth in order. Few scholars have the encyclopedic attainments, combined with powers of analysis and generalization, adequate to master and marshal this vast accumulation of materials. Those familiar with the progress of literature are aware that the production of such a work has been the aim of the most comprehensive learning, and of the loftiest philosophical speculations, in Germany, France and England. Each recent system of philosophy has had this in view. The various, almost innumerable, productions on the history of civilization, of literature, of art and the arts, of the different branches of science, of philosophy in all its departments, and of morals and theology, are contributions to this result. And masters in the sphere of thought have endeavored to combine all these in one general view, which should exhibit the rationale and the end of human progress. The elaborate researches and speculations of Schelling and Hegel, of Comte and Buckle, and of many others, bear upon this question, attempt to solve this problem.

One of the most striking facts now, about this new work

of Dr. Draper, is, that he seems to ignore, or to be ignorant of, all that has been done by previous explorers. Ever since the time of Vico, and in every cultivated nation, there have been men of the ripest qualifications devoted to this task, and yet they are here hardly recognized even by name : Condorcet, Herder, Schlegel and Guizot, besides Schelling and Hegel, Comte and Buckle, are not mentioned in this treatise. Even Mr. Dove's work on the *Theory of Human Progression* contains a more careful scheme, better worked out, than the one here presented.

It may be said, that the scheme is new, that the theory is original, and therefore could not receive much aid or elucidation from the labors of others. But so far as we can get at the theory of Dr. Draper it seems to us, in its main drift, quite identical with that which Comte, Buckle and Mill have been elaborating for the last quarter or third of a century ; though it is not so carefully or logically stated by him as by either of these three masters of positive science. Differing from them in some points, his tendency is in the same direction. Human progress in general is confounded with progress in the so-called positive sciences. The substance of the age of reason, according to him, is an increased knowledge of the laws and forces of nature, brought into the service of man. In morals, theology and metaphysics, he sees no progress, and finds no hope for the future. In fact, all the ground of intellectual progress which seems to him to remain is in the advance of physiology. And this he indicates as the main discovery and fruit of his researches. This position is so strange, that it deserves a somewhat fuller examination. Here, too, he leaves the broad ground of other positivists, and defines and circumscribes his main object. Comte and Buckle make induction from facts subject to the senses to be the main instrument of progress, but they do not condition the advance of intellect upon any one science ; Dr. Draper finds in physiology the source, test and law of the intellectual development of Europe.

In the Preface he announces his theme : it is " a history of the progress of ideas and opinion from a point of view heretofore almost entirely neglected".   " Social advancement is as completely under the control of natural law as is bodily growth. The life of an individual is a miniature of the life of a nation. These propositions it is the special object of this book to demonstrate."   " No one, I believe, has hitherto undertaken the labor of arranging the evidence offered by the intellectual history of Europe *in accordance with physiological principles,* so as to illustrate the orderly progress of civilization, or collected the facts furnished by other branches of science with a view of enabling us to recognize clearly the conditions under which that progress takes place.   This philosophical deficiency I have endeavored in the following pages to supply."   "Seen thus *through the medium of physiology,* history presents a new aspect to us.   We gain a more just and thorough appreciation of the thoughts and motives of men in successive ages of the world."   The same general propositions are reiterated at convenient stages throughout the volume, which is in fact only an expansion of the last chapter of the author's Physiology.   How far are these views original ?   How far are they true ?

The propositions are these three : the life of the individual is completely under the control of natural laws : society, made up of individuals, is under the control of the same laws : and these laws are physiological.   Hence, physiology is the science of the sciences—all development is to be explained by it.

Is the life, now, of each individual, under the control simply and solely of natural laws ?   Is that a demonstrable proposition ?   Has Dr. Draper proved it ?   No ; he just assumes it as an axiom, as if it were incontrovertible ; and he nowhere examines or defines it more specifically.   And yet, in his own view, every thing hinges just here.   He seems to identify the whole life of the individual with his physical life.   Physical life, bodily growth, physiology, if you please, is under the control of natural law, or rather, is a part of the system of natural laws.   But is there nothing more in man to be developed than his bodily structure, his anatomical and nervous system ?   The latter may be first developed, it may be the substratum of the other developments ; but is it identical with these other developments ?   In short, has man a soul as well as a body, and a soul distinguishable from his nervous system ?   If he has, and if that is developed, and developed according to its own laws—then the whole theory of the book is null.   And the author concedes that man has a responsible, immortal soul.   This concession is fatal to his theory.   He says (p. 589), "while man agrees with inferior beings in the type of his construction, and passes in his development through transformations analogous to theirs, he differs from them all in this, that he alone possesses an accountable, immortal soul".   Further (p. 594) : " Animals remember, man alone recollects.   Every thing demonstrates that the development and completion of this instrument of intellection has been followed by the *superaddition* of an agent or principle that can use it". " From the silent chambers and winding labyrinths of the brain the veiled enchantress looks forth on the outward world, and holds the subservient body in an irresistible spell." Now if there be in man a soul distinct from the body, a soul which uses the body only as an instrument, a soul with an immortal destiny, then we say that there is no sense or reason in the position, that the whole development of man is under the dominion of bodily or physical laws. On the contrary, reason demands of us the assumption, that the soul may have its own law of growth and progress equally with the body. Physiology is not, and cannot be, all ; there is also a psychology—there is a psychological as well as a physiological development even of the individual life.

And this is still further evident as soon as we come to a closer analysis of the growth of the individual man. By what physiological laws can you explain perception, memory, imagination, logic and reason ? What analogy even is there between the processes of reasoning and any physiological processes that can be named ? A body, in this life, may be needed for all these mental operations ; but the operations are quite distinct from any of the laws of bodily growth and development. The mind does not grow in the same way that bones, flesh and nerves grow. The law of the one cannot be the law of the other. What is there in the nervous system that resembles the phenomena of consciousness—the distinction of subject and object ? Can our ideas of universal and immutable truth be derived from aught of which the senses are directly cognizant ? In sensation itself is there not an element which cannot be deduced from any properties of the nerves as a material substance ? Nay, in the very idea of natural law itself, as constant and orderly, is there not a factor, which reason alone, and not the senses, can recognize ? And when we attempt to educate and develope the soul of the individual in art, in morals, in religion, even in science, are we not obliged to resort to very different methods from those we make use of in training and unfolding his bodily powers ? Where then is the sense of saying, that the laws which control man are bodily or physical or physiological ?

This first proposition then of Dr. Draper's book is unproved, and is inconsistent with his own concessions. That it is original, we suppose neither he nor any body else would dream of asserting. It is the common place of all material-

istic philosophy.   It can be proved only as materialism is demonstrated.

The second proposition is, that society, being made up of
individuals, is under the control of the same laws with them.
Individual and social life, he tells us over and over again,
" are physiologically inseparable from one another ; the
course of communities bears an unmistakable resemblance to
the progress of an individual ; man is the archetype or exemplar of society".   " Nations like individuals are born, proceed
through a predestined growth and die.   One comes to its end
at an early period, and in an untimely way ; another, not
until it has gained maturity.   One is cut off by feebleness
in its infancy, another is destroyed by civil disease, another
commits political suicide, another lingers in old age.   But
for every one there is an orderly way of progress to its final
term, whatever that term may be" (pp. 615–16).   " The march
of individual existence shadows forth the march of race existence, being, indeed, its representative on a little scale."
" A national type pursues its way physically and intellectually through changes and developments answering to those of
the individual, and being represented by Infancy, Childhood,
Youth, Manhood, Old Age, and Death respectively" (p. 11).
And upon this general view, the author rather prides himself,
as his consummate work : " Whoever has made the physical
and intellectual history of individual man his study, will be
prepared to admit in what a surprising manner it foreshadows
social history.   *The equilibrium and movement of humanity
are altogether physiological phenomena.*   Yet not without hesitation may such an opinion be frankly avowed, since it is
offensive to the pride, and to many of the prejudices and
interests of our age" (p. 2).   This is what he calls " primor-
dial law".

It is difficult to believe, that any scholar at this day can
imagine that there is in this general scheme the slightest
degree of novelty ; or, that it helps us one jot in understanding the intellectual development of the human race.   Certainly from the time of Pascal this idea has been one of the common
places of literature.   Vico brought it out distinctly in relation to each nation, marking the stages of growth and decay.
All historians of any reflection have made use of it.   The
analogy is on the very surface of things.   You have mastered
all there is in it, just as soon as you have said to yourself that
nations and races begin to be, grow, become mature and pass
away.   This is one of the most trivial reflections which school-
boys are taught.   And the analogy with the individual life is

just as common and tells us just as little.   The analogy holds about as well of animals and plants, as it does of men : these all have a beginning, a youth, a maturity, and at last die.   A fact common to botany, zoology and history, can hardly be a very special fact in history, or tell us much about its laws and order.

How much does it tell us ?   Only what nobody ever doubted, or ever could doubt : that all that exists in this world, in space and time, has had and will have a beginning, a growing and an ending, in the individual form in which it is here manifested.   And when we have learned that, what have we learned about the specific nature, characteristics and growth of that which thus appears and thus passes away ?   Why, just nothing at all.   We have still to find out all that from a study of the objects themselves in their interior structure.   The analogy does not help us here at all.   What the plant is, what the animal is, what man is, what society is—what are the laws and developments of each and all these—we are still to discover from a particular examination of each by itself.   The analogy is then, just good for nothing, as a help in the most important part of our investigation.

Is human society, as a whole, under the same laws as the individual, and under no other?   How can we answer this question ?   Manifestly only by studying society itself, as developed in different times, races and nations, and seeing whether there is that in the whole which is not in the parts ; or, rather, whether any thing is developed in the social state, in nations, in races, which could not, and would not, be developed by the individual alone.   Society may come and go like individuals ; but in coming and going it may unfold powers, capacities, and ends which the individual alone could never attain unto.   All men may be alike in living, growing, and dying ; but that does not prevent one man's history from being a very different sort of development from that of another. Society may live, grow, and die like the individual ; but then its development may have resulted in something more than can be comprised in this abstract formula for transient existence in time and space. This physiological law, protruded with such parade of science, as the culmination of thought, is in fact one of the most barren schedules of human progress that can well be excogitated.

Society is indeed made up of individuals, but there is that developed in the combination which could not be developed in the parts.   Even chemistry might teach us that atoms combined produce entirely different results from what they ever would, or could, in their isolation.   Doubtless there is that in each atom which fits it for such combination; but yet the combined result is a new and different product.   Still more must this be the case when the elements brought together are human souls, with all their boundless capacities and infinite possibilities of union, conflict and adjustment.   The result must be such as we can find no strict analogy for in the individual life.   Even in the narrow sphere of the family, in its relations of parents and children, brothers and sisters, there is an unfolding of the moral nature and of the affections, of the principles of love and duty, such as the merely individual life cannot attain unto. And in the ordering of human society, in its government, laws, and institutions, in the progress of art, science, and religion, and in the aims which every great nation has in view, there are principles, means, and ends involved, which far surpass any possible analogies drawn from the individual life, and still more from physiology.   And when we come to the vast and unfolding drama of human history, as this has been developed in the successive races and nations that have led the march in this grand and solemn procession, there are, and must be, principles, aims, and ends that will forever elude the grasp of him who tries to hamper and contract our vision by crude formulas about "physiological laws".   Schelling has well said that "There can only be a history of such beings as have before them an ideal which can never be realized by the individual alone, but only by the race as a whole".

The analogy between individual and social life also fails in another aspect.   All individuals die; nations rise and fall; but individuals and nations are not all that we have to consider in history.   There are also the different races, and there is also the race as a whole.   The races of men do not die out, as do the separate nations.   With few exceptions, they reappear under other national forms, and perpetuate their life from age to age.   And the human race, as a whole, has had, and must have, a continuous being until the great end of its creation and historic growth is reached.   Now, it is just with this progress of the race as a whole that the philosophy of history and the law of its development have to do; and it is just here that the analogy with the individual life cannot be carried out. There is as yet no decay, but rather progress, of the race as a whole.   And this there must be if we can have any general scheme of human history.   And even when particular nations lose their geographical boundaries and limits, and are said to die out, this is true only in a very partial and limited sense. Their descendants mingle with, and help to make, other nations. Their laws, literature, arts, and science survive, and become the property of other generations. And there is thus a continuous life of the human race, which abides in the midst of all the changes of the individuals. What is natural and physical decays; what is moral and spiritual survives, and shapes the future.

This analogy, then, between the individual and social life, and the attempt to explain all history by such an analogy, must be barren and fruitless. It can only issue in eliminating from the life of the race its most essential and important developments and ends. It narrows our view of man's whole historic career. It is difficult to reconcile with the view that Providence is educating the race for moral ends, by means of a moral government, and that the physical is subordinate and subservient to the moral. In fact, as we shall see, the author excludes the moral element from his theory of the progress of the race.

The third proposition of Dr. Draper's theory is, that individual and social life is under the control of physiological laws. History is to be read by the light of physiology. The history of "the intellectual development of Europe", it is claimed, is here written for the first time "in accordance with physiological principles". "The equilibrium and movement of humanity are altogether physiological phenomena." To show this is the main object, that it is shown is the grand pretension, of the volume. The author has written a work of physiology of considerable repute; and this is the complement of that work, treating of man in his social relations, in the light of physiological principles. This claim struck us as so unique that we have examined the volume with special care, in the hope of finding some light cast upon the bewilderment into which we must confess the project cast us. We could not at all understand what the writer meant, and we have searched for explanation and evidence. But our investigations have been utterly fruitless. After reading the volume, its arguments, its summaries, we are still as much in the dark as ever. It will scarcely be credited, yet it is still a fact, that there is not in the whole work any attempt to explain what is meant by applying physiology to history; there is no enumeration of the "physiological principles" by which history is to be elucidated; there is no proof, and no attempt to prove, at any point or juncture of the historic series, that the development has been of a physiological sort. And, upon reflection, we think we can see a reason for this; and that is, that it could not possibly be proved; that there is no way by which it can be shown, and that there are no facts to show, that history is a branch of physiology—that historical laws and physiological laws are identical. In the first place, the author has not proved this thesis; in the second place, he could not if he tried; in the third place, if he did, it would lead to a variety of absurdities.

He has nowhere, we say, proved his prime position—that history moves according to physiological laws. The only appearance of an attempt at this is found in a few passages, in which he repeats over the formula about Infancy, Childhood, Youth, Manhood, Old Age, and Death, as applicable to societies and nations as well as individuals; and, as if parallel with this, the division of the progress of Greece and Europe into periods of Inquiry, of Faith, and of Reason. But the analogy here is of the slightest. Infancy may be credulous, childhood inquiring, youth believing, manhood rational. But are the laws by which childhood is led to inquire, or youth to believe, the same with the laws by which the body of the child is made and the physiology of youth is developed? The physical transition from youth to manhood is in accordance with certain well-known physiological laws regulating the growth of the body. Now, is it these same laws, and no other, which regulate the transition in a nation from the age of faith to the age of reason? Is there any thing in the age of faith which resembles the structure and laws of the human body when that body is in its youth? Is there any thing in the age of reason which resembles the structure, functions, and growth of the human body when it is about forty or fifty years old? Is reason developed out of faith by the same process by which a man of forty-five is developed out of a man of thirty-five years of age? Physiology, as Dr. Draper treats it, in his manual on that science, is "a branch of natural philosophy", and is divided into two parts—"statical physiology", containing "the conditions of equilibrium of an organized form", and "dynamical physiology", or the "development" of the organized form, its "course of life". Until history can be resolved into some definite organized form, with members and functions physically connected, it can never be shown that it is only "a chapter in physiology". As soon as it is attempted to make the analogy strict and scientific, it evaporates into a fancy.

Not only does the author thus neglect the proof of his cardinal position, but, we add, he could not possibly prove it if he tried to do so. No human ingenuity is sufficient to show that history is controlled by physiological laws. All that there is in it is the simple fact that the human beings who go to make up history are in part animals, and, so far forth, each one of them is under the laws of physiology. But that the historic laws are the same with the physiological laws which shape their bodies, is a very different sort of a proposition. Take, for example, any of the main interests of society on whose progress the welfare of the body politic is conditioned, and try to find out the amount of physiology which is contained in it. There are in history, says the author, "five intellectual manifestations to which we may resort—philosophy, science, literature, religion, government". Now, what physiological principles are illustrated and exemplified in the progress of mankind in any one of these higher intellectual manifestations? The growth of philosophy, for instance, is conditioned upon the discovery and organization of ideas and truth. What physiological law is illustrated by the processes of induction and deduction, which are necessary to the unfolding of truth? What is there akin even to the inductive formula in any of the laws by which the nervous system is fashioned and grows? What physiological law is exemplified in those intuitions by which we recognize, and rest in, ultimate and universal truths? Do we pass from the premises to the inference in a logical argument in the same way in which digestion is carried forward in the bodily system? The subjects compared are manifestly so disparate that we cannot conceive of even a fugitive analogy, much less of an identity, between them. So, too, it is with literature, religion, and government. The fundamental ideas in each are entirely different from the fundamental idea of physiology, and consequently the laws of their growth or development must be different. The idea of animal life is the germinant idea of physiology; the idea of God is the essential idea of religion; the idea of justice is the controlling idea of government; and until it can be shown that animal life, God, and justice are all identical, it cannot be shown that physiological laws control the progress of religion and of government.

And this also in part establishes our third remark upon this remarkable scheme, that is, if it were proved that physiological laws are the same as the laws of history, we should be landed in a variety of absurdities. One absurdity is this—that physiology is the queen of the sciences; that all art, ethics, politics, and religion are but branches of the science of animal life. For if physiological laws make and control all historical developments, then whatever appears in history is but an efflux of this stream of animal life. We should have to reform all our processes of education, and all our theories in art and morals, to say nothing of religion. The central idea of philosophy would henceforth have to be that of the growth of a physical germ.   Instead of discoursing of the laws of beauty, we must talk about the physiology thereof; instead of enforcing the moral law we must enjoin obedience to physical law; instead of commending religious duties to the conscience we must insist upon our physiological duties.   The category of physical development must displace that of an immutable rectitude.   And how would the other sciences fare in the light of such a theory?   Can they, too, be reduced to physiology? Might they not also set up equally good claims to such universality?   Why not just as well attempt to explain all history on chemical, or astronomical, or mathematical principles, as on physiological?   We recommend the attempt to the experts in these sciences, not doubting that they can show as many and as good reasons in their favor, as this volume adduces in support of its physiological hypothesis about the intellectual development of Europe.

Such are the main propositions of this volume, so far as it lays claim to originality; and we have dwelt upon them more fully because they fall in with some tendencies of the times which the author may not wish to favor, but which such vague and unscientific treatment of the most momentous theories surely encourages.   There may be in some religious thinkers what scientific men call cant and prejudice; but there is also among some of the devotees of science a flippancy in talking about moral and religious truth which is far more detrimental to the best and highest interests of man.   Religious convictions have a strong background in the nature and necessity of religion itself.   Religious truth is vital; scientific truth is valuable.   Science will vindicate itself; the tendencies of the times, the progress of investigation, favor it.   We have no quarrel with it, and no fear of it, in its proper sphere.   But yet it must learn and know its own metes and bounds, and not obtrude its partial principles into other and different spheres. Just as soon as it takes up the assumption that natural science is all in all, that induction is the only road to truth, that all history and progress are conditioned by physical laws, and these alone, just so soon it arrays, and must array, against its pretensions, not only the religious convictions and belief of the race, but also the prescripts of the moral sense, and likewise that instinctive belief in the reality of spiritual truth, which has led the greatest thinkers of every age to elaborate systems of metaphysics.   We are far from classing Dr. Draper with those sceptical materialists who deny moral truth, the immortality of the soul, the being and government of God, and the beneficence of the Christian faith.   There are incidental statements

40

scattered through his work which imply that he holds to these. But yet the undoubted drift of his theory is to encourage those speculations which run in a different direction, and enthrone physical laws as supreme. His better nature may here be inconsistent with his philosophy; but it is with his philosophy that we have to do in criticising his labors.

And there are several points in which this tendency is manifest, besides the main theories on which we have already commented. One is in expressly subordinating the moral to the intellectual, denying in fact the reality of a proper moral development of the race. A kindred error, involved in this, is, that he makes intellectual development, especially in the domain of the natural sciences, to be the aim and issue of the whole historic course. He also casts contempt upon all metaphysics, properly so called, taking the position, that metaphysics is to be fashioned and reformed by physiology.

As to the subordination of the moral element in human progress, the broad ground assumed is, " that the aim of Nature is not at moral, but intellectual development". " The intellectual has always led the way in social advancement, the moral having been subordinate thereto. The former has been the mainspring of movement, the latter passively affected. It is a mistake to make the progress of society depend on that which is itself controlled by a higher power. In the earlier and inferior stages of individual life we may govern through the moral alone. In that way we may guide children, but it is to the understanding of the adult that we must appeal " (p. 591). What the author means by ' moral ' and what by ' intellectual ' it is somewhat difficult to say, for he nowhere defines the terms; but taking them in their ordinary sense, we have here the theory of Comte, Buckle and the positivists expressed in an unqualified way. How a believer in God and a divine government, and in man's immortal destiny, can advocate such a view we cannot conceive. Morality, from its very nature, sets before us as our ideal the great end of human life — a life of love to God and love to man, of justice, truth and righteousness. The objects for which states labor, in their highest functions and aims, are essentially moral objects. Unless intellectual and scientific progress contribute to the development of human rights and the establishment of justice, freedom and civil equality, they fail of their best end, and may only entail evil upon society. In constructing a scheme of human life and of human society, the intellectual must subserve the moral, for the moral includes the great and permanent interests of mankind. Still more emphatically is this the case, when we turn from human to divine government and laws. By the consent of the conscience and reason of the race, God is essentially good and holy; and to diffuse goodness and establish righteousness is the great end of creation. Nobody can believe that God's chief end for man is to develop his intellect. Even Plato taught that to escape evil we must be like God, and that to be like God we must be righteous. God's government of his rational creatures is essentially a moral government; and as soon as we doubt or deny this there remains for us no God to love, worship and obey, but only some blind force or unconscious and impersonal reason. Only materialism or pantheism can consistently subordinate moral to natural or intellectual ends. It is indeed true that there is not in human history such a development of new moral principles, as there is of new scientific facts and laws: but this rather attests the glory of moral truth, and proves the real dignity and worth of human nature. New moral truths are not discovered, any more than new intuitive truths are discovered; for these prime principles are the original endowment of man as a moral and rational being. But there are as conspicuous and new applications and developments of moral truth in the progress of society, as there are of scientific and of intellectual truth. The truths are unchangeable in their nature and evidence, but ever varying in their applications to human society and life. Human rights, justice among men, forms of government, the principles of benevolence and charity — are not these advancing in their application to society as the race advances? Is not here very much of the real progress of the race to be found? Dr. Draper tells us that moral motives are for "inferior stages" of culture, for children and youth. But what kind of a culture is that which leads a person to put the moral virtues, such as justice and love, below intellectual attainments? In spite of the positivists we must still hold, that a man may know all chemistry, geology and even physiology, and yet if he have not charity he is nothing. The fallacy here seems to consist in this, that because science brings to light some new facts and principles, and morals remain immutable in their nature and obligations, therefore there is progress in science and none in morals. But in the development and application of moral truth there may be as conspicuous progress in human society, as there is in the growth of the knowledge of physical laws. Bishop Butler might still give a few useful hints even to men of science: "Knowledge is not our proper happiness. . . . Men of deep research and curious inquiry should just be put in mind not to mistake what they are doing.   If their discoveries serve the cause of virtue and religion in the way of proof, motive to practice, or assistance in it, or if they tend to render life less unhappy and promote its satisfactions, then they are most usefully employed ; but, bringing things to light, alone and of itself, is of no manner of use any otherwise than as an entertainment or diversion". (Butler's Works. Sermon xv.)

Kindred with this theory, is that which makes intellectual development, especially in the domain of science, to be the aim and issue of man's historic career. The refutation of the above scheme in fact includes the refutation of this.   We do not doubt that the physical sciences are to advance and prosper, and contribute to the well-being of mankind.   We welcome every addition to this stock of human knowledge, and neither contemn nor fear its progress.   Natural philosophers are aiding in the great work of giving man dominion over nature.   But to make such conquest of nature the great end of the race is to restrict our view of man to his earthly and temporal condition — to cut him off from God and immortality.   Dr. Draper makes "the improvement and organization of national intellect" to be the aim of the social progress of great communities, and chiefly through and by the advance of science. This he insists upon in the last chapter of his work, in a curious and artificial comparison of Chinese with European civilization, as if these were the two great types.   There is a double error here : one, that of making intellectual development the main thing ; another, that of confounding intellectual progress with the growth of physical researches.   Of the former we have perhaps said enough.   As to the latter, it shows in a striking way, how a proficient in one branch of investigation is inclined to assign to it an undue prominence. The author's whole argument runs into the conclusion, that the age of reason is identical with the age in which the positive sciences are most fully developed — that reason is unfolded fully and consciously only or chiefly through the progress of physical discovery.   That some intellectual faculties are fostered and developed by the study of the natural sciences is indisputable.   But the intellect of man has a wide scope. It includes the art of reasoning ; but we do not always find our most expert logicians among the geologists and physiologists.   It embraces imagination also : but our highest poets are not necessarily deep in anatomy.   Intellect, too, should be conversant with ultimate truths ; yet we cannot say that the natural sciences directly contribute to elucidate such truths.

The highest effort of the intellect must be in the attempt to construct a complete system of truth, to organize the realm of ideas in one scheme.   Of that scheme, the natural sciences may give an important part, but yet not the most important. To reduce all reason and intellect to the attempt at understanding physical law alone is to degrade and not ennoble human nature.   Such a reason would not be reason in any recognized or intelligible use of the term.

In harmony with this theory is Dr. Draper's contempt of metaphysics, and his strange assumption, that future metaphysical systems are to be written on physiological principles alone.   In giving his sketch of the Greek culture he introduces a superficial account of the Greek philosophy, evidently drawn from second-rate sources.   But in his whole narration about European civilization, he totally ignores its mental, moral and metaphysical sciences.   A man who can write a history of " the intellectual development of Europe", and say nothing of the systems of Descartes, Malebranche, and Spinoza, pass over Leibnitz and Kant with a word or two, utterly neglect Fichte, Schelling and Hegel, not refer to Cousin, and pass by in silence Reid, Stewart, Mill and Hamilton, must have a very singular notion of the task he has set before himself.   In fact, the last part of his work is really not much more than a sketch of the progress of the natural sciences. He says himself, " the reader has doubtless remarked that, in the historical sketch of the later progress of Europe given in this book, I have not referred to metaphysics, or psychology or mental philosophy. . . . It is only through the physical that the metaphysical can be discovered".   This deficiency, if there were no other, stamps the volume as really worthless in respect to its professed object.   For the intellectual history of Europe is in great part summed up in its psychologies and metaphysics.   The author might just as well write a physiology without alluding to the circulation of the blood, or a botany without allusion to sap.   It would be no more of a blunder.   And from the specimens he has given us of his knowledge and acumen about metaphysical systems, we are inclined to think that there is some reason for this silence. He does not know or understand these great speculative attempts of modern thought.   He is not able to grapple with the subjects which they present.   Thus his account of Kant is all a mistake.   He ascribes to him the view (p. 172) " that there is but one source of knowledge, the union of the object and the subject — *but two elements thereof*, space and time". This is an inexcusable blunder.   So, too, in his speculations

on the criterion of truth, he comes to the conclusion, " that in
the unanimous consent of the entire human race lies the human criterion of truth". What a valuable criterion! With
all deference to the author's scientific knowledge, we must say
that he is not the man, qualified by either his attainments or
his grasp, to pass sentence on the works of the great thinkers
of modern Europe, to scoff at metaphysics, or proclaim the decrepitude of theology.

He intimates, indeed, that metaphysics is to be reformed by
physiology. This crops out in several passages. But the
idea is not further developed. We wish he would undertake
the task. We should like to see the result. Metaphysics on
physiological principles would certainly be a novelty. Metaphysics is the science of truth and being : physiology is the
science of natural organisms. Has the author any idea of
what he means when he says, that all truth, all ideas, the
philosophy of being, can be evolved from physiology, and developed on strictly physiological principles? We should just
as soon think of developing the moral law from geology, or
constructing the science of government by means of botanical
principles.

There are some other incidental points in this work which
we had intended to comment upon, but we can only make a
passing reference to them. His judgment on Lord Bacon is
absurdly unjust, describing him as " a pretender in science, a
time-serving politician, an insidious lawyer, a corrupt judge,
a bad man". His judgment on the Baron of Verulam may
perchance react on himself, that "with the audacity of ignorance, he presumed to criticise what he did not understand".
Of Milton's Paradise Lost, we are told, that, " a Manichean
composition in reality, it was mistaken for a Christian poem".
His account of the early Christian controversies, the Athana-
sian and Augustinian, is loose and incomplete — giving the
mere surface of the matter; as is the case too with his allusions to the scholastic theology, and the central question of
nominalism and realism. He repeatedly discredits miraculous
interventions. His sketches of early Christian and mediæval
history do not betray any acquaintance with the latest and
best literature of the subject. He talks of the " grim orthodox productions of the wearisome and ignorant fathers of the
church". His estimate of the value and power of the Mohammedan influence is greatly exaggerated. It is only in the
account of the progress of the natural sciences, and in some
of his speculations, analogies and groupings in this department, that the volume can be considered as having added to

our stock of knowledge, or can be recommended for use.   In its main theory and aim it is a mistake and a failure, and in some of its principles it favors pernicious tendencies.

Theology and metaphysics have interests to guard, as sacred, to say the least, as those of the positive sciences.   Both these high branches of thought have their own history, their fitting methods, their proper domain.   Science also has its rightful sphere, its appropriate methods, its legitimate principles and results.   It is to study and interpret nature.   Let it do its work well and thoroughly.   But it has no right to impose its processes and principles upon the spiritual world.   Spirit cannot be explained by matter, nor the laws of spirit by the laws of matter.   Physiology is excellent and useful in its place : but it is not ethics, it is not metaphysics, it is not theology — nor does it give the law even to history.   History includes it, but it includes a vast deal more, the development of man's whole nature, under a divine guidance, towards the highest moral and spiritual ends.   And this development and these ends are to be explained, if at all, not on physiological, but on moral and spiritual principles.   Providence, and not natural law controls the course of history and determines the destiny of the race.

Art. VI.—THE CHINESE CLASSICS.

By Prof. Roswell D. Hitchcock, D.D., New York.

The Chinese Classics : with a *Translation, Critical and Exegetical Notes, Prolegomena, and Copious Indexes.*   By James Legge, D.D., of the London Missionary Society.   In seven volumes.   Vol. I. containing *Confucian Analects,* the *Great Learning,* and the *Doctrine of the Mean.*   Vol. II. containing the *Works of Mencius.*   Hong Kong and London.   1861.   8vo.   Pp. 376, 497.

By the kindness of the Rev. Dr. Cox, a friend and correspondent of Dr. Legge, we have been permitted to examine these most interesting and important volumes.   The author went as a missionary to the East in 1839, having previously bestowed some months of study upon the Chinese language, which he appears since then to have thoroughly mastered.   He no sooner found himself face to face with the civilization of the Middle Kingdom than he felt the necessity of investigating for himself " the whole field of thought through which the sages of China had ranged, and in which were to be found the foundations of the moral, social, and political life of the people". But of the several translations which had from time to time been made from the writings of Confucius into the Latin, French, and English languages, not one seemed 'to him sufficiently critical and exact to answer his purpose. He therefore resolved at once upon the gigantic task of translating the entire collection of the Chinese Classics, to be published with the original text and annotations upon it, so that nothing might be wanting to occidental scholars in order to a full acquaintance with the whole Confucian system. Twenty years of diligent study have at length borne their first fruits in these two stout octavos which are now before us. A richer contribution to science, more sure of bringing solid and lasting fame to the author of it, has not been made for a long time. The Chinese, who have been called "the Yankees of the Orient", are at once an ancient and a modern people, constituting full a third part of the present population of the globe, with a history and a literature, and with deeply ingrained characteristics, which render their conversion to Christianity one of the most perplexing and stubborn problems of our age. This great work of Dr. Legge, when completed, will be accepted as the most important contribution yet made towards, first the appreciation, and, finally, the solution of this problem.

The Chinese Classics, which are to that utilitarian people what our Bible is to us, consist of nine books: " The five *King*", and " The four *Shoo* ". " The five King ", or canonical books, are: The *Yih*, or "Book of Changes"; the *Shoo*, or "Book of History"; the *She*, or "Book of Poetry"; the *Le Ke*, or "Book of Rites"; and the *Ch'un Ts'ew*, or "Spring and Autumn", a chronicle of events from 721 to 480 B.C. These have all been ascribed to Confucius; but only the last-named is wholly his, the fourth but in part, while to the first he added only appendices, and had no hand at all in the second and third.

" The four *Shoo*", or " Books ", are: The *Lun Yu*, or "Analects of Confucius ", made up chiefly of the sayings of the sage; the *Ta Hĕŏ*, or " Great Learning " by Tsăng Sin, a disciple of Confucius; the *Chung Yung*, or " Doctrine of the Mean ", ascribed to K'ung Keih, the grandson of Confucius; and the " Works of Mencius ", who lived between 371–288 B.C.

These four *Shoo* in the original Chinese, with an underlying translation abundantly and carefully annotated, prefaced by all the historical and critical apparatus required in order to an understanding of the Books themselves, occupy the two volumes now published. Of the first volume, 136 pages are devoted to the Prolegomena, 218 pages to the "Analects", 27 pages to the "Great Learning", and 52 pages to the "Doctrine of the Mean", to the whole of which are appended seven indexes, occupying 79 pages. The second volume is devoted to Mencius, whose works in seven books occupy 378 pages, leaving 246 pages for the Prolegomena and Indexes. From this statement it will be seen that less than half the matter contained in the four *Shoo* belongs to Confucius and his disciples, and that nearly three fourths of this Confucian part of the collection are embraced in the "Analects". Nor will "The five *King*", promised by Dr. Legge in at least eight more volumes, give us any great additional amount of matter from Confucius himself. The "Analects" must accordingly stand as our chief witness on all points pertaining to the Confucian system.

In the Prolegomena to the first volume Dr. Legge has given us a biography of Confucius, which claims to be more correct than any which has yet appeared in any European language. He was born 551 B.C., in the north-east part of China, in the State Loo, within the present province of Shan-tung, where also, after a life of much wandering and many sorrows, he died 478 B.C., at the age of seventy-three.* China was then in its feudal state, composed of thirteen principalities, in many respects independent of each other, with a large number of smaller dependencies; the central imperial sovereignty, as in Europe during the Middle Ages, being hardly more than nominal. The family to which Confucius belonged was of high rank, but at the time of his birth was reduced to poverty. At the age of twenty-one he set himself up as a teacher and reformer. For about twenty years of his life, at different times, he was wandering from province to province, striving to secure the application of his principles to the affairs of state. Several times he was in office, and accomplished important reforms. From 515 to 501 B.C., and again from 483 to 478 B.C., when he died, he resided without office in his native province, devoting himself to study and teaching. On the whole, his career was one of hardship, disappointment, and defeat. He had, indeed, many disciples, at one time, it is said, as many as three thousand; but he died under a cloud, complaining that, "of all the princes of the Empire, not one would adopt his principles and obey his lessons". But no sooner had he died than his name began to receive that reverence which finally culminated in worship. At first he was worshipped only in his native province of Loo, but in 57 A.D. it was enacted that sacrifices

---

* The dates commonly given are 552 and 479 B.C.

should be offered to him throughout the Empire; and since 628 A.D. the custom of erecting temples to him has prevailed. In every city of the Empire, down to those of the third order, there is now a temple to Confucius.*

There are three religions in China: the mystic Rationalism of *Taou*, who was born about fifty years before Confucius; Buddhism, which was imported from India in 65 A.D.; and Confucianism. The first two are tolerated by the Government, and embrace, no doubt, a decided majority of the people; but Confucianism is the State religion, and determines the character of the Chinese civilization. There is but one path to public office, of whatever grade, and that lies through the schools and colleges of the Empire, whose only text-books are these nine classics, which Dr. Legge is now translating. To understand China, therefore, one must master the system of Confucius, as embodied in these works.

As to the classes of persons to be benefited by these editorial labors of Dr. Legge, foremost of all stand, of course, the managers and patrons of Christian missions, and especially the candidates for missionary service, amongst the Chinese. Hereafter they may go less blindly to their work, having gauged intelligently both the strength and the weakness of the system to be encountered. The Christian apologist is also helped. Of late the most formidable attacks on Christianity have been directed against it not as absurd or worthless, but only against its lofty assumption of absolute and exclusive authority. As *a* religion it is praised, but denied to be *the* religion of the race. Permission is given it to take its place amongst other religions of the world, all of them more or less worthy of acceptance; but it can have no throne of undivided dominion. The man of Nazareth may continue to have his disciples; but so also may Zoroaster, Sakyamuni, Confucius, Socrates, and Mohammed. Thus, instead of striking Christianity down in the open field, the plan now is to smother it in a new Pantheon, steaming with incense to all the gods. Hence, in certain quarters, a greatly increased enthusiasm in regard to the lives and teachings of the heathen sages. Hence, also, in the interest of this new eclecticism, an immense exaggeration of the merits of these sages. Something has even been said of a new gospel, to be culled from the teachings of these men, which shall rival the Gospel of Christendom. To meet and frustrate this changed strategy of our adversaries, we must explore thoroughly for ourselves the sources from which this new gospel is threatened

* See Davis's China, 2 : 6.

to come. So far as concerns Confucius and his system, Dr. Legge, if his life and strength are spared, will leave us nothing to be desired. Meanwhile, it may be well to call the attention of Christian scholars to those more important points, which have already been brought out with refreshing distinctness.

And, first of all, it is clear that Confucius cannot justly be called a great philosopher, nor can he be regarded even as a great man. The Chinese brain, as indeed the brain of the whole Mongolian race, is not speculative, but intensely materialistic and utilitarian. And Confucius, as Dr. Legge says, "was a Chinese of the Chinese". On no subject whatever, whether in physics or in metaphysics, did he speculate. He never concerned himself about either the origin or the end of things. He had no theory of creation. About man even, he never inquired either whence he came, or whither he was going. He not only added nothing to philosophy; he did not even pursue it as a study. Indeed, there was no philosophy in China to be studied; and all he aimed at was the revival of certain ancient traditions of his race. What those traditions were, how meagre, cold and formal, we shall notice presently.

Nor can Confucianism be looked upon as a religion. Doubtless there was then in China, handed down from the earliest times, a worship of God, as well as of departed ancestors; but Confucius put no emphasis upon it. The personal name of God, *Te* or *Shang Te*, in use before his time, Confucius nowhere employs, but always the word "Heaven" instead. If no atheist himself, as probably he was not, certainly he so ignored religion in his teachings as to prepare the way for the atheism which has, since his day, gained so strong a foothold in China. In regard even to the continued conscious existence of human spirits after the death of the body, he refused to speak explicitly. When inquired of once, whether the dead have knowledge of the worship rendered them, his answer was: " If I were to say that the dead have such knowledge, I am afraid that filial sons and dutiful grandsons would injure their substance in paying the last offices to the departed; and if I were to say that the dead have not such knowledge, I am afraid lest unfilial sons should leave their parents unburied. You need not wish to know whether the dead have such knowledge or not. There is no present urgency about the point. Hereafter you will know it for yourself." Not that he would do away with this worship of ancestors, which had been practised for centuries; he commended it rather as " an institution to be devoutly observed". But his faith had no fervor in it. Of religious feeling in any direction, he gave no sign. Spiritual things had no charm for him, no power over him. In the "Analects" [6 : 20], when asked, "What constitutes wisdom?" he replied: "To give one's self earnestly to the duties due to men, and while *respecting* spiritual beings, *to keep aloof from them*, may be called wisdom". His own departure out of life was one of the most melancholy on record. He died apparently without one thought about his future, without consolation, and without hope. Some days before the event he was heard singing to himself:

> "The great mountain must crumble;
> The strong beam must break;
> And the wise man wither away like a plant."

Constitutionally unreligious himself, like the race to which he belonged, he passed away without leaving behind him one new impulse to faith, one new aspiration after God, one new hope for eternity. The system has proved too cold and barren even for China. Hence the imperial embassy during the first century of our era in quest of a new system, resulting in the introduction of Buddhism, whose adherents now outnumber the disciples of Confucius.

And this leads us to remark, in the third place, that the Confucian system is only ethical, and poor at that, concerning itself much more with manners than with morals. The rules of propriety are far more prominent than the rule of right. Artistically elaborate and painful ceremony constitutes no small proportion of the lessons taught. But there are still graver defects. The proverbial deceitfulness of the Chinese people is not without its warrant in the example of the sage. It is written of him, without rebuke, that he once deliberately broke a solemn oath on the ground that it was extorted from him. Once, according to the "Analects" [17 : 20], he feigned sickness in order to avoid an unwelcome visitor. "Joo Pei wished to see Confucius, but Confucius declined, on the ground of being sick, to see him. When the bearer of this message went out at the door, he took his harpsicord and sang to it that Pei might hear him." And yet he praises sincerity and truthfulness. The *lex talionis* is also laid down in the writings of Confucius in the strongest terms and in its greatest extent. When asked, "What course is to be pursued in the case of the murder of a father or mother?" Confucius replied: "The son must sleep upon a matting of grass, with his shield for his pillow; he must decline to take office; he must not live under the same heaven with the slayer. When he meets him in the market-place or the court, he must have his weapon ready to strike him". This bad lesson of the sage has not been lost upon his countrymen. The Chinese are noted as a revengeful people. With all their submissiveness to government, they are ever prompt to take the law into their own hands, and so whole districts are often distracted by private feuds. There are seven grounds of divorce in China, among which are ill temper, thieving, and *talkativeness*. That Confucius put away his own wife, as alleged, in order to have more time for study, Dr. Legge thinks has not been proved.

Man, according to Confucius, is *naturally* virtuous. His vices come chiefly of ignorance and bad example. What he needs, therefore, is not Divine assistance of any sort, but only a good teacher and pattern of virtue. The duties of universal obligation are determined by the five relationships of life : between sovereign and minister, between father and son, between husband and wife, between elder brother and younger, and between friend and friend. These duties, Confucius said, had been best taught and best observed by "the ancients". His ethical injunctions assumed accordingly the form of traditional precepts. Humanity at large was ignored in his system. He knew no world outside of China. He labored for nothing but Chinese virtue on the basis of Chinese example and precedent. The best feature of the system is the emphasis which it puts upon personal character. If a sovereign would have wise and good subjects, he must first be wise and good himself: then his ministers and subjects will also be wise and good. So in the family, a wise and good father will have a wise and good son. In treating of husband and wives, however, the duty most insisted upon is that of the submission and obedience of the wife to the husband. Nor is the relation between parents and children so much that of mutual affection, as of dignified and stately authority on the one side, and distant reverence and fear on the other. In short, formality and coldness characterize the whole system from beginning to end. There is no tender regard for womanhood, and no place for the sweeter charities of life. The eulogists of Confucius have indeed boasted, that he gave utterance to the Golden Rule of doing to others as we would that others should do to us. This is a mistake. The famous maxim of Confucius, which occurs twice in the "Analects", is altogether negative in its character, not enjoining beneficence, as does the Golden Rule of our Saviour, but only forbidding injury. In the "Analects" 15 : 23 it is written: "Is there one word which may serve as a rule of practice for all one's life ?" And Confucius answered : "Is not *reciprocity* such a word? What you do not want done to yourself, do not

do to others." When asked what was to be thought of the
principle that injury should be recompensed with kindness, he
replied: "With what then will you recompense kindness?
Recompense injury with justice, and recompense kindness
with kindness". ["Analects" 14 : 36.]

That Confucius has accomplished much for China, is not to
be disputed. The zeal with which he insisted upon personal
culture, even though that culture contemplated so exclusively
the mere proprieties of life, has not been without its fruits in
the lives of the people. But his tone was cold, and his range
was narrow. His final aim was the state. And his theory
was, let the individual be first reformed, then the family, then
the province, and then the empire. He looked no farther out
than China, no higher up than the ground. No mere moralist
ever had so large an audience as Confucius has had for these
twenty-three hundred years in China. And the result is, these
two national virtues most remarkably developed: submission
to government, and obedience to parents. It is to these virtues that the nation is indebted for its marvellous longevity.
So much has Christianity to build upon, but it has no more.
It has to confront in China a race of men more moral by much
than the heathen average, but intensely conceited, scornful towards all outside Barbarians, and exceedingly torpid in feeling,
and dull of vision, in regard to all things unseen and eternal.

We might have dwelt at much greater length upon the
points touched upon in this brief notice of the Chinese classics.
But those for whom more especially we have written, will of
course make the acquaintance of Dr. Legge for themselves.
The final result must be: for the Church, a deeper sense of the
difficulties to be overcome in evangelizing China; and for the
world at large, a much lower estimate of Confucius and his
system, than has prevailed amongst those who have tried so
hard to find another master than Christ.

Art. VII.—ROGER BACON IN THE LIGHT OF NEW DOCUMENTS.*

By EMILE SAISSET, Prof. of the History of Philosophy in the Faculty
of Letters, Paris, &c.

IN the last century there still existed at Oxford, beyond the
town, in a suburb on the other side of the river, an old tower
which was pointed out to strangers as having once been the
study and observatory of Friar Bacon.† According to tradition, it was to this place that he retired in order to study the
heavens and read in them the secret of the affairs of earth.
It was there that he sought the *great work* in the society of his
good friend Friar Thomas Bungey and other necromancers and
sorcerers whom the legend associates with him :

> " The nigromancie thair saw i eckanone,
>   Of Benytas, Bengo and friar Bacone," &c. ‡

It was, without doubt, in the most hidden corner of this
mysterious retreat § that Bacon and his friend constructed that
famous head of brass, which spoke and delivered oracles. Tradition describes the two monks as questioning the miraculous
head : they ask for the revelation of some way of surrounding

* This article was written for the *Revue des Deux Mondes* upon the appearance
of two recent publications : *Roger Bacon, sa vie, ses œuvres, ses doctrines, d'après
des documents inédits*, par M. Emile Charles, Paris, 1861. *Fr. Roger Bacon Opera
quœdam hactenus Inedita*, London, 1860.   [The article is reprinted in Saisset's
Précurseurs et Disciples de Descartes, Paris, 1862.   Of the author's work on *Modern Pantheism*, 2 vols. Edinburgh, 1863, we gave a notice in the April number of
our *Review*.   For the translation of this valuable essay on Bacon we are indebted
to Col. Joseph Howland, Matteawan, N. Y.   EDS.]

† This tower was used as a post of observation during the civil wars, and an en-
graving of it may be found in Joseph Skelton's work : *Oxonia antiqua restaurata*,
t. ii, p. 2, Oxford, 1823.

‡ See the *Enchanted Mirror* of Douglas, a Scotch poet of the end of the fifteenth
century.

§ Mr. Gordon, an Englishman of great learning and courtesy and formerly a student at the University of Oxford, writes us as follows : " I give you a story which
when I was a boy used to be current among my comrades at the university.   Doctor
Cyril Jackson, dean of Christ Church and later tutor to the Prince of Wales (George
IV) never passed under the arch of Roger Bacon's tower without fearing it would
fall in and crush him.   The fact is there was an old prophecy to the effect that this
tower would fall whenever a greater man than Bacon should pass beneath it."

their precious Albion with an impregnable wall. At first the head remains mute ; then, just at the moment when the dis- couraged magicians allow their attention to be distracted by other cares, the head suddenly speaks and reveals the great secret. Alas ! they did not hear it. Who knows but that more than one worthy Englishman of our own time, in meeting with this legend, will not regret that Friar Bacon's brazen head was not preserved to these days that it might tell its secret to the attentive ear of Lord Palmerston. How many false alarms and how much needless expense would have been spared the English admiralty! From what an amount of anxiety would the mind of Mr. Gladstone have been relieved. But every thing in these singular traditions, in which national feeling con- spires with the fancies of the legend in order to caricature a man of genius into a sorcerer, ought to be thrown aside. Roger Bacon was an Englishman in his genius and in his sym- pathies, as he was by birth. His great idea, that which com- mends his name to posterity and brings him near the illustrious chancellor, his fellow-countryman and namesake, is profoundly British : it is the idea of the genius of man subduing nature to his will—the conquest of the universe by his industry.

How happens it that England, so celebrated for the pious worship she pays to her great men, should have for so long a time allowed the thoughts and writings of Roger Bacon to re- main forgotten, and have abandoned the memory of one of her most illustrious children to the caprice of tradition? I do not venture to assert with M. de Humboldt, that Roger Bacon was " the greatest apparition of the middle ages " ;* but, unques- tionably, he is worthy of a place, in the age of St. Louis, beside St. Thomas, St. Bonaventure and Albert the Great. His two compatriots, the monks Duns Scotus and Ockham, have their monument, while the greatest of all the English monks still waits for his.

We must pass from the thirteenth century to the eighteenth before we can meet with any serious work relative to Roger Bacon. In 1733, Doctor Samuel Jebb, a clever and learned man, at the solicitation of the court physician Richard Mead, published the first edition of the *Opus Majus*. His work is creditable, though not without faults of both commission and omission, since he inserts chapters in the *Opus Majus* which form no part of the work and suppresses, by some un- accountable oversight, the whole of a book of the highest im- portance, the seventh, containing the ethics. This is all that

* *Cosmos*, t. ii, p. 398.

England has done for Roger Bacon up to the present time; she has left to a Frenchman, to one of our countrymen, an enthusiastic scholar as well as an eminent philosopher, the task and the honor of taking up the labors of Samuel Jebb and of initiating an activity of research in favor of the illustrious Franciscan of Oxford which will not cease, God willing, till full justice shall have been done and Roger Bacon shall have recovered the place he merits in the history of the human mind.   In 1848, M. Cousin, while absorbed in his labors on the philosophy of the middle ages, discovered in the library of Douai an unpublished manuscript of Roger Bacon.   This valuable memorial interested him.   " We cannot forget ", he says, " that ingenious and unfortunate Franciscan, who, at the end of the thirteenth century, appreciated the great importance of languages, enriched the science of optics with a map of valuable observations and experiments even, pointed out the imperfection of the Julian Calendar, planned the Gregorian reformation, either invented gunpowder or discovered its composition ; who, finally, for being more enlightened in physical science than his age, received the name of *Doctor Mirabilis*, was reputed a sorcerer and suffered the long and absurd persecution which has made his memory sacred to posterity.   We attached the more value to the discovery of an unpublished work of Roger Bacon, because a careful examination had convinced us, that if Roger Bacon belongs to England by birth, it was in France and at Paris that he completed his studies, took his doctor's degree, taught, conducted his experiments and discoveries, and was twice condemned to a more or less just confinement by the General of his order, Jerome d'Ascoli, in that famous monastery of the Franciscans or Cordeliers which occupied the spot where the School of Medicine now stands.". *

With his mind filled with these great recollections, M. Victor Cousin applied himself to the study of the Douai manuscript and was not long in recognizing it, under an incorrect title and in the midst of other documents, as one of the principal works of Roger Bacon, the *Opus Tertium*.   It was known that after sending the *Opus Majus* to his protector, Pope Clement IV, Roger Bacon wrote a second book entitled the *Opus Minus*, intended as an epitome and complement of the first ; but it was less well known, and the fact had been lost sight of since the time of Samuel Jebb, that Roger Bacon had made a third and far greater endeavor to collect the entire body

* *Journal des Savants*, March, 1848.
41

of his thoughts and discoveries in the form of a sort of encyclopedia. This last effort of his genius is the *Opus Tertium*.
To M. Cousin belongs the credit of having first brought it to
light and of having made public its most interesting features.
This is not all : since 1848 M. Cousin has rendered additional
service to the memory of Roger Bacon by discovering, in the
library of Amiens*, a manuscript containing a sort of commentary by Roger Bacon on the natural, philosophy and metaphysics of Aristotle. This manuscript is an important one.
In it we see Roger Bacon struggling with the great problems
of metaphysics. Now this gives us a view of his genius which
has hitherto been completely unknown to us. For this reason, M. Cousin, having concluded his researches respecting
the unpublished manuscripts of Roger Bacon, addressed a
noble appeal to the learned men of France and England.
He called upon some young and conscientious student of the
philosophy of the Middle Ages to undertake seriously the
study of the manuscript of Amiens, promising him an ample
and rich harvest as his reward ; he stimulated the patriotism
of the scholars of Oxford and Cambridge in beseeching them
to complete the publication begun by Samuel Jebb. Neither
England nor France was deaf to these pressing entreaties.
The works of Roger Bacon have been included in the vast
collection which is publishing by order of the English parliament.† Still more recently, a professor of the University of
Dublin has recovered in part the complement of the *Opus
Majus*, and we are given to expect the early publication of
the entire fragment.‡ Finally, we have a French scholar,
M. Emile Charles, who gives us a complete monograph§ on the
life, works, and doctrines of Roger Bacon. It is the fruit of
six years of industrious research. Nothing was able to weary
the patience or dampen the ardor of this young Benedictine
of philosophy. Long and expensive journeys, toilsome tran-

---

* Amiens has been enriched with the books and manuscripts of the ancient
abbey of Corbie. See the *Journal des Savants*, August, 1848,
  † The title of this collection is: *Rerum Britannicarum medii œvi Scriptores*, or,
Chronicles and Memorials of Great Britain and Ireland during the Middle Age,
published by the authority of Her Majesty's Treasury, under the direction of the
Master of the Rolls.—The publication of the inedited writings of Roger Bacon
has been confided to Mr. J. S. Brewer, professor of English literature in King's
College, London. As yet we have only one volume, which appeared in 1859 and
contains the *Opus tertium*, the *Opus minus*, the *Compendium philosophiæ* and, as
an appendix, the tract *De Nullitate Magiæ*.
  ‡ *On the Opus majus of Roger Bacon*, by John Kells Ingram, fellow of Trinity
College, professor of English literature in the University of Dublin. Dublin, 1858.
  § *Roger Bacon, sa vie, ses œuvres, ses doctrines, d'après des textes inédits*, by
Emile Charles, professor of philosophy in the Faculty of Letters of Bordeaux ;
1 vol. 8vo.

scriptions, laborious decipherments—no species of trial dis-
couraged him.   No known manuscript escaped his researches.
He sought for new ones in all the libraries—in the Bodleian
Library, the British Museum, the Sloane Collection, the Ash-
mole Museum, the Imperial Library, the Mazarin Library,
in all the colleges of Oxford, and in all the collections of
London, Paris, Douai and Amiens.   The result of so much
care, labor and study is a work of the highest character,
which, after a brilliant defence at the Sorbonne, the Faculty
of Letters of Paris crowned by a unanimous vote.

But the subject is far from being exhausted, and much
remains to be done before the form of Roger Bacon can be
brought out distinctly from the obscurity of centuries.   It
has seemed to us, however, that we have already sufficient
material to warrant an attempt to sketch the character of the
Admirable Doctor, to recount the vicissitudes of his destiny
and set forth the nature of the work, too long forgotten, of
the most daring genius to which the Middle Ages gave birth.

1.—*The Life of Bacon.*

The birthplace of Roger Bacon is known with certainty :
it was Ilchester, in Somersetshire.   We are in comparative
doubt as to the year of his birth, though it was probably
1214.   He belonged to a noble, rich and honored family.
His elder brother played a part in the civil discords of the
reign of Henry III, taking the side of the King against the
barons.

Roger, as a younger son, and being ardently devoted to
study, was destined for the church, and was sent by his family
to the University of Oxford.   Merton College and Brazenose
College still contend for the honor of having educated him.
Even at that distant day Oxford was noted for its taste for
languages and the mathematical sciences, and especially for a
particular spirit of independence and liberty, in speculative
inquiries as well as in practical matters.   Roger found there
the masters who best suited the natural bent of his genius and
character—Robert Bacon, a member of his own family (probably his uncle), Richard Fitzacre, the Dominican, Adam de
Margh, Edmund Rich, and, above all others, Robert Grosse-
teste, Bishop of Lincoln, a theologian passionately devoted to
letters, of an energetic and bold character, so well known on
account of his quarrels with Pope Innocent IV, whom he
finally went so far as to pronounce a heretic and antichrist.

Roger Bacon's spirit freely expanded itself in this atmosphere
of curious science and unrestrained criticism.   We find him

figuring by the side of his kinsman Robert in a solemn scene, in which his political boldness is a prelude to the more dangerous temerities of his later life.

In 1233, on St. John's day, King Henry III had an interview with his discontented barons. He was obliged to listen to a long sermon and severe reprimand. The preacher who had been chosen for this duty was the friar Robert, Roger Bacon's kinsman. The sermon barely finished, the monk directly addressed the King and declared to him that a permanent peace would be impossible unless he banished from his councils the Bishop of Winchester, Peter Desroches, the object of English hatred. "The audience cried out at such audacity;— but the King, by a strong effort, was enabled to restrain himself. Perceiving that he was calm, one of the clerks of the assembly, even then celebrated for his wit, ventured to address him with the following raillery: 'My Lord the King,—Do you know which are the dangers to be most feared in navigating the open sea?' 'Those know', replied Henry, 'who are in the habit of making such voyages.' 'Well, I will tell you', said the clerk,—'those dangers are rocks and reefs' (*les pierres et les roches*), thereby intending to designate Pierre Desroches, the bishop of Winchester." *

This audacious jester was no other than Roger Bacon, at that time nineteen years of age. Having finished his studies at Oxford, he went to Paris in order to complete his education. This was the universal custom of the time. The University of Paris attracted the Englishman, Roger Bacon, as it had attracted the German, Albert, the Italian, St. Thomas, the Belgian, Henri de Gand. We are not in possession of any details respecting Roger Bacon's first sojourn at Paris; but it is certain that during it he applied himself to profound study, received the degree of doctor, and began to acquire a great reputation.

It is not known whether Roger Bacon entered the order of St. Francis during his first residence at Paris or only after his return to Oxford. That such a man should voluntarily have become a monk, and a Franciscan monk, was utterly incomprehensible to an illustrious scholar, to whose venerable old age the men of the writer's own generation may have had an opportunity of personally paying their respect, and who knew by experience what fetters and what regrets a calling prematurely adopted bears along with it. "What did he among the Franciscans?" exclaims Daunon, with an accent which seems

* Chronique de Matthieu Pâris, p. 265.

to reflect a secret and bitter remembrance of his own experience. "What place had a man of genius, eager to discover the light and to unveil it to others, among these monks?" * The reflections which the old Oratorian adds are not less curious. "Roger Bacon, if he wished to embrace the monastic state, would have done better to have connected himself with the Dominicans, inquisitors, it is true, and persecutors outside their convents,—but ambitious of attracting to and retaining within their order all who distinguished themselves by scientific or literary, religious or philosophical productions. Of such they have possessed, encouraged and honored a very great number, while directing· the intolerant zeal of their institute against those who did not belong to them. The Franciscans, on the contrary, always governed, if St. Bonaventure be excepted, by generals of slender talents and little learning, felt only humiliated by the presence and the reputation of the men of merit who had strayed in among them, Roger Bacon suffered more than any other from the effects of this envious malevolence, and it must be admitted that no one ever gave greater provocation, since he was then, and is still, by the scope and splendor of his genius, the most illustrious of the Franciscans."

Something might perhaps be said to tone down the rather vivid coloring of this picture of the two rival orders of St. Francis and St. Dominic; but how is it possible not to sympathize in the pathetic regrets of old Daunon, when we reflect on the persecutions which are about to assail our Franciscan, trouble his whole life, restrain the flight of his genius, check the course of his labors and attack his writings and even his memory?

It is now certain † that Roger Bacon suffered two distinct persecutions,—one which lasted about ten years, from 1257 till 1267, St. Bonaventure being general of the Franciscans; and another still longer and more cruel, from 1278 till 1292, during the generalship of Jerome d'Ascoli, who became pope (in 1288) under the name of Nicholas IV. What was the reason of these repeated severities? If we interrogate the historians of the order, Wadding for example, we find them almost silent on the subject. It would appear as though they wished to bury in the same forgetfulness ,both the sufferings and the

---

* See the article by M. Daunon, interrupted by his death, in the *Histoire littéraire de la France*, t. xx, p. 230. A worthy inheritor of his learning, M. J.-V. Le Clerc, has completed it with learned bibliographical research.
† See M. Cousin, *Journal des Savants*, numbers of March, April, May, June, 1848. —Compare M. Emile Charles, *Roger Bacon, sa vie*, etc., p. 11, *et seq.*

glory of their victim.   Did Roger Bacon sin against morals?
No, his life was pure and innocent.   Did he assail the dogmas
of the faith?   Far from it—Christianity never had a more sincere believer nor the church a more devoted adherent.   Had
he refused to recognize the authority of the holy see?   Not at
all.   He even went so far as to rely upon a pope, who was a
friend of letters, in his efforts to rid himself of the bonds in
which his convent held him.

What then was his crime?   A few words in Wadding, very
discreetly chosen, tell what it was.   He was condemned, he
says, *propter quasdam novitates suspectas*.   In truth, Roger
Bacon was essentially an innovating spirit.   Like all of his
kind, he was dissatisfied with his age.   He complains especially
of the exclusive authority which is accorded to Aristotle.   Instead of studying nature, he says, twenty years are lost in
reading the reasonings of one of the ancients.   "As for me",
he boldly adds, "if I had the disposal of the works of Aristotle, I would burn them all up, for this sort of study is only a
loss of time, and it engenders error and propagates ignorance to
an extent which passes all conception".[*]   Not that Roger Bacon
fails to appreciate the genius of Aristotle ; but, he observes, it is
necessary to understand him before you can admire him, and
in order to understand him you must read his writings in the
original, and this is what the most reputed doctors of this time
are incapable of doing.   They admire a false Aristotle, dis-
figured by imbecile translators.

Roger Bacon spares no one.   Some have imagined they discovered in his attack upon Albert the Great and St. Thomas a
trace of the nascent rivalry between the monks of St. Francis
and the followers of St. Dominic.   This is a mistake.   Roger
Bacon is not less bitter against Alexander of Hales, the oracle
of the Franciscans, than against Albert the Great.   "I except
no Orders", he remarks, in these very terms : *nullum ordinem
excludo*.[†]   He has no patience with the subtlety, dryness, and
prolixity of the theologians, with their stupid, interminable
Summæ.   According to him, all that is valuable in Albert the
Great might be condensed into a treatise of not one twentieth
part the bulk of his writings.   And elsewhere, in even a
sharper tone, he says : "Very high commendation is bestowed
on the Sum of Friar Alexander of Hales, and indeed it is ponderous enough to break down a pack-horse ; but this greatly
admired Sum was never written by him".   And as for St.

* *Compendium Theologiæ*, pars. i, cap. 2.
† See M. Charles's book, p. 107.

Thomas— *Vir erroneus et famosus*, is what the irreverent
Franciscan calls the Angel of the School.   Without pity for
the Christian theologians, he treats the Arabians hardly any
better : Avicenna is full of errors ; Averroes has borrowed
from others all that is good or true in him — from his own resources he has drawn only errors and chimeras.   "And people
pretend ", exclaims Roger Bacon, " that nothing remains to be
done in philosophy, that it has been perfected in these latter
days, quite recently, at Paris " !   What an illusion !   Science
is the fruit of time ; and, moreover, it can never become either
an easily acquired or a common possession.   " What the vulgar praise is necessarily false ",* harshly observes Roger Bacon.
Neither does he hide from himself that it is the destiny of men
of genius to be despised by the multitude and to suffer persecution.   What matters it ?   We can reciprocate the contempt
of the vulgar.   " The multitude has always been despised by
the great men it hás disowned.   It was not present with Christ
at the Transfiguration ; only three disciples were chosen.   It
was after the multitude had followed the preaching of Jesus
for two years that it abandoned him, and cried out, ' Crucify
him ' ".†   But there is nothing in such a prospect to shake the
courage of Roger Bacon.   " Those who have sought to introduce any reformation in science have always been exposed to
opposition and liable to meet with obstacles.   Yet the truth
has prevailed, and always will prevail, till the day of Anti-
christ ".‡
We can easily understand how a spirit and character of this
order were out of place in a convent.   The monks could make
nothing of this strange brother, who passed his life in his tower
at Oxford, observing the stars and making experiments in
physical science.   They suspected some horrid mystery—perhaps a secret intercourse with evil spirits.   They whispered to
each other, that Friar Roger boasted of having invented wonderful machines—an apparatus by which a man could rise into
the air, and another for moving over the water without row-
ing, and with a speed never before heard of.   They talked
about incendiary mirrors, capable of destroying a whole army
in an instant, and an automaton possessing the faculty of
speech—an android of most prodigious power.   Now, could
all this be accomplished without a little magic ?   Could a man
having such intimate relations with the infernal powers be at
the same time a disciple and servant of Christ ?   Had he not
borrowed from his friends the Arabians, followers of Mohammed,

* *De mirabili potestate*, 47.   † *Opus Majus*, p. 6.   ‡ *Ibid*, p. 13.

the horrible and devilish doctrine, that the appearance of the prophet and the origin and progress of religions are determined by the conjunctions of the planets,—that the Christian dispensation, in particular, depends on the conjunction of Jupiter with Mercury; and, finally—O, prodigy of error and iniquity!—that the conjunction of the moon with Jupiter will be the signal for the destruction of all religions?

Such were the rumors of the convent, and, as is usually the case, a little truth was mixed with a great deal of falsehood. The Superiors, being informed of these charges, sent the accused friar from Oxford to Paris, where a system of severe surveillance and meddlesome inquisition was commenced which lasted ten years, and was occasionally pushed so far as to include the most humiliating punishments. One must hear Roger Bacon himself relate his tribulations to his Holiness in the preface to the *Opus Tertium*, discovered by M. Cousin, and which recalls the *Historia Calamitatum* of Abelard. In the first place, he was not permitted to write, nor, with greater reason, to teach. What a trial for a man who was devoured with a passion for imparting his ideas, and who continually repeated the saying of Seneca: " I love to learn only that I may teach others ". He was reduced to solitary meditation; no books were allowed him, and his mathematical instruments were taken away. If he employed himself in the simplest calculations, if he wished to prepare any astronomical tables, above all, if he tried to lead any young novices to the observation of the planets, he caused great fright, and found all these noble and innocent exercises interdicted to him as the works of the devil. The least punishment he incurred in case of disobedience was fasting on bread and water.

While Roger Bacon wasted away in the midst of these indignities a ray of light suddenly came to illuminate his cell and rejoice his heart. The inauguration of a new pope is announced. He is a Frenchman, Guy Foulques,* a generous and liberal spirit, a friend of letters and Bacon's friend. Before entering the church he had had experience in both war and jurisprudence. Chosen by St. Louis as his secretary, he rapidly became archbishop, cardinal and afterwards the pope's legate in England. While there he heard of the monk of Oxford

* I do not know why M. Charles italianizes the name of Foulques and constantly calls him Guido Fulcodi. Fulcodi may pass, but why Guido? Guy Foulques was born at St. Gilles on the Rhone. He took orders after the death of his wife, was archbishop of Narbonne in 1259, cardinal-bishop of Sabine in 1261, was sent to England as legate by Urban II for the purpose of healing the quarrel between Henry III and the barons, and was finally made pope in 1265. See the notice by Daunon and M. Cousin's writings.

whose labors excited admiration mingled with jealousy and fear. Not being able to communicate directly with the friar, he made use of a common friend, Rémond de Laon, and learned through him that Roger was preparing a great work on the reformation of philosophy. When Roger was exiled to Paris, Foulques wrote to him several times but without success, the prohibition of the superiors being absolute.

We may imagine how great was the joy of the poor Franciscan, when he heard of the exaltation of his protector. Hope once more entered his soul. The evidence of this joyfulness may be found in the *Opus Tertium*. "Blessed be God, the Father of our Lord Jesus Christ, who hath raised to the throne of His kingdom an enlightened prince desirous of serving the interests of science! The predecessors of your Blessedness, occupied with the affairs of the church, harassed by rebels and tyrants, had no leisure to give to the encouragement of liberal studies; but thanks be to God, the right hand of your Holiness has displayed its triumphal standard, drawn the sword from its scabbard, thrust the two contending parties down to hell and given peace to the chutch. The times are propitious for works of wisdom."*

Notwithstanding the strict watch kept on all his actions, Roger managed to send letters to the new pope: a knight named Bonnecor undertook to deliver them and add all necessary explanations. Clement IV was not long in replying; we possess his letter,—Wadding, the historian of the Franciscans, having copied it from the archives in the Vatican:

LETTER FROM POPE CLEMENT IV TO ROGER BACON.

"To our beloved son the friar Roger, surnamed Bacon, of the order of the Franciscans: We have received with gratitude the letter of your devotion, and have carefully noted the verbal remarks which our dear son the knight Bonnecor has added by way of explanation, with as much fidelity as prudence. That we may better know what you desire to accomplish, we will, and we command you, in virtue of our apostolic authority, that, without regard to any contrary injunction of any prelate whomsoever or any constitution of your Order, you send us without delay the work we desired you to deliver to our dear son Rémond de Laon, when we were legate. We desire you, moreover, to explain yourself in your letters respecting the remedies, which ought to be employed in those dangerous diseases you describe to us, and that in the most secret manner and without delay you apply yourself to the performance of this duty."

"Given at Viterbo, the 10th day before the Calends of July, in the second year of our pontificate."

---

* *Opus tertium*, cap. 2, Douai manuscript. The extracts from the *Opus tertium* may now be compared with the edition lately published in London, previously alluded to.

In reading this letter, which reflects so much honor on Clement IV, it will be remarked that he does not venture to require the release of his favorite.   He, the vicar of Christ, the successor of Gregory VII, humbles himself so far as to request secrecy on the part of a monk of St. Francis,—so great was the prestige of this formidable order, which forced the heads of the church and emperors and kings to keep careful accounts with it : an immense army, at once disciplined and factious, whose destruction was planned by several popes, who had neither the courage nor the power to accomplish it, and which at one time thought itself on the eve of overturning the settled order of things in Europe by the establishment of a sort of universal republic of which the general of the Franciscans was to be the head.   Thus the letter of Clement IV was far from putting an end to Roger Bacon's trials.   It re-animated his courage, but instead of improving his condition it rather made it worse.

He was not allowed to see any one ; all communication with the outer world was forbidden him, and his strength began to fail under the amount of fasting and penance required of him. With all this he applied himself to the execution of his task, but the great question was how he should obtain the books, money and parchment even which were necessary.' He needed assistance in his experiments and calculations, but it was refused him ; he required copyists and he knew not where to find them.   If of his order, they would have handed over his writings to the superiors ; outside of his order there were only the copyists of Paris, a set of mercenary creatures noted for their faithlessness and who would not have failed to make public those writings whose first perusal was intended for the pope alone.   Finally, he needed money, and this was the most difficult want to supply.   A simple monk, Roger possessed, and could possess, nothing.   He excused his Holiness, "*who, seated on the throne of the universe and burdened with a thousand cares had not thought of remitting a small sum*"; but he cursed the agents who had not had the wit to say any thing to the pontiff and who were unwilling to spend a single farthing. He in vain promised to write to the pope and assure them of the repayment of any advances they might make.   He wrote without success to his brother, who had been very rich but whom the war had ruined, and to numerous prelates, to *those people whose faces, but not whose hearts, you know*, he bitterly wrote to the pope, but everywhere he met with refusal ; even his honesty was suspected.   "How often have I been taken for a dishonest man !   How often have I been turned away, and how often deceived with vain hopes !   What shame and anguish have devoured my very soul!" In desperation, he finally applies to some of his friends who were almost as poor as himself; he induces them to sell a portion of their modest estate and to mortgage the remainder at an usurious rate, and by dint of such efforts and through such humiliation he finally succeeded in raising the miserable sum of sixty livres!

And all this time, as the last historian of Roger Bacon pointedly observes,[*] while the poor Franciscan in his cell by the Porte Saint-Michel was wearing himself out in efforts of every kind, his rivals in glory and genius were living in the favor of popes and kings. St. Thomas was dining at the table of St. Louis, and Albert the Great was bestowing on the Emperor that ostentatious hospitality, which tradition has so fantastically embellished.

In addition to these indirect hindrances, there was added cruel personal treatment. Any course of action was considered admissible which might have the effect of making him renounce his projects. Bacon, supported by the letter from his Holiness, refused to submit. In this struggle, violence was pushed to the last extremity; it was so serious that he did not dare tell his story in a work which had to pass through the hands of copyists. "I will perhaps reveal to you", he says to the Pope, "some true particulars of the cruel treatment I have received, but I shall write them with my own hand, on account of the importance of the secret".[†]

It was in the midst of all these obstacles, and this treachery and violence, that Roger Bacon contrived to write the *Opus Majus*, and to transmit it to the Pope by a young man named John, his beloved disciple. The Pope finally decided to interfere. By his order Roger Bacon was released; he was at liberty to revisit his native land, see his dear city of Oxford once more, and resume the execution of his vast scientific projects in the society of his friend Thomas Bungey. Unfortunately, this period of favor and liberty was very short. Hardly a year had passed when Clement IV died, and his successor was a pope who owed his tiara to the influence of the general of the Franciscans. Deprived thenceforth of all support, Roger Bacon again fell beneath the weight of the spirit of prejudice and hatred he had for an instant exorcised.

Persecution had in no way changed him. He continued to both speak and write, and, to his reprobation of the popular philosophers and the authorized theologians, he added the bold-

[*] Emile Charles, 25, *et seq.*   [†] *Opus Tertium,* cap. 2.

est attacks upon legists and princes, upon prelates and the mendicant orders, daring to denounce even the ignorance and dissolute manners of the clergy and the corruption of the Court of Rome. The storm which had been gathering burst over his head in 1278. To St. Bonaventure, who, in spite of his surname of "Seraphic Doctor", had not shown any especial tenderness towards Roger Bacon, but who at least imparted to his rule a portion of his own comparative elevation of mind and gentleness of character, had succeeded Jerome d'Ascoli, a man of energetic, narrow, and inflexible character. Jerome proceeded to Paris for the purpose of convening a general chapter of the order. The first person obliged to appear before was Friar Pierre Jean d'Olive, accused of participating in the errors of John of Parma, and of the *Eternal Gospel*. After him came Roger Bacon's turn. We know nothing of the trial except that the opinions of the rebellious friar were condemned, and that he himself was thrown into prison.

In vain Roger Bacon addressed himself to Pope Nicholas III. Jerome had anticipated him with his Holiness, and the unhappy Franciscan's cries of distress were stifled. This new and most terrible trial, respecting which we have no particulars, lasted fourteen years. It was not till 1592, after the death of Jerome d'Ascoli—who had been Pope since 1288, under the title of Nicholas IV—that the new general of the order, Raymond Galfred, or Gaufredi, gave Roger Bacon his liberty. The unfortunate man was no longer in a condition to abuse it; he was nearly eighty years old. He died at Oxford very soon afterwards. The hatred which had persecuted him all his life pursued his writings after his death. His books were nailed to boards, so that they could not be read, and were left to rot amidst dirt and dampness.

II.—*The Method of Bacon.*

We must not expect to find a general system of philosophy in the *Opus Majus*, or in any other of Roger Bacon's works. There is in this respect a striking resemblance between the monk of Oxford and his great namesake, the Lord Chancellor of England. Read the *De Argumentis* and the *Novum Organum*—you will look in vain for a new system of metaphysics, but you will find a superior method and superior views respecting the reformation of philosophy and the constitution of the human mind. And so in the writings of Roger Bacon you will meet with a method and views of a general character; but what claims our admiration is the fact that the Franciscan of the thirteenth century extols the same method and rises to the same views as the contemporary of Galileo and Kepler.

There is, however, a remarkable difference between the two Bacons, and the advantage is entirely on the side of Roger. The Lord Chancellor possessed unquestionably a great mind, and was a great promoter of science; but it cannot be denied that he lacked an essential gift — one which Descartes and Pascal possessed in the highest degree—he lacked that gift of invention which gives to the human mind the power of penetrating the mysteries of nature. Bacon of Verulam discovered nothing of real importance. Admirable when he is describing the true method—when he praises its advantages and prophesies its conquests—it might be said that he loses his wings as soon as he attempts to enter the sphere of application. He does not cease to be ingenious and brilliant, but great in invention and really fruitful he is not.

Roger Bacon possessed greater fertility of genius. He was not only a promoter of science, he was an inventor. Even if he neither understood nor described the method of observation and induction with that clearness, coherency, and power which we cannot sufficiently admire in the later Bacon, it must be admitted that he made use of it with more assiduity and greater success. The genius of the Lord Chancellor observed nature from a height above it; that of the Franciscan dwelt with it in intimate and familiar intercourse. So nature confided some of its secrets to him. If Roger Bacon had been born in the sixteenth century, he would have been a Kepler or a Galileo. Add to this, too, that Roger Bacon, without showing much originality in metaphysics, is a greater metaphysician than Bacon of Verulam, who is not one at all. Roger certainly did not invent a new system respecting the nature and origin of things; but he took part in the great metaphysical controversies of his time, and there also he has left traces, of which the history of the human mind ought to take note.

What is perhaps most extraordinary in him, is the clear and profound perception he had of the views of the philosophy of his age. Remember that this was the thirteenth century. This was the golden age of scholasticism, the heroic epoch of the great doctors,—of Alexander of Hales, their refragable doctor and of St. Thomas Aquinas, the angelic doctor; drawing after them Duns Scotus, the subtle doctor, and Henri de Gand, the solemn doctor. The Aristotle of Boëtius, and the petty combats of the dialectics of the eleventh century, are forgotten. The horizon has become enlarged; all the essential problems of philosophy and theology have been set forth ; Aristotle is still venerated, but it is the Aristotle of the Arabians—no longer only the logician of the Organon, but the author of the treatises on the *Soul*, *Physics*, *Metaphysics*, and the *History of Animals*—Aristotle the psychologist, naturalist and theologian. We see St. Thomas, the master of masters, with Aristotle in one hand and the Bible in the other, preparing to sum up all the labors of his age in one gigantic encyclopedia, and to write for the instruction of future ages that immortal *Summa*, in which all the problems of science and faith are resolved into their elements, regularly discussed and magisterially solved ; and in which profane wisdom, represented by *Philosophy*, contracts an apparently indissoluble union with sacred science—a unique monument in its order, proportions and the greatness of its general design, as in the delicacy, abundance and precision of its details.

Truly, if science ever held forth the image of the eternal and the definitive, it was in the age of St. Thomas. Yet there was one man wearing the habit of a monk of St. Francis, who was not deceived by these magnificent appearances ; who, in examining the foundations of the edifice, was able to discern and lay his hands upon those portions which were weak and decayed. And this same man, sketching in his prophetic thought the plan of an edifice far more vast and substantial, in complete self-reliance also vigorously commenced its execution.

Roger Bacon brings forward three principal accusations against the scholastic philosophy. He reproaches it, in the first place, for its blind credulity as regards the authority of Aristotle ; then, for its gross ignorance of antiquity, both sacred and profane,—reaching such a point that even its Aristotle is a counterfeit Aristotle ; and, finally,—and this is his chief complaint,—he accuses it of moving in a circle of abstractions, of ignoring all that is real, and of entirely neglecting the observation of nature ; of being, in consequence, artificial, subtle, disputatious and pedantic ; and of shutting up the human mind within the schools, far away from nature and God's works. We have here in fact the groundwork of the victorious polemics, which the revival of letters and a later age have directed against scholasticism. Bruno, Campanella, Ramus, Bacon of Verulam himself, did not more clearly perceive the vices of the philosophy of the middle ages. They made the same charges against it. Only Bacon the Franciscan lost his case against his age, because he was too soon in the right, whilst Bacon the Lord Chancellor gained his, not because he pleaded better, but because he found better judges. Nothing can equal the vehemence of Roger Bacon when he protests against the yoke of Aristotle. What is more arbitrary, says Roger, than to declare on a certain day that a certain philosopher is infallible? "Hardly half a century has passed, since Aristotle was accused of impiety and banished from the schools. And to-day he is our sovereign master. What is his title? He is wise, it is said;—be it allowed; but he did not know every thing. He did for his age all that it was possible to do, but he did not reach the farthest limits of wisdom. Avicenna has committed serious errors, and Averroes is open to criticism on many points. The Saints themselves are not infallible; they often made mistakes and often retracted; witness St. Jerome and Origen."* "But, the schools say, we must respect the ancients."—"Oh! unquestionably, the ancients are venerable and we ought to show gratitude to them for having prepared the way for us; but we ought never to forget that these ancients were men and that they often fell into error: and, moreover, the more ancient they are the more errors they commit; for, in reality, the youngest are the oldest; the men of this generation ought to surpass in wisdom those of ancient days, since they inherit all the labors of the past."

This is the language of a monk, about the year 1267. As at this day we encounter this saying, then so new, bold and ingenious,—*the youngest are in reality the oldest,*—does it not seem as though we heard the author of the *De Augmentis* exclaiming: *Antiquitas seculi juventus mundi,* or the author of the *Pensées,* comparing the human race. to one man who never dies and who is constantly learning and advancing?

In this common resistance to Aristotle, Roger Bacon has this advantage over the men of the Renaissance and those of modern times, that he has profoundly studied the great philosopher whose tyranny he repudiates and that he renders full justice to his labors. He remarks: "I would more readily pardon the abuse which is made of Aristotle, if those who invoked him were able to understand and appreciate him; but what makes me indignant is, that they praise Aristotle without having read him. Besides", adds Roger, "it is no easy matter to understand the philosophy of Aristotle. We possess only portions of his writings and even many of these are mutilated. There are many works of an infinite value which cannot be recovered. Did not Aristotle write, according to Pliny, a

* *Compendium philosophiæ,* cap. 1

thousand volumes? Only a very small number of them is known to us. Even the *Organon* itself is imperfect. The original of the *History of Animals* consisted of fifty volumes; the Latin copies have only nineteen. Only ten books of the *Metaphysics* have been preserved, and in the translation which is best known a host of chapters and an infinite number of lines are wanting. As to the sciences which treat of the secrets of nature, we have only a few miserable fragments. And is there any one capable of understanding these scattered fragments of Aristotle? They are read, but not in the original, which is not understood. The Latin versions are referred to. Now, who are more unworthy of confidence than the Latin translators of Aristotle? In the first place, we have Michael Scot, who, ignorant of Greek, employed a Spanish Jew named Andreas; then we have Gerard of Cremona, who understands neither Latin nor Greek nor his own translations; then we have Hermann, the German, who acknowledges that he did not undertake to translate the *Poëtics* of Aristotle because he did not understand it; and, finally we have William of Morbecke, the most ignorant of all, though he is now flourishing and furnishing translations to his friend Thomas Aquinas. And it is thus that this Aristotle, who is made the incarnation of all human wisdom, and who, so it is pretended, is in harmony with divine wisdom, is not understood. And is divine wisdom, is sacred antiquity, better understood? Not in the least. And what is the reason? The reason is that Hebrew is no better understood than Greek. Of the sacred text there are parts badly translated and others entirely wanting. Two books of the Maccabees are missing; we no longer possess the writings of Origen or St. Basil, or Gregory of Nazianzen. Besides, the sacred books are full of obscurities, and St. Jerome himself was not always able to understand them. And what ought to be done? Instead of disfiguring the Bible more and more, and putting it into those miserable verses with which children's memories are burdened, a serious study of grammar and the languages ought to be established in the schools. And when readers capable of understanding the original texts have been trained, search should be instituted for the monuments we have lost. Why do not the higher clergy and the wealthy send learned men to Italy and the East, to collect Greek manuscripts? Why not imitate the holy bishop of Lincoln, Robert Grossetête, who at great expense commissioned a number of competent persons to travel in search of the records of both profane and sacred antiquity? Would not this be a worthy object of solicitude for the holy see? The conversion of infidels by missionaries speaking their own tongue; the reconciliation of the Greek church — what a magnificent prospect, without taking into account the advantages of this acquaintance with languages as regards the commerce and friendship of nations! The four philosophical languages—that is to say, Greek, Hebrew, Arabic, and Chaldee—ought to form part of common education. From these all the sciences have proceeded; they are the ancestors whose children and heirs we are. God gives wisdom to whom he pleases; He did not see fit to give it to the Latins, and philosophy has been attained only thrice since the beginning of the world: by the Hebrews, by the Greeks, and by the Arabians." *

Who is it that speaks thus, who is it that so enthusiastically and vehemently commends the study of Greek and the oriental languages, the restoration of the monuments of antiquity and a criticism of texts based on an exact philosophy and universal erudition? Does it not seem as though we were transported to the School of Florence, under the auspices of the Medici, in the society of Marsilius, Ficinus, Pico della Mirandula, and Politian, or even into the full assembly of the College of France in the time of Turnèbe and Budæus?

Like these great renovators of the human mind, Roger Bacon is full of enthusiasm for all that is beautiful and noble in antiquity. He even goes so far, Christian as he is and monk by vocation and mode of life, as to place the moralists of Greece above the doctors of the school. "It is strange that we Christians should be incomparably inferior in morality to the ancient philosophers. Let us read the ten books of the *Ethics* of Aristotle, the innumerable treatises of Seneca, Cicero, and so many others, and we shall perceive that we are in an abyss of vice and that the grace of God alone can save us. Zeal for chastity, gentleness, peace, constancy, and all the virtues was great in all the philosophers; and there is no man so outrageously corrupted by his vices as would not renounce them at once if he were to read their works, so eloquent in their praises of virtue and their invectives against vice. The worst of all vices is anger, which destroys all men and the whole universe; yet even the most passionate man, if he were to read with care the three books of Seneca, would blush to give way to it." † Roger Bacon has an especial liking for Seneca. He cannot praise him enough for having recommended an examination of one's conscience every evening. Behold, he exclaims, what an admirable argument for morality! A pagan, without the light

* *Opus tertium*, cap. 10, Douai manuscript.
† *Opus tertium*, cap. 14.

42

of grace and faith has reached this point, led thither only by the force of his reason.*

But if the study of the ancients, when conducted with independence and enlightened by erudition and criticism, is a fruitful study, there is one still more fruitful and far more necessary: this is the study without which all others are vain—the study of nature, the contemplation of God's works. Here it is that we meet with the deadly vice of the scholastic philosophy. It consumes itself away in vain disputes, it sharpens and refines and confounds itself in subtleties; it ignores life. There is but one remedy for this evil, experimental science. On this subject Roger Bacon wrote some memorable pages, which, four centuries beforehand, successively announced the *Novum Organum* and the *Discours de la Méthode*. We will call attention in the first place to a few detached thoughts which would hold their own perfectly well among the best aphorisms of Lord Bacon.

" I call experimental science that which disregards reasoning; for the strongest arguments prove nothing so long as the conclusions are not verified by experience."

" Experimental science does not receive truth from the hands of sciences which are superior; she alone is mistress and the other sciences are her servants."

" In effect, she has the right to command all other sciences, since she alone establishes and consecrates their results."

" So experimental science is the queen of all the sciences and the limit of all speculation." †

These are only rapid glances and, as it were, flashes of genius. The following thoughts are more connected and more fully developed: "In all research we must employ the best possible method. Now this method consists in studying the different parts of a science in their necessary order, in placing those in the first rank which actually ought to be found at the beginning, the easier before the more abstruse, the general before the particular, the simple before the compound; in addition, the subjects of our study should be those which are most profitable in view of the shortness of life; finally, we ought to exhibit the science with all clearness and certainty, without any mixture of doubt and obscurity. Now all this is impossible without experiment, for we have many different ways of becoming acquainted with truth, namely, by authority, by the exercise of our reason and by experience; but authority has no value if we do not recognize it, *non sapit nisi detur ejus*

---

* *Ibid.* cap. 75, Douai manuscript, fol. 82.
† *Opus tertium*, in the Douai manuscript.

ratio, it does not make us understand any thing, it only makes us believe ; it imposes itself upon the mind without enlightening it.   As to reasoning, it is impossible to distinguish sophistry from demonstration except by experiment and practice."   What admirable words ! This proud independence, this hatred of obscurity, this need of clear and distinct ideas, this love of order and simplicity,—are not these distinguishing traits of the *Discours de la Méthode* and the very expressions of Descartes himself ?

Roger Bacon makes a distinction, as the *Novum Organum* did later, between two sorts of observation : one passive and vulgar, the other active and learned. The latter alone deserves the name of experiment. "There is a natural and imperfect sort of experiment", he says, "which is unconscious of its power, which takes no note of its processes and which is fit for artisans and not for learned men. Far above this, far above all speculative science and all arts, there is the art of making experiments which are neither feeble nor incomplete".*   But under what condition will experiment attain precise results, dealing, as it always does, with fugitive and changing phenomena?. Under the condition that it always calls to its aid instruments of precision, and, before every thing else, mathematical calculation. "Natural philosophers ought to know", says Roger Bacon, "that their science is fruitless unless the power of mathematics is applied to it, without which observation languishes and is incapable of any certainty".† Bacon himself had progressed so far on this new and daring course that in a tract *De multiplicatione specierum*, which had occupied, so he states, ten years of labor, he had attempted the work reserved for Descartes and Newton—the reduction of all the phenomena of the reciprocal action of bodies to mathematical laws.

Armed with experiment and calculation, science may rise above facts; for facts, considered in themselves, are not the object of science. Facts have their proper utility, but science aims at something higher than the useful : it aspires to truth. It is not satisfied with facts, it must needs lay hold on laws and causes, *canones, universales regulae.* "If Aristotle, in the second book of the *Metaphysics*, pretends that the knowledge of reasons and causes is not to be attained through experiment, he speaks of experiment of an inferior kind. That which I have in view extends as far as causes, and by the help of observation it discovers them. Then only is the mind satisfied, all uncertainty vanishes and the philosopher reposes in the intuition of truth." ‡

* *Opus tertium*, cap. 13.   † *Opus majus*, Jebb's edition, p. 199.
‡ *De Cœlestibus*, cap. 1, Mazarin manuscript.

The laws of nature once discovered, speculation has finished its work and the application of those laws is the labor which remains.   We must allow that here the ardent imagination of Roger Bacon carries him beyond what is reasonable and possible.   As he admits no limits to man's possible knowledge so he places none to his power.   No force in nature is so hidden that man's intellect cannot discover it and his will master it.   The universe once known is the universe subdued.   " Machines will be made for sailing over the water without rowers and for navigating the greater ships, with only a single man to manage them, faster than though they were filled with sailors ; carriages which will rush along without any horses ; machines for flying, in which a man may take his seat, touch a spring and set in motion artificial wings, beating the air like those of birds ; a little instrument three inches wide and as many high capable of raising or lowering incredible weights.   By the aid of this last machine one could raise himself and his friends from the bottom of a dungeon far up into the air and then come down to earth when he felt inclined.   Another instrument will possess the power of dragging any resisting object over level ground, enabling one man to drag a thousand persons against their will.   There will be an apparatus for walking at the bottom of the sea and of rivers without the least danger ; there will also be machines for swimming and for enabling people to stay under water, bridges over rivers without piles or columns—in fact all sorts of marvellous machines and apparatus."*

The modern reader should be on his guard against dealing too severely with these brilliant promises, in which a few wild fancies are mingled with more than one prophetic expectation. Neither Kepler nor Descartes nor Leibnitz himself were able to keep themselves entirely free from illusions, and, even for superior minds, it may be necessary, in order to attain an end within the reach of human power, that they should aim to reach a point above and beyond it, and soar towards the inaccessible and infinite.

III.—His Discoveries.

Among the innumerable discoveries (we speak of those discoveries which are properly scientific), which a not too strict criticism, from Wood to M. Pierre Leroux, attributes to Roger Bacon, which are those which certainly belong to him ?   This is a delicate and complicated question,—one, however, respecting which the recently discovered documents are able to fur-

* The material for this sketch is obtained from the tract : *De Mirabili* and from an unpublished fragment of the *Treatise on Mathematics.*

nish us with more than one valuable piece of information ; but we shall refer to these with great discretion, leaving the discussion of the subject to special and competent judges.

The best established scientific claim of Roger Bacon is to the reformation of the calendar. The fact is now incontestable that the Franciscan monk proposed this reformation to Clement IV. Copernicus also advocated it in his time, but it was accomplished only under Gregory XIII, in 1582.

"The defects of the calendar", says Roger Bacon, "have become intolerable to the wise and are the horror of the astronomer. Since the time of Julius Cæsar, and notwithstanding the corrections which the Council of Nice, Eusebius, Victorinus, Cyrillus, and Bede endeavored to introduce, the errors have only become aggravated ; they have their origin in the estimate of the year, which Cæsar made to consist of 365 days, and intercalating a whole day every fourth year ; but this estimate is exaggerated, and astronomy affords us the means of knowing that the solar year is less by one one-hundred-and-thirteenth of a day (about eleven minutes) ; and hence follows that every one hundred and thirty years * one day too much has been counted, and this error would be corrected if one day were omitted after this period."

" The church", Roger Bacon further says, " in the first place fixed the vernal equinox at the 25th of March, and now it has it at the 21st ; but the equinox does not arrive at this date. This year (Roger was writing in 1267) the vernal equinox took place on the 13th of March, and it advances one day about every 125 years. Moreover, the church made a mistake at the beginning ; 140 years after the incarnation Ptolemy discovered that the vernal equinox took place on the 22d of March ; 1127 years have elapsed since then. It now takes place on the 13th, that is to say, nine days too early, and in dividing 1267 by 9 we obtain 124, which is the number of years at whose expiration the equinoxes have advanced one day. The church pretends that the winter solstice took place on the day of the nativity of Jesus Christ, the 25th of December : this is an error. The verification of Ptolemy having fixed it, in the year 140, at the 22d, it could not in the first year of our era be late more than a little over a day—that is to say, from the 23d to the 24th. Neither could the vernal equinox be the first year, on the 25th of March, since Ptolemy fixed it for the year 140 at the 22d of this same month ; still less can it be, as is now considered, on the 21st, according to the custom of the church ; in reality it comes on about the 13th, since it advances one day

* Accurately, one hundred and twenty-eight.

in 124 years. Thus we perceive the equinoxes are not fixed
since they do not take place on the days designated by the
church".

The errors relative to the lunations are commented on by
Roger Bacon with not less sagacity and precision. "The present calendar", he says, "badly indicates the new moons; in
76 years the new moon gains upon the time fixed by the calendar 6 hours and 40 minutes; * at the expiration of 365 years
the error will amount to one day". In adding other errors
to this one Roger Bacon arrives at the conclusion, that after
4266 years the moon will be at the full in the heavens and new
in the calendar, and he concludes by addressing to the pope
this energetic and eloquent adjuration : "A reformation is
necessary. All persons versed in calculations and astronomy
know it and laugh at the ignorance of the prelates, who maintain the present condition of things. The infidel philosophers,
Arabian and Hebrew, the Greeks who live among Christians,
as in Spain, Egypt, and the countries of the East and other
places, abhor the ignorance which Christians evince in their
chronology and the celebration of their solemnities. And yet
Christians now possess sufficient astronomical knowledge in
order to build upon a sure foundation. Let your Reverence
give orders and you will find men capable of remedying these
defects, those of which I have spoken, and others besides (for
there are thirteen in all), without counting their infinite rami-
fications. If this glorious work should be carried out during
the pontificate of your holiness, the result would be the accomplishment of one of the grandest, most beneficial, and most
beautiful enterprises which was ever undertaken by the church
of God".

Roger Bacon does not confine his astronomical views to the
single subject of the calendar. He attacks the system of Ptolemy at all points, and, which is greatly to his credit, he attacks
it on the side which at a later day attracted the severe notice
of Copernicus, finally calling forth the new system of the world.
The Cosmos of Ptolemy, with its infinite articulations, with its
eccentrics and its epicycles, seemed to him artificial, complicated, too much under subjection to the outward appearance of
things and infinitely removed from the simplicity of nature.

If in astronomy Roger Bacon is the forerunner of Copernicus, it may be said that in optics he prepares the way for Newton. It is perfectly true that the works of the Arabians in
both sciences, particularly those of Alpetragius and Alhazen,
were of the greatest service to him; but he has the distinction

----

* With greater exactitude: 6 hours, 8 minutes.

—an eminent one for the time—of having described the delicate and complicated mechanism of the eye with rare precision and of having suspected the action of the retina. Neither is the service slight of having held the position against Aristotle that the propagation of light is not instantaneous, * and that the light of the stars proceeds directly from themselves and does not come to them from the sun, and, in addition, of having made an attempt to explain the stellar scintillation, and also the very curious phenomenon, still so much discussed, of falling stars. In his opinion these meteors are not real stars but are bodies comparatively small, *corpora parvæ quantitatis,* which traverse our atmosphere and become ignited by the rapidity of their motion.

In optics the invention of spectacle glasses and of the microscope and telescope has been attributed to Roger Bacon. And, in fact, we discover in the preface to the *Opus Tertium* that, in sending his work to Clement IV, Roger charged John, his beloved disciple, to deliver to his Holiness a lens of crystal; † but this suggestion is rather vague. What is beyond dispute is that Roger carefully studied the phenomena of refractions, particularly those which combine to produce the rainbow, and sought the law of the deviation of luminous rays traversing the atmosphere.

We find greater difficulty in deciding how far he advanced in chemistry. Did he discover phosphorus, manganese, and bismuth? Did he invent gunpowder? The chemical formula certainly is in his writings, but he may have taken it from the Arabians, as he did many other recipes and observations. Professional men know, besides, that between even a fortunate observation of details, an exact chemical formula, a prophetic presentiment — between all this and a genuine scientific discovery there is an infinite difference. The fact is that the alchemists, in their rather unphilosophical search for the philosopher's stone,-which was never to be found, came across a great many truths which they were not looking for. Roger Bacon is far oftener an alchemist and an astrologer than a real astronomer or a chemist worthy the name. He believes in the transmutation of metals and in the influence of the 'celestial

---

* M. de Humboldt having attributed the honor of this discovery to Bacon of Verulam (*Cosmos*, t. iii, p. 86), I will cite the text of Roger Bacon: "All authors", he says, "including Aristotle, hold that the propagation of light is instantaneous; the truth is that it takes place in a very short time, which is, however, measurable". (*Opus majus*, pp. 298 and 300.)

† Puer vero Johannes portavit crystallum sphaericum ad experiendum, et instruxi eum in demonstratione et figuratione rei occultae". (*Opus tertium*, ch. 81 of the Douai manuscript.) Compare pp. 110 and 111 of the great London edition, edited by Mr. J. S. Brewer, London, 1859.

conjunctions upon human affairs. The Arabians had assured him that Artephius lived one thousand and twenty-five years, and that the chemical elixir could prolong life even further. He gives us electuaries into whose composition enter potable gold, herbs, flowers, *sperma ceti*, aloes, serpents' skin, etc.

An alchemist and an astrologer, he required nothing in order to be a magnetizer. In fact, we find in Roger Bacon the great discovery of the eighteenth century—animal magnetism; so that, while he has the glory of having been the forerunner of Copernicus, and Descartes and Newton, he has not escaped the misfortune of having anticipated Mesmer. "The soul", he says, "acts upon the body, and its principal act is speech. Now, speech uttered with profound thought, direct exercise of will, great desire and strong consciousness, retains in itself the power which the soul has communicated to it, and bears it to the exterior; the soul acts by it both upon physical forces and upon other souls which bend to the will of the operator. Nature yields obedience to thought, and man's acts possess an irresistible energy. In this consists the power of symbols, charms, and sorceries; we have here also an explanation of the miracles and prophecies, which were only natural events. A pure and sinless soul may thus command the elements and change the order of the world; it was in this way that the saints performed so many wonderful things".*

We must forgive Roger Bacon, who three centuries ago anticipated the great ideas of modern times, for resembling in more than one unworthy respect, the adventurous geniuses of the sixteenth century. We must acknowledge that he has some features which recal Cardan and Paracelsus; but there is greater justice in tracing a resemblance to Kepler. Like this great astronomer, he associates precise calculations and the speculations of genius with the caprices of an excited imagination. Like him, also—and we find this same weakness in several of our contemporaries, rather tardy disciples of the ingenious and chimerical renaissance—he introduces mathematics into religious and moral matters, explaining the Trinity by geometry, and perceiving the most beautiful analogies between the effusion of grace and that of the luminous rays. But perfect sincerity, candor, and artlessness entirely redeem these flights of fancy. The source whence Roger Bacon draws his ardor is not a foolish ambition to astonish the vulgar, nor a desire to possess material riches; no, it is a noble ambition to comprehend and render co-ordinate all parts of the immense body of truth, and to make truth itself a help and a blessing to the human race.

* *Opus majus*, p. 251. Comp. *Opus tertium*, cap. 27.

IV.—Bacon as a Metaphysician.

Was Roger Bacon an original metaphysician as well as a promoter of the true method and a discoverer in science? M. Émile Charles would willingly have us believe that he was, and to M. Charles belongs the credit of having been the first to study, in the entire collection of manuscripts, this side of the genius of Roger Bacon, first pointed out by M. Cousin, but still little known, and of rather uncertain character. We can readily understand why M. Charles should regard his subject with somewhat excessive partiality and admiration, but we ask to be excused from going with him beyond certain limits. We admit that Roger Bacon is not simply a learned man. No one can resemble less than he what we may call a specialist (*homme spécial*)—the grand metaphysical controversies of his time attracted his attention, and this is an interesting and noteworthy fact, serving to complete the idea of his character. It belongs, therefore, to the history of philosophy to inquire what were his opinions on matter and form, on individuation, on sensible species and intelligible species—and this is what is done by M. Charles, who presents us with an immense amount of matter relative to the subject, a curious collection of texts courageously gathered. But was Roger Bacon a really original metaphysician, equal or superior to his contemporaries Albert the Great and St. Thomas Aquinas? M. Charles ventures to affirm that he was, though he occasionally contradicts himself. I believe he is nearest the truth when he contradicts himself.

The learned interpreter of Roger Bacon states the metaphysical problem of substance remarkably well; he states it in the same terms in which the thirteenth century expressed it—that is to say, in starting from the distinction between matter and form ; but M. Charles has scarcely pointed out, in a somewhat superficial manner, this celebrated distinction established by Aristotle, before he hastens to declare that for him it possesses only a logical value. In his opinion, in the reality of things, the idea of substance is a simple idea. But this is a matter which calls for elucidation and proof. After having stated the question of matter and form, M. Charles expresses the opinion that the solution of it given by Bacon *is certainly the most original of his age ;* then, while maintaining this high commendation, he explains it by saying that the principal merit of Bacon's ideas on substance is *that of being of the most negative character possible ;* for, adds the learned author, the best theory of matter and form is that of Descartes, who suppresses the problem. Did Descartes really suppress the problem, and can the greatest philosopher in the world suppress a problem which has its root in the nature of things and in the constitution of the human mind? It was not lightly that the profoundly penetrative genius of Aristotle imposed upon whoever would penetrate the intimate nature of any being whatsoever these two questions: "What is the substance of this being?—that is to say, the bottom, the foundation, the subject of its attributes and its modes; and, further, What is the essence of this being?—that is to say, its distinctive, characteristic attribute. Substance is what Aristotle calls matter; essence is what he speaks of as form. It is clear that the problem is perfectly serious and absolutely inevitable, unless we suppress metaphysics—a way of simplifying things very popular at the present time, but one which Descartes never used.

Even when the question is only the explanation of the material world, Descartes finds himself confronted by the problem of matter and form, and he solves it in imagining an indefinite extent, movable, figurable, and divisible, a first matter which becomes all species of bodies in receiving determinate figure and movement. So, let Descartes do his best, he was unable to suppress the problem; and if he had really banished it he would not have been a great metaphysician. How, then, can Roger Bacon have the right to be proclaimed the author of the most original doctrine on substance which appeared in the thirteenth century, if he confined himself to banishing an inevitable problem? It would be necessary, in order to justify this praise, to demonstrate either by Bacon's assistance, or by new arguments, that the problem of matter and form does not really exist.

And the same may be asserted of another problem bearing close relations to this—one greatly agitated during the middle ages—the problem of individuation or individuality. These two questions have an appearance of being new ones in the time of St. Thomas and Duns Scotus. Words alone cause the error. The human mind is ingenious; when contempt falls upon some metaphysical problem, under a certain pedantic and antiquated form, it feigns to give up the contest, and assumes an air of modesty; it then artfully invents new formulas, covering up the problem which had been set aside; and now the metaphysicians again resume their labors, and new generations take a passionate interest in their systems and their strifes. I fear that M. Charles has not discovered that the problem of individuality is no other than the problem of matter and form, which itself is nothing but one aspect of the eternal problem of the realists and the nominalists.

But let us glance at what Roger Bacon says in relation to matter and form. M. Charles admires the clearness of his theory—which proves he is not hard to please in the matter of clearness. What I, for my part, manage to see in this obscure and doubtful doctrine is, that every real individual, spirit or matter, dead matter or living body, human soul or angelic spirit, so far as it is real, so far as it is substance, possesses matter and form—that is, may be regarded by the reason from the point of view of indetermination or possibility, or from that of determination or actuality. There is, therefore, spiritual matter and corporal matter, angelic matter and human matter. Consequently, it is not true that form is the sole principle of difference between beings, as many celebrated doctors contend, nor that matter, in man, is the principle of individuation,* as it pleases others to maintain.

This theory appears to be very acceptable to the historian of Roger Bacon. I should have preferred better grounds for my admiration. He says that it possesses the advantage of explaining the existence of the general laws of nature, while the other systems make these laws impossible. This is simply irony; for, according to Roger Bacon's theory, each individual having its own matter and its own form, I do not see what relation of analogy it possibly can have with other individuals. On the contrary, in the writings of St. Thomas, for example, which teach that the principle of identity among men is form, or the soul, and the principle of difference matter or the body, the general laws of the human race are explained by the identity of form ; and as to individuals, they find their principle of individuation in substance or matter.† Or, if we accept the doctrine of other teachers, that all complete beings proceed from a common matter, we still have an explanation of general laws, for in this case matter is the principle of analogy and form the principle of difference. M. Charles claims that the theory of Roger Bacon has the merit of avoiding the *separated forms* (*formes séparées*) of the Angelic Doctor, a very singular and very dangerous conception, and several other difficulties which attach to the Thomist theory of individuality. Let this be granted, yet other difficulties take their place. How would Roger Bacon explain the union of the soul with the body, each having its particular matter and particular form, thereby con-

* See the extracts from the *Communia naturalium*, given by M. Charles, taken from the Mazarin manuscript, p. 368 *et seq.*

† St. Thomas is very changeable in the matter of this exceedingly abstruse question of the principle of individuation. Consult the learned work of M. Charles Jourdain, *La philosophie de Saint Thomas d'Aquin*, tome i, p. 271, sqq.

stituted two widely separated beings, without any real analogy or conceivable union? And how, we ask, are we to understand the immutability of God, if God himself is matter in as much as he is substance? I do not push the argument; but really I do not see why Roger Bacon deserves the praise for metaphysical originality which it is desired to accord him. Roger Bacon errs in attempting to suppress a problem which is inherent in metaphysics; then, instead of suppressing it, he adopts a peculiar solution, liable to a thousand objections.

The following remarkable passage from Roger Bacon, respecting the universal appears to me to contradict entirely the theory relative to matter and form which his historian attributes to him: "There are sophists", says Roger,* "who endeavor to prove that the universal has no existence, either in the soul or in things, and they argue from such an idle notion as this: That every thing that is in the particular is particular. According to them, the universal does not exist in things, and the only relation between individual objects consists in analogy, and not in participation of a common nature; between one man and another man there is no other relation than an analogy . . . . . ."

This is in very truth the doctrine of the universal as rightly deduced from Roger Bacon's principles concerning matter and form; this doctrine is well known: it is called nominalism. And what happens? After having pledged himself to it, Roger changes his mind, and attacks it; he distinguishes in the individual two sorts of characters—one sort absolute and individual, the other relative, resulting from the relations of this individual with all those who are united to him by a common nature, such, for example, as humanity. But if this is the case, if Socrates and Plato, besides their individual nature, participated in a common nature, it is no longer true that every being has its particular matter and its particular form. Either the matter or the form must have a general character, and, moreover, there must be something besides a purely logical and artificial difference between the matter and the form. I am astonished that so penetrating a mind as that of M. Charles should not have discovered this contradiction. He congratulates Roger Bacon upon having discarded the problem of individuation and upon having almost said as Ockham did later: *Et ideo non est quærenda causa individuationis.* This is easy to say, and I also can imagine Ockham turning into ridicule the hæcceities of Duns Scotus, the *magister abstractionum*, and

---

* Extract from the *De Communibus naturalium*, third part of the *Opus tertium*, according to the Mazarin manuscript.

the universals of realism. He only admits the existence of individuals, or rather phenomena—a very simple doctrine, I will allow, and a very convenient one, especially ; one which clever men, disguised followers of Condillac, present to us at this time as the final achievement of Hegelian science ; but to deny substance is not to get rid of the problem, it is to solve it in the sense of absolute scepticism.

For these reasons I cannot by any means admit the pretended originality of Roger Bacon's doctrine respecting either matter or form, or the universal, or individuation. I will allow that Roger Bacon, inclined as he was by vocation and by genius to devote himself passionately to science, possessed the rare merit of comprehending the importance of metaphysics ; I will allow that he applies a taste for simplicity and a force of good sense to these matters which often inspire him very happily, as when he rejects the useless medium which scholasticism established between the mind and its objects under the appellation of sensible and intelligible species. To disperse the phantoms of abstraction is exceedingly creditable, but only under the condition that we do not proceed so far as to deny inevitable problems and certain realities. Roger Bacon inclines towards nominalism, but he so inclines without knowing it. In this respect he has not the boldness and distinctness of Roscelinus or the ingenious delicacy of Abelard; he is an undecided nominalist, and, as proof that he is not fully aware of the tendency of his system, he is of the most perfect orthodoxy in theology, truly a monk in this respect, and a monk of the thirteenth century, setting the faith above every thing else, accepting all the mysteries with humility, and, in addition, the supremacy of the pope and the superiority of canonical law over civil law. How far this is removed from the logic of one like Ockham !

This mediocrity of the metaphysical sense in Roger Bacon, conjoined with this exact theological orthodoxy, completes his character and places him in true relation to his century and the centuries which have followed. To one who should think of only the persecutions he suffered in his order, he might at the first glance appear simply as a monk in open revolt ; and so also, if the boldness of certain of his opinions were all that were looked at, there might be an inclination to regard him as a free-thinker and libertine. Both views would be erroneous. Roger Bacon is neither a Luther nor a Bruno. In the midst of the most audacious of his flights towards the future he remains a Franciscan and a contemporary of St. Bonaventure. The explanation is simple enough. A man always belongs to his age on one side or another. To suppose one who had no point of resemblance to his contemporaries is to suppose something more than a prodigy—it is to imagine a monster, an inexplicable and useless apparition. Roger Bacon submitted to the conditions of the moral life of the thirteenth century, and, going even further, he freely accepted them. He assumed the calling of a monk, and he remained a monk in the most profound depth of his belief. For him, the truth was to be found in Holy Scripture; all that remained to be done was to extract it thence or to connect it therewith; this was the service of philosophy. Holy Scripture is the closed hand; .philosophy is the open hand. Why did the ancient philosophers have presentiments of the highest truths of Christianity? In the first place, because they collected through mysterious channels that first revelation which the patriarchs transmitted one to another and of which fragments were distributed to the wise of all lands. And besides, there is another simpler and more profound reason for the necessary accord between philosophy and theology: it is that they have the same origin. They are two rays from the same sun, for the reason which enlightens philosophers—that *active intelligence*, as they call it—which excites and enkindles all intelligences, is the very Word of God, the Word which was made flesh and dwelt among us.*

This is indeed a very elevated way of conceiving the harmony between science and faith. But who does not instantly perceive that this doctrine is the very same as that taught by all the great theologians of the thirteenth century? Why, therefore, does Roger Bacon manifest so profound a disdain for the work of Alexander of Hales, Albert the Great and St. Thomas, and for what reason did he devote his life to opening a new way for his contemporaries? The following is, in my opinion, the solution of the enigma.

Roger Bacon thoroughly understands the Christian theology and believes it to be absolutely true. Now, what is theology but the regular and rational solution of all the great problems which concern humanity? In the dogmas of Christianity, and even among the obscurities of its mysteries, there is a secret metaphysical science. Is the Trinity any thing else than an explanation of the nature of God,—an incomplete explanation, it is true, light mingled with shade, but accommodated to our feeble vision, while we wait till it be capable of supporting the full glory of the truth seen *facie ad faciem*. Do we desire to conceive the origin of man and of all things? Theology explains it by the creative power of the word. And as to the

---

* *Opus majus*, p. 28. Comp. *Opus tertium*, cap. 24.

earthly condition of the human race, does not religion present us with the first cause in original sin,—a formidable dogma, and yet one which is fast tied to the consoling doctrines of the incarnation and the redemption, pledges of our salvation and future happiness? To gather together, and, as far as reason allows, to understand these dogmas, to seize their mutual relations and regular connection is in truth to understand the first causes and first principles of things. This knowledge is what is properly called metaphysics. If this be so, what is the most fruitful labor which human science can propose to itself? As to first causes, theology alone knows them and teaches them. There remains the region of second causes, that of man and the universe. Now, in order to understand the universe and man, is it necessary for us to speculate in an abstract manner about the material cause and the formal cause, to invent *intentional species, hæcceities, entities*—a fantastic world in which the spirit labors fruitlessly and wears itself out in vain conflicts? Or ought we to torture the writings of one of the ancients, who has been made an oracle, without knowing how to read or understand him, in order to accomplish the corruption of the faith through Aristotle and of Aristotle through faith, under the pretext of conciliating the two? No, there remains something better for us to do: it is to leave where they are the disputes of the schools and the books of Aristotle and to contemplate the universe. The great book of nature lies open before us. God has placed it before our eyes that we may be induced to read it unceasingly and seek in it the plans of his wisdom and the secrets of his omnipotence. This is the object of true philosophy.

It is thus that Roger Bacon's work appears to me. I do not find him a pantheist, intoxicated with the infinity of worlds, as was St. Bernard; still less does he appear to me as one of those narrow-minded and unyielding observers who are determined to see nothing beyond mere phenomena. His was a great and bold spirit, capable of embracing the whole horizon of the human mind, but repelled by the vices of the metaphysics of the schools; one who had a presentiment of the natural sciences to a degree at which presentiment becomes genius. Though it has at times seemed to be fading, the glory of Roger Bacon is sure. Instead of being diminished through the late researches of French erudition, this imposing figure has been at once illuminated and made grander. Roger Bacon still remains the most extraordinary of the great minds of the middle ages. A truly marvellous doctor, as well on account of the extent and variety of his knowledge on all subjects, as for the bold independence and heroic energy of his character, he possessed, in addition to the gift of perceiving general principles, another and a superior privilege—that spirit of invention and discovery which is the portion of only the greatest among the great. It is indeed glorious to be a St. Thomas Aquinas—I mean by this, to be the exponent of a great age, its majestic voice heard through the centuries which follow; but there is a privilege still more glorious, as surely it is more dangerous: it is that of combating the prejudices of a man's own age at the price of his liberty and repose, and of constituting himself, by a miracle of intellect, the contemporary of men of genius yet unborn.

Art. IX.—THEOLOGICAL AND LITERARY INTELLIGENCE.

FRANCE.

THE *Bulletin Théologique* is a quarterly supplement or pendant to Pressensé's *Revue Chrétienne.* The first two numbers, 1863, contain several valuable articles : Godet on the Organization of the Theological Sciences (encyclopedia); Pronier on the same topic, criticising Godet's scheme ; C. Malan (fils) on the Supernatural as the Reëstablishment of True Nature —a chapter from a work he is about to publish on Miracles ; a review of the Theological Literature of Germany for 1862, by Lichtenberger, and of recent French works by De Pressensé ; Tissot's Analysis of the Introduction to Schleiermacher's System of Faith ; a reply by Pressensé to Coquerel's objections to his article on Inspiration as not quite liberal enough ; Bost on Geology in Relation to Revelation ; Arnaud on the Divinity of Christ and the Trinity in the Fathers of the Church—a well studied summary. Arnaud's new Commentary on the New Testament is well spoken of by the *Bulletin*, as a good book for popular use: it will be in 4 vols., of which three are announced. Godet, in his article on Encyclopedia, gives the following scheme : I. SPECULATIVE THEOLOGY : 1. *Exegetical,* comprising Sacred Criticism, Hermeneutics, Bibl. Theology, Bibl. Archæology, Exegesis. 2. *Systematic* subdivided into Dogmatics, Ethics, Polemics. 3. *Historical,* viz. History of the Theocracy ; of Bibl. Theology ; of the Church ; of Doctrines ; Statistics ; Symbolism. II. PRACTICAL THEOLOGY. 1. *Ecclesiastical Economy ;* comprising (1) Applied Ecclesiology : (2) Theory of the Ministry—the latter subdivided into Liturgies, Homiletics, Catechetics, and Pastoral Care. 2. *Theory of Missions.* 3. *Apologetics.* Pronier propounds a modified arrangement, putting Polemics into Practical Theology, under Apologetics, and the Theory of Missions under the same head, and adding Irenics. His two divisions of *Practical Theology* are Apologetic Theology and Ecclesiastical Economy. He also, in the first division, puts Historical Theology before Systematic.

Annales de Philosophie Chrétienne, April, May, and June, 1863, gives the text of the Pope's Pastoral of Dec. 11, 1862, condemning various works of Frohschammer of Munich, as teaching doctrines on the authority and independence of philosophy, subversive of the claims of Rome ; it takes the broad ground that all philosophy must be subject to the church. Tamizey de Larroque criticises, in two articles, several points in Martin's History of France. Abbé Mansuet contends that Peter sent St. Mansuet to Toul. The editor, Bonnetty, continues in two articles his learned notes on the Knowledge which the Romans had of the Jewish faith. Abbé Blanc gives an account of a Temple of the Druids in the Department of Gard. M. de Borghgrave contributes an article on St. Willebord, the apostle of the Netherlands. Abbé Faydit's attempt to prove, 1695, that the Gauls knew Christianity before any other country [in the North and West of Europe ?] is reprinted with notes.

The Imperial Library has purchased for 90,000 fr. Count Bédoyère's magnificent collection of works on the French Revolution, Empire and Restoration, consisting of over 100,000 different " articles"; 4,000 vols., 2,000 newspapers, 4,000 engravings, MSS., etc.—the most important library on the subject in France. The Catalogue is a vol. of 688 pp.

M. Oppert has received from the Academy of Inscriptions the prize of

43

process against him, or to oblige the priests of the Seminary of St. Sulpice, at Montreal, to testify against him; and it was necessary to remit the case to his bishop or the grand vicar to punish him by ecclesiastical penalties, or to arrest him and send him back to France by the first ship". According to this, Fénelon was actually in Canada; there was not then in France any other Abbé of the name.

Theological Works. Abbé J. B. Christophe, *History of the Papacy in the Fifteenth Century.* 2 vols. M. Walter, *Life, Writings, and Doctrines of Swedenborg.* The works of the Emperor Julian, translated by Talbot, and published by Plon, with notes and explanations. A. Gratry, *Commentary on Matthew,* 1st Part. Luquet, *The Sanctuaries of Rome,* fol. 50 fr. Ed. Reuss, *History of the Canon.* Abbé Guettée, *Schismatic Papacy, or Rome in Relation to the Eastern Churches.*

A new translation of all the works of Spinoza has been begun by L. G. Prat, to be comprised in 5 or 6 vols. The first volume contains the lives of Spinoza, by Lucas and Colerus, and a translation of his Principles of the Cartesian Philosophy, and Metaphysical Meditations.

A new work on Joan of Arc, refuting various errors, has been published by Villaume. Michaud and Poujoulat published her life in 1861, and Wallon in 1859.

The *Revue des deux Mondes,* May, has an article by Réville, on the School of Tübingen, giving its reconstructions of early Christian history; an interesting account of Savonarola, by Geffroy; and a Comparison of the German and French Schools upon the philosophy of Roman History, by stitutions in Mexico about the beginning of our era. Other migrations continued to the 12th century. The Peruvians received their religion from the Toltecs. The volume is beautifully printed, with plates, at 25 francs.

The collection of Inscriptions made by Wescher and Fourcrat from the Cyclopean wall surrounding the temple of Apollo at Delphi, numbering about 400, will soon be published. Didot's new volume of Greek Anthology, edited by Dübner, contains poems ranging through fifteen centuries, and embracing 321 Greek authors : they comprise collections made by Jacobs, Boissonade, Bothe, and others, with the criticisms of Hermann, Meineke, Bergk, Hecker, and others, who have written on the Anthology after the two works of Jacobs. *Correspondance Littéraire.*

Abbé Thibaudier, Professor at Lyons, has published a tractate on the Vital Principle, discussing the various theories, and advocating the position that what he calls *animism* is the only orthodox view : That is, the *soul* of man is the vital and informing principle of the whole organism. This is in opposition to *duodynamism*, which recognizes a vital principle distinct from the soul ; and to *organicism*, which makes life to be the result of organization. He claims that this is the view of the church, and cites in evidence the papal (Pius IX) condemnation of the works of Günther and Baltzer. Augustine says : "The soul vivifies this terrestrial and mortal body by its presence." Apollinaris was condemned for teaching that there was in Christ's humanity a vital principle alone. The fourth council of Constantinople, and that held at Francfort in 794, condemned the theory of two souls. In the Clementine Constitutions, the opinion was denounced "that the substance of the rational and intellectual soul is not truly and of itself the *form* of the human body". The Catholic church has held with Aquinas : Anima rationalis est forma sui corporis. Francésque Bouillier has also written in advocacy of the same view.

Rationalism in the Lutheran Church of France. Some years since, M. Leblois, a preacher at Strasbourg, declared in public that the worship of Christ was idolatry. For this he was mildly rebuked by the Pastoral Association. Colani, editor of the *Nouvelle Revue de Théologie*, an open opponent of orthodoxy, was appointed in 1861, Professor in the Protestant Seminary at Strasbourg. Hosemann, a Lutheran pastor at Paris, wrote a pamphlet exposing Colani's rationalism, to which the latter replied in vindication of his "Position in the Church". Inspector Meyer, President of the Paris Consistory, declared in the *Espérance* (July, 1861), that an honorable man could not hold office in a church, whose fundamental dogmas he opposed : and has since published a Simple Exposé du Debat, 1862.

The largest publishers in the world are MM. Mame & Son, of Tours; they employ 1000 hands, 700 in binding alone. They have in stock 8,000,000 books, bound or in boards, besides an immense reserve in quires. At the late London Exhibition, their bindings carried the palm for cheapness and taste.

Abbé Glaire's French version of the New Testament, Paris, 1861, has been approved by the Congregation of the Index. Scio's Spanish version, Martini's Italian, Alliole's German are also sanctioned.

M. Curmer, the editor of the charming edition of the Imitation of Christ, and of the *Livre d'heures* of Anne de Bretagne, is preparing an illustrated work, *Evangiles des dimanches et Fêtes de l'année*, in the highest style of art, with miniatures and drawings from the most beautiful illustrated manuscripts of France, Italy, and Germany.

A beautiful Missal, made in the fifteenth century for Jaques Juvénal des Ursins, Archbishop of Rheims, a chef d'œuvre of the early French miniature painting, of 227 leaves, was purchased by Prince Soltikoff in 1849, for

10,000 francs. It has been recently sold to the eminent bookseller, Firmin Didot, for 36,000 francs, and presented by him to the city of Paris. The agent of the British Museum bid against him, but Didot had determined that it should not leave France. He has also just published a treatise on this Missal.

The first 13 vols. of the Recueil des historiens des Gaules et de la France, par Dom Bonquet, etc., are to be reprinted—250 copies only, for 468 francs. These vols. have become rare; Graesse gives their value at 2,500 francs. The first vol. appeared January 1, 1862, to be completed in two years.

M. Renan's Life of Jesus is making a great sensation in France and England. Less critical than Strauss, less destructive than Baur, it is still imbued with the pantheistic tendency—making Christ to be a moral enthusiast, somewhat after the French type. An English translation is announced for publication in New York.

ITALY.

The French government is publishing the works of the epigraphist, Count Borghese, deceased the last year in Italy. His chief work, the Fasti Consularii, has been expected for a long time.

A History of the Popes has been published at Florence in 6 vols. : *Storia de' papi* esposta dal Professore Stanislao Bianciardi. The author is said to be a man of learning and ability; he has previously written *Veglie del prior Luca,* and *Gallo de Ouifasso.*

Giaciato Macri, *Metaphysical Principles of Ethics.* Palermo.

Abbot Bernardi, of Florence, has found a number of letters of Alfieri, which are to be published.

L. Molino, Realismo razionale, ovvero Filosofia pura, religiosa, sociale. Napoli, pp. 302.

C. Greeth e P. G. Ulber, Antropologia, pp. 444: Logica, pp. 308.

E. A. Cicogna's extensive work on Venetian Inscriptions is completed by the publication of the 25th fasciculus.

Church and State. The last Italian Parliament had an animated discussion respecting the theological faculties at the Italian Universities. In all the universities of Italy there are but twenty-one theological students, because the bishops prohibit clerics from studying theology in the universities, and therefore the expense of maintaining some fifteen theological professors is, it is alleged, superfluous. The deputy Giorgini proposed a middle course, which has been accepted, and these chairs will gradually cease to exist.

Waldensian Periodicals. Since the withdrawal of the *Buona Novella* from the field as the organ of the Waldensian Church and of Italian evangelization, Dr. Revel has begun to edit a little quarterly—*Evangelical Messenger of Italy*—with the letters of colporteurs and evangelists.

The Provedenza del Popolo, of Bologna, has been discontinued, owing to the vexatious sequestrations to which it was subjected. Naples sends out a new evangelical periodical, *La Civilta Evangelica,* edited with much ability, and arranged to suit the popular taste, by Signor Perez, the ex-Jesuit, who has been for some time evangelizing in the South. The news of the work that is going on in all quarters is given in an unsectarian spirit.

The number of codices of the Divina Commedia of Dante exceeds 500—the larger number being from the middle of the 14th to the middle of the 15th century. The larger part of course are in Italy; next comes England with 60; France has 40; Spain and Portugal 12; in Germany are very few. The Oxford Bodleian Library has 15; the British Museum 12. Florence has 159, of which 87 are on the Laurenziana. Rome has about 70. Professor Witte, of Halle, has collected 407 of these codices, and has published the Inferno, based on 4 MSS., at Rome, Florence, and Berlin, with various readings, and a photographic portrait of Dante.

SWITZERLAND.

M. Gaussen, of the Theological School of Geneva, died June 18, aged 73 years. He was the successor of Cellerier, at Satigny, where he wrote his *Parables of Spring*. At Geneva, 1815 to 1830, he was the leader in the religious awakening and the revival of a better theology. He was universally honored for the purity of his life, and his fidelity to his convictions. He is best known in this country by his *Theopneusty*, and his work on the *Canon*. He also published *Daniel*, and volumes of *Sermons*. He was a thorough mathematician.

Professor De Candolle in *La Semaine Religieuse* (Geneva) gives a list of all the foreign members of the French Academy since 1725, restricted to eight at a time. From 1725 to 1861, there have been eighty-one, and one remarkable fact about them is, that not more than fifteen have been Roman Catholics—all the rest were Protestants, with the exception perhaps of one from the Greek-Russian Church. Of these, ten were from Switzerland, five from Holland, twenty-seven from England, nineteen from Germany, ten from Italy, two from the United States, etc.

SCANDINAVIA.

J. Clausen, *The Life and Writings of Laurentius Valla:* a Contribution to the History of Humanism, pp. 302, Copenhagen: B. E. Malmström, *Literary and Historical Studies*, Upsal; Andr. Fryell, *Contributions to the Literary History of Sweden*. Part 7, Stockholm.

A Scandinavian literary periodical, under the auspices of Professor Dietrichson, of Upsala, has been started. It is written in Danish, and bears the title "Northern Periodical for Literature and Art."

BELGIUM.

The *Acta Sanctorum*, 54 vols. folio, is to be reprinted at Brussels, at 25 francs the volume for the first 500 subscribers, and 35 for later purchasers. The work is not completed, reaching only to the 15th of October in the saints' days. It is edited by J. Carnandet, aided by the Bollandists.

Baron Kervyn de Lettenhove has brought out the missing part of the First Book of Froissart's Chronicles, which he discovered in the Vatican library.

Gachard's History of Don Carlos is completed—a work of research.

The 3d Part of Laurent's work on Church and State has been published at Brussels; it is on *Revolution*.

The first volume of the rare and valuable Memoirs of Francis d'Enzinas has been published in Latin and French by the Société de l'Histoire de Belgique, Brussels. Enzinas, the learned Spaniard, published it at the request of Melancthon; it was translated into French, in 1558, revised by Calvin. The new edition is edited by Campana. The *nom de plume* of Enzinas was Dryander. In these Memoirs he gives an account of the persecutions of the Protestants in the Netherlands.

SPAIN.

Nicomedes Mt. Mateos, published at Madrid, 1861–2, 3 vols. 4to, on *Spiritualism*, a Course of Philosophy.

Mr. Rivadeneyra, an eminent printer and publisher of Madrid, is preparing for the press a new edition of *Don Quixote*, carefully edited by a collation of the old editions. He has conceived the whimsical idea of printing this edition at Argamarilla de Alba, in the prison in which Cervantes wrote the famous romance. He considers it a species of monument to Cervantes, and will issue a limited number of copies in two forms—the first in 32mo, in four volumes; the second in large handsome type, and on paper which is being made expressly, in imitation of the old hand-made paper, in 8vo.

The works of the Spanish Reformers are being republished by two learned men, Don Luis de Usoz y Rio and Benjamin B. Wiffen. Twenty volumes have appeared already, and in the series are to be found a great number of publications which in consequence of being condemned by the inquisition, and burnt by the executioner, have become extremely rare. Very few of our readers would care, perhaps, to procure, much less read through, the whole series. Those, however, who wish to see a *Compte Rendu* of the whole, may find such a series of articles which M. Guardia is now writing in the *Revue Germanique* (published in Paris). Much new light will be thrown on this part of the history of the great Reformation.

GERMANY.

Theologische Studien und Kritiken, Parts 3 and 4, 1863. The first article by Professor Erdmann, of Halle, is an admirable account of the theology and philosophy of Duns Scotus, bringing out the main points of difference between the Thomists and Scotists. He makes the emphatic point in the system of Duns to consist in this—that he criticised the scholastic method, he reflected upon its processes. Written by an acute philosophical critic, it is of value to the student of the history of doctrines and of thought. R. Baxmann, of Bonn, reviews the question as to the time when the Book of Daniel was written, in view of the criticisms of Bleek, Auberlen, Dorner, Hofmann and Zündel; he advocates the period of the Maccabees. Rüetschl communicates several letters of Zwingle, Farel and Viret, not before printed. Pfeiffer examines the vexed question of the site of the city of Gadara. The new edition of Credner's New Test. Canon is reviewed by Weiss, and Ranke's Hymnological Studies by Justi. The 4th Heft contains an excellent treatise by Ullmann, prepared for this country, on some features of the History of the Heidelberg Catechism; Achelis on the subject of Rom. vii; Düsterdieck on 1 Cor. xi, 12—"The woman having 'power' (veil or headdress) on account of the angels", as illustrating Paul's use of the mysterious doctrine about the angels; Rösch, the Date of the Building of the Temple in 1st Book of Kings, vi, 1, a polemic against Lepsius, Bunsen and Brugsch; several unpublished Letters of Zwingle, and reviews of some recent works.

The third and fourth parts of the *Zeitschrift f. d. hist. Theologie*, 1863, are filled with the continuation of Ebrard's elaborate investigations on the history of the Culdees; their theology and religion, church government and monastic life, and miracles, are here handled more thoroughly than in any previous treatise. The two last chapters are on the propagation and dispersion of the Culdee church.

Zeitschrift für wissenschaftliche Kritik (Tübingen), 2d and 3d Parts, 1863. Johann Major, the Wittenberg Poet (1533–1600), by G. Frank.   A. Merx, continuation and conclusion of a Critical Investigation upon the Laws about Sacrifice, Levit. i–vii.   L. Paul, Historical attestation of a Real Resurrection of Christ, after the New Testament accounts—two articles, clearly put and strongly reasoned, defending the resurrection as a historical fact.   A. Hilgenfeld, conclusion of an Examination of the Theology of John, and the latest works on it.   The most curious article of the number is by Dr. F. Strauss, the author of the noted work on Christ's life—upon the parable of the planting of the Seed, in Mark iv, 26–29—as compared with the analogous parables in Matthew xiii.   The parable as given in Matthew, speaks of an enemy as sowing tares at the same time, etc., of which Mark says nothing.   Strauss now says, that in the conflicts of the Petrine and Pauline parties in the early church, the Petrites were wont to call Paul 'the enemy', an 'evil one', and the like; and that they probably used the parable in Matthew in this way (even if Matthew's Gospel were not written in this sense, which Strauss concedes would be a rather violent supposition).   Now, Mark has a parable about the seed sowing, and says nothing about an 'enemy' sowing tares, and the like.   Consequently, Mark's Gospel was written by a pacific sort of man, who did not wish to engage in or fan these dissensions.   And this is the "higher criticism" !   The 3d Part contains Hilgenfeld on the Prophet Ezra, in reply to Volkmar, and on the Gospels and the historical Character of Christ, in reference to recent criticisms, and the views of the school of Baur.   Strauss contributes another short article on the miracle of the piece of money found in the mouth of a fish by Peter (Matthew xvii, 24–47).

The *Zeitschrift für Kirchenrecht*, edited by Dr. Richard Dove, of Tübingen, now in its third year, is one of the best periodicals on ecclesiastical law.   The second and third parts for 1863, contain Friedberg on the History of Marriage Contracts; Schumann on Ecclesiastical Administration in Bavaria; Hundeshagen on the Theocratic State, and its Relation to the Church; Sarwey on the Legal Nature of Concordats; Jacobson, the Reformed in Prussia.

Theologische Quartalschrift, 2d Heft, 1863, (Roman Catholic).   Dr. F. Speil, The Genuineness of the Book of Daniel—a long article of 60 pages. Hefele, Pope Gregory and Emperor Frederick II—a review of their relations and conflicts, with the author's wonted learning and skill.   In the review of books, Ritter's Church History of Rom. Cath. is sharply criticised by Reifer; Patritius' new commentary on Mark is highly commended; Wutterich's Pontificum Roman. Vitæ (A.D. 872 to 1198) is praised for its thoroughness; and Tauner on Tradition, is eulogised as an offset to Holtzmann's work on that subject.   The 3d Heft for 1863, has a long article on the Epistle to the Hebrews, by Dr. Jos. Langen, contending against Wieseler, that this Epistle was addressed to Palestinian, and not to Alexandrian readers.

We have received the following notes on lectures and books, from a Professor in a Theological Seminary, who has recently returned from studies in Europe.

"From the last official catalogue of the University of Berlin it appears that during the last semester 2708 students have attended the lectures.   Of these 1925 were matriculated—432 in the Theological Faculty—515 in the Law—338 in the Medical—and 640 in that of Philosophy.   The Theological Faculty now consists of Drs. Twesten, Nitzsch, Hengstenberg, Niedner, Dorner, and Steinmeyer.   Drs. Benary and Piper, Licentiates Vatke and Messner, and others, give instruction as *Professores Extraordinarii.*

"Dr. Niedner is issuing for his pupils, to be used in connection with his lectures, a new and enlarged edition of his Church History. Dr. Twesten gives no promise of completing his Dogmatik—(one of the best works, of this kind, so far as it goes, Germany has given us), but lectures with his usual clearness and vivacity. Dr. Dorner has given through the winter semester two parallel courses of lectures, one upon Apologetics, the other upon the Theology of the Old Testament. These lectures are preparatory to three other courses upon Special Dogmatics, Christian Ethics, and the Theology of the New Testament.

"*Apologetics* is treated, by Prof. Dorner, as an integral part of the System of Christian Doctrine, as the first part of Dogmatic Theology. Its ground lies in the claim of Christianity to be eternal Truth—lies in Christianity itself. It is the justification of Christianity in its claim to be the final, absolute religion. It is the justification of Christianity to thought; it shows, or tries to show, that there cannot be conceived a more perfect Religion. Christian Doctrines, it attempts to prove, are to be received not merely as given, but as Truth. The energy and convincing power of Truth is an axiom of Apologetics. It seeks to reconcile the Logos of the first creation, with the historical work of the Logos in his absolute Revelation. Apologetics thus conceived differs from Christian Apologies. It started, indeed, with repelling attacks. But these attacks were merely the historical occasion of its existence. It exhibits the Christian Religion as self-grounded—self-dependent. It has an offensive as well as defensive work. It seeks to show the inner lack of Truth in all thinking which is not Christian. It differs also from a mere Philosophy of Religion, inasmuch as it draws from historical monuments. The essential peculiarity of Christianity is the historical Person—the God-man. Prof. Dorner makes no attempt to construct religion or ethics out of pure thought. His lectures upon Theology are ready for the press, and will be published, though not immediately.

"In the department of General History Prof. Droysen has lectured upon Historical Methodology and Enclycopædia, and upon Modern History since the year 1789. The influence of the Amer. Revolution and of our institutions, he appreciates and acknowledges. 'When God gave America Washington, he thought also of Europe', remarked in our hearing a distinguished Professor in Berlin. The veteran historian Ranke has also been lecturing upon recent history, and with an appreciative interest in this country. We may remark, also, in passing, that one of the most brilliant and popular courses of Lectures at the College de France has been upon American Liberty from Prof. Laboulaye. The Lectures have been given on successive Mondays to crowded audiences composed largely of the most intelligent and cultivated residents of Paris. The enthusiasm of the students has been very noticeable.

"At Halle the usual high standard of philological and theological instruction has been maintained. Dr. Müller's health has been so far reëstablished that he has assumed his usual share of labor. With Profs. Tholuck, Hupfeld, Müller, Jacobi, Guericke, have been recently associated Profs. Wuttke, Beyschlag, and Riehm. Prof. Wuttke is favorably known by a volume upon the History of Heathenism, and by a Manual of Christian Ethics, the second volume of which has recently appeared. Dr. Beyschlag was called from a pastorate. He has published a charming memoir of a brother of unusual promise, together with sermons and essays. He has lectured at Halle upon the Life of Christ, the synoptic Gospels, and the Epistles to the Corinthians, and has presided over homiletic exercises. Prof. Riehm was called from Heidelberg, where he published a valuable commentary upon the Epistle to the Hebrews. He is a warm friend and admirer of Prof. Hupfeld, without accepting many of the results of the latter's Biblical criticism.   He has given, the past winter, a thorough and interesting course of lectures upon the Messianic prophecies, which we are glad to hear are soon to issue from the press.

"Dr. Richard Rothe, of Heidelberg, has collected his theological essays published chiefly in the *Studien und Kritiken*, and issued them, revised and enlarged, in one volume.   A new edition of his Ethik, for some time out of print, it is said, will shortly appear.   Neander's Lectures upon Ethics are also to be published in Berlin from the notes of pupils.   In this way Dr. Chr. Fried. Schmid's *Christliche Sittenlehre* (Ethics) and also his *Biblische Theologie d. Neuen Testamentes* have been issued, two works which well deserve translation into English.

"As Herzog's Encyclopædia approaches completion, preparations are making for a new Encyclopædia of Science (Wissenschaft) in which each subject is to be treated from a historical point of view.   It is to be issued at Munich, and promises to be of great value.   Prof. Dorner is preparing for it a History of Protestant Theology.   The thorough Encyclopædia of Education, edited by Dr. Schmid, of Stuttgart, with the coöperation of Professors Palmer and Wildermuth, of Tübingen, has reached its thirty-fourth Heft—article Lesenunterricht.   It is a work of the greatest value to all who are engaged in teaching."

Zeitschrift für die lutherische Theologie, Drittes Heft, 1863.   Delitzsch, Remarks on the true Masoretic Representation of the Text of the Old Testament, with reference to Bär's edition of the Psalter, 1861.   C. M. Laurent, Criticism of the text of Clement of Rome, in the recent editions. K. Ströbel on the Union Formula of the Legitimists, with respect to Stahl. Rudelbach's Letters to Guericke, 1846 to 1850.

At a meeting of the clergy of the Kingdom of Hanover, in April, Prof. Ewald presented a proposition in favor of the union of all the Lutheran and Reformed churches of Germany in one National German Church, with a Synod.   It was adopted.   Dr. Dorner favors the movement.

Dr. Frederick Strauss, court preacher and professor at Berlin, died May 19.   He was born 24th September, 1786, was pastor in Ronsdorf, 1809, in Elberfeld, 1814, and was called to Berlin in 1822, where he was intimately associated with Schleiermacher and Neander.   He is known by his Glockentöne, Helon's Pilgrimage to Jerusalem, Baptism in Jordan, and other works.

The Archduke Maximilian, called to the Mexican throne, is one of the "royal authors", having published an account of his journey to Brazil, illustrated in the highest style; only one hundred copies were printed.

Berlin is well provided with institutions for education, besides its great university.   The number of public academies and schools is 80; of these, seven are gymnasia, one progymnasium, seven schools for practical arts, twenty schools are under churches, three are Jewish, six for orphans, etc. The number of private schools is 102.   Besides these, there 116 for the poorer classes.   The teachers in the public schools number 1,341 males, 469 females, 57,213 scholars, (of whom, 30,843 were males, and 26,870 females). —*Berliner Blätter für Schule.*

A new edition of the great work of Chemnitz, Examination of the Council of Trent, in Latin, has been edited in Berlin, by Preuss.   Taken all in all, it is, perhaps, the best and ablest Protestant work against Romanism.   It develops the Scriptural argument with great fulness and clearness, and also the theological arguments and positions.   It is a capital book for training in the Roman Catholic controversy.   Our young ministers would do well to make a study of it.   The editor has added an account of the dogma of the Immaculate Conception, and a list of the works in that controversy.

Buxtorf's Concordance is republished in a more convenient 4to form, in five volumes, at two dollars each, edited by B. Baer. A Concordance of the particles, which is wanting in all the concordances, is among the welcome additions. Dillmann, author of the Æthiopic Grammar, is about to publish a Lexicon Æthiopicum—cost $24. The Berlin Academy has projected an edition of the works of Albertus Magnus (fl. 1193–1280), to be edited by Dr. C. Jessen. Dr. A. Pohlmann (Braunsberg) has published a commentary, Part I, on the text of the commentaries of Ephraem Syrus, in the Vatican manuscripts and Roman edition. Brugsch, Recueil des monuments Egyptiens, dessinés sur lieux. Partie I, 4to, 50 plates. $8.

A manuscript found in the University Library of Bonn, published by Prof. Braun, establishes the fact that Charlemagne was born at Ingelheim, on the Rhine, and not at Salzburg or Aix-la-Chapelle. It is written by John Butzbach, prior of the convent of Laach.

‡A large number of Luther's letters, in ms., have been discovered by Dr. Burkhardt, librarian of the Grand Duke of Saxe Weimar. They were found in the archives of the Ernestine House of Saxony. They are to be published.

A Life of Uhland is in preparation, by Dr. Notter, of Stuttgart. His works are to be edited by Vischer.

The first volume of Max Wirth's History of Germany, from the most ancient times, promises a work of great value, viewing history as the product of great causes, and not as the mere narration of incidents and accidents.

Humboldt's Correspondence with Berghaus about his *Cosmos*, is to be published in three volumes.

ENGLAND.

Herbert Spencer's Theology. A writer in the *National Review* having taken Herbert Spencer to task for maintaining "the darkening influence of sacred ideas upon the human understanding", he denies the charge in the *Athenæum* and quotes the following statements from his *First Principles:* "We have found à priori reason for believing that in all religions, even the rudest, there lies hidden a fundamental verity" (p. 23). "The truly religious element of Religion has always been good; that which has proved untenable in doctrine and vicious in practice, has been its irreligious element; and from this it has been ever undergoing purification" (p. 102), etc. To this the Reviewer replies, that Mr. Spencer teaches that man can "know only the finite" and that "the infinite is the sphere of nescience and also of religion"; that with him "religion resolves itself into the acknowledgment of an inscrutable background in front of which the luminous shapes of knowledge have their play". To this Mr. Spencer rejoins, that he agrees with Aristotle, Augustine, Kant, Sir Wm. Hamilton, Mansel and others, that "we can know only the finite". He says that Theism, Atheism, and Pantheism, severally "involve symbolical conceptions of the illegitimate and illusive kind"; but in saying this, he "goes no further than Mansel". He also asserts that he believes in "the omnipresence of something which passes comprehension"; and that, better than Mansel, he holds that our consciousness of this is "positive" and not merely "negative". Further, that "in this consciousness of an Incomprehensible Omnipresent Power, we have just that consciousness in which Religion dwells. And so we arrive at the point where Religion and Science coalesce" (p. 99 of *First Princi-*

ples). This has "a higher certainty than any other belief whatever". The discussion is profitable as showing the way in which Mansel's views are made use of by those who reject the Christian revelation.

Mr. G. A. Bergenroth, the only foreigner ever permitted to consult the Spanish Archives at Simancas, collected by Charles V, succeeded in deciphering the various mss. and has made copies of what pertains to England, now deposited in the Record Office, London. In a work just published he gives a Calendar of Letters and Despatches, between 1485 and 1509.

The Sinaitic Manuscript. Kallinikos Hieromonachas of Sinai writes to Mr. Davies, that he never wrote or saw the letters published in his name in defence of Simonides; that the latter never was in Mount Sinai; and that Simonides "lies, when he positively affirms that the ms. published by Tischendorf is his work". His letter is published in the *Literary Churchman.*

· Dr. Edward Greswell's *Objections to the Historical Character of the Pentateuch*, and his *Three Witnesses and Threefold Cord*, are among the ablest replies to Colenso. The "threefold cord" in the latter work is the day, the month, and the year, to show that the three coincide at 4,005 B.C. as the starting point, and that the calendars of all nations point to the same beginning. Another able work is *History against Colenso*, two parts, by a Barrister.

The Literary Churchman, London, says "that as long as a contest is continued by the North American States which is sustained by a principle far more ferocious and unjustifiable than any thing yet perpetrated in the history of slavery in the South, English hearts will naturally so strongly condemn the greater injury, that for a time they may appear partially insensible to the less". This is in a notice of Prof. Goldwin Smith's able pamphlet entitled, *Does the Bible sanction American Slavery?* which ought to be republished here. The *Literary Churchman* represents the tone of thought and feeling among English churchmen.

The *British Quarterly Review*, representing the Nonconformists, has an article in its July number on the *Moral Aspects of the American Struggle*, written entirely in the interest of the Southern Confederacy. It protests against the Reply to the Letter of the French Ministers, which has recently been brought to this country from England. It contemns the idea that the North is fighting in the interest of freedom, and argues that reünion will defer emancipation. It speaks of the North as "besotted and blood-thirsty", and makes it alone responsible for the guilt of the war. "It is the most heart-rending and we cannot help thinking the most guilty war the world has known." And these are the words of the transatlantic descendants of the English Puritans!

Rev. N. Houghton, under the title *Rationalism in the Church of England*, reviews some of the works and positions of Alford, Arnold, Colenso, Donaldson, Jowett, Maurice, Milman, Powell, Stanley, and Williams—as representing the rationalistic tendency—a bishop, two deans, four professors and three doctors.

Geo. F. Maclear's *History of Christian Missions in the Middle Ages*, is one of the series of manuals published by Macmillan and Co., and is a very thorough and useful book.

In the Oxford Library of the Fathers, the Works of St. Justin Martyr, translated, with Notes and Indices, have been published, at 8s. The 6th vol. of Chrysostom on the Epistles, containing his Homilies on Timothy, Titus and Philemon, have also appeared in the corresponding Oxford Bibliotheca, containing the original texts.

Bagster has published, edited by Tregelles, the Codex Zacynthius, from a Greek palimpsest found in the island of Zante, containing fragments of Luke's Gospels.

New parts have appeared of the Catalogue of the Bodleian Library, Oxford, viz. Part viii of the Manuscript Codices, devoted to the Æthiopic, prepared by Dillmann; and Steinschweider's Catalogue of the Hebrew Books, 2 vols. 4to, 5*l.*; a Conspectus of the latter is on sale for 3*s.*

The History of the Martyrs in Palestine. By Eusebius, Bishop of Cæsarea. Discovered in a very ancient Syriac MSS., and edited, with an English translation, by W. Cureton, D.D. 10*s.* 6*d.* This is the 4th part of the most ancient Syriac MSS. yet known with a date, viz. History of the Palestinian Martyrs. It contained Clement's Recognitions and Titus of Bostra against the Manicheans, both of which Dr. De Lagarde has edited; Eusebius on the Theophany, which Dr. Samuel Lee edited, 1842; and the above work, referred to by Eusebius (viii, 13), and now first published in Syriac, no Greek or Latin copy being known.

B. H. Cowper has also published from the Syriac manuscripts, Miscellanies on the First and Second General Councils, etc, containing a remarkable Greek list of the bishops at Nice, and at Constantinople; a version of the Nicene canons, which "is from the oldest MSS. of them yet known;" fragments from Diocles, "the first historian of Rome, from whom Plutarch tells us Fabius Pictor drew largely"; with fragments from Christian and other writers.

America before Columbus. A writer in the *Gentleman's Magazine* advocates anew the theory that America was known before Columbus, on two grounds. 1. A chart of Andrea Bianco, dated 1436, having an island in the Atlantic named *Brasil.* But this, as Mr. Bolton Corney shows in the *Notes and Queries*, was undoubtedly one of the Azores, now called Tercera. 2. That trade was carried on with Brasil two centuries before Columbus. But the only evidence here is, that trade was carried on in brasil-wood, or in something called brasil; and Mr. Corney shows that this wood was in use for even a longer period before Columbus.

The Irish Archæological and Celtic Society have published, Book of Ancient Irish Hymns, edited by Rev. J. H. Todd; Adamnan's Life of S. Columba, edited by Rev. W. Reeves; Irish Glosses; Fragments of Annals, edited by Donovan.

Mr. Edwin Arnold of University College Oxford, has published the Book of Good Counsels, from the Sanskrit of the *Hitopadesa*, attractively illustrated by Weir. The prose is at least as old as the Christian era, and the interspersed verses from the *Mahābhārata* date back to 350 B.C., and from the Rig-Veda to about 1300 B.C.

In the *Evangelical Christendom*, the London organ of the Evangelical Alliance, there has been an interesting correspondence, between Dr. Dorner and Bishop Fitzgerald (of Cork), looking to a better understanding between German and English divines. Dorner objects to the English theology that it lays too much stress upon the external evidences for Christianity, and cites Maurice as saying that this has led to wide-spread unbelief. (Evang. Christendom, April, 1860.) Dr. Fitzgerald replied in the same magazine, Jan. 1861, asking how we can prove that the testimony of the Holy Spirit, on which Dorner lays such stress, can be shown not to be merely subjective; and how, for example, the resurrection of Christ can be proved in any other way than by external testimony? "Our divines say that it can be proved by stringent external evidence; and can the German theologians give a better answer?" He puts the case thus: The truths of revelation are *facts;* not self-evident; not to be demonstrated *à priori;* nor to be proved by saying it were best that such facts should have occurred; nor yet, by the assertion that the Holy Spirit leads to a belief in them.   In this sense, Dr. Fitzgerald's essay in the Aids to Faith is also written.   Dr. M'Cosh has also a "letter to the Churches of Germany", published in the *Jahrbücher für deutsche Theologie*, 1861, giving an account of the various theological parties and movements in England.   In the same periodical, Dr. Dorner reviews at length, and ably, the whole Mansel and Maurice controversy.   The position of Mansel he says, and shows, "involves a great and thorough contradiction", as a result of his theory about the nature of our ideas of the Absolute and Infinite.   He also replies to the positions of Dr. Fitzgerald, stating the German ground, that external evidence and authority can never produce real, living, saving faith, and vindicating "the testimony of the Holy Spirit" from the charge of being merely subjective. That the word and faith are inseparable, he says, is the principle of the present evangelical theology of Germany.   Neither *à priori*, nor merely logical proofs are sufficient; we must have the living presence of Christ in the soul, and the witness of the Spirit.   Here alone is the final ground of assurance.   The authority of the Scriptures depends on the authority of Christ, and not the converse.   The essay of Dr. Fitzgerald in the "Aids to Faith", has some reference to these views of the German divine.   It is a good thing that the matter is mooted between two such candid and able disputants.

Theological Works.   Wm. Cunningham, *Discussions on Church Principles, Popish, Erastian, and Presbyterian.*   Published by his Literary Executors.   F. D. Maurice, *Correspondence with a Layman on the Claims of the Bible and of Science.*   Rev. D. Moore, *Divine Authority of the Pentateuch Vindicated.*   John Rawlings, *History of the Origin of the Mysteries and Doctrines of Baptism and the Eucharist*, as introduced into the Church of Rome and the Church of England.   R. A. Thompson, *Christian Theism.*   Eben. Soher, *History of the Christian Church to Constantine.*   James Stark, *Westminster Confession of Faith compared with the Scriptures.*   The object of this work is to show that the Confession needs to be altered to suit modern science, etc.   G. L. Brown, *Lectures on the Gospel of John*, 2 vols.   Milman's *History of the Jews*, 8 vols., 3d ed., revised and extended.   Alford's *Four Gospels*, 5th ed.   Life of William Chillingworth, by Des Maizeaux, translated by James Nichols.   Life of Bishop Thomas Wilson, by John Keble.   2 Parts.

Professor Stanley of Oxford has aroused public attention by a forcible Letter to the Bishop of London, advocating the discontinuance of the subscription in the Church of England and the Universities.   The formularies, he says, "offer no solutions" of modern inquiries and doubts. Archbishop Whately urged the same matter twenty years ago.

The Religious Tract Society of London offer their Commentary in 6 vols., published at 24s., for 12s. to ministers and teachers.   It contains the substance of Henry and Scott, with notes from Clark, Horne, Greswell, Poole, Lowth, and others.

The *British Quarterly* has an interesting article on Bishop Butler and his recent critics.   It reviews Miss Hennell's Essay on the *Sceptical Tendency of Butler's Analogy*, 1859 ; the objections urged by Rev. James Martineau in his Studies on Christianity, and by Mr. Bagehot in an article in the *Prospective Review.*   The four objections considered are, 1. It is merely an argumentum ad hominem.   2. The difficulties found in nature are only incidental, but the difficulties involved in Christianity comprise the essence of Christianity.   3. Revelation should explain difficulties, and not merely give us the same over again.   4. Butler defends the immoralities of the

Bible, and so comes in conflict with the moral sense.   These are all shown to be irrelevant, or to rest upon a misunderstanding of Butler's work.

The Journal of Sacred Literature.   Edited by B. H. Cowper.   July. Canon Stanley's Lectures on the Jewish Church.   Isaiah xviii, Translation and Notes.   A Sermon by the Rev. Gilbert White of Selborne—author of the Natural History of Selborne.   Exegesis of Difficult Passages.   The Betrayal of our Lord.   Aethiopic Liturgies and Hymns, translated by Rev. J. M. Rodwell.   Inspiration, by Tholuck, translated from Herzog's Encyclopedia.   Contributions to Modern Ecclesiastical History, No. 1, giving extracts from the Bohemian mss. of Rev. Jos. Procházka on the Helvetian church of Lissa, above the Elbe.   Introduction to the Rabbinic Bible, by Jacob Ben Chajum, translated from the Rabbinical Hebrew by C. D. Ginsburg—a valuable and curious paper.

Dr. Raffles, recently deceased, was born in London in May, 1788.   His father was a highly respectable solicitor in that city.   At an early age he entered the old college at Homerton, near London, and on the completion of his studies, in 1809, was appointed to the pastoral office over the church of the Congregational denomination at Hammersmith.   This position he occupied for three years, at the end of which he removed to Liverpool. Among his works is a volume of poems, published in connection with his brother-in-law, the late Dr. J. B. Brown, barrister at law, and J. H. Wiffin, the translator of Tasso's "Jerusalem Delivered".   This was followed by a "Memoir" of the life and ministry of his predecessor, the Rev. Thomas Spencer, which has passed through many editions.   In 1817 appeared his "Letters during a Tour through some parts of France, Savoy, Switzerland, Germany, and the Netherlands".   To these publications should be added two volumes of lectures on religious subjects, a great variety of sermons, and many contributions in prose and verse to the pages of fugitive literature.

UNITED STATES OF AMERICA.

Mr. Scribner will publish in a few weeks Prof. Shedd's Lectures on the History of Doctrines, delivered when he was at Andover.   They will be found to be a rich addition to our theological literature.   The method pursued is in some respects different from that in kindred works.   The Introduction discusses in a philosophic manner the subject of Methodology, as applied to history.   The main divisions of the work are, 1. Influence of Philosophical Systems upon the construction of Christian Doctrine.   2. The History of Apologies, or Defences of Christianity.   3. History of Individual Doctrines—the bulk of the work subdivided into General Dogmatic History, and Special Dogmatic History.   4. The History of Symbols.   5. Biographic History as related to the History of Doctrines.

Professor Schaff is to edit Mr. Scribner's edition of Lange's Bible Work, which we have repeatedly recommended.   It could not be in better hands. The Gospels are well under way, revised with additions, from the Edinburgh translation.   The other parts will be translated in advance of the Edinburgh edition.

Gould & Lincoln (Boston) have in press, The Mercy Seat ; or Thoughts on Prayer, by A. C. Thompson, D.D.   Lectures on the Evidences of Christianity, delivered before the Lowell Institute, by A. P. Peabody, D.D. Music of the Bible ; or Explanatory Notes upon all passages of the Sacred Scriptures relating to Music.   With an Essay on Hebrew Poetry, by Rev. Enoch Hutchinson.   Also, Life and Times of John Huss ; or the Bohemian

Reformation of the Fifteenth Century, by Rev. E. H. Gillett, 2 vols. 8vo. This last work will prove one of great interest and value.   We rejoice in its speedy appearance.

Brownson's Quarterly for July has an elaborate article on Orthodoxy and Unitarianism, arguing against the latter, on rational grounds, in support of the Trinity, the Incarnation and Redemption.   He gives a philosophic construction of the *Trinity*.   He says, " in the divine interior eternal progression, the Father is the principle, the Son is the medium, and the Holy Ghost is the end or consummation".   The divine essence beholding itself, is the generative of the Word.   Some of his terminology, borrowed from Gioberti, must be perplexing to youthful inquirers.   *E. g.* he says that heterodox philosophers " do not understand that methexis is methexis, that is, a participation in the Divine Ideas, or essence, *mediante* his Divine creative act, so that the methexic is as much a creation as the mimetic or the individual".

Ralph Emerson, D.D., died at Rockford, Ill., May 20.   He was born in Hollis, N. H., Aug. 18, 1787 ; graduated at the head of his class in Yale College, 1811, became pastor in Norfolk, Ct., 1816 ; and from 1827 to 1854 was Professor of Ecclesiastical History in Andover.   He translated Wiggers on Augustinism and Pelagianism, and contributed to the *Bibliotheca Sacra* and other periodicals.

Francis Patrick Kenrick, Archbishop of Baltimore, died Wednesday morning, July 8th.   He was born in the city of Dublin, Dec. 3d, 1797. He came to this country at the age of twenty-four ; had charge of an ecclesiastical seminary in Bardstown, Ky., for nine years ; in 1830 he was consecrated as Bishop, and became coadjutor to the Rt. Rev. Dr. Conwell, of Philadelphia, and upon his decease in 1842, succeeded to his episcopal functions.   In 1851, he succeeded to the archiepiscopal see of Baltimore, upon the death of Archbishop Eccleston.   He was appointed by the Pope apostolic delegate to preside over the first plenary council of the United States, which was called in Baltimore in 1852, and in 1859 received the title of Primate of Honor, conferring upon himself and his successors the precedence over all other Roman Catholics in the United States.   Among his more elaborate works are *Theologia Dogmatica* (4 vols. 8vo, 1839–40), *Theologia Moralis* (3 vols. 8vo, 1841–43), which are used as text-books in numerous Catholic Seminaries ; " The Primacy of the Apostolic See Vindicated", " Vindication of the Catholic Church", and the article " Roman Catholic Church", in the *New American Cyclopædia*.   He is still better known by his writings on Biblical subjects, and especially by his translation of the Old and New Testaments, which are held in great favor in the Catholic community.

ART. X.—CRITICISMS ON BOOKS.

THEOLOGY AND RELIGION.

Aurora, sive Bibliotheca Selecta ex Scriptis eorum, qui ante Lutherum Ecclesiæ studuerunt restituendæ. Edidit F. G. P. SCHÖPFF. Tom. I–VII. Dresdæ, 1857–'60. This is a valuable collection of the tracts of some of those mediæval writers, whose general spirit prepared the way for the Reformation. They are published at a very moderate cost, only $1.65 for the series thus far; and the works are such as are good for all times. The first volume (or tract, pp. 15) contains Hugo St. Victor's Libellus de Laude Caritatis (which Schöpff has also published in German translation); an exquisite essay, full of the spirit of love as the highest of the virtues. E. g. "Nescio si quid majus in laude tua dicere possim, quam ut Deum de coelo traheres et hominem de terra ad coelum elevares." "Vulnerasti impassibilem, ligasti insuperabilem, traxisti incommutabilem, æternum fecisti mortalem." "Caritas omnem animæ languorem sanat, caritas vitiorum omnium radices extirpat, caritas omnium virtutum origo est. Caritas mentem illuminat, conscientiam mundat, animam lactificat, Deum demonstrat." "Reliqua igitur gratiarum dona largitur Deus etiam iis quos reprobat, solam autem caritatem quasi seipsum iis tantum, quos diligit, in præmium servat."

The second tome, pp. 50, contains Nicolas de Clamengis De Studio Theologico, not contained in Lydius' edition, 1613, of the works of this bold theologian, but taken from the Spicilegium of Dacher, 1723; full of useful hints, and earnestly insisting on the study of Scripture, and making theology to be a practical science. Its suggestions still deserve to be well pondered. "Summa igitur illius, qui theologicum recta intentione amplectitur studium, ea sit, ut formam se virtutis ad imitandum cæteris præbeat: nisi enim amicus Dei sit, sua sibi secreta non manifestabit; nisi foris luce virtutis effulgeat, alios opportune ad virtutem aedificare non poterit."—The third tome, pp. 61, contains Savonarola's Meditations on Psalms li and xxxii, written in the last years of his life, and breathing his most elevated and chastened spirit, which Luther published in 1523; and also Savonarola's Oratio in Articulo Mortis, when he received the sacrament—a most simple, touching, and appropriate prayer.—The fourth tome, pp. 50, contains extracts from the works of Hugo St. Victor, who died 1140. The first essay is on the theme, that the Christian faith is not only to be believed with the heart, but confessed with the mouth, addressed to the archbishop of Seville who had denied the necessity of such confession, saying, "Christianum non facit lingua, sed conscientia". In reply, Hugo says, among other things: "Crux in fronte, confessio in ore: utrumque debetur, utrumque exigitur. Totum Christus vindicat sibi; cor ad fidem sui, os ad confessionem sui". Another extract is on faith, which is thus defined: "Fides est certitudo rerum absentium supra opinionem, et infra scientiam, constituta". It comprises *cognitia* and *affectus:* "in affectu enim substantia fidei invenitur: in cognitione, materia". It is even called a "sacrament", so loosely was the latter term still used. On the contemplation of God, he says, that this is threefold: "in seipso, in operibus suis, et in judiciis suis. In seipso bonum; in operibus suis magnum; in judiciis suis justum. In seipso amabilem, in operibus suis mirabilem, in judiciis suis metuendum". That alone is Scripture, he says, which is inspired by the Spirit of God: "In qua, quidquid docetur veritas: quidquid præcipitur, bonitas: quidquid promittitur, felicitas est. Nam Deus veritas est sine fallacia, bonitas sine malitia, felicitas sine miseria". Similar gems of thought are scattered through these selections from this admirable mystic.

The fifth tome, pp. 76, contains Gerard of Zutphen's (Zerbolt's) plea for the Scripture and prayers in the vernacular language; the testimonies of John Gerson and Peter d'Ailly about the Brethren of the Common Life; and Gerard Magnus' Sermo de Focaristis et notariis Fornicatoribus, pars prior. The first of these works is by one of the Brethren of the Common Life, edited from a ms. at Deventer, and it is an admirable exposition of the topic, by a man of piety and learning, with abundant illustrations from patristic literature. The value of the testimonies of Gerson and d'Ailly as to the character of the Brethren is well known. The last work is edited from Dutch sources, so that it appears in a better form than before. The corruption of the church and the need of reform are presented in a bold and clear light. The sixth tome, not yet published, will contain a sermon of Gerard. The seventh has three rare works of Ratherius, bishop of Verona, viz. Itinerarium, Liber apologeticus, and a Sermon.

Joannis de Wiclef Tractatus de Officio Pastorali. E Codici Vindobonensi primum edidit GOTTH. VICTOR LECHLER. Lips. 1863. pp. 48. Wycliffe, by his pastoral labors and evangelical zeal, was amply qualified to write a practical treatise on the pastor's office. He wrote about 300 sermons. He trained many men as preachers. There has been known, as coming from his pen, a short *Epistola ad simplices Sacerdotes*, published by W. W. Shirley, in the Fasciculum Zizaniorum, 1858. Another tract, *De Sex Jugis*, bears on the same topics. In various works mention has been made of a larger treatise: it is referred to by Lewis in his *Life of Wycliffe*, though not by Vaughan in his *Life and Opinions of Wycliffe*. Dr. Lechler, guided by the directions of Michael Dénis in his Codices MSS. Bibliothecæ Vindobonensis, has at last exhumed and published the work so long neglected. The manuscript is from the fifteenth century. Dr. L. supposes it was written in the earlier part of Wycliffe's career, since it contains no traces of his polemics against transubstantiation; and all of Wycliffe's works after 1381 are full of this subject: nor has it any allusion to Wycliffe's version of the Scriptures, completed in 1380. It falls then probably between 1367 and 1378. It was found in a codex containing 50 other tracts of W., probably written in England and brought to Bohemia, and now in the Vienna library. It is a valuable treatise—as much so as any written on this subject before the Reformation; full of evangelical sentiments and weighty counsels. The pastoral office he views as intended to purge men of sin and to care for their souls. Pastors should love men more than the things of men. In the second chapter the worth and dignity of the office are finely set forth. The authority of the sacred Scriptures is largely dwelt upon, and they are cited with great frequency. The life of Christ is held up as an infallible mirror in contrast with a degenerate church. The style is vivid and lucid, and sometimes there are gleams of irony. The whole treatise is a worthy addition to the literature of the reformers before the Reformation.

A Critical History of Free Thought in Reference to the Christian Religion. By ADAM S. FARRAR, A.M. New York: Appleton. 1863. pp. 487.

44

The Bampton Lectures are bearing ripe fruit year by year. This new course for 1862 is one of the most scholarly, laborious and useful of the series since 1780. The works of Lardner and Leland, Rose and Pusey, and the translations from Tholuck and Kahnis, have been the chief English helps to the understanding of these controversies. But Mr. Farrar traverses a much wider field. He gives the history of free thought from the beginning. Lecture I. is on the subject, method and purpose of the whole course: he here divides the history into four crises, in the struggle (1) with heathen philosophy A.D. 160–360; (2) with sceptical tendencies in scholasticism 1100–1400; (3) with the literature of the Renaissance in Italy 1400–1625; (4) with modern philosophy in the three forms of English Deism, French Infidelity and German Rationalism. Lect. II. is on the literary opposition of heathen writers: Lect. III. on the Renaissance: Lect. IV. on English Deism, one of the best: Lect. V. Infidelity in France, and unbelief in England after 1760: Lect. VI. Germany from 1750 to 1835: Lect. VII. Germany since 1835, and France during the present century: Lect. VIII. England during the present century, with a summary and inferences.

On the score of learning the author shows assiduity and comprehensiveness. A very useful part of the book is the copiousness of its literary references, to fortify his own positions and to guide students in their investigations. The plan of the work does not of course allow any very extended criticism of individual authors, or many extracts from their works. But they are described with fairness and intelligence. Mr. Farrar writes, too, in a candid spirit; with an evident anxiety not to do injustice to any, even the most violent opponents of the Christian faith. His general divisions, groupings and summaries are good, and such as the subject-matter demanded. It is not a philosophical work; it does not discuss the fundamental differences of philosophical schools with sharpness or thoroughness. It is rather a literary and historical work, written by a sincere Christian, a good thinker and a fair-minded man. His account of the German schools is open to the objection, that he has not fully mastered the systems he describes, and trusts to second-hand accounts rather than consults the original authorities. He could not, e. g., get access to Rothe's works. One difficulty is imposed upon the writer by the form of lectures in which he was compelled to treat his subject; he is obliged to banish to notes at the end of the volume some of the more important elucidations and developments of his positions, which should have been wrought into the text in such a historical composition. He would have made a much better and more symmetrical book could he have recast the whole in the form of a consecutive narrative, freed from the rules and trammels of the lecture. But even in its present shape, it is an indispensable work to all interested in the conflicts between revelation and philosophy.

Palmoni : or, the Numerals of Scripture a Proof of Inspiration. A Free Inquiry. By M. MAHAN, D.D. New York: Appleton & Co. 1863. pp. 176. The Professor of Ecclesiastical History in the Episcopal Seminary, New York, here enters upon a course of recondite investigations into the mystic and typical significancy of the numerals of Scripture. He certainly brings to light some very curious and unexpected parallelisms, symmetries and results. Patience and ingenuity are here, as elsewhere, rewarded. The Old Testament history is divided up into six periods, or days; these again are subdivided by signal epochs; and then, in the names and dates of the epochs are found striking applications of certain numerals, which are supposed to have a fixed sense. Thus the number 8 signifies the resurrection, and 7 rest; 3 is the symbol of essential, and 4 of organic perfection; 6 of earthly imperfection, 5 of military organization, 9 of paternity, etc., etc. The work will be consulted by the inquisitive; but these mystical significancies, when carried so far, are so slippery, and each new writer assigns such different significations to the numerals, that we can hardly hope that the laudable desire of the author, to construct an argument for plenary inspiration on this basis, will meet with any considerable success.

The Work of Preaching Christ. A Charge. By Bishop McIlvaine. New York: Randolph. 1863. An excellent discourse on the central theme of the Gospel, by one whose evangelical eloquence and venerable years lend weight to all his utterances.

Sermons Preached before His Royal Highness the Prince of Wales, during his Tour in the East, 1862. By ARTHUR P. STANLEY, D.D. New York: Chs. Scribner. 1863. pp. 272. Published by arrangement with the Author. Besides the fourteen sermons contained in this beautiful volume, about half of it is taken up with an account of some of the localities visited during the tour—containing careful and interesting notices (with plans) of the Mosque of Hebron, the Samaritan Passover, Galilee, Hermon and Lebanon, and Patmos. The sermons were preached, three in Egypt, four in Palestine, three in Syria, three on the Mediterranean, and one in Windsor Castle. They are very short, averaging some seven pages only in length; but they are very much to the point, and each one of them breathes the spirit of the land or scene in the midst of which it was written and delivered. There is no attempt at oratorical effect, but a simple and earnest unfolding of truth, with faithfulness. Such a unique series, so well composed, is worthy of publication. By his previous journeys and studies, and by his remarkable talent for description, the author was admirably fitted for this work, which will win for him the favor and thanks of a wide circle of readers in this country as well as in England.

HISTORY AND BIOGRAPHY.

The Capital of the Tycoon. Three Years' Residence in Japan. By Sir RUTHERFORD ALCOCK, K.C.B. 2 vols. New York: Harpers. 1863. The position of the author of these interesting volumes as Envoy Extraordinary and Minister Plenipotentiary to Japan, gave him unusual opportunities for acquiring information, and also lends weight to his positions. The work is well got up, with maps and numerous engravings. It describes the social customs and habits of the Japanese with minuteness and fidelity, and gives entertaining notes of travel. But as even the Daimios do not visit each other, a foreigner cannot get admission into the private life of this secluded and jealous people. The history of the events of the last few years shows the perplexities and difficulties that attend the European attempt to force the subjects of the Mikado into some kind of sociability and intercourse. Sir Rutherford counsels warlike measures. His book means, that England needs a market in Japan, and intends to have it. He speaks contemptuously of the Japanese power of resistance. The events now transpiring lend new interest and value to all the facts here presented. That the resistance of Japan to the European projects will be obstinate cannot be doubted. Some vague accounts of the Government are given in chapter xxxiv, but little really is known of the details about officers and administration. The Mikado, the spiritual head, has only the shadow of power. The Tycoon is the real lord. Some 600 Daimios—princes, give a kind of feudal character to the government. The three great obstacles to progress are said (ii, 301) to be, "a *political economy* opposed to free trade; a *religious intolerance*, founded on purely political considerations; and lastly, a rampant *feudalism*". The style of the work is cumbrous.

Memoir of the Life and Character of Hon. Theo. Frelinghuysen, LL.D. By TALBOT W. CHAMBERS, D.D. New York: Harpers. 1863. pp. 289. The numerous friends of the honored and lamented Frelinghuysen will find in this excellent biography a worthy portraiture of one whose memory will be long held in honor in the records of patriotism, philanthropy and religion. He was distinguished as a lawyer, as a senator, and as a thinker; but his crowning glory was in his high Christian character, kept unstained in the midst of all the temptations and struggles of political life. Dr. Chambers has executed his task with taste, fidelity, and judgment. It would have been easier to make a larger volume. It is a biography which will be cherished, and the example here embalmed will bring forth fruit for years to come. Would that the work might be put into the hands of every aspiring young man, embarked amid the perils of a legal and political career. Mr. Frelinghuysen's faithfulness to his political associates was extraordinary. His letters to Henry Clay are admirable in spirit and manner. The account of the closing scene of his life, when faith triumphed over all fears and doubts, touches the deepest sympathies of the Christian heart.

The Foundations of History, a Series of First Things. By SAMUEL B. SCHIEFFELIN. New York: A. D. F. Randolph. 1863. 12mo. pp. 264. The author of this work is a Christian merchant of New York, widely known for his literary tastes, extensive travel, and philanthropic spirit. This work was prepared by him in furtherance of a plan of the Board of Publication of the Reformed Dutch Church to furnish a series of Christian school books, designed to restore Christianity to its proper place in education. It is a brief outline of History from the stand-point of the Bible. It is the fruit of extensive reading, and gives a large amount of valuable instruction in a condensed and well arranged form. Parents and Sabbath-school teachers, especially, will find this an excellent help. The maps and embellishments add to its value. The publisher has brought it out in a very attractive form.

A Sergeant's Memorial. By his Father. New York: Anson D. F. Randolph. 1863. pp. 242. This is a book of rare interest. It is a brief memoir of John H. Thompson, son of Rev. Joseph P. Thompson, D.D., of this city. Under a high sense of Christian duty he gave himself to his country, and died in her cause. His was a sweet and lovely character; and delicately and affectingly does a father's hand portray it in these pages. Would that "The Sergeant's Memorial" were in every household in the land! It is a fit companion to Dr. Stearns' touching memoir of his son, Adjutant Stearns.

The Bivouac and the Battle-Field; or, Campaign Sketches in Virginia and Maryland. By GEORGE F. NOYES, Capt. U.S. Volunteers. New York: Harper and Brothers. 1863. pp. 339. Capt. Noyes belonged to the army of the Potomac, and followed its fortunes till the close of the campaign under General Burnside. He records simply his own personal experiences and observations, the every-day incidents of camp life and battle-field. The narrative is graphic, and affords many hints and details which render the book valuable to the multitude of volunteers who are called into their country's service.

MORAL AND POLITICAL QUESTIONS.

The Social Condition and Education of the People in England. By JOSEPH KAY, Esq. New York: Harper and Brothers. 1863. 12mo, pp. 323. This volume gives a very dark picture of English society. The facts stated, the statistics given, and the result reached are full of painful interest. And yet the testimony is from a source which entitles it to full belief. The author was "commissioned by the Senate of Cambridge University, England, to travel through Western Europe, to examine the comparative social condition of the poorer classes of the different countries. His book was published in London in 1850". We have here only the portion which relates to England's poor. His summing up we give in his own words: "The poor of England are more depressed, more pauperized, more numerous in comparison to the other classes, more irreligious, and very much worse educated than the poor of any other European nation, solely excepting Russia, Turkey, South Italy, Portugal, and Spain". The statistics of pauperism tell a fearful tale. In England and Wales alone 450 millions of dollars were expended in seventeen years (from 1832 to 1848) for the relief of "abject paupers", and this does not include the extensive relief afforded by private charity, and by the different "unions". And from 1851 to 1861, England's and Ireland's paupers had increased about *five per cent annually* before the cotton famine commenced, and since then, in consequence of so many being thrown out of employment, the ratio has undoubtedly been larger still. The educational interests of England are in a most deplorable state. The schools for the common people are wretched in the extreme; so miserably conducted and supported, and so wretchedly arranged, furnished and ventilated, and having such incompetent teachers "as to make it certain that in many cases they are doing very great harm to the children who frequent them". And less than half the children between the ages of five and fourteen are attending any school. The author gives the number who cannot read and write in England and Wales at nearly 8,000,000. The ignorance and moral and social degradation of the peasantry almost exceed belief; *one half* of them cannot read or write, have no moral or religious culture or convictions, and indulge in the grossest forms of sensuality. The tables of crime given by the author show a rapid increase of crime among the laboring classes, and what is remarkable, they establish the fact that the rural districts are more immoral than the cities, and the manufacturing and mining districts. And Mr. Kay affirms, "that the greatest part of immorality is the direct and immediate effect of the utter neglect of education". From 1836 to 1848, nearly 450,000 were committed for crime, in England and Wales; and more than 90 in 100 of this number were "uninstructed" persons. If England continues to neglect the education of her masses much longer, the results will prove most detrimental, if not destructive to her social and religious condition. The social condition of the laboring class in this country, as it respects the means of education, intellectual and moral development, and independence, comfort, and thrift, is immeasurably superior to that of England's masses. Our readers will be interested in Dr. Wines' article in the present number of this REVIEW, on the "Sources of Crime". Bad as we are in this country, we are yet far better off than England.

Life on a Georgian Plantation. Journal of a Residence on a Georgian Plantation, in 1838–1839. By FRANCES ANNE KEMBLE. New York: Harper and Brothers. 1863. pp. 339. Nothing that we have read on the subject of slavery has given us a more vivid and painful impression of the essential evils and cruelties of the system than this calm, frank, and severely faithful testimony of an impartial and intellegent observer. The position and character of the witness, and her relations to the system at the time the Narrative was written, as well as the testimony itself, impart peculiar interest and value to the work. It cannot fail to make a decided impression on the upper classes in England.

Dr. Joseph P. Thompson's discourse on *Christianity and Emancipation* sa clear and concise exhibition of the argument against American Slavery from the spirit of the Old as well as of the New Testament, and from the history of the Christian Church. John Jay's address on the *Great Conspiracy* (second edition), is a forcible argument against the rebellion, and in favor of the Union. Mr. S. Cromwell's letter on *Political Opinions* in 1776 and 1863, bears on the question of arbitrary arrests, and adduces instructive historical parallels. The above pamphlets are published by RANDOLPH, who is doing a good work in this way.

Government and Administration. A Sermon by Rev. WILLIAM AIKMAN, Wilmington, DeL. A timely discourse, in which the duties of citizenship are clearly set forth, and forcibly urged, in the light of the Bible ; and the distinction attempted in certain quarters between the administration and the government itself, is shown to be unscriptural and groundless.

The Righteousness, the Satisfaction, and the Reward of a True Soldier's Life. A Discourse by Rev. J. S. HOYT, Port Huron, Mich. The character and service of Lieutenant Vandeburg—another Christian hero who has fallen in the defence of his country—are beautifully and eloquently delineated in this memorial sermon.

EDUCATION.

Science for the School and Family. Part I. Natural Philosophy. By WORTHINGTON HOOKER, M.D. New York: Harpers, 1863. Illustrated by some three hundred engravings. A new book by Dr. Hooker will be welcomed by all teachers and pupils. This work is carefully prepared for instruction—simple, clear, and fully illustrated.

The Elements of Arithmetic. Designed for Children. By ELIAS LOOMIS, LL.D. New York: Harpers, 1863.

Primary Speller. By MARCIUS WILLSON. New York: Harpers, 1863. Both these work are well done.

A Class-Book of Chemistry. By EDWARD L. YOUMANS, M.D. New York: D. Appleton & Co., 1863. pp. 460. The author's series of works on Chemistry are highly appreciated by those most competent to form an opinion of their merits.

GENERAL LITERATURE.

An Outline of the Elements of the English Language, for the Use of Students. By N. G. CLARK, Professor in Union College. New York: Scribner, 1863. pp. 220. Professor Clark has produced an excellent and useful work, in which his aim has been to bring out "the vital connection between the language and the physical and intellectual elements of the English character". It will serve as an introduction to the larger treatises of Marsh, Müller and Craik, at the same time that it initiates the student into the subject in an attractive way. It is just the book for profitable use in academies and colleges, and for the general reader. Though it goes over a good deal of ground, it is clear and simple. We hope that the author may find encouragement to proceed with his project of treating the literature in the same general method. The Illustrative Specimens, chiefly from Craik, are well selected. The book is very neatly got up.

Pearls of Thought. Religious and Philosophical, gathered from Old Authors. Second Edition. New York: Anson D. F. Randolph, 1862. pp. 252. An excellent little book. The selections are made with good taste and judgment, and the choice thoughts gleaned are conveniently arranged for reference.

Peter Carradine, or the Martindale Pastoral. By CAROLINE CHESEBRO. New York: Sheldon & Co.; Boston: Gould & Lincoln. 1863. pp. 399. Miss Chesebro's writings are pervaded by a sound and elevated moral sentiment, and by a noble purpose, which impart to them a value not often found in works of mere fiction. "PETER CARRADINE" strikes us as superior to any of her former works. "The story seldom wanders beyond the limits of the country neighborhood wherein the scene is laid, but among the 'Martindale folks', we find a variety of character, motive and action that calls the author's best talent into vigorous play." The story is one of homely experience, but it is well told, and the impression it makes is strong and good.

Romola. A Novel. By GEORGE ELIOT, Author of "Adam Bede", "The Mill on the Floss", etc. With Illustrations. New York: Harper & Brothers, 1863. 8vo, pp. 250. "ROMOLA" is less exciting than the former works of the author, but on some accounts more interesting. The scene of the novel is the city of Florence at the close of the fifteenth century, and it brings into view some of the historical characters and events of that turbulent period. The plot is simple and well executed; the delineation of character shows decided genius as well as the practised hand; the flow of the narrative is natural, and the conclusion, although very sad, is highly instructive. On the whole we consider it the least exceptionable and the ablest of all Miss Evans' works. Among historical novels it takes a foremost place.

Live it Down. A Story of the Light Lands. By J. C. JEAFFRESON. No. 233 of Harper's Library of Select Novels. Fifty cents. pp. 248. A novel, with a decided religious bent; exalting the established church in contrast with "the connection"; full of incident and minute description; prolix and yet interesting. Aunt Adelaide is a beautiful, saintly character; the villain of the book is described with spirit; its hero is natural, and its heroine attractive; and Mr. John Brownhead is a genuine specimen of English nonconformity, dissatisfied with its social position.

The Young Parson. Philadelphia: Smith, English & Co. 1863. 12mo, pp. 384. This book describes the experiences, especially the trials and tribulations of a "Young Parson" from the time of his first settlement at "Gainfield" till his dismissal, after four years of faithful and unappreciated labor. The picture is a dark one, but we fear it has too many counterparts in ministerial life. The story is admirably told. The sketches of clerical and parish life are faithfully made; the characters are set forth with discrimination; and there is a mingling of humor, satire and pathos, which makes the book a very readable one. "Little Phœbe, the cripple", is an original character, and most touchingly drawn. "The Young Parson" will revive recollections of "Sunny Side" and "Shady Side" in many a Pastor's family, and cannot fail to contribute to the exposure and correction of evils as common as they are trying in ministerial experience. We heartily wish the book might find its way into every parish in the land, and be read and noted, and its lessons inwardly digested.

INDEX TO VOL. I. NEW SERIES. 1863.

American Presbyterian and Theological Review.

NUMBER IV.

CONTENTS OF THE OCTOBER NUMBER, 1863.